The Ideal Worlds of Economics

THE **IDEAL** WORLDS OF ECONOMICS

Liberal, Radical, and Conservative Economic World Views

BENJAMIN WARD

Basic Books, Inc., Publishers   *New York*

Library of Congress Cataloging in Publication Data

Ward, Benjamin N
  The ideal worlds of economics.

  Includes bibliographies and index.
  CONTENTS: book 1. The liberal economic world view.
—book 2. The radical economic world view.—book 3.
The conservative economic world view.
    1. Comparative economics. 2. Liberalism.
3. Marxian economics. 4. Conservatism. I. Title.
HB90.W37   330   78–54497
ISBN 0–465–03199–4 (cloth)
ISBN 0–465–03926–X   (v. 1) pbk.
ISBN 0–465–06818–9   (v. 2) pbk.
ISBN 0–465–01396–1   (v. 3) pbk.
ISBN 0–465–03198–6   (v. 1, 2, 3) pbk.

Contents

Preface   *vii*

BOOK ONE

THE LIBERAL ECONOMIC WORLD VIEW

PART I / The Optimal Liberal Economic World View   *I*

PART II / Variant Liberal World Views   *93*

NOTES   *161*

SUGGESTIONS FOR FURTHER READING   *167*

BOOK TWO

THE RADICAL ECONOMIC WORLD VIEW

PART I / The Optimal Radical Economic World View   *173*

PART II / Commentary   *267*

NOTES   *307*

SUGGESTIONS FOR FURTHER READING   *319*

BOOK THREE

THE CONSERVATIVE ECONOMIC WORLD VIEW

PART I / The Optimal Conservative Economic World View   *323*

PART II / Commentary   *417*

NOTES   *451*

SUGGESTIONS FOR FURTHER READING   *459*

EPILOGUE: A Final Personal Note   *461*

Notes   *470*

Index   *471*

Preface

I HAVE HAD four main goals in writing this book. The first has to do with liberalism. Intellectually speaking, liberals are an endangered species these days. The first major aim of this work, therefore, is to persuade the reader that liberalism continues to be a substantial and persuasive intellectual position. The argument is direct; that is, in the first part of the book an attempt is made to convince the reader of the correctness of the liberal economic world view. This is done by characterizing an "optimal" liberal interpretation of major contemporary issues in which the economy plays a central role, followed by a section of description and commentary on various liberal alternatives to that optimal position. I have tried to make the account as persuasive as possible, subject to certain constraints. No known fact should be contradicted. The arguments should be coherent and mutually compatible. The account should be comprehensive, covering such major issues as the behavior of the market in affluent capitalism, the economic behavior of the state, the problems of developing countries, the nature and performance of socialism, international relations, and future prospects. The emphasis should be on the economy, though political, moral, and other considerations should be brought in whenever they are important in making the case. And, finally, the presentation should be nontechnical and of modest length.

Radical economics has been growing by leaps and bounds over the past two decades. The number of professional economists working primarily in this area in the United States has increased by an order of magnitude over this period. Nevertheless, a great many economists continue to believe that there is no such thing as radical economics, and that consequently the assertions of radical economists should not be taken seriously. A second major aim of this book, therefore, is to persuade the reader that radical economics *is* a serious and plausible venture. The format of this argument, contained in Book II, parallels that of the liberal section. Once again a direct attempt is made to persuade the reader as to the value of an optimal radical economic world view, subject to the above-noted constraints, and is followed by a commentary on radical variants.

The third part of this book serves my third major aim, namely, to persuade the reader that the conservative economic world view is serious and plausible. One might add that a goal here, as in the other two books, is to persuade the reader that the conservative world view is also humane, i.e., that it is fully consistent with conceptions of morality that are very widely recognized. Though contemporary liberals and conservatives have common intellectual ancestors, conservatism has come to differ in a number of ways from its relative, in ways that seem quite fundamental and that, as the commentary section of Book III attempts to show, have produced a distinctive world view whose variants now appear to have a strong central tendency. Again the argument parallels that of the other two books.

I undertook this work because I could find no presentation of any one of the world views that met the tests suggested above. But filling this gap was not my only motive in writing the book. For my fourth and final aim is to persuade the reader that economics is thoroughly permeated by ideology in its structure, in the ways it asks questions and answers them, and in the ways policy implications are drawn from it. However, the discipline is striking and distinctive in that there are three ideologies that are widely held by professional practitioners and whose implications for these most fundamental aspects of the subject are very different from one another. If the work is successful the reader will find that each world view is worthy of being taken seriously. As the epilogue suggests, if readers have anything like the author's experience they will also find each world view persuasive. Each world view does pass the test of being statable in ways that contradict no known facts. In terms of policy implications, each is consistent with reasonable codes of morality. Furthermore, each is coherent, the parts being mutually compatible and usually mutually reinforcing. And yet when discussing the same problems, such as the economic activities of government or economic development or socialism, the shift from one world view to another is really like shifting from one world to another.

Although each optimal world view is followed by a section of commentary, these commentaries stay within the framework of the world view being discussed. The liberal commentary is designed to assist the liberal in choosing among alternative liberal positions on particular issues, and the same applies to the radical and conservative commentaries on their respective optimal world views. This procedure is followed because there is in fact no fourth alternative in economics today. These are the only world views we have; as the reader will see, the variants tend clearly to fall within one or another of the world views. I could of course have stated my own views on each issue, but that would be inconsistent with the aims of the work. Though the author is never entirely irrelevant to the book, here I am trying to say something about the state of economics, not about my own state.

Hopefully this work will serve as a warning to students of economics. When they pick up a textbook or walk into a classroom, they should not expect to receive the truth about the economy in the same sense in which they get it from the textbooks and teachers of physics or biology. They should understand that communication across world views does not occur with great frequency in economics and that almost every attempt to communicate across world views is essentially an attempt to alter value systems. They should find it useful to become familiar with the world view they find most compatible, both as a defense against these communications and as a means of understanding them. They may even find it useful to become familiar with opposing world views for the same reasons. Though with somewhat less optimism that they will find general acceptance, this work and these last remarks are also addressed to professional economists.

BOOK ONE

THE LIBERAL ECONOMIC WORLD VIEW

Contents of Book One

PART I
The Optimal Liberal Economic World View

1. Introduction   3
2. What Is Liberalism?   7
3. Affluent Capitalism: Some Basic Facts   12
4. Markets and Affluent Capitalism   22
5. Political Business   36
6. Management and Planning   48
7. Developing Along the Main Line   58
8. Socialism: Development and Utopia   67
9. International Relations   74
10. The Future   86

PART II
Variant Liberal World Views

11. Liberal Economic World Views in Perspective   95
12. Basic Liberal Values   102
13. The Galbraith Variant   108
14. Drucker's Liberal Discontinuities   126
15. Power and the Survival of Liberal Government   135
16. Wars and the Failure of Issue Structure   142
17. Dissent on Development   149
18. Ecological Cassandras   154

NOTES   161
SUGGESTIONS FOR FURTHER READING   167

PART I

The Optimal Liberal Economic World View

ACKNOWLEDGMENTS

I would like to thank all my liberal colleagues, past and present, for their help. In this book I have tried to be no more than amanuensis to their thoughts, expressed and implied.

CHAPTER 1

Introduction

ECONOMISTS do not like to talk about ideology. We think of ourselves as a pragmatic bunch, concerned with improving the state of the world through scientific study of its economic processes. Being open-minded is an important ingredient in the successful practice of this trade, because if you aren't you are likely to be missing a good research bet, and in the competitive environment of modern economics, such mistakes of omission are soon pointed out by one's colleagues. Because of such pressures—not to mention the openness of our society—ideology is not felt to be an important constraining factor to the development of the science.

But something very much like ideology seems to be a part of even the "hard" natural sciences, judging at least by what we know of the history of these disciplines. Through their training, scientists in a particular field all tend to be given a set of research-relevant attitudes, of implicit beliefs that one sort of approach will work, while another sort won't, that this assertion may be true, while that one is nonsense. Even relatively solid experimental results may be suppressed, that is, not published, if they fly in the face of such strongly held views. Does economics really escape this kind of congealing of the group mind?

I think not, nor is it at all plausible that a policy-oriented discipline could escape such influences. Recent events, and particularly the efflorescence of ideological combat during the sixties, have served to emphasize for all of us the hold that ideology has on our minds. And it has come to be widely accepted that, especially in the United States, liberalism is the ideological heart of the belief system cherished by the overwhelming majority of practicing economists.

However, this newly emerging self-consciousness among many economists has come at the same time as a growing belief among intellectuals in general that liberalism is a moribund creed. Economists seem to be rather ill-equipped to deal with this phenomenon. Since they do not take ideology too seriously, they have not developed any very explicit defense against such a challenge. And outsiders are not well equipped to deal with the specific charges against the economic side of liberalism because, by definition, they do not have a professional understanding of what makes the science of economics go. A growing response among economists has been to stick their heads a bit further into the sand, leading to an increasing inflexibility, an inflexibility that is indeed a serious threat to continued viability in a changing world.

This little book is an attempt to respond to this situation in a constructive way. It is my belief that the liberal economic world view continues to be a sophisticated and plausible ideological contender for economists and students of economics. I have tried to substantiate this claim by providing a succinct presentation of that ideology in the form of an interpretation of how the contemporary world works in those areas in which resource allocation is an important consideration. This presentation occupies Part I, "The Optimal Liberal Economic World View." I expect the reader of Part I to agree that this view is not beneath contempt, not so devoid of contact with contemporary reality as to be dismissible without debate.

Nevertheless, the reader may think that, though roughly acceptable, parts of the world view are in need of revision. There are in fact a number of variants of liberal economic ideology that are defended these days by writers whose liberal credentials are fully in order. Several of these alternatives are discussed in Part II, with explanations as to why I made the particular choices of Part I, and why I believe that Part I does contain the optimal liberal economic world view.

Some readers will already have rejected liberalism for some other ideology. For such readers the present work offers a challenge. I hope that they will be convinced that liberalism is a serious interpretation of the contemporary world. I hope further that they will take it seriously enough to put it up against the optimal version of their own world view, to attempt self-consciously to appraise the strengths and weaknesses of each. Perhaps tests will emerge from further research that can actually be used to resolve some of the differences. However, it should be noted that I do believe viable and plausible radical and conservative economic world views can also be constructed to explain the contemporary world.

Long before he reaches the end of this book, the reader will have noted its unscientific character. It does not contain serious attempts to establish the truth of empirical assertions or to prove theorems. In addition, the language is somewhat less than scholarly; in fact, it is quite clear that a pitch is being made for the liberal economic world view. Taking this approach has made me feel a bit uneasy, but not uneasy enough to choose another mode of presentation. Part of the problem stems from the nature of the assertions being made. They are, for the most part, not capable of being tested by the canons of contemporary applied economics. They tend to be broad statements about how businesses or governments or families in general function and interact. These are assertions that not only cannot be tested on present data; often we do not even know how to design such a test in principle. But, despite all this, most of us have fairly strong views about their truth or falsity, and converts to pro and con positions continue to be made with regularity. For the most part, we are not dealing directly with economic science when describing economic world views.

Obviously, some intuitive process is involved in lending persuasiveness to the various parts of a world view. Three elements seem to be of central importance. One is an appeal to those implicit views that our experience, both direct and vicarious through such things as parents and school and reading, have inculcated in us. If the assertion seems justifiable on such grounds, and lacking decisive scientific evidence, we are predisposed to accept it. Second, there is the question of the general compatibility of the parts. If one version of a chapter in the liberal story seems easier to fit into the story as a whole than does some alternative, we are more inclined to accept the first. And, finally, there is the question of what we want to do with society. Working backward from our general policy orientation, we are inclined to accept that version of the story that most helps us to "throw the rascals out," to defend most effectively any policy we already believe to be most desirable.

Not a very scientific basis for decision making! On the other hand, it is by no means arbitrary, for each of these considerations is in fact a positive recommendation for the preferred alternative. Given the nature of the subject being considered, these seem to be the best tools available at present.

But if that is the case, why not accept the fuzziness, the inherently unscientific nature of the subject of world views, leave them for the most part implicit, and get back to serious economics? The answer lies partly in the already-noted challenge under which liberalism stands at the moment, a challenge that includes not just negative comments on liberalism itself but rapidly developing alternative world views put forth by radicals and conservatives. World views have turned out to be powerfully persuasive instruments. A liberalism that refuses to use the instrument is damaging its own cause. In a time of challenge such continued naiveté could be disastrous.

Second, implicit world views may not be optimal ones. Since there are various versions of liberalism floating around, there is some opportunity for choice. And if the choosing is not done with deliberation, explicitly, there is some chance of inefficient choice, and of a consequent unnecessary loss of faith in liberalism.

But perhaps the best argument for taking world views seriously is that they affect the course of economics as a science. Becoming a member of an economics department is a bit like becoming a member of a club: Among the candidate's qualifications, compatibility with the other members of the department is given something more than zero weight, and a single blackball, if put in the urn by an influential member who is competent in the candidate's field, will probably suffice to kill the appointment. If such departments are already predominantly liberal, there is some reason to believe that selection procedures will tend to keep them so. Much the same thing may be true of the topics chosen by economists for study and research. If they do not have a "liberal" structure, perhaps they will not be taken seriously. What liberal ideology does in economics is provide a substantive justification for at least limited continuation of this liberal bias. *Essentially, the argument is that economics is a more productive science just because it is dominated by the liberal economic world view.* The reason for this, in turn, is that the liberal framework fosters the division of issues into problems that are in a form most easily dealt with by the tools of economic science. But surely such a procedure needs defense; the structure of the science should not be determined by implicit and unspoken notions as to which candidate or topic is most useful to the profession, for such an uncontrolled procedure can become a cloak for using subjective and unprofessional considerations, such as ethnicity or sex, as the effective criterion. This book is in part such a defense.

CHAPTER 2

What Is Liberalism?

WE SEEM to be living in an age of Cassandras. Contemporary society is being blasted from all sides. From the left it is claimed that the exploitation of the lower classes, the racism and sexism and imperialism, are all the product of capitalist society and that the one can be eliminated only with the demise of the other. From the right we are told that big government is becoming Big Brother and that we must go back to older and simpler ways of life or be doomed to slavery. And even from the center our society is lambasted by outraged environmentalists, frightened zero-growth proponents, and the like, whose doomsday predictions about today's capitalism are no less cataclysmic.

This is a rather odd state of affairs. The truth is that the pragmatic, centrist methods of contemporary liberalism not only have been guiding most of the Western world's policy making for two or three decades but have produced an unparalled record of successes. The post-World War II era has posed the most difficult series of tests ever set before human society. The avoidance of nuclear war, decolonialization, modernization, the return to affluence and growth in Europe and the United States after the economic debacles of the interwar period: These challenges have been recognized and met at a level of performance that cannot be matched by any other era in history. Furthermore, there is no reason to believe that the approaches that generated these results will not work in dealing with the problems we will be facing during the rest of the century.

How could so great a disparity between what is actually going on and what intellectuals have to say about it develop? No doubt there are many reasons, such as the strong tendency for Western intellectuals to view themselves as outcasts in a philistine society. But a more important reason may well be that the very success of contemporary liberalism has tended to silence its defenders. Doing, participating in the resolution of real world problems, tends to be more appealing than merely writing about them. And for those who are participating, it soon becomes clear that they share a basic system of values with their colleagues. There is no need to go over the fundamentals again because they are not problematic.[1] Thus the central liberal position tends to be undefended just because of its great strength as an interpretation of how the world works. Instead, efforts are directed at problems of detail, whose solutions, piled one upon the other, have produced this astonishing achievement.

Liberalism today is both centrist and pragmatic. It avoids the risky extreme solutions, preferring those that involve step-by-step movements from the existing situation. It is pragmatic in the sense that it is not some rigid ideology that forms the basis of liberal action, some idealized utopia toward which it strives to move the world, but a continuing desire to make things a bit better than they are.

However, this is not to say that there is no theory, no set of values that informs the liberal position. Far from it. In fact, the liberal position has evolved out of a centuries-old tradition, which first reached maturity in the eighteenth century. Its history is roughly coincident with that of the rise of the modern world and of the establishment of basic freedoms for the individual as fundamental constraints on the actions of the state. The doctrine has continued to evolve over the last two centuries. Some areas are now better understood, especially those relating to the economy, but in other areas, such as the nature of man, there has probably been little change. This is not because liberalism has fallen behind the times, but rather because the major thinkers of liberalism seem to have had a solid, workable view as to what human nature is like.

However, we are not concerned with the eighteenth century or with Locke, Berkeley, Hume, Bentham, Smith, Mill, and the rest of that long and eminent line. Our aim is to show how liberalism explains the workings of the modern world, especially in those areas where economic considerations tend to be very important. So instead of starting off with philosophy, we begin our exposition of liberalism with four questions. These questions and the answers that follow should provide a brief overview as to how a liberal economist views the world around him and his place in that world.

Four Liberal Questions and Answers

1. *Where in today's world do we see the closest practical embodiment of liberal ideas?* The liberal answer to this question is quite unequivocal: We see it in the developed Western countries, most notably the United States and Western Europe. Opinions may differ as to which among these is best of all, in some overall sense, but it is unquestionably in those countries that liberalism is most actively practiced. We see it manifested first and most noticeably in the affluence of these societies. This affluence is not the product of pure chance, but of a population that took advantage of its opportunities by dint of hard and creative work over a period of generations. Equally, the affluence is not

restricted to a few very rich families. Its most striking and historically unique feature is that even the median or typical family has command of resources far beyond the basic necessities for survival, and there is reasonable assurance that a given family's slice of the pie will not be suddenly and arbitrarily snatched away.

A second practical embodiment of liberal ideas lies in the openness of these societies. Once again, nowhere else in the modern world can one find societies in which tolerance for dissidence and nonconformity is as high as in these societies. This too is no accident, no gift of some great leader, but the product of generations of struggle, and tolerance consequently is deeply rooted in the values of most of these societies, particularly the United States and the United Kingdom.

A third central embodiment of liberal values lies in the importance of welfare in these societies. In each of them the government is engaged in a massive effort to provide security for its citizens, security against starvation and avoidable illness and death, security against substantial loss of income and against massive unemployment. This effort is largely a product of the twentieth century and is by no means complete in all these societies, but once again it has sunk deep roots in the consciousness of the peoples of these nations, having been won in a series of political struggles over the decades.

A number of other aspects of these societies is worthy of note, but these three items, affluence, openness, and welfare, are the Big Three, the factors that in combination distinguish these societies from all others, and the factors that most centrally embody the ideals of contemporary liberalism.

2.   *How can these societies be further improved?* The liberal answer to this question is: Starting from where we are, from the status quo, try to make things a bit better here and there, concentrating attention on those areas where the productivity of effort is likely to be greatest. Current practice is the appropriate starting point, rather than some utopian vision, because liberals are pragmatic and distrusting of those who claim to have a magic formula for the elimination of the world's problems. The piecemeal approach is preferred because, once again, it is the pragmatic way; it is the little problems that we are likely to know how to mitigate. And over the longer pull, a series of such little successes can add up to quite a dramatic change. No better example of this exists than the process of economic growth itself, which has consisted essentially of adding a bit here and a bit there, year after year, to our productive capacity, until our economy has become unrecognizably more affluent than it was only a few decades before. And, finally, the emphasis on the productivity of the effort at improvement is based on the notion that improvement is costly, so costly in fact that we can't do much of it at one time; from that it follows quite directly that the urgent problem we don't know how to solve should take a back seat to the many little problems we *can* deal with (or perhaps that urgent and intractable problems can be divided into a number of little problems, some of which can be dealt with).

3.   *What specifically ought we to do next?* The liberal answer here

is: There is *no* right answer to this question. People are bound to disagree as to what ought to be done next, with what priority and with what level of allocation of resources to the effort. That is because we humans have different life experiences and different felt wants and needs. When we project these out onto society, we get different pictures as to where action is most needed. So the liberal feels that controversy over what ought to be done, and what is currently being done, is a mark of the success of a society, not of its failure, an indication that wants are being given genuine political expression. The function of the social, economic, and political institutions of a liberal society is to contain this conflict and direct it into reasonably productive channels. One important thing these institutions can do is to eliminate proposals that nearly all can agree are not worth pursuing, and to restrict the conflict to those disagreements that can survive exposure to the known facts. Another thing the institutions can do is see to it that most people get at least some of what they want; this results from a simple recognition of the fact that truth is not something possessed by only a single segment of society.

Of course, there are certain general propositions about needed social change on which liberals can agree. In the United States at the present time there is general agreement among liberals, for example, that there is too much inflation, unemployment, discrimination, and crime. This agreement serves to point the search for solutions in the right general direction. But the serious search for policies to implement brings us immediately into controversial realms: Should the economy be given more stimulus in the form of government spending? Should specific affirmative action regulations such as Title IX be made tougher? Should the negative income tax be put in, and if so at what level of subsidy? As one gets closer to the actual, implementable policies, the controversy tends to emerge more clearly. But that is the relevant level, if one is seriously interested in social change.

4. *Isn't what has just been called the liberal answer to the above three questions the only sensible way to look at social problems?* Judging from the response of a number of my students, I suspect many readers will feel that the correct answer to this question is yes, that all sensible people want these things and look at the social world in this way. But that is not the case. Such people, I submit, are the Monsieur Jourdains of liberalism, who have been speaking liberal prose all their lives without knowing it. There are many people who act and speak and write as if they disagree with this liberal position.

Consider first the libertarian conservative. He tends to be appalled at contemporary capitalist society with its big government, its constant intervention in the lives of the people, with the very notion that an essentially coercive government can bring "welfare" to the people. Contemporary capitalism is just not his model society. He also tends to believe that the second question above is entirely misconceived. One can make no sense of the notion of improving a society. For him society is a collection of individuals, and they have different wants. A government policy typically makes some better off and some worse off, and there is no such thing as striking a balance, which, he would say, implies that a society is some sort of organism, transcending the individuals who are its parts.

Next consider the radical. He is at least as appalled as the conservative at our pragmatic models. He believes that affluence is a sham, covering a deep malaise, that the governments run these societies for the benefit of a tiny minority of the population, so that welfare too is a sham. He also believes that the openness and conflict in these societies are a superficial manifestation of a fundamental ailment, namely, alienation, that can only be eliminated by a dramatic transformation of the social structure. And in his vision of this transformed society conflict too is transformed into a "dialectic interaction among nonantagonistic contradictions," or some such thing.

No, these *are* liberal answers, distinguishable fundamentally from those offered by the other ideologies that exist in the world today. In fact, the questions too may be liberal, tending to formulate issues in ways that favor and reveal the liberal orientation. This too is conceded, and the same liberal orientation that formed the questions will continue as we look a bit more deeply at the structure of the contemporary world political economy in the next few chapters.

CHAPTER 3

Affluent Capitalism:
Some Basic Facts

SUPPOSE we take a very large number of people, tens of millions of them, out of their traditional, or at least accustomed, abodes in the countryside and small towns, and crowd them together in large, cramped cities. Then expose them through daily contacts and newly devised media of communication to the vast range of differences in affluence among the citizens of these cities as compared with our group, most of whom will be starting out within striking distance of the bottom of the pile. Explain to them that there are not enough goods and services to go around, and that it is essentially up to them to get what they can of the pie, and that although illegal behavior is deplored, it is not really very effectively deterred by the system of justice.

Surely such a situation is a formula for social disaster, one in which life would quickly become nasty, brutish, and short. But it *is* substantially what has happened in the twentieth century in the United States and, for the most part, in the other affluent countries as well. And although modern cities are not unexciting places to live, the level of violence is actually quite low by historical or comparative standards; for example, numerically it is just not in the same league with automobile casualties. And although robbery and other forms of illegal expropriation of property are common enough, again it is the rare inhabitant of the city whose fortunes are dramatically and lastingly affected by such acts. The disaster did not occur.

Why not? Well, the central fact of the twentieth century has been the emergence of affluent capitalism as the dominant form of national social organization. This is a new form of society that has no real counterpart in earlier times and that in its own time sets the tunes to which others dance. There is thus some presumption that its emergence helps to explain the disaster that should have occurred but did not.

The present chapter describes some basic features of this relatively newly emergent social form. To show how dramatic the change has been we compare two points in time that are quite far apart, namely, the turn of the century and the present; for the same reason our comparison emphasizes that archetypal affluent capitalist country, the United States. However, the United States is not the only such country. There are at least fifteen countries that can qualify, and later in the chapter we look at some important respects in which all these countries are similar and suggest some of the reasons why.

The United States Then and Now

Consumption and leisure

Since the decade of the 1890s, output per capita has about quadrupled in the United States. This suggests that we entered the age of affluence during the decades since then. However, this figure, as is often the case, is a bit misleading. Per capita consumption of basic goods such as food, clothing, and shelter has increased less than half that much. Already in the nineties the average American had a lot of meat in his diet, was relatively comfortably housed, and was warmly if not dressily clothed. In this sense affluence had already been achieved.[1]

The fundamental changes in the economic situation of American families have been those of quality rather than quantity. Of these qualitative changes, a standout surely has been the increase in leisure. The average work week has declined by perhaps a third. Child labor has been virtually eliminated. Though female participation in the labor force has increased dramatically since World War II, in the nineties a majority of American wives were engaged in vigorous and highly productive lives as farm wives. Probably for both male and female, work demands are also much less physically exhausting than in the past. So, all in all, adult Americans have acquired an additional ten or fifteen hours a week of nonwork time, and have greater energy available for use during this time.

Of course, the supply of goods and services to typical families has also increased dramatically, if rather selectively. Household appliances have had substantial effects on housework. Movies, radio, and television have created a whole new and central form of entertainment at the same time that related but more traditional forms—such as attending lectures and reading—have also been increasing. Goods-intensive recreational activities, such as boating, skiing, bowling, and travel, have increased phenomenally. Obviously, increasing affluence has meant a substantial shift in relative family expenditures away from those basics that were already being widely bought at the turn of the century toward items that, while not necessities, also have come to be regarded as essential features of the good life.

In almost every area of consumption there have been substantial changes in technology that affect both the quality of the good and its relative scarcity. Not all quality changes are wholly in the right direction, of course. For example, technical change in agriculture and food distribution has greatly lengthened the season for many fresh fruits and greatly widened the area over which they are available. But the availability of tree-ripened fruit to the population has actually declined, partly as a result of urbanization and partly due to the very nature of these technical changes. There are those today—a rather small minority, to be sure—who claim that they would prefer the simpler and poorer situation of eighty years ago because of these negative changes in quality. Such desires are, in fact, still realizable to a considerable extent, and clearly this is something less than a mass movement.

One of the truly fundamental consequences of greatly increased production of goods and services has been the tremendous expansion in the range of choices offered the contemporary individual as compared to eighty years ago. Not only can he choose to go back to subsistence farming, he can also choose to buy his dinners already prepared and frozen, to be washed down with, say, Red Chinese beer, while watching a hang-gliding exhibition on television. Or, on the spur of the moment, he can find, probably within a few miles of his home, the ingredients for preparing a complete *haute cuisine* dinner, to be consumed the same day, if the recipe permits. For food alone there are tens of thousands of significantly different meals that are at the consumer's almost immediate beck and call. This situation is to be contrasted with that of the rural family, which was still the typical American family of the turn of the century. And, of course, this range of choice applies to most other areas of life as well, including all those that had no counterparts in earlier times, such as the hang-gliding just mentioned. Once survival needs are satisfied, it may be that meaningful increases in the range of choice of individuals are almost the same thing as an increase in their affluence.

But an increase in choice is not without its cost. One has to make those choices. This might seem like a trivial matter, but it is not. It takes quite a lot of effort, often including a certain amount of experimentation, in order for an individual to determine which of a particular class of goods or activities is the best one for him. This is time and effort removed from that increase in leisure time, at least to the extent that search is not in itself a pleasurable activity but merely a means to the end of enjoying the leisure time. The proliferation of enthusiast magazines for photographers, skiers, surfers, hi-fi users, and the like, with their emphasis on the properties in use of relevant products, is testimony to the complexity of choice (and also to the pleasures of choosing). This is especially true since, though advertising revenues are important to such publications, they are not inexpensive to buy; consumers of complex modern services are willing to pay for assistance in making their choices.

The move from town to city has also served substantially to increase the complexity of choice. It was not until the 1920 census that more than half of Americans were reported as living in cities rather than on farms; by now almost everyone is a city dweller, either in fact or by virtue of the changes wrought in rural life by the transport and communications revolutions. This move to the city, combined with the technological changes, has produced two clearly dramatic but still rather hard to evaluate effects. The first is a very large increase in the number of human contacts that the average individual experiences, and an equally dramatic increase in the number of different people he contacts. This occurs in the workplace—contrasted once again with farm life—in the city streets, and through the media, from telephone to television. It is certainly plausible that a consequence of all this is a sharp increase in "other-directedness," the dependence of individual criteria of choice on the behavior and approval of others, particularly of others outside the family. Given the great increase in the range of choice, this is possibly one of the organizing devices by which the costs of choice are reduced. One goes skiing initially because a new group of friends goes, and because the media suggest that it is the thing to do. But after one gets out on the slopes it turns out to be great fun as well. A second major consequence of this highly contactful environment is the impairment of the individual's environment through noise, pollution, and the like.

This set of facts about changes in leisure and consumption over the past eighty years or so clearly holds part of the answer to the problem posed at the start of this chapter. Increased leisure has provided families with more time to enjoy the fruits of their labor, while the vast increase in both discretionary income and the things that can be done with it has made possible a much finer tailoring of the pattern of individual consumption to the pattern of individual wants. Such an increase in opportunity for the overwhelming majority of the population must have been a vital factor in muting the conflicts and tensions of this great transformation.

However, an interesting anomaly has occurred during the last quarter of a century. It appears that since shortly after World War II there has been little or no increase in leisure time available to families, despite the fact that output per capita, and consumption per capita, has increased by more than 50 percent. In addition, the range of choice in consuming discretionary income has surely been increasing at least as rapidly as in the past. This seems strange. One would have thought that increasing affluence would make further income increases relatively less desirable as compared to additional leisure in which to enjoy the affluence. How can this be explained? We will return to the issue later, but one possibility may be mentioned now. Suppose that conditions have made feasible an increase in the intensity of consumption, so that more activities can now be carried out in a given time span than was true in the past. This greater "efficiency" of consumption could produce the observed effect, as for example in the case of the Californian who can now have his skiing weekends while continuing to play tennis after work during the week. His need for additional money to support the two habits may exceed his need for more time off to practice them.[2]

Risk

The twentieth century has brought with it quite dramatic changes in the nature and intensity of the risks associated with human existence. Perhaps the most dramatic has been the improvement in the health status of the population. Eighty years ago about one child in every six who was born live was dead before it reached its first birthday, or about seven times the present rate. Substantial but less dramatic declines in death rates have occurred for all the younger age cohorts. The live population of today is made up of individuals who on the average are bigger and healthier than their earlier counterparts. Not only is this change unequivocally in the right direction, but it is also sufficiently fundamental to have very substantial indirect effects on the attitudes of the population. Early death is a traumatic experience for all who are close to the victim, and so a major cause of enduring sadness has been much reduced.

The reduced risk of death and loss of health is more fundamental, but probably the reduction in the risk of loss of income that has occurred in the twentieth century is quantitatively much greater. Life and accident insurance, pensions and social security, unemployment insurance and relief, and property-loss insurance have come in this century to be a part of the daily life of the average citizen. On the whole they offer reasonably good protection against catastrophic income loss—loss that threatens physical survival—and typically give the family a cushion of protection against the unexpected, which at least provides time to make some adjustments. Once again it is difficult to appraise the effects brought about by this increased level of security on the attitudes of the citizenry, but surely it is plausibly very great.

One important risk has moved the wrong way, namely, the risk of war. A wag has suggested that the risk of war varies directly with the size of the armed forces. He is probably right on the whole, though that does not mean that reducing the size of the armed forces will always reduce the risk of war. But the *proportion* of our citizens in the armed forces is twenty times higher now than it was in the 1890s, and they are provided with many times more equipment per soldier now than before. Furthermore, the nuclear age has changed our very notion of the word disaster, which now embraces the possibility of destroying the human race during the course of some war. Again, the effect of this on attitudes is unknown but plausibly very great.

Another kind of risk whose change is rather hard to evaluate is associated with opportunity. Equal opportunity is a slogan that most Americans take seriously, while recognizing that in fact the probability of a given level of success in society varies greatly with the circumstances into which one was born. Has this changed much since the turn of the century? Unfortunately, the available information does not give a clear-cut answer. Rather rough data on intergenerational mobility suggest that things have not changed greatly. In both periods there was quite a good chance that a son could rise above his father's station a bit, but sharp rises in economic status are quite rare.[3] The economy was growing in both periods, and in both periods the proportion of relatively higher status jobs was increasing; both these factors contributed to upward mobility. There was, of course, one major qualitative difference in changes in economic status: A far higher proportion of the earlier generation improved their lot—or at least hoped to—by a move from farm to city. We also know that in both periods there were special barriers to advance raised before certain ethnic groups and women, but that these barriers are now much lower for most, perhaps for all, of these groups.

Organization

Turning now to changes in the organization of social life, there has been, first of all, an important change in that primary organization, the family. It has become smaller; the average number of children per family has declined; three generations live under the same roof far less frequently; and the proportion of unattached adults in the population has increased. Two of the probable causes of this development are of special interest. The first is that the smaller size is a consequence of the changed economic status of children, combined with the increased range of choice modern society provides. The farm family welcomed the additional hand to the family table, one who could be put to useful work only a few years after birth. Urbanization has largely destroyed the economic productivity of children, and the increased range of choice, particularly of mobility, has reduced the chances that children will be of much financial support to parents in their old age. And the range of choice affects the parents, too; they have options for doing other things than raising children with their time. The second factor of interest is that in earlier times the large family was a sort of social-security institution, helping to insure the individual against some of the economic consequences of disaster. That is less true today (we of course are not discussing the emotional and psychological support provided by family life), so one of the more important traditional functions of the family has been substantially reduced in importance.

This reduction in risk-bearing by the family has, as noted above, been more than compensated by risk-bearing by other organizations; otherwise, the risks of health and income loss could not have been reduced. And this brings us to the other organizations of the modern world, whose most notable feature as compared with earlier times is their large size. Risk clearly has played an important role in the desire of private organizations to grow. As with the extended family, the larger the unit, the better the chances—other things equal—that it has the resources to protect itself against some given catastrophe. Growth is a form of self-insurance, and this desire to reduce risk is clearly a part of the story.

But it is far from being the whole story. A few hundred large corporations, each employing many thousands of workers, produce perhaps half our manufactured goods and supply a dominant proportion of many other services, from banking and insurance to air travel. But there are also many medium-size and smaller businesses, hundreds of thousands of them, who survive and grow in the modern environment. If risk were the only factor, they would no longer be around.

However, compared with eighty years ago, it is the ubiquity of large organizations in the contemporary United States that stands out. There were some monopolies then, but the more dispersed character of American economic life ensured that there were far fewer instances of a single firm controlling a substantial portion of the sales in a national market. And, of course, daily contacts with the products of large organizations are almost unavoidable to an American today, while being far from typical then. Large private organizations are not restricted to profit-oriented business. Universities, political parties, even charities now tend to come in the large economy size.

But in terms of relative change, perhaps even more striking has been the growth of government. Federal and state governments can control a quarter of the national output of goods and services as a consequence of the flow of funds through their treasuries. Eighty years ago it was about a fiftieth, and the idea of stabilizing the economy through short-term variations in government policy was unheard. Indeed, given government's size, such a policy could not have been of significant effect even if the desire had been there. Nowadays even conservatives speak of the federal government as managing the economy. Education, defense, welfare, health: each of these is a service that is provided on a massive scale to its citizens by American government. Learning to live with—and probably to work in—bureaucracies is one of the new lessons that the twentieth century has required Americans to learn if they are to function effectively in their new environment.

Bureaucracies not only have to be lived with; they also have to be managed. And this is yet another of the major changes between then and now. The management of large groups of individuals who are cooperating in the carrying out of complex tasks is itself a difficult and complex art, which has come into its own in the twentieth century. A hundred years ago the Prussian state bureaucracy was considered by many to be the very model of efficient management. But a new style, developed essentially by American industry and drawing upon a variety of new sciences and technologies, such as operations research and the computer, has given an entirely new perspective to the idea of management.

Finally, it should be noted that science-based technology lies at the heart of most of the transformations wrought in our lives over the past eighty years. Technology is not a *deus ex machina*, an exogenous force that manifests itself from time to time to bring some new change to our lives. It is instead an integral part of affluent capitalist society, which fosters technical change and then also fosters social adaptation to the new possibilities released by the technical change. This interactive process, historically unique in its breadth and depth, is perhaps the most basic fact that must be understood if the nature of affluent capitalism is to be grasped.

The Affluent Fifteen

The affluent society may have first appeared in the United States, but if so we have not retained our monopoly. Other societies have been growing rapidly and narrowing the gap between the situation of their citizens and Americans; indeed in one or two cases the United States may already have been overtaken. Because any two countries adjacent on the scale of affluence tend to be rather close together, there is no sharp dividing line at the margin between the affluent and others. But, roughly speaking, there are about fifteen nations that can reasonably be said to have entered the charmed circle of affluence.[4] In addition to the United States, they are: the Scandinavian countries (Sweden, Norway, and Denmark), Britain, France, West Germany, Switzerland, the Low Countries (Belgium and Holland), the Commonwealth countries of Canada, Australia, and New Zealand, Austria, and perhaps Japan and Finland.

Unlike the United States, many of these countries' average families were anything but affluent at the turn of the century. In many other ways too these countries were very different one from another. One would not have wanted to put very many of them in one classificatory box in those days, though our contemporary list does include five of the six leading industrial countries on the eve of World War I (Russia is missing), and at least a certain amount of economic modernization had already occurred in all of them.

However, at the moment we are interested in the similarities among the affluent fifteen. In the first place, all of them *are* capitalist in that around two thirds to three fourths of their output is controlled by private-market-oriented production and distribution organizations. Second, they are all genuine parliamentary democracies in which officials chosen in competitive elections play a central role in political decision making. And third, they are all open societies with an important range of civil rights granted their citizens; the openness of these societies is sometimes questioned, but in comparison with any other group of countries in the world today on the openness dimension, the affluent fifteen would come out on top.

Government plays a similar economic role in all these societies. It engages in massive efforts in support of health, education, and welfare and serves to exert some control over the distribution of income among its citizens. Also, these governments engage in very similar processes of economic management, designed to control the level and rate of change of economic activity and the rates of inflation and unemployment. Though they grow at different rates, all of them have been growing rather steadily for many decades, and all have achieved a substantial portion of their recent increases as a consequence of the application of technical innovations to industry and trade.

This is a rather striking collection of similarities. However, there are also some differences. There is a variation of at least 50 percent in levels of output per capita, much greater variation in the population size, considerable variation in the extent of nationalization of industry and public welfare programs, the size of the armed forces, the quality and quantity of higher education, and so on. Nevertheless, given the the diversity that exists in the world today, it is the similarities among these countries that really catch the eye.[5]

Probably it is fair to say that these countries are much more nearly alike today than they were eighty years ago. Is this an accident, or are there some forces pushing them all toward sameness? Let us look at another small list of facts that seem relevant to this question. First and most obvious is the similarity in technical change in all these societies. Throughout the twentieth century, this group of countries has been the world's center for both scientific and technical progress. And each country draws on essentially the same pool of basic knowledge in designing and producing the machinery, the buildings, the vehicles, and all the rest of the paraphernalia of modern life. Of course, any given new process originates in one country and is introduced on a practical scale at different times and rates in the others. But affluent capitalist countries tend to be the world's leaders in introducing new processes and also tend to use basically the same processes. Clearly this promotes similarity.

Second, there is considerable evidence that a family's specific demands for goods tend, as income rises, to be determined more by the level of that income than by cultural or national background. Even the casual observer has noticed the rapid move toward automobiles, the new household durables, and packaged foods in Western Europe, and his insight is supported by more comprehensive studies of demand. This is not to deny differences, but the big story of the last few decades is the increasing similarity in the patterns of demand between these countries and the United States.[6]

Another feature of the affluent fifteen has been their relatively high level of political stability over the last quarter of a century. Despite the challenges of the sixties, perhaps only France among them had its political regime seriously threatened during that period (though it suffered two crises, in 1958 and 1968). This record cannot be matched by any other group of countries. Continued political stability, particularly in open societies, suggests two things: that the direction and pace of change is acceptable to broad ranges of the population, and that underlying processes are being given the chance to work themselves out undisturbed by undue institutional rigidity or fragility.

The political stability issue can be looked at from the opposite point of view with revealing results. Thus, one might ask whether there are any countries that, though not yet within the charmed circle of affluence, are nevertheless within striking distance, and if so, what sorts of political institutions and stability they possess. The answer is that institutions comparable to those of the affluent fifteen are possessed by a majority of the ten or twelve countries in the on-deck circle. But perhaps most interesting are two of these countries whose institutions are strikingly different. It appears that the very different institutions can only be maintained in those countries by the presence of foreign troops on their soil. The two are East Germany and Czechoslovakia.

As a final point on our list, the interdependence among the affluent fifteen should be mentioned. They trade far more with one another than with any other group of countries. Their businesses are intermingled, with a great deal of investing by the citizens and firms of one country in the productive activity in other countries (with, of course, the United States taking the lead in this activity). They are intimately involved in various kinds of governmental cooperation, serving as the central members of the Common Market and of NATO and playing the dominant role in the management of the world's monetary system. There is a tremendous amount of movement of both goods and citizens from one country to another. Their economic processes are, as a consequence of all this, highly interdependent, holding out the promise of still more coordination of future behavior.

There is one overwhelming change in the relationships among these countries now as compared with eighty years ago. Instead of the desperate rivalry that led many times to the brink of war, and finally in 1914 to the real thing, these countries have shifted to a pattern of mutual cooperation. No pair of them has come close to a serious risk of war in the past quarter of a century or so. This, of course, could change, but once again there is the suggestion that underlying forces are pushing in the direction of greater rather than lesser levels of cooperation. Indeed, there appear to be some respects in which all, or at least most, of these countries are becoming a single social entity.

Conclusion

In their general thrust the factors associated with affluent capitalism in the United States—increased leisure and consumption and range of choices for consumption, decreased risk, especially of loss of health and income, and increased large-scale organization—are equally associated with the other nations we have called affluent capitalist. And of course the five traits we have just assigned to the affluent capitalist group— increasingly similar technologies and tastes, political stability, increasing cooperation and interdependence with the other affluent capitalist countries—also apply to the United States. One cannot avoid the suspicion that the basic organizational traits shared by all of these countries— predominantly private-market economies and parliamentary democracies —have something to do both with the generation of affluence and with the development of these various traits. Over the course of the next three chapters a discussion of basic institutions should nurture that suspicion, and perhaps turn it into firm conviction.

CHAPTER 4

Markets and Affluent Capitalism

SELECT the twenty or so most affluent countries in the world today. Eliminate from the list the rich oil states, and then the remaining fifteen or so countries will *all* be capitalist democracies. The oil states are eliminated from the list mainly because their wealth is not the product of a generations-long process of economic, social, and political transformation, as has been the case with all the other affluent countries. So unequivocal an association of affluence with a particular set of institutions must have some power to explain events, and particularly the events and patterns that we noted in the last chapter. In the present chapter we take a look at markets, in order to see what their contribution has been to the rise of affluent capitalism, and how it in turn has come to affect them. We begin with positive aspects of market operation and then turn to the various ways in which markets malfunction in the contemporary world.

Markets and Deals

In essence, a market is a collection of deals; some of them are merely offered, but many of them, billions in the United States every year, are actually closed. And every deal has the aspect that any one of the parties can say, "No deal." Thus, in a well-functioning market society there is a tremendous amount of essentially voluntary activity going on. It seems quite plausible that this aspect of the market is most central to the resolution of much of the potential conflict that resides in modern society.

The voluntary nature of deals is closely related to another aspect of a well-functioning market. This has to do with the special position of the status quo in a market society. Each participant tests the deals he may be interested in against his present situation. At any point in time he can preserve that situation by refusing to make a deal, and so any deal he makes must be a little better for him than what he already has. From the point of view of conflict resolution this is fundamental, since it tends to tie behavior to the existing state of affairs. In effect, the little deals constantly being made for the millions of goods produced in an affluent society carry with them an implicit acceptance of the status quo as the position from which each participant will try to better himself. And the voluntary nature of the market limits each participant to those ways of bettering himself that will also better the lot of some others, for if he cannot do this he is not going to be making any deals. This tends to eliminate potential deterioration in the status quo for some members of society.

However, there are limits to the stability of this status quo. Very few members of our society have made deals for the permanent supply of essential goods, and even fewer produce such goods for themselves. Consequently, the participants do have to come onto the market from time to time in order to survive. The special status of the status quo holds at the margin, so to speak, and provides the basis for those deals that involve, for the participants, at best a modest change in their current situation. If one is coming onto the marketplace because survival is at stake, any deal is likely to seem highly involuntary. However, as noted, this is not a frequent occurrence for families under affluent capitalism.

Small-scale adjustment, or adjustment at the margin, is really the central feature of the market. Its institutions are adapted to this purpose, and its strengths and weaknesses stem from that fact. For example, consider the role that prices play. The great advantage that prices and money offer is increased understanding by the participants of their alternatives. Because all those millions of goods have their price tags attached, when someone tells you that the price of a good is ten dollars, you immediately can relate this to the other deals that are available to you. Ten dollars spent to buy this good is ten dollars not available to buy three of those or twenty-five of those others. Generally, that kind of information can greatly improve the individual's ability to make the right decisions. In thinking about this point, it is worthwhile to remember the changes in consumption noted in the last chapter. The tremendous increase in the variety of goods and services available to the contemporary consumer makes heavy demands on the decision maker's information-processing capacity. In such an environment the market-based price system can be a real timesaver, thus allowing more time for the enjoyment of the goods in use.

But pricing is also extremely important in generating the meeting of minds between buyer and seller, of facilitating the market process itself. In negotiating a deal, each party will be seeking persuasive comparisons in order to convince his potential partner that the deal he proposes is the right one. These are of the familiar "I-can-get-it-down-the-street-for-less" sort, but the point is that the market throws up a tremendous body of information about just what in fact *is* going on down the street. Facing participants with a well-structured reality, so that they do not have to waste a lot of time shooting down obvious pipe dreams of their fellow dealers, is something that the market system tends to do very well.

This property, too, is most significant for the market when it is serving as a marginal adjustor, for then the available price information is at its most relevant. A very big, complicated deal, a deal to take effect over a long time span, or a deal made when the status quo is changing very rapidly: These are situations in which expectations tend to be created that some prices will be very different from current market quotations. In this situation knowing what is going on down the street is of much less decisive importance, and the price system structures reality less effectively.

Prices and money are important facilitators of market processes, but one must bear in mind that they are just that: facilitators. What people want is goods and services, and the market and its attendant institutions are the social devices by which these goods and services are produced and allocated.

A similar facilitating institution is competition. One of its most important if rather simple functions is the pressure it creates for prices for the same kind of good to become equal. If there is a wide price spread for a good, the word will get around. The buyers who had been paying higher prices will go looking for lower-price sellers, and vice versa for the lower-price sellers. The result is the generation of relatively coherent information to the users of markets. Competition also tends to weaken opportunities for sellers to discriminate by finding those people who are willing to pay more for the good and charging them more.The relative stability of the prices of many consumer durables —such as washing machines and television sets—over a decade or more of rising price levels in the fifties and sixties is no doubt a product of the intense competition among the major producers and marketers. Given the complexity of modern economic life, this simplification of the information about available alternatives is in itself a major facilitator of exchange.

But there is another feature of competition that is at least as important. This is its incentive effect. The competitor who does not keep up with his rivals in terms of quality and price tends to lose customers. This aspect of competition has been borne in on Americans very strongly in recent years by the emergence of German and Japanese automobile manufacturers as extremely effective competitors for American producers. When not carried to destructive extremes, competition seems to be one of society's most useful processes for generating energy. In the voluntary marketplace these energies are directed by the system itself to serving the demands the participants have brought with them.

All in all, the market is really an extraordinary social mechanism.

It has been with us for thousands of years. Parts of ancient Greece and Rome used it extensively, and the industrial revolution brought markets to the fore in Western society along with the factory and machine, substituting steadily for the more traditional devices of social allocation. We have had a great deal of experience with the operation of many different kinds of markets. They are the central object of study of economists. They are by no means perfect. But perhaps this brief description suggests some ways in which they can serve as fundamental resolvers of conflict in society. Armed with these general notions, we now turn to twentieth-century markets under affluent capitalism to see how, in fact, markets have been performing.

Markets and Affluent Capitalism

Markets nurture affluence in a very direct way. Each deal tends to improve the economic situation of the parties to the deal without reducing that of others. This can, of course, happen simply by redistributing a fixed quantity of goods among participants in the economy through the market's voluntary processes. Usually, however, there is production involved as well. The seller has done something to the product to make it more valuable. The completed deal is his hallmark of success, for someone has demonstrated a willingness to pay for the more valuable product, to give up other things in order to get it. The summing up of all these increases in value as measured by the prices at which the deals were made is our conventional measure of the national product of an economy. So markets are indissolubly linked to the growing affluence.

Two additional features of the market system that foster affluence should also be noted. The first is the way in which markets divide up incentives. Individuals who are looking for groceries or skis or an apartment or a car can concentrate their search on one item at a time, and of course the same is true of producers and distributors. The producer of skis need not concern himself with groceries—except when he himself is hungry—but can concentrate his attention on getting out a useful and profitable pair of skis. This may not seem like anything very startling, but consider for a moment the only known alternative to markets. That is a bureaucracy, which plans the output of the entire economy and also plans how much will be allocated to the various distributive outlets. In this case the production agency whose attention is constantly being diverted to problems of the production of many different kinds of goods—from steel to computers to soap—must also plan the production and distribution of skis. The basic link between producer and consumer, provided by the profit incentive in the market system, is much diluted in a bureaucracy. The result is predictable: a relatively inefficient search of the consumer's wants by the system of production.

For example, a few years ago the Soviets reduced the price of bread in a subsidized attempt to give the consumer a break. As a result, farmers found it profitable to feed the bread to pigs rather than to the intended consumers.

Corollary to the market's division of incentive to match the size of consumer demand for the goods and services wanted is the way information, too, is effectively organized in a market economy. The consumer and the producer can limit their investigation of market conditions to those markets in which they actually expect to deal. Furthermore, as noted above, prices contain a great deal of information about the alternatives available, and in a form relatively easy to process. In a bureaucratic economy neither planner nor consumer can escape a more intensive and less efficient accumulation of information, for prices, not being the product of deal making, cannot convey the same kind of information to them. Given the amount of information consumed in a modern economy, this is no mean saving. Visitors to the Soviet Union and Eastern Europe are struck by the importance in those bureaucratic economies of knowledge of the *availability* of goods. When word gets around that fresh meat or wool sweaters are available, the queues form swiftly. A Czech study indicated that the average household spent a dozen hours a week standing in line. Also it should be remembered that these extra information and acquisition costs are being borne by consumers who are far from affluent.

Affluence generated by a market system has a kind of piecemeal structure to it. Growing affluence means that a deal here and a deal there are securing the increased value of goods in the hands, in each case, of only a few participants in the economy. In a very real sense affluence is viewed not as an entity, not as a property possessed by the nation, but as something that is gradually being accumulated by the various individual participants in the economy. Once again the market captures the essence of the liberal notion that what counts is not nations but individuals and that big changes are made up of a large number of small ones.

In addition to supporting affluence and its growth, markets also have a role to play in supporting political stability. For example, markets have a way of turning a potentially highly divisive economic allocation process into one in which a strong harmony of interests seems to emerge. The divisive potential stems from the fact that much of the economic activity often seems to be simply a matter of pie slicing, in which more for one party means less for someone else. The market tends strongly to mute the divisiveness for the same reasons that it promotes affluence. In the first place, a growing pie is easier to slice without hurting some participants. But most important is the division of incentives and the focusing of attention on deals made one at a time. In this situation each party to a successful deal is in contact with someone who is also a party to a deal—and others who are not party to the deal are not hurt, in the sense that they remain as they were, in the status quo. Because of this, pie slicing turns out to be a bad metaphor for what is happening in a market system, and certainly one that the participants in the deal-making process do not see as central.[1] For example, the redistributions carried out by the market exchange process are the product of wholly voluntary exchanges, in which all rational participants are gainers and none are losers. Thus there emerges out of apparent conflict a kind of harmony of interests.

Consider the following market redistribution. Suppose a key factory burns down, resulting in a considerable scarcity of some good. Prices for this good will rise, and income will be redistributed away from consumers of the good and toward the remaining producers and holders of stocks. This is, in a sense, an unfair redistribution. But there is no coercion involved. The consumers are not required to cut back their consumption of other goods in order to obtain this one, and many of them do not; those who do are revealing just how badly they want this good, and each individual consumer is free to make this decision. Of course, there is likely to be some resentment. But that resentment is also likely to be relatively short-lived, because of the market's self-correcting mechanism. The higher price stimulates the owners to try extra hard to get the destroyed factory at least partly back into service as soon as possible, importers seize the opportunity to make some extra profits, producers of substitute products try to enter the market, and so on. As boycotters swiftly learn, "direct action" is not of much use against the forces of the market, which, acting impersonally, has great powers to defuse potential conflict.

Of course, the market does not always produce a harmonious pattern of perceptions in the participants. At bargaining time for a new labor agreement in the automobile industry, each side clearly perceives that much of the gains obtained by one side will be at the expense of the other. But the importance of such situations to the economy should not be exaggerated. In the first place, much of the bargaining has to do with how expected productivity gains are to be shared, so that in fact neither side is "giving up" anything more substantial than expectations. And second, this particular bargaining situation does not fit our standard description of deal making, for there is no status quo to which each side has free access. If the company says "no deal," what it gets is not the status quo but a strike. So for this rather big deal the market does not work quite as we have described it. Bargaining of this kind is especially prominent in affluent capitalism, and so inevitably the question is raised: Has not the nature of markets changed fundamentally with the rise of affluent capitalism?

It is certainly true that things have gotten a good deal more complicated in the twentieth century. Affluent capitalism has grown in almost every way imaginable. Organizations have become bigger, markets have become larger, deals have become more numerous and more complex, the time horizons of market participants have expanded, and technical change has proceeded at unprecedented rates. All of these things have implications for the functioning of markets, so we must try to get a feel for the extent to which the changes may have made it more

difficult for markets to function as effective resolvers of conflict, pre-
servers of social cohesion, and generators of general affluence. We turn
now to the various ways in which markets can fail to do their job.

The Five Malfunctions of Markets

1. First we have the familiar problem of **monopoly**. Monopoly
eliminates the incentive effect of competition, opens the door to discriminatory practices against classes of consumers, concentrates resources
in a few hands, and probably reduces the incentive toward technical
change. It conjures up images of stagnation and corruption, of lack of
vigor and conservatism. How has the problem of monopoly been dealt
with under affluent capitalism?

It is important to note at the outset that monopoly is not really all
that common. Studies of concentration in manufacturing industry suggest that, on balance, the degree of concentration has not changed
dramatically in the United States in the twentieth century.[2] The reason
is in part that the markets have grown along with the firms. Today's
giants in any given industry are several times larger than their earlier
counterparts, but so are the markets they serve. The typical pattern is
not monopoly but oligopoly, in which a handful of large producers generate a large fraction of the sales of a given product. And the opening
of the European Common Market has probably meant an intensification
of competition in that other major segment of affluent capitalism.

One reason for this preservation of at least small-group competition
has to do with the interaction of technical change with the degree of
monopoly. For any given product there tends to be a number of sufficiently close substitutes so that the single monopoly producer cannot
afford to behave as a monopolist without risking a massive loss of business. And if there are not close substitutes and the producer is reaping
super profits as a result of its monopoly position, the word could not
help but get around—capital markets function as major purveyors of
just such information. This, in turn, would offer a powerful incentive
for some other firm to try to invent a close substitute for the monopolized product in order to carve out a share of that lucrative market. In
a dynamic economy there are many firms familiar with the process of
developing and marketing such new products. So the dynamism itself helps to inhibit both the formation and the persistence, once
formed, of monopoly. And the competition can come from sources that
are apparently quite different in nature.[3] Under the leadership of a
large, complacent firm, U.S. Steel, the American steel industry compla-
cently languished technologically for several decades. But this complacency has disappeared in the last decade or two, mainly because of
competition coming not from within the industry but from other materials, especially aluminum and plastics, and even to some extent

from competition by foreign steel manufacturers. And U.S. Steel has paid the price of complacency in falling profits. In a dynamic economy there are few monopoly havens.

Nevertheless, there are some monopolies, and there are circumstances under which others might have formed and survived—for example, by controlling available supplies of basic minerals—were it not for government intervention. It is very difficult to appraise the effect of antitrust laws; clearly, their direct effects have not been very great. But powerful businessmen have a strong propensity to know what the antitrust laws say, and what sorts of cases are prosecuted successfully by government lawyers. Probably their mere existence on the lawbooks has had a considerable inhibiting effect. In a number of cases the government has resorted to regulation in the attempt to control the bad effects of monopoly, which is often cheaper than attempting to eliminate it entirely.

In sum, monopoly is always a threat in a market economy because of the prospects of large gains it holds out to the successful monopolist. But the market system itself has a number of checks on the generation of monopoly, and these tend to be relatively more effective in a growing society oriented toward technical change. And, in addition, there are various ways by which government can inhibit monopoly without abolishing the market system.

2. A second though related market malfunction is created by unequal bargaining power. For example, the starving family without enough salable resources to survive may be able to postpone the final disaster by making a few deals, but that does not make the market look good. Its very impersonality becomes a part of the problem in such cases, the problem being that the market, working from the status quo, takes the existing distribution of income as given and then supports marginal movements away from it in which no one loses. But this is too little to help those whom circumstances have stripped of their ability to earn income. However, this is not a central issue in affluent capitalism, partly because affluence has raised the ability of the overwhelming majority of families to withstand catastrophe far better than before, and partly because of government intervention to provide a material welfare floor for the poorest citizens. Essentially what has happened is that there is now general recognition that this *is* an important type of market failure, and affluent capitalist governments have stepped in to compensate for the failure.

The opposite kind of unequal bargaining power is also troubling. The largest hundred or so firms outproduce all the remaining manufacturing enterprises combined: They produce half or more of total manufacturing output. This is an issue with important political implications, to which we will return in discussing government in the next chapter. At the moment, however, we are concerned with economic power that the top hundred firms may use in the marketplace against the rest of the market economy.

It is important at the outset to distinguish between relative size and absolute size. As noted already, large relative size is nothing new, and there are comparatively few markets that are effectively monopolized. Deals are much bigger than they used to be, especially where the top hundred firms are concerned, but even the large individual deals are still relatively insignificant. The billion-dollar deal is still a rarity—and even it is a small fraction of a percent of the trillions of dollars worth of deals made every year in the United States. And, most important, deals still have at least two parties to them, and each side, by general agreement, is still concerned to get the best possible deal, which means getting more for less—the same as ever. Firms may be relatively more growth-oriented than before—though that is a controversial point—but by all accounts profits remain a very important consideration, and growth and profits often point the businessman in about the same direction. In all these respects, then, the market remains, generally, very much as it was before, despite the very large increase in the size and number of deals and in the size of the larger firms.[4]

But this is not to argue that there have been no significant changes in market behavior. The increase in designed products and in design change, and the complexity of modern production, have forced both an extension of business time horizons and an attempt to deal somehow with the uncertainty that increases rapidly the farther you look ahead. Increase in size of firm and in numbers of different products is one effective response. The large firm's advantage is similar to that of a gambler coming to the table with a big stake to play, rather than a small one. His risk of ruin for any given amount of play is diminished the larger his stake. Also increasing the variety of product markets a firm enters helps to average out the risks that are specific to individual markets. But these are not the only ways a firm can reduce the uncertainty under which it operates. An obvious risk reducer is advertising, which attempts to supplement the consumer's favorable attitude toward the product by various psychological devices, some of which are informational, some of which, by establishing reputability, are aimed at increasing the consumer's reliance on a standard of product quality, and some of which are simple attempts to play on snob appeal, impulse, and the like. Much of this advertising may be defensive rather than offensive, aimed more at preventing rivals' advertising campaigns from luring away customers than anything else. However, it should be emphasized that each of these large firms is in competition with other firms for the consumer's dollar, and that moving the goods out and the money in is still basically what it's all about.

Probably the most fundamental change brought about by the development and institutionalization of big business in its present multiproduct, basically oligopolistic form has been the emergence of an inchoate form of planning. Planning in this sense has grown out of the expert negotiators' awareness of the vital interests of their opponents. Remembering that these modern deals do tend to be fairly large and complex on average, and so require some, often considerable, negotiation, it becomes clear that a good deal maker needs to have a sensitive awareness of the limits to which his potential partner in the deal is willing to go. Beyond that line lie the opponent's vital interests. Any threat to these is a survival issue for the opponent and will be met with great hostility. Deal making is essentially striking a compromise. One may at times subtly threaten, but the ultimate deal will not be worth much unless it preserves the vital interests of both parties.

Though he was not operating on markets, Henry Kissinger's celebrated "shuttle diplomacy" gave the world a series of lessons in this aspect of deal making. A hard-headed defender of American interests, he was nevertheless extraordinarily sensitive to the wishes and political necessities under which his bargaining opponents had to operate. And each successful conclusion of a deal tended to be preceded by a brief period of crisis, in which success hung very much in the balance. A series of less significant but otherwise similar marketplace examples are familiar to sports fans, namely, the process of bargaining between star players and team owners and the negotiations associated with shifts in team franchises.

In this framework, the rise of a fairly large number of giant firms has meant that serious threats to the vital interests of opposing firms, of potential partners in deals, is excessively costly. Size brings with it great power to defend—and to attack. And this is the heart of the system of business planning, a kind of mutual understanding that the competitive game will be played out in such a way as to preserve the vital interests of each party. Achieving institutionalization—that is, general acceptance among big businessmen—of this kind of rule of the business game was no doubt a difficult and long-term process. Its story has never really been told, and perhaps it cannot be since so much of it occurred in the process of negotiations behind closed doors. But we know something of how this same process has operated in other parts of society and will return to it later. At the moment it is enough to note that this business-planning system does not seriously inhibit the intense competition among large firms for lucrative contracts. Nor does the ultimate basis of business planning—preservation of the vital interests of the parties to a negotiation—represent a fundamental departure from the bargaining of earlier times.

3.   One of the most important lessons the twentieth-century affluent capitalist societies have learned is that the market system is not stable. This is a third way in which markets can malfunction. Left to their own devices and seeking their own benefit, the participants in the marketplace will produce not an optimal economic outcome but a chaos of economic ups and downs. Some controls on market functioning from outside the system have become generally recognized as necessary in order to keep overall supply and demand in balance at a level close to full employment. In recent decades government techniques of intervening in financial markets have been developed so that, when properly used, they are capable of varying the level of economic activity as a whole, while having a relatively balanced impact on most sectors of the economy.

However, the question of economic stability can be raised in areas other than that of the overall level of market activity. For example, if income distribution is substantially affected by market activity, the concentration of wealth in a few hands might increase to the point at which monopoly does in fact become widespread, which could pose an obvious threat to the stability and survival of the market system. This has not happened; by and large, affluent capitalist societies have quite an unequal distribution of income, but the relative shares going to the various income groups have not changed dramatically over time. The economy behaves as if there were some underlying tendency for *relative* opportunities (that is, the opportunity to increase present income by some given *percentage*) to be quite similar in all reaches of the income distribution except the very bottom. But though that may be true, and may be substantially a product of the operation of market forces, there is no very satisfying explanation of the phenomenon. We do not know enough about the distribution of opportunities to be able to say with confidence that they have had that sort of distribution or that the distribution will persist. But there is a plausible political explanation for this relative stability to which we return in the next chapter.

The farm problem, which is still very much with us, illustrates the way instability can raise issues of public policy. Because the demand for food is relatively inflexible (price inelastic, as economists would say) and harvests somewhat volatile, the market prices of farm products tend to fluctuate sharply. The fluctuation in price serves to reduce variations in amounts consumed as, for example, stocks are drawn down and the level of exports reduced in response to a price rise, and therefore is socially useful. However, this price volatility can be the ruin of the farmer, particularly the family farmer who rarely has the financial power to survive a few bad years. This creates pressures from farmers for government assistance, and since farmers almost everywhere are still quite numerous and politically well organized, the politicians are willing to listen. Because markets are so hard to control effectively by bureaucratic regulation, especially highly decentralized ones, regulation often does not work very well. But clearly the more productive farmers have been greatly helped by the farm subsidy program, and there is a case for intervention of some sort to protect the efficient farmer from extremes of price volatility.

4. A fourth way in which the market can fail to do its job properly is through what economists call externalities. Essentially these amount to violations of the rule that deals start from the status quo. When a factory begins to emit noxious smoke, it is changing the status quo for those who breathe the vapors, even though there has been no deal made between factory and breathers. When the deals that produced the factory are made between the factory owner and machinery manufacturers and other owners of goods relevant to the factory's production, the presumption that operation of the market is not affecting nonparticipants to the deals no longer holds. The more externalities there are, the less well the market is doing its job of welfare-increasing resource allocation.

Externalities have become a major and increasing problem as the twentieth century has progressed. A principal reason for this has been urbanization, for in cities individuals have many more contacts that are not mediated by deal making; for example, that factory smoke would cause little trouble if factories were few and widely dispersed in the countryside. Also, participants in the marketplace generally do not have much incentive to take externalities into account in their deal-making behavior. It is almost impossible to get the citizens who live near a polluting factory to band their resources together to make it profitable for the polluting factory to desist. The costs of putting together such a deal are just too great. Nor can one expect profit-oriented enterprise to engage in much voluntary action to reduce externality costs if, as is usually the case, doing so would cut into profits and growth. This is one of those areas in which the market cannot reasonably be expected to do the job.

The automobile emission-control issue illustrates the way in which an interactive relationship between markets and government regulation can improve economic outcomes. The profit-oriented automobile companies were unwilling individually to undertake substantial emission-control research, for the higher costs would hurt their competitive position. When controls were mandated, government and private research produced some answers. But then along came the oil crisis and dramatically increased the cost of fuel, thereby changing the tradeoff between atmospheric pollution and fuel economy. This signal produced responses by both the companies and government, altered the control standards, and is, at this writing, bearing fruit in a whole series of new, cost-efficient, low-pollution automobiles. The various private companies took different tacks in dealing with the issue so that, under competitive market pressures, we are in effect carrying out a vast experiment to determine the most effective solution, while continuing to use automobile transportation.

5.   A final way in which markets may malfunction results from the nature of the information available to users. It is always costly to become informed. We have already noted that the ideal market tends to organize information efficiently; but that does not always hold in practice. If markets are volatile it costs much more to collect enough information to be able to predict future prices and availabilities. At times the future is so uncertain as to be virtually impenetrable; then information is of little use, no matter how much you have of it. In between the ideal and this extreme lie the situations typically encountered in practice, in which you can find out more about the future, but only at increasing cost. Also there have been times, some of them quite recent, in which the malfunction of markets has reduced the value of information that can be obtained, on the one hand, while the complexity of operations on volatile markets has increased the cost of obtaining useful information, on the other. The stock market and most commodity markets have been behaving this way in recent years. The resulting increase in the level of uncertainty is clearly a market malfunction.

But informational malfunctioning of markets goes beyond the costs and benefits of extracting the classic price-quantity bits from the market. There are important problems of knowledge and understanding that can affect market functioning also. The most frequently mentioned of these has to do with demand manipulation, the asserted ability of large firms with large advertising budgets, and the capacity to design products to suit the needs of the corporation rather than the consumer, to structure consumer tastes. To the extent that this is possible, the market becomes a sort of sham operation, in which the consumer is simply snookered into buying what the corporation wants him to buy, even though the good gives little real satisfaction.

A still deeper attack on the knowledge malfunction of markets comes from those who assert that the market inculcates crass and commercial incentives into its participants. The very act of dividing up incentives so that the individual concentrates only on what is useful to him has its other side: Consumers are in effect taught by the market not to consider the social consequences of economic behavior. The impersonality and unconcern that results is, assertedly, of devastating impact on the quality of life under capitalism.

There is no question that corporate advertising budgets are far higher today than they have ever been in the past. Nor can anyone doubt that the consumer frequently has been led down the garden path by false or misleading advertising, or that business attempts through such things as "institutional advertising" to inculcate probusiness beliefs into the citizenry. These have all been areas in which the malfunctioning of markets in the twentieth century has been quite generally recognized. Then too it will be remembered from chapter 3 that one of the most fundamental changes in twentieth-century society has been the rise of a welfare concern by affluent capitalist governments. Recognizing the relatively selfish motives that inevitably come to the fore in market behavior, society has expanded dramatically the role of government in protecting citizens against the income losses that can result from participation in the market sector. The increased relative power of producers over consumers has been compensated for by a continuing series of legislative acts designed to make the producer tell more of the truth, and to hold him more responsible in cases of failures of his products.[5] Once again, this is an area of market failure that has come to be widely recognized by the citizenry of affluent capitalism and that has led to substantial efforts to design a political framework to mitigate or eliminate the consequences of such malfunctions.

Conclusion

Perhaps enough has been said to convince the reader that the market is a powerful and effective but by no means flawless social device for the allocation of resources. The twentieth century has posed new problems of complexity and scale for the market to cope with; but basically it seems that the market has proved capable of coping, capable of

handling trillions of dollars a year in deals in a way that seems almost routine, at least to the outside observer.

But the twentieth century has also brought with it in increasing
strength problems that the market has not been able to deal with effectively. These are our Five Malfunctions: monopoly, unequal bargaining power, instability, externalities, and imperfect information. As a
consequence government has assumed a rather steadily increasing role
in economic decision making. Some of this increase has been the result
of an increase in our knowledge of how to deal with market problems
that have always been with us. The control of economic instability
through monetary and fiscal policy is perhaps the leading example of
this kind of increased government intervention in the economy. But
some of the increase has also been the result of increasing malfunction
of markets. Perhaps the best example of this is the large body of laws
and regulations protecting the consumer from the consequences of using a far more complex bill of goods than was available in the past.
In concluding this chapter on markets it is essential to note that everywhere in affluent capitalism, even though government has become
much larger, most goods and services continue to be produced and
distributed through the private-market sector. That this allocation system continues to do the job better than any known practical alternative
does not seem to be seriously in question in these societies' political
discussions.

CHAPTER 5

Political Business

ONE of the liberal economist's standard stories explains the allocative function of markets in terms of the political mechanism. Consumers come to the marketplace with their dollar votes, casting them for the various goods they desire, up to the limit of dollar votes available. These votes are tallied, and the producers respond to the results of a series of such elections by producing the goods that are getting the dollar votes. The analogy is, of course, imperfect, but it serves to suggest that there are democratic elements in the market process, that there really is a sense in which the people choose the allocation of resources that results.

Suppose we try to turn the analogy around and, using what was said in the last chapter about markets, appraise the functioning of parliamentary democracy. The results are not the same; indeed, it is now the differences between the two processes that seem to stand out. In the first place, in the political marketplace choice is far more limited. The dollar voter chooses among thousands of items and can usually see and feel and operate the item before deciding to cast his votes. But with real votes one is typically choosing among a very few, often only two, candidates, and even then there is only very limited information as to just what package of policies the candidate will support. Second, coercion is a much more central aspect of the political decision. Of course, the dollar votes of others do affect my market options via the cost of the good and even its availability—very few kinds of goods will be produced solely to satisfy my dollar votes. But in the political arena the policies that you vote against will be put into effect nonetheless, if you are in the minority. In the marketplace you can say "no deal," but not in politics. This means that the status quo does not have that central place in the political analogy that it does in market theory. Consequently, there is a constant threat of having one's position worsened by the political action of others. Also the political process has some inherently nonmarginal features to it, that is, situations in which alternatives are being compared that are very unlike one another. Situations involving coercion often have that property, but especially noticeable is the existence of big decisions in politics. War or peace is perhaps the best example; it is largely an either/or proposition, it being hard to have just a little bit of war, and the costs in both lives and treasure can never be called marginal. And finally there is the indirectness of politics. The formal decisions are not made in the market by the participants but in the political buildings of the national capital by politicians who may or may not represent any given participant's interests.

These features of parliamentary democracies have led to strong criticisms of the institution from both the left and the right. But in fact the marketplace provides a bad analogy to politics. It grossly understates the ability of the political system to respond effectively to the wishes of the citizenry. Parliamentary democracy in its various forms has displayed a high degree of flexibility and adaptability in practice, and especially so over the past quarter of a century. The problem with the market analogy is that it neither shows how people in a democracy are actually organized for political decision making, nor does it capture the various devices by which the parliamentary system does in fact use the status quo and marginal change as the basis for its decision making.

The heart of the political success of affluent capitalism lies in the institutionalization of an establishment that contains within itself the main interests that have aroused the concern of the citizenry of these countries. This of course is not to say that every group has gotten what it wanted. It would perhaps be closer to the truth to say that under establishment politics *no* group gets exactly what it wants. The essence of the operation is compromise, based on the status quo, the compromises being negotiated in an open environment where prime facts do tend to become known. There are many parallels with the operation of the market, but there are also differences stemming from the nature of the services supplied by each institution. Striking the appropriate balance between market and polity, by taking account of the strengths and weaknesses of each, has been one of the central social tasks of affluent capitalism in the twentieth century.

The Establishment in Politics

Our discussion of the political process in affluent capitalism, and particularly in the United States, begins with two definitions. An *interest group* consists of a group of individuals who are more or less organized for the purpose of protecting and developing a limited range of interests they have in common. An *establishment* is a collection of interest groups who recognize one another as being influential and who operate through government in protecting and serving their interests. Interests may be highly organized and affluent groups with paid lobbyists, a national organization, and even a number of legislators in their pocket.

Or they may be loose groupings of individuals who obviously have certain interests in common and whom legislators recognize as important because they supply votes and perhaps precinct work at election time. To qualify as an established interest, a group merely needs to be recognized as influential by the other participants in the political decision process.

The establishment interests are the key political actors who serve to convert the formal political process into an essentially marginal political adjustor, that is, an adjustment process that tends to avoid dramatic changes in the short run. A sort of ideal-type picture of the process goes as follows: An issue comes up one way or another, and this results in a proposal to the legislature, formally introduced by a legislative representative (de facto) of an affected interest group. Legislators, following that body's formal rules, look over the bill to see how interests with which they are concerned are affected. Some may propose alternative legislation. Some of these are immediately seen to be unacceptable to important interests and are discarded. But those remaining are all likely to have the property that some interests benefit and some lose if the proposal is enacted. This leads to amendment of one or more proposals. It may also lead to packaging and logrolling—that is, one way or another to combine the given bill with bills dealing with other issues until one finds a package that benefits some interests and causes no substantial harm to any other established interest. In this form our original issue has produced a piece of legislation.

As an example of the process we may consider the Food and Agriculture Act of 1965. The major element of the bill called for a four-year program of price supports and production controls for half a dozen major crops. Favored by farming interests such as the National Farmers' Union and the Grange, the bill was first proposed by the administration and constructed under the supervision of Agriculture Secretary Orville Freeman. The House Agriculture Committee, whose members consist of representatives of interests strongly affected by agricultural legislation, made certain changes in the original proposal, for example by adding a price-and-production control scheme for cotton. When the bill reached the floor, however, opposition developed, and its passage seemed uncertain. At this point the Democratic leadership agreed to tie the bill to one proposed by liberal Democrats to repeal state authority to pass right-to-work laws. This changed the votes of enough House liberals (i.e., urban representatives), who were afraid of the effects of the farm bill on consumer prices, to ensure passage. Many other aspects of the bill came under intense bargaining and were adjusted accordingly, though the final bill bore a fairly close resemblance to the initial administration proposal.[1]

With our establishment now put into the voting game, we can return to the question of marginal adjustment. Consider first that vital property of effective markets, the use of the status quo as a starting point in deal making. One of the most notable features of parliamentary systems is the existence of so-called veto groups, which are claimed to be a very wide variety of interests who have the power to prevent any particular piece of legislation from being enacted. At times this power to prevent legislation has perhaps been exaggerated by proponents of the veto-group thesis, but there is obviously a variety of devices open to an interest that opposes a piece of legislation.[2] These run from proposing an alternative that has wider appeal to logrolling to prevent passage, from the many delaying tactics permitted by legislative practice to mounting a national publicity campaign. It does not always work, of course, but we are not dealing with perfection when we talk about markets, either. There are declining industries just as there are declining interest groups. The point is that a recognized interest has great power to deflect any particular piece of legislation. And this clearly serves to keep the status quo in the foreground of legislative deal making.

A second facilitator of marginal responses has already been mentioned—namely, the overwhelming dominance of economic issues in modern legislation. If one is to build a legislative package that meets the establishment specifications, it must be possible to add a little bit here and take away a little bit there. This kind of divisibility is essential to compromise packaging. And it is a feature that is typically present with economic issues. When measured in dollar terms, one can have a little bit more or less national defense, even a little bit more strategic defense and a little bit less limited-war defense—and, in fact, the breakdown can get much finer than that. The same applies to education, health, and welfare. Very important in all of this, of course, is the element of time. Initial legislation may establish some fundamental new government activity but at the same time provide very little financial support. Time then serves to delay, but it also serves to turn substantial change into a series of marginal changes, with some forms of deflection or sidetracking feasible at each step of the way. That is why a serious establishment legislator has a lot of homework.

As mentioned, the market sector of society does not function as a perfect marginal adjustor of the status quo either. The twin issues of unemployment and inflation serve to illustrate this particular problem, for in their more virulent forms they can destroy the status quo as a datum. There is now essential consensus that control of these phenomena in affluent capitalism is a proper function of national government. Clearly, the establishment interests as a group have a stake in performing this task with reasonable success, since having a well-defined and stable status quo is essential to the legislative process we have just been describing. Can inflation be effectively controlled by government? The first thing to note is that the less serious the problem, the easier it is to control it, a relatively minor problem being more amenable to marginal adjustment. It is probably also true that larger scale unemployment is easier to deal with than, say, double-digit inflation, because the necessary spending can be packaged relatively easily so as not to hurt any established interests. But once inflation gets going, it is harder to stop, and it becomes more difficult to design a package that does not hurt an established interest.

This is a still-unresolved issue in the political economy of affluent capitalism. However, one should not make too much of it. The under-lying structure of these societies has proved to be extraordinarily stable, and this provides a substantial cushion in dealing with any given problem. For example, in a recent issue of the *Wall Street Journal*, a proposed solution to the continued 7 percent inflation rate called for labor to forego wage increases for one year. This, it was asserted, would end the major pressure on costs and permit businesses to hold prices steady. Having done this once, inflation would be broken and no special restraint on the part of either business or labor would be re-quired to keep prices reasonably stable in the future. Even assuming it would work (among other things it does nothing directly to mitigate oil and other commodity price rises) such a program is unlikely to get past the representatives of wage earners in Congress.[3] On the other hand, it might be possible to build some sort of package, along the lines of the farm bill logrolling operation mentioned above. Broader unemployment coverage, expanded union organizing rights, favorable modification of almost any of the relevant laws currently on the books: These might be thrown into the hopper to obtain general acceptance of the affected interests. But clearly this would have to be a very big package, and its consequences for the affected interests would be relatively uncertain. Such a program would be much more difficult to put together than a conventional package involving marginal adjustments only. On the other hand, labor, management, and all the rest of us are hurt by in-flation. Given the underlying stability of our political economic system, there is a reasonably good chance of enacting occasional packages of legislation of this magnitude. Besides, most of the time the inflation-unemployment issue is divisible into much smaller packages—basically of levels of government expenditure and taxation—for purposes of political bargaining.

One final point about the establishment—perhaps the most funda-mental point of all. This is the question of how an interest comes to be established and how it preserves its position as part of the establish-ment. The answer is really very simple, and it parallels the answer given for the comparable situation in the marketplace. An interest becomes accepted by the establishment when it acquires the ability to seriously threaten to damage some important establishment interests. The—again, ideal-typical—establishment response is to bring its panoply of bargaining tactics to bear on such an interest with a view to coopting it into the establishment. The most recent example of such cooptation in the United States is discussed later in the chapter.

For an interest that is already in, the underlying establishment rule is recognition of mutual vital interests and acceptance of a pair of self-denying ordinances. The first ordinance says that a political deal must not seriously affect the vital interests of an established interest group. The second says, given that the first rule is honored, an estab-lished interest will not threaten the stability of the regime. The system is then built around a continuing acceptance by the participants that it is always in each group's interest to accept a marginal solution rather than try to improve its lot by threatening the regime, the establishment structure.

It is this aspect of establishment politics that explains labor's peculiar position of limited opposition. Labor as a political interest accepts the rules of the game, the constraints of the self-denying ordinances, and in return is recognized as an established interest. This gives labor regular access to marginal adjustments in its favor and something approaching veto power over legislation that would seriously damage its position. The resulting balance of power has paid off for labor in terms of many different types of legislation, most recently including substantial improvement in the status and security of workers' pension rights. In appraising the consequences of labor participation in the establishment game, it is important to look at gains over a period of many years, for they can, and I think do, add up to a dramatic transformation in the influence and security of organized labor vis-á-vis business. Furthermore, this tendency seems to be built into the structure of affluent capitalism, since it has been occurring in the other affluent capitalist societies as well as in the United States.

Some Major Interests

Everywhere under affluent capitalism business is the major established interest. There are not very many pieces of proposed legislation that do not affect business, and money and power are obviously related in these societies. In the United States, business has been the most powerful interest since the turn of the century. In some other affluent capitalist societies, most notably Germany, business has acquired this central position during the course of this century.

This situation has led some observers to charge that business is the dominant interest in these societies, that, in fact, it is business alone that really runs the show.[4] But, once again, this mistakes the way in which political business is done in a parliamentary democracy. The marginalization of political issues by the political process serves strongly to emphasize a situation that should be clear enough anyway: On a great many issues business is divided within itself. Even radicals have been speaking recently of a major split between businesses supplying strategic weapons to government and those supplying limited-war weaponry. Exporters and importers are often at odds on specific issues, as are businesses doing primarily domestic business and those extensively involved in foreign trade. Any given pollution issue tends to concern directly only a limited number of businesses, and usually there are firms who expect to profit from supplying whatever goods will be needed to control pollution. Public housing affects everybody's taxes, but a number of businesses will profit from the contracts. And so on.

In addition, at the margin legislation is unlikely to be a general threat to business. There certainly are times when most of big business will want to put on a more or less united front, but that is not the typical case.

A second interest, labor, is also everywhere a part of the establishment. Its influence cannot be doubted by anyone familiar with the legislative history of labor-related bills in these countries in recent decades. The process of its establishment as an interest is a central part of the history of all affluent capitalist countries during the course of the last hundred years. There has been a strong trend to secure the organizational status of labor unions, to protect the bargaining position of labor against management, and to provide, secure, and extend various kinds of income support, from unemployment compensation to health protection, from minimum wages to pensions. The details of the legislation vary widely from country to country, but the general thrust is very similar. Each year sees a variety of mostly marginal attempts to change various aspects of this large body of legislation, some of which are successful and some of which are not. Nevertheless, both the trend and the gross state of affairs are unequivocal and quite similar as one moves down our list of affluent countries. Labor has the power to obtain much legislation that has substantially improved its economic situation.

In some affluent capitalist societies, such as Sweden and Britain, labor-based political parties have come to power and had majority control of their parliaments for a period of years. One of the most striking consequences of this is the very limited effect it has had on the relations between labor and business. One might perhaps be able to make the case that labor is relatively better off in such societies than in societies where a labor-based party has never held such a commanding position, but it would not be at all an easy case to make. The marginal adjustment process continues, and although the weights assigned various interests may change, the outcomes are not strikingly different. This suggests strongly the underlying stability of the major interests in these societies; it also suggests that there may be similar underlying forces generating this structure. And, most important for us at the moment, it suggests that once this establishment is institutionalized, the electoral process is unlikely to produce results that will actually put one of these interests in a position to ignore the other interests in formulating and passing legislation.

An interest need not be tightly organized in affluent capitalist society in order to function effectively. In each of these societies there is probably a major interest that has nothing to match either labor or business in the way of organization, and yet that has been a major force shaping the structure of much current legislation. This has sometimes been called the meritocratic interest, since much of its thrust has been to provide relatively more equal opportunities for access to the better jobs in the society for the children of people in the broad middle reaches of the society's income spectrum. From the point of view of this group, educational reform to provide access to professional schools and colleges has been perhaps the major vehicle for expressing their political desires, but other issues, such as the expansion of jobs and the provision of general basic security, have also been very important considerations.

The process by which the meritocratic group has made itself felt politically has varied from country to country. In nations that already had a labor party, this was the group that had to be won over to labor's side if labor was ever to obtain a majority. In other societies, this group's interests were felt partly because of their power as a voting bloc on some issues, partly because they could supply both work and money to the parties; in other words, once this common body of central political wishes became known, the interest became effective without a central organization. Often, of course, temporary alliances were formed, for example with the teachers' lobby, whose interests overlapped. It is largely out of this meritocratic group that the ecology interest has been formed in recent years. But the variability of its forms of organization and the ubiquity of the opportunity-enhancing legislation favoring this large middle group do suggest that the existence of such an underlying interest was responded to by politicians, who of course themselves tended to be members of that group.

One other ubiquitous type of established interest needs to be mentioned—namely, the executive agencies of government. Far more than business, these agencies rely on instruments other than votes at election time to influence the outcomes of the governmental process. Their advantages are considerable. They have much control over the execution of policy, with consequent ability to delay and distort the lawmakers' intentions. They are located close to the seats of power, and often possess far more of the information relevant to legislative decisions of interest to them than do any of the other participants. And, being largely staffed by civil servants, they have greater continuity of tenure than politicians, with the advantages of experience and knowledge that this brings.

These are formidable advantages, but there are real limits to their exercise in the face of a hostile political establishment. Civil service jobs are not *that* secure, changes at the top of these hierarchies are well within the reach of elected officials, and all political agencies have perforce developed their own information services. Nevertheless, they are a set of powerful interests, perhaps none more so in recent years than the bureaucracy that contains the armed forces. Defense issues inevitably have nonmarginal components, there is a loose but at times powerful alliance among business, labor, and the defense agency, and there are personal attachments formed by legislators as a result of their own military service.

However, in appraising this troubling phenomenon it is important to keep some perspective. Defense plays an important though variable role in all affluent capitalist countries but, except perhaps in France, it has not thrown up a "man on horseback" as a serious threat to the political structure. For nowadays defense, even in the United States, is embedded in a very large and very complex body of interests. Once again critics tend to focus their attention on the stability of the status quo—in which large defense expenditures are "institutionalized"—when in fact that is an admirable quality of the system; they then ignore the changes at the margin, where the defense establishment always gets less than it wants and not infrequently suffers genuine defeats. The supersonic transport, the B-1 bomber, the giant aircraft carrier, nuclearization of the navy: These are a few of the most recent examples of defeats; the full list would run over almost every area of procurement. With well under 10 percent of the national product to work with, even during the Vietnam war, the defense interest, though firmly established, seems thoroughly tamed by the establishment game.[5] The other interests retain the power to circumscribe defense, while still providing the defense establishment, at the margin, with an incentive to accept a little bit of what it wants rather than running the destructive risk of going for higher stakes.

There are other established interests in these societies, and it is no doubt useful to emphasize once again that the interests identified above are by no means monolithic. But enough has been said to suggest that interests play a similar role in all affluent capitalist societies in supporting marginal processes of change and that there are very striking similarities in the structure of interests across these societies.[6]

The Why of Stability

Let us run briefly through the phenomena that seem to be most important in producing this underlying structure of stability in contemporary liberal societies. These phenomena are important not only in understanding affluent capitalism, but also in understanding the rather different situations in other parts of the world.

Perhaps most important is an attitudinal symbiosis between market and polity. To put it less pompously, the marketplace gives citizens of affluent capitalism a training in economic deal making that is precisely what is needed for effective political deal making. In both cases the essence of deal making is the art of compromise, and this in turn requires each participant to develop some awareness of the interests of others. Further, it encourages him to accept the marginal process of change and to resist the temptation to threaten to overthrow the regime as an instrument for improving his own position. There is, of course, a high transfer value of these skills when one turns to politics. There are many differences of procedure and much information that is highly specific to the political deals currently at issue. This must be learned by any marketeer turned politician. Once it is acquired, however, the actual processes of negotiation are strikingly similar. Game theory is a very esoteric branch of social and mathematical theory. But it has also been a topic of very great interest to students of the actual operation

of government and market. This is not because powerful theorems have
been developed in this field that could be applied directly to understanding the real world, but because much of its terminology captured the
great similarities in bargaining behavior in *both* situations.

It might be difficult to overestimate the importance of this kind of
marketplace indoctrination in keeping the political system functioning
as primarily a marginal adjustor. Of course, it is also very difficult to
appraise empirically. But it seems quite clear from what we know of
other societies that the art of deal making is not something we are
born with, and that to do it effectively is no mean accomplishment. To
live in a society that is constantly giving one lessons—though, of course,
not always free ones—is to have a long leg up toward keeping things
running smoothly.

A second phenomenon, to which we have referred a number of
times already, is the importance of maintaining the status quo as the
point of departure for deal making. Nothing more will be said at the
moment about it, except that it is probably best appraised by thinking
for a moment about the unsettling effects something like a depression
has on an individual's future expectations, and the effect this in turn
may have on his political orientation.

One aspect of the process of marginal adjustment from the status
quo is quite distinctive, and often is unappreciated. Our knowledge of
the consequences of various social policies is always limited. Such
knowledge as we do have tends to be heavily concentrated on understanding what things are like at or close to the status quo. Thus, a
political process that keeps us close to our best knowledge of consequences tends to be stabilizing. By keeping changes marginal we are
less likely to generate substantial ill effects as a result of some unexpected consequences of any particular political deal. This is, for
example, a major reason why Clausewitz was wrong. Going to war is
definitely a nonmarginal decision, fraught with uncertainty as to consequences, and so much more than the continuation of foreign policy by
other means.

Economists in their work have responded enthusiastically to this
environment. Their tools of analysis are adapted primarily to just this
kind of appraisal. The burgeoning of forms of analysis of alternative
government policies relies heavily on measurements of cost and benefit
derived from the marketplace, and which are of real use primarily for
making comparisons of policies that are not too far removed from the
recent past, which provides the data on which the measurements are
based. This relatively new branch of economics has provided more
effective analyses of the consequences of making alternative marginal
adjustments in the status quo and so has lent added weight to this
knowledge phenomenon as a relatively stabilizing political force.

If the status quo is important, so, too, is the direction of movement from it. Clearly, the marginal adjustment process works more
smoothly when the economy can be expected to generate an increasing
flow of goods and services. Adjustments to the needs of all groups can
be kept positive while still permitting the relatively more powerful to

obtain their aliquot share. That economic growth which does not entail sudden dramatic structural changes supports the political process and tends to preserve stability, there can be no doubt. And this is a benevolent circle; a stable political process tends to make it more likely that fairly steady economic growth will be achieved.

A final phenomenon, which no doubt rivals the first in importance, is the adaptability of affluent capitalism's political system. When people's allegiance shifts a bit in the direction of labor or business, this is reflected in the relative strengths of the established interests in the parliamentary decision process. But even rather dramatic shifts in electoral strength do not imply substantial shifts in the political decision-making process itself. Rather, they mean that those marginally adjusted deals will have more and more subordinate clauses favorable to the group whose power has increased. This kind of adaptation is no doubt a major factor in keeping such economic parameters as the distribution of income in such a relatively stable state.

But there is also a second kind of adaptability in the system, and one equally as important. This is the process by which the establishment accepts and co-opts a new interest into membership in the establishment. One of the best examples of this process has been the recent political history of black Americans. A few decades ago, blacks were a group with special political interests but with essentially no access to the establishment to get them considered. The process of assimilating blacks into politics did not begin until they were able to make themselves felt as a threat. This came partly as a result of legal processes, and partly as a result of the civil rights movement, which was led at first by whites. But as the process continued, blacks acquired sufficient experience to take control of the political organizations and the new leaders tended to be more radical, threatening serious disruption of society if their demands were not met. These demands were *not* met. Instead, forces were assembled to make clear that society's defenses were in order. But signals also went out that black needs would receive political consideration if presented by a leadership that was willing to follow the basic establishment rules. The incentive to form this leadership was strong, and what we have been witnessing in the last decade is the institutionalization of the black interests as an effective, though not yet a major, interest in the American political establishment. That this process closely parallels familiar processes of deal making in the marketplace cannot be doubted.

Perhaps the best overall test of the stability of functioning of this political system comes from the evidence on income distribution. As was noted in chapter 3, over the postwar period in the United States there has been a rather puzzling stability in the shares of total income going to each segment of the income distribution. However, this is not surprising, given an effectively functioning establishment. There is, of course, no strict proportionality in the sharing of benefits and costs among interest groups as determined by the political process. Such an outcome is precluded by variations over time in the relative influence of groups, in the structure of issues, and in knowledge of the consequences of implementing any particular policy. But roughly, one would expect the establishment to work so that no major segment of the population that is effectively represented would suffer substantial relative loss at the hands of the political decision process. And that is exactly what has happened. Since there is no other very plausible explanation of this phenomenon, we may take it as positive support for the thesis that an establishment, consisting of a number of interests, no one of which is dominant, has in fact been at the center of political decision making in the postwar United States. And somewhat similar phenomena have been observable elsewhere in affluent capitalism.[7]

The Limits of Marginalism

The above list of contributors to the stability of affluent capitalism's political process can also be turned on its ear so as to become a list of things that, if they go wrong, can promote instability. It must be emphasized that this stability, this basically effective functioning, is not a product of impersonal forces that we can perhaps analyze but cannot influence. It is, instead, the product of more or less deliberate human action. If the human participants do not perform their parts in the drama with reasonable skill, the system cannot survive, however favorable the "underlying forces." It is in the nature of deals for the negotiators typically to reach a crisis point when each party is pushing very hard to improve its position and using the threat of "no deal" to the utmost. Getting across this minicrisis takes skill and determination and experience. And when the deal is more than marginal—for example, when the system must adapt to the rise of a new interest—the quality of management must be relatively high if the process is to function effectively. The system is operated by individuals and its success depends on individual performance. What we have seen in this chapter is that the environment of politics in affluent capitalism is favorable to effective decision making. The opportunity to build a better society is there, but not the certainty that it will be achieved. That depends on individuals.

CHAPTER 6

Management and
Planning

THE SKYSCRAPER has become a central symbol of modern life. All over the world, but particularly in the downtown sections of affluent capitalism's major cities, there are these tiered workplaces of modern business and, to a lesser extent, government. What they symbolize is one of the great revolutions of the twentieth century, for neither the skyscrapers themselves nor most of the activities that go on within them existed at the turn of the century.

A less visible but even more important manifestation of this revolution is suggested in a few American statistics. Around the turn of the century about 10 percent of the population of high school age was in high school. Now the figure is closer to 80 percent, and over a third of the college-age population is in college. The occupational structure of the country has changed dramatically, too: a doubling in the proportion of professional and technical personnel in the work force, a near doubling in the proportion of managers, officials, and proprietors outside farming, a threefold increase in the proportion of clerical workers, a 50 percent increase in the proportion of sales workers, a fourfold increase in the proportion of federal civilian employees, and a twentyfold increase in the proportion in the armed forces.[1] All affluent capitalist countries have experienced similar, if not always quite so dramatic, changes.

In the last chapter the meritocratic pressures toward supplying better access to education were mentioned. This strong belief that education opened opportunity's door was an important impetus on the supply side to the above changes. But that would have counted for little if there had not also been a very large change in the kinds of workers that the economy demanded. Working together with forces tending to increase the proportion of more skilled workers among manual occupations, these were major factors in producing the dramatic increase in realized opportunities that has also been a hallmark of twentieth-century affluent capitalism.

These phenomena are essentially a product of the revolution of organized knowledge, a revolution that is itself a product of the twentieth century and of developing capitalism. It has a strong technological base in computers and other modern information processors. And it has a vital base in the accelerated accumulation of knowledge about how the world works. But the catalyst that puts these things together and makes them work is modern management. Modern management itself has three basic components. One is a change in the nature of large-scale organizations. There are not only many more of them, but they operate in ways very different from how they used to. Another is the rise of planning, a great increase in the making of deliberative choices among complex future courses of action. And, in a sense sandwiched between these two and supporting both, is control, the development of detailed and complex understanding of what is going on and what has been going on in a complex organization. This chapter is a brief survey of the nature and significance of these phenomena.

The Corporation

A hierarchy is a pyramid, each successive layer smaller than the one below. Eighty years or so ago, the Prussian state bureaucracy was widely regarded as a model large-scale organization, and the pyramid was a good metaphor for its structure, suggesting durability and neat, well-defined relations of command running through layer after layer of officialdom until finally at the apex was to be found the prime mover, whose orders set the whole structure to functioning. It looked very good on paper, but in practice this form of organization tended to become extremely unwieldy and inefficient beyond a certain rather modest size. There were many reasons for this. One was that the people in the middle of the pyramid typically had little or nothing creative to do and were so hamstrung by the flow of instructions that taking any nonroutine action was made very difficult; it also tended to be costly because, since there was no effective way to tell whether some unit in the middle of the pyramid was doing its job very well or merely fairly well, the criterion tended to be: If you have heard nothing bad about the unit, it must be doing all right. And officials had a tendency to report information that reflected well on their unit but to distort any possibly unfavorable information, the result being that a piece of information starting from the bottom of the pyramid frequently reached the top in unrecognizable form, if at all. It was very difficult for the leader of such an organization to take effective action when facing these obstacles.

The table of organization of a contemporary corporation might still have, vaguely, the pyramidal shape, but neither the metaphor nor the facts is very relevant for this new form. The modern organization is a far looser, more flexible institution, with a strong task orientation and a very different role for top management. Of these factors the most important for the rise of modern management was the recognition of the possibilities and requirements for task orientation within a large organization. There is a natural unit in a large business corporation—namely, the factory. It is a natural unit of control, and, of course, every organization that contains several factories will tend to have a manager for each.

But from the point of view of a business corporation, the important thing to recognize about the factory is that it can be not just a technical unit, defined essentially by the technological and organizational requirements for getting the goods out, but can also be an economic unit—that is, a unit responsible for the procurement of the materials that flow into the factory and for the sale of the products that flow out, as well as for what happens inside. Once this was accepted, the power of the factory manager was, of course, greatly increased, since procurement of inputs and sales of outputs are both complicated and crucial tasks. But there was one special advantage to increasing authority in the middle of the pyramid, which made it worth the risk in terms of potential power loss by top management. This was the fact that—in principle—quite a simple criterion could now be used to judge the manager's performance—namely, the principle of profitability. From a technical job whose appraisal required a complex analysis of esoteric engineering and organizational details, the position of factory manger had been transformed into an economic job whose performance could be appraised in terms of dollars and cents.

This change turned out, in fact, to have a very important side effect; it dramatically changed the motivation of our middle-level bureaucrat. He now had a relatively well-defined responsibility and a relatively free hand to act in the factory and in the marketplace. He responded—or, rather, those who succeeded in getting these jobs responded—with a burst of energy. For many people challenge tends to bring out their best efforts, and people of this kind can be selected in advance with some success. Certainly these jobs were now challenging. Anyway, the shift to task orientation dramatically reduced the seriousness of the problem of the stagnant middle in these large organizations.

It might seem but a short step from this reform to letting the task become wholly autonomous—that is, to going back to the era of relatively small independent business. But nothing like that has happened, and for good economic reasons for the most part. In the first place, the survival risks for single-factory firms are very serious. Acts of God and similar phenomena peculiar to a particular plant or region or industry can bankrupt even the well-managed smaller firm; armed with the resources of a large firm with many factories under its control, these difficulties are averaged out and the well-managed factory survives despite short-run reverses.

Second, there is a variety of supporting activities that a large firm can supply more effectively than a smaller one. Among these research and development stand out; the larger firm can afford to look ahead farther and to invest more heavily in such activities. Also, a large firm can usually borrow money at far less cost than a smaller one, yet another scale economy.

This brings us to the new role of top management. Stripped of its day-to-day control of production and marketing, what is left for it to do? The activities mentioned in the last paragraph are, of course, very important. All major investment decisions, including investment finance, are typically made at this level. To be made well, such decisions must reflect an overall appraisal of the prospects of various sectors of the economy, and the resources to do this are simply not available to the smaller businessman. Some control is exercised by top management over price policy, especially in oligopoly markets where the zeal of the managers might threaten to lead to a destructive price war. And, of course, top management is centrally concerned with personnel. This becomes one of its most potent weapons both in improving performance of the firm and in controlling the behavior of the autonomous units. Freed from excessive concern with detail, it appears that the broader tasks remaining to management can be performed more effectively, so that decentralization has served to increase rather than decrease top management's ability to affect outcomes in desired directions.

Finally, the increase in flexibility needs to be noted. Given the kinds and rates of changes in almost every sector of the economy, this is a fundamental desideratum. Compared with the older form of bureaucracy, there is a strong aura of the experimental about the modern corporation, a willingness to reorganize units, change the criteria of performance, raise or lower the level at which a particular decision is made—in effect, to respond to problems by making a wide search for potential answers. No doubt this is related both to the looser, more open nature of the organization as well as to the broader horizons and reorientation of both top and middle management.

General Motors was a pioneer in developing the techniques of running a decentralized corporation. First applied under the leadership of Alfred P. Sloan in the twenties, they have spread to most large American corporations by now.[2] Indeed, they are well on the way to conquering Europe, as Anthony Sampson's delightful book, *The New Europeans*, attests.[3] Of course, there have been many refinements of the basic concept over the years. For example, there has been a good deal of experimenting with alternative bonus schemes for rewarding management, though the trend in recent years is to emphasize managerial performance in terms of the key variable, rate of return on investment, and product-market share. And adapting to the computer has wrought a dramatic new change in the nature and structure of corporate management. The real managerial revolution continues.

Planning and Control

By now it has probably occurred to the reader to ask: If this new form of business organization is so effective, then why do we have all those new skyscrapers full of people pushing paper around? The answer is straightforward: first, there is a lot more going on these days, and second—and much more important—what is going on is much more complicated. A not untypical product these days will have many of the following properties: (1) it took a few years of experimental work to design; (2) it took comparable amounts of work to design efficient methods of producing it; (3) a hundred or more different kinds of products are either used up in producing it or are fitted together as part of it; (4) these parts come from factories, mines, and the like scattered all over the globe; (5) marketing the product involves delivery to thousands of points all over the globe; (6) marketing also requires much market research, advertising, and sales effort; (7) because of the continuing improvements made in competing products, a winning combination of the preceding items will not last long, unless they are continually adjusted. One of those autonomous, task-oriented units we were just talking about may easily produce quite a number of such products.

Home office tasks are not exactly simple, either. Managing a financial position in today's world involves literally hundreds of daily choices. Deciding whether or not to put up a new plant to do some perhaps wholly new thing involves at least as many and complex issues as those described in the last paragraph. And someone has to handle the thousands, perhaps tens of thousands, of employees—not just keep their files in order, but keep *them* in order, willing and able to do the best job they can, and see that they are adequately rewarded when they succeed.

The central step in getting hold of all this is usually called control. The term comes from modern accounting and refers to the routinized procedures by which the operations of an enterprise are described. The task of the designer of a control system is to construct an efficient language by which each unit and subunit of an enterprise can communicate to others, but particularly to the home office. The special property of efficiency is the crucial item. To be efficient the language must be set up so that people talk only about things that are relevant for decisions that have to be made, that these things are talked about in a way that conveys clear understanding of relevant alternatives, and that all this communication is done in the simplest and least time-consuming way.

There is no need to attempt a description of such a language here. Obviously, it takes much organized information generation and processing to control the operations of a corporation that has, say, a billion dollars' worth of sales a year, produced in several dozen factories, has a few hundred million dollars invested in building new plants, and has some tens of thousands of employees. Such a firm will have hundreds of points at which decisions will be made that have a significant influence on the firm's future. The right information must get to each point at the right time, and the decision points themselves must be coordinated. The employer will have thousands of contacts with outsiders every day, and many of these too will have a significant influence on the firm's future. And the firm must monitor its environment carefully, from consumers to suppliers to governments in a dozen lands in order to prepare those decision points properly. Control is a massive as well as a complex problem.

The computer and its various support devices nowadays are often put into a large-scale organization as the "management information system." The information system organizes, processes, generates, and produces decision-relevant information, supplying in principle every decision point in the organization with the information that is available and relevant to that point's set of decisions. But, of course, the concept of control is what lies behind the design of such a system. Combining the computer-based information system with decentralized management has proved revolutionary in its impact on the efficiency of large business organization.

However, one central property of control languages must be mentioned because it seems to be missed by many observers of the business scene. Oddly enough, it is probably the single most central fact about the control of business. And that is that control systems are fundamentally based on the market, and particularly on the prices that the market economy generates. Comparisons of technical productivities of alternative processes make no sense; inputs and outputs are always a bit different as you cross over to a new process, so you are comparing apples and pears (which one is rounder?). But when you can compare costs in terms of dollars and cents, you have something to work with—namely, the same ingredient the business is set up to generate, dollars of profit. The information saving is tremendous, and that seems to be the real bottleneck commodity when it comes to the control of modern business.

That a very great deal of planning is necessary in the kind of environment we have been describing goes without saying, planning being the design of one's behavior in such a way as to make the future come out as profitably as possible. What *does* need to be noted is the way in which planning grows naturally out of control. In a rapidly changing environment much, perhaps most, of what we know about the consequences of various courses of action will be obtained from information on what those consequences have been in the recent past. And that is exactly what the control system is all about. Furthermore, it is oriented toward the making of decisions, so the information flow tends to support the development of hard information about all except those alternatives that are very substantially different from anything that has been tried before. Without an effective control system, there can be no effective planning.

But this brings us back to the role of prices and markets. If they are central ingredients of control, they can hardly fail to be central ingredients of planning, and indeed they are. Once again information on costs and sales, the ingredients of profit, are not only wanted in order to measure profitability but because of the tremendous efficiency in information processing they offer. For a relatively trivial decision a manager may only want a profitability appraisal of the alternatives. If the decision is a more important one, and particularly if there are differences among the staff as to which alternative is to be preferred, the manager will, of course, have to go some ways behind this calculation to appraise the differences. But he can choose the amount of effort he puts into the process because at almost every step of the way there is a summary of the situation in dollar and cents terms that he need not try to penetrate if he does not want to.

All this is true, provided the prices that are the basis for measurement really do reflect the terms on which alternatives are offered the decision makers. That is, the prices must be generated on markets, be the product of genuine deal-making behavior, if they are to reflect what, in the short run, one can do with a given amount of money. When that is no longer the case, as in wartime rationing or under central planning such as occurs in the Soviet Union, prices lose much of their usefulness for planning and control. This is a major reason why cost overruns become epidemic in such situations. Management's goals are shifted toward getting the goods out, and price-based costs are no longer viewed as much of a constraint. And much of the staff becomes less interested in monetary reward, seeking perks or payment in kind as money becomes less able, acting through prices, to command goods. If such a situation is allowed to continue for any extended period, the whole accounting system tends to become less and less relevant to business decisions. And those decisions become much more complicated, for there is now no simple way to compare the value to the firm of alternative combinations of outputs or inputs. Control has been lost.[4]

Of course, to some extent prices can be simulated, developed artificially from mathematical models of the environment, but in practice this has only worked for very limited groups of prices in very limited areas of decision making, such as some internal corporate decisions. The general environment must be based on real, deal-based prices for effective planning to develop.

It is often suggested that mangements of contemporary corporations are at least as interested in growth as they are in profits. The issue remains somewhat controversial, but it does not affect anything we have been saying about planning and control. For the measurement of growth, too, in a large corporation producing many products is inevitably carried out in terms of dollars and cents, and market shares in terms of proportion of total dollar sales. Those market-based prices also loom as a fundamental input to a growth-oriented corporate management.

Management in Government

This modern, task-oriented, flexible, decentralized organizational form is not entirely the product of industry. The armed forces of several countries were also pioneers in its development. Military interest probably grew out of the peculiar military requirements of the tank and airplane, which created opportunities for mobile warfare that could not be effectively controlled in detail from headquarters. A system of organization strikingly similar to that of the corporation came into existence during World War II, perhaps most notably in the case of the U.S. Navy, with its task forces serving as counterparts of the corporation's factory division and with headquarters in Honolulu and Washington serving the new top management functions.

In this different governmental environment the new organizational form has one major disadvantage and one major advantage as compared with the typical corporation. The disadvantage stems from the fact that the criterion of performance can no longer be profit and loss. The mission of the armed forces is not easy to specify; phrases such as "ensure the survival of the nation" or "deter aggression" are unspecific in their implications. War is what you are trying to avoid, but you cannot really tell if the armed forces are effective without a war. The corporation is always at war, and last year's balance sheet describes the results of the action.

The advantage the armed forces offer is a kind of commitment to the "product" that is fundamentally beyond the reach of the corporation. Young men will risk their lives for the nation, but not for soap. This means that the armed forces can rely on dedication as at least a partial substitute for the carefully designed incentive systems of business. Naturally, material incentives to performance are present in the promotion systems of all armed forces. But the tests of performance are weaker; hence the need for greater reliance on commitment.

Affluent capitalist governments today have quite a variety of agencies in addition to defense; perhaps the most central are those dealing with education, health, and welfare. Each of these possesses the same relative disadvantage and advantage as the armed forces. But many of them suffer from yet another disadvantage—namely, a far less effective personnel policy. The top management of a government agency in the United States is changed as a matter of course when the political party controlling the presidency changes, and this regardless of whether it has been doing an effective job or not. And the new management is further constrained in that civil service regulations sharply limit its ability to make substantial changes farther down the line. Inevitably, this means less effective control at the top, though there is general agreement that this is preferable to the spoils system that would result if the management of government agencies were given a free hand in hiring and firing personnel.

The important point to note about this situation is that it is not a product of inefficient organization but of the nature of the service provided. The services provided by government typically came under government control because the profit criterion could not be expected to provide delivery at acceptable levels. Such services often do not lend themselves as well to autonomous task specification as does the production of marketable goods, and even people with relatively similar political orientations may disagree sharply as to the quality of the service being provided. Fundamentally, the problems associated with the delivery of these services stem from the nature of the services themselves, not from the nature of government bureaucracy.

Nevertheless, it must be admitted that the management revolution has come to government rather late, really only in the past ten years or so in a few affluent capitalist countries, aside from parts of the armed forces. It seems likely that the tools of modern management can be brought to bear to improve substantially the effectiveness of government service delivery. For example, even though outputs of these agencies are not measured very effectively, the measurements themselves can be much improved by the development of a genuine control system. And on the cost side prospects are not so bad, since the basic criterion of government service is recognized in principle to be delivery of the appropriate level of service at a minimum cost measured in dollars and cents. The old-fashioned formal hierarchy in many of these agencies can be restructured to reflect a much greater measure of task orientation than presently exists. But in a political environment all this takes time, because these agencies are also caught up in the process of maneuvering for favorable positions in the deal-making process.

Conclusion

This chapter has described the heart of the "planning system" of modern affluent capitalism. There is a basic interdependence linking the internal decision-making processes of corporations to the processes of interaction among businesses. On the one hand, the usual market processes generate prices that reflect the results of intense bargaining among the participants and give all interested parties a dollars-and-cents measure of the terms on which alternative are offered them. On the other hand, these prices are used within the corporation to control the efficiency of the operation, and through future decision making to move the corporation in the direction of greater profitability and growth. Each part depends on reasonably effective operation of the other for its own success; in that respect it is a system.

And that brings us to one of the most exciting things about modern liberal society, namely, the scope that is offered for creative talent. The management operation we have been describing requires at almost every point and level skill, experience, and creative energy if the task at hand is to be carried out successfully. Deciding to do this rather than that is not a routine operation; or rather, after such decisions as *are* routine have been put onto the computer, it turns out that there is a vast array of decisions requiring the above traits. Whether in government agencies, the political arena, the corporation, or the marketplace, crisis points are continually emerging in the deal-making process, and only a relatively high level of skill will suffice to get across these points successfully. Of course, this means that each generation must face the prospect that success is not assured by the performance of those who went before. All we have really learned is that there is tremendous *potential* for dealing with basic human problems in an open, tripartite society fundamentally based on markets, democracy, and modern management.

CHAPTER 7

Developing Along the Main Line

The Main Line

AS YOU GO about the world these days you will find increasing reminders of home. That is really the theme of this chapter. But let us start with just one of those reminders; at least it is one for an economist—namely, the national income and output statistics. All over the world nations have economic statistics agencies collecting very similar kinds of information. Among these, especially among the nonsocialist countries, there are very roughly comparable data on national output. So let us take the dollar figures for output per capita for each country and, using that value as the criterion, line the world's capitalist countries up in ascending order according to it. This is what we will be calling the main line.

Again very roughly, we find that the main line runs from well below $200 per capita per year to well over $3000 per capita per year. For the moment we ignore those countries below the lower figure; we have already discussed those above the higher figure, for that is about where affluence sets in at 1975 prices. We can now begin to notice some of the properties of this fifteenfold range of the main line. The world's economies are pretty well strung out along the line so that any point on the line is quite close to a point representing an actual country. And second, if we consider per capita growth rates over the last decade or so, most countries are growing at a fairly rapid rate, historically speaking, so that any point on the line is fairly close to a country that has been growing. Figure 1 shows a selection of these growing countries. Clearly, rapid economic growth is being achieved by some countries all along this line.[1]

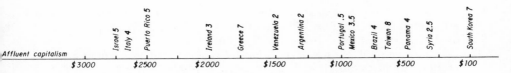

At this point an economist who concerns himself with such numbers speaks up: "We can do better than that. The main line can be used to predict the structure of production in a developing country. Give me just the country's place on the main line, its output per capita, and I'll predict fairly accurately the proportion of the country's output that is produced within its manufacturing sector and the proportion produced within its agricultural sector. I'll also predict the proportion of the employed population working in those sectors. In fact, I can go farther if you don't demand too much accuracy. I can even predict the level of per capita output at which the first paper mill is likely to be built, the first steel factory, the first modern plant in a dozen or more industries."[2]

Continuing in the same vein, our economist finds a number of differences in consumption patterns in these countries. But, he says, these differences are in considerable measure purely superficial, reflecting the differing distributions of the numbers of people in each income class. If you compare consumption patterns of families in roughly the same income bracket in countries over our spectrum, you are again far more struck by the similarities than by the differences in the proportion of consumption going to broad groups of expenditure.

The burden of these numbers will come as no surprise to the tourist who has visited several developing countries. In each country there is a big city with a downtown area that looks very much like the one back home, with similar buildings and layout, similar transportation, similar items in the stores, even similar programs on radio and television. The more developed country's cities are more numerous than the less developed one's, and the countrysides may be much different. But modern times are coming to all these countries via their cities, and in the cities it is similarities rather than differences that dominate. In cities and their inhabitants there is, above a certain income level, a universal demand for modern fabrics, modern foods, modern durables, cars, even for "modern" forms of recreation, from skiing to bowling and golf. Not since the days of the Roman Empire has this level of reproduction of the center's facilities in the periphery been seen.

But we still have not exhausted the properties of the main line. There are also connections, less close to be sure but nontheless there, between it and political and social factors. Affluent capitalist societies are all parliamentary democracies. Of the dozen or so countries closest to affluence, perhaps half are genuine parliamentary democracies; below that group democracy becomes relatively rare, and in the lowest group on our scale perhaps only India has recently qualified. This association may come as a surprise to many. But it will be no surprise to find rates of urbanization and literacy and the like fairly strongly associated with position on the main line, for clearly the process of modernization entails changes of that kind.

The general picture is now clear. Economic development can be, crudely perhaps but not inaccurately, characterized as a process of making "Them" more like "Us." Furthermore, it seems to be working in precisely that sense: By and large, developing capitalist countries are rather steadily becoming more like us. It may sound patronizing but, judging from both the statistics and observations, to become more like us is what "They" want.[3]

The Why of It

A discussion of the causal factors generating and sustaining the main line must begin with technology. Clearly, the developing countries are borrowers of the technology that is generated in the already highly developed countries, technology that overwhelmingly comes out of the affluent fifteen. There are engineers and scientists in developing countries, but they do not as yet have the skill or the facilities to engage in major research and development work. Indeed, the situation is often even worse than this, in that much of the most creative talent in developing countries receive their training abroad and then remain abroad to practice their skills, exercise their creative energy, in the only places where that is feasible.

Furthermore, it appears that modern technology is relatively inflexible. It tends to be so complex that it is quite costly to introduce substantial variations in the processes, since doing so may mean experimental testing of variations on literally thousands of variables. This means, in effect, that an opportunity to increase productivity in the modern sector in a developing country almost always refers to an opportunity to do something quite similar to things that have already been taken advantage of elsewhere. A plant turning out a given product will tend to look very similar from one country to another; the chief determinant of variation is likely to be the date of installation, since technology in affluent capitalism is itself undergoing rapid change.

A second major factor in generating and sustaining the main line is less obvious. To put it in economists' language, the major determinant of changes in the structure of production in developing countries is change in the structure of domestic demand. When economic development produces an increase in the incomes of a broad segment of the population their demand for goods goes up, of course. Businessmen are likely to seize the new opportunity for profits by expanding production of the goods whose demand has increased. What our proposition says is that, even for relatively poor developing countries, it is what goes on inside the country that is most important in this process. The rise in domestic incomes tends to have more effect on the nature of domestic production than does demand for the country's exports. Of course, there are wide variations in involvement in international trade by developing countries, and some international developments can certainly be crucial. What we are talking about here is the average relative causal effect over many countries and over a long stretch of recent history.

The implications of these two factors, technology and domestic demand, when taken together are very great. We have already discussed the similarities in the patterns of demand among people of comparable incomes. This means that if domestic demand dominates, then these countries as they grow will tend to be moving in the same direction in terms of the new production facilities they add. So production and consumption both will tend to be moving along the main line.

Not a great deal is known about income distributions in most of these countries. Almost certainly income is more unequally distributed than in affluent capitalism. Probably the patterns of distribution in the urban sectors follow the main line, so that as countries get into the upper reaches of the main line, inequality is reduced to levels nearer those of the affluent fifteen. At any rate, there is sufficient similarity in the distributions for those income classes able to demand modern goods that even the overall structure of demand, not just that by income class, is similar for countries near one another on the line.

These properties of the developing countries have a dramatic implication for the process of economic planning. Since one can say, crudely, that the vision of a country's future can be had by taking a look at countries only a little way farther along the line, there is really little need for dramatic long-range plans to totally revamp the society. Such visions have a tendency to be built on speculative sand, to capture the imagination but not to occupy the minds of the actual makers of policy. And for reasons we have discussed in earlier chapters. What we know about economic and social change tends to be concentrated on the present and on situations not too different from the present. All large organizations, including governments in developing countries, must plan these days. But effective planning tends to be a matter of working out the details of the next few paces forward.[4]

To put it another way, what the main line tells us is that the marginalist approach to the problems of economic development in a given country is just the one that is most likely to work. Armed with domestic and world market information and with a good knowledge of the special situations faced by their country, the planners can be expected to design a policy for the next few years that has a reasonable chance of working. The techniques for doing this are not so different from those being used to control affluent capitalism; that is, they are relatively well known. To try to capture a picture of the society a generation or two hence, or even a decade away, seems to be beyond the reach of currently effective planning techniques. Once again, the secret of success lies in the existence of a situation in which primary attention can be devoted to selecting the best ways to make relatively marginal adjustments in the status quo.

Stretches and Bends in the Line

The picture we have presented of economic development so far has been a very optimistic one, certainly a far cry from the kinds of statements current in the popular press these days, where gloom abounds. The truth, in fact, lies somewhere in between. The picture of economic development offered by the main line is the story of basically favorable underlying forces. The message is that with skill and dedication, and a bit of luck, the task can be accomplished. But it is in no sense a sure thing. What we need to do now is briefly review the more important of the things that can go wrong with the process of economic development and their consequences.

The first point to make is that the process of economic development, under the best of circumstances, is a distressingly long one.[5] While it is going on, there is a great deal of human misery induced by the poverty, the lack of development. One would like to relieve it, but unfortunately we do not know how, in the short run. Health care can be improved and food supplies better distributed, but when such policies are carried out, there is still a great deal of deprivation left. Only economic development will cure this residue, and that seems to mean that several generations must pass before current levels of the affluent societies can be reached by most developing countries. For example, a country growing at an annual rate of 2 percent per capita, the lowest rate among those countries listed in figure 1, is growing substantially faster than did Great Britain in the nineteenth century. But even so, it will be thirty-five years before that country's output per capita has doubled. Among the best performers a quadrupling of output per capita has been achieved in a quarter of a century, but so far few countries have been able to sustain such a rapid rate.

The length of time this takes will be strongly influenced in each country by its population policy. The process of absorption of the population in the traditional sectors of a developing country into the modern urban service and manufacturing sectors is very rapid in absolute terms. But when population is growing at 3 percent a year—more than twice the rate in major affluent capitalist countries during comparable periods of their growth—the development process can actually produce an increase in the misery of the traditional sector even though economic growth is rapid. Since in most developing countries the continuation of misery is largely a consequence of the still relatively small size of the modern sector, there is a straightforward connection between the rate of population growth and the length of the main line.

Countries in this situation can be given some outside help. The technology of birth control, like most other technology, is a product of the developed countries, and further technical improvements and breakthroughs must come from there. Assistance in the effective delivery of birth control and family-planning methods can also be provided from outside. But population policy for a present-day nation is primarily a matter of domestic policy. The decision to do nothing is in effect a decision to stretch out the main line. Even so, the longer run prospect for most countries is favorable. True, there is a fairly strong tendency for rapid economic growth and rapid population growth to go together, and the population part of this ratio does stretch out the main line, other things equal. But there is also a tendency for the rate of growth of population to decline as growth proceeds, so that there is a reasonable prospect that in time population growth will be reduced to a point that permits the completion of the basic processes of modernization. And, of course, it should be emphasized that the primary policy instruments that can prevent stretching of the main line are under domestic control. Special forms of aid, such as famine relief, require outside assistance, but even these will only work if the domestic society and polity is adequately organized and motivated.

In recent years the energy crisis has imposed a new stretching of the main line for many developing countries with no domestic sources of oil. This stretching has been particularly poignant because of the connection between oil and fertilizer. A major input to most commercial fertilizer production, oil's price has increased several-fold, with the consequence that agricultural modernization based on fertilizer-intensive cultivation has had to be abandoned, at least temporarily, in a number of countries. These are distressing events, but they need not be catastrophic. In fact, in recent years increases in world agriculture production have been able to keep up with increases in world population. It appears that even the food problem can be solved in the long run if those basic organizational and motivational conditions for tying a country to the main line can be established.

The State

This brings us to the relationship between politics and economic development.[6] The state has played a very central role in the development of most affluent capitalist countries, far more in fact than the student of British or American history is prepared to expect. This is no less true in developing countries today. The first function of the state is to establish a framework within which a system of national markets can function effectively. Given the primarily domestic causation we have been discussing, this particular framework function becomes especially crucial. Second, the state must have an orientation favorable to economic development, since its economic policies can be a *sine qua non* for successful development. And third, the state must have an administrative apparatus capable of reasonably competent execution of established policies.

These institutional conditions for successful development explain the lower cutoff point of the main line. Many countries below that line, and some above it, have not yet established one or more of these conditions, and consequently are unable to set the development process in motion. Some of these countries may very well be nonviable political economic entities, so that some substantial change of boundaries or the like will have to precede movement onto the main line. This most intractable aspect of the issue of economic development still eludes attempts to work out practical policies for overcoming it.

Turning back to countries already on the line, there is the question of the decreasing incidence of parliamentary democracy as you move away from affluent capitalism. What domestic political factors in these countries could produce such an outcome? Our discussion of politics in affluent capitalism becomes relevant here. First and most important is the very different nature of the establishment in a developing country. The range of interests in such a country is very great, with tradition-oriented big landowners tending to oppose most development policies at one end of the spectrum, and representatives of firms interested in getting the goods out without much regard for domestic impacts at the other. In between lie all the groups familiar from affluent capitalism, but in very different mixes. Representatives of modern, domestically financed and controlled business are relatively weak. Labor may be weak or strong, but tends to represent only a small fraction of the labor force—namely, that part which is working in the modern sector. The military is likely to be very strong, the government bureaucracy to be large. Peasants may or may not be organized. Students may be organized and politically effective.

Some fraction of this motley crew of interests will be formally dedicated to overthrowing the existing regime. And many groups that are reformist in orientation nevertheless feel little commitment to the existing regime, and are not at all averse to threatening its survival if that seems to be an effective tactic. Because markets are not as well developed, there is far less experience in deal-making behavior. Because the political regime is not likely to have been around too long, there is far less experience with the political art of compromise. Because of the great range of interests in existence, it is less likely that a proposal even exists that could effectively compromise all the influential interests. And finally, because the country is by definition poor, there is a much smaller pie to be carved up among all these interests. One way or another, almost all our conditions for the effective functioning of parliamentary democracy seem to be violated, and the violations are the greater the farther down the line we move. There is really no mystery to the positive association between incidence of parliamentary democracy and level of economic development.

So until they get very far along the main line, developing countries tend to be governed by authoritarian regimes. This fact seems to be built into the structure of the situation, and there seems to be very little that can be done about it. For one thing, when parliamentary democracies do exist in these countries, they may be quite ineffective. It is always very risky, from the point of view of some interests, to move from the status quo, and this tends to be an immobilizing influence on government policy. So in practice the main political questions for most developing countries are: (1) how to get an authoritarian regime to accept a strong growth orientation and (2) how to get reasonably effective policy implementation.

The first question is not a trivial one. When they first make their appearance as objects of development policy, these countries tend to be under the domination of a coalition of big landowners and merchants whose orientation to a traditional life-style usually excludes any serious concern with modernization. If significant economic progress is to occur, this group must either be converted to the idea of modernity or overthrown. By and large, it is the latter tactic that has been followed, though the traditional groups tend to maintain considerable influence even after this "bourgeois" revolution.

What are the souces of concern for modernity and economic growth? The principal effective domestic sources are probably located in business and the military. Some businessmen perceive, in their contacts with other parts of the world, the opportunities for profit that inhere in the process and have the flexibility to make the necessary adaptations. The military learns about modernity from the modern weapons it must have to be an effective force, and which are available to all such countries through political alliance or simply in the international marketplace. In both cases, making effective use of the new technology requires some degree of mastery of modern organization. These reorientations create a modernity interest. The implication is not particularly attractive but is unavoidable: In many developing countries an alliance between a military regime and a modernizing business elite holds out the best hope for reasonably swift movement along the main line. This choice looks unattractive to those steeped in democratic traditions, but only until one looks at the alternatives, which entail slow movement along the main line, perhaps even retrogression, and continuing misery for the many. The generation or so of turmoil and increased misery that precedes communist revolutions also means a substantial stretching of the main line.

Of course, the above paragraph has its exceptions, and there is no implication that attempts to establish a working, growth-oriented democracy should be inhibited by policy emanating from either within or without the developing country. But thinking of the history of democracy and growth in developing countries that have attempted to use this political form—countries such as Greece and Chile and India—there is no reason for optimism about democracy's prospects in the short or even the medium run. However, in the long run the story is very different, and once again optimistic. Democracy tends to become more frequent as one moves up the line, and *all* those that have crossed the line into affluence have also crossed the line into democracy.

Conclusion

Perhaps a balanced picture has now emerged. There is a process for economic development, a sort of recipe book, that on the average is capable of producing a successful outcome, of modernizing the country, and of providing a decent standard of living for most of its people. Given a reasonably favorable international environment (which we discuss in chapter 9)—that is, one not less favorable than that of the last two decades or so—the process can work. Whether it does in fact work depends more than anything else on the organization and ability of the domestic leadership in these countries. Despite that recipe book of things that "on the average" work, this is no simple task. It requires courage and skill and common sense and practical vision. It is difficult, but no superhuman effort is required.

CHAPTER 8

Socialism: Development and Utopia

WHAT are the three most significant phenomena of the twentieth century? Surely the institutionalization of affluent capitalism has to rank as the greatest achievement of twentieth-century social progress. Next to it in importance is probably the tying of the main line to affluent capitalism, the stabilizing of reasonable hopes that affluence can be a part of most of the world's future. The third major development of the twentieth century might well be the rise of socialism. Thinking of the Soviet Union, China, Cuba, and the remaining East European and East Asian communist countries as the "socialist camp," to use the militaristic term that they prefer, there are almost as many socialist as affluent capitalist countries, and their population is about three times larger.

A supporter of these countries would probably claim two major achievements for twentieth-century socialism: the speeding up of the process of economic development and the creation of a basis for the good society. A planned society, he would claim, will avoid the fluctuations in the level of economic activity that are an inevitable part of the working of the "anarchic" market. And planning permits the concentration of economic forces on the primary task of developing the economy, which will produce faster growth. With respect to the creation of the good society, the key step these countries have allegedly taken is the substantial elimination of exploitation by placing the means of production under social control. The worker can then feel that he is entering "his" factory gate, that the capitalists are not skimming off the cream from the top of his work day. Let us take a brief look at contemporary socialism in order to appraise these claims.

Development

Lenin's revision of the Marxian expectation that revolution would come first to the most advanced capitalist countries was certainly a prescient one, since *none* of the socialist countries has reached the stage of affluence. A rather natural corollary to Lenin's revision is that the efforts of socialist countries would have to be very heavily concentrated on bringing about economic development. Forced draft industrialization has tended to be the order of the day.[1]

The first thing to note about socialist development is the extent to which socialist leaders have accepted basic tenets of the main-line theory in their development policies. In the first place, it was recognized that the goal was economic catch-up—that is, the task was to make the productive apparatus of the economy over in the image of that of the more advanced countries, all of whom, of course, are capitalist. At times this aspect of the policy was exaggerated to the point of parody, as countries like Bulgaria and Rumania appeared to be trying to develop an industrial base as broad as that of the United States. That a very great deal of Soviet industrial policy has been little more than mimicry of the United States is well established.

Not only did the socialist leaders accept, de facto, the main line, they also accepted the two underlying notions of the necessity of technological borrowing and of the dominance of domestic forces. The borrowing needs no explanation; the question of national economic autonomy was, in fact, central policy. It was partly conditioned by political notions, by fears of dominance through trade relations, many socialist countries being as afraid of this dominance stemming from the Soviet Union as from capitalism. But clearly the leaders felt that the process of rapid development would create domestic demand for the goods they planned their new industries to produce, and that domestic demand would be by far the most important one.

The main difference between main-line and socialist policy stemmed from the socialist leaders' belief that they could shrink the line, could sharply accelerate their countries' movement toward developed country status. Supporting this belief was the policy of extensive growth, which all these countries followed for at least a number of years. The policy called for a massive increase in national savings—and a consequent massive reduction in the proportion of output available for consumption. These saved resources were to be devoted to investment, of course, and especially to investment in basic industry, the industries that produced the capital goods and energy for the economy. Behind this policy lay a rather vague notion that, concentrating on a very rapid increase in the production of the goods that produced the goods that were ultimately to be consumed, there would be a kind of multiplier effect on the eventual rate of growth of the latter goods. Rapidly increasing "roundaboutness" of production, combined with very high investment rates, were to be the keys to shrinking the main line.

How well have these countries fared in performing this central task? The statistics suggest that "not bad" would be an accurate answer. On the average, they have grown at rates comparable to the more successful of the capitalist countries. However, they are not necessarily world record-breakers. The leaders in the world's growth race tend to have capitalist names like Japan and Brazil and Taiwan rather more often than socialist names like Rumania and the Soviet Union. In comparing East with West Europe, growth rates of the former have been about 1 percentage point a year higher than the latter, with industry growing significantly faster in the East and agriculture growing a bit faster in the West. But though their performance has been "high average," there have been some slow growers, such as Cuba and Czechoslovakia. Also, the quality of the goods produced in these countries tends to be quite low, often too low for them to compete successfully on world markets. Taking account of this would probably result in some lowering of the growth rates. One cannot help but wonder if "not bad" is a sufficient result to justify revolution.[2]

Utopia

But, of course, development is not everything. There is also the very serious question of whether or not these countries, or at least some of them, have found the path to a better world. Surely a collection of fourteen socialist countries, all of which have been in existence for at least two decades, and one of which has been around for six, offers enough evidence on this issue to make quite a good appraisal of the tendencies toward utopia that may be built into their social structures. If socialism has nothing to show after all that experience, even the most hardened revolutionary might want to reevaluate his options.[3]

However, the situation is not that bad. Socialism has some undeniable achievements to its credit. Most of the socialist countries have succeeded in providing, most of the time, a more equal distribution of income than have capitalist countries at comparable stages of development, and they may also provide relatively better income security for the poorer portions of their populations. Then, too, they have demonstrated their capacity to master the most complex modern technology, Russia and China both having developed fusion bombs and rockets.

Against this short but significant list, there must also be placed a list of failures. The frequent resort to terror and the tightness of political controls are readily apparent to the most casual visitor to any of these countries (excepting perhaps Yugoslavia and, for a few months, Czechoslovakia). If the *Guinness Book of World Records* had a tabulation for "most citizens of own country deliberately killed in pursuit of domestic policy aims," that record would be held by socialism, by Stalin's Russia, not by Hitler's Germany. The sorry stream of refugees that flows in larger or smaller currents from these countries, one year from Hungary, another year from Czechoslovakia, yet another year from Viet Nam, is further grim testimony on this point. The year in which this paragraph is being written is a year of the Soviet Jew, representing yet another kind of failure of these societies.

One might expect that a more wholesome domestic environment would produce more wholesome international relations, especially relations between socialist states. Here, too, one must report a considerable dearth of favorable signs. The Soviet Union maintains troops in several socialist countries, at least partly in order to prevent the local populations from revolting. It has invaded two socialist countries to put down such revolts and has threatened others. The relations between China and Russia are not exactly models of correct relations between socialist states and involve mutual recriminations of a caliber more appropriate to a burgeoning barroom brawl. The Soviet Union sharply restricts the amount of trade it permits East European countries to engage in with the West, in order to protect the flow of machinery and other key goods from these countries to the Soviet Union.

But perhaps international affairs are a rather indirect basis for appraisal of domestic utopian achievements. There is a more direct claim, made especially for China and Cuba—namely, that in these societies a process of transformation of man has been set in motion, a process that is on the way toward the generation, for the first time, of a truly socialist man. This is a very fundamental claim. Furthermore, there is a good deal of truth in it. A substantial transformation of man has probably been occurring in all of these socialist societies.

There is also a fundamental misunderstanding. The transformation that is occurring is generating *modern* man, and it is occurring in all developing societies. Max Weber is the scholar who first drew serious attention to this process.[4] He claimed that the rise of capitalism brought with it a fundamental change in attitude. This change is based on the rational calculation of the costs and benefits of alternative courses of action that is made feasible by the development of market and price relations. In response to this new environment, man in Weber's view became much more oriented toward deliberative choice, and in this sense became more rational.

This thesis seems to have a good deal of truth to it; however, one should add that it is not just markets but technology too that tend to induce this kind of deliberative choice. Even a peasant faces decisions with respect to the distribution of crops to plant and has many choices with respect to inputs to make in a modern environment. As these choices emerge and the peasant begins to respond to them, he may well tend to become a somewhat different person. He is aided in this process by the tendency of modern society to destroy the traditional culture. Vast numbers of peasants move to the city and are removed from serious contact with the propagators of the old values. Also, there is a strong trend toward nationalization of culture. Village culture, despite its resort to culture-wide myths and history, nevertheless had a

strong element of the particular attached to it, based on family and village traditions and the relative lack of contact with outsiders. In the new
environment national media and mobility tend to extend the bounds of
commonality of culture in many directions. And finally, there are the
specific elements of the new attitudes, based on the discipline of the
modern workplace, the relative intensification of nuclear family relations, and the development of modern habits of consumption.

All these changes are in the direction of restructuring attitudes to
be more like those to be found in affluent capitalism. The collectivization of agriculture under socialism has meant rather stronger pushes
toward this kind of transformation of man even in the countryside.
Much of Chairman Mao's thought, especially in the form of the slogans
in the little red book, can be interpreted as an attempt to instill the
attitudes of rational man.[5] If the aim were stated in these terms, one
would probably rate at least a number of socialist societies as relatively
successful in transforming man.

But as the role of markets in generating rational man suggests,
there remains an important respect in which socialism and capitalism
differ—namely, in the widespread elimination of markets as the mediators of relations between production units. Socialists tend to have high
hopes that the elimination of markets will in itself generate a much
more wholesome society, arguing that markets tend to foster narrow
materialism, egotism, and vulgarity, and the treatment of other men as
objects to be manipulated for one's own advantage. How has socialism
fared in this respect?

Planning and Utopia

One of the most interesting discoveries of liberal economics has been
that from the point of view of efficiency, a centrally planned economy
can do no better than to simulate the kinds of outcomes that would
occur in a competitive capitalist economy. The socialist environment
entails a more equal distribution of the national income, no doubt, but
when that has been accomplished, a pricing system that reproduces the
results obtainable on markets would be essential to effective planning.
These prices would do the same thing in a planned economy as they do
under capitalism—namely, tell people what the opportunity cost of
doing one thing rather than another was—and in the case of the
planned economy they would measure socialist opportunity cost. Of
course, the actors are different; in a planned economy the prices are
telling the central planners about their alternatives, not the individual
consumers and producers. Behind this lies the basic and elementary
notion that in both societies scarcity is what requires careful choice,
and scarcity works the same, in principle, in both types of economies.

One might think this result implies that a centrally planned economy is perfectly feasible. If so, the socialist countries, with their clear political preference for highly centralized, controllable structures, would certainly adopt full central planning. But they have not. There is something rather like markets for labor and consumer goods in most of these countries, and there appears to be strong and continuing pressure to move in the direction of more decentralization. Their younger economists seem largely convinced that socialist markets (that is, with the means of production still nationalized) would be the best policy. Even China uses many marketlike practices in the relations between rural communes and the city marketing organizations. This seems inconsistent with our economists' result.

The answer to the puzzle lies in the spheres of incentives and information. These two key factors do not play much of a role in that competitive theory, but in practice they turn out to be crucial. The great advantage of the market system is that it focuses actors' attention on those problems that are most relevant to themselves, and forces them to bargain with others whose interests are engaged very directly. But a central planner cannot get too excited about whether an order of women's shoes will reach Omsk this month or next. Even a dedicated planner is likely to feel that he has other, more important things to do; and that is where information comes in. It has not proved possible to collect the detailed information necessary to produce a full central plan in one spot. Instead, the central planners work with aggregates, product groups, and rely on others farther down the line to break down the aggregates in an appropriate way. At no step in the procedure is there a close connection between the basic decision makers and those who need or make the goods.

The consequences of this are quite predictable, and have, in fact, occurred. The centrally planned economies are able to get the goods out in a few key areas to which they devote very high priority. But in other spheres there is a great deal of confusion and mismanagement. General appraisals of performance indicate that communist countries generally require far more inputs to produce a given amount of output than does a capitalist country such as the United States. Also, as noted, the quality of the socialist-produced goods tends to be inferior. No wonder their younger economists look eagerly to markets to solve their problems. In this particular area the costs of deviance from the structures decreed by the main line have turned out to be quite large.

A major defect of the planning mechanism as a substitute for markets is the downplaying of the deal-making process. Instead, bureaucratic relations are substituted, and the essential learning process that has proved so effective in generating high-quality management in both business and politics under affluent capitalism is substantially underdeveloped. One might well be inclined to think of this as a failure of the process of transforming man that occurs under socialism, and that may account for much of the observed crudity and inefficiency in the functioning of these societies.

Conclusion

In sum, socialism does not yet offer a very challenging alternative to the capitalist way to modernization. In the first place, socialist development policies are similar to those followed by growth-oriented capitalist countries. Second, achievements in terms of growth rates and the structure of production are also not strikingly different. The great hope of socialism was that it offered support for the poorer people whose lot in turn-of-the-century capitalism was miserable indeed. It has done just that; but so has capitalism. As we noted, a fundamental change in the United States then and now lies in the tremendous increase in income support and in the health of the poorer portion of the population. Socialism has achieved a great success in this area; it just turns out that it is not a *socialist* success, for essentially the same thing has happened under capitalism. Improvements in health and reduction in the risk of income loss for broad segments of the population is a world-wide trend in the twentieth century.

The vision of a planned, marketless society is fading under the very impact of socialist experience with the large nonmarket segment of its economies. There are only two known ways to mediate relations among producing and consuming units in modern society—namely, markets and bureaucracies. And bureaucracies in this area have tended to be too bureaucratic to be very appealing, not to mention the implicit centralization of political life that accompanies them. Perhaps many would feel that socialism in the twentieth century has done too well to be called a "disease of the transition," in Rostow's phrase; but it certainly has done far too poorly to be called "the wave of the future," if its future is to be determined by the free choice of the world's citizenry.

CHAPTER 9

International Relations

HARDLY a day passes without the news reports reminding us in one way or another of the parlous state of international relations. There is always a war going on somewhere, so there are some battered bodies to look at—usually, given the nature of modern war, bodies of civilians. There is usually a war about to begin, or at least threatened, so there are pictures of busy diplomats talking it over in one capital or another. Not infrequently a coup has just changed regimes somewhere, so we have a clutch of grim-faced generals to look at. And two or three times a year the United Nations meets, and we see pictures of speakers who are probably reminding us in strident tones that that body has belied the hopes that it would be a great bulwark for peace.

The economist who checks out the financial news can find plenty to worry him, too. There will be a piece reporting, for the thousandth time, that worldwide inflation has not yet been brought under control. There will be an expert announcing that the world monetary system is in danger of collapse. Yet another study will show that seventeen— or is it thirty-seven?—developing countries will be bankrupt before the year is out.

And so on. It would be a foolish person indeed who denied that the world was at risk. Nevertheless, the picture that emerges from all these nightmare stories *is* quite one-sided. And, more important, much of the other side of the story deals not with the daily news, but with the underlying forces that are shaping that news and with the many events that are not striking enough to make the news. That story is very much different. In dealing with these forces we will start with the rather pedestrian level of foreign trade and move gradually back up toward the more spectacular issues of war and peace.

Trade and Economic Dependence

Underdeveloped countries trade very little with one another; the vast majority of their trade is with the more developed countries. The latter, on the other hand, have a relatively small volume of trade with underdeveloped countries; the vast majority of their trade is with one another.[1]

The implications of this persistent structure of world trade explain a good deal. Of course, one implication is clear enough. The underdeveloped countries need developed-country trade much more than the developed countries need the underdeveloped. This dependence is even greater in practice because a typical underdeveloped country probably has a very large fraction of its trade, especially its exports, with a single developed country. And it has a number of developing-country rivals who would be very happy to take its place in that market. It has never been proved, but this situation certainly leaves one with the feeling that there are elements of imperfect competition in the relations between developing and developed nations.

What does the developing country get from trade, given this unfavorable basic environment? Well, foreign trade is like domestic trade: It is the product of deals. The deals are not made at a loss, in terms of opportunity cost—almost every developing country does more trade than is necessary for its simple survival—so there is a presumption built into market relations that foreign trade deals provide benefits to both sides.

Less obviously, but probably a good deal more important, trade brings investment. Again typically, as a country's trade expands, there will also tend to be an increase in foreign investment. The implication of this is that there are indeed profitable deals being made on the underdeveloped-country side of the market, and that the profit rates are higher, at the margin, than alternative investment projects in the developed country. And investment is typically not a one-shot affair; once it starts, it has a tendency to grow, suggesting that the base of profitable deals is expanding. And, again typically, this base is expanding simultaneously for both foreign and domestic investment in the developing countries.

Foreign investment is, of course, far more than just an indicator of profitability; it is also the bearer of modern technology. The entering firm will not be putting up indigenous factories. And nowadays it will not typically be staffing the better jobs exclusively with foreigners. So with the new factories come the beginning stages of the development of domestic ability to deal in an economically effective way with modern technology.[2]

In fact, there appears to be a kind of pattern to international technological development these days, a pattern consisting of four stages. In the highest stage are industries in affluent capitalist countries that are the latest product of science and technology, the pioneers in developing new products and techniques. At the second stage are national industries, usually also in affluent capitalism, that have specialized in taking these new techniques and improving them so that cost is lower and quality higher under mass-production conditions than in the early factories. The third stage involves industries in countries where the capacity to alter technologies is very limited; existing technology is borrowed and operated, perhaps only producing for domestic consumption, perhaps taking advantage of lower labor costs to compete a bit internationally. The fourth stage involves industries in countries where modern technology has not penetrated so that no domestic capacity to operate it exists. Many American industries operate in the first stage, though so do many other countries for one product or another. Germany and Japan stand out as countries that have, at one time or another, for one product or another, occupied all of the stages, though in recent years they have perhaps most frequently been found playing the stage-two role. By and large the developing countries occupy the last two stages.[3]

The point is that countries can and have moved upward from stages three and four. The *sine qua non* of this progress is past experience with technology, with developing the domestic skills and experience and organized creativity to handle these kinds of tasks. The only way to acquire such skills is through extended contact with the technology and with the people who know how to operate, maintain, and improve it. Contact with the people is so important that socialist countries such as the Soviet Union seem willing to violate basic tenets of their ideology in order to obtain technology from affluent capitalism in much the same way as developing capitalist countries already do.

The twentieth century has had one of its most profound technological revolutions in the areas of transport and communications. People, goods, and messages can now be transmitted at a tiny fraction of previous time and cost, and are moving about in truly massive volume. This has meant a rather powerful increase in pressures on developing-country leaders to get on the main line, to acquire a growth orientation and reap the benefits that are displayed daily by the media. It has also greatly facilitated the transfer of modern ideas and technology, as broad reaches of the citizenry of developing countries are exposed to modern orientations. For the investor all this means that to be a success he must have a truly international outlook, the implication clearly being that he may find his best deal in a developing country. And if he does look there, he is also much more likely to find facilities and cost calculations favorable precisely because of this drastic shrinkage of the economic significance of distance. The underdeveloped countries are already massively caught up in modern times, and even the great autarkic socialist countries such as China and Russia clearly feel that they lose out on something vital when they remain aloof from the world market.

This brings us to the last implication of that original characterization of the structure of trade between developed and underdeveloped countries. The implication is that as a country grows economically, its trade will also grow, and probably the trade will grow faster than the domestic economy. As this happens, it will trade more and more with the more developed countries, and will also tend to concentrate its trade structure less on one or two countries. On the average this change does in fact occur as you move up the main line; and it is very roughly equivalent to developing one's way out of economic dependence. That is the real message of international trade in the modern world. Unfortunately, it is not the whole story.

Aid and Intervention

There is such a thing as economic imperialism. There is nothing esoteric about it; it has existed in all ages of history, and is neither more nor less than the powerful using their leverage to obtain economic benefits at the expense of the less powerful. Changes in the nature of society and economy do change the instruments of economic imperialism, and some ages and situations are more favorable to its exercise than others. To appraise contemporary economic imperialism, we must look briefly at present-day instruments and situations.[4]

History's longest continuous economic squabble has probably been that between creditors and debtors, and a traditional backdrop for the squabble has been monetary policy. Creditors want hard money and stable or declining prices, and debtors want the reverse. Our contemporary international monetary system is an arena for this sort of debate, and by and large the policies in this area have reflected the balance of interests between creditor and debtor. The developing countries have major problems with rising debt, and the international monetary authorities are continually after them to harden up their currencies. The overhang of debt for many such countries is near crisis proportions. And the creditors, overwhelmingly from the ranks of affluent capitalism, clearly have some leverage on the governments of such countries that goes beyond the pressure of monetary authorities.

On the other side of the ledger there is economic aid. The United States particularly, but also a number of international agencies, and notably the United Nations, have offered at times massive amounts and great varieties of technical and economic assistance to developing countries. It was hoped that aid could be self-liquidating—that is, that the aid would stimulate economic growth and that the growth, following the process described in the last section, would improve the international position of the developing country to the point at which it no longer had any need for aid. This has happened to several countries— among them Greece, Taiwan, and Yugoslavia stand out—and under favorable conditions could happen to many more countries.

Unfortunately, the total amount of aid being offered has been declining recently. Also, much of the aid has been wasted from an economic point of view. Instead of being applied to countries who are prepared to use it to foster their own economic growth, most of it has been used in the service of other foreign policy aims. Aid is potentially a very important instrument for assisting economic development, but most aid has not been used for that purpose.

The multinational corporation is often treated these days as if it were a foreign power rather than a business.[5] The bigger ones are certainly very powerful, and they do indeed have considerable leverage in dealing with a developing country or with its businessmen. Some of this leverage does stem from its frequently close associations with political policymakers back home, so perhaps it is well to discuss it in the "intervention" section. However, one should not lose sight of those economic properties of multinationals that are of benefit to the developing countries. In the first place, multinationals are likely to be the only effective vehicle of modern management in the developing country. As such, and especially since they are likely to employ substantial numbers of local citizens in positions at least up to middle management, they are a training ground for one of the most important of modern skills. Second, and related to this, they seem to be especially successful, with high profits rates, quick and effective access to modern technology, and great flexibility of response to changing environments. The impact of the multinational cannot be assessed with any confidence on present evidence, but it is quite possible that it offers many developing countries an opportunity to shrink the length of the main line at least a bit.

One problem with the multinational corporation is that it has a considerable ability to elude effective control by playing the divide-and-conquer game in developing countries. And the ability of the developed countries to control some dimensions of multinational behavior has been called into question, too, as the rise of the special dollar markets in Europe and Asia testifies. But one should watch for the inherent bias in available information about multinationals. One hears the individual horror stories of their political interventions in developing countries, but since balance sheets rarely make the evening news, one hears much less of the continuing story of the economic results of their worldwide operations. Both sides of this story must be appraised before the multis can be properly understood.

No one could deny that American and other developed-nation interventions in the Third World have had in many cases strongly negative consequences. But it should not be forgotten that the last quarter of a century has seen the most rapid worldwide economic growth that history has recorded. The very vision of modernity that inspires change in the developing world, as well as much of the means to achieve it, can only come from sufficient interaction to permit effective transfer of technology and organizational forms. And, once again, the longer run prospect for successful developers is growth out of dependence and into interdependence within a framework of genuine national sovereignty.

Socialist Revolution and Socialist Intervention

Surely in no previous century has the word "revolution" been bandied about so much. And yet there have not been more than a bare handful of genuine revolutions in the twentieth century. Most countries became socialist as a result of the imposition of a socialist government by forces external to the country. Only in Russia, Yugoslavia, China, Cuba, and Vietnam have indigenous revolutionary groups succeeded in coming to power. Well, perhaps we should add two more countries to our list—namely, Hungary and Czechoslovakia—where attempts at a humanist revolution against Soviet-imposed regimes succeeded domestically, only to be put down by the Soviet Union's own military forces.

The five indigenously based revolutions all had one common feature: The revolution succeeded not so much because of the power of the revolutionary forces as because of the weakness of the existing government. In Russia, Yugoslavia, and China the indigenous government had been brought to its knees by war and corruption. A revolutionary party of relatively modest size, in each case clearly representing a small minority of the people, was able to push the weak central government aside. In Cuba there was no war to weaken the government, but there was enough corruption to fully compensate. In China the forces of Chiang Kai-shek were nominally large but, riddled with corruption and discredited by the failure to fight effectively against Japanese invaders, they were unable to make the numbers of their soldiers effective. In Yugoslavia the partisan movement was not very large, but toward the end of World War II it was growing rapidly, with large-scale material support from its capitalist allies and substantial military support from its Soviet allies. The weakness of the South Vietnamese government needs no comment.

These five revolutions give one *no* sense of a tidal wave of history sweeping across the twentieth century. Rather, they sound like a series of historical accidents. The formula for revolution they suggest is: Wait until your country's government is too weak to defend itself effectively, and then find some capitalist or socialist powers that are willing to support you in your campaign. Without odds of that kind in your favor, you might as well forget about revolution, unless its function is merely to serve your death wish. And the odds are probably lengthening against revolution in the future. For the process of decolonialization has only temporarily created weak, poorly legitimated governments in many lands. As their domestic political processes develop and become institutionalized these countries will become less susceptible to revolutionary overthrow.

However, there is one important exception to this generalization about the potential of revolution. The Hungarian and Czech revolutions mentioned earlier do not have the same features as the other revolutions. Indeed, both of them managed to succeed without any assistance from outside. Both were also relatively spontaneous mass movements, striking a chord deep in the desires of broad sectors of the population. So far, within the Soviet bloc, such forces, most likely forces that exist elsewhere in the socialist camp, have been kept effectively under control. But as yet in this century the message of history is that revolution is more likely to be a substantial historical force in the socialist than in the capitalist world.

That the Soviet Union responded strongly to threats of regime change among its satellites is, of course, to be expected. The Soviet Union has an impeccable record of using its power to the hilt against weaker powers. Two of the most interesting applications of economic aggression in the postwar period have been the Soviet boycotts of Yugoslavia and China. In both cases close socialist allies were viewed in Moscow as not toeing the line sufficiently closely, and so strong economic sanctions were brought to bear, the intent clearly being to bring about a change of domestic policy or, better yet, a change of political regime in the two countries. That the policy failed in both cases reflects the basic weakness of the boycott instrument in the modern interdependent world, and is of a piece with the American boycottt of Cuba. These are striking instances of the dominance of great power status over the structure of ownership of the means of production in determining behavior. Hence they provide the most striking support for the liberal notion as to the real basis of imperialism.

There is one important difference between the Soviet Union and affluent capitalism in terms of relations with developing countries. The Soviet Union does not engage in direct foreign investment in the sense of acquiring property rights to assets in the developing countries. However, the importance of direct foreign investment probably does not have much to do with levels of influence on the developing countries. Instead, it probably reflects the much more limited capacity of the Soviet Union to transfer competitive modern technology to developing countries. Because of the long period of international economic isolation it has chosen to undergo, there are relatively few areas in which the Soviets are capable of producing commercially competitive technology. Even the much more highly developed—at the time of communist takeover—Czech economy suffered so great a deterioration in its relative position in modern technology that by the late sixties it was no longer competitive in areas in which only a few decades previously it had been a world technological pacesetter. The implication is clear: A Soviet decision to engage in direct foreign investment would not improve its ability to control developing countries much because it does not have a great deal to offer them in the way of modernization.

Perhaps now we are in a position to summarize the basic nature of the effect of socialism on the twentieth century. As we have seen, it has not made a fundamental contribution to our understanding of the process of economic development. It has not provided us with a vision of a better society that reasonable people, rich or poor, are likely to find very attractive. It has not shown us by the foreign policy of its leaders how a decent foreign policy can be constructed and implemented in the modern world. Essentially, socialism has played a disruptive role, destabilizing the balance of power, constructing governments in a fourth of the world whose domestic support requires terror to sustain, and unlearning, or at least not learning, the lessons of compromise and deal making that have been the basic glue of modern society for generations in both economics and politics. As we will see in the next section, the hope of the world, and perhaps even its expectation, is that we will be able to lead the socialist world back toward acceptance of the bargaining principles of this two-centuries old institutional main line.

The Prospects for Peace

A crude extrapolation of the experience of the three post-World War II decades would predict for the next three decades many small wars but no nuclear war.[6] However, such extrapolating of the facts of those three decades carries little weight, because the situation has been changing substantially over that period. Instead, we must look at the causes both of wars and of their absence and then to relate them to the changing environment in order to form a more plausible picture of the prospects for peace.

The easiest factor to deal with is the primary cause of half or more of those fifty-odd postwar wars. They were associated with the process of ending political colonialism and of establishing reasonably stable boundaries for the newly emerging nations. This involved a tremendous readjustment all around the world, but particularly in Africa and Asia, and its effects were quite enduring. One of these wars, that in Vietnam, the product, primarily, of an attempt to reimpose a discredited colonial regime and displace an already existing national government was, for a variety of reasons, fought more or less continuously for the whole of those three decades. Elsewhere, as in Algeria, there was a long and costly war, but with a sharply defined beginning and ending. In still other areas, such as much of French and British Africa, the process was of much shorter duration and much less violent. In some cases, as in the series of wars between India and Pakistan, the former colonial government played no direct role, but the fact of colonialism and the need to establish legitimated and recognized borders tied the military action closely to the process of decolonialization.

That process, though not yet over, is nearing its end. Clearly, this particular cause of war will have very much less influence on international events in the coming three decades than it had in the last three. So we have the reasonable prospect of a substantial reduction in the number and intensity of the wars we are about to experience.

Unfortunately, the other primary cause of these so-called limited wars is not a one-shot affair at all. To appraise its significance we must go back to the institutional structures of the developing countries. As we saw, under both capitalism and socialism these structures are relatively fragile. Leaders are often frustrated in their attempts to satisfy the demands of the various interests in their society, partly because in developing countries resource availability is by definition relatively limited, partly because the arts of compromise are not well developed as yet. In such circumstances it is all too natural for leaders to attempt to develop international threats as a device to divert attention from domestic tensions. Capitalist and communist countries' leaderships vie with one another in the intensity of their expressed fears of, respectively, communist and capitalist infiltration. Historically and culturally based grievances are aired and utilized to the point of war and massacre; and people whose own lives are fraught with the tensions of the transformation from traditional to modern culture are only too responsive to these appeals. Indonesia, Biafra, the remnant Jews of communist Eastern Europe, ethnic "intruders," Chinese, Indian, and others—all form part of these sad stories.

Behind the stories lie the tensions of economic development. They will not disappear until the institutions of affluent capitalism have taken sufficient grip on the world to offer a clear and peaceful alternative to bloody strife.

Can affluent capitalism really offer the kind of hope laid out for it in that last paragraph? Let us start with a few facts about the postwar period and then turn to attempts at explanation. First, there has been an extraordinary lack of serious conflict among the affluent capitalist states during this period. The contrast with the pre-World War II and pre-World War I situations could hardly be more striking. Of course, part of this is attributable to the overwhelming military dominance of the United States. But that cannot be the whole story, because there have hardly been serious rumblings at lower levels of conflict. The most serious such conflict has probably been between the United States and France, but this dispute was not strong enough to end continued military cooperation or even basic agreement on the proper deterrent threats needed to keep the common enemy in line, militarily speaking.

Second, there is the behavior of the leading affluent capitalist power of this period, the United States. In the first place, despite the fact that during the first half of this period (1945–60) it possessed the capability of destroying the military potential of the Soviet Union at modest to near-zero cost to itself, it at no point came even close to exercising that nuclear option. This self-restraint was based apparently on the feeling of the top leadership that such strong measures were unnecessary to preserve American institutions; this, in turn, seems clearly to imply that the Soviet threat could be met by the traditional marketplace and domestic political skills of compromise.

Third, there is the growing interdependence among affluent capitalist states. Though official sovereignty is preserved, the economic and political interdependence is reaching the point at which in some senses they can be treated as a single entity. This is a product of the need for common action in such spheres as money and credit, regulation of competition internationally, environmental controls that steadily intensify interactions with the developing transport revolution, and the internationalization of consumer demand and of, as noted in chapter 3, the media. The basic conflict-resolution message from interdependence is that each nation has acquired such a strong ability to hurt the other that no one can afford to exercise brute power. And the institutions of affluent capitalism are peculiarly appropriate for the propagation of this message, as we have seen.

It is this last message and its import that brings us back to the relations between the superpowers. There are, and will remain for at least a decade, only two superpowers, only two powers with the capacity to inflict unacceptable levels of damage on any other power, regardless of the defensive measures the latter may take. In the last fifteen years there has been a dramatic change in the relations between the two superpowers. Essentially what has happened is that each is now prepared to recognize the vital interests of the other in situations of international conflict, and, in addition, each is prepared to seek an optimal outcome for itself, subject to the constraint that it does not thereby threaten the vital interests of the other. This orientation has been learned, though there has been a good deal more learning necessary by the Soviet Union than by the United States. The first learning occurred in the process of resolving the Berlin issue, an issue in which the vital interests of both sides were almost immediately engaged by any change in the status quo. The Cuban missile crisis deepened the understanding, this time in a situation in which American interests were more threatened than Soviet. And at the present writing there appears to be a genuine attempt by both sides to work out the Middle East conflict, essentially by the Berlinization of Israel. It is a rather more complicated issue, and the resolution is far from being stabilized, but learning from the past the two superpowers are now able to tackle such more complicated issues with some confidence.

Essentially what we have been describing is the acceptance by the Soviet Union and the United States of a fundamental limitation on their respective sovereignty—namely, a willingness to forego attempts to improve their own situation at the risk of the other nation's vital interests. *A world establishment is developing, and the threat of nuclear war is the basis of its constitution.* That is, the common desire to avoid nuclear war provides the impetus toward accepting lower levels of conflict and higher levels of compromise in settling disputes. That sounds frightening, but effective coercion lies as a threat behind every successful constitution, and one suspects that a threat less massive than nuclear war could not serve as a constitutional base for world affairs.

The institutionalization of this slowly and haltingly emerging world political order requires the development of mutual interdependence, for only such mutual involvement will offer the opportunity for making all those marginal political deals that keep interests from threatening the regime itself. Other nonsuperpower, even nonnuclear, interests have their role to play on this world political stage, for like their counterparts among the established interests of the domestic political order of affluent capitalism, they have their power leverages in the economic and even the political sphere. Fostering this order is the best hope for peace we have.

Conclusion

The basic message from the underlying structure of contemporary international relations is positive. Developing countries start with the handicap of dependence, and the big economic powers take advantage of that dependence. Iran used to be the great example of this kind of behavior; her oil resources were being looted by the West, and back in 1952 an Iranian government that tried to gain some control of its own nation's resources was brought down by blockade and domestic intrigue on the part of the United States and others. Today Iran stands as an example of the process we have been describing, a country with land reform behind her, with very rapid industrialization underway for a decade and more, and possessing full domestic control of her oil resources. The oil makes Iran's current situation more favorable than average, but then in her dependence phase oil made her a special target.

Developing countries cannot avoid strong interaction with the more developed. Again, this means opening the gates to dependence; but it also opens the doors to escape from dependence as modern technology filters into the society and creates the conditions for modernization of skills and attitudes. Much the same can be said of economic aid, though it appears at this writing that aid will be less a factor, for both good and ill, in the immediate future than it has been in the past.

When it comes to war and revolution, the world, at times in part, at times as a whole, can expect to be seriously threatened by such events from time to time. Successful revolutions seem rather less likely to occur, but political stability for countries undergoing development seems by and large only to be found in authoritarian regimes; and they are by no means highly stable regimes.

Even so, limited wars should be of less frequent occurrence over the next few decades, for two reasons. The first is that decolonialization is largely completed. The second is that there is an emerging world establishment, based on the powerful mutual threat of nuclear war wielded by the two superpowers, and which has been the basis for producing a recognition of mutual vital interests that represents an important step toward the defusing of future crises. This basic fact, combined with growing interdependence everywhere, including especially growing economic interaction between East and West, suggests that substantial beginnings have already been made toward the creation of a world establishment, in which the negotiation of marginal changes from the status quo would gradually become the basis of international conflict resolution.

Any prediction of the future, however, must be hedged with a special condition beyond the admission that all social theories are rather speculative in nature. This special condition relates to the fact that each crisis involving the threat of war suddenly throws up a small handful of men whose behavior will determine the outcome. A favorable underlying environment means that when such crises occur, there will probably be a compromise deal available that can be made acceptable to all parties. But unwillingness or inability to recognize this possibility can prevent the deal from being made. The quality of international leadership will have a fundamental influence on the amount of violence the world will be forced to undergo.

CHAPTER 10

The Future

THE basic message to this point is that behind the tremendous technical change that has occurred, and despite the wars and revolutions, the twentieth century has developed surprisingly stable organizational forms. Essentially representing a modernization of the social orientations of liberalism, these forms have shown themselves able to adapt to all of the change and not only survive but thrive. Furthermore, this wholly novel technology-organization-attitude combination is universalizable to countries beyond the affluent fifteen where it first took root.

Very well then, the combination has done well with the kinds of change it has faced hitherto; but will the future bring different kinds of change, kinds that seriously challenge the adaptability of this new social organism? Certainly grave doubts have been expressed by many contemporary thinkers as to the viability of the liberal orientation as the basis for avoiding future catastrophes. The semipopular literature abounds these days with predictions of imminent disaster. Perhaps the most popular visions of our collapse are via the population explosion, nuclear proliferation, resource exhaustion, overcentralization, and ecological degradation. We have already discussed the first two of these in chapters 7 and 9, so attention here can be concentrated on the last three. Our aim is not to predict future technological environments but to appraise the capacity of the underlying organizational structure we have been describing to cope with these kinds of problems.[1]

Resource Exhaustion

There is a tendency for many people to think of a resource as if it were a box of candy. You eat away merrily until suddenly you open the last layer and realize that it is almost gone. Then you must make some dramatic readjustment in your eating habits. But this is a bad analogy. It fails to take account of the combined roles that technology, markets, and government play in providing a much more flexible reaction to this problem.

In practice, when a resource shortage begins to develop, the first sign is likely to be a persistent increase in the price of the commodity. Of course, the prices of most resources fluctuate quite widely in response to short-run changes in immediate availability, but the knowledgeable buyer or seller will be able in time to perceive any durable change in the market situation. As a consequence of such a price rise, people start looking around. Some look for new stocks of the resource; some look for more efficient refining processes; some look for substitute products that can do the job about as well. The desire for more profits or less costs tends to intensify these searches as the price continues to rise. Modern technology has produced a situation in which there is a tremendous variety of processes available, which makes it quite likely that the search will produce commercially viable results along one or more of these dimensions. After adjustment to the declining stock of that particular resource has proceeded for a while, one is more likely to be struck by the smoothness of the process and the speed with which acceptable substitute methods have been introduced than by the disruptions.

But this is not quite the whole story. Nowadays our knowledge has proceeded to the point that we can back up the initial phase of response to resource scarcity. There is enough information around now so that, for example, government agencies can make some tentative predictions as to where the next shortage is likely to hit, and more basic scientific and technological search and research can be instituted. The society that was able successfully to predict how long it would take to generate the technology and skills and hardware to put a man on the moon can enter into these search processes with reasonable confidence of success.

Much of the discussion about resource exhaustion these days is a consequence of this last and relatively new stage in the reaction. Students of such problems are bound to differ as to the seriousness of the problem, and governments probably tend to be overly reluctant to face some new unpleasantness, some new claim on the political system's time and resources. So the experts or the popularizers of their views take their case to the public. This is often a useful way to get the government moving, but it does tend to have as a secondary effect the generation of excessive fears as to the risks entailed in the situation. One should expect to do a little discounting when reading this sort of material, while at the same time recognizing its potential usefulness.

It might be objected that the smooth marginal adjustment process we have just been describing bears little resemblance to the major resource-exhaustion crisis of recent years, namely, the energy crisis. It is certainly true that the crisis itself did not follow a very smooth course, though nobody's worst fears were realized and recovery has been, for the most part, swift. However, the important thing to note is that the energy crisis of the early seventies was not in fact a resource-exhaustion problem. Everyone agrees that there is enough easily accessible oil available to satisfy the world's conceivable needs for at least two or three decades. Oil is getting scarcer and we are beginning to tool up for the initial phases of the adaptation process described above, but that is not really what all the excitement has been about.

What happened is that oil suddenly became a central part of the Middle East crisis. As economic development has proceeded in the Middle East the Arab governments have matured, become more stable, and found it relatively easier to act in concert among themselves and with other oil producers. They were aided in this by the twin factors that oil could be a potent bargaining weapon with the West, and especially the United States, in shaping a favorable Middle East settlement, and by the tremendous revenue increase that would result from a coordinated sales policy.

This new development has produced a number of serious problems It means that Israel will probably have to be content with a less favorable settlement than she might otherwise have had. It means that the West will have to live with higher costs on a permanent basis, not because of resource exhaustion but because of monopoly. It means some very serious adjustment problems for a number of developing countries, in effect stretching out the main line for them. And it means that that emerging world establishment must face the prospect of admitting a new interest group to its inner councils.

All this has created a crisis, with the risks that a crisis entails, including, as always in the case of the Middle East, some risk of a nuclear confrontation. But once again the underlying message is a more confident one. In this case two factors stand out. First, the more mature behavior of the Arab nations suggests they are acquiring a stake in the modern world, that they are aware that deals short of war may be feasible, even favorable, from the point of view of their vital interests. And second, the introduction of oil into the Middle East equation is probably basically stabilizing in its impact on that crisis. Oil is an economic resource, highly divisible, easily valued in money terms. It is a first-rate item to have in a central place when deal-making time comes, just because of these flexible, marketplace properties. These factors don't guarantee peace, they do nothing for the less influential developing countries who are being hurt badly; but they do point to new opportunities in this most complex of current world problems.

An example of a resource problem that is relatively intractable largely because of contemporary organizational forms is the control of ocean fishing. Some powers derive more gain individually from a relatively uncontrolled situation than from a controlled one, even though the former implies a steady reduction in the size of the world harvest. And because the world establishment operates only in a few limited areas and has no effective formal organization, it is not possible to engage in the issue-packaging devices such as logrolling that could tip the balance of interests favorably. Without issue packaging unanimity cannot be attained, and without an effective world organization unanimity cannot be effectively sought. The more problems of that kind we have, the bigger the trouble we are in.

But most environment problems can be dealt with reasonably effectively within the existing structures, unless we are very unlucky indeed. And even those that require global agreements are not without hope if it is possible to continue the move toward broader areas of international negotiation. For as the interactions continue to cut across lines of international interest and rivalry, new potential packages emerge, and these are the stock in trade of the political deal maker.

Environmental Degradation

In this area the list of disasters is a long one. Some are already problems such as air and noise pollution, crowding and the near death of some lakes; others are only possibilities, such as the death of the oceans, the melting of the icecaps, and the destruction of the earth's atmosphere. Though most of the doom mongering on most of these topics is of quite recent origin, and has some of the properties of a fad, some of these issues are becoming major social problems, and other ecological problems are likely to become serious as time goes on. Do these pose novel challenges to our institutions?

As far as the great catastrophes are concerned, they all represent possibilities whose prospects are very little understood. The main thing that is needed is much more research to understand them better and, for those problems that survive the research test, to develop solutions. It might also be useful to organize research in such a way as to generate awareness of new problems of this kind and get them into the appraisal system a bit earlier.

But all this requires no dramatic change in existing institutions. Research is a substantial part of the effort of all the more developed societies. But only in affluent capitalism, among existing societies, can an effective early-warning system be applied, because only where there is an open society does the scientist who cannot get an effective response from government or colleagues turn to the public for support. A Paul Ehrlich or a Barry Commoner would not be tolerated in a socialist country.

There is a risk that we will not find out about some of these catastrophes, or will not be prepared to act, until too late. It is true that the system will not tolerate a massive crash program designed to deal with a controversial off-chance. That is probably a quite rational constraint, for we simply live in too risky an environment. To follow such leads could easily use up all our resources. In other words, there is a minimum level of risk that we cannot eliminate just because our resources *are* scarce; what we can do is allocate our resources in such a way as to minimize social risks, given the resource constraint.

Another kind of environmental degradation problem seems to be frequently misunderstood, at least as far as it concerns the responsibility of various institutions. The problem of the automobile and pollution illustrates this.

It is now well established that automobile manufacturers did not rise to this challenge until compelled to do so. In fact, they seemed not only to sit on the problem but actively to discourage those who were trying to make an issue of the possibilities of reducing pollution by modifying automobiles. But surely that is to be expected. Management's responsibilities are to pursue their goals of profits and growth, subject to law and the constraints of the marketplace. Clearly, they cannot be allowed the power to silence critics, but primary responsibility for dealing with a problem of national scope like pollution lies equally clearly with government.

But government's response must be a bit subtle. There is a good argument against nationalization of the industry on efficiency grounds, and also on the grounds that quite a lot of the American economy is already centrally involved in making automobiles, providing them with roads, and otherwise supporting them and the motorist. And, most important of all, there is the argument that government should not be allowed to become any larger than necessary, partly on grounds of efficiency, but mainly because a government that is too big is bound to be too powerful, a threat to continued liberties.

So what is needed is a market-framework solution. That is, the research effort, which can be shared between companies and government because of the strong elements of competition in the industry, should be organized around the design of a system of laws that changes business incentives in desired directions. Available as tools in this effort are the full panoply of government instruments from tax incentives to outright prohibitions to the setting of standards of performance. The practical operation of the latter instrument was instructive, because it provided the basis for the decision by the major automobile companies to engage in a massive research effort to develop and appraise the commercial feasibility of alternative forms of emission control. Of course, much of this is already in place or well underway, including notably government-mandated emission controls, and a massive automobile company research effort, triggered by the combination of the government's rules and the companies' continuing search for profits. Once again the system of affluent capitalism seems able to demonstrate that it has in place effective institutions for dealing with problems of environmental degradation. But, as always, they will not be set to work automatically, but will require a substantial political input by concerned citizens.

Overcentralization

All of the examples of environmental degradation we have considered so far, and most of the issues dealt with elsewhere in this book, seem to require adding to the government's scale of operations in order to deal effectively with them. As long as the economy continues to grow government too can grow without perhaps posing a serious threat of overcentralization. Bringing the new management forms in with their decentralization impact may substantially increase the possibility of a much larger government operating with tolerable efficiency. And the problem of power concentration is probably more one of relative than of absolute size. But all these new operations, and particularly the kinds discussed in this chapter, do raise the substantial possibility of increasing relative size of government. What can one say about the relation of this problem to the survival value of democratic institutions in the United States and throughout affluent capitalist countries?

In addition to decentralization through modern management, there are also substantial possibilities of decentralization to lower levels in the American federal system. Also, issues that require market-framework solutions are relatively less threatening than those that require direct government operation of a system. The major government effort is expended in setting up a market-framework system of controls. After that, maintenance and adaptation require much less government effort. Indeed, given the already high levels of government framework control of the marketplace, one might argue that more legislative policing in this area makes relatively little difference in terms of government size and threat potential, since more than likely it is already engaged in some regulation of the newly affected markets. This has certainly been true of the automobile.

There is another and more troubling type of overcentralization possibility, namely, the erosion of the properties of the market system by developing monopolies in the private sector. The growing dominance of a rather small number of institutional investors in the stock market may be taken as an early warning of this possibility. And it can probably be said that if this problem cannot be dealt with by the standard marginal-adjustment processes of the political system, it probably will not be dealt with without some sort of governmental crisis. If such a problem should develop, the structure of incentives in the marketplace and the structure of power in the establishment would both be unfavorable to serious action. The fact that there are no known attractive alternatives, that we either make affluent capitalism work or simply revert to the much more common authoritarian forms, is little consolation. Clearly, this is a potential catastrophe of environmental degradation that should be taken at least as seriously as the others. And the sooner it is taken seriously the more likely it is that marginalist responses will work.

Conclusion

Our future is not determined. We know of no grand forces that serve to fix in stone the fate of our civilization. We do know that we have many problems and that many of those will have to be solved if anything like our contemporary ways of life are to be preserved. We also know that our ways of life themselves have been undergoing change and that those changes will in turn change the nature of some of the problems we face. A fluid and no doubt dangerous situation!

But we know something else, too. We know that in the world today we, Americans, the denizens of affluent capitalism, are the world's true revolutionaries. We are the ones who pioneered that new social entity, affluent capitalism, in which first basic goods and services and then substantial discretionary income was made available to the overwhelming majority of the citizens. We are the ones who created modern science and technology and are, overwhelmingly, the ones who lead its continuing development. We developed the medical science and the health-delivery systems that reduced the risks of death and illness from disease by an order of magnitude for our citizens. We developed that most flexible and adaptable, and complex, of human institutions, the interacting market and democratic state that is the central mediator of social relations in our society. We have generated history's first set of powerful and durable open societies, societies whose openness is preserved even for dissenters in time of war.

And our revolutionary tradition continues. Technical change itself has not slackened and is forcing new adaptations on us. Adaptation to the management revolution continues, and still has far to go, especially in government. We are in the early stages of life-style experiments that hold some promise of eliminating racial discrimination while preserving cultural difference, of transforming the relation between man and woman while accepting full equality of opportunity for all, of seeking acceptable social alternatives to the life of the nuclear family. And we have begun only dimly to perceive the outlines of a system of collaborative international relations in which nations very much different in their economic and political structures can survive and change without using war as the arbiter of conflict. In the twentieth century so far it has been in the United States that these various, decentralized, groping revolutions have tended to make their homes, but increasingly the other affluent capitalist states have joined in. In fact, their increasing interdependence makes affluent capitalism an entity that increasingly when called upon to bear witness responds with an "I" rather than a "We." Others watch, when they can, and copy some of the successes. We have created a social structure that has made it possible to live with, and enjoy, permanent revolution.

PART II

Variant Liberal World Views

CHAPTER 11

Liberal Economic World Views in Perspective

IN PART I we presented the optimal liberal economic world view. It is optimal at least in the opinion of the writer, providing the best selection of liberal arguments in order to make a persuasive, coherent, and comprehensive defense of the liberal orientation and liberal procedures in dealing with those social problems in which resource allocation plays a central role. Naturally, given our interpretation of liberalism, many thoroughgoing liberals will disagree with some of the selections, though I believe all should accept the general thrust of the presentation. It is quite possible that some mistakes in selection have been made. The function of Part II is to assist the reader in appraising this claim to optimality. In chapter 12 we look at some of the philosophical fundamentals of liberalism, and in chapters 13 to 18 consider a number of alternative arguments to the ones we have chosen. The present chapter draws a few general conclusions from Part I and sets the stage for what follows. It contains three primary assertions about the liberal economic world view, and each assertion is followed by some commentary.

  1. *There is a coherent and plausible and contemporary liberal economic world view.* In other words, conventional liberalism is far from dead as a social and political phenomenon. As was noted at the beginning of this book, it seems a bit odd to find it necessary to make statements like this, but they are occasioned by the writings, if not the behavior, of a great many liberals. Some of the strongest attacks on conventional liberalism have come from within the camp. For economists, the name of John Kenneth Galbraith stands out among the

liberal critics of liberalism, but the list of liberals whose thrust is often strongly critical of liberalism includes the names of most of those who have dealt with ideological issues in recent years. Indeed, one of the most puzzling phenomena in this whole area is the strongly critical stance of liberal ideologues.

Of course, if conventional liberalism really is moribund, then such a critical posture is entirely explicable. But that just is not a plausible position. Part I is a defense of that assertion. The basic arguments of Part I are neither original nor esoteric; they tend to be part of the equipment of the liberal practitioner. And yet that same practitioner, often together with his students, is among the major consumers of the critics' product, assigning these works in classes and tending perhaps to criticize the economics but not the general thrust of the arguments. This despite the fact that the conventional arguments are plausible rather than ridiculous, and the package is coherent, relying consistently on a relatively traditional conception of human motivation and behavior in its various parts and unmarred by blatant contradiction.

There is a possible liberal explanation of this puzzle. Remembering once again that we expect people to have disagreements over what ought next to be done, we would certainly expect liberal critics to speak with more than one voice. But, more than that, even self-conscious liberals who wholly agree with the Part I formulas will differ over policy issues. How will they try to make their case? Of course, part of the effort consists in developing the scientific part of economics in directions that help; but we are not much concerned with that here. The other thing they can do is to take their case to the public. But the public has a much shorter attention span for economic affairs than does a professional economist, so the standard approach may have been to hoke things up a bit. Exaggeration, a bit of wolf crying, some mildly apocalyptic prose: There are the stocks-in-trade of the liberal economic politician, just as they are of the liberal ecologist. If some distortion, explicit or implicit, of liberal ideology results, it is in the service of a good cause, namely, that of making our liberal society work a bit better in some of its seamier areas.

If this is the most important reason why Bigthink liberalism tends to be couched in strongly critical terms, there is another factor that helps to explain the relative dearth of serious attempts to present the liberal position in a straightforward way. As mentioned in chapter 1, it is simply that there is a somewhat different process at work inculcating liberal ideology in economists than that by which, say, econometrics or fiscal economics is learned. Casual reading, the coffee-klatsch interplay of jokes and ideas, the gradual emergence in the student of an implicit awareness of which assumptions and approaches are acceptable and which are not: It is in these ways that the liberal ideology most American (and Western) economists have absorbed at home and school as children has become revised and sharpened to support the edifice of contemporary scientific economics. This revised ideology needs no coherent defense, or even explication, unless it is seriously challenged. And the critics referred to in the above paragraph are recognized as being pseudo-challengers, whose dramatic postures of despair or indignation will evaporate with a few marginal policy changes—or will be transformed into a new set of postures appropriate to the next policy discussion. Getting serious about the world view may only serve to hamstring efforts at change that conventional economists generally support.

There are some other possible explanations of this puzzle; for example, ideological writers are like other people in their desire for respect, influence, and even for money. Product differentiation is necessary in the ideology market; when successful it can make one's name almost a household word and may generate quite a good income as well. But human motives are generally mixed, and the product differentiation is typically related in some positive way to beliefs that actually are strongly held by the writer.

But today there *is* some need for a straightforward presentation of the conventional liberal view. The challenges have become stronger, from both right and left, and the corruption that has become manifest in liberal government has tended to generate cynical attitudes of rejection of basic liberal values. The corruption is probably quite a bit more important than the challenges in Western affluent capitalism; certainly that is the case in the United States, and may explain much of the criticism coming from the liberal center itself. A restatement may not rejuvenate the cynics, but it can serve at least as an intellectual prop when such rejuvenation becomes feasible. Without it there is some risk that the liberal critics will be taken literally, and liberalism would then be in serious trouble.

Let me emphasize that the above remarks should not themselves be read as a kind of cynicism. Or rather, as no more than marginal cynicism. It is my belief that liberalism is a powerful, an inspiring, and an effective ideology over a range of issues that covers a good deal of the spectrum of current conflict over economic policy. To argue that people do not say literally what they mean is not necessarily to call them liars; the world is a bit more complicated than that. The question suggested by all this, and which should be put to liberal critics is: Do their analyses and policy proposals conflict with basic liberal values at any point? If so, are these conflicts fundamental? That is, can one obtain the result desired by the critic from within the liberal framework? Questions of this kind will be put to some positions of several liberal authors in the chapters that follow.

2.   *Part I describes the optimal contemporary liberal economic world view.* Certainly there are some assertions in Part I that are controversial among liberals, most notably perhaps the choice of a relatively conventional neoclassical interpretation of the functioning of the market instead of Galbraith's "planning system," in which the market is replaced by planning and cooperation among the top corporations. The picture of an essentially marginalist approach to ecology would be rejected by many liberals as well, as would the relatively "hard" line

on international relations. Some defense of these choices is clearly in order, and will occupy several of the following chapters. But first it is necessary to consider the grounds on which one might choose between two such positions.

The arguments of Part I, and the alternative arguments to be considered shortly, almost all have a peculiar feature that we may call "puzzlelessness." Economic research and controversies within it tend to develop a particular form, in fact to appear as puzzles. This means that the problem is formulated relatively clearly—What will be the effects on decisions by economic actors of a change in a tax of type X?—and, at least as important, that the practitioners are in rather general agreement as to what sorts of research will help to answer the question. No doubt the puzzle will take skill and ingenuity to solve—if not it would not be a scientific puzzle—but the problems tend to look much more like those found in chess than those found in soap operas.

But when we turn to the kinds of issues that divide advocates of economic world views, this property of being relatively well structured tends to disappear. Consider the issue of demand manipulation. Galbraith argues that consumers are being manipulated by advertising into buying goods that they do not really want or need and that will not give them much satisfaction. Neoclassical economists argue that advertising tends mostly to be defensive, designed to protect a company's market share, and informative, and that people show little sign of having their demand manipulated. It is not immediately clear exactly what distinguishes the two positions. Both sides agree that it takes information to make decisions and that advertising does convey *some* information. Both sides agree that such things as mistaken purchases and impulse buying occur, after which the consumer may not derive much satisfaction from the purchases. Both sides agree that businesses will try fairly hard to get consumers to buy their products. But at what point does ordinary market behavior become transformed into manipulation? It is by no means clear.

Furthermore, even if the above problems were overcome and we did have a clear picture as to what constitutes a manipulated and an unmanipulated consumer, conceptually speaking, what sort of research would reveal the incidence of the two kinds of behavior? Since some demand manipulation leads to repeated purchases of the same unsatisfying product by the consumer, and since it is likely to be assumed that sometimes consumers may not know consciously that they have been manipulated, the research design is rather unclear, and certainly would be rather subtle. One would not approach this issue with high expectations that there could be prior agreement by members of the two schools of thought as to which experiment would constitute a decisive test of the issue.

However, even though many Bigthink controversies are, like the issue of demand manipulation, relatively fuzzy and not capable of resolution through the normal processes of economic research, this is not to imply that the issues are meaningless or without relevance for economics. Typically, even serious professional economists have quite strong views on these questions; and typically, they are rather contemptuous of defenders of the opposing school. They seem to behave as if the issue is a simple matter of common sense, so that what is actually in question is not the issue itself but only the good judgment of the protagonist. Furthermore, these choices are quite important for our understanding of how economies work. If the neoclassicals are wrong, then a good deal of the consumer theory that is taught in the classroom is irrelevant to actual human behavior, antitrust policy is substantially misdirected and even when used in the right place it applies the wrong remedy, and economists have put themselves into the de facto position of pitchmen for the big corporations. Is it possible that the heat generated by such issues stems from implications such as these rather than from the obviousness of the "correct" position in the controversy?

I think the answer is yes. There is inertia in everyone's life, and academics too resist the idea that they might have a substantial amount of unlearning to do. Hence the neoclassical resistance to Galbraithian demand manipulation. And the opponents' problem is equally severe. Price theory takes a while to learn. It is not just a matter of memorizing a few propositions; rather, it is a way of looking at the world that takes considerable time and effort to assimilate. Inertia works on this side of the picture too. Also there is the political aspect of the question. Probably most policy proposals can be defended from either position on demand manipulation, but the neoclassical is reluctant to give up his framework of argument because it does other things so well, while the Galbraithian is reluctant to give up the public acceptance such manipulation theses have in broad segments of the population. For each side it seems politically more expedient to stick to their guns.

But what about substance? Is there really no way to resolve such controversies? It seems to me that there is one important possibility. Of course, any efforts at "puzzlification" should be encouraged. For example, sometimes the issue can be divided up into several components, some of which can be dealt with within the puzzle framework of economic science. And sometimes some especially relevant tests can be found—it is my feeling that the socialist-auto test noted in chapter 13 [1] is one such test—which, while never likely to be decisive, do shift the relative strengths of the positions somewhat. But even when nothing further can be done along such lines, another test can often be applied. This is the test of compatibility with the rest of the optimal ideology. To make such a test the world view must, of course, be specified, and there must be some agreement among the parties to the particular controversy regarding essential features of the optimal world view. Given this, it should be possible to restrict substantially the range of acceptability and the relative plausibility of alternative versions of segments of the world view. This sort of *ceteris paribus* coherence test will play an important role in the appraisals to follow. For example, it was central in determining the choice between Galbraith and the neoclassicals for the optimal liberal world view.

3. *There is a strong central tendency among liberal economic world views.* Behind the liberal economic world view there lies a conception of human nature and society that has been developed over a period of three centuries and more. This conception, which we sketch very briefly in the next chapter, sets some not so terribly fuzzy limits to economic liberalism. As was noted in chapter 2, it is possible to be illiberal in the modern world, but in developed capitalism it is not terribly common. What seems to have happened in the nineteenth and twentieth centuries is a bifurcation of classical liberalism, with the libertarians going their separate way. But among the remaining liberals, there does appear to be a strong tendency for views to become ever closer. This in turn suggests that something like an optimal liberal economic world view may have some meaning as a position toward which contemporary liberalism is itself tending as a result of accumulating experience.

This is clearly a Bigthink proposition, which means that it is itself somewhat fuzzy and incapable of any real scientific test. The arguments for it tend to be of two kinds. First, there is the question of the relation of fundamental liberal conceptions to the particular liberal variant. What one might ask of a writer's arguments is the following: When apparent contradictions of the fundamental propositions of liberalism are asserted, are qualifications also made that suggest the writer is striving to stay within the liberal fold? To the extent that the answer is positive, this suggests that the fundamental conceptions do tend to set outer limits to the trajectories of liberal world views through time. Galbraith's qualifications of the scope of demand manipulation are a case in point.[2]

The second kind of argument is more direct: One simply asks if two alternative liberal economic world views are really all that far apart. The trouble with this argument has already been noted. Not only is there the fuzziness, there is also the tendency toward exaggeration and product differentiation built into the kind of audiences liberal Bigthinkers are after. This leads the appraiser into the murky waters occasioned by the need to ask: What does the writer *really* mean? We will face this task bravely, but not very hopefully. The reader will probably not be surprised to learn that my conclusion is that some current liberal world view writers are much less far apart than appears at first glance.

All these difficulties in resolving controversy suggest that many of the disagreements will survive even the best attempts at resolution. Indeed, one would be surprised if that were not the case. For even in science a powerful test of the viability of the discipline is its liveliness. Even where puzzles are well formed there are many disagreements; the essential function of normal science, as Thomas Kuhn has called it, is to try to resolve such differences, while recognizing that resolution tends to put new controversies in the place of the old. Part of the way in which a scientific puzzle becomes well-formed is for a few alternative solutions to be proposed. So too the liberal economic world view will not survive long if there are not differences as to which is the optimal version of it. Human differences over policy and variations in life experiences will see to that.

Essentially, the chapters to follow are an attempt to show that the situation is not hopeless. It is possible to argue plausibly that some positions, even though not directly refutable by scientific research, are nevertheless substantially less likely to be true than others. I think the broad similarities among liberal variants will also emerge clearly.

CHAPTER 12

Basic Liberal Values

PART I did not specify a complete liberal world view. Only those positions were considered that helped to interpret the workings of economies in the contemporary world. For example, no use was made of the long—and voluminous—tradition of philosophical liberalism that has developed not only a political philosophy but theories of ethics, of the nature of reality and causation, and of the nature of man. In this chapter we briefly outline this tradition, or rather those portions of it that have some reasonably direct relevance for the Part I arguments. To someone who knows that tradition it will seem like a caricature, but even in this form it can serve the useful purpose of indicating the compatibility of the Part I arguments with the basic thrust of philosophical liberalism, and also of suggesting the sorts of arguments that are not compatible.[1]

The real foundation of liberalism is to be found in its theory of the nature of man. This theory, in turn, can be summed up in three more or less philosophical terms: hedonism, rationalism, and atomism. The first refers to the seeking of pleasure and the avoidance of pain, to human motivation as having a very strong materialistic, sensate side. This side is sufficiently strong that it can be used as the basis for social analysis, though without losing sight of the nobler qualities that motivate humans from time to time.

Rationalism is the tendency toward deliberate choice. Armed with his hedonistic criterion of choice, a rational man assembles information about the alternatives open to him and their expected performance in terms of his criterion, as the basis for his choice. And having made the choice, he acts on it. Finally, atomism has to do with the essential separateness of humans. The criterion of choice always belongs to an individual and is tied very closely to his own personality. It is, of course, true that others can influence the criterion, but fundamentally it is autonomous, a basic and durable part of the individual.

Taken together, these three properties tend to suggest that the basic element of social analysis might well be the decision to act. If these are the three most fundamental properties of human beings, then the decision to act is easily characterized in terms of these three traits, as we have just seen. And a society, or a portion of society, may then be char-

acterized as a collection of individual actors, each distinguished by his
criterion of choice, the actors being in interaction through the environment that generates alternatives, to which they in turn react. Even the
most modern and sophisticated branches of psychology and economics
can reasonably be classified as applications of this general pattern of
analysis.

A second fundamental aspect of liberalism is its theory of the
state. One of the primary aims of early liberals was to demystify this
area of political philosophy, eliminating such notions as the divine
right of kings and the autonomous, organic nature of the state. Instead,
they characterized it as a supplier of services to the population. Since
that is its function, that is also the way to appraise its performance. A
good government provides the appropriate goods in the appropriate
amounts and with as little cost to society as possible.

But the problem arises as to how to specify the word "appropriate"
in the above formula. The liberal answer comes in three parts. First, the
state is the primary instrument of legitimate coercion in society, and
nobody likes to be forced to do anything. Anarchists respond to this by
wanting to do away with the state, but liberals point to a very important
class of services that, given man's nature, can only be supplied by an
agency capable of enforcing its policies. These are the services that
generate the so-called free-rider problems. A classic example is the
taxpayer in modern society. He may approve heartily of the current
national defense policy and of the level of expenditures that support it.
But if taxes were voluntary, he would have no incentive to pay them. His
rational calculation would be that the difference in the quality of
national defense resulting from his paying his full share of taxes, as
compared to paying none at all, is an entirely insignificant fraction of
the tens of billions of dollars being spent each year on defense. Thus he
will get a level of national defense that is completely independent of
his own behavior. His optimal strategy is to talk all his friends and
acquaintances into paying, if possible including those who do not support current policy, but to pay nothing himself.

Fortunately, our individual has another choice open to him. He
can support the idea of enforcing tax payments, so as to get closer to the
policy he wants. Since the liberal view of man implies that there is at
least a bit of the freeloader in all of us, there is also widespread support
for the idea of compulsory taxes in order to get some of those services
that have this free-rider property.[2]

A second aspect of determining appropriate government-supplied
services has to do with the framework of the society. The central liberal
argument for liberty is a negative one, stemming once again from the
characterization of man. It says that individuals should be left as far as
possible to make their own decisions because of two defects that others
almost always possess: They do not know as much about the individual
as he himself does, and they do not care about him as much as he
himself does. Since our concerns are with broader aspects of policy, we
can leave members of the same family as an exception to this rule. But
in considering interactions with those in not quite so close a relationship,

it seems clear enough that the criterion of choice, being the property of the individual, is likely to be something that, for the most part, the person knows more about than anybody else. Given his autonomous nature, a person is also likely to care more about what happens to himself than to others, and particularly all those others he has never seen.

The implication is that government should be restricted to the supply of those services that clearly cannot be provided effectively by noncoercive means. The general regulative or framework functions of government clearly fall within this rubric, as do the supply of many services, such as national defense, in which the free-rider property is abundantly present. But a major function of government is to take each demand for service separately and consider its appropriateness. The government in effect is a collection of services, not an organic whole. An important modern technique, cost-benefit analysis, is designed to appraise the efficiency of alternative kinds and levels of supply of a particular government service precisely within this framework. Of course, there is a prior decision that must be made—namely, whether this kind of service is or is not appropriately supplied by government.[3]

The third specification of "appropriate" deals mostly with an overall appraisal of government. Suppose an individual has looked over the various kinds and amounts and efficiencies of the government services being supplied and finds them totally unacceptable. What should he do? The answer is clear enough: He should consider changing the government. It is, of course, most important to have a polity that is responsive to growing dissatisfaction by the citizens. That is, by our principles, the *only* appropriate test of government performance. But given the negative argument for liberty, there is good reason to believe that government officials, elected or not, are not nearly as eager to supply services as the citizenry are to receive them, and that this relative indifference will from time to time produce poor performance by government. So a vital desideratum for an effective government is a means for changing it.

But our rational liberal will not stop here. He will be concerned to evaluate the costs and benefits of changing government in making this decision. What is needed is a low-cost method of change that moves government in the direction of correcting growing dissatisfaction but is not disruptive of daily life. An established electoral system of government, parliamentary democracy, provides us with most of the historical examples of such low-cost change. One might note in passing that revolution as a means of changing governments typically has a very high price tag attached to it, but one can certainly imagine situations when our liberal's rational calculation would justify it.

The liberal attitude toward the economy applies the same principles of human nature. Our hedonistic citizens have a very great potential for conflict over the inevitably scarce goods that the society is producing. Each wants to get more and give less, and there is never enough to go around. Perhaps the central triumph of social development in the liberal view is the institution of the market, which·turns this conflict into a basic harmony of interests. The trick is performed by dividing the problem up into little bits in such a way that each individual, in order to get the best deals for himself, must seek out individuals whose own interests and his are complementary. The market does this, and, furthermore, it is essentially a voluntary mechanism, thus supporting those properties of man the liberal considers to be essential. When Jeremy Bentham, one of the great names in the development of political theory, first read Adam Smith, he decided there was no need for him to do further analytical work in the area of economics. Smith's characterization of the marketplace as a system of natural liberty was itself a natural for the liberal philosopher. We have learned much about markets since then, and, generally speaking, the idea that they tend, over a wide and roughly specifiable range of human activity, to provide effective and voluntary resource allocation has survived since Smith's day essentially intact.

Finally, there is the liberal orientation toward progress. This is perhaps a less fundamental notion than the others, but it serves to illustrate once again the way liberal principles tend to be mutually reinforcing. There is a liberal belief in progress. It is to be expected that over the long run men will make mistakes; but rational men will learn by their mistakes and will tend to act on what they have learned. So underlying the liberal message is also an aura of optimism. That is not to deny that the world is a risky place; it is not to deny that men, societies, the world as a whole can take sharp turns for the worse. It is simply to point to an underlying mechanism that offers some support to an optimistic attitude.

That, other things equal, it is better if you can be optimistic is hardly a controversial assertion. And this, in turn, suggests some rational appraisal of the kinds of social structures that will lend greater credence to the idea of progress. One rather obvious candidate is the open society. People make mistakes because they think that what is in fact false is true. Even after making the mistake, they may be unwilling publicly to face an admission of error. In an open society this negative process can be brought under control. In a relatively free competition of ideas there is some presumption that our rational and deliberative choosers will tend more often than not to be influenced by the truth. And this, in turn, will offer encouragement to those who are trying to tell it. Of course, arguments of this kind have to be pushed in terms of averages and in terms of behavior over the longer run. But once again, they reveal the inner coherence of this collection of fundamental liberal principles.

Compatibilities

The general compatibility between the remarks in this chapter and in Part I should be apparent. However, in relatively detailed aspects of the argument Part I arguments are often in even closer harmony with this version of philosophical liberalism. The example of establishment political decision making from chapter 5 may serve to illustrate this point.

Consider first a proposal to alter marginally the status quo. It is put forward by an interest group and so serves to promote the interests of some segment of the citizenry. After appropriate modification the adopted proposal will tend to make some—possibly expanded—segment of the population better off and leave the rest of the population very little affected. This is the typical pattern of political decision making.

Several aspects of this process are worthy of note. In the first place, the fact that the decision is a small one, affecting a limited number of people in less than fundamental ways, makes it relatively easy for the participants to concentrate on the effects of the legislation on themselves rather than on others. The material-interest aspect of the consequences comes to the fore, and so there are less likely to be very strong moral objections to a marginal change that might contradict individual reaction based on a what's-in-it-for-me? type appraisal. So atomism and hedonism are served.

Second, rationalism seems also to be served. Most social conflict resolution on a national scale is very complicated. The marginal approach isolates limited aspects of big problems, making it somewhat easier to grasp the implications of change. Furthermore, as was argued in Part I, we best understand the consequences of doing things that are similar to things we have done before. That understanding has been at least partially codified in, for example, applied economics. So once again our knowledge of consequences tends to be at its best, and the requirements of deliberative choice met about as well as they can be, when change is restricted to marginal alterations of the status quo.

Furthermore, a government that operates in this way lends itself to a liberal appraisal of its performance. The citizenry is not being hoodwinked by grand organic philosophies about the mystic union between state or party or political leader and the masses. Rather, the citizenry is faced, at election time, with a choice between a government that has carried out in the recent past a series of political actions and an opposition that tries to indicate how segments of the citizenry have been hurt by those acts. Even without any research, and despite the natural tendency toward fuzziness in political speeches, it is not all that difficult for the citizen to decide which party is more likely on balance to move in directions compatible with that citizen's interests. Thus governments are appraised and changed on the basis of the services they offer and the costs those services entail, a very liberal conception of what government should be. And once again the marginal nature of the changes assists the citizen in his appraisal.

Finally, we may remember those who are not represented in the establishment. Their appraisal of the political process is likely to be rather negative; getting little or nothing out of the governmental process, with the routine process of change of government holding out little hope for improvement, these are the people who are likely to be giving thought to revolution. In an open society there will be those who see a political opportunity in this situation and who will try to organize to resist or even overthrow the unresponsive government. If they begin to organize successfully the liberal government then faces one of its strongest tests. Will it try to co-opt the group into the establishment or will it try to suppress the group? Probably it will at first ignore the group, then make some efforts to destroy it, and only then try co-operation. Good liberal government will be staffed by people who are making rational judgments about such threatening groups, who are trying, after the group does have some threat potential, to find the deal that will give the group enough of what it wants so that its own rational appraisal of the expected net benefits of revolt will turn negative. Once again the process both uses and generates liberal attitudes in the participants by its very structure. The establishment political game, when played rationally, is liberal all the way.

Much the same can be said of other Part I arguments. Most obviously, economic deal making parallels political deal making so closely that essentially the same appraisal of it can be made. But then are there any arguments offered by liberals that are in fact illiberal? The answer is yes. In the last chapter we discussed the argument that large corporations are able to manipulate the consumer into a situation in which he or she is unable to exercise free choice in the decision to purchase corporation-supplied goods. If a substantal fraction of the population cannot make deliberative choices effectively with respect to an important segment of its activities, then liberalism's values are being fundamentally contradicted. We know that this view is widely held, so this is no straw man that is being held up.[4] It might be noted that supporters of this notion are often willing to concede two important points: First, the consumer misspends only his discretionary income, not that portion of his income needed to assuage hunger and thirst and cold; and, second, he can be persuaded that he is being deceived so that essentially liberal political processes can be used to correct the social malfunction. A core of illiberalism remains in the argument, but it becomes much less worrisome with these important qualifications.

CHAPTER 13

The Galbraith Variant

JOHN KENNETH GALBRAITH may well be the world's best-known living economist. Certainly few people anywhere in the United States can have taken more than a course or two in economics without having acquired some familiarity with his views. His four main works, *American Capitalism* (1952), *The Affluent Society* (1958), *The New Industrial State* (1968), and *Economics and the Public Purpose* (1973), have a high degree of mutual consistency and, taken together, present a unique and fairly comprehensive economic world view. Though one or two reviewers have suggested some anomalies in his more recent work, most readers would have little difficulty in classifying him as a liberal. Furthermore, his writings and his political advocacy are mutually compatible, and his liberalism in politics can hardly be questioned. To what extent then are his expressed views and the liberal world view of Part I in conflict? That is the question to which we now turn.[1]

A problem immediately arises to confront anyone who embarks on an appraisal of Galbraith's work. The problem is that Galbraith provides a kind of extended appraisal of his own work in the form of a critique of conventional economics, and this critique thoroughly penetrates and colors his more constructive remarks. Furthermore, I believe he provides a highly distorted characterization of neoclassical economics. Consequently, an appraisal of Galbraith's criticisms of conventional economims would be tedious and ultimately unrewarding. Fortunately, we can avoid this exercise because we already have before us in Part I a characterization of liberalism at about the same level of generality as Galbraith uses. So we can simply ignore his anti-neoclassical strictures and concentrate on his views as to how the contemporary economy *does* work.

Unfortunately, even this is less straightforward than it sounds. Another question arises as to what level is the appropriate one to read Galbraith. His style seems to encourage a relatively casual approach: Sit back and run through the text, enjoying the jokes and getting the general hang of the argument. At that level one can hardly avoid the conclusion that Galbraith is quite an unconventional thinker, not only an iconoclast of economic science, but a thinker with a constructive view of what society could and should be that is very much different from our present tendencies. But one can also plod through Galbraith, checking out the subordinate clauses for qualifications and looking carefully at the arguments. This is not an easy task, for Galbraith's attempts at persuasion are very different from those found in the pages of a scholarly journal. But of course it can be done, and I think the reader who perseveres in this effort will come away with a rather different impression from that of the more casual reader. When the qualifications are put in, Galbraith looks much more like a Part I liberal than one might expect.

There is one difference between Galbraith and Part I that needs emphasis. Galbraith is trying to persuade the reader that a fairly specific direction of social change should be embarked upon in the United States. Many of the policies Galbraith advocates could easily be supported by the optimal liberal of Part I. But though they may do so, Part I liberals need not agree with Galbraith's policy recommendations. As was noted in chapter 2, there is a considerable variety of thoroughly liberal views as to what ought to be done next at any point in time. Galbraith's is only one of these. Consequently, disagreeing with Galbraith is not the same thing as denying that he is a liberal, and this chapter will have the twofold task of both defending the optimal liberal where there is disagreement with Galbraith and determining whether or not Galbraith's alternative is essentially liberal.

Our attention will be concentrated on the most important parts of Galbraith's position, and with more emphasis on the more recent of his four main works. The reader will probably find it helpful to bear in mind that there is a single general thrust in Galbraith's work that does distinguish him from most conventional economists and accounts for some of the differences in emphasis. If one were restricted to a single word in describing that thrust, the best choice would probably be "populist," in the traditional American sense of the term. Galbraith believes that a small number of giant business corporations have acquired excessive power over American life, and he appraises politics and economics as if he were seeking ways to reveal that power and control it. Whatever their views about corporate power, conventional economists tend to ask not about power but about efficiency: Whatever the power configuration, does this aspect of the system work reasonably effectively, and if not, what can be done about it? This difference in the question asked explains many of the differences in the answers offered.

Motivation of Management

In *The New Industrial State*, Galbraith offers a view of motivation that emphasizes factors not given heavy weight by conventional economists. This is the book in which we hear of the technostructure, the people whose specialized knowledge relating to the making of decisions is organized in the modern large corporation. They ("it" Galbraith would say) are motivated especially by two factors that are largely ignored by conventional economic theory, namely, identification with the aims of the organization and adaptation to the organization with a view to influencing those aims. In addition, Galbraith claims that economists exaggerate the influence of income on effort among executives.

He certainly has a point here. Though the motives of identification and adaptation would not be denied by conventional economists, they clearly are not integrated into economists' thinking about how corporations and other economic agents interact. But there is a reason why economists have tended to stick to a rather simplistic theory of motivation. Clearly, there is a large body of research on the internal organization and behavior of bureaucracies, including business corporations. This work has not been very successfully tapped by economists because they have not found a way to tie generalizations about what goes on within the bureaucracy to generalizations about the interaction among corporations and other economic actors. But understanding this interaction is the real basis of the economist's interest in the internal working of the corporation. Both Galbraith and conventional economists share a primary interest in the working of the economic system.

Has Galbraith then succeeded in this task and finally brought a more sophisticated theory of motivation to bear on the analysis of interaction among economic institutions? In fact, the major conclusion Galbraith draws from his special theory of motivation in the technostructure is that firms in the planning system will try to maximize growth, subject to the constraint that an appropriate level of profits is attained. "A secure level of earnings and a maximum rate of growth consistent with the provision of revenues for the requisite investment are the prime goals of the technostructure."[2] The technostructure wants the organization to survive; hence the "secure" rate of profits. But, given that security, maximum growth is desired, with internal financing preferred because it gives the technostructure more autonomy.

This is a somewhat anticlimactic conclusion to some hundred pages of supposedly highly unconventional comments on the corporation and its officers' motives. For the criterion that Galbraith comes up with is very similar to, and in practice is probably indistinguishable from, the criterion proposed by several leading economists, such as Robin Marris and William Baumol, who are working within the neoclassical tradition.[3] Galbraith's unconventionality turns out to be very much at the margin.

Once this difference is recognized as one between schools of thought within conventional economics, it is possible to draw on a body of conventional research on the criterion of choice that corporations appear to follow, and on its implications. We need not follow that controversy here except to note one point. A new theory of motivation is not needed in order to explain an orientation toward growth by corporations. We live in a technologically dynamic environment, and new technology is tied to new plants, which means growth sensitivity on the part of management. Institutional aspects of our environment, such as the tax laws, also give some push in the direction of growth orientation. The alternative theory, that corporations continue to act basically like profit maximizers, can also explain the gross facts of corporate behavior. Galbraith, for example, puts emphasis on the firm's desire for autonomy as a consequence of the adaptation and identification and notes that self-financing by corporations is best explained in this way. But there has been considerable variation in the degree of self-financing in recent years, which suggests that this desire for autonomy is in conflict with other goals, which at times become more important in the changing environment. One possibility is that it was more profitable to resort to less self-financing and to a greater use of debt financing.

We need not choose between these two positions here. Probably at the moment there is not decisive evidence in favor either of constrained growth maximization or profit maximization. There are considerable difficulties in distinguishing clearly observable differences in behavior that would result from using one or the other criterion.[4] But perhaps enough has been said to support our conclusion: Galbraith's version of the criterion of choice used by corporations is one of the variants under serious consideration by conventional neoclassical economists. To the extent that profit and growth maximization are indistinguishable, and that covers a very broad area of corporate behavior if not all of it, Galbraith's view is equivalent to the conventional view, which is of course the view adopted in Part I.

The Planning System

The heart of Galbraith's characterization of the contemporary American economy lies in his account of the planning system. This consists of the several hundred largest American corporations. Operating individually in accord with his theory of motivation, they assertedly employ an entirely different method of coordination of their activities than is conventionally believed. Let us follow Galbraith's own most explicit account of that process.

We have here, an important point, the essential mechanism for the coordination of production plans by different firms in the planning system. The market, the traditional and revered mechanism for such coordination, does not work. As elsewhere noted, a higher price does not reliably accommodate supply to need within any predictable period of time, and this is especially so as products, components, materials and manpower become more specialized and technical. The contract, projecting the buyer's requirements for months and years—and specifying prices and terms—does ensure response. The firm's planning turns on prospective growth as the primary goal. From this, requirements are readily adduced. Along with similar information and guarantees from others the supplying firm is provided with the information required for *its* planning. It is then able to meet the needs of its customers in accordance with their schedule.

From the foregoing circumstances comes one of the most remarkable and also one of the most curiously unremarked features of the planning system. This is the vast web of interlocking contracts that it involves. The contract that secures the price and supply for one firm secures the price and sales for another firm. With increasing development and increasing technical complexity of products and the processes by which they are manufactured, this web of contracts continuously extends and thickens. In consequence millions of contracts are in existence at any time; tens of thousands are negotiated each week. Contract negotiation in the planning system is a major preoccupation that rivals concern for production or sales. A businessman, at any given time, is negotiating a contract, assembling the information that allows him to do so, contemplating the renewal of a contract or considering the cancellation of a contract. Business in the planning system, it can be said with only slight exaggeration, is mostly contract negotiation.

The contract accorded by the manufacturer or supplier of end products to those that supply him solves, or goes far to solve, the problem of vertical coordination in the planning system. The firm producing automobiles or weapons uses its power to plan its own output; by use of contracts it allows those on whom it depends to plan their production and thus ensure that the requisite components are forthcoming when and in the amounts needed.[5]

This is Galbraith's description of the process of coordination among firms within the planning system. How does it compare with conventional accounts? Basically, except for his initial remark that the market "does not work," there is nothing in this description that a conventional economist would object to, nothing that contradicts the account of markets in chapter 4 above. Deals and their making are the natural and basic elements of price theory; they are also the basis of the chapter 4 account of markets. Contracts are those deals in which agreement and performance on the agreement are not simultaneous. Contracts have been around for a long time and in very large numbers, far longer than the planning system. The development of contract law over recent centuries into a highly sophisticated doctrine is ample testimony to this fact. That extending and thickening web of contracts Galbraith mentions is a nice metaphor for the interdependence among producers and consumers that is the staple of the conventional economic theory of markets. The passage reminds one strongly of Leon Walras's characterization of markets as a general equilibrium system in a classic work of a century ago.

Thus the central competitive element that conventional economists see in the market is also present in the planning system. There is a considerable literature describing how this coordination process works. Clearly, Galbraith's planning system is less distinctive than he would have us believe. But there remains the question of overt cooperative behavior. As was noted in Part I, such behavior does occur in effectively functioning markets as participants seek advantage by learning more about their competitors' and clients' tastes and what the limits to their concessions will be. This leads in turn to that basically stabilizing element, the establishment game, in which participants generally avoid behavior that threatens the vital interests of other established participants. This provides an important added device by which the planning system is coordinated. What it does not do is distinguish Galbraith from the conventionals.[6]

If the above is true, then it would seem that a different puzzle becomes salient, namely, how did Galbraith come by his position? Part of the answer may be explained by his background, which is compatible with populist, anti-big business rhetoric. And part of it may stem from an intellectual trap that many populist and institutionalist economists seem to have fallen into. We might call it the marginalism trap, because it is based on a failure to distinguish the relationship between structure and marginal change in ordinary market behavior. At any particular point in time most people are operating in only a very few markets. They are not collecting information about most markets, they expect that tomorrow they will be doing pretty much what they did today, the quantities they expect to buy and the prices they expect to pay are about the same as they are currently paying. This vast structure of habitual behavior, many times the size of the deals made in any one day, is largely ignored in the conventional theory of markets. If one concentrates one's attention on this structure, people can be discerned who are behaving "irrationally"—not buying when the price suddenly falls, not looking for a new job when some good ones are available, or impulsively buying in a market where the price is higher. A long list of deviations from the conventional theorist's picture of behavior will emerge.

But what has not emerged from this sort of study of structure is any theory as to how that structure changes. The neoclassicals, with their emphasis on a few relatively simple variables whose action is mediated by the relatively small number of agents who are, at a particular time, monitoring a market closely, *do* have such a theory. It always seems implausible to one steeped in the lore of the structure that this should be so, but the twentieth century has been the period in which the neoclassical theory has grown into dominance in Western economics. It happened in an environment of intense competition with other orientations, and though there are still a few adherents to these latter, mostly a bit ancient by now, scattered around the academic scene, they clearly lost the battle with the neoclassicals because they could not explain change effectively. Galbraith seems to fit into the institutionalist mold, not only in his attitude toward markets but also in his emphasis on power rather than efficiency as the object under study. And, of course, one cannot avoid another speculation on this subject: Galbraith's fuzzy descriptions, tied officially to no part of developed economic science, offer him a much freer ground on which to push his political ideas.

Market System vs. Planning System

Galbraith divides the economy roughly into two production sectors, which he calls the market system and the planning system. The latter consists of those several hundred large corporations, the former of the

millions of enterprises that comprise the rest of the economy. These
are mostly the tiny and the weak, who have little control over their
environment, who find merger difficult, and who at times have attempted
to defend their interests by combining for political action, as for example
have the farmers.

Conventional economists too have a crude dichotomy, their terms
being "oligopoly" and "competition." This dichotomy is roughly equivalent to Galbraith's, though the conventional economist's emphasis on
what is going on in individual industries may put a number of somewhat smaller firms into the oligopoly box because they dominate relatively small industries while not themselves being giant firms. Furthermore, both parties agree that the weakness of the "market-system" firms
is a product of their relative inability to control the prices of their
outputs and inputs, and of the greater risk of ruin that a relatively
small firm runs in a volatile economic environment.[7]

Differences between these two dichotomies are mainly a matter of
emphasis. The conventional economist is centrally concerned with
appraising the efficiency of the two market forms, while Galbraith is
more interested in the problem of power. However, there is some
difference on the efficiency front too, with Galbraith emphasizing the
inefficiencies that result from the volatility of competitive markets,
and conventional economists emphasizing the efficiency of the response
to changing market conditions. But power is the main issue in Galbraith's view, and weakness makes for visibility: "Firms in the market
system get much attention for accomplishing very little by way of setting aside market constraints or otherwise modifying the economic
environment to which they are subject. And the large firms in the
planning system get no attention for accomplishing much."[8] The large
bureaucracies, and the cooperation among a relatively small number of
units, give a privacy to the combinations of big business that is denied
to the small, and so further imbalances the power relations. This view
would not be denied by a conventional economist, but once again he
would not give it much emphasis, preferring to analyze the efficiency
costs and benefits of both small *and* big combinations.

One distinction Galbraith makes between market system and
planning system calls for comment. He asserts that there is a tendency
for market-system participants to be playing a zero-sum game, in which
one party's gain is always another party's loss. When one party makes a
gain, a dealer selling a car, for example, another dealer in hot competition with the first one has lost a car sale. Members of the planning system tend to be able to avoid this outcome, he asserts. I think Galbraith
overstates this case a bit. One of the most striking of the zero-sum
games in modern business history occurs with defense contracting,
which is right at the power center of the planning system. Boeing either
gets the contract to develop the new bomber or it doesn't, and the net
difference may be a billion or so dollars that goes to one of its two or
three competitors.[9] Formal conventional theory exaggerates in the opposite direction, holding that in competitive markets a seller is totally

indifferent with respect to any particular sale, since he can sell all he wants to someone at the going market price. The markets that Galbraith is talking about in the market system, like nearly all real markets, have some imperfections in them, so that the seller is not entirely indifferent as to whether he makes a specific sale or not. But the specific sale only becomes centrally important when a seller makes only an occasional sale. And this is not a property that is typical of the market system, perhaps occurring there with even less frequency than within the planning system. Galbraith's distinction, designed to arouse sympathy for market-system participants, does not seem to hold water.

But once this qualification has been made, it is important to emphasize that there are some very important differences between typical firms in the planning and the market systems. The first one is the defining characteristic itself, namely, size. As Galbraith says, size provides security in many ways, reducing the firm's risk of ruin from such things as the business cycle by means of financial strength, product diversification, and a variety of other properties. Important among these properties is one emphasized by Galbraith, namely the ability of the individual firm to exert some influence over price. This trait is shared by many market-system firms, and there is price competition in many planning-system industries, but few economists would disagree with the main thrust of this particular argument.

Of course, it is also true that affluent capitalist societies have long been aware of these differences and have introduced a variety of measures designed to redress the balance. Operating through antitrust laws and a variety of other legislation, there have been continuing attempts in the United States to control extremes of concentration within the planning system by devices from the regulation of prices to the regulation of excessive interlocking of control, from jawboning to dismemberment of corporations. The liberal tendency of piecemeal intervention has been especially evident in these acts. Many students of the subject have doubts that the measures have had a very substantial effect; but probably on balance they have served to inhibit a good deal of potential cooperation against the public interest.

There has also been a variety of interventions designed to give a little more protection to market-system firms than the market itself provides. These too have taken a variety of forms, from a special program of government-secured loans to small business to fair-trade acts permitting some cooperative price setting, from agricultural subsidies to government-sponsored increases in the demand for medical services. There has been a good deal of discussion among economists as to the most effective ways to intervene in these situations. The main thrust of Galbraith's arguments would seem to be: Forget questions of efficiency and think only of relative power. That is, having rejected the conventional economist's way of testing efficiency and having put nothing in its place, we are left only with the Galbraithian dichotomous test of power: If you're in the planning system, you're too strong; if you're in the market system, you're too weak. Taken at face value, that is a rejection of the liberal approach, which is the approach that has in fact been followed in the many attempts of recent decades to deal with specific problems of the functioning of the market and planning systems. Whether Galbraith *should* be taken at face value on this issue we will consider later in the chapter.

A final point. In the days before writing this book, when I read Galbraith casually, obtaining that peculiar mixture of pleasure and frustration that he generates in an economist, a particular interpretation of his basic notion of the distinctive operation of the planning system seemed most plausible. This might be called the Implicit Big Deal thesis. The idea is that the interactions among corporations has so circumscribed the effectiveness of the market that firms merely go through the motions of competition to satisfy the politicos, while in fact engaging in thoroughgoing collusion. Contracts made by firms in the planning system tend to differ from their counterparts in the market system in several ways. They are, of course, bigger and often of far longer duration. They are more complex, not infrequently looking more like a book than a broadsheet, covering hundreds or thousands of terms relating to the nature of the goods and the timing of delivery. Since there are only a few hundred firms in the planning system, there is a considerable likelihood that a firm will be in continual contract negotiation with one or another subsidiary of the corporations with which it does business. This expectation means that a contract, instead of being an autonomous deal with essentially no implications for others or for nonprescribed future behavior of the participants, is merely a small part of a Big Deal that links a number of firms in a stable, long-term relationship. A planning-system contract then would really be more like a new piece of legislation than a conventional contract, part of an elaborate structure of laws that substantially restricts the significance of this one law. Government, and perhaps some other actors such as investment bankers, would serve the role of brokers and mediators of disputes. What economists see when they observe industry in action in the planning system is, then, merely a facade, making economists somewhat like Plato's cave dwellers in their relation to reality.

Something like this hypothesis is probably held by most radicals. But judging from his recent writings (and from a less casual rereading of his other works), Galbraith does not subscribe to it. His comments on the role of contracts within the planning system suggest that the contracts themselves are the coordinators. As we have seen, this does not distinguish planning and market systems, since both make very extensive use of contracts. Nor does it distinguish Galbraith from the neoclassicals, for whom contracts—deals—also serve this coordinating function. Galbraith does emphasize the special scale-related properties of many planning-system contracts, but he does not draw the conclusion that a given contract does not represent the true relationship between the parties.[10] But perhaps more important than this, his discussions of policy do not seem consistent with this interpretation. We return to this question below.

The Consumer as Patsy

In Part I we emphasized the profit- (or growth-) oriented producer's incentive to provide goods consumers will be willing and able to buy. Galbraith's "revised sequence," in which the producer is also able to profit from "managing" the consumer into buying goods he would otherwise not buy and that do not meet his real needs, must also be recognized. The guileful horsetrader of tradition was a manager of demand, as is his descendant, the used-car salesman. Everyone is familiar with this phenomenon today; probably everyone with an income has been its victim. The issue that divides economists is not whether but how much.

Galbraith has two main theses regarding demand manipulation, both of which cast the planning system in the role of principal villain. The first assertion is that the ability to manipulate demand is primarily in the hands of the planning system: Lacking control over prices and under strong financial pressure, the producer in the market system is relatively powerless. The second assertion, which Galbraith calls social imbalance, is that this manipulation extends into the choice between public and private goods, so that the individual is maneuvered into accepting a much higher ratio of private to public goods than is socially needed. More recently Galbraith has added a corollary principle that has certain sectors of public goods, especially defense, over-supplied relative to such areas as health, education, and welfare.

Once again Galbraith's principal purpose in raising this issue seems to be to contribute to his general argument about the excessive power wielded by the corporations in the planning system. In this case the manipulation of private demand is viewed as controlling volatility, making future demand predictable, and so making it possible to engage effectively in long-range planning. This seems rather substantially to overstate our ability to predict demand, whether it is manipulated or not. These days the ability of economists to make accurate forecasts is not much praised, and with good reason. If anything the ability to forecast demand for individual products and product groups is weaker than for general economic variables. This part of Galbraith's argument carries much less weight than conventional economists might have been willing to accord it a decade ago.

Nevertheless, the general argument about demand manipulation must be appraised. Beyond some limit, the revised sequence becomes inconsistent with the basic liberal idea of the autonomy and rationality of the individual. Galbraith's language is sufficiently vague that opinions will probably differ as to whether he has stepped over that liberal line in dealing with demand manipulation, but clearly he believes that this sort of thing is much more important and ubiquitous than do Part I liberals or the majority of conventional economists. Wherein do the differences lie?

First, we might note the variety of ways in which a consumer, for one reason or another, may act against his own interests, buy goods that do not meet his needs optimally. In the first place, he may be denied access to goods. If the trains no longer stop at his town, or a producer no longer turns out his preferred good, the consumer is forced to accept a second-best substitute. And if the government decides on a particular level of national defense with which he disagrees, our consumer is once again stuck with a level of goods that is wrong for him.

Information can also create obvious sorts of problems. The producer may mislead or lie directly about the quality of the goods, or simply may avoid providing key pieces of information. Furthermore, the consumer may not be able to process effectively the information he does get, whether because of the expertise required or simply because of the time and effort involved in making his myriad purchase decisions accurately.

The criterion of choice can also cause problems. A consumer may enjoy the act of choice so much that he neglects the consequences, as with much gambling. More important, he may be misled into believing in the wrong criterion of choice, for example by thinking that a big automobile is more satisfactory for him when in fact a small one is much better. This might happen if the advertisements led him to overemphasize status and underemphasize operating cost in choosing a car.

But these various ways in which the consumer can act against his own interests are not all to be blamed on planning-system misbehavior. In the first place, the typical consumer is very likely to buy his home, his car, his household durables, and his recreational equipment from a firm in the market system. The wiles of the salesman, from blandishments to threats, from misinforming to simple salesman's ignorance, are thus in large measure a part of the market system. It is certainly not obvious that the market system is powerless; presumably Galbraith is thinking of a comparison between the local store and Standard Oil, a relevant consideration when talking about political power but not when appraising demand manipulation. Ten thousand hungry used-car salesmen may have a power to manipulate demand comparable to General Motors itself. Surely one must conclude that there is power to manipulate demand in both parts of the private economy.

There do not seem to be any easy ways to appraise demand manipulation using economic research. The factors involved are too fuzzy and subjective for that. But one or two points can be mentioned in order to put the problem into perspective. For example, as the discussion in chapter 3 indicated, there has been a tremendous increase in the complexity of choice faced by consumers in the twentieth century, and particularly with respect to ways of spending their discretionary income. This gives the producer increased opportunities to exploit the consumer, to be sure, but it also makes it a good deal harder to demonstrate irrationality. Let us take the automobile as an example. Clearly, Detroit has wanted consumers to buy big, gas-guzzling cars and has tended to put a good deal more emphasis on style than on safety. And the automobile and oil companies have been active in Washington and the state capitals in support of highway construction, the stretching out of engine emission control deadlines, and in opposition to the use of automobile-related tax revenues to support urban mass transport development. Probably most readers find much of this deplorable. But does it really imply that consumers have been fundamentally manipulated, that for example what consumers really need is a modest number of small cars and many mass-transit systems?

There is not much point in dwelling on the convenience of the automobile in providing point-to-point, unscheduled transportation. But one might note that there has been a trend toward smaller cars in the United States for over a decade, and that it is accompanied by increasing costs of owning and operating larger cars, factors that, combined with lower incomes, produced the European small car long ago. This suggests that consumers are responding rationally to a changing environment. One might also remember the chapter 3 discussion of the increasing goods-intensity of leisure time consumption activities. The automobile plays a central role in allowing the individual to move swiftly enough from work or home to playground to permit this increased intensity. The fact that this is valued enough by consumers to slow or perhaps even halt the secular trend toward increasing leisure time and away from work time suggests the importance of efficient time management for many consumers. Clearly, the automobile is vital to keeping the time between activities at a minimum.[11] And finally, one might note the development of demand for the automobile in Eastern Europe and the Soviet Union. There were no car advertisements at work there, and government policy long favored the very solution of the Western, control-minded liberals, namely, a low level of supply of vehicles, modest development of the road network, and mass-transit systems for urban travel. But the consumers in these countries, subject to a monolithic control of their media far beyond the capabilities of even a General Motors, have clearly revealed the strength of their desire for a private car and all the things that go with it; and the state has recently been responding.

Attitudes toward demand manipulation by the private sector hinge ultimately on subjective considerations, given the absence of relevant research. However, the above points should serve to suggest that there are two sides to the question. Given the fundamental presuppositions of a liberal society, perhaps one should be very careful in imposing consumption patterns on consumers, whether via the private sector or via public controls.

But we have, along with Galbraith, neglected one rather vital point. As in other areas of twentieth-century life, it has come to be generally recognized that the uncontrolled market economy can lead to harm consumers substantially by leading them to act in the marketplace against their own interests. As a result a great variety of consumer protection legislation has been gradually built up over the century.[12]

In fact, a basic change in the attitude of government toward the consumer occurred in the first decade or two of this century in the United States. As a larger fraction of the population moved to the city and acquired a much less direct relationship, on the average, to the production of the goods it consumed, the old legal doctrine of "let the buyer beware" became recognized as obsolete. In a series of laws passed in this era foods, pharmaceuticals, and a variety of dangerous substances came under government control. The idea was to compensate for the complexity of consumer choice in modern life by, in effect, depriving the consumer of access to goods that might cause him harm. Regulation steadily increased and new types of control were instituted to improve their effectiveness, such as requiring prior testing before marketing some goods and by a periodic increase of the number of goods under control. Some of this legislation was passed in the interwar period, and still other series of laws came into effect in the ten or fifteen years that preceded the publication of *The Affluent Society*. Of course, legislation of this kind has continued to increase in scope, and no doubt Galbraith, along with Ralph Nader, has had some effect on the political process.

There have been other kinds of consumer protection against acts of producers as well. For example, there has been a general tendency in many affluent capitalist societies to expand very substantially the range of third-party liability for damage caused by defective consumer goods. The famous case early in the century of the driver of a Buick whose steering wheel came off in his hand is a classic case whose scope of coverage has been steadily broadened and deepened, covering new products like swimming pools and power saws with their special problems, and extending the liability in various ways. The tendency of the legislation has been similar in many countries, whether the legal system is that of common law or of law codes, whether the Galbraithian and Naderian voices are heard or not.[13] It seems clear that this has been a very strong reaction to a universal problem. The consumer *does* require substantial extramarket protection in modern affluent capitalism. However, the nature of that protection tends to vary depending on the nature of the product, among other things. Consequently, this is yet another area in which the piecemeal social-engineering approach has been applied. No doubt many additional areas of application will be found as our society continues to change. Galbraith is advocating change in an area in which much change to protect the consumer from the producer has already occurred. That sort of liberal, marginalist approach is quite consistent with the beliefs of our optimal liberal.

Social imbalance is similar to private demand manipulation in that the consumer-voter can act against his own interests, and in similar ways. However, the situation is changed somewhat by the intervention of the political process. For example, consider the case of urban transit. Once society, say a particular metropolitan region, has decided on a level of urban transit, all consumers get that same level, regardless of their individual demand. Of course, scheduling and route selection will be based on consideration of prospective demand, but still, the fineness of choice is much less than in the case of private goods purchases. On the other hand, unequal bargaining can manifest itself through the price system, with the poor being priced out of the automotive transport market. In this case urban transit gives the poor a far wider range of choice than would the private system. It is on such issues of reduced scope that social choices are most efficiently made, because research can effectively be brought to bear on the appraisal of alternatives.

But even so, hard information about alternatives is not so easy to come by. Public-transit delivery systems are extremely complex technical and social mechanisms. As a consequence, the individual consumer is relatively helpless in choosing among different types of transit systems, certainly far more helpless than in choosing among alternative cars. He must rely on his political representatives to make these choices in his interest, and that opens up a substantial area for his interests to be given the kind of modified attention that occurs in the political arena. Furthermore, these choices often involve alternatives that are far different from any hitherto familiar to either the consumer or his political representatives. As a consequence, it may be difficult to know even what criterion of choice is relevant.

All this is to suggest that once again we are in a very complex area of contemporary social decision making, and that easy generalizations are not likely to be too helpful in appraising the nature of the results we have been getting. Nevertheless, there is one generalization that is easily substantiated and that perhaps suggests the proper way to view Galbraith's opinions on the subject of demand manipulation in general. The fact is that liberals are generally agreed that there has been substantial social imbalance and that an increase in the relative level of government activity vis-à-vis private activity has been necessary. In general a trend in this direction is visible in affluent capitalist societies, and is certainly evident in the United States over the whole of the twentieth century. Indeed, in the United States the relative level of federal government activity has increased to the point that we have almost the highest such ratio among affluent capitalist societies. This in turn has led to a counterargument to Galbraith: Since we are getting relatively fewer effective public services for our relatively greater expenditure, the best means of further improvement now is efficiency in government rather than expansion.

And so we reach the conclusion to this section on the consumer as patsy: Galbraith might be called a conservative among liberals. For what he is advocating is a continuation of a decades-long trend in American society, toward both an increase in government regulation of the marketplace to protect the consumer against abuse and an increase in the relative role of government services as opposed to those of the private sector. This view is shared by many liberals, but others feel that a change in direction is called for. The policy of incrementalism is certainly not opposed by Galbraith, or by his liberal opponents, and it would seem to be the most effective means for compromising and resolving differences in these areas of public policy.

Economic Policy—the Five Socialisms

"The central problem of the modern economy is unequal development." [14]
The biggest firms in the planning system are too powerful, and many
segments of the market system are too weak. This is Galbraith's central
theme and the basis for his policy advocacy, at least in his latest book,
Economics and the Public Purpose. It is essentially considerations of
power that lead him to propose five major policies: (1) public operation
of weak parts of the market system such as housing, the railroads, and
urban transportation; (2) government intervention to assist firms in the
market system to become bigger and to organize to countervail the
planning system's power; (3) nationalization of the major military contractors and of the biggest corporations; (4) establishment of government planning of the planning system, with such instruments as wage
and price controls and other direct interventions in corporate decision
making made available as necessary to the government planners; (5)
establishing a strong and universal guaranteed income and minimum-
wage law, and dropping full employment as a goal. The key to the
success of these policies, Galbraith believes, lies in the gaining by the
public of effective control over the government via an upgrading of
the relative power of Congress, and of course a shift in the balance of
power in Congress and the government away from the planning system.

This is quite a potent set of policies. By no stretch of the imagination could the policy package, taken as a whole, be considered a proposal
for marginal change, because an either/or decision on this package of
proposals might well upset the stability of the establishment political
game described in chapter 5. So once again we must face the question,
Is Galbraith straying from the liberal fold?

Once again I think the answer is no. Galbraith goes to some lengths
to indicate his support for the usual processes of competitive persuasion
and political decision making. Clearly, he does not envision any sort of
extraconstitutional process of change. Nor is there real reason to suppose
that Galbraith expects any such all-or-nothing treatment of his proposal.
The five policies are notably separable: Any one of them could be
introduced without the other four. Furthermore, the level of introduction
of each is subject to considerable variation. The number of firms to be
nationalized, the scope of the planning authority, the cost of the
guaranteed income scheme, and so on, are all subject to substantial
variation. Galbraith is presenting us with a list of policies, each of
which is incremental in its social impact, and each of which can be
brought through the established political process without threatening
the stability of that regime.

But nonetheless it *is* a package, one that embraces a vision of
substantial change in American society. What can one say of the package
itself? Perhaps the best generalization is that it is an attempt to move us
from one end of the spectrum of existing affluent capitalist societies to

the other end. For example, many European capitalist countries have nationalized a number of their industries. In many of them railroads and urban-transit systems are operated by the government (and often appear to be substantially more efficient than their American private counterparts). National planning is done in a national agency in a number of these countries, their income-support programs are more comprehensive than the American counterparts, and they have had more experience with wage and price controls. To put it crudely, with this revision the United States would look rather more like Sweden or Great Britain and rather less like Germany.

Thus even after adopting the whole package the United States would still possess a political-economic framework similar to some other affluent capitalist societies. Of course, that is not to argue that all liberals should agree with Galbraith's proposals. Britain and Sweden are not fashionable objects of emulation at the present time. But, more important, judging from foreign experience a post-Galbraithian America would still be a very liberal America.

The history of policy in the United States over the past half century is one of a steady encroachment on the power of corporations to act freely. The Republican Party, which is the most consistent representative of business interests, has been in a state of secular decline and only rarely in the postwar period has managed control of even one house of Congress. A simple measure of the decline of corporate political power is Galbraith's set of proposed policy measures themselves. A quarter of a century ago they would have been unthinkable for a mainstream politician, as Galbraith himself notes; but no longer.

And much the same thing can be said of the market system. The problem of unequal bargaining power is a recognized basis among liberals for considering political intervention into the market process. But there are enough examples of just this kind of government intervention to suggest that there is already quite a bit of influence that can be brought to bear on politics from outside the planning system. Some of these interventions have been sufficiently costly to consumers that one may also question Galbraith's relative lack of concern for efficiency in dealing with the problems. At any rate, the general point is that one could easily read the last half century of American political history as the story of a substantial relative decline in the political influence of the planning system.

Nevertheless, there is some reason to fear the increasing proportion of productive assets that are coming under the control of the top 200 corporations. There is little reason to feel that, so far, this has served to enhance the monopoly power of corporations in the market-place directly, and it does not seem easy to make the case that this growth in relative size has been accompanied by increased political power. But the potential is there, and will increase with further concentration. As was argued in chapter 10, this *is* a situation that should concern all liberals, but it is one that can still be dealt with through the incremental liberal procedures.

Conclusion

We have taken a fairly extended look at Galbraith, partly because his works have become so well known and partly because his works have appeared to contradict our Part I version of liberalism at several points. These differences with Galbraith are of three kinds: those that may be fundamentally illiberal, those that are essentially liberal, and those that are apparent rather than real. In sum, our appraisal has concluded as follows.

There are two areas in which Galbraith's views may contradict the fundamentals of liberalism as described in chapter 12, namely, the Implicit Big Deal hypothesis (described on p. 116) and demand manipulation. Our tentative conclusion is that Galbraith does not subscribe to the former hypothesis. As for the latter hypothesis, when the qualifications Galbraith offers are noted he has a quite muted view of the scope and depth of demand manipulation, one that remains within the liberal ballpark and is consistent with the Part I liberal policy approach of incrementalism. But Galbraith's arguments in this area seem relatively unpersuasive, given the inevitably poor quality of the relevant evidence.

Social imbalance seems to have been the state of the American economy throughout the twentieth century, for there has been a steady trend toward increasing the relative role of government. Whether that relative trend will continue at past rates is a question upon which liberals divide. Galbraith's views no doubt will be found persuasive by some, but many liberals will also find an acceptable basis for disagreement. This is an area where substantial controversy is inevitable and will continue.

Galbraith's description of the operation of the planning and market systems provided the area for our most substantial disagreement with his stated views. Paradoxically, this was also an area in which, after suitable interpretation, he was found to disagree only relatively mildly with conventional economists, and with the optimal liberal position. The solution to this paradox seems to lie in the different fundamental orientation of Galbraith and the conventionals, with Galbraith emphasizing differences in power and the need to correct power imbalances, and conventional economists emphasizing efficiency and looking for efficiency failures as the basis for public action. Liberals can reasonably disagree as to how powerful the large corporations are, but there has been a fairly persistent and continuing tendency in the twentieth century for them to agree that corporate power should be restricted. This feeling has been reflected in a good deal of legislation and puts Galbraith and the conventionals basically on the same side of the issue.

There is one more Galbraithian paradox for which we can now suggest a solution. This is the surprising response of conventional economists to Galbraith's extremely strong attacks on the relevance and productivity of their efforts. Their response has been to assign his works

to their students and to elect him president of their professional association. But as we have seen, Galbraith differs from liberals far less
than he would have us believe. As an influential person in Washington,
he made no attempt to fill the capital with unconventional economists;
quite the contrary, he was part of an otherwise quite conventional
group that consulted in Washington during the years of his influence.
And when the portions of his work that criticize the neoclassicals are
ignored, Galbraith comes on as quite a main-line liberal, one who has
put together a picture of where American society is heading that is, in
most important respects, acceptable to liberals. Professional economists
—excluding Galbraith—seem to project in the public mind an image
as being rather conventional, perhaps even square. But they also seem
to have sufficient self- and professional confidence to be able to recognize a fellow traveler, especially an influential one, even when he is
attacking them.

Drucker's Liberal

Discontinuities

PETER DRUCKER plays liberal-from-the-right to Galbraith's liberal-from-the-left. A professor of business and successful management consultant, he first acquired a public name with his paean of praise to the modern corporation, *The Concept of Corporation*, published in 1946. Our optimal liberal's account of management draws considerably on his views, which is to say Drucker was one of the leaders in developing the contemporary liberal economic world view. However, his latest book of Bigthink, *The Age of Discontinuity* (1968), seems to strike a discordant illiberal note, with its emphasis on the dramatic and discontinuous changes he claims we must prepare for, and which are to happen very soon. At times one might get the impression one is reading Paul Ehrlich or some other Cassandra, except that Drucker has a different set of "discontinuities" to display. He is thus a representative of that peculiar group mentioned in chapter 2 that appears to attack liberalism from a firmly liberal base. In appraising Drucker we begin with a short characterization of the main line of argument of *The Age of Discontinuity*, and then compare it with the optimal liberal economic world view.[1]

The Age of Discontinuity

Predicting the state of the world around the year 2000 is all the rage these days. But it is a futile exercise, for we can clearly see four fundamental discontinuous changes already making their impact on contemporary society. The world is going to change in essentially unpredictable ways over the next few decades; in such a context the appropriate way to confront the future is to specify these discontinuities and develop the policies needed to cope with them, not to try to predict the new structure that will result after the long-run adjustments have all been made.

There has been a basic stability in the structure of production in the advanced industrial nations since World War I. Despite the social and political cataclysms of the twentieth century, including the destruction of a good portion of the industrial plant in some of these countries, this has been a basic continuity in economic life. Its nature can be seen most clearly from the impacts of three of the dominant industries of the era, steel, automobiles, and agriculture. Steel has been very important throughout the twentieth century; already in 1913 it was the centerpiece of modern industry. But demand for steel as an almost universal material of modern life roughly speaking just kept pace with economic growth in the succeeding half century. Steel grew with the economy, but because it was already important steel thereby contributed importantly to that growth.

The technological basis of the automobile industry was well established by World War I, though it was relatively insignificant in size then. In the succeeding half century it was perhaps the major growth industry, rising to truly dominant importance in the peacetime American economy by the nineteen fifties, for example. Over that period automobiles grew from "established insignificance" to dominance.

Agriculture was a relatively declining industry and lost large numbers of workers. Nevertheless, it was a major growth industry in its indirect impact. Productivity per worker rose more rapidly in agriculture than in any other major industry, starting from a very low level. At the same time, demand for its output was not growing rapidly. The effect was a dramatic transfer of workers from low-productivity work in agriculture to much higher productivity work in industry. This transfer effect was a major factor in the economic growth of industrial nations.

These three phenomena entailed dramatic change, but it was change of a kind that was already experienced and understood as the twentieth century was getting underway. The scientific basis of these industries was laid in the nineteenth century; the twentieth-century story consisted in elaboration of the basic ideas and expansion of the basic production. As a consequence, simple extrapolation was a good basis for economic prediction a half century ago, even a quarter of a century ago.

But no more. New industries are coming along now that will dramatically change this familiar basis of production. Most important is the development of the information industry. Based on the computer and related techniques and paraphernalia, the information industry is bringing about a revolution in our conception and use of knowledge, and it still has fundamental changes in store before its potential can be realized. Another is the materials revolution, as we shift away from steel and toward the design of each material to fit the needs of the particular job. The oceans as a major source of raw materials will bring dramatic changes in industrial structure. And dealing with the megalopolis will require entirely new systems of production, distribution, and consumption. This still unpredictable change in the basic structure of production constitutes the first of the four great discontinuities.

The policy challenge of this discontinuity is to develop once again the almost forgotten nineteenth-century art of entrepreneurship, but this time within the framework of the modern corporation. As we leave that stable age in which corporations essentially developed the ability to respond effectively to the need to perform routine tasks, corporations must leave the stable command structure that suited that age but has been proved too conservative to meet these new challenges. Craft-skill unionism must also go, for it has the same conservatizing tendencies, especially with respect to production techniques. And tax policies that encourage retained earnings by double-taxing dividends must be abolished so as to increase the risk capital available to the economy. Finally, the corporations, the great investors, must take their basic price signals from the world market, because these are the only markets today whose price structure is unrigged by distorting government policies.

The second major area of discontinuity lies in the international sphere. There is already today a world economy that differs dramatically from the past in that appetites, demands as the economist would say, have been universalized. The French want Coca-Cola, communists want automobiles. This involves a dramatic break with the past, but the impact of the discontinuity lies especially in the absence of institutions to support the new unity of demand: "The present world economy is one of perceptions rather than institutions." [2]

Associated with this discontinuity is another: Before World War I just about every decade saw the emergence of a new nation into the ranks of the advanced industrial economies. Since that time there has not been a single new entrant. In other words, in recent decades economic development has been a failure. There has been much growth of output, cities all over the world have their modern districts, but no new nation has played catch-up successfully.

The reason for this is that the old policies no longer work. For example, in the nineteenth century the developed countries had a relatively underdeveloped agricultural sector. This made it possible for the new-land countries that could produce cheap grain using preindustrial methods to sell this grain to the advanced countries in order to finance their own development. But today the productivity gap between advanced and developing countries is relatively greater for agriculture than for manufacturing. No significant economic development can be financed by selling grain to the United States or Western Europe today.

Another change relevant for development has come in the sphere of foreign capital's impact. In the nineteenth century it went mostly to develop the capacity of extractive industry in the developing countries. Consequently, the borrowed capital could be paid off out of the profits from the exported commodities. But nowadays much capital import is used to support import-substituting manufacturing production that has little export potential. Consequently, there is no natural basis for paying off the loans, and balance of payments' instability is the inevitable result.

Foreign aid in principle could be used to cover this problem. But in practice it doesn't work. "Aid, by its very nature, will flow toward problems rather than toward opportunities." [3] Also aid, being a political process, is subject to the wastes inherent in politicized economics; for example, quite a lot of it is used up in providing the local military with their peculiar toys.

The fundamental prerequisite for economic development is development-oriented domestic leadership that recognizes that the main task is to make the poor *productive*, and that this is best done by a strong profit orientation and by the development of human capital. Given the world commonalty of demand, this means a strong orientation toward world markets and modern technology—though not the most advanced industries; agriculture, steel, and automobiles are major developing-country growth industries even today. Support for this can come from developing a strong world monetary system and from elimination of advanced-country protectionism. Foreign aid can be a useful stimulant to deal with short-run problems of structural adaptation, as worked so well in South Korea and Taiwan. "The most effective agent of rapid human development in the economy has been the multinational corporation," [4] which kills two birds with one stone by also being strongly profit oriented.

There is inevitably a dangerous period in the early stages of economic development when takeoff has occurred but the leaders continue to act in traditional ways. When that has been overcome policies like the ones mentioned above can begin to once again produce development successes. If we do not succeed in this, and fairly soon, there is a serious risk of a global race war, since the affluent are mostly white and the poor colored, and the media make us part of a single worldwide perceptual system.

The third area of discontinuity consists in the emergence of a society of organizations in which "every single social task of importance today is entrusted to a large institution organized for perpetuity and run by managers." [5] Corporations, governments and government agencies, and even universities are all run in this manner. But these organizations are coming under increasing criticism, partly because their central role in modern society is not understood, partly because they are still often organized along lines appropriate to a different age. The organizations are all strongly interdependent and we have as yet no real theory as to how they work. Nevertheless, there are a few principles that can be applied, most of which have developed from the experience of the large business corporation.

First, today's large organization is principally a knowledge organization in that it exists to make productive a variety of specialized kinds of knowledge. Second, the business rule of separating governing from doing, as exemplified in the distinction between top management and division management, applies to all modern organization, including government. Third, organizations must be limited in purpose or there will be no basis for assessing their performance, with appalling inefficiency the inevitable consequence. Fourth, in a pluralistic society of organizations, freedom is largely to be assured by the countervailing power exercised by such limited-purpose institutions.

The implications of these principles are clear enough. Government must be stripped, not of its power to govern, but of its gigantic and inefficient bureaucracies. Reprivatization captures the idea, but this does not mean that owners of capital should be the controllers of every organization, only that autonomous organizations must be given the tasks that government defines. This is not really decentralization, since government retains its governing function; it is simply the right way to solve problems in a world of large knowledge-based organizations.

The final discontinuity is the most fundamental one. "Knowledge, during the last few decades, has become the central capital, the cost center, and the crucial resource of the economy." [6] Nowadays it is the only true factor of production, and it is by far the most mobile of economic ingredients. "The systematic and purposeful acquisition of information and its systematic application, rather than 'science' or 'technology,' are emerging as the new foundation for work, productivity, and effort throughout the world." [7] This is to be contrasted with the economy of the past where everything from training to innovation grew out of experience. The essence of this change is captured in scientific management, which is the application of knowledge to work. Frederick Taylor, its inventor, thus was also the creator of the knowledge economy, and along the way provided the way out for the growing conflict between labor and capital toward the end of the nineteenth century.

Several dramatic structural changes are required by the universalization of the knowledge economy. First, knowledge opportunities exist primarily in large organizations, for only there can a variety of disparate bodies of information be organized for the solution of some specific problem. But this means that the professional of today becomes the successor of the employee of yesterday, rather than of the independent professional of the past, which creates a major problem of social adjustment in status and orientation. Second, in the postwar period the tremendous upgrading of educational requirements for jobs has been far more a supply-side than a demand-side phenomenon; that is, job prerequisites have been upgraded to satisfy the growing demand for knowledge-based employment rather than because of changes in the nature of the work needed. But now we must face the real task of creating the genuine knowledge jobs that will be compatible with the underlying social forces.

Third, the process of learning itself has not yet been adjusted to the requirements of the knowledge society, or even to our present understanding of learning. Three principles are essentially important: (1) Dumb students are made, not born; they are the product of bad teaching, which ignores diversity in learning rates and styles. (2) Learning is both mechanical and cognitive; both drill and insight or perspective are essential to true learning. (3) Teachers are not so much unproductive as engaged mostly in nonteaching activities, such as advanced baby-sitting. Finally, our institutions have not adapted to the requirements of the knowledge society. The university stands out as a bastion of conservatism, subject-matter orientation, and archaic teaching methods.

Essentially, dealing with these problems requires two things: (1) implementation of the principle of task orientation, for example, using teams rather than command structures in the business corporation; and (2) development of moral codes that define the responsibilities of the majority of actors in the knowledge society, the knowledge workers.

Drucker and the Liberal Overview

At first glance Drucker appears to be in fundamental opposition to the liberal overview, with his discontinuous knowledge society, shift to a world economy, and failure of the underdeveloped countries to catch up. However, there is more illusion than substance to this appearance. In the first place, there are several important areas in which agreement between the two positions is quite explicit. Drucker agrees that the advanced industrial nations are a unique group, as is indicated by the significance he attaches to the failure of catch-up and to the leadership these countries provided in establishing his "pluralist world of organizations." Second, even with respect to the developing countries, he concurs on the issues of domestic demand dominance, the universalization of demand patterns, and the occurrence of a great deal of growth following implementation of more or less traditional policies. Third, he accepts the idea of an underlying stability that has governed economic change in the twentieth century up to the late sixties. And finally, though he has little to say about socialism, his remarks strongly suggest pressures within those countries pushing toward the Western pluralist model.

Drucker's central conflicting claim is that the knowledge society is upon us and that this requires a dramatic, "discontinuous" restructuring of ideas, policy, and organization. Of course, futurologists always admit the existence of a substantial risk of dramatic diversion from their most likely scenarios; they also accept the idea that even gradual change occurs at varying rates, now faster, now slower. Unfortunately, Drucker never specifies his notion of discontinuity; it is in fact not at all clear that his notion is inconsistent with gradual adaptation of existing structures. We may take an example or two to illustrate the point.

Following the concepts of knowledge work and output used by Machlup and the Commerce Department,[8] Drucker shows the dramatic rise in this type of activity which, extrapolated, puts more than half the American economy in the "knowledge activity" box by the late seventies. This is certainly a dramatic change, but it has been underway for decades, already occupied a quarter of the economy by the mid-fifties, and has not shown signs of accelerating. This characterization sounds rather like Drucker's picture of one of those "stabilizing" industries such as the automobile industry, whose basic technical structure was established some time ago and which has contributed to growth by growing more rapidly than other industries after starting from a small base. That is, the statistics will not reveal any discontinuity, nor does Drucker adduce any reason to suppose that they will in the future.

One might easily argue that technical change in the knowledge industry is far more dramatic than it was in the case of the automobile. Certainly within the industry there is a much higher mix of highly educated technicians and professionals, and automobile production probably never went through the kinds of swift and dramatic technological changes that have occurred in the knowledge industry, as for example the shift in production of computer components from vacuum tubes to transistors to integrated circuits over a period of little more than a decade. The structure of production in the seventies is clearly and strikingly different from that in, say, the twenties.

How fundamental is this structural change from the perspective of the liberal overview? Actually, it is the product of a series of gradual changes over a period of decades in the kinds of work being done and the kinds of training and education needed to prepare people to do it. Again this looks very much like the kind of structural change that Drucker associated with stability in discussing the last half century.

Another area the knowledge revolution affects is that of organization. Here the basic change to a world of large organizations occurred long ago and adaptations to the new requirements have been underway for decades, as witness the transformation of the university into a large bureaucratic organization in the postwar United States. The adaptations that Drucker asserts are required, such as greater use of team organization in corporations and greater orientation toward tasks other than subject matter in universities, have been rather steadily growing features of the organizational scene. In the universities the transformation is far from complete, but the proliferation of new, relatively small scientific departments and the rapid rise of interdisciplinary research in social science are two examples of organizational adaptation that has been carried out gradually and with a minimum of those inconveniences we usually associate with the word "discontinuity."

Turning to Drucker's views on development, there are two primary discontinuities proposed: the absence of successful catch-up after World War I and the failure of the nineteenth-century development strategy to work in a world in which the advanced countries are especially advanced agriculturally, and in which much of the capital demanded by developing countries is for import substitution and infrastructure rather than for export-oriented production. The first of these puts very heavy emphasis on the effect on developing countries of relative as opposed to absolute backwardness. Drucker points out that many developing countries have fairly high growth rates and modernized cities. The fear he expresses is that if the primarily nonwhite populations of the developing countries appear doomed to relative backwardness as compared to the primarily white populations of the advanced countries, then race war is a likely outcome, even though output per capita is growing at a pretty good clip absolutely.

Who could deny that this is a possibility? However, Drucker makes no real attempt to argue the case, and the counterargument of the optimal liberal overview seems rather more plausible. It goes as follows: In its domestic impact economic development has always been a trickle-down process. A small segment of the population engages in modern production activities and becomes relatively affluent. From then on development means making that small segment both bigger and its individual members more affluent. When it is relatively small there is a good deal of political instability, and this is, as Drucker claims, a dangerous time. But as it grows it acquires steadily more resources that are available to co-opt threatening groups. So absolute economic growth as it continues and trickles down promotes stability. This is not to deny the importance of relative deprivation, but it is to deny its dominance. When an individual or a group has a choice between a risky revolution or international venture on the one hand and membership in the establishment with concomitant income security and gain on the other, nearly all will choose the latter. In a word, Drucker has blown a transition difficulty out of proportion and missed the very strong forces promoting the continuity of change in the modern world.

As for the problem of financing development, clearly there is a difficulty, since debt/export ratios have been growing too rapidly in many economies. Furthermore, the sharp rise in oil prices, which occurred several years after Drucker's book was published, has made the problem a good deal more serious for a number of countries. It is quite likely that this will result in dramatic financial crises for some developing countries, which will mean a debt moratorium, some losses to government and commercial lenders, and a stretching of the main line for the defaulting countries. But this does not imply any necessary "discontinuity" for the world as a whole. World currencies are managed, debt moratoria have been survived in the past, and both debtor and creditor have a stake in continued and growing productivity in the defaulting countries. There are ways of handling such crises, based on both past experience and economic science. But they will have to be handled well if a genuine "discontinuity" is to be avoided. In this sense Drucker presciently put his finger on a potential threat to continued stable development of the international system.

There is a basic continuity in Drucker's orientation that he clearly, if implicitly, expects to survive the challenge of the four discontinuities. That is the market system. In his pluralist world of organizations profit orientation is central, indeed should be strengthened by tax revision in the United States, and more generally by the "reprivatization" of tasks.

He does not even consider the possibility that the knowledge revolution would threaten the viability of the market as the basic resource allocation signaler for the advanced countries. His comments on what is needed to cope with the rise of an integrated world economy are in the same vein. What is wanted is a strong world monetary system and institutional support for the further development of the multinational corporation as part of a worldwide pluralist society of large organizations. In this context he finds world market prices the best available measures to govern trade and investment policy. And this framework too is claimed to be best as a support for the developing countries, or at least for those whose leadership is growth oriented.

It seems after all that Drucker might legitimately have engaged explicitly in a bit of futurology. For implicitly he certainly says a number of things about what the year 2000 is going to be like, and they do not appear to conflict fundamentally with the optimal liberal view. Much the same can be said about his analysis of the last half century, though here the similarities are, even overtly, much greater. In light of all this, Drucker's use of the word "discontinuity" takes on a different perspective. His discontinuity emerges if you compare the situation at one point in time with that at a point in time two or three decades removed from it. In that sense his four discontinuities should indeed be substantial. But so are the differences that would emerge from extrapolation of existing trends. That is, Drucker's discontinuities are of the benign variety that can be accommodated by gradual adjustment of existing institutions, much as a good world monetary system, in his view, might emerge gradually via the further development of devices like special drawing rights. Such discontinuities abound in liberal analyses of the twentieth century, for "discontinuity" has now become a synonym for "change." Drucker follows the fundamental liberal orientation in which there is a basic continuity to change brought about by the strong underlying stability of the fundamental institutions of the twentieth century, namely, the market system, the large organization, and parliamentary government.

CHAPTER 15

Power and the Survival
of Liberal Government

A MAJOR consequence of Galbraithian demand manipulation is social imbalance, the starving of the public sector to the benefit of the private sector in resource allocation. This happens when the consumer has been falsely led to make excessive demands on the private sector and falsely taught that government can do him little good and much harm.

There is another argument that produces about the same result, namely, the free-rider argument of chapter 5. In this case the rational consumer, possessing a clear view of his own interests, makes the decision for relatively too much private-sector production on grounds of personal productivity. If he works a bit harder and makes a bit more money he has obtained a straightforward increase in his spending power. But no matter how hard one individual works in the political arena, it is highly unlikely that he will be able to point to a definite change that he has brought about in government supply of services. It is rational for our consumer, however badly he wants the government service, to allocate his time toward obtaining more private services.

It is odd that Galbraith makes no use of this argument, for it is a good liberal one and perfectly compatible with his general orientation. Furthermore, it seems to have similar implications for policy. Galbraithian policy calls for the creation of a coalition that can get political control away from the planning system. Major groups who are victims of the planning system's operation are already, for the most part, organized into the Democratic Party in the United States. Galbraith wants to add to this segment of the party the members of the technostructure and the market system's direct victims, the small businessman. That sounds like a majority coalition, and if effectively organized, one that could certainly change the trajectory of government policy away from big business. Some of these policies, like nationalization of a segment of the planning system, are designed, at least in part, to strengthen such a coalition's hold on government once acquired.

But suppose now we ignore the demand imbalance of Galbraith's kind and turn to free-rider imbalance. Assuming there is such a thing, what are its policy implications? Under free-rider rules one would expect government to favor big business. The situation of large businesses is just the opposite of the consumer. They have things that can be directly gained from government action and that are important enough to business for even individual corporations rationally to assign resources to the task of persuading government. This is all the more true when their ability to work through government agencies rather than the Congress is noted, for there the costs of getting desired results are likely to be smaller.

Hence the problem posed once again is how to get control of big business. A coalition of non-big business free riders, based on the already organized left-of-center groups, certainly seems like a good bet. The key is getting majority power, and this means obtaining the votes of the middle reaches of the citizenry for this coalition. Professional and technical workers and the more threatened of the small businessmen are the people who tend to occupy this position in affluent capitalism, whether in the United States or elsewhere. The response turns out to be about the same. Indeed, much of the history of affluent capitalist politics in the last quarter of a century is the history of attempts to build and sustain just such a coalition. In some cases they are successful, as in Sweden and Britain, and may manage to hold power for some years. The policy outcomes no doubt have been more favorable to members of the coalition and less favorable to big business during such periods than would have been the case had they not come to power. That is to say, in practice they have changed the trajectory of government but have wrought no great revolutions in government policy. And it is probably safe to say that in all affluent capitalist societies big business remains the most powerful single interest.

Which of these two arguments about social imbalance is the correct one? There is no scientific way of settling such an issue, because a rather difficult set of assumptions about human intentions is at issue. One is likely to feel that there is some merit in both views. However, this is one of those cases in which the truth need not be known because the policy implications of the two positions are so similar. It is possible that the Galbraithian will be more eager to bring to bear some controls on advertising and even education that the free-rider theorist would not particularly favor. But Galbraith himself has not included this in his bill of policies. The point is that the liberal, marginalist argument of Part I is perfectly capable of doing the job of the structuralist argument. Since the former is compatible with the rest of the liberal world view while the latter is not, this is in itself an argument in favor of the marginalist view.

A Conservative Reaction

If that were the end of the story, liberal policy would be quite unequivocal, and all affluent capitalist societies would seem to need a substantial "liberalization" in the same general direction. But this is not the case. There is in fact a large body of the citizenry in the United States, for example, that believes government is too big and offers liberal arguments in support of that view.

There are three main strands to this position. The first is the direct contradictory of both Galbraith and the free-rider arguments. Once it is recognized that government policies are designed as responses to the pressure of organized interests rather than individuals, the free-rider problem is turned on its ear, so to speak. Each interest brings forth its proposal, which essentially calls for a particular benefit to be conferred on its members, the costs to be borne by a small increase in the general tax burden. These proposals, when put together into a package, provide benefits broadly across established interests. Of course, the total tax cost may now appear to be quite high. But tax legislation is passed separately, and there is always deficit finance. Thus, given the way government actually works, there is a built-in tendency for too much rather than too little government spending.

The second strand argues that big government is the major cause of big business power. Among the major policy items of interest to big business is the preservation of its power position. This can be secured by various kinds of tax breaks, subsidies, tariff concessions, and the like, which are conferred massively just because government is so big and powerful. But this argument also implies that all interests will attempt to gain the same kinds of benefits, and that unions in particular have succeeded. The consequence down the line is that big government forces the private sector and, of course, particularly the consuming and working family, to bear the brunt of its policies in the form of constraints on private behavior that promote inefficiency.

The third strand of the argument is perhaps the most fundamental. This is the claim that continuing growth of government is creating a monster that will destroy the system. Clearly, there is a point in the relative growth of government as a controller of a share of output at which the private sector is dominated by government. At that point the marketplace can no longer serve as the primary arena for converting conflict into harmony. This primary task will have to be assumed by government, and it is not clear that it can bear that burden. The basic structure of political democracy will also be threatened. Adherents to this theory believe we are getting close to that point.

The policy implications of these arguments are clear enough. They imply a substantial cutback in the role of government in favor of private-market decision making. The government would retain its traditional functions of defense and protection of the helpless. It would also continue to serve as the regulator of economic activity, though the use of deficit finance as a control instrument would be sharply restricted. Strong cases of externality would still be legitimate objects of government policy, but again, in order to counter the interest-bias of government, each individual case would have to be very strong. Drucker's notion of reprivatization is an example of one possible response. Government concentrates its activity in policy formulation but farms out implementation as far as possible, either to private business on a contract basis or to autonomous public corporations. The aim would be to obtain the efficiencies of modern management and markets while achieving the social purposes that a pure market system would ignore. Perhaps that "conservative" view is not so very different from Galbraith.

The range of disagreement between Galbraith and Drucker over economic policy is substantial. However, there seems to be an underlying acceptance of the basic institutions, combined with a willingness to make incremental adaptations of those institutions to meet our changing social and physical environment. The survival of liberal government, of course, depends fundamentally on the ability of the political process to accommodate the different policy aims at a level acceptable to both the Galbraithians and the Druckerians, "acceptable" meaning that they continue to be willing to use the legitimated political process as the mechanism for obtaining different outcomes. So long as society does not become polarized to very different views, so that the adjustments of the centrist orientation to changing relative weights are perceived as unsatisfactory by a large fraction of the participants, the basic environment will tend to promote the stability of liberal government. Whether the Druckerian or the Galbraithian coalition can in fact be formed is a matter of secondary importance compared to this.

Education, Liberal-Style

The liberal theory of government leads to the prediction that liberals will differ on many counts as to the proper role and level of government activity. This is especially noticeable with government policies because there is only one possible level for government activity in any one area. All those who want more or less are to some extent dissatisfied. This is in sharp contrast to the marketplace, where everyone wants more (or at least no one wants less, given the opportunity to throw away the surplus), and where the market tends to divide incentives so that getting more or less is fairly closely tied to individual effort, talent, and skill. But in almost any area of government policy, many will have much less than they want, and many others much more, and it is all too clear that they aren't getting more or less because other groups don't want them to have it. This is, of course, a central problem for any government and, despite the attempt at simulating aspects of the market via creation of an establishment of interests and a system of marginal political adjustment, it is a major problem of stability for affluent capitalism.

Clearly, central aspects of contemporary democracy rely heavily on the liberal picture of man as essentially rational and atomistic. But we have seen a variety of arguments, by men of undoubted liberal orientation, to the effect that vast reaches of humanity do not understand their own interests and consequently do not behave rationally. This raises a question of compatibility with liberal ideas; it also raises the question as to the proper role of government-supported education in an affluent capitalist society.

The liberal criterion for responding to this problem seems to be twofold. In the first place, there is nothing wrong with believing people are misguided so long as you retain the belief that they can be guided back to the truth via persuasion in an open environment, that the truth can afford to compete with falsehood. This principle does not seem to be under threat from the groups we are discussing. Though Galbraith at times has treated the issue of freedom rather lightly, he clearly accepts the principles of free discussion in an open environment.[1]

However, there is a second principle, which serves to qualify the first. It states that there are circumstances involving peril to the liberal structure of society when restrictions on the right to persuade are legitimate. Wartime and the threat of serious civil disorder seem to be widely legitimated as satisfying that condition. But this problem has become much more salient in contemporary affluent society because there information and education have become much more central. The suspicion arises in some quarters that many people think the way they do about government because the government is their educator, supplying schools and paying teachers' salaries, and because major interests controlling government consequently have a preponderant role in defining the aims and procedures in education and information dissemination.

It would be hard to deny that any such thing happens in the United States today. Furthermore, education is an area in which concrete facts are very hard to come by. So it is also bound to be one of those areas in which there will be substantial disagreement as to how serious the problem is and what needs to be done about it. Liberal underpinnings offer strong support for nonintervention in this process except where distortions are proved. But government is already massively intervening in the process of forming young (and adult) minds, so the principle seems to offer no clear-cut guidance. Proposals range from giving educational professionals more power to giving more power to local communities of parents, from a voucherized government subsidy of private education to the creation of a system of uniform national education.

This is a central and unresolved problem in contemporary liberal society. One does notice that the great variety of educational institutions extant in various affluent capitalist societies do not produce strikingly different patterns of political belief. This might be attributed to universal dominance of the educational process by essentially the same interests; or it might be attributed to the ability of people in a variety of institutional environments to perceive clearly enough their own various interests. These attributions probably boil down to much the same thing. That is, for the overwhelming majority of the citizenry of affluent capitalism, their own interests have been relatively well represented by the established interests. The great stability shown by liberal governments in affluent capitalism over the last quarter of a century represents the strongest evidence in favor of this coincidence.

An example of this kind of negative appraisal of the working of contemporary affluent capitalism, but one that our optimal liberal would reject, is provided by a recent argument of Charles Lindblom. He suggests that issues can be divided into two kinds, grand and secondary. Grand issues, such as "commitment to private enterprise, peace in most circumstances, high levels of employment, and public education" in the United States, will be accepted by all the major participants in the political process and so are not challenged politically.[2] It is on secondary issues, such as income tax reform, foreign aid, gun control, that there will be differences. Since only the grand issues are fundamental, this means that the political process does not deal with fundamental issues. What Lindblom never seems to realize is that a series of decisions about secondary issues can add up to a substantial change in the structure of society, a de facto political decision about grand issues. Furthermore, that change will probably be accompanied by a change in the general public's attitude about the grand issue. After this change, a new apparent stalemate would then be attributed, by a student applying Lindblom's dichotomy, to what is in fact a dynamic society. We have already discussed a counterexample in chapter 13, where it was pointed out that public attitudes toward private enterprise have changed dramatically in the last quarter of a century, as both Galbraith and his recently proposed "five socialisms" attest. The relative stability of those grand issues is a product of the establishment game, is essential to the successful political appraisal of secondary issues, and is a far cry from petrifaction or ideological dominance of our thought patterns by big business.[3]

One last point might be made about the relation of stability to freedom. Clearly the connection is quite close. And that in turn is one of the reasons why use of an essentially marginal adjustment process for politics tends to be stabilizing. There will always be disagreement about the desirability of a given government policy. But so long as it represents only a modest move away from the status quo, those who disagree are not likely to entertain thoughts of overthrowing the government in response to such a move. And the tendency for the establishment's orientation to hunt a place on the political spectrum within striking distance of the median voter again serves to mute the disagreements of most of the citizenry, when placed against the alternative of threatening the stability of the regime.

These processes are thus mutually supporting. Policy discussions in a relatively free atmosphere tend to promote government responses that are broadly desired; the promotion of modest but broadly desired policies tends to promote political stability; and political stability tends to be supportive of greater freedom. This is yet another way in which the underlying structure of affluent capitalism tends to be stabilizing despite the need for continuing social change.

CHAPTER 16

Wars and the Failure of Issue Structure

PROBABLY the most intense disagreements in liberal debate in recent years have dealt with foreign policy. The hard liners, whose views by and large are the ones represented in Part I, suffered a substantial erosion of their popular strength during the sixties, as increasing numbers of people felt that fundamental mistakes were being made. Among the various opposing opinions the following claims stand out:

"The Cold War is over; indeed, it was always about half fiction."

"The 'free world' can live with communist regimes in the Third World, if that is what the people in those countries want."

"There has been almost no point in time after 1954 when the United States should not have immediately gotten out of Vietnam."

"The United States should not intervene to bring down governments, or to support right-wing coups, in places like Guatemala, Cuba, the Dominican Republic, and Chile. And it should have been able to live with democracy in Greece."

"The United States has far too many military bases abroad."

"The domino theory is nonsense."

Behind these claims and behind the arguments that support them, there is clearly a rather optimistic assumption, namely, that an American withdrawal from its active policy of defending anticommunism will tend to be stabilizing for the international arena. A few governments may change, the argument goes, and there may be a civil war or two, but that has been going on anyway. No massive shift in the balance of power will result. A basic reason for this is assertedly that only a few people, mainly generals and defense contractors, have any real stake in war; almost everyone else wants peace. Once it is apparent, as a result of a few practical peaceful gestures, that the United States is seeking peace too, the world will be more or less free of major confrontations.

Certainly some of the individual arguments of this soft liberal position seem to have been vindicated, even to many former hawks. Nevertheless, in some fundamental respects it is no longer a very popular position, and recent trends have been strongly in the direction of winning new converts to a tougher American foreign policy. For example, many of those who espoused the soft liberal position always made an exception of the Middle East, arguing that only a strong American stance there, including a willingness to back up our position with the nuclear threat, could keep the peace. And more recently there have been relatively strong liberal reactions against talk of "a generation of peace," with much accompanying comment on the limits of détente with the Soviet Union. Of course, there have been switches in the opposite direction too, the policy of détente with both Russia and China having been assiduously promulgated by one of America's most prominent former hawks, Richard Nixon.

The end result of all this backing and filling seems to be a foreign policy whose main lines are closer to being consensual than has been the case in several decades. Arguments nowadays tend to center around the pace of efforts and the effectiveness of particular bargaining counters. For example, the current discussion is not over whether our European troop strength should be reduced but whether to start the reduction off unilaterally or only with negotiations.

What has brought about this change? Our answer, as usual, looks to underlying structures and says: There has been a change in the issue structure for fundamental foreign-policy issues, combined with some learning. In exploring this answer some further light will be thrown on liberal processes of conflict resolution and on the role of the economy in contributing to solutions.

Vietnam, an Illiberal Issue Structure

The central problem with Vietnam as an American political issue during the sixties was that there was no feasible compromise solution. Unless the United States continued to increase its involvement up to a massive commitment of troops and material, the South Vietnamese government would be eliminated. And considerations of the vital interests of opposing great powers set upper limits to American involvement—for example, precluding the conquest of North Vietnam—which meant that defeat of the opposing forces was not possible. The typical liberal response to such a situation is neither to accept defeat nor to seek victory at excessive cost, but to find a compromise that leaves the major parties to the dispute in something like the status quo. But that is only feasible if the status quo itself has some stability. There was no such position between the two extremes; governments and citizenry were forced to choose between two dramatically different alternatives in a situation in which neither choice could be very pleasing to very many.

That this was indeed at the heart of the Vietnam issue is suggested by the fact that as soon as even a rickety compromise package could be effected, that is, as soon as South Vietnamese forces could be trained and equipped well enough to control no more than modest-level attacks by their opponents, the compromise was swiftly negotiated, and by one of the war's major hawks. That this issue structure was an important part of the problem is also suggested by the tendency for both major sides in the American debate to conceal the harsh fact. The government's public position continually attempted to suggest a nonexistent willingness to compromise, and peace packages from the opposite side tended to have stages in them that suggested a rather more tender concern for the South Vietnamese government than the substance of the package could support. As time wore on these fictions tended to wear off; but only after some stabilizing of the military and political situation in the south was any compromise feasible.

In retrospect, and especially with the Pentagon Papers as a guide to government thinking, the decision process does not look very effective. As many have pointed out, this was not because of lack of understanding of the military and political situation by government officials. Basically, the problem seems to have stemmed from continued hopes by American leaders that some kind of a deal could be worked out that would not require a substantial change in the status quo. Even when quite forlorn, these hopes seem to have guided the words and deeds of the politicians. One emerges from a perusal of the Pentagon and related papers with the feeling that the decision process has itself gone awry.

That much seems almost noncontroversial today. The art of compromise can only work when the potential for compromise exists in the environment of alternatives. Trained in the arts of compromise, liberal government officials find themselves at a loss in dealing with issues having a no-compromise structure; their arsenal of weapons just will not reduce this fortress. In the case of Vietnam, the very process of dividing up the issue tended to be further destabilizing, entailing as it did periodic incremental escalations of threats and of actual involvement. This too is a typical property of the issue in which no middle ground for compromise exists.

The lesson of Vietnam seems to be that liberal governments will tend not to perform too well when issues have this particular structure. If true, it becomes important to appraise the frequency of occurrence and importance of this type of problem, and to consider what might be done to reduce its frequency of occurrence. One answer has already been suggested in chapter 8, namely, that war often has this property. That is especially true where war is related to the rapid deterioration of some institutional structure, for then the status quo is changing and may prove impossible to sustain. Indeed, the rapid deterioration of an institutional structure that has in the past sustained a balance of power among competing interests is probably a fairly comprehensive description of the origin of no-compromise issue structures.

The disturbing fact about this definition is that it describes situations we are likely to encounter again more than once in the rest of the twentieth century. There are many rickety governments—as we have seen, the underlying structure of developing countries favors their occurrence—and plenty of domestic and international conflict to create just this kind of situation from time to time. Does that mean we must expect to have to endure more Vietnams?

Packaging Once Again

One of the most common devices in the development of a difficult deal is the introduction of a new, hitherto unconsidered factor as a means of bringing the parties together. Often a developing deal will reach a stalemate point at which, say, A's final proposal does not offer B enough to be acceptable, even though both parties feel that if the deal could be made it would be a very good one. The new factor that can convert such a stalemate into an agreement can take many forms; very likely it will involve some additional ingredient that is worth relatively more to B than to A. This is an aspect of bargaining that is not well captured in abstract models because it involves a creative changing of the payoffs during the course of the game. But it is nonetheless central to much deal-making activity.

The key to using this device is, naturally, the frequency of occurrence of that ingredient with the characteristics needed for putting together the deal. And this is one of those places where the market shows one of its great and frequently unrecognized strengths. Not only does the openness of markets support a rather wide-ranging search by the parties to the deal for such a property, but the market valuations offer a relatively firm basis for appraising the value of a wide variety of such properties. It also permits maximum use to be made of the physical divisibility of goods and services in preparing the property for offer and in ensuing negotiation. Operating in such an open environment the negotiator can with reasonable confidence seek to use this technique in attempting a breakthrough in any negotiation involving the market economy in a central way.

As we have seen, much of the political process in affluent capitalism is broken up into units that have properties similar to our market deal. Politicians too are ready to use this "new-ingredient" weapon. But then why can't the instrument be used to turn our no-compromise issue structures into deals that are merely temporarily stalemated? The answer is that they often can, and, further, that the process of generating these properties is underway in central areas of foreign-policy deliberation today. Much of such détente as currently exists between the United States and the Soviet Union is a product of the development of just this technique for "destalemation." No detailed defense of this argument will be attempted, but a brief outline of the way to tell one recent foreign-policy story follows.

Détente: Generating the Compromise Structure

The Cuban missile crisis and Berlin played a central role in defining the developing relationships between the two superpowers. The former produced in each power a quite explicit recognition that his opponent has vital interests that in the nuclear age must not be challenged. The latter provided a model of superpower conflict resolution that, in at least some of its broad outlines, can motivate the search for solutions in other areas. Among its features the acceptance of continued but restricted conflict is a central ingredient. Modest levels of interference with traffic by the East and modest changes in the nature of West German political action in Berlin are accepted, but are by tacit agreement kept under careful control. Once expectations are established that this approach will work, the prospects for further steps toward stabilizing East-West relations in Europe became more attractive, both parties realizing that this is an area in which vital interests become quickly engaged, so that stability is of mutual benefit. The level of stabilization achieved in this area in the last decade, despite some unfavorable events, represents a substantial achievement, and can reasonably be called détente.

Superpower operations in the Middle East seem interpretable as an attempt to apply the Berlin model to this much more complex and fundamentally less stable area. Achieving stability in the status quo in Berlin required some tests of the American ability to resupply the city, and also some tests of the American willingness to defend it. Stabilizing the Middle Eastern environment is more difficult, and no high degree of success can be expected. But one of the major steps has been the achieving of dominance over the Palestinian guerrillas by the leading Arab governments surrounding Israel. Until that was accomplished, there was no one to negotiate with in several of these countries, no one who could enforce an agreement once made. The key step in this process was undoubtedly King Hussein's defeat of the guerrillas in pitched battle. From that point on Arab countries could make and have the power roughly to keep agreements on limitations on the use of force. The recent resurgence of Palestinian power is in a very different context, since the states surrounding Israel now all have the power to effectively control guerrilla activities within their borders. Relatively random acts of terrorism by the more extreme groups are largely ineffective in this context.

A second key element of stabilization needed was the achievement of some balance of power between Israel and the Arab states. This was

partly a matter of domestic legitimation of several of the Arab governments, of making compromise politically feasible for them, and partly
a matter of institutionalizing restricted conflict that would not immediately involve the superpowers. In this sense the last Arab-Israeli war
represented another major step toward stabilization. Obviously though,
to be stabilizing the relative increase in Arab military power must be
limited.

The third step in achieving some stability in the area involved the
superpowers themselves. Most important once again was the acceptance of some fairly well-defined notion of the opponent's vital interests in the area; for example, it now seems accepted that neither side
is prepared to accept catastrophic defeat of its allies. Second, there
must be a willingness on the part of each superpower to negotiate and
to encourage negotiation by its allies on the properties of a stabilizing
settlement, one that would inevitably set fairly low upper limits to
expected future gains by either superpower in the region. This too
seems to have been largely achieved and to be able to survive such un-
toward destabilizing events as the Cyprus confrontation.

Into this complex situation, which was moving slowly toward
some sort of resolution, the oil crisis was suddenly injected. Its effect
is strongly destabilizing in that it brings a wholly new element into the
bargaining process, and changes relative power calculations. Furthermore, it shifts one of the major seats of negotiation away from the
superpowers and toward a relatively separate negotiation between the
oil producers and the most affluent capitalist states.

At this writing there is no resolution, but the familiar negotiating
dance is well underway, complete with the use of threats and counter-
threats in a way that would be very frightening if the two superpowers
were directly involved as the opponents. But this is all part of a rather
different game, namely, the process of co-opting the oil producers into
the more powerful ranks of the slowly emerging world establishment.
The process was outlined in chapter 4; it is always a tricky one just
because it springs from the destabilizing fact of a substantial change
in the relative power of an interest. No doubt its effect will be to postpone the process of conflict resolution in the Middle East. But successful negotiation of acceptance of the new power status of the oil-
producing states could have a substantial and positive effect on many
aspects of world stability. Also a longer-run force is basically positive
in its impact: the increasing oil-based affluence rapidly expands a
middle class that has a stake in a stable and prosperous future. But
clearly, the quality of the management of the negotiations by both
sides will be a very important factor in the outcome.

Just because economics is so centrally involved in this particular
act of attempted co-optation, there is some underlying reason for optimism. Vital interests are at stake on both sides, the West needing the
oil and the Arabs needing the West to make its oil revenues of value.
Oil and money are infinitely divisible, so there should be no problem
in packaging compromise deals. And if the crisis of cooptation is

successfully hurdled, oil may well become the lubricant that then speeds up the continued process of negotiating a durable Middle East political-economic structure. It is always reasonable to be frightened by these crises, but there is underlying reason for optimism that they can be controlled. And each step toward control creates both a more stable framework and many new opportunities for packaging when the next crisis comes along.

CHAPTER 17

Dissent on Development

THE institutionalist orientation to economic development offers an interpretation of the problems the Third World faces that is fundamentally liberal but nevertheless an alternative to the optimal liberal world view. Institutionalism has several variants but some frequently occurring claims are the following.

    1.   There is a vicious circle in which developing countries are embedded. It was symbolized by Ragnar Nurkse in terms of the poor peasant who is weak because of lack of food; being weak, he cannot work very hard and so he produces less and continues to have a poor diet, which keeps him weak. The same phenomenon writ large generates the vicious circle of underdevelopment, though additional contributory factors stemming from the traditional attitudes and institutions in these countries make the circle even more self-reinforcing.

    2.   Once a country has broken out of the vicious circle, the factors that were previously vicious tend to become benevolent in their impact. Having become stronger, the peasant not only works harder, he begins to apply new techniques to his productive activity. This produces more income, which provides him with still more resources for the next effort. And institutions too tend to adapt in the direction of success. If something tried tentatively seems to work, one can expect pressures to try more of it the next time. This applies to the import of technology, to modern education, and to management practices, among others.

    3.   Getting from the vicious to the benevolent circle may require a "big push," that is, an extraordinary concentration of resources on the task of moving the society far enough along fast enough for the benevolent circles to begin to catch hold.

    4.   A fundamental threat to successful development lies in the population problem. Many developing countries are growing at more than twice the rate of the populations of affluent capitalist countries during their development phase, and even a big push may not suffice to move these countries into the benevolent circle. However, once they have broken through the underdevelopment barrier, a benevolent circle

involving a "natural" decrease in the rate of population growth comes into effect.

5.   The impact of affluent capitalism on development has tended to be pernicious. Foreign investment ties an enclave of the economy to the world market, leaving the rest of the country behind. International currency policies and protectionist policies at home reduce the desperately needed foreign exchange income of these countries. And foreign aid tends to be allocated on the basis of military alliance rather than need.

6.   Structural, institutional change is the centerpiece of successful development in the modern environment. This requires an effective government, capable of planning and administering economic development; in many countries it also requires a land reform, and a dramatic change in attitudes in the population itself, a sort of general mobilization of will and energy for the task.

A leading exponent of the institutionalist approach, Gunnar Myrdal, would subscribe to most, perhaps all of the above points.[1] But one should be clear also about the limits of Myrdal's and other institutionalists' disagreements with conventional economics. Myrdal, for example, believes that the market is a necessary and central institution for development in most countries. He believes that pragmatic planning devoted to isolating problems in a broad framework that takes account of institutions and attitudes but does not fail to put heavy weight on conventional considerations of scarcity is another vital feature of successful development. In short, Myrdal's institutionalism is unconventional primarily in its emphasis on the problems of breakthrough, of getting out of that initial "low-level equilibrium trap."

And this in turn suggests that much of the disagreement between institutionalists and main-liners has to do with the kinds of countries they are talking about. Myrdal's major work on economic development dealt with Asian countries that were all toward the lower end of the main line; many of them in fact lay well below our (rather arbitrary) cutoff income. Countries caught up in that vicious circle are countries that main-liners recognize as not yet ready for the application of their prescriptions. For such countries institutional change, it is agreed by almost everyone, is the primary desideratum.

It would be nice to report that the institutionalists have a line on how to get such countries going. But beyond the claim that various things have to be done, there is very little in the way of detailed proposals for implementation, given the institutional situation in these countries. Almost every student of development believes India should do more about birth control, and the techniques and methods of effective delivery to the population are also fairly well known. What is not known is how to make this knowledge and skill work, given the existing institutions and apathetic attitudes. Institutionalists and conventionals are at a comparable loss when faced with issues like this.

Clearly, the main line is a rather crude notion, especially when characterized in the few pages devoted to it in chapter 7. Economic planners in any individual country are, if they are competent, aware of the specific features of their country that set limits to the rigidity with which they can follow the main line's gross prescriptions. Policies relating to land reform, migration, foreign investment, and many others are constrained in unique ways as you move from one country to another. Indeed, effective economic development planning is fundamentally a detailed operation that must emphasize very heavily the specific relative scarcities of a given time and place. The primary elements of economic development programs are investment projects, detailed appraisals of the feasibility of installing highly specific productive capacity and infrastructure, given the particular conditions of scarcity in the country. Some of these projects are developed by national planners, some by local business, and some by foreign businessmen. Developing these projects and developing an appropriate private/public decision process for selecting the ones to be implemented: This is what economic development planning is all about. And no conventional economist would suggest that all you have to do to know whether the time has come for a steel plant is look at the country's position on the main line.

But if this is true, what is the use of the main line? The answer is that it serves as an orienting device, a suggestion that after those initial institutional requirements are met we have reason to be confident that the step-by-step or marginal-adjustment procedure will work in the long run to produce successful modernization of the country. Instead of telling you when to build the steel plant in country X, the main line thesis tells you that, following standard criteria of judging costs and benefits in a basically market context, you will be able to make a correct decision as to whether or not to put the plant in over the next few years. It tells you that the most useful information for *current* decision making, which is also the most easily obtained, is the kind of information you need in order to make correct longer-run decisions. This is a fundamental insight, and roughly speaking it seems to be generally shared among development economists, whether institutionalist or conventional. Differences over the main line's significance lie more in the language used than in the substance of the arguments.

Nevertheless, there are differences among development economists that amount to more than the phrases they use. At the heart of these differences there probably lies a fundamental dilemma faced by the liberal in trying to come to terms with the issues of economic development. In a way modernization is a quite illiberal process. Vast numbers of people who have lived and thought within their own distinctive cultural institutions for centuries are suddenly confronted, through no choice of their own, with modern man. He enters their countries looking for resources and bringing with him money, the media, and his own way of life, which is then reproduced in their territory. Through their contacts with him, some of the members of the traditional culture become converted to modern ways, cast off their heritage, and begin, with substantial aid from modern foreigners, to remake the country in this modern image. There is an underlying implication to this process that the "natives" don't know what is best for themselves—until they decide to modernize. And the interdependence in the contemporary world virtually prevents that from being a choice because of the deadly impact of modernity on almost every traditional culture.

Liberals tend to react in different ways to this dilemma. Some tend to minimize the interaction between modern and traditional society, and especially to minimize interactions brought about by coercive institutions such as governments. Others, noticing the terrible human costs of the transition to modernity, want to use every feasible effort to ease and speed the transition. And, of course, almost every position in between these two extremes is also occupied. Clearly, the process of interaction has gone beyond the point of no return these days. But the issue of the extent to which essentially illiberal transformations of cultures can be justified remains, and at times lends some air of inconsistency to liberal argument. Let us look very briefly at a few major differences that persist among liberal ideologues, even after differences in linguistic styles have been controlled.

Literally hundreds of millions of people, nearly all residing in the underdeveloped countries, suffer serious dietary deprivation. To put it bluntly, they are hungry most of the time, sufficiently so that children's growth is stunted. This appalling fact has led many otherwise liberal economists to advocate additional massive interventions in developing countries. Better organization of the system of distribution of the world's food has been one of their proposals, and, clearly, a number of things can be done in this area. A well-organized standby system of emergency famine relief could save the lives and health of millions, and is perfectly feasible. Expansion of the food crop output in the richest lands of the world and subsidization of its transfer to improve the lot of the malnourished is also technically feasible, might well help break vicious circles in some countries, but would be costly to the developed countries. A modest shift in diet among the affluent away from meat could in itself have a considerable effect on the availability of food grains. And technical assistance for agricultural modernization could be multiplied many times over its existing level. More indirect approaches such as food enrichment programs and the more rapid development of local pesticide and fertilizer production could also help greatly. And over the longer run, a massive effort to get population growth under control could greatly shorten the length of time these people are condemned to a miserable existence.

These are examples of some of the ways in which one might react to all this human misery. One cannot doubt the humane concern of many economists and others who have dedicated themselves to increasing the role of affluent capitalist governments in improving outcomes in the developing countries; many of them have dedicated their lives to the problem. But it is not the only possible position for a liberal to take. An alternative view might go something like the following: Doing good is certainly beneficial when one is assured of the productivity of the instruments one is to apply. The trouble with economic development is that we still do not know a great deal about it. The instruments are quite uncertain in their impact. The idea of bringing elementary medical care to developing-country populations is a case in point. In practice, it has substituted one kind of misery for another and may actually have increased the total number of the miserable. The instruments economists wield are far more equivocal in their known positive effects than is basic medical care, and their possible negative side effects are no less frightening. Here one might mention the impact of the Green Revolution. Introduction of these new agricultural techniques led to a very large increase in food grain output but, because they could not afford to buy the fertilizers, tube wells, and other things that the new methods required, the Green Revolution tended to make life more difficult for the poorer farmers in many regions. And, as noted, the dramatic rise in the price of oil has meant that many farmers who switched to the new techniques are unable to continue with them because of the uneconomic cost of the large amounts of fertilizer they have been using; for them a return to older ways means a substantial capital loss. Many, though not all, of the other items on the interventionists' agenda face rather greater problems of uncertain impact than these.[2]

This argument between those favoring more and those favoring less intervention could continue far into the night. It could pick up on broad areas we have not yet touched in this chapter, such as the political interests of the intervening governments that lie beyond humane concern, and the various policies themselves could be discussed in great detail. But perhaps enough has been said to suggest the basis for the substantial liberal disagreements in this area. Faced with the appalling misery, many liberals wish to suspend somewhat their liberal distrust of paternalism as an effective basis for social policy in the hope of speeding up the developing countries' breakthrough to that benevolent circle. Probably all liberals are prepared to take steps in that direction. Differences remain as to where productivity considerations set their limits to effective intervention. In practice, liberal governments have tended to take an intermediate position between the two extremes just described. And it seems that the possible types of aid to developing countries are sufficiently divisible that future policies will be discussed in essentially incremental terms. Just possibly that "liberalization" of the issue of economic development will have the usual outcome of keeping the discussion firmly tied to policy alternatives whose consequences we are best able to judge.

In conclusion, the most important point is that once a country gets onto the main line, liberal, incremental processes come into their own, and the dilemmas we have just been discussing become progressively muted. That is the message of underlying liberal optimism that informs the optimal liberal economic world view.

CHAPTER 18

Ecological Cassandras

IN the last decade or so a new concept has emerged that might be called global specialization. Problems of resource exhaustion, pollution, and issues associated with the atom and energy all seem to have in common a sort of global relevance. It takes specialized technological knowledge to understand the physical processes that generate these problems; it takes biological knowledge to understand the interaction between these processes and the environment and human beings; and it takes knowledge of economics and politics to understand the policy implications and possibilities associated with these problems. A number of scientists, of whom Paul Ehrlich and Barry Commoner are perhaps the best known, have become leaders of this specialization, which is now taught to many university students.

It seems too that there is an increasing tendency for practitioners of global specialization to have a particular orientation toward economics and politics. The Ehrlichs are among the most vehement on this subject, and so they state the position most explicitly: "The story of the energy mess underlines the utter incompetence of our institutions and leaders at dealing with dislocations that, compared with the coming food-environment-economic-human-relations problems, were easy to foresee and avert." [1] Barry Commoner seems to agree:

In tracing the origin of the energy crisis, and its relation to the crises in the environment and the economy, we have found that these arise from some as yet unspecified fault in the economic system which may be so basic as to suggest that the system is self-contradictory and fated to collapse. . . . All this suggests that it may be time to view the faults of the U.S. capitalist economic system from the vantage point of a socialist alternative—to debate the relative merits of capitalism and socialism. [2]

The problems are viewed as fundamental, seriously threatening our survival as a society, and the required remedies are believed to be drastic.

The problems that produce this rejection of our central institutions are undeniably serious. Nuclear war, waste, and proliferation, smoggy air, foul water, a limited and rapidly diminishing supply of petroleum:

No one denies that these are serious problems and even that some of them have the power to bring down our civilization if we do not react to them effectively. One more thing is probably true: There is not a single person around with any understanding of these problems who believes that our response to date has been wholly satisfactory.

Certainly the situation described in the last paragraph is consistent with the conclusion that our institutions are utterly incompetent. But is that the only, or even the most plausible conclusion to reach? The answer to that is no, and the reasons for it are revealing. Let us begin with a metaphor.

In the recent past—and for at least the near future—the greatest scourge in our society has been cancer. Not only is it the leading cause of death, the nature of the death it causes tends to be among the most unpleasant imaginable. And yet I think it safe to say that despite a steadily increasing intensity of research effort over the past decade or two, not a single serious research worker is devoting himself to finding the cure for cancer! Should we conclude that our institutions are utterly incompetent? Of course, the answer is no. Early in the game there were hopes that *the* cure for cancer might be found. But as research progressed it became clear that cancer is a multivariate phenomenon, that there are many different kinds of cancer, and that ending the scourge will require a many-sided effort to deal with this many-sided phenomenon. In some of these areas substantial progress has been made in effecting actual cures. In other areas the best news is nothing more than a steady accretion of information, of more accurate descriptions of the course of some of the diseases we call cancer and of the conditions under which they occur. And, of course, there are areas in which inter-mediate stages have been reached. No doubt many mistakes have been made. Some of them have been political-economic in nature, involving the allocation of resources for research to the wrong areas. But outside of the lunatic fringe, the fundamental failure to find *the* cure for cancer is not regarded as a product of utterly incompetent institutions.

The analogy with ecological problems is fairly close. Basically, ecological problems are externalities, costs and benefits that the actions of some citizens impose on others but that are not mediated by the market economy. The general property that distinguishes externalities from other resource allocations is that the market-based price system will not in general lead to an efficient resource allocation in the case of externalities; indeed, the market tends to create incentives that prevent efficient resource allocation in these cases. Economists at first began looking for a general solution to this problem in the form of some sort of overall price-generating scheme that would create the appropriate incentives among the actors in an economic system. But such a solution did not manifest itself. Instead, it turned out that there are many different kinds of ecological or environmental problems, each requiring a different pattern of research to understand and a different pattern of policies to control. Furthermore, there are wide differences in the level of our understanding of different ecological problems, a fact which in itself has important differential policy implications.

The conclusion that one should then draw, to complete the analogy with cancer, is that researchers no longer search for *the* solution to the ecological problem. But unfortunately at this point our analogy fails us. We see that Cassandras abound, and that they feel there is a fundamental flaw in the system such that *the* problem of ecology calls for *the* solution, namely, a fundamental transformation of our basic social and political institutions. At some point all metaphors fail; however, in this case the failure itself is revealing, because the metaphor should not break down here. What has happened?

The first point to note is that there is a basic contradiction in the notion of a "global specialization." The world long ago became too complex for universal minds to grasp all its workings at a detailed level. But that seems to be the way human ecologists describe their discipline. They have, in effect, defined themselves as jacks-of-all-trades, but that carries with it the consequent, They are masters of none. Perhaps more important, this global way of defining a field predisposes the practitioner to global solutions. Lacking the expertise to deal with problems in a detailed way, the ecological Cassandra is also unable to deal with policy in a detailed way. Forced to an overall consistency in his level of discourse, he tends strongly to look for solutions that match the global generality of his characterizations of technology and biology.

Furthermore, the biologist/ecologist turned eco-Cassandra is likely to bring with him some of the basic preconceptions of his scientific field. And the ecologist's field is conserving in its general orientation. In his professional life he is looking for the conditions that define ecological balance, the state in which a variety of organisms can interact and continue to coexist with no tendencies for some species to die out and others to become dominant. Transferred to the realm of the human environment, this search for balance tends to bias him against the growth of humans in both numbers and affluence. For inevitably that means that other aspects of the environment, from whooping cranes to mercury ores, will tend relatively to decline. Also associated with this notion of ecological balance is the idea of harmony, which seems to manifest itself in an immediate distrust of the motives of those who disagree with his own prognoses and diagnoses. The ecologist's picture of the world in a state of harmonious balance has no place in it for those who may think they prefer another world.

The Liberal Response

All this sounds rather illiberal, even radical. However, eco-Cassandrism seems to be widely believed by many people who in other respects, in their nonecological politics and their personal lives, are thoroughgoing liberals. However illiberal it may sound, it is a critique of contemporary affluent capialism that has grown up from within liberal ranks. Furthermore, because economists who have been concerned with ecological issues have not caught the public eye, there has not been a very effective response.

The general liberal response to these charges has already been outlined in chapter 10. Emphasis was placed there on the fact that the ecological problems we face do not differ in essence from other failures of the market that have come to be understood and controlled during the course of development of affluent capitalism in this century. Also emphasized was the fact that many market externalities are already under substantial control, and that the process of controlling externalities does not pose any fundamentally new challenges to the system. Marginal change, incrementalism, is the process that makes best use of available knowledge and is also the process that the political-economic institutions of affluent capitalism are best able to implement effectively.

It may be useful at this point to describe one of the typical liberal policy responses to certain ecological problems, so as to convey some notion as to how, within the liberal framework, processes often ignored by noneconomists can be brought to bear effectively to produce a relatively decentralized, limited, but nonetheless effective abatement of environmental degradation. This is the use of an effluent tax as a substitute for regulative prohibition of pollution.[3] The idea is to levy a tax on the direct polluter at a rate that varies with the rate at which he emits the designated pollutants. Such a system can have several advantages. In the first place, it has consequences somewhat like those of the marketplace. The polluter is now forced to consider pollution a cost of doing business. This leads him to search for ways to reduce his cost, among which such things as finding alternative, less polluting production processes and sponsoring the development of new technologies will have some priority. It tends to locate the focus of concern in a place where something can be done about it. It tends to tie penalties for pollution to the benefits that also accompany pollution, namely, the goods whose production generates the pollution as a side effect. Thus the consumers of polluting products will have to pay a higher price for those products, and they too will be seeking out alternatives. Also the tax recaptures for society resources that are the product of the social cost of pollution and that enhance the government's general ability to deal with social problems. And finally, the administrative cost is often relatively small, since no elaborate apparatus is needed beyond the actual metering of pollutant flows.

Such a system will not deal with every problem of environmental degradation. For example, land-management issues such as preservation of wilderness areas cannot be solved by a metering-and-taxing system alone. And some activities are easier to tax than others. Nuclear wastes must be carefully monitored, but taxing the emission of a fission reactor will not do much for either nuclear proliferation or waste disposal. The problem here is that the first is primarily a political problem and the second a problem of technological design that cannot benefit much from decentralized search for solutions by the operators of power plants. But in some areas, such as water-basin quality control and perhaps in automotive smog control, the effluent tax either has already quite a good track record or considerable promise. And there is no reason to suppose that our institutions are too incompetent to be capable of appraising and implementing a control scheme of this kind.[4]

So this is the liberal model: Try to break up the problems into manageable units and then try to find a way of dealing with them, one by one, that will yield reasonable results. There is no evidence in the works of the eco-Cassandras that demonstrates that this method, proven already in a hundred areas of social control in this century, will not also be capable of dealing with the ecological problems we face that are capable of human solution.

But some features of the solution, as indeed of the mode of operation of liberal political economy, need to be borne in mind. It is quite possible that even after the most successful application of this technique to a pollution issue, there will not be a single actor in the system who is wholly satisfied with the result. For the result will be a particular level of supply of each of several pollutants and of each of several goods associated with the pollutants in production. Probably nearly everyone will feel that some levels of pollutant supply should be lower or some levels of goods supply should be higher (or at least their prices lower); probably no one will feel that the political and economic process has gotten things exactly right. But that, as has by now been argued many times, is the way things work when the population has diverse tastes and technology decrees that only one level of pollution is available to society (because there is only one Lake Erie). In such situations, the perfect society unfortunately just does not exist. The measure of success is whether enough people are sufficiently satisfied that they are not actively trying to change the government because of this particular issue.

However, there appear to be some government policies toward ecological problems that have inhibited an effective liberal approach. One of these has to do with training. Half or more of our legislators were trained as lawyers. This tends to predispose them toward regulative solutions, which they have come to understand because of the nature of their profession. By the same token, they tend to be mistrustful of economists' approaches just because of their lack of education—and no doubt because of the failure of economists successfully to educate. Perhaps even more serious an impediment to dispassionate consideration of possibilities such as the effluent tax is the fact that it *is* a tax. A congressmen usually wants to be reelected. Supporting higher taxes is a good way to lose votes. And regulation does not impose direct and immediate costs on the citizenry, as do taxes. So there is a bias against the one and in favor of the other approach that can produce the bad outcomes of big bureaucracy, corruption, and, ultimately, ineffective control of pollution.

That this is a problem cannot be doubted. That it cannot be overcome *can* be doubted. In fact, help is already on the way. The very expansion of the activities of economists into nearly every area of government operation has tended to increase the knowledge of economics among civil servants. Trainee programs in the universities, such as the recently developed schools of public policy, put far more stress on economics than in the past. And a number of economists have been acquiring expertise in specific aspects of externalities, so that the economist's voice will be increasingly heard. Finally, despite their reluctance, congressmen have many times been willing to levy a tax once the favoring arguments have persuaded a sufficient number of their constituents. In the ecological area much needs to be learned before definitive solutions can be devised. But it is already clear that the economists who are joining the fray are adding their voices to the cause of incrementalism, not to that of eco-Cassandrism. Liberalism is once again rapidly becoming as lively in ecology as it is elsewhere in the realm of economic policy.

In Part II we have seen a variety of partial dissents from the optimal liberal position of Part I. On the whole it seems that when the apocalyptic prose is discounted the actual proposals turn out to be quite liberal and evolutionary in their thrust. Our ecological Cassandras represent something of an extreme, since they do appear to believe that the institutions of affluent capitalism are corrupt beyond repair. However, they have nothing to offer in its place. Commoner's suggestion that it is time to take a look a socialism is a bit tardy: A whole field of neoclassical economics is devoted to this topic. It is called comparative economic systems and studies, via both theoretical and utopian models and empirical study of existing socialist economies, the properties of this set of institutions. The field has been flourishing for a quarter of a century and though this is not the place to report the results of its investigations, one can at least point out that it has had a high propensity to turn students of the subject into nonsocialists. Affluent capitalism can approach the prospect of Commoner's test with great confidence.

Drucker and Galbraith and Myrdal are more typical of the partial dissenters from the optimal liberal perspective. When stylistic and terminological difficulties are overcome, Drucker and Galbraith deal in reforms that are tailor made for the establishment game and are thoroughly liberal in their thrust. Galbraith and Myrdal are very critical of neoclassical economics, the conventional economics of American academe, but as we have seen the questions they ask can be quickly adapted to the neoclassical framework without substantial distortion, and these questions can probably be studied much more effectively within that framework than from the rather vague perspectives the authors would put in its place. Both men have helped economists to widen their perspectives, but they have done so without offering a substantive or constructive alternative to the optimal liberal approach to problem solving. And on our translation of their remarks the substantive differences with the Part I version of liberalism are not so great after all.

This strong central tendency among liberals is no accident. We humans tend naturally to gravitate toward success. It is the success of affluent capitalist societies in dealing with the great issues of the most dynamic era in world history that makes us reluctant to tamper in sudden and drastic ways with our social mechanisms. And as we have seen, the structure of affluent capitalist institutions is such that success tends to breed success. Success with problems of the recent past gives us models to emulate in dealing wih the future, and it also gives us more knowledge about the structure of current society with which to confront the new problems. There will always be problems to face, but our survey in chapters 10 and 18 indicates that the ones we currently face are not fundamentally different from those we have been dealing with. Liberalism is the correct perspective with which to confront our future problems.

Notes*

Chapter 2

1. I might note, somewhat regretfully, that this assertion has been confirmed by the reaction of one liberal reader of this volume. "Why go over it all once again?" he asked. For one who is exposed daily to colleagues who clearly have absorbed it already, it seems incredible that the contemporary liberal economic world view has not yet been systematically articulated.

Chapter 3

1. The numerical data on the United States in this chapter, unless otherwise noted, is taken from *Historical Statistics of the United States,* U.S. Department of Commerce, 1960, the 1965 publication, *Continuation to 1962,** and recent issues of *Statistical Abstract of the United States.**
2. Staffan Linder [Burenstam], *The Harried Leisure Class* (New York: Columbia University Press, 1970).
3. For a survey of the evidence, including international comparisons, see Reinhard Bendix and S. M. Lipset, *Social Mobility in Industrial Society* (Berkeley, Calif.: University of California Press, 1959).
4. Data for this section was culled from the *Statistical Yearbooks* of the United Nations, from the *Economic Surveys of Europe* volumes of the United Nations' Economic Commission for Europe, and from Simon Kuznets, *Modern Economic Growth* (New Haven: Yale University Press, 1967).*
5. Some interesting analyses of these differences and similarities can be found in Frederick Pryor, *Property and Industrial Organization in Communist and Capitalist Countries* (Bloomington: Indiana University Press, 1973).
6. Edward F. Denison was so struck by this growing similarity that he made a statistical test in his *Why Growth Rates Differ, Postwar Experience in Nine Western Countries* (Washington: Brookings Institution, 1967),* which, though controversial, suggests strongly that patterns of European demand are rapidly converging on those of the more affluent United States.

Chapter 4

1. John Kenneth Galbraith in his recent book, *Economics and the Public Purpose* (Boston: Houghton Mifflin, 1973),* makes pie slicing (zero-sum games) the major property of conventional markets. We return to this peculiar argument of his in chapter 13, but note here that few economists would find it acceptable.
2. For a short survey of the evidence on concentration, see Richard Caves, *American Industry: Structure, Conduct, Performance,* 3rd ed. (Englewood Cliffs, N.J.: Prentice-Hall, 1972).*
3. For an appraisal of evidence on the relation between technical change and monopoly, see Edwin Mansfield, *The Economics of Technological Change* (New York: Norton, 1968).
4. See pp. 111–16 for a negative appraisal of Galbraith's claim that the market has been replaced by "the planning system."
5. Some of this legislation is discussed at p. 120. For a short history of this substantial and steadily growing body of legislation, see *Congressional Quarterly: Congress and the Nation, 1945–1964,* vol. 1, 1965, pp. 1159–85.

* Starred items are available in paperback editions.

Chapter 5

1. *Congress and the Nation, 1965–1968*, vol. 2, pp. 558ff.
2. As an example, a national health bill has been kicking around Congress for years and as of this writing is still some way from passage. This reflects the power of the American Medical Association and allied interests, who in this case have proved to be an effective veto group. But their power is far from total even in their area of primary interest. Several recent bills that have very substantially increased federal expenditures on and control over aspects of the supply of health services have passed despite AMA opposition, most notably the Medicare bill. In these cases the best the AMA could do was obtain some modifications of the laws. Cf. ibid., pp. 751–56.
3. This proposal is a promanagement cousin to the European-style national wage bargain. Obviously, for it to work there must be some organization that can represent essentially all of labor, and another organization for all of management. The European experience with such systems is mixed, but worth considering.
4. This seems to be the view of Charles Lindblom, *Politics and Markets, The World's Political-Economic Systems* (New York: Basic Books, 1977), chaps. 13–14. Lindblom apparently does not feel that the massive body of prolabor legislation enacted during the past four decades, over persistent business opposition, constitutes serious evidence against this view. For further comment on the nature of this misunderstanding, see p. 140. Lindblom presents a variety of evidence that, however, makes clear that business is the leading private interest group, with labor running a fairly distant second. Of course, on specific issues this pattern may not hold; see note 2 above.
5. The doubter might compare the political position of the U.S. military with that of the military in countries other than the affluent fifteen—the Soviet Union, for example, or China.
6. An excellent account of the workings of establishments in various affluent capitalist nations can be found in Robert A. Dahl, ed., *Political Oppositions in Western Democracies* (New Haven: Yale University Press, 1966).
7. Perhaps the best way to make the point about stability is to cite a recent radical appraisal, in which the reluctant conclusion drawn was that there was just not much movement in the relative shares of the plutocrats and the wage slaves over the postwar period. See Richard Edwards, Michael Reich, and Thomas Weisskopf, eds., *The Capitalist System, A Radical Analysis of American Society* (Englewood Cliffs, N.J.: Prentice-Hall, 1972),* chap. 5.1, pp. 207–218.

Chapter 6

1. These figures were taken from *Historical Statistics of the United States, Continuation to 1962,*,* and *Statistical Abstract of the United States.*,*
2. The pioneering work describing this organizational change is Peter Drucker's, *The Concept of the Corporation*, Mentor, 1964 * (first published in 1946). Organizational developments in several large corporations are described and analyzed in Alfred D. Chandler, *Strategy and Structure: Chapters in the History of the American Industrial Enterprise* (Cambridge, Mass.: MIT Press, 1962).*
3. Anthony Sampson, *The New Europeans* (London: Hodder and Stoughton, 1968).
4. A readable textbook survey showing how managerial calculations are supported by the information system of the enterprise is Jack Gray and Kenneth Johnston, *Accounting and Management Action* (New York: McGraw-Hill, 1973).

Chapter 7

1. These numbers were obtained from various issues of the *Statistical Yearbook* of the United Nations, and from *World Bank Atlas* (Washington, D.C.: World Bank, 1976).
2. The most substantial effort along this line has been completed recently at the World Bank: Hollis Chenery and M. Syrquin, *Patterns of Development, 1950–1970* (New York: Oxford University Press, 1975).
3. The idea of the main line was really first articulated by Walt W. Rostow in his famous book, *Stages of Economic Growth, A Non-Communist Manifesto* (Cam-

bridge: Cambridge University Press, 1960).* However, it has undergone considerable modification since. One of the critics of Rostow's book, Simon Kuznets, has gone on to produce several volumes—of which *Modern Economic Growth, Rate, Structure and Spread* (New Haven: Yale University Press, 1966), is the most central—which show the broad similarities in patterns among modernizing countries, though Kuznets is very cautious in drawing conclusions from his massive data collection. Sophisticated tools of economic analysis when applied to the statistics have further confirmed and elaborated these patterns in the work at the World Bank, mentioned in note 2.

4. In a recent article, "Lessons of Twenty Years of Planning in Developing Countries," *Economica* 38, n.s. (May 1971), Stanley Wellisz has argued that longer-term planning has proved to be largely a failure, because the plans tend to be ignored wherever the market—and the more detailed political bargaining—determine that the proposed project is not worthwhile. Essentially, the experience of the last quarter of a century suggests that the market is relatively more valuable as a signaler of appropriate investments than was thought to be the case. But of course there still remain many projects that require government sponsorship and support, especially in the area of infrastructure development, that is, the creation of the transport network and other backups to industrial development.

5. One must always be careful about generalizations of this kind. For example, Robert Heilbroner in his *The Great Ascent* (New York: Harper and Row, 1963), expressed great pessimism that the development process could proceed at a sufficient rate to relieve poverty even in a few generations. Then, as growth began to spread and continue in a large number of Third World countries, the pessimism began to be rejected by many, and the examples of Japan, Brazil, Mexico, and others were cited as examples of the favorable possibilities. More recently some measure of caution has returned, as some unfavorable distributional consequences of growth have been surfacing. But a mood of cautious optimism can still be held by the well-informed expert; see, for example, Hollis Chenery et al., *Redistribution with Growth* (New York: Oxford University Press, 1974). The optimism is now based partly on the performance of some countries and partly on our increased understanding of the process of modernization.

6. For a useful account along the general lines of this section, see Walt W. Rostow, *Politics and the Stages of Growth* (Cambridge: Cambridge University Press, 1971).*

Chapter 8

1. Probably the single best source of information and interpretation of the nature of socialist economies today is Peter Wiles, *Economic Institutions Compared* (New York: Wiley, 1977).

2. Useful growth comparisons can be found in Frederick Pryor, *Public Expenditures in Communist and Capitalist Nations* (Homewood, Ill.: Irwin, 1968), p. 32, and Wiles, *Economic Institutions Compared*, p. 402.

3. A very nice appraisal of the policy dilemmas posed by communist orientations can be found in Richard Lowenthal, "Development vs. Utopia in Communist Policy," in Chalmers Johnson, ed., *Change in Communist Systems* (Stanford: Stanford University Press, 1970).

4. See Weber's *General Economic History* (New York: Free Press, 1950).

5. John Starr in an unpublished paper, "On the Possibility of a Pragmatic Ideology: Pragmatic Elements in Maoist Ideology," has argued for the presence of a strong thread of Deweyan pragmatism in Mao's thought. Mao may actually have heard Dewey lecture in Peking around 1920. According to Edgar Snow's report of his interviews with Mao in 1937, by that relatively late date in his intellectual development Mao had still not read Marx's *Capital*, which had not yet been translated into Chinese.

Chapter 9

1. Nobel laureate Jan Tinbergen, in his *Shaping the World Economy* (New York: Twentieth Century Fund, 1962),* describes the structure of trade and proposes policies for improving the terms of trade for Third World countries. Chenery, in *Redistribution with Growth*, shows the general tendency for such countries to grow toward interdependence in the structure of their foreign trade.

2. The multinational corporation's role in the transfer of technology is assessed in Raymond Vernon, *Sovereignty at Bay, The Multinational Spread of U.S. Enterprises* (New York: Basic Books, 1971).

3. The product-cycle theory is discussed in ibid., pp. 71–82.

4. A careful appraisal appears in Benjamin Cohen, *The Question of Imperialism* (New York: Basic Books, 1973).

5. See Vernon, *Sovereignty at Bay,* and Charles Kindleberger, ed., *The International Corporation, A Symposium* (Cambridge, Mass.: MIT Press, 1970).

6. Herman Kahn is the person to go to for extrapolations related to war. For a recent effort, see Herman Kahn and B. Bruce-Briggs, *Things to Come, Thinking About the 70's and 80's* (New York: Macmillan, 1972).

Chapter 10

1. Herman Kahn, in *Things to Come* and in his *The Year* 2000, *A Framework for Speculation on the Next 33 Years* (New York: Macmillan, 1967), coauthored by Anthony Wiener, has developed futurology into something more than an occult art. Of course it is indeed speculation, but his various attempts do give one confidence that the Cassandras in this business *need not* turn out to have been right. Already since Kahn's work was published we have been treated to the rise and fall of the doomsday work of the Club of Rome group's futurology: It turns out that they got their overly pessimistic results simply by making overly pessimistic assumptions.

Chapter 11

1. See p. 119.

2. See chapter 13, pp. 117–21.

Chapter 12

1. See Harry Girvetz, *The Evolution of Liberalism* (New York: Collier, 1963),* for an account of early liberalism and its development during the nineteenth and twentieth centuries.

2. One is reminded here of President Carter, an ardent tax reformer who wants to close the loopholes, but who felt justified in taking advantage of a large loophole for the benefit of his own peanut business. Most of us, certainly including the writer, have no doubt acted as free riders from time to time.

3. A lucid exposition of cost-benefit analysis, in the framework of a discussion of some interesting specific studies, can be found in Robert Dorfman, ed., *Measuring Benefits of Government Investments* (Washington, D.C.: Brookings Institution, 1965).* The Brookings Institution now publishes annually a volume analyzing priorities in the federal budget in more or less cost-benefit terms and with respect to issues formulated specifically for public policy discussions.

4. We will return to this argument again in chapter 13.

Chapter 13

1. Galbraith has, of course, held the attention of the economics profession since the publication of the first of the above-mentioned works. *The American Economic Review* has sponsored symposia on several of his individual works, in which leading economists have offered their appraisals: "On American Capitalism and the Concept of Countervailing Power" in the May 1954 issue (vol. 44) by George Stigler and John Miller, and "On the New Industrial State" in the May 1968 issue (vol. 58) by Walter Adams and H. L. Nieburg. Among the many reviews appearing elsewhere, that by Robert Heilbroner in the *New York Review of Books* 8 (June 29, 1967), on the new industrial state is especially worthy of note. For a good account of the development of Galbraith's ideas, see chap. 3 of Leonard Silk, *The Economists* (New York: Basic Books, 1976).

2. John Kenneth Galbraith, *The New Industrial State*, (Boston: Houghton Mifflin, 1967), p. 176.

3. See Robin Marris, *The Economic Theory of 'Managerial' Capitalism* (New York: Free Press, 1964) and Robin Marris and Adrian Wood, eds., *The Corporate Economy; Growth, Competition and Innovative Potential* (Cambridge: Harvard University Press, 1971). Readers of these works will notice two major differences in the presentations as compared to Galbraith: They aren't nearly as witty and, perhaps more important, the main-line economists consider it important to try to find fairly specific links between their concept of motivation (or the criterion of choice of the actors) and the resulting, economically relevant behavior.

4. The paper by Robert Solow in Marris and Wood, eds., *The Corporate Economy*, attempts this as, in a less technical way, does Solow in his now-famous exchange with Galbraith that appeared in the magazine *Public Interest*, Fall 1967, and Spring 1968, and in which the wit is almost entirely supplied by the more conventional protagonist.

5. John Kenneth Galbraith, *Economics and the Public Purpose*, (Boston: Houghton Mifflin, 1973),* pp. 126–27.

6. We have already come across this line of argument twice in the present book. It occurs first in chapter 4, where the cooperative tendency in deal making is discussed. Each party wants to get more for less, of course, but in negotiation each tends to accept the right of the other party to survive, and to tailor serious offers in such a way as not to threaten a relatively powerful opponent with catastrophe. We also encountered it in chapter 5 as the establishment game. The political process thus works in a wholly symmetric way, the established parties recognizing a restriction on their own political deal making, namely, that other established interests may not be seriously hurt by a given deal. The misunderstanding that arises so frequently among analysts of these processes stems from a failure to note that a long series of deals, each of which accepts the above "marginalist" constraint, can have a very large effect on the underlying structure, including the emergence of some major new established interest, and the decline of others. For example, in many affluent capitalist countries over the last century, essentially this process has brought about the rise of labor and the decline of organized religion as major established political interests. This issue is discussed further in chapter 15.

7. For a parallel discussion of these issues by a conventional economist see Richard Caves, *American Industry*.

8. Galbraith, *Economics and the Public Purpose*, p. 50.

9. For a fascinating account of how some specific big deals in defense have been negotiated in recent years, see Anthony Sampson, *The Arms Bazaar, From Lebanon to Lockheed* (New York: Viking, 1977).

10. It might also be noted, à propos the question of scale, that the occasional billion-dollar deal is not much indication of "planning" in a trillion-dollar economy.

11. Again Staffan Linder's *The Harried Leisure Class*, (New York: Columbia University Press, 1970), is the place to go for arguments along this line.

12. For a short history of this legislation, see *Congress and the Nation, 1945–1964*, in *Congressional Quarterly* vol. 1, 1965, pp. 1159–85.

13. For these general legal trends in twentieth-century capitalism, see especially the chapter on torts in W. Friedmann, *Law in a Changing Society* (Berkeley: University of California Press, 1959).

14. Galbraith, *Economics and the Public Purpose*, p. 276.

Chapter 14

1. Like Galbraith's, Drucker's basic works have showed a broad consistency over the years. Drucker's first synthetic work, *The New Society, The Anatomy of Industrial Order*, (New York: Harper & Row) appeared in 1949.* *The Age of Discontinuity* (New York: Harper, 1968) covers more ground, putting greater emphasis on international affairs and the emerging "knowledge society," but clearly is a close relative of that earlier work. Hence we deal only with *The Age of Discontinuity* in this chapter.

2. *Age of Discontinuity*, p. 83.

3. Ibid., p. 118.

4. Ibid., p. 130.

5. Ibid., p. x.

6. Ibid., p. ix.

7. Ibid., p. 266.

8. Fritz Machlup, *The Production and Distribution of Knowledge in the United States* (New Jersey: Princeton University Press, 1962).

Chapter 15

1. See Galbraith, *Affluent Society*, chap. 18, and *New Industrial State*, pp. 397–98, where Galbraith's view is summed up: "The danger to liberty lies in the subordination of belief to the needs of the industrial system."
2. Charles Lindbolm, *Politics and Markets, The World's Political-Economic Systems* (New York: Basic Books, 1977). The discussion of grand vs. secondary issues occurs in chaps. 10, 15, and 17.
3. Ibid., p. 142.

Chapter 17

1. Myrdal's theory of development, couched mainly in the form of a critique of conventional neoclassical conceptions, is perhaps best stated in appendix 2 of vol. 3 of his massive work, *Asian Drama* (New York: Random House, 1968).
2. See Keith Griffin, *Political Economy of Agrarian Change, An Essay on the Green Revolution* (New York: Macmillan, 1974). For a serious and concerned liberal interpretation of the issues of agrarian transformation, see Bruce Johnston and Peter Kilby, *Agriculture and Structural Transformation* (New York: Oxford University Press, 1975).

Chapter 18

1. Paul and Anne Ehrlich, *The End of Affluence, A Blueprint for Your Future* (New York: Ballantine, 1974),* p. 87.
2. Barry Commoner, *The Poverty of Power, Energy and the Economic Crisis* (New York: Knopf, 1976), p. 237.
3. A carefully argued policy antidote for eco-Cassandrism is provided by Allen V. Kneese and Charles L. Schultze, *Pollution, Prices, and Public Policy* (Washington: Brookings Institution, 1975).*
4. For arguments dealing with these and similar areas, see also Joe S. Bain, *Environmental Decay, Economic Causes and Remedies* (Boston: Little, Brown, 1973).

Suggestions for Further Reading*

Aron, Raymond. *The Imperial Republic, The United States and the World, 1945–1973.* Englewood Cliffs, N.J.: Prentice-Hall, 1974.
    A pragmatic appraisal, showing the inevitability of a fairly deep involvement of the U.S. in the affairs of some other countries if a stable international order was to be achieved.
Campbell, Robert W. *The Soviet-Type Economies, Performance and Evolution,* 3rd ed. Boston: Houghton Mifflin, 1974.*
    A straightforward and accurate account of these nonutopias.
Caves, Richard. *American Industry: Structure, Conduct, Performance,* 3rd ed. Englewood Cliffs, N.J.: Prentice-Hall, 1972.*
    A lucid textbook answer to the Galbraithian charge that conventional economists do not understand, teach, or interpret the facts about large-scale economic organization in the United States today.
Chapman, Janet G. "Consumption." In *Economic Trends in the Soviet Union,* edited by Abram Bergson and Simon Kuznets. Cambridge: Harvard University Press, 1963.
    Offers then-and-now comparisons as well as us-and-them comparisons, and shows how economic security (but not affluence) has become a part of *both* capitalism and socialism in the twentieth century.
Cohen, Benjamin J. *The Question of Imperialism.* New York: Basic Books, 1973.
    A careful, liberal interpretation of the question.
Commoner, Barry. *The Poverty of Power, Energy and the Economic Crisis.* New York: Knopf, 1976.
    A pessimistic reading of the problem and its prospective solution.
Congress and the Nation. Washington: Congressional Quarterly, vol. 1 (1945–1964), 1965; vol. 2 (1965–1968), 1969; vol. 3, (1969–1972), 1973; vol. 4 (1973–1976), 1977.
    A massive survey of the process of proposal, development, modification, and passage of the thousands of pieces of legislation that have occupied the attention of Congress in the postwar years. Perhaps the most penetrating single source for understanding just what contemporary liberal government is really about.
Dahl, Robert A., ed. *Political Oppositions in Western Democracies.* New Haven: Yale University Press, 1966.*
    Shows through a variety of examples that variations in the form of parliamentary government in affluent capitalism are much greater than variations in the substance of the political decision process.
Downs, Anthony, Allen V. Kneese, et al. *The Political Economy of Environmental Control.* Berkeley: University of California Press, 1972.*
    Downs's contribution lays out the liberal economist's alternative to the drastic approach of the ecological alarmists.
Drucker, Peter F. *The Concept of the Corporation.* New York: Day, 1946.*
    How General Motors moved toward modern management and its implications; a classic work in the management literature.
———. *The Age of Discontinuity, Guidelines to Our Changing Society.* New York: Harper and Row, 1969.
    Richard Nixon thought it was great and we think it is very liberal.
Ehrlich, Paul R., and Anne Ehrlich, *The End of Affluence, A Blueprint for Your Future,* New York: Ballantine, 1974.*
    More popular in tone and also more shrill than the following book; this is vintage eco-Cassandrism.
———, and John Holdren. *Human Ecology, Problems and Solutions.* San Francisco: Freeman, 1973.*
    A cogent posing of the problem in terms that permit only drastic solutions.
Galbraith, John Kenneth. *A Theory of Price Control.* Cambridge: Harvard University Press, 1952.

* Starred items available in paperback edition.

Galbraith's account of his wartime contacts with the planning and market systems.

————. *American Capitalism, The Concept of Countervailing Power*, rev. ed. Boston: Houghton Mifflin, 1956.* Pp. 137, 151–52 and 167–68 are useful supplements to his latest book.

————. *The Affluent Society.* Boston: Houghton Mifflin, 1958.*
Probably his most influential book.

————. *Economic Development in Perspective.* Cambridge: Harvard University Press, 1969.
Based on his Indian experience, Galbraith sounds very "main line" in this one.

————. *The New Industrial State.* Boston: Houghton Mifflin, 1968.*
A turn toward populism/institutionalism in troubled times.

————. *Economics and the Public Purpose.* Boston: Houghton Mifflin, 1973.*
A whiff of socialism, but still liberal at heart.

Girvetz, Harry. *The Evolution of Liberalism.* New York: Collier, 1963.*
The title is descriptive.

Heilbroner, Robert L. *An Inquiry into the Human Prospect.* New York: Norton, 1974.
The liberal who is exhausted by the struggles and uncertainties of the past decade will appreciate this one. The message, here and in some others among the author's brilliant and sensible works: We are stuck with marginal processes of change and the problems may be too big for that process to handle.

Kahn, Herman, and Anthony Wiener. *The Year 2000: A Framework for Speculation on the Next 33 Years.* New York: Macmillan, 1967.
Both dated and flawed, the basic argument—that inertial forces, pushing societies to continue to go in the same direction they have been going, are powerful—survives as the liberal approach to futurology.

Kerr, Clark, John T. Dunlop, et al. *Industrialism and Industrial Man.* Cambridge: Harvard University Press, 1960.
An analysis of the roles of management and pluralist decision making in aiding advancement along the main line.

Kneese, Allen V. and Charles L. Schultze. *Pollution, Prices, and Public Policy.* Washington: Brookings Institution, 1975.*
The liberal economist's answer to ecological Cassandras.

Kuznets, Simon. *Modern Economic Growth, Rate, Structure and Spread.* New Haven: Yale University Press, 1966.*
In this and his later *Economic Growth of Nations* (Cambridge, Mass.: Harvard University Press, 1971), Kuznets presents the results of his massive data collection effort in dozens of countries, which tell the story of the main line and its links to the growth processes of the affluent fifteen.

Monsen, R. Joseph, Jr., and Mark Cannon. *The Makers of Public Policy: American Power Groups and Their Ideologies.* New York: McGraw-Hill, 1965.
How established interests make the general case for policies that reflect their wants.

Myrdal, Gunnar. *The Political Element in the Development of Economic Theory.* London: Routledge & Kegan Paul, 1953.*
Originally published in Swedish in 1929, this is the first of Myrdal's many appraisals of the ways in which belief systems have constrained the development of economics.

————. *An International Economy, Problems and Prospects.* New York: Harper, 1956.*
An institutionalist's pessimism pervades this account of prospects for international integration. From two decades of hindsight, Rostow's more optimistic view, based on the idea of the main line, seems nearer the liberal truth.

————. *Asian Drama,* 3 vols. New York: Random House, 1968.*
Our dissenter of chapter 17 on the institutional obstacles to development in very poor countries. Read vol. 3, Appendix 2, pp. 1843–1940 (sic.) for his general views on development. A principal actor in the Asian drama, China, is missing from this massive work.

Parkin, Frank. *Class Inequality and Political Order.* New York: Praeger, 1971.
The interaction among social stratification, ideology, and power in both capitalist and socialist countries are neatly and liberally analyzed.

The Public Interest, no. 34, Winter 1974. A special issue entitled "The Great Society: Lessons for the Future."
Appraisals by a number of liberal authors of the programs of the sixties and how to improve them.

Rostow, W. W. *The Stages of Economic Growth, A Non-Communist Manifesto.* Cambridge: Cambridge University Press, 1960.*

A classic and initial statement of the main-line thesis, which has been somewhat modified by the later works of Simon Kuznets, Hollis Chenery, Irma Adelman, and others.

Sakharov, Andrei D. *Sakharov Speaks*. New York: Knopf, 1974.*
The Soviet physicist is clearly a liberal. That is hard on him, but hopeful for the rest of us. See our chapter 9.

Samuelson, Paul A. *Economics*. New York: McGraw-Hill.
Ten editions, beginning in 1955, that epitomize, in an elementary survey, the fruitful melding of liberalism with economic science.

Schultze, Charles L., Alice M. Rivlin, et al. *Setting National Priorities: the 1973 Budget*. Washington: Brookings Institution, 1972.*
This pioneering volume and its annual successors contain some of the best marginalist appraisals of public-policy alternatives available to the interested citizen.

Seliger, Martin. *Ideology and Politics*. New York: Free Press, 1976.
Though somewhat obsessed with the problem of defining the term, this book provides a useful account of current views as to how ideologies work and what they are like.

Shonfield, Andrew. *Modern Capitalism, The Changing Balance of Public and Private Power*. London: Oxford University Press, 1965.*
Public bureaucracies tend to do similar things in similar ways throughout affluent capitalism: a classic work of liberal, the-present-as--history scholarship.

Silk, Leonard. *The Economists*. New York: Basic Books, 1976.
Describes the views of five contemporary economists. Especially fine is the account of the development of Galbraith's ideas.

Vernon, Raymond. *Sovereignty at Bay*. New York: Basic Books, 1971.*
One of the major stories of the growing interdependence in the world, the spread of the multinational corporations, is told and appraised.

BOOK TWO

THE RADICAL
ECONOMIC
WORLD VIEW

Contents of Book Two

PART I

The Optimal Radical Economic World View

1.	Introduction	175
2.	Contemporary Capitalism: The Charges	180
3.	The Structure and Tendency of Societies	187
4.	Monopoly Capitalism: Structure and Tendencies	196
5.	Exploitation Under Monopoly Capitalism	205
6.	Government and Monopoly Capital	214
7.	Instability and Crisis	222
8.	Development and Imperialism	229
9.	The Rise of Socialism: The Soviet Union	238
10.	The Rise of Socialism: Yugoslavia and China	246
11.	Transitions	254
12.	The Future	262

PART II

Commentary

13.	Radical World View and Radical Economics	269
14.	Baran and Sweezy	274
15.	Stagnation and Surplus Absorption	284
16.	Alienation	288
17.	Horvat	293
18.	Technical Economics vs. Radical Economics?	299
19.	The Role of Revolution	304

NOTES	307
SUGGESTIONS FOR FURTHER READING	319

PART I

The Optimal Radical Economic World View

ACKNOWLEDGMENTS

Someone who, like myself, came back to the serious study of Marxist interpretations of contemporary capitalism in the sixties is bound to have been strongly influenced by younger students of the subject. Of the many who have taken time out from other activities to continue my education, I would particularly like to thank George Evans, Bob Harris, David Kotz, Michael Reich, Richard Roehl, John Roemer, and Alan Shelly. A considerable number of dissertations have been completed in recent years at Berkeley that deserve broad circulation among students of the political economy of contemporary capitalism, and which inform the present work. These include Marilyn Goldberg's study of the sharing of housework, Louis Green's study of the economics of establishing a separate black state in the United States, David Kotz's study of the influence of finance capital on industrial corporations, John Roemer's study of Japanese-American competition in other countries, Sam Rosenberg's study of labor market duality, Don Shakow's study of economy-based political power in the Soviet Union in the twenties, Alan Shelly's study of the macroeconomics of depression, and John Willoughby's study of the relation between trade structure and imperialism. Taken as a group, these works demonstrate the viability of radical orientations in supporting scholarly interpretation of the major economic problems of our time.

CHAPTER 1

Introduction

THERE ARE two basic defining qualities of a radical. The first is a commitment to the wretched of the earth, and with it a recognition of their humanity, their dignity, their rights. Sometimes the commitment is acquired abstractly by reading and thinking and in discussion. But attitudes formed in this way have little real force until they are grounded in experience, until in some social sense one has become a part of this large and still growing community of the dispossessed. But, of course, the great majority of those possessing a commitment to the wretched of the earth acquired it by the simple act of being born into membership.

That commitment can make a social worker or even a priest as well as a radical. To become a radical, a second quality is also necessary. This is a firm belief that the wretchedness of much of humanity is unnecessary and that it cannot be eliminated within the framework of existing society. This notion can be acquired intuitively by almost any observant person living in capitalist society. There are those constant contrasts between extremes of deprivation and wealth, and that peculiar phenomenon of scarcity in the midst of plenty, of idle hands together with shortages.

But unless this insight into the basic insanity of capitalist institutions is buttressed by a firm grounding in radical thought, it may not survive. Radicals who do not possess such knowledge are subject to rather violent swings in orientation in the face of changing times, and particularly of adversity. For there are too many comfortable theories around explaining why things have to be as they are, and there are times when it is very convenient to accept one of them. Theoretical grounding is an essential defense against this. But, of course, abstract understanding plays a more substantive role too. It is out of a radical understanding as to how the world works that one acquires a successful strategy for changing the world. Radical thought is not an object of esthetic beauty, but it is a fundamental tool in the service of these two aims.

Radical political economy is at the heart of radical thought because material deprivation is at the heart of most of the misery in the world today. Alienation need not be accompanied by material deprivation; however, the sense of meaninglessness typically grows out of the inhumane aspects of both production and consumption activities, and of the dehumanizing effect on affluent and poor alike of living with such continuing misery. The central task of radical thought is to understand these problems and to understand what to do about them.

Essentially, radical political economy offers a general view of how the world works in the economic and related spheres of human action. This view must simultaneously vindicate the defining qualities of a radical, be consistent with the known facts, be persuasive, and provide an agenda for action. It is not a branch of technical economics, though it draws on research results, from whatever area, that are useful for its purposes. Basically, it tells the big story of how the world works, but in such a way that the little stories of how countries, classes, and even individuals function can be fitted in. It has been in process of development for two centuries, at least since the French Revolution, but its main concern must be to understand the contemporary world, that being the only one we can change.

At the moment of writing (1978), radical political fortunes in many parts of the world of monopoly capitalism are at a relatively low ebb; this is particularly true of the United States. Also, there have been recent setbacks in some developing countries, most notably perhaps in Bolivia and Chile. This sort of thing has happened before, and it is important to understand why it happens, why it will be followed by an upsurge, and why each upsurge tends to surge up farther than the one before. Today hope, confidence in the victory of socialism, lies in three facts. First, there is the fact of the existence of a number of socialist countries who have established their ability to defend themselves successfully against capitalist depredations without destroying the essence of socialism within their societies. Second, there is the fact of the size and power of socialist movements around the world. We are living at a time of very high-low tides, one that is accompanied by surgent socialist forces in many parts of Africa, the Arab world, southern Europe, and East Asia. The radical base is growing larger and even though in the best of circumstances not all of these movements will bear immediate fruit, even the superficial trends are favorable.

Third, and not to be undervalued, there is the fact of the upsurge in radical economic thought. Radical intellectual fortunes have had their ups and downs in the twentieth century, just as radical political fortunes have. However, the causal factors are somewhat different. Obviously they are connected; for example, political oppression of radical intellectuals and the constraints imposed on radical intellectual dialogue by the demands of political action have taken their toll. But there are important underlying factors that have affected the course of twentieth-century radical thought. Most important of these is the history of monopoly capital itself. Created, roughly speaking, around the turn of the century out of capitalism's first major survival crisis and itself bringing great disturbance to the world, it has taken a long time for monopoly capital to reveal its fundamental properties to the radical analyst. However, by the mid-fifties enough evidence was in, and several broad-gauge appraisals of contemporary society from the perspective of the radical economist were published. The first of these, Paul Baran's *Political Economy of Growth*,[1] contained a general theory of the tendencies in modern capitalism, with emphasis on the interaction between developed monopoly capitalism and the Third World economies. Later Baran collaborated with Paul Sweezy in producing *Monopoly Capital*,[2] a survey of the processes of waste and exploitation in contemporary America and of their implications. A Belgian Marxist, Ernest Mandel, in his *Marxist Economic Theory*,[3] provided a general historical analysis of world economic development in the nineteenth and twentieth centuries, based both on Marxian theory and on recent empirical research. He has recently updated some of these views in a large work, *Late Capitalism*.[4] And Yugoslav economist Branko Horvat in his *Toward a Theory of Planned Economy*[5] offered a theory of the underlying processes of change in the contemporary world with emphasis on the emergence of participation as a central part of recent social-economic development.[6]

These works demonstrate the power of radical analysis in exposing fundamental processes in contemporary society; they also demonstrate the viability of Marxism as a basic tool of economic analysis. But, of course, such works are synthetic in nature. They cannot provide a detailed picture of the problems we face today or offer a detailed analysis of proposed solutions. Work of this kind can now be found in considerable abundance in a variety of journals that deal with radical economic analysis, such as the *Review of Radical Political Economy*, published in Ann Arbor, *Socialist Revolution*, published in San Francisco, *Monthly Review*, New York, *New Left Review*, London, and *Cambridge Journal of Economics*, Cambridge, England, to mention only the most interesting of the Anglo-American journals. And so, for the first time in half a century, a rich new intellectual base has been emerging, one on which further upsurges in understanding can be built.

Another central factor in the resurgence of radical economic thought came from the policies of socialist countries and their defense by socialist leaders. Their insights into the nature of society are an amalgam of their practical experience in organizing both revolution and socialist society, and of their intellectual experience in assimilating the major works of radical thought. Though their writings are typically not scholarly in quality, these leaders' works are a major source of insight into the problems posed by the transition to socialism and the establishment and stabilization of socialist momentum in postrevolutionary society. At least one of them, Mao Tse-tung, has fundamentally redirected the radical analysis of the process and needs of economic development.

The socialist countries, of course, publish a great variety of relevant materials for radical economics. Perhaps of most interest in the context of this chapter are the general works appraising contemporary world economy from the perspective of the respective leaderships of these societies. For example, the Soviet Union's Communist Party publishes an English-language version of their *Political Economy*, which gives special weight to the role of the Soviet Union in shaping twentieth-century experience. Chinese views are captured in their political economies of capitalism and socialism, one of which has recently appeared in English translation,[7] and especially in the works of Mao. His *Selected Works* are available in a cheap five-volume English language edition.[8] Horvat, mentioned above, offers a perspective on Yugoslavia, and some important aspects of the Cuban revolution are to be found among the speeches of Ché Guevara, collected by John Gerassi in *Venceremos*.[9]

A third source of resurgence in radical economic thought has been the radical youth movement of the sixties. Of course, the forte of activists within that movement was not so much radical economic analysis as it was a well-articulated awareness of the contradictions of monopoly capitalist society. As a consequence of their work, many millions of people who do not think of themselves as radicals have had permanently etched on their minds the great gap between the civics textbook ideals of a liberal society and the facts of liberal action in dealing with such things as racism, sexism, inequality, and war.

The undogmatic nature of this movement had its effect on radical thought. The distinction between the Old Left and the New Left, very striking, for example, in the United States in the early sixties, has essentially disappeared with the changing circumstances of economic and political life, and with a recognition of fundamentally common goals. An environment has thus been established in which radical dialogue on central issues of radical thought can once again take place productively.

These factors in combination have generated an unprecedented interest in radical economics. Not only are there a large number of young men and women seriously engaged in the effort of developing a powerful radical instrument of economic analysis, but the intellectual quality that they bring to bear on that effort is extremely high, far higher, I believe, than in any previous generation. One can reasonably expect that the next decade will bring a revolutionary improvement in the breadth and depth of radical economic thought.

But that is not to suggest that consensus will be reached on every major point. At present a genuine dialogue does not yet exist between the radical economists of most socialist countries and their Western counterparts, or even among economists in different socialist countries. The work of Third World and Western economists is only in an early stage of mutual interaction. And among Western radicals there is a great variety of views; some of the few remarks that have so far been made in this introduction would certainly be disputed.

This situation suuggests the opportunities that exist for further development of radical thought. It also says something about the dialectical nature of current radical political economy. A serious student of radical political economy will have an overview. She [10] considers this overview to be optimal in the sense that it characterizes better than the radical alternatives the ways in which the contemporary world works. But such a student must also recognize that many of those alternative views are not to be dismissed from further consideration. Rather, they are a part of radical political economy, the subject matter of the dialogues that, in combination with further study and experience, will resolve portions of the disagreements. Thought is as dialectical as life; contradictions must be recognized and built upon. The views expressed in this work are, hopefully, one side of a discussion, and will no doubt require revision in the light of even initial responses.

CHAPTER 2

Contemporary Capitalism: The Charges

CONTEMPORARY MONOPOLY CAPITALISM has a number of achievements to its credit. For example, putting a man on the moon was a very neat trick. No one would deny the great effort and skill that went into the performance of that trick. However, perhaps a majority of Americans have felt that this effort was undertaken only because of a mistaken notion of appropriate social priorities. A radical, on the other hand, would be likely to claim that it was no mistake but was rather a typical manifestation of the peculiar inhumanity of monopoly capitalism, in which it was decided to leave millions of American citizens hungry, ill housed, their massive health problems largely untreated, while performing this little $20 billion feat of technical wizardry.

This example suggests why in the present chapter no attempt is made to offer a "balanced" picture of the achievements and problems of contemporary capitalism. Instead, we in effect bring the defendant to the bar and detail her crimes, in order to determine whether these crimes are of sufficient magnitude that he be deemed a menace to public safety. The crimes are not mitigated by the achievements because even they are all tainted by this distorted sense of values. Putting a man on the moon is of no relevance to the case, not because there is no intrinsic interest in the episode, but because it was bought at the expense of a continuation of capitalism's failures. Its significance is to be measured by those failures.[1]

Inequality

The defendant is unlikely to contest this charge.[2] In absolute terms it refers to the 20 to 30 million Americans who fall below the poverty line and whose lives clearly are rendered nightmarish by the various forms of material deprivation they must endure. The official American poverty line was drawn with a political aim of "ensuring that very few of those who were listed as living in poverty would not in fact be," [3] so that the true figures probably are much higher and have been rising alarmingly in recent years. Furthermore, the line captures the basis of material deprivation in a complex modern society only in a very crude way, so that it is quite possible that as many as 50 million Americans find their own and their children's lives stunted by serious deprivation, most likely of adequate health care or housing. And all this in the world's richest country.

But this is only the beginning. Recent estimates put the number of the world's citizens who suffer serious effects from hunger and malnutrition at well over half a billion, with the upper limit possibilities getting close to a billion.[4] And these figures, it should be emphasized, refer to serious malnutrition, the kind that stunts growth, creates mental retardation, and generates susceptibility to the many diseases that shorten life dramatically. Furthermore, this hunger is not a product of the inadequacy of the world's food supply. It is rather a matter of its distribution, which is a social property of the problem, determined by the kind of institutions that govern economic life. In this case, of course, the institution is capitalism.

The reason for associating capitalism with these problems can be suggested by looking at the other end of the spectrum in American society. Here we find 1 percent of the populace owning well over a quarter of the privately held wealth, over two thirds of the corporate stock in private hands, and almost all the municipal bonds. Here we find over five hundred citizens reporting an annual *income* of over a million dollars. The very rich tend to have inherited much of their wealth and to hire skilled professional administrators to increase it for them and to reduce their tax liability. The results suggest that under capitalism the distribution rule is the familiar one: Those who have, get. A large segment of the poor—a fifth or so—have negative wealth; that is, they owe more than they own.

In the "developing" capitalist countries, the situation is generally much worse. The top 5 percent tend to have up to twice the proportion of national income as in the developed countries.[5] Presumably the wealth distribution follows the income distribution too, though it is much more highly skewed. Private ownership of the means of production is clearly the key to these appalling figures. Those little pieces of paper that give a citizen the legal right to some portion of a firm or government's income are what generate the extremes of opulence and misery.

Inequality of wealth and income provides the basis for reproducing the social structure of a society generation after generation by creating very great inequality of opportunity. The children of the affluent are better eduucated in better schools and, through parental influence, are likely to be given preference in entry to privileged jobs, such as the professions. Children of the poor suffer the handicaps of material deprivation compounded by the unequal treatment they receive in the marketplace. Once again, at the heart of the inequality of opportunity is the inequality of wealth, and at the heart of the inequality of wealth is the system of private ownership of the means of production.

Imperialism

Imperialism is another charge where the evidence is decisive.[6] In the first place, there are a number of overt acts that cannot be concealed. In a long list of countries, including Chile, Brazil, Vietnam, the Dominican Republic, Lebanon, and many others, the United States has assisted in the generation of a regime favorable to its interests. In some cases this has meant sending in the marines (Lebanon, Dominican Republic), in some a systematic financial boycott (Chile), in other cases various forms of clandestine assistance to fascists (Greece), in some massive military intervention (Korea, Vietnam), and in almost all cases success of the political venture is followed by opening American coffers, in the form of aid and loans, to the new anticommunist, procapitalist government.

What is all this in aid of? One thing does stand out—the tendency for a large increase in American foreign investment to follow closely upon the success of such ventures. This investment is made by private American business, mostly large multinational corporations, and is done for a single reason, namely, to make profits. The association between intervention and investment is strong enough to suggest, even without any theory, that there is some sort of a causal connection.

Second, of course, there is anticommunism. That this is a distinct aspect of American foreign policy there can be little doubt. Even if one cannot quite take seriously the speeches innumerable influential public figures make in support of this policy line, there is the more direct evidence of the connection between military and economic aid and the containment of communism. American's vast giveaway programs were mostly spent around the periphery of the communist world and were aimed at sustaining appropriately reactionary and procapitalist governments in power as a buffer against any further communist expansion. Yugoslavia, a major aid recipient, was an exception to the rule but not to its spirit. More typical were the suppression of revolution in Greece, the massive support for Chiang's Taiwan, and the far more massive investment in General Thieu and South Vietnam. This buffer, as long as it lasts, provides a barrier around the foreign investment operations that have proven so profitable to monopoly capital.

The consequences of this sort of behavior for the ordinary people of the world are very great. Militarization diverts over $200 *billion* worth of resources a year to the sterility of the arms race and indoctrinates millions in the arts—and the practice—of violence.[7] Industrial development is oriented toward profits, which automatically precludes doing anything about the misery of the poor, who, of course, cannot pay a profitable price for the things they need. Social revolutions are suppressed, or prolonged, or distorted, by the appalling scale of the violence and oppression engendered by the worldwide capitalist system of economic organization.

Racism and Sexism

Racism and sexism, of course, antedate capitalism. The charge here is that capitalist institutions have tended to support and enhance existing forms of discrimination. One evidence of this lies in the wage data, which show blacks and women obtaining less than two thirds the pay of men. In some capitalist countries the figure drops below one half. There is often a substantial direct discrimination discount for people doing the same work, but most of the difference reflects the low skill and temporary nature of the jobs into which the discriminated groups tend to be forced.[8]

Beyond this direct material effect of discrimination lies the subtler generation of inequality by means of stereotyping, by establishing in young children's minds low upper limits to their prospects if their sex or skin color differs from the "norm" of the white male. Added to this are a variety of legal and quasi-legal disabilities, which control black access to middle-class housing, female access to abortion, and the like. Among the nastiest of these is the treatment accorded blacks who are caught up in the criminal and penal processes of American society.

Behind racist and sexist behaviors lies the phenomenon of class. This is reflected in the high incidence of black- and women-headed families who show up in the lowest ranks of the income distribution. It is reflected in the low-wage history of the South, where racism has been used as a most effective device to keep wages of both whites and blacks down and to prevent effective unionization. And it is reflected in intergenerational mobility, where poverty is shown to breed poverty in the next generation via the effects of material deprivation and stereotyping.

Alienation

The settlers' town is a strongly built town, all made of stone and steel. It is a brightly lit town; the streets are covered with asphalt, and the garbage cans swallow all the leavings, unseen, unknown and hardly thought about.

The settler's feet are never visible, except perhaps in the sea; but there you're never close enough to see them. His feet are protected by strong shoes although the streets of his town are clean and even, with no holes or stones. The settler's town is a well-fed town, an easygoing town; its belly is always full of good things. The settler's town is a town of white people, of foreigners.

The town belonging to the colonized people, or at least the native town, the negro village, the medina, the reservation, is a place of ill fame, peopled by men of evil repute. They are born there, it matters little where or how; they die there, it matters not where, nor how. It is a world without spaciousness; men live there on top of each other, and their huts are built one on top of the other. The native town is a hungry town, starved of bread, of meat, of shoes, of coal, of light. The native town is a crouching village, a town on its knees, a town wallowing in the mire. It is a town of niggers and dirty arabs. The look that the native turns on the settler's town is a look of lust, a look of envy; it expresses his dreams of possession—all manner of possession: to sit at the settler's table, to sleep in the settler's bed, with his wife if possible. The colonized man is an envious man. And this the settler knows very well; when their glances meet he ascertains bitterly, always on the defensive, "They want to take our place." It is true, for there is no native who does not dream at least once a day of setting himself up in the settler's place.[9]

These two paragraphs are a black French psychologist's account of the effect of colonialism on a human community. It describes succinctly the way in which a class society distorts the values of the participants. The oppressed dream of acquiring the status of oppressor, the oppressors strive to continue the oppression, while minimizing their contact with its inhumane consequences. Both end up in an alienated state, unable, within the context of their society, to find a means of expressing themselves through normal human relations.

But, of course, this account is not relevant only for Algeria; it fits the situation in capitalist society everywhere. The ghettos of the poor are to be found all over the United States, the leading capitalist country, as are the attitudes of "settler" and "native." But in the heartland of monopoly capital the alienation is extended in a variety of ways. In large-scale business one may think of the shift from management to administration. That is, the captain of industry shouting out her dictatorial orders to underlings who have no doubt as to who is boss and how powerful she is has become an anachronism. In her place is the almost anonymous administrator, who creates a complex web of carrots and sticks, each one of minor significance, that guides the underlings and serves to shield the individual's awareness of the brutal coercion and oppression that continues to sustain the system.

Or one can think of the subdued pluralism of a one-dimensional, uncritical democracy. In the "democracy" we know in the United States, one can find deeply critical books, but they turn out to be irrelevant in the institutional context of our political system. In the latter a massive effort is undergone to make a choice where there is no choice, to select among candidates whose effects on policy are virtually indistinguishable. Or one can think of the technocratic environment of the worker, whose worklife is dominated, not by his needs as a creative human being, but by the need for certain kinds of manual assistance by the machines a profit-oriented capitalism tends to design.[10]

Or one can think of the vulgar and commercial world of leisure time, in which the fundamental settler-native structure of society presses its members to ever greater paroxysms of consumption in the effort to preserve their hard-won status, whatever that may be. In all these cases alienation, the sense of fundamental meaninglessness, of lack of a strong commitment to some coherent set of values, is the product of living in an environment in which the individual has no feeling of being a participant in making the basic choices that shape her life. The property of that society which generates these various kinds of alienation is its class nature, which is, of course, an inherent property of capitalism.

Irrationality

The irrationality of capitalist society lies in the insane contrasts in which it abounds. There is the contrast between those who are deeply deprived and those who are alienated by the very quantity of goods they possess and the intense activity required to display them to friends and neighbors. There is the ever-present contrast between the ever-increasing size and "quality" of the armed forces, usually called the instrument of national "defense," and the increasing incidence of war and of the threat of nuclear war. There is the contrast between the increasing need of the growing body of the world's deprived and, under current institutions, helpless peoples, and the increasing lack of manifested concern for other humans. And so on.

And this list deals only with the visible contrasts. Lying behind it is the fundamental contrast between ideals and actions in modern capitalist society. The ideals of mutuality and respect are not dead; they are a part of the inner nature of all the actors in our drama, dope fiends, alcoholics, housewives, tycoons, and all the rest. But they have been suspended by pressures stemming from the institutions under which they all live, under which, as individuals, they are constrained to live.[11]

Conclusion

This brief sketch of the charges against contemporary capitalism indicates the depth and breadth of the failure of its institutions to deal effectively with basic problems of human life. It also indicates the poverty of such measures as output per capita or "real" income, which are typically used by conventional economists to measure progress under capitalism.

The conventional economist reading this list reacts by saying, One thing the charges do not indicate is whether another form of society can do better than this. That is quite true, aside from the feeling one must get that there *has* to be a better way than this just because this is so bad. One way to respond to that objection is to point to one of the obvious and uncontested achievements of socialist societies: They have dramatically reduced inequality of income distribution. And they have done it by taking a very simple step, namely, by placing the means of production under social control and thereby eliminating at a stroke all those little pieces of paper that entitle the most affluent of capitalist citizenry to continue to enrich themselves simply by virtue of possessing the bits of paper. Many of the legion of toilers in the service of the former capitalists, lawyers, tax men, brokers and the like, were put to useful work. And the proceeds from this operation were used largely to provide a basic material cushion for the citizenry, so that hunger, for example, is not a phenomenon to be observed in these societies. That may not be a full answer to the objection, but it goes quite a ways.

Another objection is that the charges in themselves are of little help because they do not establish causation, do not establish the necessary connections between capitalist institutions and these facts. Much of the rest of this book is devoted to filling this gap.

CHAPTER 3

The Structure and Tendency of Societies

KARL MARX has been dead for ninety years; to put it another way, you can look all through her massive collection of writings without finding a single fact about life in the twentieth century. Since he put great emphasis on the flow of history as a basis for social understanding, even a Marxist is bound to feel that there are serious inadequacies in her works as descriptions of contemporary society. But not only has history thrown up new facts, social thinkers have been at work in massive numbers interpreting these facts and unearthing and interpreting new ones about earlier times. Here too Marx's work necessarily displays some inadequacies.[1]

Nevertheless, Marx still has some fundamental things to say to the student of contemporary society. One of these is his emphasis on broad, underlying, long-run forces that condition even the daily life of humans for entire historical eras. Another is her emphasis on changing labor productivity, or the forces of production, as he called it, as creating conditions favorable for new social developments. A third is an analysis of the role of class in conditioning the ways in which new social developments affect the relations of production, that is, the ways in which human beings interact while creating the social product. Yet another is Marx's emphasis on the way in which the upper class of a society is able to use the relations of production as a device for stripping those who create the social product by their work of any excess product beyond their essential consumption. A final factor is his emphasis on a nonlinear dynamics in all societies, that is, a process of change that proceeds at times steadily, at times with increasing instability, at times with cataclysmic change.

This small list by no means exhausts the durable portion of Marx's work, but it does capture the central ideas.[2] In discussing and illustrating them with some selected aspects of historical development up to the eve of the twentieth century, we will not follow Marx's own analysis rigidly. Instead, an attempt will be made to modify the orthodox Marxist picture wherever new facts and analyses suggest that is necessary.[3] But this chapter is not aimed just at illustrating concepts; the historical movements are relevant for understanding contemporary times because today we are in the midst of two of history's most fundamental eras of change: the era of the industrial revolution and the era of the rise of socialism.

The Peasant Revolution

The first great revolution in labor productivity occurred some thousands of years ago. Previously, humans had existed by harvesting the fruits of nature through hunting, gathering, and fishing. The new ingredient was settled agriculture, the planned and deliberate cultivation of the things that were later to be harvested. The result was a potential increase in output per person of manyfold and a fundamental transformation in the relation of people, both to nature and to one another.

Consider for a moment one of its manifestations, namely, the great river valley civilizations of Egypt, Mesopotamia, India, and China. The creation of massive irrigation works led to an increase in output per person of over tenfold as compared with simpler production techniques. This in turn made it possible for the surplus beyond the peasants' own needs to be used to support a large population engaged in other pursuits, from priestly duties to craft production to military activity to city building. Large cities were built to house a substantial class of rulers and their hangers-on and of workers producing goods not essential to human survival.

For all this to take place, some system of distribution had to be created. The details of the system are still unknown, but roughly the palace or temple obtained the right, backed up, of course, by force, to a share of the peasants' output. In return for this the peasant was presumably given some assurance of participation in afterlife existence and was given some protection from famine by the palace storage facilities. At any rate it does not seem that the peasant family itself retained any significant portion of the surplus it created.

The forms and the stability of life varied considerably from one such civilization to another. Egypt enjoyed extraordinary stability—it was perhaps the most stable society known to history. In southern Mesopotamia, on the other hand, such things as the high water table and the nearness of the sea meant that irrigation canals silted up and land became saline and unusable after three or four generations, bringing about the periodic decline of one city and the rise of another. Also the modest size of cities on the Mesopotamian plain seemed to prevent any one city from maintaining a durable control over the others, so that Mesopotamia's ancient history is an extraordinarily bloody one.

In Mesopotamia and elsewhere one sees some almost cyclical structural movements, an alternation between periods of imperial hegemony and feudal dispersion. This may have been related to the limits to effective control that could be exercised, given the military technology of the day, and the tendency for the best military leaders to be raised and trained near the borders of an empire after a generation or two, thus creating a favorable environment for a revolt. These great cycles of the rise and decline of kings and emperors provide the stuff of political history. They also dramatically affect the lives and well-being of the peasantry that probably comprised four fifths to nine tenths of the population, as lands were ravaged, soldiers conscripted, captured, and enslaved, women and children carried away into slavery, and the like. But they had no great effect on the basic organization of society for a period of two to three thousand years, the same processes of production and surplus extraction providing a stable and durable structure even to the rapidly changing southern Mesopotamian political-geographic scene.

Greek and Roman societies represent a later and somewhat "modernized" version of the river valley civilizations. The status of the peasant in Mesopotamia and Egypt is clearly that of a human being under substantial coercive restraint; however, it appears that her status is not that of a slave, in the sense that he could not be bought and sold at the whim of his master. Rather, she seems to have been bound to the land and to the performing of certain duties outside his own plot of land, including probably the building of irrigation works and possibly the building of temples and tombs. Roman and Greek slaves are "slaves" in the sense made familiar to us from, for example, the history of the American South, where elements of markets were well enough developed for a money price to be placeable at almost any time on a slave. But statuses and obligations, such as the rights and abilities associated with manumission and the breakup of families, tended to vary widely over time and place. The main element of continuity in these societies lay in the fact that the slaves performed the basic labor of the society, and the ruling class, one way or another, extracted the surplus of the slaves' production and put it to their own uses. These uses too varied widely over time and place, reflecting, among other things, variations in culture, the productivity of the land, and the threat of invasion.

As one moves down through history and across cultures, a great variety of institutional forms for extracting surplus from peasant populations emerges. Serfdom of the Western European kind is one method, probably growing up as a reflection of the relative surplus of land and scarcity of peasants in economies where some market relations have come to exist. The nobility is able to control runaways fairly effectively by force, and so uses the fiction that the peasant is "bound" to the land and cannot be bought and sold separately from it or allowed freely to leave it as the device for keeping him at work and getting a portion of her labor product. An alternative form, when labor is relatively less scarce, is share tenancy, in which the land "owner" allows a peasant to work the land and reserves for himself some substantial fraction of the product. Peasant freehold farming has occurred throughout history but as a durable form has been largely restricted to peripheral and less productive areas, such as the mountains, where physical control of the peasant is difficult and the surplus product relatively small.

As one comes closer to modern times, one finds increasing portions of the world's peasant labor force caught up at least marginally in the money economy. This produces some central tendency toward a fairly specific structure of agrarian production relations, often known as debt peonage. In such structures there is a fraction of farmers who own fairly substantial farms and are relatively free of debt and a fraction of farmers who own no land and must either rent land or work as wage laborers on the farms of others. But most peasants lie between these two extremes, owning some land, which is heavily burdened with debt and insufficient for a livelihood, and renting the rest, perhaps combined with some off-farm labor by one or two members of the family. From the point of view of surplus extraction, this form had two key advantages: (1) the ideal of debt-free ownership is held out as a carrot to the farmer and provides a strong motivation to work hard; and (2) debt is an effective instrument for surplus extraction from this hard-working citizenry.

This form of organization has proven to be extraordinarily durable. Of course, a major reason is its efficiency as a resource extractor. The moneylender in less affluent societies often is also a farmer. In China, for example, she would have been either a rich peasant or perhaps a member of the literate and cultured gentry who owned farmland but also had other sources of income. In such more highly developed peasant societies banks can also arise to serve this function, thus transferring the surplus more or less directly out of agriculture.

But other features of this system enhanced its durability. For example, the moneylender was not the only person who could prey on the farmer. Often the middlemen who handled the transfer of the agricultural product to the cities were able to obtain—always in part through the use of coercion—monopoly power over the sale of crops, thus ensuring a minimal price to the actual producer. Yet another feature of this debt-peonage system was that it avoided agglomerations of peasants into large groups who might pose a serious revolutionary threat to the regime. When conditions became intolerable, which happened frequently, there were endless peasant riots and petty revolts. But organization was extremely difficult to achieve on a mass scale among such a dispersed population, and where the material condition and culture of the peasantry might vary quite considerably from one locale to the next. Consequently, a peasantry bound to the production task by this particular set of relations of production has tended to persist almost everywhere except where economies of scale have led to an entirely different mode of farming, or where a conquered people can be effectively bound to a latifundia system of large estates. Debt peonage, a relatively late product of history's first great technical revolution, is still playing a central role in contemporary history.

The Industrial Revolution

The last two centuries have witnessed the rise and spread of world history's second great quantum leap in the productivity of labor. Closely associated with factory production and the use of machines, the first major steps in this social and technical revolution were taken in English cotton and iron and machinery production during the eighteenth century, spread to most of Western Europe, the United States, and Japan during the nineteenth century, and have been reaching out to most of the world's peoples during the twentieth. Once a country gets caught up in this process, an annual average rise of output per person of several percentage points is sustainable over a period of decades, to say the least.

The industrial revolution has some features in common with its predecessor, the peasant revolution. In both cases the change transforms the lives of the overwhelming majority of human beings. In both cases the process has changes in the forces of production, changes in known ways of transforming nature, as an essential precondition. In both cases class differentiation plays a central role in fixing the structures of the new societies, though a wide variety of social forms remain feasible. And in both cases societies that have not made the transition are substantially affected by those that have.

We are still in the midst of this great revolution. Almost all the world's societies are presently changing at unprecedented rates. The longer-run outcomes of the process are still probably not to be discerned with any clarity. Nevertheless, some features of even the earlier phases of the industrial revolution are helpful in understanding the contemporary world.

In the few centuries just preceding the industrial revolution, several factors combined to set it in motion. First there was the development of the world's most effective military technology in Western Europe, combined with the improvement of sea transport to the point at which victorious military force could be transferred to almost any seaside point on the world's surface. The Atlantic nations used this power to loot much of the treasure that great peasant civilizations had accumulated, after which still more treasure was extracted from mines and plantations set up in the conquered areas. This primitive capitalist accumulation was one of the keys to the origin of the industrial revolution.

However, there were equally important domestic developments in Europe. A more stable domestic life had given its usual stimulus to trade. The increased trade, probably assisted by a period of relative scarcity of labor induced by the Black Death and, perhaps, climatic change, and by the influx of monetary metals from the New World, accelerated the movement toward the more modern form of peasant exploitation, debt peonage. This increased mobility and greatly stimulated the development of markets and the money economy, a factor still further enhanced by the rise of the early modern state under the influence of the new military technology. Cities flourished, demand increased, and the greater cultural interactions made many aware of the variety of possibilities in human existence. This heterotic vigor has been a typical feature of such times of relatively intense crosscultural contact. But the creativity, shaped by the emerging new environment, tended to be strongly focused on new ways of making money. These various factors were most strongly combined in post-Civil War England, and so England became the home of the industrial revolution.

A second important aspect of the industrial revolution is the illustration it provides of the strong interdependence between the forces and the relations of production. The industrial revolution is closely associated with the concentration of large numbers of workers in a factory full of machinery. However, in its early phases the new technology did not require such concentration, particularly in textiles and machinery production. It would have been perfectly feasible to continue to use the putting-out system, in which various operations were farmed out by a merchant entrepreneur to workers dispersed in farms and small shops. The rise of the early factory seems to be more a matter of the advantages it offered from the point of view of surplus extraction. Workers could be kept at the job for long hours and their manner and intensity of work subject to close control. The very extensive and extremely brutal use of women and children in these factories was no doubt in part because they were more easily disciplined, though of course they came a good deal cheaper too.

The point of this story is that technology did not determine the outcome. What it did do was open up the possibility of dramatically increasing labor productivity, a possibility that could have been realized under several alternative systems of production relations. The particular one that was chosen was a reflection of the existing relations of production in early modern society, a class society in which an upper class of merchants, petty producers, and putters-out had established, on a small but extensive scale, a market system of exploitation via small-scale production and trade. Their interests dictated the move to large-scale production in factories, and they had the power to implement their desires. The relations of production and the forces of production in combination produced the industrial revolution.

There is yet another, perhaps even more fundamental aspect to the industrial revolution, namely, the line of causation running from the relations of production to the forces of production. Once the factory system was established and had demonstrated the fantastic opportunities for surplus generation that were inherent in it, further efforts at technological change were likely to be slanted strongly toward devices that could be used in factories. The later history of technological change enhancing the productivity of labor is thus in all probability very strongly conditioned by the social environment in which the search was embedded. As time went on the technology clearly became such that in most industries high productivity could only be achieved in large factories. But to the extent that this line of causation was effective, the outcome was by no means strictly necessary. It was a trajectory to some unknown but perhaps very substantial extent determined rather by the social relations of production. The supreme relevance of this point for the analysis of contemporary society needs no emphasis.

As a final contrast between the peasant and industrial revolutions, there is the difference in the distribution of population over the earth's surface. Essentially, the peasant revolution, while permitting an order of magnitude increase in population, permitted only relatively small concentrations of population. Some particularly fertile plains, such as the Nile Valley, acquired large concentrations, but on the whole under 10 percent of the population was concentrated in cities. The industrial revolution, of course, has had just the opposite effect, with the proportion of population engaged in agriculture being reduced below 10 percent in the most advanced countries. The concentration of the exploited class in cities, and in factory agglomerations where they were in close contact with one another, made possible the rise of mass movements of the exploited. The process by which this occurs is a complex one, and there have been all too many ways in which worker organizations have been subverted into tools of the exploiting upper class, but in general terms urbanization of the direct producers has posed a fundamental threat to the stability of the factory system as a method of exploitation.

The Crisis of Nineteenth-Century Capitalism [4]

The unprecedented growth of productive resources and the concomitant rapid social transformations that accompanied the growth have turned the industrial revolution into an era of great social turbulence. The uprooting of traditional modes of life, the throwing of vast numbers of people onto impersonal labor markets, the insecurity of wage labor as a basis for sustaining a family, and the violent swings in the level of economic activity that accompanied the growth trends all contributed to this turbulence. During most of the nineteenth century the growth itself, with the promise of ultimate plenty that it held out, probably played a substantial role in muting social conflict in much of Europe. There were upsurges of revolutionary activity in 1830, again in 1848, and again in 1870, and the level of violent but localized disruption in individual economies waxed and waned throughout the period; but basically nineteenth-century societies undergoing industrial development seemed to retain some tolerable measure of underlying stability.

However, as the nineteenth century drew to a close this situation began to change. Several factors combined to produce a fundamental threat to the newly emergent industrial capitalist system. One of the most important of these was the growing and intensifying rivalry among capitalists. The rivalry took a number of forms. For example, in the

United States it was in considerable measure a consequence of the creation of nationwide markets, which in turn were brought about by the rise of the railroad. Businesses that had been able to maintain local monopolies because of the high transport costs potentially rival factories had to pay suddenly found themselves faced with competition. Often, in a market where several firms operated under negotiated price agreements, these cartellike arrangements tended to break down as the number of sellers to that market increased substantially. In England the process was less intense, partly because of the slower pace of growth, partly perhaps because in a number of areas it was possible to sustain gentlemen's agreements for market sharing and price fixing, and partly because of the relief to local market entry offered by the burgeoning opportunities for foreign investment. The pressure increasingly came from factories in other industrializing countries. Each country had its own unique story to tell in this regard, but intensifying competition was nevertheless a ubiquitous feature of the capitalist scene.

A second factor was economic instability, which seemed to be increasing sharply as the century wore to a close. Business cycles in the anarchic market system are rather like hydrodynamic turbulence: The general lines of causation are understood but a well-developed theory still eludes the theorist, in both cases because of the great variety of factors that can impinge on a given situation. Inventory cycles, construction cycles, cycles of expectations that stimulated over-investment, financial crises induced by rigidities in the monetary system; all these played their role in generating the business cycle. The intensification of the cycle was related to the accumulated growth, which tended to put a steadily larger amount of productive activity into relatively volatile sectors of the economy, such as investment and the production of other goods whose purchase is easily postponable. The very rapid development of financial markets, an extremely volatile sector in which prayers and promises and chicanery are major "means of production," no doubt played its role as well.

Another major factor in intensifying the cycle was the internationalization of the capitalist system, which was proceeding rapidly during the second half of the nineteenth century. From the eighteen fifties on business cycles in the various industrializing countries became interdependent. In practice this meant that a crisis in one part of capitalism's geography was quickly transmitted to the other parts. Consequently, some potentially stabilizing factors such as foreign investment could not be brought to bear because prospects were simultaneously bad all over.

But the internationalization of capitalism had a far more serious effect than that, for it also generated the era of imperialist rivalry. The economic expansion of capitalism was never separated from the use of violence; the two were linked during the age of primitive capitalist accumulation, and this linkage continued during the period of colonialization of the world. But this deadly competition for raw materials and markets abroad forced capitalists into competing national groups, each with its own fleet and army. This rather substantial conversion of capitalist states into the instruments of national coalitions of capitalists operating internationally created a period of almost annual international crisis. It also led to a very substantial and increasing diversion of resources into the competitive development of the rival fleets and armies.

One more factor needs to be put into the crisis equation, and this the most fundamental of all. In the later nineteenth century labor began everywhere in the developing industrial world to mobilize for economic and political struggle. The factory system was beginning to negate itself as the class consciousness of workers developed their awareness of the basically exploitative structure of the societies in which they lived. Unions were growing everywhere and were becoming more militant. But, even more alarming to the ruling class, workers were also forming political organizations. Social democracy in Germany, the Labour party in England, the Socialist party and the IWW (International Workers of the World) in the United States, and a variety of other political organizations in these countries and elsewhere signified the intensification of the domestic class struggle everywhere.

From the point of view of the stability of capitalism, this struggle could not have occurred at a more unfortunate time. Not only were there the problems of instability, and the threat of war, which would have to be fought with the working classes as cannon fodder, but a sort of economic climacteric had also been reached. The diversion of resources abroad and into military expenditures at home, and perhaps other factors as well, such as the intense rivalry among capitalists, had led to a stagnation in real wages under capitalism. Workers were well aware that labor productivity was continuing its growth but that they were obtaining no share in the increase. Labor turbulence of all forms was increasing at a dramatic pace as capitalism moved through these years and into the early twentieth century.

Such was the scene of crisis. Some sort of explosion seemed clearly imminent, and desperate measures indeed would be required if basically capitalist relations of production were to be preserved by the ruling class. The twisted and brutal adjustments that were made ushered in the era of monopoly capitalism and that bloody, transitional period that we call the twentieth century.

CHAPTER 4

Monopoly Capitalism: Structure and Tendencies

MONOPOLY CAPITALISM is not a rigid structure that was created in the year 1900 and has remained unchanged ever since. Rather, it has come into being piecemeal in response to specific crises and opportunities and, once created, has made numerous adaptations to its structure in the face of newer events. Nevertheless, it will be useful to start the discussion with a description of the principal adaptation to each of the aspects of the first general crisis of capitalism as these were given at the end of the last chapter. Then we will follow monopoly capitalism's course through the century in order to assess its role in the great events of our era and to appraise the tendencies built into it.

Emerging Structure, A Response to Crisis

The first element of crisis discussed in the last chapter had to do with the intensifying rivalries among capitalists.[1] Though the process varied from country to country, the outcome tended to be much the same. There was a strong trend toward substantial concentration, in many cases to the point of monopoly or industrywide cartel, accompanied by a dramatic centralization of the capital markets on which new securities were issued. This was the era of the Sugar and Tobacco Trusts and of the emergence of U.S. Steel. The first of these developments, the emerging industrial concentration, served effectively to inhibit price wars, an important matter because the wars tended to permit a considerable portion of already extracted surplus to be siphoned

back to the mass of producer-consumers. This development also sig-
naled a shift, particularly in the United States, toward recognition that
the greatest mass of surplus would be extracted from continued productive operations of firms rather than from looting ventures such as
had characterized much of nineteenth-century railroad history. The
second measure, performed by J. P. Morgan and the other big investment bankers, organized capital markets to support this operation and
also simplified market-sharing arrangements and the like through in-
formal regulation of new stock and bond issues.

A revealing development occurred in the United States, namely,
the domination by big business of the growing collection of congressional and regulatory "controls" over business activity. Because of the
existence of a large and politically relatively organized commercial
farming population, the operations of the growing monopoly capital
sector did not go unchallenged. A variety of regulative agencies, such as
the Interstate Commerce Commission, had been created and in the
early twentieth century several of the biggest monopolies were broken
up by political and judicial action. These events served as an important
educational experience for the monopoly capitalists. They discovered
that despite the voting power of the farm bloc, Congress in particular
and the government in general remained firmly in their hands. Even
in those days it took a fair amount of money to get elected, and
monopoly capital had overwhelmingly the largest pool of this in the
land. So it was possible to establish an extremely effective political
regime. Elected officials were "responsive" to mass voting pressure by
passing legislation that appeared to be in the interests of such groups;
but as a result of the powers of appointment, appropriation of funds
and administrative powers, vested in officials whose future depended
on the favor of monopoly capital, this legislation could be kept as
only a little more than window dressing. The regulative agencies, for
example, often turned out to be a blessing in disguise, permitting more
overt collusion and price fixing than would otherwise have been
feasible.

And so it was with trust-busting as well. An element of competition among firms, it was found, made for more efficient operation and
consequently for more effective surplus extraction. At least that was
true so long as prices could be kept quite close to their monopoly levels.
But, of course, that was just what the new form of competition was designed to do. And as technology produced new products, monopoly
capital could move in, confidently expecting that the combination of
the already existing trade arrangements and the regulation of the
capital market would prevent competition for shares of new markets
from getting out of hand. Consequently, movements in the direction of
increasing productivity, instead of being a threat to the system, were
merely an effective way to increase the surplus. Thus was born the
system of oligopoly in industry that was to dominate the century's
surplus-extraction process.

Naturally, the precise chronology of these developments varied
from country to country. In Germany concentration was high from the

first and investment banks were deeply involved in industrial regulation well before the turn of the century. In Britain these developments came more slowly, the crucial change probably occurring as a result of economic controls and the resulting cooperation among industrialists brought on by the First World War. But long before World War II this basic structure was established in all the major capitalist countries.

Adaptation to the problem posed by the domestic business cycle is a familiar story, and it too has been universalized. The first step involved getting a better understanding of the functioning of money, and particularly of bank credit, in the economy and then developing instruments for effective control. The Keynesian revolution introduced a new set of fiscal instruments and a new theory of control. It took a while to convince many capitalists that this kind of economic intervention should be permitted—indeed it took some of them quite a while even to understand the basic argument—but they finally came around, and monetary-fiscal regulation of the level of economic activity is a standard feature of contemporary monopoly capitalism.

Adaptation to the growing economic interdependence among capitalist nations has been later in coming and far less substantial. The international monetary organizations have no effective power to follow the control procedures used domestically, but liberal theory indicates that that is approximately what is needed. Coordination of monetary policies in the general interest has also been conspicuous by its absence at key crisis points in recent years.

The Pax Americana certainly eliminated significant and overt imperialist rivalries among the great capitalist nations during the postwar period. Of course it was not really much of a pax, given that over fifty wars occurred during the period.[2] But the overwhelming military dominance of the United States within the imperialist camp, together with the felt threat from the Soviet Union, combined to suppress the sort of behavior that dominated the scene before World War I. What this suggests is that an adaptation has not been made in this area, only that circumstances for a while created relative stability. These circumstances are easing in the seventies, and so a test as to whether a significant adaptation of the system has been made is probably in the cards before too long.[3]

Finally, there is the adaptation to the great domestic threat posed by the rise of an organized working class. One factor made life a bit easier for monopoly capital, namely, the continued and substantial upward trend in labor productivity. This allowed resources to be devoted to modest increases in real wages and to the buying off of potential militant leaders within the labor movement. For example, in the United States the building trades have tended to exert far more than proportionate influence both within the labor movement and on the political scene. Their conservative and politically nonmilitant orientation has made them most effective in dealing with the ruling class, since in effect they help to stabilize the basic institutions of monopoly capitalism.[4]

Other adaptations were made in this central area of conflict, an area that did pose a genuine survival threat to the capitalist system.

Union influence within the business sector was accepted, and workers in big business factories were granted a relatively high degree of economic security, medicines well-known for their antimilitancy properties. An elaborate system of division of status among workers was instituted within business and government with a similar aim in view. And the development of military and police technology and training to control domestic disorder was also instituted. Many of these adaptations came later in the United States than elsewhere, but, once again, they are today universal features of the monopoly capitalist scene.

The Dynamics of Lurching

One of the stocks-in-trade of bourgeois economics is the fragmentation of research. By dividing big issues into many little ones, a false sense of manageability is conveyed to the student. Furthermore, some of the most powerful interactive forces in modern society are completely ignored by this approach. That makes for a very comfortable ideology but for a gross distortion of the truth.

Nowhere is this strategy more effective, or more pernicious, than in the liberal attempts to analyze twentieth-century capitalism. The problems of wars, revolutions, even major depressions, all seem to be treated as if they were exogenous; indeed, one can find liberals even heaping praise on the system of advanced capitalism for its ability to withstand the "shocks" that "circumstances" have forced it to endure since the turn of the century.

Nothing, of course, could be further from the truth. Wars, revolutions, depressions, and all the other forms of crisis are endogenous to monopoly capitalism, products of a class society undergoing rapid change that its social science is incapable of understanding. And so the giant lurches from one great catastrophe to another as a fundamental part of its nature. Figure 1 charts key aspects of this lurching movement, which is described in more detail in the following text.

The stabilization of domestic capitalist rivalries via monopolization had proceeded quite far by 1914. But other elements of the crisis remained, in particular the ruinous rivalry between national coalitions of capitalists. Indeed, domestic monopolization may even have intensified this particular contradiction between the class and regional interests of monopoly capital. At any rate, such rivalries, abetted by attempts to use nationalism to defuse the increasingly militant working class, were the dominant causes of the First World War, with its tens of millions of dead, one of the most impersonal of the humanly directed slaughters known to history.

A caused event itself has consequences. World War I is an endogenous part of the world monopoly capitalist system, both caused by it and setting in train forces that were strongly to condition its fur-

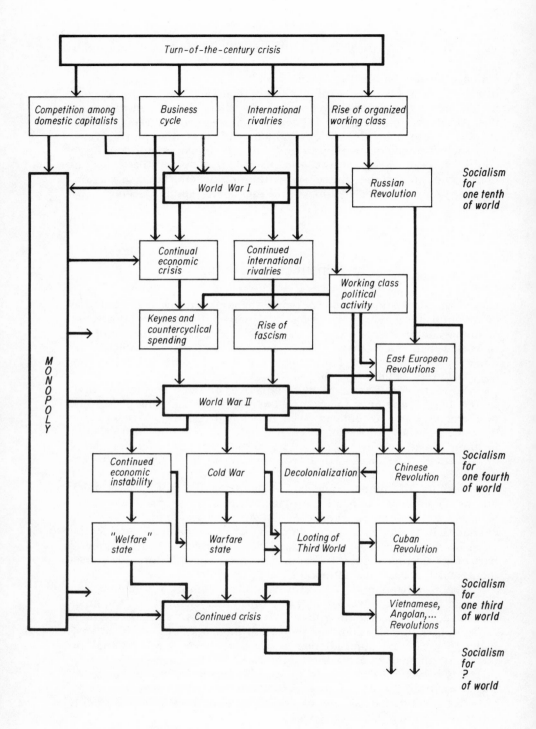

ther development. Perhaps most important of these was the direct political threat represented by war weariness, the collapse of the German government and the establishment of the world's first socialist government in the Soviet Union. The early stages of the overthrow of capitalism as a whole seemed to have been reached for a few brief months in 1918–19, with revolutionary governments being set up in parts of Germany, for example. Though the crisis was survived it left a strong mark. Social legislation and repression were used in varying combinations in the different countries, depending on their internal situation. For example, the former was predominant in Britain, the latter in the United States, and Germany used both, combining a social democratic government with military suppression of revolutionaries. Efforts were made to overthrow the Soviet government too, but these were beaten back, and domestic fears prevented any large-scale direct intervention beyond a few events such as the American occupation of eastern Siberia, the British occupation of Murmansk, and a French-Polish military advance toward Moscow. As a consequence, some unknown but considerable portion of the social-security benefits obtained by workers under monopoly capitalism can be laid at the door of the continuing specter of a functioning socialist society where the means of production are no longer under private control.

Serious as it was, the Soviet threat was not powerful enough to unite the national coalitions of capitalism, and international instability continued to be a major weakness of the system. Attempts to loot the defeated German coalition by means of "reparations" payments symbolize this continuing conflict, as do the nationalistic trade and monetary policies of the thirties. But the disruptions of the war had major domestic impact as well. Unemployment was a serious problem in these economies in the twenties. In some, such as Britain, it was a desperate problem, and the capitalists could agree on no measures that would resolve the problem for fear of eroding their own individual shares of the loot. The trend toward monopoly in an uncertain environment seemed to produce some stagnationist tendencies. The brittleness of a society based on this combination of monopoly capitalist features was revealed in the Great Depression. The resort to fascism provided a means for the German capitalist coalition to return to its "rightful" place at the international surplus trough, while other governments struggled against total collapse of their domestic economies. No relief via acceptable domestic policies seemed to be in sight; for example, in the later thirties the American economy was heading back toward the desperate and protorevolutionary situation of 1931 to 1933.[5] Not surprisingly, the technique of international scapegoating suggested itself as a solution, and belligerency in foreign policy began to increase markedly. The United States "abandoned" neutrality, sent destroyers to Britain, and decreed a boycott on Japanese import of vital American scrap iron. After all, this solution—escape from revolution through war and preparations for war—had worked before, both in 1933 in Germany and in 1914 all over Europe.

And in a sense it worked again. Unemployment was ended for a time, as was domestic class conflict. However, world war is a rather myopic policy from the point of view of the survival of monopoly capitalism. The end of the war found the European capitalist economies in a state of deep crisis. American economists and politicians were in general agreement that, shortly after the war's end, the American economy would probably sink back into a depression similar to that of the thirties. Colonialism was plainly on its last legs, promising a fundamental readjustment in the relations between imperial and dependent states. Domestic communism posed a serious challenge to the French and Italian governments. And not only was the Soviet Union a victorious power in the war, having assisted in the new defeat of the German and Japanese coalitions of capitalists, but socialism was again on the march, heading for power in a number of East European and East Asian countries.

Once again the solution to one crisis sent the monopoly capitalist system lurching off into another. However, the solution tried this time was more effective, at least for a while, than had been some previous ones. For one thing, the Keynesian lesson had been learned, and by and large monopoly capitalists had come to accept the idea that a program of economic stabilization could be designed so as to increase the surplus accruing to each major capitalist group. Second, the military and political dominance acquired by the United States served, for a while at least, to eliminate one of the major weaknesses of the system, namely, imperial rivalries. In fact the United States, acting partly to support domestic capitalists by providing them with orders and partly to meet the threat of the Soviet Union, offered substantial economic aid to help start up the European economies once again.

Another major response was the Cold War. This too had several dimensions. First, the Soviet Union, of course, by its very existence posed a threat to the capitalist system, though the threat was much weakened by war losses and by Stalinism in the late forties. Second, there was the fear that communism could not be contained before it swept across the decolonializing Third World, and even perhaps southern Europe as well, where a civil war in Greece was already underway. Third, there was now ample evidence that government military spending could be a very profitable business, while war tended to blunt domestic class conflict. The Cold War was a more efficient version of a hot war, permitting the suppression of dissent in the interests of "national survival" ("clear and present danger" was the phrase much used by liberal Supreme Court justices), while at the same time permitting the economy to operate without inconvenient economic controls.

This system worked reasonably well, from the point of view of the monopoly capitalists, for a decade or two. It even provided one or two bonuses, which had perhaps not been fully appreciated at the start. The large-scale military spending made massive resources available to control the process of decolonialization in such a way as to be minimally disturbing to established capitalist relations in the Third World; at the same time the spread of "communism" was checked for a while after it had reached out to cover not much more than a fourth of the world's population. Indeed, the opportunities for extracting surplus from the newly emerging Third World may even have been increased, as the national bourgeoisie in these countries could be used as a screen for monopoly capitalist operations. The Pax Americana was a bloody and frightening time, full of war and misery for hundreds of millions of the world's citizens, but from the point of view of monopoly capitalism it was a stable and prosperous period.

The Current Crisis

To paraphrase one of those Hegelian triads, with monopoly capitalism success breeds failure. The Pax Americana was in a certain sense a time of stability and prosperity for monopoly capitalists, but by now at least the stability side of it has come to a close. Europe and Japan have been playing successful economic catch-up to the point at which they can once again begin to challenge the American capitalists. This affects stability in the same two basic ways. First, it makes international financial control difficult, as complex negotiations affecting different coalitions have to be worked out in a rapidly changing situation. And, second, it makes the renewal of imperialist rivalries feasible as Japan, Germany, and other groups accelerate their foreign-investment programs.

Success has bred failure in other areas too, notably in the challenge that some developing countries are able to offer monopoly capital. The oil crisis needs no comment, and however the oil-producer consortium works out it suggests fundamental problems of adaptation among competing regional coalitions of capital.

Yet another area in which success has tended to breed failure is that of the new government-business alliance. This alliance offered opportunities to buy off labor and to socialize some of the costs of doing business, while at the same time stabilizing the economy. However, it has developed instead into an additional arena for combat among competing capitals. A consequence of this has been the development of inflation, whose rate has actually been on the increase for over a decade. And in political-economic terms, inflation is far more difficult than depression to cure, because cutbacks are difficult to allocate among the competing domestic capital coalitions. Those highly touted seven or eight years of steadily rising real GNP in the sixties were preparing the way for the instability and uncertainty of the seventies.

Another frightening underlying aspect of the Pax Americana has been the steady militarization of the world. Not only is there more than one gun per capita in private ownership in the United States, but American and other nations' arms sales, direct and indirect, have spread weapons of destruction and the capacity to produce them in truly massive quantities all around the world. The result has been that the cost of war has gone up for all sides, as have the expected levels of destruction that a war will achieve. The burgeoning crews of military technicians, of citizens trained in the arts of war, of the military in high political positions, all suggest that war is much more on the minds of the world's leaders these days.

The waste, the irrationality, the insanity of this, the most stable era of monopoly capitalism, cannot but affect deeply the lives and attitudes of everyone who willy-nilly is a part of it. The malaise of life in urban and suburban America needs no retelling here, but surely it reflects the generalization of Marxian production-process alienation to every corner of life in monopoly capitalist society. The revolt of youth in the sixties was but one—though at least a rational one—of the manifestations of this deep sickness in society. Out of the disenchantment with traditional liberal ideals that spread so widely during the sixties will perhaps come both the understanding and the commitment to toss this intolerable social system into the historical ashcan.

CHAPTER 5

Exploitation Under Monopoly Capitalism

THE AVAILABLE EVIDENCE on human history shows that when a surplus begins to be produced in a society, attempts will be made to extract that surplus from the producers for the use of others. It seems natural enough to call this exploitation. The success of the attempts tends to vary over time and place and the method of extraction used. There does appear to be a very broad and powerful tendency for the rate of extraction to increase more rapidly than the productivity of labor; that is, as societies become more productive, the direct producers tend to benefit relatively less from the improvement than do those to whom the extracted surplus is allocated.

It is important to note that we are commenting on a widely observed historical tendency, not on some rigidly deterministic theory. Throughout history nonexploitative microsocieties have coexisted with exploitative ones. Some of these nonexploitative societies have been too poor for a significant surplus to exist. In the early nineteenth century the western Shoshone Indians searched in nuclear-family groups for acorns and bugs as their basic diet. Occasionally they came together to hunt rabbit or fish. At such a time some surplus over essential consumption no doubt was often created. Just as obviously, this surplus was typically retained by the quasi-community of producers. Relatively low productivity or technical difficulties in surplus extraction seem to have been the main reasons for the survival of such groups; of course, the same factors tend also to account for their relatively small numbers.

Among societies where surplus extraction was practiced as a central feature of social life, the particular extraction process also varied widely over time and place. This was noted in chapter 3, but it becomes relevant again as we look at this aspect of monopoly capitalism. There has been an important change in the structure of exploitation with the shift from capitalism's nineteenth- to its twentieth-century versions.

The industrial revolution wrought a great change in the opportunities for surplus extraction. Exploitation in peasant societies was based essentially on the control over land exercised by a ruling class, but this process was affected by the relatively close ties that tended to exist between the producer himself and the land, stemming both from cultural considerations and the uniqueness of individual plots of land. The industrial revolution brings produced means of production to the fore as the control instrument for surplus extraction. But these capital goods are not unique in the same sense; items of machinery are often mutually interchangeable, and most any factory is reproducible. This made it possible to wholly separate the producer from any long-run connection with the basic means of production he was to use.

Out of this grew the generalized system of wage labor, and with it the so-called law of value, a concept that gives some quantitative expression to this highly impersonal system of surplus extraction. For a given state of the forces of production the new market system tended to generate, in the long run, prices that reflected the labor content of the goods produced. This is a simple consequence of the long-run reproducibility of goods, including capital goods and labor, and continues to hold so long as there is no major resource exhaustion. Ruling-class control of the means of production permitted that class to keep the price, the wage, the exchange value of labor at a level that, roughly, was minimally consistent with productivity and the replacement of aging workers. The surplus accrued to the capitalists by letting the market compel the worker to work for much longer each day than was necessary to recreate the value of his labor. The actual rate of surplus extraction might vary from industry to industry, but the process of extraction was governed by these same impersonal factors, operating under the primary influence of the capitalist class's monopoly control of the means of production. The worker's choice was simple: Work for very low, monopolist-induced wages or starve.

Of course, this was not a wholly novel process of surplus extraction. Factories and shops employing labor for wages existed in many earlier societies. However, in these earlier instances the process was embedded in a very different kind of society, and this affected many aspects of its operation. For example, there was often a paternalistic element to these earlier forms, though this may have meant in human terms no more than that there were social processes oriented toward establishing feelings of loyalty in the worker and that these feelings were one of the devices by which surplus was extracted. At any rate, the newly generalized system of wage labor essentially eliminated such master/servant ties. And this in turn was one of the factors generating alienation and fractured personalities in the new society, as people were impelled by the new environment to treat one another as mutually interchangeable and exchangeable objects.[1]

There are, of course, many other consequences of this transformation of the central process of resource extraction in modern society. But enough has been said to suggest the fundamental aspects of the transformation. This process continues to operate in contemporary monopoly capitalism, and remains a fundamental source of surplus for the ruling class. However, monopoly capitalism has brought new processes of surplus extraction to the fore and has brought about yet another generalization of the process of surplus extraction. It is to these new processes that we must now turn.

Surplus and Its Growth

Celebrations of capitalism always place rates of growth of output as the centerpiece of accomplishment. Since the turn of the century in the United States, this story will go, output per capita has increased almost fourfold. Undeniably that is a great accomplishment, signifying a genuine increase in the level of the forces of production and offering the technical possibility for tremendous further accomplishments that are more directly relevant for human beings.

Unfortunately, the measure of output used by economists is hard to relate to the ways in which human lives are changed by the output increase. That is precisely because it is not really a measure of achievement but of promise, of what might be done. The distinction was brought out most clearly in a little calculation made many years ago by Paul Baran that relates to the changes wrought in the American economy during World War II. In 1944, for the first time since World War I, there was approximate full employment. However, of the 66 million members of the officially designated labor force, some 11 million were in the armed forces and thus not engaged in productive labor. And about half of the officially designated output produced by the remaining four-fifths of the labor force was military goods. This massive mobilization and reordering of the economy from its gross malfunctioning of the depressed thirties, you would think, must have called for a tremendous material sacrifice by the population. But there are strong indications that reality was very different, and that in fact the general standard of living of the mass of the population actually improved. The implication is clear: The American population could be brought to a peak standard of living by using only half the "output" of the economy. Output per capita has at least doubled in the thirty years since Baran's calculation. Also, in those days not much more than a third of working-age women were officially in the labor force; nowadays the figure is more like one-half. When one adds these facts in, and makes some allowance for the need to maintain and perhaps increase the stock of factories and durable goods in the economy, it would be a conservative estimate that our current population could be maintained at a decent, "American" standard of living with the use of well under a half of our "output." [2]

That is quite an astonishing figure. We are deluged these days with complaints and comments by politicians and pundits to the effect that "there is no free lunch," that there is no way we can provide for the environment or for the poor. We must live, even our "liberal" politicians tell us, for years with our 25 million officially poor, people who by no stretch of the imagination have a decent standard of living. We must also live with inadequate medical service, with poor schools, with commodity shortages, even with inadequate and overcrowded jails. What are they doing with that half to two-thirds of our potential output?

It's a good question. You will not find the answer in any official statistical table, because such figures are not considered respectable by our eminently respectable economists. As a consequence, we can't put numbers to the various amounts of misuse of our economic potential. However, we can at least make a list of the things that happen to prevent the tremendous promise heralded in the "output" figures from becoming achievements. As we go through this list, it might be well to remember not only that there is this tremendous promise in the United States, still the world's richest country in its economic potential, but that there is really no social accounting for the goods that represent that potential. We are reduced to qualitative and speculative comments precisely because this great secret is being kept from the American people by a massive obfuscatory flood of irrelevant statistics and commentary by politicians and economists alike.

The question we have just referred to is, How can we resolve the contradiction of scarcity in the midst of plenty? On one side we have tremendous productive capacity, holding out the promise of a society of abundance; on the other side we have tremendous unmet needs, needs that seem to be getting more intense even as the capacity to satisfy them grows. On one side we have the economists' statistics that show "consumption per capita" rising more than threefold over the era of monopoly capitalism in the United States; on the other we find tens of millions in poverty, children hungry and their illnesses untended, and all around us signs of a deteriorating environment. Of coure we want to know why such things happen; but first there is the simple question of fact: What is happening, where is the promise gone? Here are some clues to the mystery.

1. Quite a bit of that potential output is simply unproduced. In an average peacetime year between 5 and 10 percent of the labor force is out of work. Average use of our stock of capital is at a substantially lower level. Because of the inherent instability of the capitalist system and of the opportunity for big profits during the brief periods of frenetic prosperity, the United States uses its stock of productive capital at an average rate of only three-fourths or so of potential. Given the expansion of the last three decades, this means that the currently *unused* plant and workers in a typical year might have produced close to half of the massive surplus generated in 1944.

2. There is a tremendous amount of wasteful production. The magnitude is suggested by a study that found that the cost of model changes in producing Ford cars over a four-year period came to over

a quarter of the purchase price of the car.[3] Basically, these costs relate to getting people to buy more cars sooner, not to improvements in the functioning of the car as a means of transportation; they represent waste. The drug industry is another one that is notorious for generating wastes of the above kind. In addition, it turns out that only about six cents on every drug sales' dollar goes to research, while twenty-four cents goes to advertising.[4] Highway accidents often produce fifty thousand annual deaths and a grand total of a million annual casualties. These damaged goods and people, of course, have to be repaired, and the repair itself is an expensive process. The above items are a small sampling of things that divert the promise of our productive capacity to waste, for they are largely avoidable and represent burdens on our capacity brought about by mismanagement.

3. In addition to wasteful production, one can distinguish wasteful occupations. That is, many jobs that contribute "value added" to the official national product use talented human beings in essentially unproductive ways. Advertising has already been mentioned. Nowadays most nonlawyers would recognize a large fraction of that crew as wastefully employed protecting clients against other lawyers' actions and generally working massively at paper combat for pay. The proliferation of bureaucracies everywhere in the towering office buildings of downtown America are eloquent testimony to the wastefulness of American business and government. Even the marketplace, supposedly a paragon of efficiency, turns out to be tremendously wasteful, given the costs of generating and organizing information in its anarchic mode of operation and in peddling the goods.[5] Literally millions of jobs are filled in these activities and, more than likely, most of them are unnecessary.

4. There is now a growing awareness of the tremendous amount of loss-producing economic activity in the United States. Urban sprawl reduces the amount of available agricultural land, and the cost of producing farm products rises as a result. The transport of goods and people and the production of goods by unsafe methods causes casualties that must be repaired. Among the affluent and well-insured the doctors prey, providing unneeded and even pernicious services, for example by performing truly massive amounts of unneeded surgery. And, of course, pollution by some factories raises the cost of production in others, and generates debilitating respiratory and other ailments in surrounding populations. Under the incentives of modern business it has often been less costly to spill oil than to take simple and even cheap preventive measures.

5. Perhaps a separate category should be allotted to the three major illegal activities, drugs, prostitution, and gambling. Losses of that promised output resulting from unproductive and degrading aspects of these activities are unmeasured but clearly very substantial.

6. It is no secret that our income distribution is highly skewed, far more so than is necessary as a material incentive for workers to generate the potential output in the economy. There are hundreds of individuals in our country who report over a million dollars of annual

income, and probably hundreds more who have it but don't report it. Over a quarter of personal income goes to less than 10 percent of the families. And perhaps three fourths or more of the privately held securities are owned by less than 2 percent of the families.[6] The diversion of our productive promise to servicing the fashionable "needs" of the wealthy, through both the private market and government favor, represents a substantial fraction of potential output.

7. There is also a major bit of information as to where the surplus did *not* go. In the last dozen years or so it did not go to the working class, since their real wages have remained stagnant.[7]

8. But there is a substantial fiction even in the statistics that show a rise in the real incomes of families in the broad mid-range of the income distribution. One telling figure is the virtual stagnation in the average amount of time worked over the last thirty years. On the face of it, this suggests that rising incomes do not permit the population to take more leisure, but that they must continue to work about as much as before simply to stay even. Much of what we think of as income increase is really simply compensating us for losses that our new environment has created. Most obvious perhaps is the expenditure for transportation. Expensive cars must be increasingly used as urban public transport deteriorates. Movement to places farther away from the job is made necessary by the decay of formerly attractive neighborhoods in town. Because of this a car becomes a necessity for security, for shopping, for recreation, where in the past these needs could be conveniently met locally. Despite all those expenditures on fancy appliances, studies indicate that housewives do not spend less time on housework, suggesting that once again the gains from the goods are eaten up by compensating expenditures.[8] Some measured increases in "real" income are fictitious, as when rising wages increase the "value" of essentially the same services provided earlier for less. The low quality and durability of many goods, substantially less than in the past or at least quite low compared with their "promise," mean that another fraction of that increased income goes to maintenance and replacement. Perhaps the most striking and important single example of this phenomenon of compensating expenditure lies in the field of health care, where expenditures are several times greater than in past years when the measured health status of this mid-range of the population was comparable to its present state.

9. Finally, there is the category of alienation expenditures. This would be the hardest to quantify, but is probably also the most pervasive, tainting almost the full range of human activity in contemporary America. Job absenteeism, reduced performance by the millions of citizens on Valium and booze, these are measurable consequences of the alienating environment generated in our society. Beyond lie less clearcut but still obvious enough phenomena. For example, the increasing failure of our schools is clearly related to their misuse as institutions for advanced baby-sitting and disciplining of youth. The "successful" product of these schools is basically certified as someone who is willing to spend endless time doing meaningless things on order. Work

has been moving in the same direction, with specialization and routinization depriving most participants of any sense of creativity or personal responsibility for the product.[9] Surrounding everyone—from the first look at television, the first day in school, the first day on the job —is the brainwashing, the incitement to pitch in and make America great by first working harder and then consuming harder. The costs of creating a whole society that is thus forced to accelerate with its brakes on is the last great sink down which our productive promise flows. One might seriously question whether the last generation or two of life under monopoly capital has produced any real increase in income at all.

Surplus and Insecurity

Defenders of monopoly capitalism have another line of defense set up behind the breached barriers of the growth ethos. This is the argument that the system has provided a tremendous increase in the security of its citizens. Social security, unemployment compensation, medical insurance: In these and other ways monopoly capitalism, it is claimed, has reduced life's risks, thus making our existence a good deal more pleasant than levels of real income might indicate.

Like other such arguments, this one is based on a half truth that grossly distorts the reality of the situation. The above programs do exist and provide coverage for a substantial fraction of the population, though the fraction varies quite a bit from one program to another. In addition, improvements in the state of the art of medicine have led to a very substantial reduction in the death rates of young children, certainly a major improvement that can be laid in part at the door of the political economic system. In this case it did in fact deliver the goods, even if still on a selective basis, providing, for example, much higher death rates for poor and minority members of the population than for rich and white members.[10]

But the half of the truth submerged in this account is not so difficult to dredge up. Capitalism is still a highly volatile economic system. Unemployment rates are both high and variable, by no means everyone is covered by unemployment insurance, and incomes tend to drop substantially when a member of the family is laid off.[11] Inflation too is high and variable and eats at the other end of the income, so to speak, producing at times large drops in the ability of families to purchase their accustomed mix of goods. The variability of commodity prices, which basically reflects the intensifying conflict between monopoly capital and the Third World, is another large source of income insecurity, affecting both the prices of goods and many jobs.

Much of the insecurity of modern life is a direct product of monopoly capitalism, all right, but is less directly connected to economic processes of the marketplace. The virtual explosion of crime, by no means restricted to cities or to the United States, is directly related to the political economy of monopoly capitalism: It breeds on poverty and alienation and hopelessness. The ruin of neighborhoods, even of whole cities, is a serious risk under mature monopoly capitalism, one for which no insurance can be bought and that government policy seems strangely incapable of abating. The lower risks to traditional causes of infant deaths are at least partly compensated for by the higher risks to the general population from cancer and respiratory ailments, whose increased incidence now seems to be quite closely tied to the deteriorating environment created by monopoly capital's great organizations. And the risk of death from war has never before in history been so high, including the serious prospect of the destruction of all human society. The age of monopoly capital is *not* an age of security, not even for Americans.

Surrounding and permeating human behavior under all these risks, giving that behavior its bizarre hues of violence and of madness, is the depersonalization of human relations under monopoly capital. We become not so much predators as objects to one another. This in turn deprives the individual of that elemental security that derives from being a member of a community, of a group of people who have some commitment for mutual aid and support of one another. The deterioration of security in this dimension may be the most fundamental risk of all. Out of it grows the tolerance for misery in others that conditions the growing risks in contemporary society. And it in turn grows out of the system of monopoly capital itself, which forces depersonalization on participants as a condition for survival within the system.

Exploitation and Monopoly Capital

This chapter began with a brief account of the classical Marxian processes of exploitation. But most of the chapter was devoted to appraising the allocation of the surplus in contemporary monopoly capitalism, in particular the various diversions from its effective use and the ways in which risks relevant to the citizen have changed. Does this mean that the subject has been changed, that we are no longer speaking of exploitation?

I think not. Exploitation in the traditional sense, the extraction of surplus from the producers by a ruling class, continues to be a central feature of monopoly capitalism. But the classical Marxist version, based on labor reproduction costs under a labor theory of value, is no longer capable of telling the whole story of exploitation under monopoly capitalism. A wholly satisfactory alternative explanation is not yet forthcoming. What we are trying to do here is to suggest some elements that must be included in such an account.

The basic thrust of the argument does not imply a rejection of Marx's theory of exploitation.[12] Our society can eliminate material deprivation as a cause of human misery. Indeed, the Baranian calculation suggests that, given time to make appropriate adaptations in our stock of capital and our institutions, we have the *present* capacity to achieve this. The promise remains unrealized, and appears to many to be unrealizable, because of the fundamental flaw in our society, which produces all those diversions of resources and increased risks of ruin. That flaw is the class nature of the society, which generates the endless series of conflicts, negotiations, truces, chicanery, and renewed conflicts that destroys the society's potential. Only by creating a new society can we achieve the promise and eliminate material deprivation as a cause of human misery. This is the only real resolution of the contradiction of scarcity in the midst of plenty.

But, clearly, contemporary exploitation differs from its predecessors. It is the incredible waste of resources that strikes the eye here, and the distortion of human behavior, rather than any quantum of material deprivation, though the latter continues to exist for many millions. True, the ruling class continues to expropriate a very substantial portion of the mammoth surplus for its own uses; but in this weird society the ruling class is itself to some extent a victim as well as an exploiter. The lives of its members too are distorted by the society's inhumane values and the behavior that is required to sustain the system. Alienation deprives many goods of much of their value for any consumer. But this in itself offers hope, as it has now become possible to recruit substantial numbers of the young from the ruling class itself to the goals of creating a new society, one in whose success they too have a direct stake.

CHAPTER 6

Government and Monopoly Capital

IN THE DAYS of classical capitalism, the functions of state and economy were fairly sharply separated. In the more advantaged capitalist countries, such as nineteenth-century Britain and the United States, one might reasonably say that the primary function of the state was to protect the legal-institutional system of private property relations. These relations guaranteed bourgeois control over the means of production and thus determined the nature of exploitation of the direct producers, which in turn was a product of ruling-class control over the produced means of production. This monopoly, of course, is the key to understanding the operation of what liberals call the free market. The state is required because ownership is quite an intangible thing, defined at law in terms of the phrasing of certain documents and protected by the threat of use of the coercive instruments under the state's control. The state could thus remain in the background, available for very tangible use whenever the "rights" and power of the bourgeoisie were called into question, but otherwise very much less active than the "private" sector of the economy, where nearly all production and exchange occurred.

Things are very different nowadays, at least on the surface. No one could accuse the governments of monopoly capitalism either of being in the background or of being sharply separated from the economy. In trying to understand these changes, it is vital not to take the static, snapshot approach of simply comparing the early capitalist state with the monopoly capitalist state. Though each of these regimes has its own special properties, understanding is only gained by looking at the process by which the properties were acquired. Here as elsewhere change is to be understood as the resultant of struggle, often of violent struggle, among a variety of contenders for power. The struggle shapes the outcomes and deprives those outcomes of their rationality, however "rational" may have been the strategies of individual contending factions. And, of course, the struggle continues, shaped both by its past history and by its present environment. In our brief look at the process of development of the monopoly capital state we will find one central, invariant theme that ties the early and the late capitalist state together: The primary function of the state continues to be the protection of the regime of private property relations.

The Rise of Big Government

At the turn of the century federal, state, and local government expenditures in the United States were $1.7 billion, or about 10 percent of gross national product. Nowadays the government expenditures figure is around $600 billion, or about 40 percent of the current value of gross national product. That is quite a change, obviously one that has had a dramatic influence on the behavior of both the state and the economy. How did it come about?

At the top of any list of explanations of the rise of big government in the twentieth century is war. The United States illustrates this process very well. Military expenditures expand at a good pace during the prewar years of increasing international tension (a 50 percent increase in 1902 to 1913 and a trebling in 1934 to 1940), then explode during the war (about twentyfold for World War I and tenfold for World War II). During the course of this explosion, business grows accustomed to military contracts and finds ways for mutually beneficial collaboration among businessmen who in the past had been at loggerheads. Consequently, the new peacetime levels of expenditures are far higher than those of even the tense prewar period (1922 military expenditures were more than three times those of 1913, and 1948 more than six times those of 1940).[1] As we saw in chapter 3, the wars themselves are no accidents of history but are natural products of the functioning of the capitalist system. So indeed is this internal manifestation of permanently rising military expenditures.

The experience of war teaches businessmen not to hate war, or especially to love it, but to appreciate the opportunities inherent in close interaction with government. But this means a different kind of government-business relationship. Government is no longer just protecting property rights and mediating conflicts among business groups. It is now collecting surplus through taxation, a form of coercive expropriation, and then allotting the surplus to various capitalists in the form of military contracts. Of course, some of this has always gone on. But at these new levels of expenditure the government becomes by far the largest demander of goods in the economy. Instead of mediating conflict among businessmen, it now becomes something more like its feudal counterpart, a direct participant in the squabble within the ruling class for a share of the surplus loot. Clearly, this represents a change of some significance in the relations of production.

The second major change in the role of government is a product of the increasing need for social-harmony expenditures, that is, for expenditures that reduce the risk of overthrow of the capitalist system. The first major increase in this sector of expenditures came in education. Expenditures on education have not only increased rapidly throughout the twentieth century in the United States, but during pre-World War II peacetime years they tended to be at least two or three times greater than national "defense" expenditures. Some of this increase is associated with a genuine need for a higher level of technical training for workers in modern industry. But as the origins of the movement for universal compulsory education indicate, and as the ideological slant of the textbooks—adopted for compulsory use—confirm, the principal motivation in this area was control and discipline of the work force. Early increases are associated with rapid urbanization and the threats posed by the concentration of large numbers of workers in towns. Increasing literacy does not seem to have been the central motivation; for example, in Massachusetts the districts whose factories required little skill tended to opt for compulsory primary education before those employing a large fraction of skilled labor.[2]

A second and later thrust of social-harmony expenditures is of course associated with the word "welfare." It should be noted that programs primarily supplying relief for the destitute have never assumed a large role either absolutely or relatively in government spending. There seems to be some feeling that stabilizing a large idle force of working-class citizens is not the way to go about preventing revolutionary ideas from spreading. Instead, the welfare budgets have increasingly been allotted to a variety of programs aimed, at least minimally, at dealing with specific problems of the poor. There has been much public housing construction, many hospitals have been built, urban services expanded to create jobs, and subsidies provided to assist the purchase of food, health, housing, and other specific services by the poor. Both relatively and absolutely the great expansions of this kind occurred in the United States after World War II, though other capitalist countries began the process somewhat earlier.

By now it is possible to discover from government statistical documents that expenditures on welfare-related items substantially exceed national defense expenditures. Monopoly capitalist governments are now often referred to as "the welfare state" and defended as instruments of mercy in a threatening world. Unfortunately, the facts belie this kind assessment. One only need remember that such expenditures stem from the nature of capitalism, a system in which the profit-oriented ruling class does not assign tens of billions of dollars of the surplus it has extracted from the direct producers as a simple act of mercy. The first impetus for such spending, as noted, comes from the fear of revolution. The ruling class is very small—substantially less than a tenth of the population on any reasonable measure. When things go wrong with the system, as during the Great Depression of the thirties, fear becomes a major factor in ruling-class reactions. In a number of capitalist societies, this reaction expressed itself in the rise of fascism. In the United States and Great Britain, the opportunity was seen to preserve power by less drastic means. And thus the "welfare" program was born. As already noted, fear of the Soviet Union also contributed to monopoly capitalist attitudes.

However, once instituted, such programs tend to take on a life of their own, again conditioned by the nature of the system. They became structured in such a way that the affluent could profit from "welfare" as much as or even more than the supposed "target populations." It has been estimated that the incomes of medical doctors increased by more than 50 percent within a very few years of the introduction of Medicare. Opportunities to profit from all sorts of construction contracts associated with welfare programs have been legion. And even job programs have a strong effect on the system. There are now several hundred thousand officials administering poverty programs.[3] The allegiance of these people to the government that employs them is a distinct plus for the ruling class. Furthermore, they now have a stake in the complex and unwieldy service systems of which they are a part and become an influence persistently working for increase in their size and scope.

What is the upshot of all this? At the present time the total welfare budget amounts to around $150 billion. If that money were simply handed out to the poorest people in the country, it would mean a gift of $3000 per year to every man, woman, and child in the poorest quarter of the population. In other words, poverty could be eliminated completely and permanently with a fraction of this sum, even given the general inefficiencies in the capitalist system. But the welfare system is so permeated with waste, corruption, and inefficiency, with rakeoffs to the nonpoor, that poverty itself remains only lightly touched by the trickle of funds that survives all these diversions. One is reminded of the Syr Darya River in Central Asia; as thriving cities grew along its banks, and with them their needs for water, the river flow steadily diminished and finally disappeared into the sands long before reaching the sea; and then the cities died.

But in a way there is an even more fundamental consequence of this development. Government and economy now become thoroughly mixed in the process of extracting and allocating surplus to the "welfare" program. Instead of simply laying down and enforcing the general rules of operation of the market economy, we now find as much as a fifth of our output funneled through the government to the welfare and defense systems. Government agencies, businesses, and elected officials are locked in continuous struggle on literally hundreds of fronts, as the various interests scramble for their share of the surplus that has been extracted from the direct producers. The outcomes of these little struggles cannot be socially effective, because the participants are not the supposed beneficiaries. They will not be very much concerned with saving on taxes because each individual program is just a drop in the bucket, given the size of government and the ability of the participants to shift the tax burden away from themselves. Powerful processes have thus been set into motion that will tend to increase both the size of the program and, *pari passu*, its level of waste, of failure to fulfill the stated objectives. It is also a very divisive, conflictful process, even for the participants. And, finally, awareness cannot help but grow among the supposed beneficiaries as to what is really happening to the "welfare" program.

There is a third major cause of the change in government's size and role in monopoly capitalism. This stems from the basic contradiction of capitalism, that between the increasing socialization of the forces of production and the private nature of the relations of production. What has been happening increasingly, as twentieth-century science and technology have continued to develop rapidly, is that the decentralized market has become a steadily less effective mediator of economic activity. If there were such a thing as stable markets, private competitive capitalism could at least have been an efficient, if exploitative, economic system. But new technologies have required a larger scale of operation and, increasingly, more complex and direct relations among producers than the arms-length bargaining the classical market processes could permit. And, of course, modern production has increasingly been generating harmful side effects on the environment that cannot be abated by resort to market processes.

Part of monopoly capital's response has been centralization of private economic organizations. In the United States this has meant, in just the last few decades, almost a doubling of the share of output coming from the largest corporations, until, for example, the top 200 manufacturing firms now control almost three-fifths of the assets employed in manufacturing.[4] Similar—in fact, probably even greater—concentration exists in firms involved mainly in financial operations, such as banks and insurance companies. To the outsider's casual glance these firms begin to look increasingly like a single entity.

But they still retain, in both legal fact and actual practice, their separate identities and autonomy. Consequently there has been an increasingly urgent need to provide mediators and arbitrators for the disputes that continually arise among these giant organizations. Government has an obvious role to play here and, through regulatory agencies and in many other ways, has been serving that role to a rapidly increasing extent. However, government, as noted above, can no longer assume the position of "outside" agent in resolving such conflicts. It is also the economy's largest dispenser of largesse to these same corporations. So increasingly government itself has become a battleground in which corporations vie with one another for a larger slice of the pie. And so the basic contradiction is further intensified, waste and corruption continue to increase, and the conflict-resolution process begins to lose much of its legitimacy. Once the battle over Richard Nixon's survival came to the crunch, the decision tended to be transformed into just such a conflict; the ruling class was itself divided over the appropriate role of government in this confusing environment of intensifying late-capitalist struggle.

These three factors then have primarily conditioned the rise of modern monopoly capitalist government: war, the need for social harmony expenditures, and the increasing socialization of production. They have turned government into a Kafkaesque madhouse of inefficiency, in which its typical functions are almost unrecognizable. Does that mean that an entirely new regime has been created? That is the question to which we now turn.

Normal Government and Crisis Government

Most of the time the monopoly capitalist state appears as the arena for innumerable conflicts among a large number of disparate interests. Business, of course, appears very prominently among these interests. But many of the conflicts are between one segment of business and another. Labor appears frequently in the arena, mostly in conflict with business, but organized labor at times can be found in collaboration with segments of business. Other interests too appear on the scene, from environmentalists to genuine representatives of the impoverished and the minorities. It is perhaps not surprising that some observers have called this process of conflict "democracy."

But that *is* a serious error. In the first place, such a claim fails to take into account the fact that all this conflict takes place within a context of acceptance of the basic operation of the capitalist system. Private property relations continue to be the basis for surplus extraction and allocation. Government actions serve to define new areas of surplus extraction, it is true, but as already noted, the process takes place in a context of continued dominance by the same ruling class, and private property remains the one principal source of personal wealth.

Related to this is the fact that the conflicts themselves are individually small in scale, mere skirmishes over marginal restructurings of the surplus process or, more likely, marginal deviations from proportional divvying up of the growth dividends. From time to time these conflicts are resolved against the interests of some segment of business. But what is lost are mostly skirmishes, only rarely are they battles, and never campaigns. When the results of several years of conflict are tallied up, the ruling class, operating through its control of all the major institutions of production and distribution, finds itself still firmly in the saddle. Consequently, a short-run viewpoint tends to produce two kinds of mistaken feelings: that many groups representing nonruling class interests are very powerful in monopoly capitalism; and that the system is relatively stable. Generating these mistaken feelings is the principal task of capitalism's apologists; an aura of scientific legitimacy is lent their work precisely by their emphasis on amassing the trivia of the daily operation of the system. All those numbers and little facts look very impressive and screen the casual viewer from the real basis of operation of the system.

But the fundamental instability of the system, whose surface manifestation is that dynamics of lurching we have already discussed, on occasion reveals itself in an internal crisis. At such times one gets a glimpse of the true structure of power in the system. The crisis of New York City has been especially revealing in this regard. For long New York has been regarded as a bastion of humane liberalism, with a government fully under the control of the people, supported by powerful organized labor, welfare groups, and other natural opponents of big capital. New York's wage structure and welfare system were apparent reflections of that power, and the high levels of pay and services, relative to the rest of the country, had grown up as the result of a long series of struggles of the kind just described.

But then the "fiscal crunch" came, the city was no longer able to find rich investors to buy its bonds, and a full-scale crisis in this sector of monopoly capitalist government came. What was the upshot? Well, first things first; and that means finding out who's in charge. Just so there would be no more mistakes on that score, this bastion of people's power was immediately taken over by a committee of bankers. Without a shot being fired the power to make budget decisions was taken away from the elected officials and placed in the hands of . . . a committee of the bourgeoisie! Once that was settled, the rest came as might be expected. Wage freezes, massive layoffs, service and welfare cutbacks. This was a minicrisis, affecting only a part of the system. But it represents a straightforward revelation of the true structure of power under contemporary monopoly capitalism.

Is it true then that somewhere in the background there actually is some shadowy supercommittee of the bourgeoisie running the show? The answer to that is no. The functions of the "committee" are handled in normal times by the structure of the system, by that basic set of private property relations to which all participants in the system must pay their obeisance. But when crisis comes one sees clearly enough the secondary and basically legitimizing role that the trappings of democracy play in the United States and elsewhere under monopoly capitalism. In their public statements capitalists in the United States usually pay homage to the democratic process. But that allegiance is only skin deep. For example, during the Watergate period, a crisis period but not one in which the survival of monopoly capitalism was at issue, one found businessmen saying things like this to one another: "This recession will bring about the healthy respect for economic values that the Depression did"; "I can't believe that social responsibility was ever invented by a businessman; it must have been made up by a sociologist." "It is up to each of us, not to some prostitute of a Congressman pandering to get reelected, to decide what should be done." "Maybe we should take the franchise away from government employees so the system can be preserved." [5] The distance between these actually expressed thoughts and fascism is not so very long.

So we find confirmation of the assertion, made at the beginning of this chapter, that under monopoly capitalism the primary function of the state continues to be the preservation of the system of private property relations. The state grows larger, the arena of struggle grows wider, inefficiency and corruption flourish more luxuriantly, as the history of the monopoly capitalist state unfolds. That sounds like a formula for intensifying crisis and instability, and it is.

CHAPTER 7

Instability and Crisis

THE LIBERAL ECONOMIST'S term for instability and crisis is "business fluctuations," a term that reveals the narrowness of the liberal perspective. It is true that business does go up and down, though it was not until the so-called Keynesian revolution that most conventional economists were willing to consider even *that* an interesting question. It is also true that there are causal links within the economy, that is, among strictly economic variables, whose study can provide some understanding. But for the liberal economist that is the end of the story; such an economist is uninterested in serious study of those aspects of instability that involve political and social links to the economy, or of those aspects of instability that are a product of longer-run political-economic forces. But, of course, that is where the radical's interest begins. The radical economist thinks of "business fluctuations" as something imbedded in a particular social system. One can throw a couple of bottles into the surf and then study the forces that nudge them this way and that, determining their positions relative to one another; a conventional model of fluctuating economic variables might do something such as that. What the radical economist tries to take account of is those towering waves that are tossing *both* bottles about so wildly.[1]

Tendencies Promoting Instability: A Short List

1.   A classic example of such a process, operating over the long run, is urbanization and the development of the factory system. The result of this process has been an increasing concentration of workers in urban centers, which in turn makes political organization easier. It also gives the worker some direct insight into the fact that his personal plight is shared by many others, and so into the general nature

of the capitalist system. This process has played a continuing role in
the economic history of monopoly capitalism, the post-World War II
migration of blacks from country to town being one of its most recent
manifestations in the United States. The result, of course, is an intensification of class struggle.

2.   The revolutionary technical developments in transport and the
media of communication have had a somewhat similar consequence.
These are usually discussed in terms of the added power they give to
the state to control dissidence. However, the physical mobility and the
ability to develop and maintain lines of communication, even among
hunted revolutionaries, has been dramatically demonstrated in recent
years. The oppressive nature of the world system of monopoly capitalism is now a commonplace, with incident after incident exposed, often
naively, in the conventional media and interpreted in the dissident
press. As a result, defenders of monopoly capitalism have been forced
increasingly into a defensive posture: The tinder has become much
dryer.

3.   There is a strong secular tendency toward increasing volatility
of demand. Investment is, of course, notorious for the volatility of its
demand, a consequence of its postponability and the uncertainties of
its profitability. But the various categories of waste and surplus in
both production and consumption are also volatile, and these are also
categories where fashion and caution can produce sharp variations
in demand over short periods of time.

4.   The internationalization of the capitalist system, combined
with media and transport revolutions, has not had the expected effect of averaging out the consequences of local catastrophes on supplies
of goods, and especially of raw materials. Instead, the interdependence, combined with very weak mechanisms of coordination, has
universalized supply uncertainty. Among the most volatile indexes to
be found in the economist's collection is that for commodity prices.
Furthermore, the synchronization of crises internationally has led to
the recent generation of multiplier effects, so that in general internationalization has tended to intensify instability.

5.   As capitalism has developed so have capital markets. Financial markets are larger, more complex and more volatile now than ever
before. There is literally no place an investor can go to secure his
capital these days, which is a striking contrast with the past.

6.   Governments have now become by far the largest organizations in the capitalist world. Consequently, they require expert management to be made to do their repressive jobs effectively. But as was
noted in the last chapter, they are so structured that by their very
nature they cannot do this job well. It is true that the rather steady
increase in government spending has had some stabilizing influence
on capitalist markets. But studies have suggested that, for example, in
Britain the effect of government policies in the fifties and sixties
was generally destabilizing for the domestic economy.[2] And, much
more important, government inefficiencies raise serious doubts as to
its ability to respond effectively in crises. The mismanagement of the

economy under the Nixon administration, a time of unusually power-ful centralization of government authority, is a case in point.

7. The tendency toward stagflation seems to be increasing strongly. The continuing intensification of class struggle has made it increasingly difficult for the usual methods of inflation and recession controls—make the workers and the poor pay—to be implemented.[3] And every proposed policy has differential effects on the various business sectors, so that the conflict among competing capitals further reduces the flexibility of government response. The problem is further complicated by strange alliances, such as those between big business and big labor to protect both labor and capital in a particular industry at the expense of the rest of the economy.

Underlying Forces

The above list is by no means complete, but it is long enough to make the point that there is a considerable variety of factors at work in the capitalist system that push in the direction of increasing instability. There have probably been two main forces pushing in the opposite direction, namely, the rise of government expenditures as a share of total economic activity and the development of monetary and fiscal policies that are designed to counter economic recession. Before appraising the currect balance of forces promoting and inhibiting crisis, however, we need to take a look at the underlying causes of instability, at the basic features of the capitalist system which are fundamentally divisive. Traditionally, radicals have emphasized three crisis-promoting aspects of capitalist relations of production.

Class structure is clearly of central importance. A society that is split into two mutually hostile groups is a good candidate for instability. Each group will try to shift the costs of a deteriorating economic situation onto the other. The more powerful will probably win, and this will deepen the hostility of the less powerful group. And since capitalism has been an unstable but growing society, the losing group is growing in numbers, and also in class consciousness. It is rather natural to expect this situation to produce a tendency toward increasing instability.

One specific way in which class conflict has manifested itself as instability is in generating strong pressures toward an economic down-turn. A persistent feature of the later stages of an economic upturn is a more rapid rise of wages than of profits. Labor tends to be at its most militant during such times, because the unemployment rate has been reduced by the earlier part of the upturn, and so the relative demand for labor has become greater. Business fears that continuation of the boom can lead to an actual downturn in profits, and so it cuts back on capital-spending plans. There is also awareness that a mild recession, which brings labor costs back into line, can be the prelude to another high surge in profits. This in turn occurs because of cost-cutting during the earlier phase of the downturn, and because labor can be rehired in such a way as to make maximally efficient use of existing plants. Thus when viewed from the perspective of two or three years, a recession may well look like the best feasible course for business. Not so for labor, of course, and history shows whose interests have tended to dominate.[4]

A traditional feature of economic activity under capitalism has thus been the ability of the ruling class to shift most of the burdens of recession onto the working class. However, this ability has tended to be eroded with the increasing political power of organized labor. The consequence has been not an end to recessions but a cost to both business and labor. Both sides become locked in a struggle to preserve their slice of the pie. The result is more inflation, an erosion of the purchasing power of both profits and wages, and a deeper recession. This process of class struggle has been one of the major causes of the recent stagflation and recession cum inflation.

Another place where class struggle has played a central role in generating instability has, of course, been in international economic activity. The class difference is most striking in this sphere in relations between the Third World and the developed capitalist countries. And the class struggle is fought mainly in the money and commodity markets. The tremendous debt overhang that requires many Third World countries to spend a fifth or more of their export earnings just to pay off the interest obligation gives much political and economic leverage to big capitalists and their governments. But it also raises the threat of bankruptcy, of nonpayment, and these factors in combination enhance the already great instability of capital markets. The intense bargaining over the terms of commodity trade needs no comment. The fact that OPEC could raise the price of crude oil over fourfold in a year is a measure of the extent of the ripoff that this trade has typically involved for developing countries. And the prospective volatility of both price and supply that is suggested by the OPEC experience is an indicator that these always fluctuating markets are about to become much more so.[5]

A second crisis-promoting aspect of capitalist relations of production consists of the effects of the struggle among competing capitals. In times of survival crisis, the capitalists can frequently manage to present a common front against the working class. But at other times their competition among themselves for a bigger share of the surplus pie can be very intense, which is to say destabilizing. Class conflicts in the international sphere are exacerbated by this factor, for all too often capitals there are also capitols, that is, whole national committees of the bourgeoisie become lined up against one another. The pre-World War I rivalries are the classic case in point, but the story today is of continued conflict, though not yet to the point of military confrontation among the major capitalist nations. Instead the battle is fought in international money markets, as nations seek advantageous situations for their exports and protection from threatening imports, and in trade competition, most notably these days in the infamous, government-supported and highly profitable international arms trade.[6]

Competing capitals also have a major role to play in preventing timely and effective domestic intervention by government to reduce the volatility of capitalism. The problem is that some capitalists profit from high interest rates, some from lower ones, some profit from government stimulus to the economy far more than others, some are helped by a general export drive, others are hurt. Compounding this are the many opportunities individual businesses have to profit from particular expansions of government activity—and on occasion contractions. The burden of all these little conflicts is substantially to tie government's hands in many directions that are crucial for economic control. And the general tendency seems to be for more government, even when there is widespread recognition that such policies are likely to be destabilizing.

Finally, there is the so-called anarchy of the market. Marketplace behavior in nineteenth-century capitalism was not only uncontrolled, there was no self-regulating mechanism. Adam Smith's invisible hand referred to what is known as equilibrium, and meant, very roughly, that once all deals that people are willing to make are made, no more deals can be made that make people better off. But neither Smith nor later writers explained how a system of markets could move dynamically, in response to continuing deal making and the changing environment, to produce this state. And there is good reason to believe that the system will not generally tend to settle down in an equilibrium. For one thing, the participants have very little information about what is going on in the economy outside their own petty spheres, and this is clearly not enough to provide an effective guiding hand. Furthermore, expectations of participants are formed on the basis of this limited information, which is obtained from markets that are both out of equilibrium and changing rapidly. That this will produce anarchic results—for example, far too much investment in one industry and far too little in another—is to be expected. And though price changes may eventually tell everyone a mistake was made, it is too late then, and besides, the new prices may very well exaggerate the situation. Anarchy is a very plausible name for the private market system, indicating just how deeply volatility is embedded in it.[7]

For many years now, liberal economics textbooks, almost the only kind available in the United States, have been claiming that the business cycle has been tamed by Keynesian economic principles. That argument has lost some of its cogency with students who have been themselves experiencing the worst recession since Keynes's major work was published. And with good reason. The failure of Keynesian policies has many dimensions, but the most fundamental stems precisely from the anarchy that continues to pervade the capitalist marketplace. Big business does not alter the fact of anarchy, for each of the hundreds of large corporations is itself autonomous and in intense and direct competition with a number of other businesses. Decisions that will affect potential profit levels for years to come have to be made in a highly uncertain environment. Furthermore, the uncertainty is increasing with all the volatilities we have been discussing. And fashion often sweeps up whole rows and banks of executives into a flurry of investment that turns out to be excessive, or of caution that serves only to justify the fears in a new downturn. Even if the government could behave as an effective economic manager, there is little reason to suppose that it could control this anarchy with the limited tools of the Keynesian policy package.[8]

The Structure Crisis

At times the capitalist system has presented the world with a relatively mild and stable surface. From the post-World War II recovery and the Korean war to well into the Vietnam war, developed capitalism seemed to be moving on a fairly smooth track. The great conflict between liberal capitalism and fascism had apparently been resolved in favor of the former. The great imperial rivalries gave way before the hegemony of the United States. And economic growth was moving along at a record pace that was marred by only relatively modest stops and downturns. Government leaders everywhere began talking like Keynesians, and economists began to speak of the possibility of ending recessions forever.

That is just about what one would expect from those bottle theorists. The radical story, of course, was very different. An appraisal of the forces promoting instability shows that an unusual combination of circumstances had produced this apparent harmony; it also shows that the interlude could not last very long, and that it may well have had some of the properties of an Indian summer.[9] Britain, the first great industrial nation, offered an example of the kinds of difficulties associated with inefficient government and class struggle combining to generate intermittent crisis. Conflicts between hard- and soft-currency nations, with West Germany increasingly leading the former group as the United States began to flag, revealed the fragility of the "international monetary order" constructed so painfully in the early postwar years. By the mid-sixties the countries who had carried Keynesian-type planning farthest, such as the Netherlands and Sweden, and other planners such as France, found themselves increasingly unable to effectively control inflation. Third World countries, whose resistance to exploitation was somewhat muted as many of them strove to gain domestic economic control in the aftermath of political decolonialization, increasingly found their international voices. They also found themselves heavily in debt and bound by the monopolistic controls of international big business over their main markets. Expanding socialism was at times a stabilizing threat, serving to unite international capitalists against the greater menace of communism, but as the Soviet Union achieved nuclear parity and then the ability to offer substantial support to national liberation struggles far from its borders, as in Cuba and Vietnam and Angola, a new type of crisis of expectations had made its appearance.

The picture that emerges is one of a crisis that has many dimensions, only some of which are purely economic. The system of monopoly capitalism has shown by its history that it can surmount crises that consist of a combination of one or two of the above factors. But the clouds seem to be darkening and the prospects increasing that a crisis soon will come that combines many, possibly even all of the instability-producing factors at a single point in time. Such a crisis would be unprecedented, and there is no theory to predict for us its consequences or to offer capitalists guidance through it. But it takes no fancy theory to show that most of these crisis-inducing factors are specific to the monopoly capitalist system, and therein lies both an additional threat of crisis and grounds for hope.

CHAPTER 8

Development and Imperialism

THERE ARE fifty or sixty nations around the world, members of the Third World, that, though they are not monopoly capitalist in their political economic structure, nevertheless have basically capitalist institutions. Some of these countries, such as India and Bangla Desh and Chad and Honduras, are desperately poor. Others, such as Taiwan and Greece and Chile and Morocco, are somewhat better off. But all use markets and private ownership of the means of production as basic resource-allocation instruments, and in all of them the state tends to show special favoritism toward the wealthier citizenry. These countries are the subject of this chapter.

One historical point should be made at the outset. In the half century before World War I, every decade or so a new country entered the ranks of the world's great industrial nations. The last country to do this was Japan, and she did it early in the twentieth century. Since World War I not a single country has entered this charmed circle of advanced, industrial, capitalist nations.[1] One of the things that needs to be explained is why there was this dramatic change in the relative progress of capitalist countries. Given the timing, the reader will have surmised that it has something to do with the rise of monopoly capitalism.

Creating Underdevelopment

Developing countries, like their more developed counterparts, have an internal dynamic of their own. In modern times much of this internal dynamic stems from the creation of national markets as a result of transport development and the creation of a central administration through the penetration of the state into the most important areas of economic life. Behind these phenomena are the familiar surplus-extraction processes, adapted to the lower levels of the forces of production in the developing capitalist countries. For example, much of the surplus-extraction operation continues to be by the traditional debt-peonage structure of the countryside; and a good deal more comes from the extractive operations of mines and plantations. Nevertheless, developing countries have their modern enclave as well, and it is here that more modern processes of surplus extraction occur.

Such a description suggests that developing countries are simply relatively poorer versions of developed capitalist lands. But that would be quite misleading. To explain why, we must first move back in history a bit and observe the process of primitive capitalist accumulation at work in these countries. There are famous stories describing the more spectacular instances of this process. The looting of India by the British in the eighteenth century is one of these, resulting in the sending back to England of sufficient wealth to support a fairly substantial part of the early investment in the industrial revolution. Another well-known case is the Opium War and its aftermath in the 1840s, when the British defeated the Chinese in order to prevent the latter from eliminating the flow of British opium into their own country. Once again the profits accruing, after the troops had created the appropriate environment, were very great. Similar if at times less spectacular developments were occurring all over the world after the voyages of discovery.[2]

However, our concern is not with the profits made by the conqueror but with the nature of the losses sustained by these Third World countries. The loss in bullion and luxury craft products was serious but perhaps not fundamental. More important was the effect on both the economy and the social structure of these countries. For example, the continued foreign demands on the Chinese government forced a reorganization of the taxation system in order to meet "indemnity" payments and sharply restricted the government's ability to engage in any productive activities at home. In India preferential rules destroyed the Indian cotton textile industry, substituting factory-made English goods for the products of Indian crafts. Important sectors of the dependent economies tended to be destroyed by various aspects of the country's "contact" with the West.[3]

But the depredations did not stop with economic stagnation and decline. There were also fundamental social effects. The national elite tended to lose its legitimacy, either directly because of the institution of colonial rule or indirectly because of its de facto powerlessness. There was no one able to think through and execute any programs of social or economic development. The internal dynamic of the nation was broken by the conquerors. Nations that had already taken a number of the basic steps that would ultimately lead to modernization were stopped in their tracks by this phenomenon. In this sense underdevelopment is not the result of *being* backward, but the result of a process *imposed* on the Third World countries by the imperialist powers.

How does this history affect the current situation in developing capitalist countries? Of course, technological backwardness and the relatively low level of labor productivity is one consequence. But the current social structure is also deeply affected. The debt-peonage land system is an efficient surplus extractor but is usually a highly inefficient system in terms of the modernity of the production processes it can utilize. This means that there is a substantial social obstacle to bringing about major improvements in this crucial area.

But the problems go still deeper. The colonial or quasi-colonial regime did provide a place for relatively affluent national landowners and merchants. These groups maintained their niches by not rocking the boat, being content with the pickings that were thrown their way. Consequently, even after so stirring an event as decolonialization they continue to represent a powerful braking force on economic development, preferring the certain income from current conditions to the uncertainty that rapid change would be bound to bring. These and other traditionalist groups in a new nation tend to promote a society fractured by differences over the proper policies to adopt.

Such countries will also have development-oriented groups too, people who perceive economic opportunities in the expansion of production facilities. However, their ability to effect change is restricted by the above factors. For example, modernizing agriculture requires a simultaneous development of industry to absorb surplus hands from the countryside; but integrated programs of development are the very things that cannot be achieved in such a brittle political structure. And much of the potential increase in labor productivity that might be achieved is siphoned off by another major interest group thrown up by the distorted social structures of these countries: the military.

Despite all these handicaps, some growth has in fact occurred in a number of Third World capitalist countries. But this growth is strongly conditioned both by the social structure we have just described and by another factor of supreme importance, namely, the role of foreign capital and imperialist policies in the domestic development of these countries. To appraise this phenomenon we must first take a look at contemporary imperialism itself.

Continuing Underdevelopment

The twin destruction of both wealth and social structure is a partial explanation of the failure of any new industrial capitalist nations to emerge in the last sixty years. Handicapped by their past, today's developing capitalist countries start from farther back and have greater difficulty establishing the needed modern institutions. If this were all there were to the story, *contemporary* capitalism would not be responsible for these countries' plights and there would be little that could be done to help them. However, clearly there is more to the contemporary story than this. For there is not only the problem of making up for the past, but also the problem of being pushed still further back by the present.

Another fact that requires explanation is the peculiar impact of technology on developing capitalist countries. Modern technology should bring the cornucopia of higher labor productivity in its train, but instead it seems more often to bring disaster. There is the all too obvious connection between modern health technology and those hundreds of millions of malnourished human beings. Another example is the Green Revolution. This new agricultural technology, combining special seed with irrigation and massive use of fertilizer and pesticide, can bring a doubling and more of output of rice and wheat. However, the poorer farmers either haven't enough land or can't afford the required inputs to take advantage of the new approach; so when increased output—by the richer farmers who *can* afford it—lowers the price of grain, their situation worsens. And, of course, the Green Revolution substantially increased the dependence of agriculture on world market prices. The dramatic oil price increase, acting through the cost of the fertilizer that petroleum is used to produce, priced the Green Revolution out of most markets, leaving the farmers to foot the bill for their investments with no return to show.[4]

Another example comes from the transport and communications revolution, which has been at least partially introduced in developing countries. By increasing mobility and, more important, by introducing the agricultural population to modern ideas, products, and behavior through radio, television, and the like, this revolution has done a good deal to create the culture of poverty, the peculiarly fragmented forms of life and attitudes that are endemic to much of the citizenry of these countries. By destroying the old culture and by emphasizing the relative goods deprivation of the masses, tawdry materialistic values are created that seem to exacerbate the commodity fetishism of traditional capitalism.[5]

Why are these distortions created? Much of the answer lies in the role played by imperialist nations in the social development processes of Third World countries. Over the last quarter of a century imperialism essentially means the United States, though Britain and France and others, including even Portugal, itself an underdeveloped country, have also been in the game. Using the modern instruments of imperialism, developing countries continue to be looted and to have their social structures gutted by outside intervention.[6]

The major instruments of imperialism are foreign trade, foreign investment, foreign aid, political pressure, subversion, military intervention and war. A century ago a favorite practice was conquest and the establishment of a colonial administration. But just as slavery became modernized in ancient times by developing an effective market in slaves, thereby increasing the extraction of surplus, so have the instruments of imperialism become more subtle and effective. Client political regimes, nominally independent, have become the successors of many former colonial administrations, with consequences that have generally been quite satisfactory to monopoly capitalists. Most large multinational corporations seem to generate far higher profit rates abroad than at home. Let us run briefly through the operations of each of these instruments to see how they affect the dependence of developing capitalist countries.

Foreign trade works in a very similar way to debt peonage as a surplus extractor. Developing countries mostly export commodities, minerals, and agricultural products. These are exported in strong competition with other developing-country suppliers, and for the most part are purchased by a highly organized cartellike group of importers, who then further process and market the goods. Such trade tends to produce rather wide fluctuations in incomes to the developing countries; being poor, they must finance their own import program by borrowing when export earnings are down. Thus through both trade and debt a pattern of economic dependence and a basically exploitative relationship is created. It is a sort of international version of the debt-peonage system.

In principle, the foreign trade instrument can be effectively applied without any imperialist presence in the developing countries. Foreign investment, however, is a very different matter. In this case a foreign company, most of the time an American multinational, establishes a subsidiary abroad. This involves importing machinery, employing local workers to construct the factory and to work as its operatives, and brings in further foreign exchange via the foreign managers and technicians who come to live near the factory. This, it is often claimed, stimulates domestic demand and so provides fundamental benefits favoring the creation of a modern industrial base in the developing country.

The true impact of foreign investment is somewhat different. In the first place, one must not forget that foreign investors expect a profit from their operations. This means that some portion of the economic benefits flowing into the country flow back out again later in the form of repatriated profits. It has been estimated, for example, that in Latin America over much of the postwar period there has been net decapitalization; that is, in most years the sum of profits repatriated exceeds the total value of new foreign investment.[7]

Developing countries try to control these losses with the limited instruments available to them. One of these is currency control, used in support of policies aimed at compelling foreign capitalists to reinvest locally some portion of their profits, and to prevent too much of the country's limited exchange earnings to be wasted on luxury-goods imports. The net result of this, given the power and wealth of the opposing interests, has been a massive illegal operation in currency and goods, which in turn means that the above assertion about decapitalization must substantially understate the true losses incurred from foreign investment.

Perhaps even more important is the impact of that new technology the foreign investment brings in. The problem here stems from the divergence between the economic interests of the importing capitalist and the development needs of the society. Much of the new technology will be oriented toward serving the world market, and so the level of operation of the factory will vary with world market profit opportunities rather than domestic needs. The new factory designed to capture the growing domestic demand for a good will probably be given a tariff wall to protect it against competition and so to ensure a monopoly price for the product. And, most important of all, this new technology will have a very high output per worker as compared to earlier times, so that labor absorption will be relatively low. These factors in combination provide a major reason why the real incomes of the poorer half of the population in many fairly rapidly growing economies are actually falling.

Foreign aid, one might think, is unequivocal in its economic impact; surely it is positive. No doubt a $100 million extra in foreign exchange is, other things equal, better than its absence. But that is about as far as one can carry the positive story. On the other side of the ledger is, first of all, the modest and recently declining magnitude of aid. A relatively minor movement in commodity prices is sufficient to cost developing countries a greater foreign exchange loss than the total of foreign aid received in most years. Second, there is its distribution. Most of it has been for military rather than economic "development," and most of it has been allocated, not to the countries that can make the best economic use of the funds, but to countries who happen to be located along the fringe of the socialist camp.

And, of course, the big problem with foreign aid lies in its political implications. Not only does it give bargaining leverage to the donor country, it has substantial impacts on the structure of the domestic country's society. Much of the military aid is not aimed at repelling invasion but rather at putting down incipient revolution. This distorts the internal dynamic of the country. The increasing power and influence of the military has the same effect. The military represents a conservative influence domestically, and is often both politically active and oriented toward modernization. In combination, this has gone a long way to explain the rise of "growth fascism," the military regimes of such places as Brazil, Greece, Bolivia, Taiwan, and elsewhere. Consequently, though foreign aid seems to have had rather little direct impact on economic growth, its political and social effects have been very substantial and very harmful.

The primarily political instruments of imperialism, such as political pressure, subversion, intervention, and war, are spectacular enough to require no description. These are also the traditional instruments of even precapitalist imperialism. The sending of marines into Lebanon or the Dominican Republic gives one a nostalgic sense of continuity with the past—unless one is among the many victims of the act. The CIA's Dirty Tricks Department provides stories to match the bedtime reading of the thriller addict—again, provided one has no direct involvement in the human costs of these operations. The massive slaughter in Vietnam can be matched, and not on a smaller scale either, in many countries whose populations are doomed to extremes of wretchedness as a consequence of the political regimes installed by such interventions. Some of the most appalling examples can be found in American imperialism's back yard, Central America, where infant mortality and illiteracy rates are among the highest in the world.

However, there is an important difference between the behavior of modern monopoly capitalist imperialism and its precapitalist forms. Basically, these direct political interventions represent a failure of monopoly capital, whereas in earlier regimes they were simply the device by which control of a dependent country was obtained. The modern practice is labeled neocolonialism. The idea is to utilize a domestic bourgeoisie to administer the state and a domestic military force to prevent revolution. Monopoly capital then works its magic via the three economic instruments we have just discussed. Marcuse might well call this subdued conquest. When overt acts of force by the imperialist nation are required, this is a sign that the basic neocolonial policy is not working. Of course, the aim of the intervention is to restore it to working order.

Once again though, the irrationality of monopoly capitalism forces a qualification of this distinction between precapitalist and monopoly capitalist imperialism. The military-industrial complex back home feeds on expanding military power. Its legitimacy requires at least occasional use of some of the massive force created over the years. Consequently, premature and irrational application of force in neocolonial areas, even from the point of view of the monopolists' own interests, is also a fact of contemporary imperialist life. Opinions may differ as to whether it was a mistake, from the point of view of effective imperial control of the Dominican Republic, to stage that intervention. To put it more precisely, the Dominican intervention was clearly a plus from the point of view of the segment of capitalists who draw their primary profits directly from the military; what is not clear is whether it was also a plus for the segment of capitalists who expected to profit from their economic operations involving the Dominican Republic. A "mistake" of that kind can be expected from time to time under neocolonial imperialism.

Uneven Development

What are the prospects for the developing capitalist countries that find themselves in this situation? To appraise this question, it will be useful to run briefly through the domestic situation of a typical developing country to get some idea of its potential as well as of the obstacles to realization.

The first thing to notice is that the relative surplus even in the poorer countries is quite large, probably somewhere between a fifth

and a third of current output. This is one of the most surprising results of the study of economic development. It was put forward by a
Marxist, Paul Baran, twenty years ago, and has since been vindicated,
most especially in the Chinese experience. After coming to power in an
area containing one of the world's most impoverished populations, the
Chinese communists have not only succeeded in delivering basic goods
to the whole population, but also in diverting a fifth or more of their
output to the expansion of productive capacity. It is now widely accepted that all but a few developing countries possess a relatively large
surplus over the basic needs of their populations.[8]

The misery in which much of the population of Third World countries is sunk has already been mentioned several times. But a few
remarks about that misery are still in order. First, there is the connection between food and productivity. Many of these people are physically
incapable of supporting themselves because of a debilitating diet.
More tragically, some portion of the 200 or 300 million children
caught up in this wretchedness are being permanently damaged by
their current levels of malnutrition. And even those who are capable
of work are likely to be substantially underemployed, either on tiny
farms or in shantytowns where there is virtually no work to be had
beyond the basic struggle for survival in an alien and unproductive
environment. Many of these countries not only suffer from all the above
problems but also face rapidly growing populations, which year after
year are compounding the misery.[9]

All of this can serve as a measure of the irrationality of developing capitalist societies. But that irrationality cannot be fully appraised
until the situation of most of the population is placed alongside the
enclave development of the so-called modernized sector of the economy.
Here in central cities there will be high-rise apartments, fancy cars,
stores full of Western goods, and factories turning out the products
of contemporary capitalist society. Workers will receive very low wages
by developed-country standards but will be substantially better off than
the citizenry described above. There will be a fairly substantial set of
fashionable neighborhoods that will contain the villas of the national
capitalists, the upper-middle class, the professionals, politicians, and
military officers, and, of course, the foreigners who occupy the key
places in much of the economic activity. In a well-set up country it
will be possible for the wives and children to go downtown to shop and
to head to the various fashionable recreation spots without ever having
to come close to the misery in which they are embedded.

This fundamental social contradiction is not unknown to past history except for one fundamental difference: Over the last ten or fifteen
years the bottom half of the population will likely have suffered a fall
in real income, while the real incomes of those in the enclave have
risen dramatically. This phenomenon is even observable in Brazil, which
possesses one of the world's fastest growing enclaves, and in India,
which sometimes claims to be socialist, and where the fact that the
poorest part of the population is worse off than it was twenty years ago
seems inconceivable.

Clearly, countries in this state are ripe for dramatic structural change. One almost wonders how things could have persisted like this for so long. The explanation of this persistence comes in two parts. The first is that extraordinary efforts have been made to preserve the enclaves intact because of their benefits to monopoly capitalism and because the alternative is feared and expected to be communism. It is one of the facts of revolution that the most wretched are not likely to play a leading role simply because their health and energy levels do not permit strenuous action even in their own interests. This tends all too clearly to blunt the enthusiasm of monopoly capitalists to work seriously to eliminate the misery.

Second, the enclave is allowed to reproduce many of the social relations of domestic monopoly capitalism; this means a substantial income differential between those caught up in the enclave and the rest of the population. This aristocracy of dependent capitalism is, of course, the group that possesses the domestically held knowledge and skill needed to run the modern sector of the society. It is also likely to be a group in which the level of alienation is quite high, since many of them have only recently cast off the traditional culture in which they were inculcated in their youth. This group forms a central element of the domestic political support for the existing regime.

In the countryside there is a smaller group whose allegiance also lies in this direction. These are the moneylenders and traders who prey on the peasantry. Their success requires the threat of force to function effectively and so, though they are perhaps typically not really a part of the modern enclave, they tend to support it politically. Then too there are the actual wielders of force in the society, the military and police. These will be trained in modern methods and probably will be fairly well-equipped to carry out their jobs. Once again, the job is protection of the enclave and its supporters from domestic threats.

Finally, lined up firmly with these groups and often orchestrating their joint efforts are the foreign capitalists and their political representatives. They bring with them the experience gained in preserving the system through the more than fifty wars that have marked the Pax Americana of the last quarter of a century. They also can offer outside support at levels essentially restricted only by the level of need.

This panoply of subversion and coercion represents the forces of law and order in developing capitalist society. It cannot succeed in preserving tranquility, given the nature of these societies, but it has so far proved able to suppress revolution with that combination of co-optation and surplus extraction that constitutes its basic modus operandi. Can it be defeated? Before answering that question we must turn to twentieth-century socialism for a look at its achievements, the nature of the alternative it offers developing countries, and the processes by which they might adopt it.

CHAPTER 9

The Rise of Socialism: The Soviet Union

THERE HAVE BEEN three great, innovative, socialist revolutions in the twentieth century, the Russian, the Yugoslav, and the Chinese. Each of these revolutions was great in the sense that it entailed a massive and sustained struggle before the leadership could be brought to effective political power. Each was socialist in the sense that the leadership was committed to the abolition of capitalist relations of production, possessed the will to carry out this massive structural change, and took the workers and poorer peasants as its primary power base. And each was innovative in that in each country a very different set of relations of production has developed out of the demise of capitalism.

There is a very important similarity among these three revolutions. All three were cases of revolution coming to an economically backward country at a time of national disintegration. As a result of this the revolutionary party was able to seize power over a portion of the country, and was then forced to spend years in armed struggle in order to obtain general control of the country. This appears to have been a very vital period, a time of molding of leadership and cadres, of the development of an experienced and disciplined body of men and women who can form the vanguard for the difficult social transitions that must follow the political success of the revolution. A necessity for the survival of the revolution, this period and process has also had a profound effect on the revolutionary process in each of the three countries.

The Russian Revolution [1]

Revolution is a very complex process, a point that is easily missed. After all, there is an overriding purpose, which is simply the seizure of state power, and this requires crude and brutal actions rather than sensitive and complex ones. And even after political success there is still a need to use the cruder forms of coercion against the substantial number of defeated but not yet quiescent enemies of the revolution. Even the economic problems are likely to loom as stark and simple issues: how to feed the population, how to reconstruct a shattered economy. The cruder economic devices of rationing and direct control of key commodities are likely to be at the center of attention.

And yet during these same years in which attention and effort is so sharply focused, a variety of things are happening that will profoundly influence the historical course of the revolution. A brief sketch of this process in the Soviet Union will serve to illustrate the key issues that arise in the creation of a new society.

The first thing to note is that the Russian revolution was history's first successful socialist revolution. There was no relevant experience to draw on. The leadership was without experience in managing either a state or an economy, and what was known of the few weeks of the Paris Commune was of little help. Furthermore, much of even the top leadership of the Bolsheviks had not worked together for any extended period of time, so that even the working understandings had to be acquired very hastily.

Beyond the uniqueness of the experience was the very limited control over events that circumstances permitted. Essentially, the revolution in the countryside ran its course with little more than verbal encouragement from the Bolsheviks. In the major cities things were at least somewhat better; but many factories were in the hands of factory committees who were not all firmly committed to the Bolsheviks. The czarist army had disintegrated, which was a great advantage, but which also provided no organized base from which a new army could be built. And within a few months of October a civil war with the reactionary elements was in full swing, posing a very serious survival threat to the Bolshevik government and demanding all its energies just to keep the troops and supplies flowing to the several fronts.

In February 1917, there were probably no more than a few thousand Bolsheviks. Their numbers, of course, expanded very rapidly after that, and experience in the revolutionary army was a very effective way to build dedicated cadres. But the Russian civil war and accompanying economic chaos were extremely destructive. A large fraction of these cadres had fallen on battlefields and from sickness during the three years of civil war. The survivors were far too few to handle the massive administrative tasks of operating the Russian state and economy during the twenties; furthermore, their war experience had not provided them with any special understanding of how to organize a socialism that would satisfy the peacetime needs of worker and poorer peasant.

Unfortunately, the leadership had learned perhaps more about how not to operate a peacetime socialist economy than about how it ought to be done. The high degree of paper centralization of the civil war economy, the so-called war communism, was in fact little more than an ad hoc requisitioning of the most desperately needed goods and their intermittent delivery to the most desperately needy potential consumers. Clearly, it was no way to operate a peacetime economy, and it had already aroused considerable suspicion of the Bolsheviks in the countryside. The retreat to decentralized market forms of operation of much of the economy was clearly a response to these factors.

Nevertheless, the state still had immense requirements for cadres, and these had to be filled from the ranks of careerists, opportunists, and Old Bolsheviks, the latter in a rather small minority. A periodic weeding out of undesirables was no doubt helpful, but the Communist party could not be a terribly effective instrument of policy, especially in areas where strong commitment to the ideals of socialism was needed. And it had no deep roots in the countryside, where most Soviet citizens lived, and where the revolution had, without Lenin's ability to affect the outcome, thrown up a system of peasant freehold agriculture whose relations of production were basically incompatible with socialism.

A final factor needs to be mentioned. When the revolution did not materialize in the rest of Europe, the Soviets were forced to accept the environment of "socialism in one country." This was a hostile international environment, one in which continuing attempts to frustrate and bring down the Soviet government were made. It was an environment in which trade was extremely limited and loans nonexistent. The Soviet efforts at reconstruction and socialist construction had to bear the direct costs of this isolation, which were substantial. They also had to bear the indirect costs, in the form of relative isolation from the worlds of science, technology, and art, as well as from social and political contacts as they were developing in the rest of the world; for many leading segments of Soviet society, this may have imposed an even greater cost.

Achievements of Soviet Socialism [2]

These days it is difficult to appreciate the spirit of creativity that permeated Soviet social life during the twenties. Just a few points will illustrate how far this spirit went and how close was the association between thought and action. In the West the women's movement reached one of its peaks around the time of the first world war, receding almost everywhere after women obtained the right to vote—and after the men returned from war. In the Soviet Union most of the social disabilities that continued to balk the liberation of women elsewhere down to our own time, such as ease of obtaining a divorce, equal legal status in handling finances, the right to abortion, and equal pay for equal work, became official policy and had dramatic effects. In education, curricula were reformed to reflect the needs for vocationally and professionally qualified workers rather than supplying essentially no more than the cultural fare of the gentleman. A statistical system was established that may well have been the world's finest of its time, and one strongly oriented toward supplying data of the kind needed by policymakers. A social welfare system was developed that was oriented toward providing a more realistic system of protection of the urban worker's economic rights than was available in far more affluent capitalist societies. And the world's first full-scale reorganization of the penal system to emphasize rehabilitation rather than punishment was instituted.

Of central importance for the survival of socialism, the problem of management of the economy was slowly being mastered. This was a very creative period in Soviet economics; indeed, in the twenties Moscow and Leningrad were probably the world's most exciting places for an economist to be; and because of the close connection between words and deeds in Soviet intellectual life, one was expected to assume responsibility for the practical consequences of one's academic work. In this environment the tools were being fashioned that would later be adopted around the world wherever at least the semblance of economic planning was practiced. Through the so-called control figures the basic ideas of managment of a relatively decentralized socialist economy were developed in practice. Through the emerging planning bodies the role of the medium-term plan in guiding the economic trajectory of a socialist economy was being developed and, in the late twenties, applied. And throughout this period cadres were acquiring the experience that would be passed on, not so much in manuals as by word of mouth and demonstration, to future generations of planners.[3]

The systematic application of science, technology, and economics in the service of a deliberate process of economic modernization is an invention of Soviet socialism. Both the economic and the political tools for this effort were developed in the Soviet Union. Economists had heard of economic development before, and some governments had engaged in piecemeal efforts to build up the national economy. But never before had an attempt been made to bring the full panoply of human knowledge, skill, and effort to bear on the problem. The result was one of history's great accomplishments: The swift reconstruction of a shattered economy that in 1920 was operating at about a fifth of its level of five years earlier, and the transformation in the following decade of the Soviet Union into the world's second most powerful industrial nation. Economists now realize that this transformation cannot be effectively measured in conventional statistics; essentially, it was a dramatic qualitative change in the nature of the heart of the Soviet economy, and it remains an effort that is probably unmatched in the capitalist world.

The demonstration effect of the existence and behavior of the Soviet Union on monopoly capitalism is very hard to appraise, except for the claim that it was extremely important. It manifested itself first in the wave of revolutionary activity just after World War I, which brought those distant events home in a very striking way. Probably the Soviet Union deserves a great deal of credit for the social welfare legislation that became a ubiquitous part of monopoly capitalism during the interwar period. And the Communist parties that were created around the world exerted a profound effect on domestic developments in tens of countries; their impact on the rise of the independence movements in the Third World is still unappraised but was clearly substantial. Also, the core of militants communism supplied to working-class movements everywhere no doubt had a profound if often indirect influence on the behavior of union and political leaderships, in addition to the impact of their dedication on other workers.

But the Soviet Union had a much more direct impact for several decades as the only major defender of socialist interests in the international arena. That American policy for a few decades was forced into the relatively defensive stance suggested by the word "containment" is attributable almost solely to the existence of the Soviet Union. Socialism in Eastern Europe and Cuba clearly owe their continued existence to the support of the Soviet Union. And adventurism by monopoly capitalism in other areas, from Egypt and the Near East to China, has clearly been inhibited by its presence. Developing the ability to carry out this policy has taken a heavy toll in terms of further development of socialism within the Soviet Union; but it is a central socialist achievement that should not go unnoticed.

One final Soviet achievement should be mentioned, and this may well be the most important of all. It was in the Russian revolution that the great political and social instrument of socialist revolution was forged, namely, the Communist party. This great vehicle for mobilizing whole nations for the task of social transformation is a distinctive feature of all successful socialist countries; and where socialism's success has been dubious, a weakness in the party tends to loom large among the causes. It takes strong medicine to overcome the tensions of fragmentation and wretchedness that abound in underdeveloped countries, and the process of change is fraught with conflict and continued attempts at subversion from both domestic and foreign enemies. One of the lessons of the twentieth century is that a Communist party, organized along the lines pioneered in the Soviet Union, can serve successfully as that strong medicine.

Soviet Failures

Collectivization was one of the most serious, as well as one of the most misunderstood, of Soviet failures. That it was a failure can hardly be doubted. In the first place, there was the terrible human cost, which must run to millions of unnecessary deaths, many of them poor peasants, the supposed clients of a workers' and peasants' state. These deaths came primarily because collectivization was imposed on an unwilling freehold peasantry who had not been brought into serious and trusting contact with the communists. Collectivization appeared to them as confiscation. It turned out in fact to be a regime that supported a brutal and exploitative extraction of their surplus, and even more than the surplus. In fact, Soviet collective farms looked like such effective surplus extractors that the invading Nazi armies decided to retain them in the Ukraine.

Political neglect of the countryside was combined with economic neglect, so that Soviet agriculture has remained a relatively ineffectual part of the economy down to the present day. The peasantry is now far better off than during the thirties and has been the beneficiary of substantial provision of communal services and a guaranteed base income to families; but the inefficiency remains as, in all likelihood, does the unpopularity.

These undoubted failures have often been attributed to all forms of collectivization, and therein lies the misunderstanding. The more gradual and humane processes of collectivization adopted in other socialist countries have produced far different results. One of the most interesting tests came in 1968 when Czechoslovak peasants, had they wished, could have decollectivized and divided up the land once again into family farms. Essentially no collective farmer took advantage of this de facto opportunity, which is quite a decisive test of popularity. In other countries the basic efficiency of the form seems established, and in some places, such as China, the results achieved by collectivized agriculture can only be called spectacular. Building on Soviet experience, later socialist collectivizations have managed to avoid the most serious of the Soviet mistakes in this crucial area.

A second basic failure of the Soviet Union is represented by Stalinism. As a consequence of the brutality of Stalin's rule, from collectivization in the late twenties to the "doctors' plot" on the eve of his death, the Soviet regime was marked by an extreme of political centralization and terrorism that is one of history's darkest pages. Part of this result was simply bad luck, namely, Lenin's early incapacitation and death and the consequent failure of the Bolsheviks to establish an effective succession policy. Part was a consequence of their failure to reach the peasants politically and ideologically. This inserted an element of fear into Bolshevik attitudes and of coercion into their policies, so that such a man as Stalin could seem to many effectively to meet the needs of socialist construction. Stalinism was in part a consequence of the extremely threatening international environment in which the Soviet Union was forced to make its way, an environment so fraught with hate and fear that paranoia seemed almost to be a rational reaction. And Stalinism was, of course, partly a product of Stalin's personality, the tendencies of which had not been fully revealed by the time he acquired power.

The environment of the time called for a very strong central government both for domestic transformation and for protection against invasion and subversion. Stalinism was not exactly an ideal answer, but there is little in the later history of socialism to suggest that he is at all a likely phenomenon under socialism. The Soviet Union has been institutionalizing a regular succession routine in which, roughly speaking, the Central Committee of the party serves as the basic constitutional organ of leadership selection. Other socialist countries also generally reveal a more flexible and open attitude toward constructive socialist dissent than would have been feasible under Stalin. This political loosening up has not gone as far as many would like, but it *has* made Stalinism a thing of the past.

A third area of disappointment with the Soviet Union as the world's first socialist state has been the undeniable manifestations of imperialist policies. The suppression of the Hungarian and Czechoslovak revolutions and the continued intervention in the domestic affairs of East European nations are obvious enough. Some of this can be attributed to defense needs of the Soviet Union, but there is obviously more to it than that. And no one would argue that socialism can develop very far while its domestic representatives can only stay in power because of the threat of foreign intervention.

The extent to which these policies are based on genuine fear of the West may be tested if a substantial troop withdrawal from Central Europe is negotiated with the United States. But there are already signs of a lessening in the use of imperialist coercion through the much greater flexibility in domestic policymaking that has been occurring in Eastern Europe. The Hungarians are continuing their ten-year-old experiment with a form of decentralized socialism, and a variety of new policies have been introduced independently in Poland in recent years. In fact, in these countries and in East Germany some of the more interesting experiments in developing socialist experience with alternative economic structures are being tried. Once again the trends suggest that there is a good deal of learning from past mistakes going on.

But the most important point about Soviet imperialism comes from a much different direction. The Soviet Union's "satellites" are put through the same social revolution as the Soviets themselves were. As a result there is an incomparable difference between life for an average citizen in, say, Bulgaria as compared with her opposite number in a "free world" dependent state such as Nicaragua. The former citizen is hard at work transforming her country, assured of a good education for his children, high-quality health care, and an increasing flow of consumer goods for her family. The latter is probably a hungry peasant whose malnourished children are unlikely to see the inside of a schoolhouse for more than a very few years and whose health will not permit much learning. For the ordinary citizen the difference is between hope and hopelessness. Imperialism is perhaps not such a good word to use for *both* these phenomena.[4]

Conclusion

The Soviet Union was at one time the hope of the world for socialists. That is no longer the case. If socialism were to come to the rest of the world tomorrow, the Soviet Union would have a good deal of catching up to do. However, the Soviet contribution to the development of socialism in the twentieth century has been very great indeed and, as we have seen, there are strong signs that some of that catching up is already occurring. We will return to the issue of reformability of the Soviet Union in chapter 10, but enough has already been said to suggest that the anomalies of Soviet behavior are likely to be more easily corrected than those of monopoly capitalism.

CHAPTER 10

The Rise of Socialism: Yugoslavia and China

THE ARGUMENT that there are many paths to socialism is based on the thesis that there are powerful long-run forces at work in a society conditioning any change that takes place. The forces-of-production concept stands for one such set, for those forces related to the productivity of labor, and in the twentieth century we have been learning a good deal about the amount and rate of change in the forces of production that is feasible. The relations-of-production concept stands for another set, those related to the extraction and allocation of surplus, and we have been learning more about changing them too, though it is inevitably a more difficult concept to come to terms with empirically. But it does seem that the unique histories of countries set different combinations of factors to work conditioning changes in both the forces and relations of production. For that reason it is not really sensible to explore the nature of socialism in a very abstract way.

In this chapter we deal with the aftermaths of two successful socialist revolutions. They suggest the great range of socialist ideas as to what a well-functioning society should look like. Neither, of course, is perfect, but both have succeeded in carrying out fundamental changes in both the forces and relations of production. The idea is to compare very briefly the approach in each country to four basic aspects of society: economic development, participation, decentralization, and the transformation of man. The aim is not to choose between paths; the idea is rather to suggest that on present evidence it seems that a well-developed socialism might contain societies practicing either or both of these approaches.[1]

Economic Development

For the first two decades after World War II, the Yugoslavs followed the Soviet strategy for economic development rather closely. Essentially, this involves a very high rate of investment, up to a third of national income being allocated to increasing the stock of means of production. It also means placing central emphasis on industry in general and heavy industry in particular. The aim, obviously, is the swiftest possible development of the forces of production to modern levels of labor productivity. Despite a four-year depression from 1948 to 1952 brought on by the Cominform boycott, the Yugoslavs followed this strategy successfully, achieving one of the world's highest growth rates of output during this period.[2]

Any strategy involving a concentration of efforts inevitably implies that some things will be left behind. That was certainly true of Yugoslavia. For almost a decade after the completion of postwar reconstruction, there was very little rise in levels of consumption. Of course, communal services such as health delivery and education expanded extremely rapidly during this period, but provision of the marketed type of consumer goods did not expand much more rapidly than population, and the service sector of the urban economy was neglected.

However, the main sector that was left behind was agriculture. At first this represented a deliberate but mistaken developmental strategy, based on the feeling that agriculture would quickly reattain its prewar position as a major earner of foreign exchange. When this did not materialize, more resources were devoted to the sector and a substantial expansion of output was achieved. However, the retention of small-scale peasant freehold land tenure, while providing a basic level of security to peasant families, did nothing to solve the social problems of the countryside or to introduce socialism into it.

Yugoslavia faced a difficult dilemma with respect to collectivization. The problem was that the initial drive coincided both with two very bad harvests and with the Cominform blockade. The need for national unity and for development made a stabilization of the rural relations of production essential. But to go forward would then have meant rapid collectivization à la Russe. Unwilling to take that drastic and inhumane step, the other recourse was to fall back, allow peasants to leave already established collectives if they wished (90 percent of them did so), and to provide security of family farm tenure. This they did, leaving a legacy of tiny farms and much technical backwardness in farming methods.

By the time collectivization could again be contemplated, the Yugoslavs had essentially decided on a different strategy for transforming rural society, namely, migration from the overpopulated countryside. This strategy has worked, in the sense that the peasantry has fallen from two-thirds to one-third of the population, mostly as a result of migration to Yugoslav cities, partly to Western European ones. Collectives may yet become the basic agricultural organization in Yugoslavia, but if they do it will probably be by a process of emergence through felt economic need for larger-scale production.

The lesser social upheaval entailed by the Yugoslav rural strategy has its appeal, but for many countries the Yugoslav approach is simply infeasible. Usually there are few opportunities for migration abroad and the domestic cities have no hope of absorbing the surplus rural population. China, still over three-fourths peasant, is one of these countries, and so the Chinese had to devise a different strategy.

The failure of economic development to relieve misery in capitalist countries occurs precisely in those countries in China's, not Yugoslavia's, situation. The Chinese have, in effect, suggested that the fundamental problem of economic development needs to be reappraised in the light of this terrible fact. Instead of being modernization, the fundamental task of economic development should be to steady-state a humane agrarian regime. This regime must be capable of sustaining the peasantry at a decent level of life during the two or three generations in which massive absorption of the peasantry into developing-country cities will not be feasible. Through their commune system the Chinese seem to have done just that.[3]

The commune—and its equally central smaller units, the brigade and team—provides basic social security for income and health to its members. It is also a cultural and administrative center for organization of nonroutine projects, such as water conservancy measures and other forms of local investment. The lands are farmed jointly by teams, and rewards are related to effort and, to a variable extent, to work attitudes. Each family typically has a small private plot and the right to dispose of its output. Small-scale industry is often developed within the commune. A substantial portion of the surplus is siphoned off by the state, partly by compulsory sales at low prices and partly by taxes, but a large—if unknown—portion remains at the commune's disposal. Clearly, this system has provided for the basic needs of the rural population and appears to be very popular. It differs from Eastern European collectives more in the successful integration of members into the system, and of the commune into the larger society, than in its basic organization.

Of course, the Chinese have not neglected modernization. They appear to have made very substantial strides in this direction as far as urban industry is concerned. But their performance in this area does not seem to be as outstanding, relative to other countries, as in their method of dealing with agrarian misery. It is this latter respect, the acceptance of the peasant as a genuinely equal partner to the urban worker in socialist society, that represents the most significant novelty in the Maoist development strategy.

Participation

Participation means playing an active role in making the decisions that affect one's life. The emphasis is on the word active. For example, voting in a capitalist democracy is *not* participation. The individual cannot affect the outcomes by casting his vote one way or another, and besides, the system is rigged in such a way that money counts for more than votes in producing government policies. By and large participation implies activity that has a significant impact both on the formulation of policy alternatives and on the choice among alternative policies. The mechanisms of contemporary monopoly capitalism simply do not fill this bill.

In China participation probably reaches its peak in the countryside. The peasant understands his production environment; he is even able to appraise many aspects of the applicability of new technology at least as well as a scientist. And he is given some control over that environment, partly through his private plot, partly through the relatively small team that is the basic socialist production unit. We cannot obtain a clear picture of how "leading" a role cadres play at this level of decision making in China, but it does appear that there is a substantial role for active participation by ordinary team, brigade, and perhaps even commune members in the decision process at these various levels.[4]

In the urban factory there also appear to be serious attempts to enlist participation by ordinary bench workers in dealing with relevant infra-factory decisions. Once again there is very little evidence based on serious and extended study of behavior in these Chinese environments, but efforts to improve communication all along the line, and particularly between the experts and the people, are certainly substantial.

However, the limits to participation in China must also be mentioned. There are sowing plans laid down by higher authorities, which are a substantial intervention in the daily lives of peasant producers. The commune and lower units have very limited ability to control the destination of the substantial portion of their output that leaves the farm. Urban workers do not decide what or how much to produce in their factory, nor are they involved in any serious participation in determining the terms on which the goods are delivered to society. The Chinese environment has a very strictly controlled information system, one that must substantially restrict worker and peasant understanding of the environment in which their production unit is embedded. State control of communication also serves to protect the entire system from serious study by outsiders, inevitably leaving open the question as to the relative de facto influence of workers and cadres. There is more participation in China than in large production units under monopoly capitalism, but much of what really happens remains very cloudy.

Yugoslavia has a very different approach to participation. Basically, the Yugoslav belief is that participation is a matter of power. Consequently, their hopes for developing a participatory society hinge on giving the workers in socialist production units the power to make the basic decisions of an enterprise. An elected committee, the workers' council, consisting mostly of production workers, not technicians and managers, is empowered to make such decisions as what to produce, how much to produce, where and on what terms to sell the output and buy the inputs, and, aside from taxes, how to distribute enterprise income among the producers and between wages and investment. These bodies have seen their de facto power increase rather steadily since the system was first inaugurated twenty-five years ago, and today they clearly are a major power in economic decision making in Yugoslavia.

There are limits to that power. The manager remains a figure with dual loyalties, both to the workers' council and to the government. Party and trade unions exert some influence within the firm, though far less than in any other socialist society. And the local government is a power to be reckoned with by most enterprises. Finally, the financial environment, including the (worker-managed) socialist banks, are able to influence enterprise policy. In Yugoslavia as elsewhere in the modern world, decision making is complex, but at every major stage direct representatives of the workers will be found actively participating in the decision process.[5]

Yugoslavs have communes too. That is the name they apply to local government, whose average population is perhaps a half dozen times larger than that of the typical Chinese commune. Here Communist party influence is relatively stronger than in the firm, but citizens selected in genuinely competitive elections also play a major role in decision making. And the communes are rather more powerful than their counterparts in either China or the West in that they are the beneficiaries of a revenue-sharing scheme that gives them a genuinely autonomous tax base, the central ingredient in participatory economic decision making within government. Once again participation on issues of central importance to commune members' lives is likely to be substantial.

Decentralization

There are only two basic forms of interproduction unit relations known in industrial societies: markets and hierarchies. It appears that all socialist societies except Hungary and Yugoslavia have chosen the latter form for their modern, larger-scale industry. Hungary and Yugoslavia are the socialist experimenters with market forms.

When Yugoslavia first adopted the market for relations between production units, it was almost universally criticized by socialists. However, since the period of economic reform in Eastern Europe, and with the growing appreciation among socialists of the alternatives, the market has become a bit more acceptable as a socialist resource-allocation device. Within the socialist sector, Yugoslavia has remained one of the world's most egalitarian societies despite use of the market for almost a quarter of a century now. And both the growth experience and the competitive quality of its goods suggest that the market has served reasonably effectively as a socialist resource-allocation device. Hungary has less than a decade of experience with the market, but there too it appears to be working successfully.

However, all this is not to deny the success of those socialist countries that have continued to use hierarchic systems of relationships among enterprises. This is a form that differs more substantially from monopoly capitalist practice than the market and so one might expect that a relatively long time period will be required to develop its full potential. But probably its greatest comparative advantage lies in its use as a mobilizer of resources in the early stages of modernization. Such a period of crash transformation of the economy bears some resemblance to the problems of wartime economy, where hierarchic controls tend to be ubiquitous.

Both systems offer substantial opportunities for preserving relative income equality, as the above facts suggest. However, it cannot be denied that decentralization produces some inequality, since localized units tend to become residual recipients of windfall gains and of natural advantages under decentralization. Yet it appears that somewhat similar processes occur in bureaucracies as well, screened by the relatively closed information processes of this form.

Emphasis is often placed on decentralization in the Chinese experiment. But the size of the country must also be borne in mind. Szechuan, just one province, has a substantially larger population than France or West Germany. A substantial decentralization "to the provincial level" means in China decentralization to the size of a typical large nation. Furthermore, the centralization of most of large-scale modern industry at levels equivalent to that of the state elsewhere is a fact of the Chinese way.

Some decentralization has occurred in China via the emphasis on development of local industry at the county and commune level. This has become important in permitting relative autonomy for these smaller units of government and production, and is also an important part of the Chinese way. And there has been some development of processes of contracting that allow limited leeway to local bodies in negotiation of the terms of exchanges; however, the extent and significance of these latter is unclear at the moment.

A major criticism of the use of markets under socialism is the same as that under capitalism, namely, its anarchic action. The Yugoslav economy has not been a terribly stable one and has had a recurrent problem with inflation and with a stop-go pattern of output aceleration and deceleration associated with balance of payments difficulties. However, a good deal of this is capitalism's instability being transferred via the world market to the Yugoslav economy. Presumably, a socialist market system has two advantages over its capitalist counterpart: (1) there is no capital market, one of the most volatile and central in the capitalist economy; and (2) the absence of the basic class division between workers and capitalists makes effective stabilization policy much easier to institute at the political level. It is not really possible to separate the relative strengths of these factors on present evidence. However, it has also turned out that hierarchic socialist economies are subject to rather greater fluctuations in annual rates of growth than earlier socialists had anticipated.

Other things equal, socialists will certainly prefer decentralized to centralized forms of resource allocation, so as to permit a maximum of participation. However, as the above remarks suggest, other things are not equal and a variety of considerations may decree relatively centralized forms for most socialist economies, at least for a while. We will return to this issue in the next chapter.

Transformation of Man

A central tenet of socialist belief has always been that man's behavior is strongly influenced by her environment. Give him a more humane environment to live in than capitalism, and human nature itself will appear to have been transformed. One of the principal tests socialist visitors apply to reputedly socialist countries is, Do you see evidence that a process of transformation of man is underway?

Socialist visitors to China tend to come away answering this question with an unequivocal yes, as indeed do many nonsocialists. The sense of solidarity, of working for the good of the society rather than for selfish aims, is very strongly conveyed, even though the barriers of language and culture are exceptionally high in the Chinese case. Certainly there is no doubt of a massive effort by cadres and media to promulgate socialist habits of thought and behavior. And major political events, such as the cultural revolution, seem aimed at continuing this process. Efforts to reduce the status distinctions among various types of work, including especially the requirement that officials spend a good deal of time working alongside the people, are also an extraordinary manifestation of this effort.[6]

The socialist visitor to Yugoslavia will most likely answer this key question in the negative. He will find rather limited efforts at best of the kind described in the last paragraph. When asked about this issue, a Yugoslav defender might reply: We too expect a transformation of man, but we expect it to emerge from unalienated relations of production, not from artificial efforts at indoctrination. The Yugoslav way to the transformation of man is to make the Yugoslav worker the master of her fate, insofar as that can be done in the modern world. Working together in a group that has genuine power over its workplace, and living in an environment in which home life, too, is participatory, we will let human nature speak for itself.[7]

The retention of a substantial private peasant sector and of a significant small-scale urban private sector no doubt sets some additional barriers to this emergence in Yugoslav society. But it is also true that much of the solidarity the casual visitor perceives in China is the result of a highly centralized control of public media of communication. Only a much deeper penetration into the real relations of production in daily Chinese life will permit a judgment as to how effective the transformation of the Chinese citizen has become.

Conclusion

Clearly, the Yugoslavs and the Chinese have very different fundamental ideas as to what developed socialism should look like. In neither case has the ideal as yet been closely approached. But in both cases impressive transformations of the relations of production away from capitalism have been achieved. Some of the differences between the two conceptions of socialism grow out of their differing situations; the Chinese did not have the Yugoslav development strategy open to them. Central to the differences are a different conception of the nature of human nature in society. The Yugoslavs are closer to the anarchist tradition, with its emphasis on voluntarism and the autonomy of the individual in an environment of equality as the basis for self-realization. The Chinese are closer to the solidarist notion that one person's nature is joint with another's so that self-realization is primarily through interaction. Perhaps the appropriate way to resolve this difference is to watch and support these two attempts at creating a new society as they unfold.

Transitions

SO FAR in this book there has been a good deal of talk about capitalism, and a bit about socialism, but none about how to get from one to the other. That is the topic of the present chapter, which considers separately the three rather different transitions: from developing capitalism to socialism, from monopoly capitalism to socialism, and from present-day socialism to real socialism.[1]

Peaceful Transition?

Can there be a peaceful transition from developing capitalism to socialism? No, there cannot. One can be quite definite on this point because of a recent and decisive test, namely, the case of Allende's Chile. Here was a country with perhaps the strongest and longest democratic tradition in the developing world. Chile is a relatively rich country, with much copper and good agricultural potential. Only a fifth of its population were engaged in agriculture, so the special problems of the countryside were not the crucial ones. The Allende government stayed within the constitution, and a portion of the armed forces, led by the now-martyred General Prats, was willing to support Allende so long as he remained constitution-respecting in his behavior. And finally, Allende came to only limited power, holding a minority of seats in the parliament, and so could effect only a sharply limited set of reforms; a full referendum would be held at the next election, which could send liberals back into power if a majority preferred.

It would be hard to design an environment more favorable to a peaceful transition to socialism than this. And it failed. The reasons for failure are simple enough. Domestically, the problem was that there was a set of parliamentary elections three years after Allende's accession to the presidency. Contrary to the constant complaints that were being voiced everywhere in the liberal world about Allende's failure, in these elections his supporters substantially increased their share of the vote. They did not achieve a majority but the threat was now clear: Allende's policies of doing something about poverty and unemployment and economic stagnation were popular. The results of this election brought the still essentially liberal or conservative armed forces onto the scene as Chile's rescuers from the will of the people.

But, of course, action to remove Allende began well before this, and not so much in Santiago as in Washington. The sorry list of measures taken by the United States, from the ITT offers to engage in subversion to the Kissinger decision to mobilize international capital in a boycott of Chile, need not be retold. Obviously, the real list is much longer than the one publicly available. But the latter is long enough to demonstrate that substantial and powerful efforts began to be made as soon as the election results put Allende in the presidency. These efforts were directed singlemindedly toward returning Chile to the "free world."

Had the story gone the other way in Chile, the issue of peaceful transition would still be controversial. For nowhere else in the developing capitalist world is there a country that could come close to matching the traits that made peaceful transition seem possible there. The failure of the Chilean transition is decisive.

At the present writing there is a great deal of talk about Eurocommunism, which many think offers a new opportunity for a peaceful transition in France or Italy or perhaps elsewhere in southern Europe. Certainly the possibility exists for a Communist party to obtain enough electoral votes to be legally empowered to form a parliamentary government. The Chilean case finds a full parallel to this point. But why, one might ask, should the rest of the Chilean script be played out once again?

Of course it need not be, at least not fully. Should a genuinely socialist party find itself in the above position, it will soon have to face the choice between becoming either a liberal, social democratic representative of the left in parliament, or of moving on to genuine socialism. The capitalists, and the history of class struggle in the country, will force that choice. We have seen many examples of one side of that choice in the twentieth century. The German social democrats of Weimar Germany are the archetypal example. The social democrats were the great revolutionary party of continental Europe, inheritors of the Marxian tradition, and after coming to power in Germany in the nineteen twenties by a similar electoral decision, they decided on the course of compromise and accommodation. This gave the capitalists time to regroup, to form political alliances, and to preserve and strengthen their control over the armed forces, and in particular the officer corps. Then if electoral politics did not suffice to eliminate genuine socialists from the seats of power, other means would be available. Furthermore, the environment of parliamentary compromise, acted out in the context of an existing regime of private property relations, tended to sap the socialist orientation of many leaders of the social democrats. Whatever they may have been originally, long before losing power social democrats had become liberals. This path is well worn, the forces that push members of the left down it are very strong, and the consequences are clear: a return to liberal parliamentarism under capitalist relations of production.

But there is another path, one that requires the elimination of the power base of the capitalists. That can only be done one way, namely, by nationalizing the means of production that provide that power base, and particularly the commanding heights of large-scale industry. Once that step is taken the door is open to movement toward genuine socialism. But it is hard to imagine a capitalist class sitting quietly while such a vote is taken, in parliament or elsewhere. This key step will be strongly resisted, will promote a great political, social, and economic crisis. The usual term for such a crisis is revolution, and it will not be resolved in favor of socialism without some elements of violence. But it is a path down which Eurocommunism *may* move, if its leaders still have the will to create a socialist society.

Revolution

A considerable number of reactionary governments have been overthrown from the left since World War II. Among them, in addition to Yugoslavia and China, have been Cuba, Vietnam, Bolivia (1952), Peru, Egypt, Algeria, Syria, Iraq, and, most recently, Portuguese Africa. The overthrown governments in almost every case were in a state of great weakness or even disintegration. The exceptions are the colonial governments, where an essential ingredient in revolutionary success has been, not so much the defeat of the colonial government and army, but the raising of the cost of continuing to operate the colonial government to the point at which the metropolitan government finds independence the less unattractive alternative. The frequency of these occurrences suggests some measure of optimism is justified that we have not seen the last of them.

But the political revolution is only the first long step toward establishing socialism. There is still—for those who made the political revolution—the wholly new set of tasks posed by the morrow of the revolution. Effective soldiers cannot be turned overnight into effective economic managers; nor do drill masters understand the way to turn workers and peasants into convinced supporters of a socialist regime. Something else is needed.

The leading proposal in the field to serve as that "something else" is the Leninist party. It has been the major tool for the mobilization of society for the great tasks of the transition in at least thirteen socialist countries. These thirteen countries have a successful record both in

economic construction, in eliminating the basic institutions of capitalism, and in successfully resisting challenges from the right to restore
those institutions. Of the countries that have had a political revolution
but have not had a Leninist party in the central place as a mobilizing
agent, perhaps only Cuba has as good a record as these thirteen; and
the Cubans within a very few years of the political revolution were
in fact making central use of a Leninist party. The association is too
strong to be accidental.

The revolutions in China and Yugoslavia stand out because of the
cadre-building that went on during the period of revolutionary struggle. On the morrow of those revolutions there was in each country a
large body of men and women whose commitment to socialism was
buttressed both in battle and in study of the basic ideas of socialist
thought. In both cases these cadres played a fundamental role in the
swift restructuring of society and have since, even in Yugoslavia, been
essential in sustaining a basically socialist structure for society. As
noted, in Cuba the melding of the 26th of July people with the regular party people was carried out over the years after the revolution, but
no student of recent Cuban history doubts the importance of these
cadres in preserving the revolution. Even in Eastern Europe, where the
party cadres often appeared to the population as alien agents, they
were central to the elimination of the capitalist class from positions
of power and to the creation and operation of the basic socialist
institutions.

This is in sharp contrast to the situation elsewhere. Not only does
mobilization of the population seem weak in the years after the
political revolution in countries such as Egypt, Bolivia, Algeria, and
Syria, but economic development seems on the whole rather less
successful, and the slipping back of institutions into quasi-capitalist
forms also seems a serious threat, not to mention the political-military
weakness that made a countercoup successful in Bolivia (Egypt too?).
In this list one should be careful not to underestimate the importance
of economic transformation of the country; economic backwardness is
one of the major threats to the survival of socialism in developing
countries.

There is another factor that suggests the strong-medicine approach represented by the Leninist party is essential. This is the reaction of monopoly capitalism to the threat of revolution. The inherently
unstable situations of the period of elimination of political colonialism
are now largely past, and regimes, often strongly authoritarian ones,
are in place and functioning as agents of the new, "nationalistic" neocolonialism. These governments are somewhat less frequently ripe for
revolution than was the case in the decolonialization period. Furthermore, the metropolis has devoted great efforts to the development of
"counterinsurgency" techniques, from helicopters to "scientific terror,"
including torture. And the imperial metropolis is prepared to spend a
great deal of money and effort in training and equipping local counterinsurgency groups. This does not by any means end the possibility of

revolution; but it suggests that the struggles are not going to become easier in coming years. What is basically needed are trained and committed cadres who are ready to seize the time when it comes.

Monopoly Capitalism

There are two important differences between developing and monopoly capitalism that argue for a different approach to generating socialism in the latter. The first has to do with civil rights. In a benevolent environment conventional civil rights are closely related to truth seeking. The truth is often threatening to established positions, even to the positions of great revolutionary heroes. In a society in which the people have the education and the energy and the humane values to understand the truth when it is spoken, that right to speak and disseminate ideas must be given full protection. Conventional civil rights are also closely related to the relations of production. Exploitative surplus extraction may occur even in a basically socialist society, and its victims, whether individuals or groups, must be in a position to make effective protest, or the exploitation will no doubt continue.

No radical would argue that monopoly capitalism represents a benevolent regime. But a well-informed radical is compelled to admit that conventional civil rights are better respected in every monopoly capitalist society than they are in any contemporary socialist society. One understands why this is true—the last section contains part of such an explanation—but conventional civil rights have only been established historically after centuries of struggle, and then where they do occur, only imperfectly. This is a fundamental value that must not be lost in the revolutionary process.

The second difference has to do with nuclear war. The United States essentially has the capacity to blow up the world. It is almost true that one man, the president, has that power. Monopoly capitalism is an irrational society, in which the values, particularly those of the narrow tier of leaders at the very top, are sharply distorted and inhumane. This situation poses something of a doomsday threat of an irrational use of nuclear weapons in a crisis situation. It is a factor that cannot be overlooked in considering alternative ways of generating socialism in the United States.

Fortunately, at least the first of these differences has a positive as well as a negative side, from the point of view of feasible transitions. Radicals obviously do not compete on equal terms with liberals and conservatives in their access to the media of communication in the United States. Nevertheless, they do have fairly substantial access, especially via the university and the printing press. Furthermore, an extended period of respect for civil rights, combined with a substantial level of education in a populace, creates an environment of rela-

tive openness to dissident ideas. This environment is not all that unfavorable to the propagation of radicalism. Indeed, one might well argue
that the hindrance to further development of the radical movement of
the sixties lay more in the relatively unsophisticated quality of radical
arguments than in suppression of the ideas. Education and propaganda
can play a central role in this environment.

But clearly by itself this is not enough. In the United States
radicals are offering a direct challenge to a class that has demonstrated
a willingness, to the occasional point of eagerness, to use force against
its enemies. The "salami tactics" of a slice at a time have produced
dramatic changes in American society: To develop a serious threat a
few generations ago of instituting the changes in society that have
come since then in a piecemeal way would surely have been to pro-
voke a strong repression by the ruling class. The problem is to design
at least interim continuation of that approach.

An example will illustrate one possible strategy. The single greatest set of oppressive acts by American monopoly capitalism are those
that generate continued misery in the Third World. This has become
very widely recognized among American liberals; indeed, they have generally led the piecemeal and ineffective fight against many such practices. But this is an opportunity to separate the process of delegitimization of policies from the delegitimization of the rule of law, of respect
for individual civil rights. The package of policies that produce these
sad outcomes are separable from others; they have to do with military
aid and training, with politically controlled foreign aid, with policies
of support for multinationals, with control of international lending
agencies, and the like. A campaign to delegitimize these policies, using an escalating series of instruments, has some chance of success.
The initial weapons in such a campaign would be those of research
and advocacy, with a view to building a base of support. Instruments
would then move to the formal arena of politics, and from there to
coordinated civil disobedience and, finally, to direct action against
agencies and individuals who continue to administer the delegitimized
policies. No doubt at least the credible threat of the latter acts would
be necessary to success; probably a good deal more than threat would
be required. But once the intolerable costs of this behavior had been
properly presented (they often are not effectively presented in radical
literature today), this could be a potent and successful action. Furthermore, it is in the tradition of revolt against the intolerable, while
it continues to respect the institutions of tolerance of dissent in their
normal spheres of action. The appeal would be to the undoubted truth
of the intolerability of this behavior by American monopoly capitalism.
Of course, support from radicals elsewhere would be most helpful; but
basically this would be an American job.

Proposals for action outside a very specific political context always have a slightly utopian ring. The above is offered partly in
the belief that it *is* both feasible and desirable and partly to point
out that there are halfway houses between nonviolence and classical
revolutionary violence. If the above program were successful in that it

substantially increased the rate of introduction of socialism to the Third World, it would no doubt have substantial impacts on monopoly capitalist countries too, and these could be made to be positive, particularly where dependence on Third World supplies of commodities are crucial to the maintenance of the structure of exploitation in the metropolis. Like all effective revolutionary strategies, it combines research, propaganda, and direct action in the service of a relatively well-defined goal.

From Socialism to Socialism

At the present time there appears to be a growing number of radicals who feel that none of the existing socialist countries are really socialist. No doubt they are correct. A socialist cannot help but be disturbed by the oppressive Soviet bureaucracy and a détente that has some of the properties of a sellout, of the growing inequality and the vulgar commercialism that are by no means minor parts of the Yugoslav scene, of ping-pong diplomacy and the apparent reversal of the cultural revolution in China, of the romantic elitism of the Cuban leadership.

But then not even radical intellectuals expect socialism to be a utopia. A socialist society is still a society with its own laws of motion, its own set of legacies from the past, its own specific set of current problems. A socialist is still a human being with the well-developed capacity to make mistakes inherent in the species. The real question is, In these socialist countries, have substantial and irreversible steps been taken in the direction of real socialism? This is a fundamental question, because no one doubts that the revolutions in these countries were real socialist revolutions, carried out by people committed by lives of desperate struggle and serious study to the promotion of socialism. If such revolutions can succeed politically, but then mostly fail in the aftermath, the case for revolution itself is greatly weakened because the cost of achieving socialism has become almost impossibly high. However, it seems that the correct answer to the question is yes.

In the first place, the elimination of the capitalist class from its power base removes a major threat to the humanizing of human relations. The nature of life in a society that is not ruled by finance capital is very much different from life elsewhere. The so-called new class is a class that everywhere in socialism has seen to it that the primary needs of the people for secure supplies of food, clothing, shelter, and health are met; this too is very much different from life elsewhere. And insofar as long-run trends in these societies can be discerned, they are favorable The time of struggle is not over because these societies have gone socialist, but the terms of the struggle are dramatically changed and seem generally more favorable. In none of these societies had any tradition of democratic politics been developed, and they still do not rank high on a conventional scale of democracy. But the elites seem to be enlarging rapidly, to have a fundamental—and virtually unique in the modern world—concern for the bottom half of the income distribution, and to be opening up politically to the serious discussion of alternative socialist policies. No doubt without further struggle there will not be much more progress. But, unlike the capitalist world, there is a serious case for reform rather than revolution as the optimal strategy in these countries.

Conclusion

Recipes for the transition to socialism are not to be found in this chapter. All that has been attempted is to appraise two or three key aspects of revolution that are of wide, but not of universal, application to the contemporary world. Leninist parties are not a necessity in every part of the world. The mixed strategy will not apply to every monopoly capitalist land; indeed, it may not apply at every point of time in the United States. And some existing socialist countries may well require a revolution to keep them on the track toward genuine socialism. These are issues that must be resolved in socialist debate, which in itself is bound to be a major factor in the further movement of the world toward socialism.

CHAPTER 12

The Future

FOR A LONG TIME, radicals were reluctant to discuss at length the problems of the future society they were hoping to create. It was felt, with good reason, that those who had successfully created the political revolution would be far better able to deal with the morrow of the revolution than were those immersed in the struggle against a capitalism whose demise was still far away. Marx wrote relatively little on the subject, and Lenin's major piece of analysis of socialism was written on the very eve of the October Revolution.[1]

However, the rise of socialism has tended to erode this attitude. There is by now enough historical experience of several socialist societies so that an analyst can develop some feel for the tendencies built into their social structures; and, clearly, there are a number of extant variants of socialism. Attempts to come to terms with this experience cannot fail to have a moral dimension, a concern with whether any given socialist society is headed in the right direction. And that in turn implies some sort of notion as to what the future ought to be like. In addition, the twentieth century is posing a number of problems in new ways, and it becomes relevant to ask whether, for example, socialist societies are well equipped to deal with such issues as ecology, resource exhaustion, the rise of a technocratic elite, and the risks of nuclear war.

There seem to have been three distinct types of utopian societies that have aroused interest.[2] One emphasizes the relation between man and nature as a creative interaction and favors a simple and wholly decentralized society of mutual cooperation in support of this fundamental, "natural" harmony. Essentially, this is a form of anarchy and is epitomized in William Morris's utopian novel, *News from Nowhere*. The second emphasizes relations between humans, solidarity or brotherly love, and finds in the community the primary supporting institution. Many of the communes formed in recent years in Berkeley and Mendocino, California, have been based on this principle. And the third emphasizes man's competitive, even combative, nature and looks to the environment of voluntary exchange as the institutional basis for a realization of this drive. Libertarian anarchists support this utopia. One can find attempts to specify each of these utopias in some detail in the literature; in fact, the student of economics will have already come across arguments in favor of the third of these, for the competitive capitalist regime is the "utopia" on which much of conventional economics (but of course not contemporary economies) is built. Those who prefer one of the other utopias as a general social goal thus have another good reason to be turned off by this apologetic literature in the guise of science.

Of course, no real world society could operate, at least in the foreseeable future, as a pure case of one of these utopias. Every society will have some elements of each of these three fundamental facets of human behavior. But with this qualification the radical position does make a choice among the three. Overwhelmingly, radical literature emphasizes solidarity and community as fundamental bases of human existence; it would be very difficult, I think impossible, to conceive of a radical solution with any other central thrust. From this context we may very briefly survey some issues the future is likely to bring and one or two properties of a radical solution.

The family has been throughout history a central human institution and a primary source of such solidary relations as human society to date has afforded. It will clearly survive into the period of transition to socialism and probably a good deal longer than that; nor is there a reason in principle to oppose the continuation of an institution whose central orientation has been so strongly communal. The basic problem seems to be not with the family but with the institutions in which it has been embedded, and particularly those of monopoly capitalism. In that society, the family has been an institution that has supported deep exploitation of women and children, and has played its role in generating the fragmented personalities that are capitalism's ubiquitous product.

However, historically the family has taken many forms. Among the more interesting have been the traditional extended families, such as the Slavic *mir* and *zadruga,* in which sometimes tens of people representing several generations and many nuclear family clusters have lived together, sharing their property, their work, and their lives. This historical demonstration that groups far larger than the family as we know it today can thrive offers considerable hope for the future. The sharing of work among families united in production units, such as teams and brigades in China, suggests, in an admittedly transitional form, the possibilities for developing social units that generate both solidary human relationships and are economically viable.

There is a crude version of Marxism that holds that the social relations of production are a deterministic product of uncontrollable changes in technology. When this is combined with the observation that the efficient scale of production of many of the most important products of modern civilization is increasing rapidly, the conclusion seems inescapable that before long we will all live under the sway of some giant bureaucracy, for only such a beast could administer the highly centralized economy. The socialist utopian would then have to build his solidary community on a truly grand scale, and serious doubts would inevitably arise as to whether genuine comradeship is truly attainable on such a scale.

However, as we have seen, this notion is rejected by most contemporary Marxists. In fact, there is a growing body of evidence that technology and technical change function as integral parts of the social system, so that changes in the latter can induce changes in the former. Centralization and increasing scale occur because monopoly capitalism finds such a technology to be a useful support for its highly centralized control of the economic system. The movement to socialism will inevitably be a movement toward a technology that is compatible with the socialist system. Once again, in China one can see successful steps being taken to disperse production, even of iron and steel, to the countryside by means of effective small-scale technologies. As countries that have more resources per capita available for the effort turn to socialism, we can expect a substantial acceleration of this process.

Closely related to the nature of technology is the ecology issue. Here the relation between humans and nature is mediated by technology, by our knowledge of how to do things. And it is likely that this interaction will become increasingly unable to be supported by such a mechanism as the price system, in which, for example, pollution costs never seem to find a market price. Can socialism deal successfully with such a fundamental question? Certainly some would say that socialism's success to date in this area has been rather mixed, with the Soviets, for example, having rather similar difficulties in controlling pollution of air and water as the United States.

However, that is a rather misleading perspective. Like other socialist countries, the Soviet Union, starting out as a relatively backward land, economically speaking, has had a lot of catching up to do before many resources could be made available for needs other than the basic material condition of the populace and the economic and military needs of survival. As these additional discretionary resources are now gradually beginning to become available, we will get a better test as to whether it can handle the problem successfully. Even then a failure would not be decisive, given the Soviet status as, at best, a deformed socialist society.[3]

No one can predict the future of a crisis-ridden world with great confidence. But major preconditions for successful action on the ecology front do seem to be built deeply into the basic principles of socialism. Fundamentally, ecology means taking account in one's own behavior of the effect of one's actions on others. Its peculiarity stems from the fact that technology—such as the polluting factory—mediates the relation of cause and effect in this social relation. But in a solidary community, that is precisely where the center of attention is located. An awareness of community is the first and the most important step in resolving any particular ecological problem. Indeed, the requirements of ecological balance will no doubt play a very important role in defining the scope and forms of community in a socialist society.

Manufacturing the capacity to wage a genocidal nuclear war is yet another of the technological triumphs of monopoly capitalist society. In a socialist world one might reasonably expect that physicists and their engineering sidekicks will find something more rewarding to do than to heap one destructive "defense system" on top of another. But the nuclear genie will not go back into its bottle and disappear. One of the most central tasks of socialist states will be to find some way to rid the world of the consequences of our having eaten this particular fruit of the tree of knowledge.

Clearly, that task will not be easy. The uneven development, both economic and in levels of consciousness, of socialist societies will continue to produce tensions well into the era of universal socialism. And obviously some socialist states have nuclear capability. Is there any reason to suppose that they will be willing to dismantle their bombs and rockets, to foreswear their use forever? There are some hints at least that this will happen. No socialist state has as yet actually used the bomb in war. Socialist states have promised that they will not be the first to use nuclear weapons. And disputes among socialist states have so far entailed a use of violence at a far lower level than has been the case under capitalism. But more important than all this is the change in attitude that a move toward socialism entails. The economic security, the level of education, the orientation toward human values, the social structure—all these suggest that tensions will be far more manageable under socialism than under capitalism. The basically defensive foreign policies of the great socialist states is a harbinger of this change, still weakened by the relatively primitive nature of contemporary socialist society, but having its effects nonetheless. Even in this most difficult area there are grounds for optimism.

A socialist world is not inevitable; clearly, it is possible that it will never make its appearance. If it does appear it will only come after prolonged and intense struggles, after a continuation for many years of the crisis we are now all experiencing. But if this analysis has been correct, then it *can* come and it *should* come.

PART II

Commentary

CHAPTER 13

Radical World View and Radical Economics

WHAT MAKES an economic world view tick? Of course, to be viable it must fill some needs of those who believe it. I suppose the most natural way for an economic world view to fill a need is to provide a correct interpretation of how contemporary political economies work. But as anyone who knows the elements of Marxism is aware, there is not a straightforward relationship between subject and object, between the material world and our awareness of it. That relationship is mediated by our experiences and by our social conditioning, as well as by hard facts. And no one, which means no Marxist, no radical as well, has as yet escaped some measure of social conditioning and some measure of exposure to unique experiences. This suggests that at any particular time the world will contain several economic world views, each of which will seem most plausible to some.

However, the collection of plausible radical economic world views has one essential advantage over any competitors, an advantage that stems from the very nature of the radical world view. As was noted in the early chapters of Part I, radical interpretations are built on an appraisal of the fundamental structure of society, and in particular on the class nature of society and its implications. By going to the root of the matter right from the first, the radical interpretations are able to avoid a good deal of the obfuscation and distortion that are entailed by attempts to paper over this most fundamental of social facts. This is the distinguishing feature of radical economic world views, and also constitutes the major advantage they possess vis-à-vis rival interpretations. As a consequence, in Part II we will not be much concerned with these nonradical interpretations.

Such a limitation will not free us from the need to appraise differences for, as the reader of Part I is certainly aware, there are other plausible radical economic world views than the one presented there.

In fact, there are several quite well-developed radical economic world views, and they tend to differ fairly substantially from one another. Essentially, Part II is devoted to looking at various alternatives to Part I and explaining our choices. Before beginning the job, however, something must be said about the process of choosing among alternative world views.

There are probably three criteria that are central to this choice. The first test of the alternatives is simply how well each one fits in terms of one's own experience of life and interpretation of history. I suspect that this criterion is mostly applied intuitively, but there is no reason why one could not make a systematic appraisal. The second criterion is a bit more precise: The question is, Do the world view's assertions fit the known facts? In practice, this criterion turns out to be rather less specific than it sounds because of the nature of the "facts" that appear as parts of so broad a doctrine as a world view. For example, one of the most striking facts asserted by Paul Baran is that in Third World countries the relative surplus is quite large. To my knowledge this thesis has never been seriously tested. The concept of surplus is itself underdeveloped, and global statistical investigations have so far been carried out almost exclusively by liberals using different concepts. Nonetheless, as was argued in chapter 8, it is a very plausible fact, and certainly has not been refuted.[1] It would be quite irrational to reject a world view because it contained this assertion as an integral part of the package.

The third test is potentially the most useful. A radical has already narrowed his range of choice to a segment of the available world views and has eliminated those that patently contradict experience. The remaining test has to do with whether or not the various parts of the world view fit together to make a coherent whole. This is not a simple criterion to apply because there is a certain open-endedness to it; for example, a revealed incompatibility may be relatively minor, or one might feel that it can probably be corrected without too much difficulty. But major incompatibilities are serious obstacles to the acceptability of a world view.

An example will illustrate the issue. Baran and Sweezy have argued that under monopoly capitalism there is a strong underlying tendency toward economic stagnation, combined with a need for the economy to expand to prevent increasing unemployment from becoming a threat to the system. This leads in turn to much waste and to the development of a fundamental problem, namely, the problem of absorbing the tremendous surplus the system is generating.

The arguments they present in favor of this thesis are in themselves plausible. However, there is one implication that is very hard for a radical to swallow: The thesis implies that there exists a reformist solution to the problem of imperialism. That is, if surplus absorption is the problem domestically, it can be resolved, for a long time to come, by a massive foreign-aid program that diverts the surplus to Third World countries. Domestic capitalists could, in effect, be bribed with guaranteed profits to develop the Third World as a response to a basic domestic contradiction of monopoly capitalism.

This reformist thesis is inherently implausible as a characterization of imperialism over, say, the last half century. And it would seem that the incompatibility is fundamental: Either buy that or reject the thesis about the wastefulness of monopoly capitalism. But the alternatives are not in fact that sharp. As will be argued in chapter 15 below, by rejecting the idea of underlying stagnation in its Baran/Sweezy form the plausible parts of their thesis can be retained without being forcibly tied to a reformist theory of imperialism.

In the world view appraisals to follow, the compatibility test will play a very important role. Unfortunately, there has been no systematic effort to appraise radical world views seriously and with a view to developing optimal versions. Though one finds book reviews and the like, these are mostly unsystematic impressions and are usually not devoted to an appraisal that is concerned with world view development. As a consequence, our efforts are inevitably selective and, I'm afraid, somewhat introductory. It turns out that world view appraisal is a fairly serious and demanding business.

What is the relation of a world view to the scientific part of economics? The notion of science is nowadays fairly well defined. It consists at the very least of theory and observation in fairly close interconnection, with serious attention devoted to the establishing of the facts as a central part of the discipline. Clearly, world views by themselves cannot pass that test. Nevertheless, as will be argued, they do have an important relationship to the scientific part of a discipline.

Scientific radical economics has been under intense attack throughout the twentieth century. The political constraints on its practice in most socialist countries are substantial. In some capitalist countries there is widespread suppression of radicals and their work. In areas where there is toleration, there is a serious shortage of resources for research, especially when compared with the resources available for those scientists whose work essentially defends the system. And radical scholarship is further decimated by the felt need of many potential scholars to devote themselves substantially to political work.

But even under all these handicaps, scientific radical economics is definitely on a strong upward trend these days. One of its major tasks is the reinterpretation of the massive body of essentially liberal work so as to reveal the true meaning of that research. And it is at just this point that a world view becomes practically useful. A good world view provides the researcher with an orientation specific enough to guide his work of reinterpretation, suggesting hypotheses and approaches and, perhaps most important, providing a firm specification as to what *is* radical to sustain her in his struggle with essentially alien materials. Much the same also holds for new, as opposed to reinterpretive, research.

The role that a world view can play in determining one's approach to problems can perhaps best be illustrated negatively, that is, by looking at a serious and intelligent appraisal of "The Political Economy of the New Left" in a very popular book of that title by the Swedish economist Assar Lindbeck. A social democrat politically and a thoroughgoing liberal in his economics, Lindbeck obviously did his homework, and even seems to have tried hard to be sympathetic in his appraisal of latter-day radical economics. Nevertheless, his book leaves the reader with the impression that the New Left economists are essentially a collection of well-meaning bumblers, of people who don't do too bad a job of asking questions, except that they never bother to answer them seriously.

This conclusion is a very straightforward consequence of the method Lindbeck uses. And the method is very liberal. It consists of dividing all questions into relatively small parts, the parts being recognizable as questions typically asked by liberals. For example, Lindbeck finds radical discussions of exploitation of Third World countries unsatisfying.[2] She points out that radicals emphasize the harmful effects of high profits made by multinationals in developing countries, when in fact high profits are merely a sign that the company is efficiently providing a desired service. Lindbeck has thus implicitly reposed the problem: He claims the issue is, Which is better, an efficient or an inefficient multinational? I suppose most radicals would not be too averse to accepting Lindbeck's answer to *her* question. But they also would not find it to be at all an interesting question. The reader of Baran, or of Part I above, will know that the efficiency of the multinationals is not a central issue when it comes to center-periphery relations. The question there has to do with the existence of a pattern of exploitation, based on a large number of different instruments, many of them political and military, many of them economic, many of them of considerable age, many of them involving deep penetration into the social structure of the Third World country. By asking the questions from within the framework of a liberal rather than a radical world view, Lindbeck both distorts the facts of exploitation and defuses the outrage that those facts tend to generate in the reader.

The main thrust of radicalism is to bring about fundamental change in an exploitative society. This goal requires that one ask different questions from those asked by liberals, and the questions in turn often require the use of different techniques in order to answer them. Liberals want to preserve society, dealing with emergent problems by making small changes that will not disturb the basic structure. Those are very different goals, and they produce a very different structure for the interpretive science of society that supports each effort.

However, there is more to the difference than the nature of the questions. These two world views are oriented toward the needs, experiences, and values of two different classes. Out of that more fundamental difference lies the gap that separates members of these two classes from one another, making communication across the gap very difficult. Since the differences are based both on life experiences and on very powerful socialization processes, they may never be fully bridged. That failure, and all it entails, is simply a cost of capitalism —but not of socialism.

A developed and integrated world view can play an important role in formulating and spreading understanding of the nature of the world among its citizenry. And that in turn is the basis upon which the elimination of exploitative systems can taken place. However, at this point a problem emerges from within the radical movement. It seems that many radicals believe that serious attention to the intellectual side of radicalism is largely a waste of time, even a cop-out: "The basic ideas are already in Marx and Lenin; what is needed is to abolish capitalism, not study it." I suppose that if you expect the revolution to be coming next year at the latest, that is a not implausible view. And in fact, the way things are going there may very well be a successful political revolution somewhere while this book is in press. But that misses the point on two counts. In the first place, there is no basis for feeling that the revolution will be coming in the heartland of monopoly capitalism in the near future; in the second place, there will still be a central need for both radical world views and scientific economics after the political revolution. A central function of radical economics is as an instrument of recruitment. But an equally central function is to provide a correct understanding of how the world works. Without that, there is no good reason to feel that radicals will be able to bring about a genine revolution. After all, it is no mean trick to pull one off. And this applies equally after the revolution. Revolutions can go astray; the revolution is itself both an end and a beginning. If it does go astray, or begins to, there must be those who can point this out, and they must have the same sort of basis for making their case as their prerevolutionary forbears did. One has only to look at the Soviet Union, where such efforts are continually and brutally suppressed, to see the nature of the need. The construction and development and appraisal of radical world views is more than intellectual game playing. It is a serious and vital part of the overall radical effort.

CHAPTER 14

Baran and Sweezy

I THINK it is not controversial to assert that the two Pauls, Baran and Sweezy, have been the most substantial and most influential radical economists writing in the United States since World War II. Baran's book, *The Political Economy of Growth*,[1] is probably the most important single work of radical economics of the postwar period. It contains an integrated characterization of the functioning of monopoly capitalism, of the functioning of capitalism in the Third World, and of the interaction between the two. The joint work of Baran and Sweezy, *Monopoly Capital*,[2] extends and to some extent revises the account of monopoly capitalism, and has also been very influential. Both authors have, of course, extended and refined more detailed aspects of their views in articles, some of which have been collected and published in book form. Sweezy, as the founder and continuing editor of the Monthly Review Press, has also provided an outlet for a large fraction of the most important radical works of the postwar era.

Because of the similarities in their viewpoints and their collaboration, it is convenient to consider these two authors together. In combination they have a coherent and broad-gauge perspective, one that can reasonably be considered to be the appropriate starting point for anyone trying to come to terms with postwar radical economics. However, that is not to say that every radical economist will find all of even their major arguments acceptable. Our evaluative procedure will consist of the following: The next section outlines the views in Baran's *Political Economy of Growth*. Then the extensions and modifications of those views as they appear in *Monopoly Capital* and elsewhere are described. The final section of this chapter indicates the major points of agreement and disagreement between Baran and Sweezy and the optimal radical economic world view. The two following chapters appraise further key aspects of their work, including some comparisons with other radical writers. In reading the next section, the reader should remember that the illustrative examples were selected by Baran around 1955. They have been included here because they in no way detract from the modernity of this prescient work.

Political Economy of Growth

The basic concept Baran uses in analyzing contemporary societies is potential surplus. This is the difference between the output that could be produced, if all currently available resources were put to use, and essential consumption. At present it is not possible to make good estimates of the magnitude of the potential surplus, though a number of important qualitative statements can be made. But first a further definition: Three things can be done with the surplus—it can be invested, consumed, or wasted. The way in which a society basically functions is revealed by the ways in which it allocates surplus among these three categories, while the size of the surplus is largely a matter of the forces of production.[3]

Nineteenth-century capitalism became a rapidly growing economic system, Baran argues, because it was able to meet four basic conditions: (1) unemployment of resources was kept to a minimum; (2) the wage rate was kept down to a level that tended to maximize the size of the surplus; (3) a maximal share of the actual surplus was plowed back into investment rather than being consumed; and (4) there were plenty of profitable investment opportunities. The effect of the first three conditions tended to counter the effect of the fourth in the capital market, thus keeping the interest rate relatively low.[4]

With the rise of monopoly capitalism, including especially a high concentration of ownership and control in the modern industrial sector, this situation changed; in fact, none of the four conditions continued to hold. The volume of unutilized resources became very high, the organized labor force was able effectively to bid up wages, capitalist and other forms of consumption increased at the expense of further investment, and the number of investment projects that were deemed worthy of realization by capitalists declined sharply. Most of this change is attributable to the change in the nature of the capitalist system itself. Thus it is not true that in a rationally ordered society there would be relatively few investment projects these days; rather, it is a matter of monopoly capitalists viewing the profitability in a different light. For example, they are rarely willing to undertake an investment project that will destroy the value of some of their existing capital stock, whereas in the older, more competitive regime, the capitalists would be forced to adopt such a project in order to survive.

Thus there is a strong underlying tendency toward stagnation in monopoly capitalism. This creates serious problems. For example, with productivity and labor force both growing at a couple of percentage points each year, either some means of using the additional hands must be found or unemployment levels may begin to create a revolutionary situation. In fact, the rise of welfare state spending tends only to occur during such crisis situations, and partly accounts for the big state under monopoly capitalism. Another reason is the finally recognized need to regulate the economy in order to try to prevent the survival threat posed by major depressions. Already by the end of Roosevelt's administration it was clear that business was taking over the administration of this new state function.

The newly emerged state system with its substantial welfare spending and the great waste of resources that nevertheless keeps unemployment rates at a manageable level, combined with imperialist operations abroad that accrue to the national benefit, creates a kind of people's imperialism, "a far-reaching harmony between the interests of monopolistic business on one side and those of the underlying population on the other." [5]

However, the stability of this system is highly precarious. The increasing waste in the form of excess consumption of gewgaws, unproductive investment in these goods, the excessive costs of organization of monopoly business, government programs of military expenditures and the like, creates an irrational society that can hardly escape the notice of the relatively deprived citizenry. Clearly, much of this kind of expenditure cannot be increased indefinitely; but increase it must if the steadily growing surplus is to be absorbed. Effective control of the economy has not yet been achieved, with inflation posing a special problem because

by causing the development of a cleavage between the interests of creditors and debtors, by dispossessing the new middle class and the rentiers, by depressing the real income of the workers, it seriously weakens the authority of the government and disrupts the political and social cohesion of the capitalist order. . . . Thus the stability of monopoly capitalism is highly precarious.[6]

The tendency toward caution and circumspection that monopoly capitalists exercise in their business affairs seems to have spilled over into their international behavior, in that they seem to prefer cold wars to hot wars; however, this line of argument cannot be pushed too far because of other structural changes in the economy. For the first time in its history the United States is now getting a "'full-time national-scale arms industry, [so that] companies . . . now treat their war output as a permanent part of their business,'" as *Business Week* put it.[7] This tends to push the government toward exerting its muscle, so as to justify the increasing arms expenditures. And the forces pushing toward war are profoundly irrational, not subject to easy control "as many big business magnates in Germany discovered to their sorrow." [8] It is this profoundly irrational system that monopoly capitalism has unleashed upon the world.

But the world had already been "prepared" for this onslaught by previous events. One of the most striking was the creation of underdevelopment. In much of the world, including precapitalist Europe, three basic preconditions for the emergence of capitalism were being created. These were: (1) a slow increase in agricultural output combined with intense feudal pressure on a servile (in status) population, and displacement and consequent rebellion of peasants; (2) the continuing process of division of labor, together with the emergence of a potential industrial labor force, the evolution of a class of merchants and artisans, and the growth of towns; and (3) a fairly spectacular accumulation of capital among merchants and wealthy peasants. And in the late seventeenth and early eighteenth centuries contacts between Europeans and non-Europeans seemed to foster the spread of science and modern technology.

But except in a few special cases, such as the United States and Japan, capitalism and the industrial revolution did not emerge in the rest of the world. Why not? In part because the military superiority of Europe permitted the extraction of resources from these countries, which served as a large fraction of the primary accumulation that fueled the European expansion while impoverishing the rest of the world. In part because the intrusion of Europe disrupted the internal dynamic of these societies, so that the social forces moving toward modernism were unable to effect their transformations. The United States, like the Commonwealth countries, escaped this process because they were, in their controlling populations, primarily European. Japan escaped because of the combination of her own earlier isolation, which protected her from the worst of the depredations and left her social structure intact, and because of the preoccupation of imperialist powers elsewhere during the key period of the Meiji Restoration. There was no escape elsewhere in the world, and the rest of the world remains what it was made by early predatory capitalism: underdeveloped.

The material conditions for rapid economic development exist in the underdeveloped world today. The first two conditions (page 275) of growth, large relative surplus and low wage rates, both apply, the first even in the countries we think of as being poor. The problem is with the latter two conditions. To see this one must first look at the class structure in these countries. The populations are primarily engaged in agriculture, where a relative surplus of perhaps one half of the output of the sector is generated. However, this surplus is appropriated essentially by four groups: (1) merchants, moneylenders, and other intermediaries; (2) local capitalists controlling industrial production; (3) foreign enterprise; and (4) the state. The first category is clearly parasitic. The second usually involves small morsels of capital and so does not use the best available modern technology, tends toward monopoly, and often is not growth-oriented. The third produces the familiar enclave, oriented toward the world market rather than domestic needs, with its managers skilled in the arts of tax avoidance and other forms of corruption. They engage in substantial political interventions aimed at generating a favorable climate for investment, which often means building up substantial armies to protect the foreigner against the pauperized masses of the country.[9]

There are three kinds of state regimes, colonial, comprador, and New Deal. The failures of colonial regimes to generate economic development is obvious enough. Typical of the compradors are the Middle East and Venezuelan oil kingdoms. They earn vast royalties on the oil extracted by foreign companies but have been spending it, for the most part, on almost anything but economic development. Much of the income slips back to the monopoly capitalist homelands one way or another. New Deal regimes are under the control of a nationalist bourgeoisie with various fringe allies. They can be growth-oriented and under favorable conditions may be able to reproduce the Japanese escape from underdevelopment. But the dice are heavily loaded against them by monopoly capital control of world markets and modern technology, and the outlook is not favorable. Their basic problem is that the high rates of investment needed to modernize can only be achieved by government mobilization of a portion of the relative surplus; but this requires heavy taxation of the regime's own principal supporters, not a popular policy among politicians.

This analysis of underdevelopment produces three conclusions that conflict with typical liberal arguments: (1) the development problem is not primarily that of a shortage of capital but that of generating investment, instead of consumption and waste, out of the large relative surplus; (2) there is no shortage of entrepreneurial talent in the developing countries, but rather there is an absence of a structure within which entrepreneurship can function; and (3) the population problem is not basically one of finding ways to control population growth, but rather of creating a rational society within which the participants will be encouraged to make rational choices about their lives.

The truth of these propositions can be examined negatively by looking at the failure of capitalist development processes in the twentieth century; it can also be examined more positively by looking at the way in which development is achieved under socialism. "The socialist camp, preoccupied with internal construction, is utterly unlikely to initiate a war." [10] The waste of resources aimed at propping up reactionary regimes in the socialist countries is converted into investment, and the high investment rates produce high rates of growth. Much of this surplus, of course, comes from the agricultural sector, where agricultural production is transformed into "specializing, labor-dividing and market-oriented industry" in which planners can control the process of surplus extraction in a rational way. The extensive policy of concentrating investment initially in industry rather than agriculture is most productive in the long run. There is still some waste in these regimes, but it stems largely from the continued threat of monopoly capitalism and the resulting deformities in military expenditures and excessive autarky to prevent use of economic leverage against socialism. Once a country has been removed from the grip of exploitation by national and foreign capital, the possibility of successful economic and social transformation in the twentieth century is no longer problematic, as the experience of these socialist countries shows.

In brief outline, this is the essence of Baran's argument.

Modifications and Extensions

The Political Economy of Growth was completed in 1955, more than
two decades ago. The years following its publication produced a great
deal more information about economic development, about the socialist
countries, and about the functioning of monopoly capitalism in the
relatively new Cold War environment. The basic ideas of Baran's book
survived, and are essentially repeated in *Monopoly Capital,* which appeared a decade later. But some new ideas and some shifts of emphasis
as well as some modifications of earlier arguments made their appearance in the later work. We will simply run through a short list of
the most important of these.

    1. In his 1962 foreword to the second edition of *Political Eco-
nomy of Growth,* Baran puts considerable weight on the forces of
production as hampering the domestic development of socialist practice in socialist countries. The political troubles of socialism he attributes to the slow rise in consumption necessitated by the need for
a rapid growth of output. Resistance to this "creates the need for political repression" and for the tension between socialism and democracy.[11] The Soviet thaw of the fifties he attributes to the further
growth of the economy. Similarly, he finds uneven development to be
the key to the problems in relations between socialist countries. The
China-Russia tensions are due to the fact that China is not yet economically ready for the thaw. Once again, further growth of the productive forces will mitigate these anomalies in socialist behavior.

    2. In *Monopoly Capital* Baran and Sweezy complement the
earlier book with respect to the impact of the managerial revolution.
They come down strongly on the side that perceives this evolution as
primarily a matter of administration and not at all a matter of the rise
of a new class. The managers are agents of the ruling class, and their
behavior reflects a continuing primary interest in generating profits.
This is quite consistent with Baran's earlier position, but in the later
context represents a firm denial of the validity of the "finance capital"
thesis that central financial institutions have come to control large
American corporations.[12]

    3. There is more emphasis in *Monopoly Capital* on stagnation
than in the earlier work. "The *normal* state of the monopoly capitalist
economy is stagnation." This is accompanied by downplaying the
Steindl thesis that had attracted Baran. Steindl was an early proponent
of the idea that the rate of innovation is closely tied to investment
rates, since the innovations can only be realized in new capital investments. He added to this thesis the inverse causation, namely, that
low rates of investment tend to inhibit the innovative process because
of the absence of expected outlets, while high rates of investment stimulate innovation. Baran and Sweezy now emphasize that there is no
necessary connection between the rate of technical progress and the
volume of investment outlets.[13]

4. Baran's strongest argument for the wastefulness of capitalism was the indirect one that, judging from the situation during World War II, the nation seemed to have from half to three-fourths of its output more or less disappear without reducing real wages.[14] In the later book the two authors develop the direct argument further, that is, by pointing to the various ways in which waste occurs within the production sector. Perhaps their most interesting story along this line comes from a study that estimated that the per-car cost of essentially cosmetic model changes in the automobile industry over seven or eight years amounted to more than forty times the advertising expenditures per car.[15]

5. In the later book much more emphasis is placed on the limits to wasteful surplus absorption under monopoly capitalism. Basically, the argument is that military-imperialist spending has had to bear the major burden of surplus absorption, and that the ability of this sector to continue to increase more rapidly than the growth of output is itself limited. Civilian government was felt to have already reached its limits as a relative surplus absorber because of the conflicts among powerful interests created by civilian spending, which tends to displace private enterprise as military spending does not. The sales effort can continue to be an absorber, but not without simultaneously generating increasing awareness in the population of the extreme wastefulness of this process. Investment cannot be relied on as a relative surplus absorber, except when a truly fundamental innovation comes along, such as the railroad. And capitalist consumption has tended not to increase relative to the growth of output. This suggests strongly that a crisis of irrationality is brewing, though it does not permit any great precision in defining its nature and timing.

6. Discussion of imperialism is extremely brief and emphasizes the military spending side. It is pointed out that successful foreign investment tends to increase the surplus that must be absorbed. However, it is in the interest of the individual corporation to make these investments, thus producing a contradiction between the parts and the whole that is of the essence of monopoly capitalism.

7. In discussing the history of monopoly capitalism, Baran and Sweezy emphasize the tendency toward stagnation as arising early; it would have been apparent by the 1880s were it not for the railroads, which absorbed almost half of American investment for two or more decades. They also emphasize the role of great catastrophes in masking the nature of monopoly capitalism during the twentieth century, and particularly the two great wars and the Cold War as concealing for extended periods the stagnationist tendency.

8. Race relations and alienation, two areas that played little role in Baran's previous work, are given strong emphasis in *Monopoly Capital*. The divide-and-conquer tactics that work to keep wages down and to prevent strong political action by buying off the black bourgeoisie represent one durable aspect of capitalist relations of production. Another argument runs from alienation to prejudice, the pressures of life in monopoly capitalism tending to find in prejudice a rather

natural outlet. But alienation affects all aspects of life, through the lack of commitment, of involvement, that is inevitable in so profoundly irrational a society.

9. Baran saw a capitalist crisis developing, but he also saw mechanisms at work that could long delay it. Baran and Sweezy do not seem much more optimistic about the possibilities of their crisis coming soon or generating an internally inspired transition to socialism. "As the world revolution spreads and as the socialist countries show by their example that it is possible to use man's mastery over the forces of nature to build a rational society satisfying the human needs of human beings, more and more Americans are bound to question the necessity of what they now take for granted." [16]

10. Sweezy's own position regarding socialism has undergone some modification in recent years. Partly as a result of an exchange with the French Marxist Charles Bettelheim, Sweezy agrees that during the long period of transition to socialism after the political victory of the revolution, markets are likely to play a large and positive role as a means of resource allocation. [17] He had been much more suspicious of markets in the past, regarding them as capitalism's Trojan horse. Also his attitude toward the centrality of participation and democratization at an early stage in the transition to prevent the emergence of merely a new form of class society has seemed to change. This is reflected in some of his critical remarks on one-man rule in Cuba, made in a 1969 appraisal of that revolution. [18]

11. As Sweezy himself pointed out in an article, the New Left may be new, but the people who provided it with its basic intellectual orientations toward contemporary society were the great men of the Old Left. This is particularly true of the United States. But with the shifts of emphasis suggested above, and particularly of those that relate to socialism, Sweezy is himself adjusting in the direction of New Left orientations. As a result this dichotomy has substantially disappeared.

12. An important extension of the Baran/Sweezy view of monopoly capital also requires some comment. Harry Braverman's *Labor and Monopoly Capital, The Degradation of Work in the Twentieth Century*,[19] is an attempt to add a characterization of changes in the labor process to the theory of monopoly capital. The degradation of work constitutes the heart of this thesis. Scientific management and its related schools of personnel administration symbolize this change most dramatically. The worker is now viewed as an object, "a general purpose machine operated by management," as Braverman describes it.[20] The worker's tasks are analyzed with a view toward designing efficiency into their execution in precisely the same way as is done for machines. The function of the industrial psychologist is to design an environment that is maximally supportive of maximum worker efficiency; that is, the worker is once again treated as an object subject to control in the service of profits. These interventions, profound in their human consequences, are also profoundly alienating. But as Braverman's research brilliantly reveals, there has been another profound consequence. The

levels of skill required to perform the broadest range of both blue- and white-collar labor has steadily declined. Braverman exposes clearly the fallacies of statistical definition that have produced the opposite impression in most observers, and enriches that discovery with a mass of detailed accounts of specific changes in the nature of work over the twentieth century. His conclusions are lent added support by the fact that Braverman is himself a worker, having spent about half his work-life in skilled blue-collar jobs and the other half in various skilled white-collar jobs.

Our Part I characterization of the optimal radical economic world view made use of Braverman's thesis, though perhaps did not give it sufficient emphasis. One problem with his work is that some of the key assertions will require further scholarly investigation before they can be accepted without question. This applies particularly to the thesis that on the whole work is more degraded now than it was, say, at the turn of the century in the advanced capitalist countries. A second problem is that Braverman essentially accepts the Marcusan thesis that there must be a dramatic change in the structure of technology itself before anything like socialism can be feasible. This thesis is discussed in chapter 16 below and, I believe on present evidence, is too extreme. But that is in no way to disparage Braverman's work. Her most impressive achievement is that, by posing a well-thought-out and carefully investigated alternative, he has revealed the poverty of a whole generation of conventional research into "labor economics."

Baran and Sweezy and the Optimal Radical Economic World View

Clearly, the world view articulated in Part I above owes a great deal to the work of Baran and Sweezy. The notion of economic surplus, which was first applied by Baran to the analysis of monopoly capital, also plays a central role in Part I, as does the analysis of waste and inefficiency, the idea that a new form of capitalism emerged around the turn of the century; and so too the Baranian analysis of underdevelopment. No analysis of monopoly capital can be complete without their contributions. Of course, some of these ideas have been floating around for a long time, but an integrated analysis, based on a clear view of the distinctiveness of this system, as well as of its similarities with classical capitalism, is the product of their intellectual labors. It is probably the most substantial intellectual achievement by radical economists since World War II.

Nevertheless we have not followed their lead in every respect. At several points, some of them important, we have taken a different tack. The most important of these, the relationship between stagnation and surplus absorption and their joint implications, was mentioned in the previous chapter and will be the topic under discussion in the next chapter. Other points of difference will be discussed later. Our criticisms are intended to be constructive, aimed at developing an optimal radical economic world view. The success of that venture depends on the development of an integrated social process of radical criticism. Hopefully, the time is past when a major work of radical economics can go essentially uncriticized in the journals for years. A world view has important dimensions other than the intellectual. But the intellectual dimension is of central importance, and that dimension must be based on a serious and critical, if basically sympathetic, appraisal of the products of radical intellectuals.

CHAPTER 15

Stagnation and Surplus Absorption

A MAJOR DIFFICULTY in developing an effective interpretation of the operation of monopoly capitalism has been the lurching described in chapter 4. Monopoly capital has proved to be an effective device for the generation of catastrophes. This in turn has tended to screen from the student's eye the basic processes at work within the system. For example, in the nineteen thirties and forties there was a general tendency to emphasize stagnation as an unavoidable property of monopoly capitalism. Not only was there the depression of the thirties, but the last quarter of the nineteenth century had come to be called the Great Depression, at least until a much greater one came along in the nineteen thirties. There were arguments that new investment opportunities were tending to dry up and that the decline in population growth had a depressing effect on capitalism, as a result of the smaller demand of the smaller population. One interesting thesis suggested that stagnation tended to reinforce itself, or perhaps even be created by a period of depression. The idea was that new inventions tended to be stimulated by the prospect of being put to profitable use. But putting them to use required new capital. If investment flagged so would the zeal of inventors.[1]

The stagnationist thesis was not implausible in those days. But from today's perspective it has lost most of that plausibility. Clearly, capitalist economies go up as well as down, and they do the former much more often than they do the latter. There have been several fairly sustained periods of growth since World War I, including the nineteen twenties, fifties, and sixties. Furthermore, if one compares the available statistics on the nineteenth-century performance of advanced capitalist countries with performance during the twentieth century, the growth rates do not support the thesis of flagging growth. Nor do the investment ratios, the proportions of national output plowed back into

the building of new plant, suggest a flagging of investment; these ratios
have tended to be higher in recent decades than they were in comparable decades of the last century. Nor does the history of technology
suggest some flagging of underlying opportunities. Not only is the information revolution in full swing, with clearly very dramatic technological changes in the offing, but the nuclear power industry is
probably still in its infancy with the long-term prospect for fusion
power promising. And at lower levels in the invention hierarchy there
has never been as much activity as at present.[2]

Paul Sweezy continues to subscribe to the stagnationist thesis, as
did Paul Baran in his major works. It is still a popular view among
radical economists of a variety of persuasions, including, for example,
Ernest Mandel. But it seems an unnecessarily restrictive view of monopoly capitalism, and one that clearly has not been established as a
product of careful and detailed empirical work. Given that fact and
the fact that the crude evidence does not support the thesis, I think
"volatility" is a better characterization of monopoly capitalism's movement through time.[3]

There is no need to repeat here the arguments of chapter 9 in
defense of this assertion. However, there is some need to relate this
difference in interpretation to the current problems of stagflation,
ecology, and resource constraints. In the first place, the effect of these
three phenomena is to reduce the potential growth rate of monopoly
capitalism. The stagnationist prediction of declining growth rates may
very well be vindicated in coming years. However, this problem is
occurring in a very different context from that of the earlier discussion.
Capitalism has lurched into a new state of crisis. This time the resource constraints reflect not a current exhaustion of resources but a
conflict between monopoly capital and the Third World, one in which
the ability of the Third World to defend its interests and its national
domain is increasing. The ecological crisis is a product of the distortions that occur in a regime where production is for profit rather than
for use. That has, of course, always been true, but it becomes a genuine
crisis only when capitalism has achieved tremendous growth, so that
we are literally drowning in the by-products of profit-seeking production activity. Stagflation is one of those turbulences in our irrational
system that is not well understood. But clearly it is in considerable
measure a consequence of irrational policies of the past, which generate premature bottlenecks, saddle the economy with a tremendously
demand-distorting overhang of debt, and divert millions of potentially
productive human-years of labor into the system's massive conflict-
resolution effort.

Perhaps stagnation is not so bad a term for this, after all. So long
as one recognizes that this stagnation has different causes and operates
in a different environment than was asserted for the earlier period,
and also recognizes that this stagnation is accompanied by increasing
volatility in the levels of economic activity, the term certainly retains
descriptive power.[4]

However, there is a more serious consequence of the earlier stagnationist thesis when it is combined with the Baran and Sweezy surplus absorption thesis. These two ideas in combination seem to produce a serious distortion of the functioning of monopoly capital. The first, and probably most important, has to do with the nature of imperialism. Let us for the moment accept both stagnation and the Baran/Sweezy version of surplus absorption as the major problem facing monopoly capitalism. And let us think of ourselves as the political leadership of an advanced monopoly capitalist country, considering ways to absorb enough surplus to keep revolution at bay at home, while the system continues to grind out its massive quantities of mostly unsatisfying products. Our problem is only made more difficult by the operations of the multinationals in the Third World, where their ripoff operations are generating and repatriating still more surplus to absorb. What to do?

The reader probably sees the capitalists' presumptive answer. Let the Third World become the sink down which the "excess" surplus flows. A massive program of loans for investment in modern industry and infrastructure, possibly even accompanied by massive grants could, in this context, be of great benefit to the monopolists at home, since they would be expanding to meet the new demand. The jobs created would keep the industrial reserve army at home at its "optimal" or productivity maximizing level, and some small portion of the increased output could be assigned for small increases in real income to domestic workers. For a generation the Third World could be kept in a state of expansion and so perhaps accepting of oppressive, if growth-oriented, political controls. The problem of surplus absorption would thus be substantially mitigated by eliminating the problem of stagnation.

A program of this kind has actually been advocated by some American leaders.[5] However, it has never been implemented. Our foreign aid and loan operations have never been on a scale that could have a significant effect in proportion to the level of relative surplus; also, they have never been increased at a rate that amounted to any significant proportion of the increase in surplus in the United States. If this obviously reformist scheme has been the way out for American monopoly capitalism, it has never been possible to convince any substantial section of the ruling class of that fact.[6]

I think that it is not the ineptness of the ruling class that is responsible. Rather, the thesis represents a misinterpretation of the situation monopoly capitalism has found itself in during the past quarter of a century. Imperialism is a problem central to the structure of monopoly capitalism; it is not something that the capitalist ruling class would be able to eliminate or substantially mitigate if only they would act rationally to serve their own interests as a class. The heart of imperialism lies in the class nature of *both* societies, center and periphery, and in the fact that it is in the interests of the center's ruling class to preserve the national bourgeoisie in power in the periphery. But far from having difficulty absorbing surplus, the various members of the center's ruling class are engaged in a keen struggle among themselves for a larger slice of the surplus pie. The nature of the society, and particularly the "bureaucratic interface" problem discussed in chapter 7, leaves no room for such foreign-aid schemes as the above. In fact, there is keen competition among the monopoly capitalists for an increasing share of the surplus that is still obtainable from the Third World. Stagnation just does not fit this picture.

Another difficulty is raised by the surplus absorption thesis in its Baran/Sweezy form. This is best suggested by the prediction in *Monopoly Capital* that went astray. Using data down through 1963, the authors stated that civilian government expenditures had already reached their peak capacity as surplus absorbers. However, the argument supporting this prediction was rather vaguely drawn and actually did not support so specific an assertion. And the facts almost immediately began to contradict the prediction. In the decade following 1963, civilian government expenditures became the leading absorber of the increasing surplus, far outstripping military expenditures in both average rates and amounts of growth. And, of course, that trend has continued.[7]

What went wrong here? As already noted, the analysis really did not support the prediction. In general, the various assertions in the book about upper limits to government spending, both military and civilian, are unpersuasive. No serious basis was laid for establishing such upper limits. However, it is very important to note that the basic idea of the existence of an upper limit to the share of government spending in total spending under monopoly capital is a sound one. As government gets relatively bigger, the time will come when the system of private property relations will begin seriously to be threatened. At that point a "negation of the negation" process sets in, in which government begins to erode its own effectiveness in carrying out its primary function under the capitalist system. That will clearly be a time of serious crisis. Substantial further relative growth of government spending beyond that level would mean an end to the system of monopoly capital. Clearly Baran and Sweezy were moving in the right direction in their analysis.

These criticisms of Baran and Sweezy obviously need further appraisal. However, that will require serious and detailed study, and cannot be undertaken here. But one point should remain clearly in view. It *is* possible to criticize even fairly fundamental aspects of widely held radical views without losing one's radical perspective. That is the meaning of "constructive criticism" within the framework of radical economics, and a good deal of it is badly needed in order to develop further the plausibility of this system of belief.

CHAPTER 16

Alienation

THERE IS a profound ambiguity inherent in the basic concepts of conventional economics. Consider a term like consumption. On the one hand, it makes a clear and positive reference to relatively easily observable things and events, such as a car or a haircut. On the other hand, it has an essentially personal and subjective meaning, referring to the generation of satisfaction in the individual, the act of consumption, or the expectation of that act. The ambiguity applies to most terms in economics, but nowhere is it clearer than in the meaning of the word "real" in the term real income. Real sounds as if it refers to the first of the above meanings, emphasizing something tangible, or at least observable. But the intent of the word as a modifier of "income" is to indicate that with this concept we are getting down to measuring the amount of the good in a way that is closely associated with satisfaction generation.

An ambiguity of this kind, embedded deeply into the center of the discipline, would seem to be profoundly unscientific. And so it is. Liberal economists are often entirely unaware of the ambiguity; however, their work tends to push them farther and farther toward assuming the objectivist meaning of the term in designing research and interpreting problems. This produces the trappings of real science, avoids difficult issues, and, as we will argue, generates a highly alienated economic "science" and an economist strongly alienated from his object of study.

Alienation has to do with separation, with a division that sets the individual apart from essential portions of her own life. This in turn stunts the individual by depriving him of the possibility of realizing important potentialities. Our economic example suggests one very broad realm in which this separation occurs in the modern world. An individual consumer finds her purchasing power, his objectified income, increasing steadily. Spending this money on an increasing amount and variety of goods, our consumer finds her sense of satisfaction decreasing, is plagued by a feeling of meaninglessness and anxiety, takes to pills or some other soporific, and in time joins the ranks of the seriously ill—but his real income was growing the whole time. Objective real income has become a totally false measure of subjective real income. As we all know, this experience has been the lot of millions of Americans, and their number seems to be growing rapidly.

The conventional economist must ignore this problem, for it would take a complete restructuring of the "science" to deal with it adequately—and besides, in a certain sense conventional economics has been constructed with the purpose of concealing such facts of life. But on this dimension Marxian economics has a very different story to tell. Very possibly Marx's first substantial intellectual achievement consisted of the adaptation of Hegel's concept of alienation so as to make it a powerful characterization of the social aspects of this separation of humans from their own natures and environments.[1] Unfortunately, her descriptive language is very difficult and he did not discuss the concept in an integrated way in her later work. Nevertheless, the basic concept is built right into the heart of Marxian economics and so has played a central role in the radical tradition. The problem of alienation emerges quite naturally in any radical discussion of contemporary economic problems.[2]

However, having once noted this fact, one must also notice an important difficulty. Alienation is a ubiquitous fact of life under capitalism. Its existence and importance is not at all controversial. But it has not proven to be an easy matter to get at the causes of alienation. Empirical research on the subject is quite spotty and superficial, and indeed there are hardly existent well-developed theories to provide a base from which such empirical research could begin. As a result, there is a considerable range of beliefs about the relationship between the extent of alienation, the nature of society, and the appropriate social processes for disalienation. We illustrate with two relatively extreme views, which may be contrasted with the more or less intermediate position argued in various places in Part I.

Marcuse represents one such extreme.[3] She argues that the social adaptation to industrial society has produced a monstrous and all-embracing depersonalization of human life, and a separation of the individual from almost every central aspect of his being and environment. Marcuse thinks of technical progress as "the instrument of domination." It works in direct ways, separating the individual from the product of her labor and from the real meaning of productive labor, in the classical Marxian sense. But it also separates the individual from his own consumption in very similar ways, depriving acts of consumption of their meaning and converting them into acts of symbolic repression of others or into means to some further end. It permeates political activity. Technological domination deprives the individual of her means of critical appraisal of serious political alternatives, turning the welfare state into "a system of subdued pluralism." It even comes to dominate language, fostering the separating, means/end dichotomy, developing an "overwhelming concreteness" to language that once again deforms and withers the human critical faculty, thus finally producing industrial society's ultimate product, the one-dimensional person.

One of Marcuse's most striking images is that of the "happy consciousness." The one-dimensional human comes to identify with his alienated state; this tends to produce a brittle and superficial happiness that seems never to penetrate beneath the surface of life. The happy consciousness believes that "the real is rational and the system delivers the goods." With this image does Marcuse have, among others, the liberal economist in mind?

Marcuse's argument is presented powerfully, the very striking imagery being most effective in conveying the sense of humans trapped in a clean, bright, chrome and plastic hell. Furthermore, she describes in abstract form instances I am sure each reader can find among his own experiences. The reader of Marcuse will find it very difficult to deny that alienation is a central fact of contemporary existence.

However, many radicals find her account of causation less persuasive. The culprit for Marcuse is the industrial society, which seems to mean any society in which modern industry dominates the forces of production. The overwhelming nature of the problem of alienation, as Marcuse sees it, seems to make attempts at change doomed from the start. At times he seems to say that anyone deeply exposed to industrial society has become too tainted to be effective in combating its consequences. At other times, she seems to feel that through education over a long period of time, enough members of industrial society can escape its thrall to bring about the needed changes. But just what those changes are is quite unclear.

Without denying any of the basic Marcusan images of alienation, I think there are more grounds for hope, perhaps even optimism, than he allows. In the first place, there is the argument that technology is endogenous to society. Thus the alienating technology that confronts us today is in part a product of the relations of production of the past, as argued in chapter 3. The implication of this thesis, that we have considerable ability self-consciously to control the directions of future movement of technological change, is that by changing the relations of production we *can* affect alienation. Second, there is no good reason to place all the blame on the forces of production. Even without a lot of fancy machinery, capitalist society was able effectively to depersonalize human relations; after all, Marx's powerful statement of the problem of alienation was written when the technological features of contemporary industrial society were almost entirely unknown. And finally, not all radicals would want to place as much emphasis on alienation as Marcuse has. They would note that Marcuse was himself not an economist, and that the kind of emphasis she places on this one issue tends to mute the role of the material conditions of production, forces and relations both, as the base from which such superstructure questions should be analyzed.

This last point brings us to our other extreme position, represented by the Yugoslavs. Yugoslav economists tend to have very little to say about alienation. When they do mention the concept, it is usually the objective form they are discussing: By alienated labor they simply mean labor power that has been stripped of control over the means of production with which it is to be combined. But that is not to say that alienation is not taken seriously. Rather, the Yugoslavs seem to have a different view as to how disalienation occurs.[4]

For this school of thought, alienation and power are very closely linked. Product and productive activity alienation result from lack of control of one's environment, and by implication consumption, political, and other more diffuse forms of alienation are similarly a product of lack of power. Hence the problem of disalienation is not one of reeducation but of providing that power to the workers. Workers' management is, of course, the major device proposed by the Yugoslavs in the service of this goal. By returning to the worker genuine influence over the conditions of work and over the nature of the products of her work, he will tend to lose that sense of separation from her environment, to become once again whole. In realizing this aim the worker must learn to understand his factory's alternatives, and learn how effectively to defend her choices within the community of workers. In this way that critical faculty that is the hallmark of Marcuse's two-dimensional human is restored.

Disalienation in this theory is an emergent property of increasing power. But it is important to note that the power must be genuine; that is, it must entail the ability of the workers to really decide for themselves about those major elements of their work environments. And this in turn means that the workers must be properly informed. There must be full access to any information *they* deem necessary in appraising their alternatives. Consequently, disalienation can only develop within a relatively open environment.

The emphasis on disalienation as an emergent phenomenon is important. The suggestion is that there is no privileged group in society that already knows what it is to be disalienated, and that can serve as a vanguard to lead the rest of society in the right direction. Rather, it is argued that the workers will define for themselves their own future states of consciousness, and that those states will be a joint product of the democratic conditions of labor and their own emergent natures. The best society from the point of view of disalienation is the most open and democratic one.

This is an argument with great appeal, and much of it has found its way into the optimal radical economic world view. However, it does seem to ignore some essential problems and uncertainties. One major problem that the above argument—though not in fact the Yugoslavs—ignore is the problem of transition, especially in a world that still contains hostile and powerful capitalist regimes. A second issue it ignores is that of the remnants of previous social structures that survive for a long time after the revolution. In Yugoslavia nationality differences have been perhaps the most persistent of these remnants. And finally, it seems a bit one-sided. In effect it ignores the difficulties raised by Marcuse. The workers by themselves do not have the capacity to design a new and disalienated technology; to do this will require a joint and self-conscious effort by broad segments of many societies. To the extent that the democratic associations of workers are constrained in their choices to essentially alienating technologies, technologies that strongly condition the environment of work, the power to choose has not really been acquired by the worker communities.

Both Marcuse and the—somewhat vulgarized in our account—Yugoslavs have important things to say about alienation. When toned down a bit, they seem more to complement than to contradict one another. But one should remember that we are still very ignorant of the causes and cures of alienation. There are a variety of modes of production operating in the world today. Careful study of alienation as it has historically affected these various societies will hopefully provide us with stronger guidelines for the future. Nevertheless, I doubt that either view described in this chapter will prove to have been fundamentally wrong.

CHAPTER 17

Horvat

BRANKO HORVAT is the most interesting and probably the best known of Yugoslav economists. Though his views are highly original, they are also strongly supportive of the basic thrust of the Yugoslav way to socialism. Horvat is well trained in both Marxism and neoclassical economics. He probably represents his generation's best shot at making tenable an eclectic socialist economics, one that mixes the strong features of both those strands of economic thought to provide an integrated socialist analysis of socialism—and of capitalism too. In this chapter we first outline some of his major arguments and then offer a few comments.[1]

Horvatism

Despite Marx's tremendous intellectual accomplishments, including unusual prescience as to future trends in the development of capitalism, there are two major trends in the twentieth century that were incorrectly or incompletely foreseen by him. The first of these is state capitalism, which may be taken either as the highest stage of capitalism or the lowest stage of socialism. Marx correctly foresaw the rise of large-scale organizations. Indeed, this rise is inevitable, meaning by inevitability that large-scale organizations are both feasible forms of organization and of superior efficiency to the petty capitalist organizations of a century ago. What Marx failed to see was the class conflict that is inherent in bureaucratic systems of control. Once the bureaucracy is established as a dominant system of economic control, a class is created with an interest in preserving its power and relative affluence against outsiders.

   As noted above, it makes little difference whether such a society calls itself socialist or capitalist. It does, however, make some difference whether it is essentially one big bureaucracy or not, and whether it developed out of capitalist preconditions. Max Weber pointed correctly both to the efficiency properties of rational bureaucracy and to the importance of rational capitalist calculation as an element in promoting that efficiency. As a consequence of the absence of a developed capitalist rationalism, a bureaucracy imposed on an underdeveloped country will be especially inefficient. However, Ludwig von Mises pointed to a vital aspect of bureaucracy that Weber ignored, namely, the absence of a basis for rational calculation within a large-scale organization that does not contain internal markets. In addition, there are the usual problems of bureaucracy: information absorption and distortion by supercautious middle-level bureaucrats, the aggregative and therefore rough-and-ready nature of the key highly centralized decisions of the top leadership, the tendency to "pass responsibility up and work down," and so on; all of which make very large bureaucracies extremely inefficient. The tendency toward capitalist concentration thus produces at first a higher and more efficient stage of society, but it also contains the seeds of its own destruction as still further growth tends to produce unwieldiness rather than rationality.

The second modification of the classical Marxist picture of social development leads to the assertion of the inevitability of worker control, inevitable again in the sense that it represents a feasible social form whose efficiency is superior to that of the historically preceding form. As to the first aspect of inevitability, there is a clear trend toward increasing worker participation in management. Partly as a consequence of the workers' natural inclinations, there has been some attempt to establish factory committees during every major revolution from 1848 through the Russian and other revolutions around World War I to those of Poland and Hungary of 1956. Partly as a consequence of the needs of state capitalist government, some measure of worker control has been introduced in a number of nationalized industries, and in Great Britain, Germany, and the United States, among others, during wartime. Partly as a consequence of the initiative of enlightened captalists, from profit sharing to production conferences, it has served to increase efficiency and therefore profits. This broad trend strongly suggests both feasibility and superior efficiency. However, it was not likely that full-scale worker control of industry would come first to a developed state capitalist society. What was needed was, first, a revolution to sweep away traditional attitudes and authority in a less-developed country, and then a developing trend toward workers' management that preceded the entrenchment of the new bureaucracy. Hence, Yugoslavia provided the first instance of this higher form of society, which realizes for the first time the ultimate Marxian aim of free associations of workers.

On the morrow of the revolution, the new society faces a number of key policy choices that, implemented over the years, will have a vital impact on the question of whether the political revolution will turn out to have been successful. Of course, in a Third World country one of these choices must be with respect to the tempo of economic development. However, many observers have failed to note that this issue is not one of consumption now vs. consumption later. A well-designed policy can actually do both. The point is that, by devoting rapidly increasing resources to investment, the general productivity of the economy can be increased enough to accommodate both an increase in consumption and the increased allocation of resources to investment. This principle was discovered in the Soviet Union in the twenties and has been widely—if not always efficiently—applied in socialist countries ever since.

Since history operates strongly through efficiency in generating new social systems, the choice of regimes of resource allocation is another crucial decision the new socialist leadership must face. The evidence favors markets as a major resource allocator under socialism. In fact, market processes generate salable levels of output and prices that reflect true levels of relative scarcity better than do bureaucracies, particularly those Third World bureaucracies that have not yet been through their rationalist purging. But, of course, markets cannot be the only planning mechanism. The society's leadership must monitor outcomes and be prepared to intervene with self-consciously planned solutions to problems in areas where the market does not, or obviously cannot, produce efficient results.

Consequently, in an optimal socialist regime enterprises will be controlled by the workers, who strive to maximize the profits of the enterprise, receiving a share in the profits as well as wages for their efforts. The profits share represents a return to the workers for their newfound function as entrepreneurs. Since the state, through the planning board, will also be involved in many investment decisions, as well as in setting overall lines of development for the economy, it too is entitled to a share as joint entrepreneur. And since this entrepreneurship is diffused throughout a socialist society, no particular workers' collective can claim title to the full profits generated by the market operations of the enterprise.

The ultimate optimal distribution of income will be egalitarian. This, of course, follows from well-known principles of socialist equity; it can also be derived from the basic assumptions of neoclassical economics. However, initially the distribution of income will be inegalitarian, reflecting the fact that in the earlier stages of a socialist regime the workers continue to have a strong personal material incentive. By paying more for more and better work, productivity is enhanced, and consequently so are both the growth rate and the current rate of consumption of the entire society. However, historical trends show that as output per capita increases, the effects of differential incomes on productivity tend to decrease. So the rule for distribution —maximum equality consistent with maximum production—will, over time, generate a more and more egalitarian current income distribution. At some point the participatory spirit becomes dominant and society begins truly to move beyond the stage of socialism.

There must be a central authority in society, both for defense against external threat and to provide domestic order. In addition, there is a third vital function for such an authority, namely, to provide basic guidelines for the further social development and to provide the educational base for that development. The Communist party is the logical agency to serve as this central authority. However, once the new socialist society has established its basic institutions and sees them functioning effectively, the party must not continue to function as if it were still engaged in a desperate and clandestine struggle to overthrow the government. Since there are many choices to be made and much uncertainty as to which course is best, the party must be an organization within which a continual dialogue takes place. Furthermore, there must be internally democratic decision processes at work, even though hierarchic structure cannot be avoided. Each level of the party must be capable of compelling the next higher level to consider seriously its proposals, and decisions at each level must involve the principle of majority rule. In this way both at the top and the bottom the social institutions are providing models of democratic and participatory decision making to the rest of society.

Commentary

Clearly, there are some very important differences of viewpoint between Horvat on the one hand and Baran and Sweezy on the other. Probably it is reasonable to say that Horvat comes much closer to a view that a conventional economist might find acceptable than do the other authors; perhaps Marcuse represents in some sense the opposite extreme from Horvat. Nevertheless, some portion of the apparent differences is attributable to different emphases rather than straight disagreements. And this in turn can mean that to some extent these authors are complementing one another's work rather than being mutually contradictory.

Consider the case of the treatment of bureaucracy. In Part I we put main emphasis on the mixing of politics and bureaucracy as the generator of waste under monopoly capitalism. Baran and Sweezy emphasize the difficulty in finding a use for the rapidly rising surplus under that regime, despite the existence of very obvious unmet needs. Horvat, in contrast, attacks the inability of a bureaucracy effectively to appraise its alternatives, to measure the net benefits of alternative courses of action, as the principal culprit in generating inefficiency. One notes that these are not mutually contradictory positions. It is quite conceivable, even plausible, that all three are at work simultaneously in producing the appalling mess that we call monopoly capitalism. It would be useful to have a more definitive view as to the relative importance of the three factors, which is of course a task for serious empirical investigation. In this area radical economics is well stocked with plausible hypotheses, and it would seem that the radical position's plausibility would not be significantly affected whichever one turned out to be the more nearly correct one.

The issue of worker control is somewhat different.[2] *All* socialists believe in some form of worker control over their own worklives and over society's productive activities. But there are substantial disagreements as to just how control is to be exercised and over which variables are to be controlled locally and which centrally. The Chinese, for example, subscribe to the vanguard-party thesis, which means that worker control is somewhat indirect. Nevertheless, the Chinese work hard to make the relationship as direct as possible by such devices as having workers and managers perform one another's work for certain periods of time, and by forming joint teams of workers, technicians, and cadres to solve enterprise problems. Horvat wants to put direct control over the key enterprise decision variables—output, working conditions, investment—into the hands of the factory's own workers. However, such worker bodies are still constrained by state policy and framework legislation, and also by the operation of the market, which determines many aspects of the consequences of alternative courses of action.

A difference of the above kind is rather fundamental. Our optimal radical takes the tack that there are many ways to socialism, that one of these may be best in one environment, the other in another; we also argue that just what should be done in the area of worker control is not yet known with full confidence, so that further social experiment is not only in order but should be respected by other socialists. That is especially true since all socialists agree that a major feature of capitalism, namely, the distortions of class, must be substantially eliminated as a precondition for meaningful worker control. Both the above forms of worker control may meet this test.

At a somewhat lower level of generality, there are likely to be disagreements with Horvat's assertion that a regime involving workers' management, in a market environment where each collective tries to maximize its own income, can be very efficient. There is a neoclassical theory that suggests this may not be the case. For example, the fact that in such an enterprise the income shares going to capital and labor are not separated by the operation of markets could cause deviations from efficient use of resources. Just how serious these deviations might be is unknown at the moment. Here once again we have an area of controversy that further experience and study can go a long way to resolve.[3]

But the most serious objection to Horvat's theory is likely to emphasize a different aspect of market socialist behavior. Some socialists argue for the slogan, Beware the market, it is capitalism's Trojan horse! The anarchic market can be very disruptive. But, perhaps more important, the market serves to inculcate selfish and materialistic values, pitting individual collectives against society in a struggle for the surplus. These issues were discussed in chapter 10, but our conclusions were eclectic and tentative. All one can say is that today the disagreement has become somewhat muted, with former "enemies" of the market such as Sweezy and Bettelheim now agreed that it does have some possibly substantial role to play under socialism.[4] That still leaves a substantial gap with respect to Horvat's views.

And so it goes with other issues, such as the role of the planning board, the role of income distribution, and the changing role of the party. Horvat has offered an integrated and thoroughgoing theory of social movement in contemporary state capitalist and socialist society. His ideas have not yet been subjected to a systematic appraisal within the body of radical literature. In this chapter our primary aim has been to show that such an appraisal is very much needed.

CHAPTER 18

Technical Economics vs. Radical Economics?

AS NOTED in chapter 1, radical economics has had a very mixed record of development in the twentieth century. Before World War I it appeared as a rapidly developing new social science. There was a strong underlying core of common beliefs, based primarily on Marx, combined with a very lively development of controversy, the central issues relating to the nature of imperialism, the rise of finance capitalism, and the possibility of an evolutionary development of socialism. But this great promise was not realized in the interwar period. The crisis of monopoly capitalism, the destruction of human life in the war and its aftermath, the rise of a socialist state that was challenged at every turn by its capitalist rivals: These were perhaps the central social factors inhibiting the further development of radical economic science and the radical economic world view. Another factor, as noted earlier, was also of undoubted importance: namely, that monopoly capitalism was lurching from one catastrophe to another while socialism was just getting off the ground in an extremely unfriendly environment; consequently, the fundamental tendencies in both these social forms were not easy to perceive.

It was not until the nineteen fifties that a substantial turnaround began to occur. Key figures in this development in the Anglo-American world were Maurice Dobb and Paul Sweezy, together with Paul Baran. They served both to keep the idea of radical scholarship alive among English-speaking economists and to develop the science further in their own works. But during much of their careers they were rather lonely voices. When once again interest in alternatives to capitalism began to be a serious matter of concern, they provided the base on which further discussion could occur.

The first stage in this new development consisted in the generation of new syntheses, new attempts to characterize the general structure and tendencies in contemporary political economies. The leading names have already been mentioned more than once in these pages, and include Baran, Dobb, Horvat, Mandel, Marcuse and Sweezy. Their works of synthesis essentially were a set of competing economic world views, posing for radical economics the question of the extent to which they could be reconciled once again, as had been the case a half century earlier, to a common core of belief. It must be admitted, however, that these works, despite their obvious differences, did not generate much in the way of attempts at appraisal and synthesis. To my knowledge, Part I of this work is the first attempt to do this, though hopefully not the last.

The next stage, naturally enough, consists in developing a radical scholarship that attempts to explore in detail various relevant aspects of the structure and tendencies of political economies. Efforts at appraising the rather general factual assertions that appear in economic world views are a part of this. So is effort devoted to resolving differences among competing radical world views. So is the development of a serious running critique of liberal economics, both at the methodological and the substantive levels. Clearly, the carrying out of each of these types of activity requires the joint efforts of a considerable number of radical economic scholars. What was still not feasible even in the sixties has become possible today, for trained radical economists now exist, perhaps for the first time, in sufficient numbers and under conditions that are not inconsistent with the carrying out of this program of scholarly work.

However, there is still an argument that questions the desirability of taking this step. It has several parts, and we react differently to these parts, so we will take them one at a time. First there is the argument that the revolution cannot wait for such nit-picking activities; making it happen requires the full-time efforts of all radicals. This seems to have been a widespread feeling among younger radicals during the sixties, but has waned considerably. The change in part reflects a recognition that the revolution may not come to many monopoly capitalist countries for a long time, but perhaps it has come mostly from a growing recognition that what happens after the revolution is connected in important ways to what happens before. Revolutions can go astray, and especially the leadership can lose contact with the masses. If difficulties such as those that have beset the Soviet Union are not to happen elsewhere, two things must be done. First, the masses must be prepared for revolution; they must understand its purpose and as many as possible of them must participate in bringing it about. Second, the leadership must understand that it is the representative of the masses, which means that it is not beyond the reach of democratic processes. Bringing about such a revolution is a complex matter and requires, among other things, that radical scholarship must be able to make its case effectively, in an environment of serious intellectual struggle with its liberal rival. On this ground the future of radical scholarship now seems secure.

A second argument suggests that radical scholarship, having a function very much different from conventional scholarship, will also have a different future history. The basic function of radical scholarship, so this argument goes, is to understand the structure and tendencies of monopoly capitalism with a view to eradicating it. But this implies that radical scholarship will lose its meaning on the morrow of the revolution. Its basic function is to put itself out of business. Such a position implies much more emphasis on political tactics rather than detailed scholarship as the primary object of study.

There are two objections to this orientation. The first is that it implies that all revolutions will be successful, or at least that the successful ones can be recognized when they occur; that sounds a bit utopian. The second, and related, objection is that it assigns a rather small significance to an intellectual movement that has had a very profound and worldwide impact over the past century. It seems more likely that radical economics has a general perspective toward the investigation of fundamental properties of political economies that, at least in part, transcends medium-term transformations of the relations of production. Indeed, I would be inclined to argue that one of the main potential supports to continuing the initial success of a revolution lies in the existence of a body of radical political economists who can continue to appraise the structure and tendencies of the system.

A third argument raises more complex issues and will occupy the remainder of this chapter. It holds that the problem with radical scholarships lies not in its purely temporary significance but in its class bias. To the extent that it embraces neoclassical economics, it is tainted with bourgeois values and elitism. To the extent that it relies on technical Marxism it, together with most liberal economics, is divorced from the world of reality. And to the extent that it apes the nit-picking of contemporary historical scholarship, it preserves "reality" at the cost of triviality. There is, I believe, some truth to each of these charges. Let us take them up in order.

The first problem with neoclassical economics is its elitism. This is inherent in the method. It presumes that there is a specialist group, the master of its arcane language and techniques, who are the only ones who can successfully solve economic problems. It is especially well adapted to serving the needs of bureaucrats, and has been spreading like wildfire in recent years as a technique applied throughout bureaucracies. Socialist societies have found their own bureaucratic classes split on the question of using neoclassical economics, but the more "progressive," i.e., technocratic among them tend unequivocally to support these techniques. It gives the bureaucracy a tremendous advantage in dealing with outsiders, such as the masses, simply because of its highly technical nature, and the large costs that must be incurred to generate a "scientific" result.[1]

If this were the only way to get at the truth about how economies work and how to design policies, then we would all be in the freedom-is-the-appreciation-of-necessity box together. But that is just not the case. In fact, much of the technical side of economics is pure mystification, self-serving to the affluent and influential economics profession. Relatively simple techniques, which can be understood by very broad segments of the population, suffice to support nearly all of our current genuine knowledge about how economies work. Further efforts could expand this demystified realm even further. For example, the Chinese at one point were teaching "people's operations research" to the peasantry. The idea was to get peasants to think in elementary quantitative terms about the cost and productivity of alternative methods of plowing or planting or machine use. A certain amount of effort spent in obtaining relevant numbers, plus a few simple calcula- tons, sufficed to give peasants who typically had no more than a pri- mary education the full basis for making their own decisions in these areas of central collective concern. By recognizing that in economics "crude is beautiful, sophisticated is bourgeois," an important element of participation, and no doubt of disalienation, was introduced into peasant life. Hopefully that movement will spread.

A second problem with neoclassical economics is that its technical structure fundamentally reflects its philosophical origins. It is the science of society of the rising bourgeoisie. As such it assumes right at its heart that individuals are what count and that the relations of production are thoroughly privatized. These assumptions come in through price theory. The efficiency properties of neoclassical "solu- tions" to economic problems are inevitably based on price theory. For example, a fundamental assumption of the theory of consumer behavior is that one person, or family, or consumption unit's satisfaction from a particular consumption package is independent of the satisfaction of other consumption units. Exit socialism right there! The corresponding assumption with respect to production, which has production carried out in atomized units, flies in the face of the trend, already noted by Marx and consequently more than a century old, toward increasing socialization of the forces of production. It is this assumption that leads to the neoclassical economist's helplessness in the face of ecological and environmental problems. Neoclassical economics is both unso- cialist and unhistorical in more than one sense of each word.

Neoclassical economics has *some* helpful things to say about how societies work. Mathematics and statistics, as is now almost uni- versally recognized by radical economists, are not apologetic wherever and whenever they are used. The problem is one of emphasis and of the nature of the particular use to which these tools are put. But con- trolling the tools has proven to be an extremely difficult job. Unfor- tunately, even though they are irrelevant, mathematical games are, like chess, fun to play. In American academia playing these fun games is, in addition, the best way to have a successful career. These pressures are very insidious and are felt by radical as well as by conventional economists who are caught up in the atmosphere of contemporary academe. Recently, for example, there has been a substantial prolifera- tion of mathematical Marxism. Much of this literature is designed to show that models derived from Marx's theories of value and of ex- panded reproduction can be brought to bear on contemporary economic puzzles as effectively as corresponding neoclassical models. Some of this work has served the useful purpose of exposing difficulties in the neoclassical models. Some of it has usefully criticized the narrowness of those models, as in debunking the notion that capital is a separate and homogeneous factor of production, or that production and distribution can be separated in analyzing economic growth. However, these models are in fact profoundly un-Marxist. They tend to accept the questions asked by bourgeois economists as the starting point for their development. This usually condemns them to irrelevance, as well as to elitist mystifying of the historical processes that generate economic development. Development of this literature distracts radical economists from their central task of developing a pragmatic and intelligible economics that will grasp the dynamic and historical nature of the contemporary crisis and the forces making for further change.

There is a third kind of trap that radical scholars can fall into. This one, perhaps surprisingly, is Marxist exegetics. Marx continues to be an author whom every serious radical economist will have read carefully. Understanding Marx for a Marxist also means understanding the historical context in which he developed his ideas. In the same way, a radical economist will feel obliged to acquire an understanding of the development of political economic thought in the twentieth century as an aid in grasping the forces at work on contemporary intellectuals. But here the radical economist must once again be careful to find the right line. Too much of too many radical journals is devoted to painstaking analysis of aspects of Marx's thought, or of that of leading Marxists of the past, without any effort being made to relate the arguments to the real problems of the twentieth century. This too it seems can be a pleasant and escapist game to play, distracting the analyst once again from the main line of effort.

A second difficulty can arise if one begins to worry about whether a particular line of argument is really Marxist or not. In many socialist countries economists have not been able effectively to deal with problems of economic valuation because they are constrained to a pricing schema that can be found somewhere in *Capital*. This misconceives Marx's own notions as to the course of development of ideas and so is self-contradictory. It also suffers from the fact, argued in chapters 5 and 6 above, that Marx's value theory is no longer an adequate characterization of the value problem in either monopoly capitalism or socialism.

These difficulties have hampered the development of radical economics in the twentieth century and have no doubt contributed to feelings that radical scholarship was perhaps unnecessary. But all they really demonstrate is that radical scholarship is difficult. Operating in a relatively hostile environment in which the structure of incentives and the intellectual milieu combine to encourage elitism and game playing, the radical scholar must have a very firm sense of purpose if she is to succeed in making a useful intellectual contribution. A well-developed radical economic world view that provides a coherent, inclusive, and integrated appraisal of the central economic issues of our time could be helpful in affirming that sense of purpose.[2]

CHAPTER 19

The Role of Revolution

ON THE LEFT, attitudes toward revolution have probably been converging in recent years. It has become increasingly apparent that Third World countries will not be allowed to embrace socialism by an evolutionary process mediated by parliamentary democracy. Violent revolution, as the Chinese are always saying, seems unavoidable as an instrument of the transition. This is not a matter of preference by the left; rather, it is an alternative chosen for the left by the forces representing monopoly capital. If the latter could establish their willingness to let such things as referenda and genuinely representative parliaments decide periodically whether to go the socialist way or not, a very large segment of the left would immediately drop its revolutionary orientation. But as was argued in Part I, this alternative is, if anything, less likely to occur now than before. Revolution is the only alternative to continued massive misery and oppression.

However, the social democratic deviation has not disappeared and at times can be a very powerful lure to leftists in one country or another. The key ingredient of this deviation is its promise of jobs and influence to the leadership via parliamentary participation. Social democratic parties retain their formal identities, and they often continue for years to use the revolutionary language of their earlier days. But parliamentary participation is a true Trojan horse for a revolutionary party. In examples from Germany to Chile, it has shown its ability to erode revolutionary interest and organization, its ability to inculcate the art of parliamentary deal making and its corollary, not rocking the boat. When the crunch comes the starch is gone; the crunch came in Germany in the early thirties and in Chile in the early seventies, and the outcomes were very similar. But the seeds of failure were in both cases sown over a period of decades of participation by the leadership in the local parliament, where the only real road open to them was that of loyal opposition.

However, the problem of revolution has become much more complicated in the homelands of monopoly capital. In all of the most advanced countries, there is a strong "democratic" left and a weak revolutionary left. There is relatively little support among the mass of the urban workers for a revolutionary program, and the peasantry tends to be relatively small and affluent. In the United States the existence of a powerful military, trained since the sixties in the arts of "riot control," complicates the problem still further, as does the existence and possible irrational use of nuclear weapons. As noted in chapter 11, there is no obvious way to describe feasible paths to revolution in these countries.

It was once fashionable to characterize stages in the development of a revolution. By such an accounting the United States is presently in a rather quiescent state. At such times the emphasis tends to be placed on movement building rather than on direct action. Some writers have suggested that it may take decades of movement building for success to become a visible prospect. Others have emphasized the state of objective crisis in which monopoly capital finds itself, a state that shows every promise of continuing and at times intensifying. For the latter emphasis, clearly there is an important immediate goal: building a movement capable of acting should a crisis opportunity emerge in the near future.

Attractive as such an approach must seem, we have argued against it, primarily on the ground that the left is not prepared intellectually for the very complex demands that revolution and its aftermath pose in monopoly capitalist countries. Programs of the splinter groups currently active run from support for institutions similar to those in each of the major existing socialist countries to a variety of policy platforms whose implementation is both dubious and essentially undefended. The conditions of revolution and the splintered state of the left would not permit any reasoned or democratic resolution of these differences. At least the groundwork for that process of resolution has to be laid first. And then there is the consideration, given great emphasis in many segments of the American left, that democracy must be an integral part of socialism in America. Surely this means that a substantial segment of the population must come to recognize the advantages of dramatic structural change of the American economy well before the revolution.

Can such an educational effort be carried out without producing essentially the social democratic deviation? Won't institutions such as schools and universities and other potential workplaces for radicals have much the same effect on their values as would participation in a legislature? Certainly it is a risk, but what is the alternative? The success of revolution in America depends on the failure of monopoly capitalism in America. If the latter doesn't happen, then the former surely won't. If revolution is going to happen, it will cast its shadow well beforehand. A successful movement will have to be one that can perceive the shadow, interpret it persuasively, and offer some realistic vision of a better world. Opinions can certainly differ as to how best to carry out such an effort. But if opinions continue to differ so substantially and bitterly over the program, the policy, then the effort is probably doomed to failure.

A central message of this book is that from the economic side there appears to be a firm base for the development of substantial unity of intellectual orientation on the revolutionary left. This base is rooted in Marxism, but involves recognition that much of Marx's analysis needs substantial revision before it can interpret successfully the events of the twentieth century. It is based on a belief that successful revolutions can occur, that they have occurred, and have transformed whole societies. It is based on a belief that there are still, as far as we can tell, many paths to socialism, and so is based on tolerance of diverse revolutionary experiments around the world. And it is based on a belief in the need for political unity in the revolutionary left within each of the advanced countries of monopoly capitalism as a precondition for success. But for that to happen there must be, to put it bluntly, further study.

Notes*

Chapter 1

1. Paul Baran, *The Political Economy of Growth* (New York: Monthly Review, 1957).* The second edition, dating from 1962, contains reactions to reviews of the book and further comments, especially on socialism.

2. Paul Baran and Paul Sweezy, *Monopoly Capital* (New York: Monthly Review, 1966).*

3. Ernest Mandel, *Marxist Economic Theory,* 2 vols. (New York: Monthly Review, 1968).* The French original was published in 1962.

4. Ernest Mandel, *Late Capitalism* (New York: Monthly Review, 1976).

5. Branko Horvat, *Toward a Theory of Planned Economy* (Belgrade: Yugoslav Institute for Economic Research, 1968). The Serbo-Croatian original appeared in 1964, and reportedly was completed several years earlier.

6. Our list, of course, does not contain the names of all seminal contemporary radical writers. In particular, the names of Jürgen Habermas, Jean Althusser, and Charles Bettelheim are missing, the first two because their contributions are primarily methodological in nature, the third because he underwent a dramatic change in orientation in the sixties. A discussion of methodological issues is beyond the terms of reference of this work, which concentrates on arguments that contribute more directly to the understanding of contemporary society. Bettelheim's name will crop up in later chapters.

7. George Wang, ed., *Fundamentals of Political Economy* (White Plains, N.Y.: Sharpe, 1977).

8. Mao Tse-tung, *Selected Works* (Peking: Foreign Languages Press, 1961–1977).

9. John Gerassi, *Venceremos* (New York: Clarion, 1968).*

10. Clearly, the time has come to eliminate an anachronism from the English language, namely, the mandatory sexual distinction when using personal pronouns. In an effort to hasten the process of elimination, I shall alternate the use of the feminine she/her with the masculine he/him throughout this book.

A brief argument in defense of this procedure is in order, even though this is by no means the first time it has been used. Given the structure of American society a century or a century and a half ago, it would have been quite convenient, certainly for whites and possibly even for blacks, to have pronouns that distinguished individuals and groups by race. The society was thoroughly permeated by racism and so it would have been "natural" for this to have become embedded in the structure of language. This did not happen because the morphology of language tends to change slowly, much more slowly than have societies in the era of the industrial revolution. But had such pronouns emerged then, radicals would unquestionably have long ago found their continued use intolerable. The subservence of women began much earlier so that there was plenty of time for the pronominal distinction of sex to become deeply embedded in the language. But surely the reasons for eliminating that distinction are as pressing as are those for the elimination of racism.

There remains the question of the specific manner of dealing with the problem adopted in this book. The first thing to note is that these days it is rarely an important distinction semantically; for example, in no single instance in the present work do ambiguities of meaning result from the assumption that all pronouns used are unspecific with respect to sex. Second, I ask the reader to bear with the usage through a reading of the book before drawing conclusions. More than one reader of the prepublication text found that by the time he had finished the text the usage no longer seemed particularly strange to her. It is a simple and effective device and involves no annoying search for circumlocutions.

* Starred items are available in paperback edition.

Chapter 2

1. Richard Edwards, Michael Reich, and Thomas Weisskopf, eds., *The Capitalist System, A Radical Analysis of American Society*, 2nd ed. (Englewood Cliffs, N.J.: Prentice-Hall, 1972) * is a collection of readings organized along the same lines as the present chapter.

2. A statistical picture of inequality and of the poverty, malnutrition, and even hunger that are a common and persistent fact of life among poorer Americans can be found in a pamphlet by Letitia Upton and Nancy Lyons, *Basic Facts: Distribution of Personal Income and Wealth in the U.S.* (Cambridge, Mass.: Cambridge Institute, 1972) and in *Ten-State Nutrition Survey* (Washington, D.C.: U.S. Government Printing Office, 1972). For a useful descriptive and statistical survey of inequality, see Herman P. Miller, *Rich Man Poor Man* (New York: Crowell, 1971).

3. Joseph Kershaw, *Government Against Poverty* (Washington, D.C.: Brookings Institution, 1970).

4. The figure is a guesstimate by the United Nations' Food and Agriculture Organization. As reported in Alan Berg, *The Nutrition Factor* (Washington, D.C.: Brookings Institution, 1973),* chap. 1, the still very high death rates for infants and small children in Third World countries are mostly a product of malnutrition.

5. Simon Kuznets, *Modern Economic Growth, Rate, Structure and Spread* (New Haven: Yale University Press, 1966),* p. 423.

6. A useful survey of American imperial foreign policy can be found in William A. Williams, *The Tragedy of American Diplomacy* (New York: Delta, 1962); see also Franz Schurmann, *The Logic of World Power* (New York: Random House, 1974).*

7. See U.S. Arms Control and Disarmament Agency, *World Military Spending*, an annual publication in recent years. Actually the figure had already reached $216 billion in 1971.

8. Two useful works on this subject are Raymond Franklin and Solomon Resnick, *The Political Economy of Racism* (New York: Holt, 1973),* and Victor Perlo, *Economics of Racism USA* (New York: International, 1975). The facts of women's subservient status in the American economy are described in U.S. Bureau of the Census, *A Statistical Portrait of Women in the U.S.*, Special Studies Series P-23, no. 58, 1976.

9. Franz Fanon, *The Wretched of the Earth* (New York: Grove, 1968),* p. 32.

10. The concept of subdued conflict is developed in Herbert Marcuse, *One-Dimensional Man* (Boston: Beacon, 1964),* esp. chap. 1–4.

11. There are two ways to demonstrate the profound irrationality of capitalist society. Novels often capture the human truth of a dying and corrupt social order most effectively. Works that inspired my generation include Robert Briffault, *Europa* (New York: Scribner's, 1935), dealing with the European ruling classes before World War I; Martin Anderson Nexö, *Ditte*, 3 vols. (New York: Holt, 1920–22), the story of a working-class woman's struggle against oppression in Northern Europe; Andre Malraux's two novels of war and revolution, *Man's Fate* (New York: Smith and Haas, 1934), dealing with the Chinese revolution, and *Man's Hope* (New York: Random House, 1938), dealing with the Spanish Civil War; John Steinbeck, *In Dubious Battle* (New York: Modern Library, 1936), the story of a great California farm workers' strike in the thirties; and Henrik Ibsen's *A Doll's House* (Boston: Luce, 1909). A second way is to contrast the reality we experience with the way a more rational social order functions. This contrast, of course, cannot yet be made for the United States, but it *is* possible to do so for China, where victims of the old society have recounted their experiences before and after the revolution. Of special interest are Jan Myrdal's *Report from a Chinese Village* (New York: Random House, 1965) * and William Hinton's *Fanshen* (New York: Random House, 1966),* the latter also showing the detailed process of revolutionary social transformation in a North China village.

Chapter 3

1. A fascinating and lucid account of the development of socialist thought in interaction with the development of capitalist and socialist societies is provided by John Gurley, *Challengers to Capitalism* (San Francisco: Chandler, 1976).*

2. Anyone who wishes to understand contemporary radical economic thought must know something about Marx's theories. An extremely lucid and simple introductory survey was produced by John Eaton, *Political Economy, A Marxist Text-*

book (New York: International, 1963).* Perhaps the best English-language account of Marxian economics remains Paul Sweezy's *Theory of Capitalist Development* (New York: Monthly Review, 1942).* These works should not discourage the reader from looking into Marx himself; many of Marx's and Engels's most interesting writings are available in the paperback *Selected Works* volume put out by International Publishers (New York: New World, 1968).* A fascinating and still useful account of Marxism-Leninism is by the two Russian revolutionaries, Nikolai Bukharin and Evgeniy Preobrazhensky, *The ABC of Communism* (Baltimore: Penguin, 1969),* originally published in English in 1922.

3. In the century since Marx a great many historians have been laboring in archives and digs, producing new information about the human past. Some of this has required a revision of Marxian ideas, though his fundamental principles of historical tendencies have not been affected by this mountain of research. The new Marxian interpretation of early history is presented in very readable form in the works of V. Gordon Childe, especially her *What Happened in History?* (London: Pelican, 1954).* The transition from feudalism to capitalism was intensively studied in Maurice Dobb's seminal *Studies in the Development of Capitalism*, rev. ed. (New York: International, 1963),* and very good accounts of key aspects of the industrial revolution have been provided by Eric Hobsbawm's *Industry and Empire* (London; Pelican, 1969) and *The Age of Revolution 1789–1848* (New York: Mentor, 1964). Much of the reinterpretation has been put together in a grand synthesis of Marxian theory and the new Marxist history in the first volume of Mandel's *Marxist Economic Theory* (New York: Monthly Review, 1968). The radical story of American economic development has been recently told in Douglas Dowd's *The Twisted Dream* (Cambridge, Mass.: Winthrop, 1974). A powerful defense of the thesis that relations of production, not technological imperatives, were the primary influences on the rise of the factory system can be found in Stephen Marglin's "What Do Bosses Do?" *Review of Radical Political Economics* 7 (1974–75).

4. A beautiful set of stories of life in the period of capitalism's great end-of-the-century crisis is to be found in Barbara Tuchman's *The Proud Tower* (New York: Macmillan, 1966).* The "climacteric" thesis was first proposed by E. H. Phelps Brown and Handfield-Jones, "The Climacteric of the 1890s: A Study in the Expanding Economy," *Oxford Economic Papers*, 1952, and has been the source of much controversy since. This era stimulated some major controversies among Marxists, of which perhaps the most relevant for the present chapter was that between the "forces of production" and the "relations of production" proponents. The former believed that the Marxian schema of successive stages of transformation of society was quite rigidly forced on societies so that, for example, czarist Russia would have to develop into a fully capitalist society before socialism could become a serious possibility. The latter, of whom Lenin was the best-known figure, argued that a socialist revolution was indeed feasible in an economically backward country. Variants of this important controversy have continued down to the present day, where, for example, in China Liu Shao Ch'i seemed to support a forces-of-production point of view in his policy of primary emphasis on the industrial transformation of China. Mao Tse-tung rejected this notion and in addition has argued that there is an important line of causation in revolutionary China running from the relations of production back to the forces of production, this being a major theoretical argument in his support of the cultural revolution. The consequent interpretation of world history has been outlined in *The History of Social Development* (Shanghai: Shanghai People's Publishing House, 1974), which will soon appear in English.

Chapter 4

1. Revisionist American historians have recently produced a new analysis of the emergence of monopoly capitalism out of the turn-of-the-century crisis. Of particular interest are Gabriel Kolko, *The Triumph of Conservatism, A Reinterpretation of American History, 1900–1916* (Chicago: Quadrangle, 1967),* and James Weinstein, *The Corporate Ideal in the Liberal State, 1900–1918* (Boston: Beacon, 1968). Branko Horvat's *Toward a Theory of Planned Economy*, as well as his *Essay on the Yugoslav Economy* (New York: IASP, 1969), contain a somewhat different theory. Instead of emphasizing the role of individuals in making key structural decisions in the Kolko-Weinstein vein, Horvat sees the emergence as a product of impersonal forces built into the structure and dynamic of early capitalism; he also finds very similar processes at work in the Soviet Union.

2. The list actually totals fifty-four just to the end of the sixties. It is provided

in Lincoln Bloomfield and Amelia Leiss, *Controlling Small Wars, A Strategy for the 70s* (New York: Knopf, 1969), Appendix C.

3. Pierre Jalée, *The Third World in the World Economy* (New York: Monthly Review, 1969), deals with one of the central processes of twentieth-century capitalism, namely, the emergence of the Third World to economic and political prominence and its interaction with developed capitalism. The emergence of the economic structures of European monopoly capitalism in response to crisis is described in several chapters of the *Fontana Economic History of Europe,* edited by Carlo Cipolla, vol. 5, *The Twentieth Century* (London: Collins, 1976). The dimensions of the current crisis are spelled out in the readings in Richard Edwards, Michael Reich, and Thomas Weisskopf, eds., *The Capitalist System, A Radical Analysis of American Society,* 2nd ed. (Englewood Cliffs, N.J.: Prentice-Hall, 1978), and indeed in the pages of almost every issue of the daily press.

4. For historical surveys of the labor issue, see David Gordon, *Theories of Poverty and Underemployment* (Boston: Heath, 1972),* and Harry Braverman, *Labor and Monopoly Capital, The Degradation of Work in the Twentieth Century* (New York: Monthly Review, 1974).

5. According to the official series, which substantially understates the actual magnitude, unemployment in 1938 was again over the 10 million mark, a 35 percent increase over the previous year; in 1939 it was well above the level of three years earlier. *Historical Statistics, of the United States,* U.S. Department of Commerce, 1960, p. 70.

Chapter 5

1. See Paul Mantoux, *The Industrial Revolution in the Eighteenth Century,* rev. ed. (London: Cape, 1961), for a number of harrowing accounts of the consequences of this depersonalization of human relations.

2. The World War II example was described by Baran in *The Political Economy of Growth,* p. 41. Additional data needed to produce the conclusion in the text was provided by the *Historical Statistics of the United States, passim.* Crudely, the calculation is based on two considerations: (1) During World War II only half the total labor force was required to produce a decent standard of living for the American population; (2) productivity per worker has doubled since then. So even after some limited refinement the estimate in the text is quite conservative.

3. See Baran and Sweezy, *Monopoly Capital,* pp. 135–38.

4. Seymour Harris, *The Economics of American Medicine* (New York: Macmillan, 1964), p. 7.

5. For a study suggesting that that paragon of competitive capitalism, the American market for wheat, has an extremely costly information system, see P. L. Schmidbauer, "Information and Communications Requirements of the Wheat Market: An Example of a Competitive System," *Technical Report No. 21,* Center for Research in Management Science, Berkeley: University of California Press, 1966).

6. For references see note 2 of chapter 2.

7. According to the 1976 *Economic Report of the President,* Table B-29, in 1965 "average spendable weekly earnings in private nonagricultural" employment, in 1967 dollars, were $91.30; ten years later they were down slightly to $90.50. Since then inflation has eroded money-wage gains to preserve the stagnation in real terms.

8. For a historical account and analysis, see Marilyn Goldberg *"Housework as a Productive Activity"* (Ph.D. diss., University of California at Berkeley, 1977).

9. For a penetrating account of the development of routinization in American work, see Harry Braverman, *Labor and Monopoly Capital, The Degradation of Work in the Twentieth Century* (New York: Monthly Review, 1974). See also below, chapter 14.

10. In 1974 white infants died during their first year at a rate of 14.8 per thousand live births; "Negro and other" at a rate of 24.9. Maternal deaths follow the same pattern but even more strongly: 10.0 for white women, 35.1 for other races. Data from *U.S. Statistical Abstract* for 1976, p. 64.

11. For a demonstration of the scandalous nature of the official treatment of the concept of unemployment, see Bertram Gross and Stanley Moss, "Real Unemployment is Much Higher Than They Say" in David Mermelstein, ed., *The Economic Crisis Reader* (New York: Random House, 1975),* pp. 32–37. Gross is a recognized expert on the subject. He estimates that the recent real rate of unemployment is about one quarter of our labor force.

12. However, it is widely believed by radical economists to require modification to fit the era of monopoly capitalism. Paul Baran's approach, developed in the two books cited in footnote 1 of chapter 1, was to estimate the size of the surplus generated in capitalist society and to show how that surplus is misused, or lies unused. Joseph Phillips made estimates that are reported at the end of *Monopoly Capital;* however, these estimates need revision. For example, they lump all profits together, though clearly it is the profits of the large corporations that represent the keys to power and influence these days, and profits of the large corporations have been increasing far more rapidly than total profits. See note 7 of chapter 15 below.

However, a fully developed and empirically applicable theory of exploitation under monopoly capitalism has yet to be worked out. Until it is, the workings of exploitation must be studied piecemeal. Among important recent writings that contribute to an understanding of exploitation are: James O'Connor, *The Fiscal Crisis of the State* (New York: St. Martins, 1973),* who provides a theory about several exploitative mechanisms for extracting and allocating surplus through the state; David Gordon, *Theories of Poverty and Underemployment* (Boston: Heath, 1972), who provides an analytical sketch of the two labor markets generated under monopoly capital to match the corporate and market sectors; and Herbert Gintis and Samuel Bowles, *Schooling in Capitalist America* (New York: Basic Books, 1976), who pin down the ways in which fundamental class biases structure American education. Ralph Nader's books provide much detailed information on the operation of the system; an interesting demonstration as to how economic power and political power go hand in hand can be found in the Nader group's recent *The Corporation State, The Monopoly Makers,* Mark J. Green, ed., (New York: Grossman, 1973).* That even so small-scale an institution as the small claims court is immediately subverted from its announced purpose by the system is documented in Dennis O. Flynn, "Reno Small Claims Court: Its Purpose and Performance," University of Nevada, Research Report #10, Bureau of Business and Economic Research, 1973.

Analysis of the class structure of monopoly capitalist society has been the subject of much recent radical discussion and research. T. B. Bottomore, *Classes in Modern Society* (New York: Pantheon, 1966), points out that a class and an elite are two different things, and that contemporary capitalism is still under class control. Some properties of America's ruling class are described in G. William Domhoff's *Who Rules America* (Englewood Cliffs, N.J.: Prentice-Hall, 1967) * and *The Higher Circles* (New York: Vintage, 1970).* The thesis that corporate America is essentially controlled by a managerial group has been accepted by some radical theorists, such as Baran and Sweezy in their *Monopoly Capital* (see esp. chap. 2). The principal opposing view, that control has largely passed into the hands of a much smaller group who, operating through a handful of banks and other financial institutions, are able to control basic decisions for the entire economy is ably defended by David Kotz, *The Role of Financial Institutions in the Control of Large Nonfinancial Corporations,* (Berkeley: University of California Press, 1977). This is one of the most interesting of the controversies among radicals these days, and has important consequences for the understanding of the nature of the contemporary crisis. See also chapters 7 and 15 below.

The issue of alienation raises fundamental questions as to the nature of man and of her responses to changes in the social structure; see chapter 16 below, and the note to that chapter, for further discussion.

Chapter 6

1. *Historical Statistics of the United States,* U.S. Department of Commerce, 1960, pp. 719, 720. Three years after the end of the Vietnam war major national security expenses were up 20 percent in dollar terms.

2. Herbert Gintis and Samuel Bowles, *Schooling in Capitalist America* (New York: Basic Books, 1976). See also Alexander Field's 1974 University of California at Berkeley dissertation, *"Educational Reform and Manufacturing Development in Mid-nineteenth Century Massachusetts."*

3. In 1975 the Department of Health Education and Welfare employed 147,100 persons, while state and local governmental employees in public welfare agencies numbered 339, 400. See *U.S. Statistical Abstract* for 1976, pp. 249, 286.

4. *U.S. Statistical Abstract,* p. 520.

5. These quotes were obtained by Leonard Silk of the *New York Times* staff and his associate, David Vogel, and reported in their book, *Ethics and Profits, The Crisis of Confidence in American Business* (New York: Simon and Schuster, 1976).

Chapter 7

1. Naturally, all broad-gauge radical writers have dealt with the question of instability under monopoly capitalism. Two major lines of argument emerged in recent decades. The first argued that the Keynesian revolution had made it technically possible to use the fiscal and monetary powers of big government to control economic fluctuations. However, it was also argued that effective control was not politically feasible because powerful segments of the capitalist class were bound to be hurt in the short run by any effective control policy (high interest rates, for example, mean more profits for bankers but disaster for building contractors). Paul Sweezy has been a major representative of this school; in *Monopoly Capital* the crisis tends to emerge in the political context of increasing and generalized dismay by the populace at the increasing irrationality of resource allocation in American capitalism.

A second line of analysis does not dispute the above arguments regarding the political and structural deficiencies of the system, but adds the important claim that there are fundamental instabilities built into the economic structure. The recent failure of economic control policies carried out by governments that were listening fairly carefully to conventional economic policy advisors has lent credence to these arguments. However, such analyses have not yet become fully developed or integrated with other aspects of radical economic thought.

2. This is the conclusion of both J. C. R. Dow, *The Management of the British Economy, 1945–60* (Cambridge: Cambridge University Press, 1964), and C. D. Cohen, *British Economic Policy, 1960–69* (London: Butterworths, 1971).

3. See Raford Boddy and J. Crotty, "Class Conflict and Macro-Policy: The Political Business Cycle," *Review of Radical Political Economics* 7 (1975).

4. Ibid.

5. See Fred Block, *The Origins of International Economic Disorder* (Berkeley: University of California Press, 1977).

6. See Anthony Sampson, *The Arms Bazaar* (New York: Viking, 1977).

7. For a characterization of the failures of conventional market theory, see chap. 2 of my *Socialist Economy* (New York: Random House, 1967).

8. Two recent University of California at Berkeley dissertations explore various aspects of the instability of Keynesian economic models: J. C. Benassy, "Disequilibrium Theory," 1973 and Alan Shelly, "A Study in Disequilibrium Macroeconomics," 1974. Victor Perlo, *The Unstable Economy* (New York: International, 1973), offers a more intuitive and institutional account of instability in the American economy. But perhaps the best evidence for this thesis lies in the extremely destructive criticism of Keynesian economics that has been developed more from the right than the left, and of which Axel Leijonhufvud's *Keynesian Economics and the Economics of Keynes* (New York: Oxford University Press, 1968) was an important contribution. At the moment it seems that conservative and liberal economists have each succeeded in destroying the policy arguments of the other side, but neither has a plausible and constructive proposal to put in the place of the defeated position.

9. In an interesting recent paper, "Stagflation and the Political Economy of Decadent Monopoly Capitalism," *Monthly Review*, 28 (October 1976), 14–29, Douglas Dowd has argued that the sprouts of our current crisis were growing rapidly during the relatively stable nineteen fifties.

A useful account of business fluctuations, with references, is Howard Sherman's *Radical Political Economy, Capitalism and Socialism from a Marxist-Humanist Perspective* (New York: Basic Books, 1972), especially chap. 7–9 and 17. Various aspects of the crisis of the seventies are discussed in the URPE collection, *Radical Perspectives on the Economic Crisis of Monopoly Capitalism* (New York: URPE-PEA, 1975),* and in Joyce Kolko, *America and the Crisis of World Capitalism* (Boston: Beacon, 1974).*

Chapter 8

1. Though no radical himself, Peter Drucker emphasizes this alarming fact in his characterization of the problem of underdeveloped countries; see his *Age of Discontinuity* (New York: Harper and Row, 1969).

2. Paul Baran's *Political Economy of Growth* * remains the primary work that has come to grips with the nature of underdevelopment and the causes of its persistence in the modern world. Andre G. Frank, in his *Capitalism and Underdevelopment in Latin America* (New York: Monthly Review, 1967), and *Latin America:*

Underdevelopment or Revolution, (New York: Monthly Review, 1969),* has told the more detailed story of the creation of underdevelopment in Latin America. Carl Riskin, "Surplus and Stagnation in Modern China" in Dwight Perkins, ed., *China's Modern Economy in Historical Perspective* (Stanford, Calif.: Stanford University Press, 1975), shows for the Chinese case just how large the relative surplus was— perhaps 25 percent of total output—in the impoverished China of the 1930s. Janice Perlman, who lived for some years among the poor people she was studying, in *The Myth of Marginality, Urban Poverty and Politics in Rio de Janeiro* (Berkeley: University of California Press, 1976), shows among other things that the shanty-town dwellers of major cities in developing countries do not escape to the more affluent parts of town over time but are condemned to permanent residence and permanent deprivation in these squalid settlements. The almost unbelievable fact of declining real incomes for the poor of India is documented in V. M. Dandekhar, *Poverty in India* (Bombay: Indian School of Political Economy, 1971).

3. See Baran, *The Political Economy of Growth,* pp. 140–50, for the argument and references.

4. See Keith Griffin, *The Political Economy of Agrarian Change, An Essay on the Green Revolution* (Cambridge: Harvard University Press, 1974).

5. Oscar Lewis, in *Five Families* (New York: Basic Books, 1959),* offers a poignant account of such fragmented lives at various levels in the income distribution in Mexico.

6. Richard J. Barnet and Ronald E. Miller in *Global Reach: The Power of Multinational Corporations* (New York: Simon and Schuster, 1974), provide a useful description and analysis of the ways in which multinational corporations inflict social, political, and economic burdens on developing countries, while raking in superprofits from the exploited citizenry.

7. See North American Congress on Latin America's publications, such as *Yanqui Dollar, The Contribution of U.S. Private Investment to Underdevelopment in Latin America* (Berkeley: NACLA, 1971).*

8. See Carl Riskin, "Surplus and Stagnation in Modern China," in Dwight Perkins, ed., *China's Modern Economy in Historical Perspective.*

9. See notes 2 and 5 above. As an indication of the human costs of American imperialism, one might note studies by the United Nations' Economic Commission for Latin America and the El Salvador Ministry of Public Health (described in *La Prensa Grafica,* El Salvador, Nos. 681204, 690122) which document the appalling deprivation, including illiteracy and serious malnutrition, of some two-thirds of the citizens of El Salvador.

Chapter 9

1. Very few American radicals are strong supporters of the Soviet Union these days. However, there is a good deal of controversy surrounding the point in time and the reasons that led the Russian revolution away from the path toward real socialism. E. H. Carr's massive eight-volume *History of Soviet Russia* (Baltimore: Pelican, 1952–76) * is generally regarded as providing the best account of the crucial first fifteen years of Soviet socialism. Maurice Dobb's *Soviet Economic Development Since 1917* (New York: International, 1948), is a very friendly account of Soviet economic history. A much less favorable account appears in chapter 15, vol. 2 of Ernest Mandel's *Marxist Economic Theory* (New York: Monthly Review, 1968).* Charles Bettelheim has embarked on a major reappraisal of the Russian revolution, of which the first volume, *Class Struggles in the USSR* (New York: Monthly Review, 1976), has recently appeared in English. The Yugoslav thesis that the Soviet Union has become a state capitalist society, not fundamentally different from its Western counterparts, is defended in Branko Horvat, *Toward a Theory of Planned Economy* (Belgrade: Yugoslav Institute for Economic Research, 1968).

2. A useful survey containing various analyses of Soviet achievements and failures can be found in the November 1967 issue of *Monthly Review,* which is devoted wholly to the reactions of a dozen leading scholars to the fiftieth anniversary of the October Revolution.

3. For a short survey of twentieth-century European economic planning, see my paper of that title in vol. 5, part II of the *Fontana Economic History of Europe,* pp. 698–738, edited by Carlo Cipolla (London: Collins, 1976).

4. Most Americans and Europeans have been exposed to the massive campaign associated with the publication of Solzhenitsyn's *Gulag Archipelago.* The many horror stories detailed in that passionate account of the Soviet labor camps often

leave the impression that all Soviet citizens are slaves. Before accepting that idea, the reader is urged to compare the situation of the average Soviet citizen, or citizen of Eastern Europe, with his counterpart in developing capitalist countries. These Soviet "slaves" have a health status unmatched in that other world, have secure incomes and assured access to the basics of food, shelter, and health care. Their children are being well educated, with illiteracy virtually a thing of the past. Even those in the remote countryside have substantial access to modern cultural events; and the prospects for their children are very bright. As a final point, one might note that a study by a team of Soviet and East European economists showed that the Soviet Union's standard of living was among the lowest of the East European socialist countries, and that in particular in the mid-sixties it was less than two-thirds as high as in East Germany or Czechoslovakia. Clearly, this is not the same sort of thing as capitalist imperialism.

Chapter 10

1. The most important thing to understand about China is the revolution itself, its basis and its thrust. This story is best told in the small in the tales of transformation of individual villages. William Hinton's *Fanshen* (New York: Random House, 1966) * and Jan Myrdal's *Report from a Chinese Village* (New York: Random House, 1965) * are detailed and moving accounts of this process. There is no one book that describes well the economic history of revolutionary China. However, basic policy and organizational issues are discussed in Franz Schurmann, *Ideology and Organization in Communist China*, 2nd ed. (Berkeley: University of California Press, 1968). John G. Gurley, *China's Economy and the Maoist Strategy* (New York: Monthly Review, 1976), describes the main features of the Maoist approach to development and of the Chinese achievement.

Yugoslavia has proved to be a difficult country for Western socialists to make up their minds about. On the one hand, it has carried the principle of workers' management of factories farther than any other country, socialist or otherwise. On the other hand, it unabashedly uses markets to mediate relations among these worker-managed firms. Perhaps most radicals have initially reacted negatively to Yugoslavia, feeling that market relations were bound in the end to subvert the beneficent tendencies built into economic participation. However, the history of other socialist countries has seemed increasingly to suggest that some measure of decentralization of the economic process is really essential; and some form of marketlike relations is about the only alternative immediately available. Perhaps typical of this changing attitude is the exchange between two of the world's leading Marxist economists, American Paul Sweezy and Frenchman Charles Bettelheim, published in the United States as *On The Transition to Socialism* (New York: Monthly Review, 1971).* Both authors seem to be agreed that for a long time during the transition, properly controlled markets will in all likelihood be an important feature of the socialist scene.

The best account of Yugoslavia can probably be found in the works of Yugoslavia's own leading economist, Branko Horvat. His *Essay on Yugoslav Society* (New York: IASP, 1969) describes the issues that have faced Yugoslav socialists in more abstract terms.

2. The most useful account of Yugoslav policy and performance is still Branko Horvat, "Yugoslav Economic Policy in the Post-War Period: Problems, Ideas, Institutional Developments," *American Economic Review* 61 (June 1971), Supplement.

3. For a good account of the development of Maoist ideas during the course of the thirty-year revolution, see Gurley, *China's Economy and the Maoist Strategy,* esp. chap. 2.

4. For a stirring account of what it is like to live on a commune in China, see Jack Chen, *A Year in Upper Felicity* (New York: Macmillan, 1973).

5. For an analysis of industrial democracy, in general and in Yugoslavia, see Carole Pateman, *Participation and Democratic Theory* (Cambridge: Cambridge University Press, 1970).

6. For a plausible Maoist account, see Gurley, *China's Economy and the Maoist Strategy,* esp. chap. 1.

7. For a collection of readings on this topic, see Branko Horvat, Rudi Supek, and Mihailo Marković, eds., *Self-Governing Socialism, A Reader,* 2 vols. (White Plains, N.Y.: IASP, 1975).*

Chapter 11

1. Transitions are not easy to write about in general terms, as each country and each crisis has unique features that are central to understanding revolutionary potential. However, *Root and Branch, The Rise of the Workers' Movements* (Greenwich: Fawcett, 1975),* is a useful account of one of the central forces at work in capitalist society that is pushing toward the transition. Michael P. Lerner's *The New Socialist Revolution, An Introduction to Its Theory and Strategy* (New York: Delta, 1973),* is one attempt at such an account. Gar Alperovitz's "Socialism as a Pluralist Commonwealth," reprinted in Richard Edwards, Michael Reich, and Thomas Weisskopf, eds., *The Capitalist System, A Radical Analysis of American Society,* 2nd ed. (Englewood Cliffs, N.J.: Prentice-Hall, 1978),* pp. 522–39, describes a socialist society in terms of goals widely shared on the American left. The best way to study transitions, however, is to read accounts of successful and unsuccessful revolutions. Probably the most useful account of the origins and development of the Cuban revolution is Hugh Thomas's *Cuba* (New York: Harper and Row, 1971). Some useful accounts of Chile can be found in Ann Zammit, ed., *The Chilean Road to Socialism* (Sussex, England: International Development Studies, 1973).* Readings on Russia and China and Yugoslavia are noted in the last two chapters, though a full and friendly account of the Yugoslav revolution has not yet appeared in English.

Chapter 12

1. For Marx, see the *Communist Manifesto* itself and the *Critique of the Gotha Program,* for Lenin, *State and Revolution.*
2. Utopian novels often provide insight into the potential inhering in human nature, though of course they should not be taken as prescriptions for the future. Some of the more interesting works in this genre are Edward Bellamy's *Looking Backward* (Cambridge: Harvard University Press, 1967, orig. pub. 1888); William Morris, *News from Nowhere* (London: Reeves and Turner, 1890); and B. F. Skinner, *Walden Two* (New York: Macmillan, 1968).
3. Once again China provides an example of the thrust that socialism provides for more humane solutions. Though unable as yet to put substantial resources into massive pollution-control technology, the dispersion of factories and the massive development of small-scale industry have constituted important antipollution measures. And of course such measures are very closely associated with effective community building. For a good account of Chinese achievements in this area, see the American Rural Small-Scale Industry Delegation, *Rural Small-Scale Industry in the People's Republic of China* (Berkeley: University of California Press, 1977).

Chapter 13

1. As was noted in note 8 of chapter 8, Carl Riskin has made an estimate of the relative surplus for China in the thirties, building on work initiated by Victor Lippitt. But this work has not yet been extended to contemporary Third World countries.
2. Assar Lindbeck, *Political Economy of the New Left,* 2nd ed. (Harper and Row, 1977), pp. 75–77.

Chapter 14

1. Baran, *The Political Economy of Growth.* (New York: Monthly Review, 1957). The revised 1962 edition contains a foreword that is an extended commentary on the reviews of the 1957 edition.
2. Baran and Sweezy, *Monopoly Capital.* (New York: Monthly Review, 1966).
3. The surplus concepts are discussed in chap. 2 of *The Political Economy of Growth.*
4. Baran, *The Political Economy of Growth,* chap. 3.
5. Ibid., p. 119.

6. Ibid., pp. 124, 129.
7. Ibid., p. 133n.
8. Ibid.
9. This classification is discussd in chap. 6 and at the beginning of chap. 7 in Baran, *The Political Economy of Growth.*
10. Ibid., p. 257.
11. Ibid., 1962 ed., p. xxxvi.
12. The case is argued strongly in ibid., chap. 2, and has been repeated by Sweezy in a number of public lectures, and in a negative reaction to the Fitch-Oppenheimer finance-capital thesis in *Socialist Revolution*, (San Francisco: no. 8, 1972).
13. The case is argued in *Monopoly Capital*, chap. 4 and 8.
14. See chapter 5 above and note 2 to that chapter for this calculation.
15. Baran and Sweezy, in *Monopoly Capital*, pp. 135–38.
16. Ibid., p. 367.
17. Paul Sweezy and Charles Bettelheim, *On the Transition to Socialism* (New York: Monthly Review, 1971).
18. See chap. 11 of Leo Huberman and Paul Sweezy, *Socialism in Cuba* (New York: Monthly Review, 1969).
19. Harry Braverman, *Labor and Monopoly Capital, The Degradation of Work, in the Twentieth Century* (New York: Monthly Review, 1974).
20. Ibid., p. 180.

Chapter 15

1. This is the thesis of J. Steindl, *Maturity and Stagnation in American Capitalism* (Oxford: Oxford University Press, 1952). In his later work Baran emphasized the dialectical interaction between the two factors, the rate of investment and the rate of innovation, rather than attributing one-way causation from the latter to the former. However, the recent increase in popularity of the idea of the Kondratiev cycle, or long swing, has tended to reemphasize that line of causation in generating longer-term booms. For an example of this type of analysis, see Robert Zevin, "The Political Economy of the American Empire, December, 1974," in David Mermelstein, ed., *The Economic Crisis Reader* (New York: Random House, 1975).

2. A good, brief account of the historical volatility of capitalism that broadly fits our optimal radical interpretation is Eric Hobsbawm, "Capitalist Crises in Historical Perspective," in Richard Edwards, Michael Reich, and Thomas Weisskopf, *The Capitalist System, A Radical Analysis of American Society*, 2nd ed. (Englewood Cliffs, N.J.: Prentice-Hall, 1978), pp. 431–40.

3. Stagnation is at center stage in Ernest Mandel's *Marxist Economic Theory* (New York: Monthly Review, 1968) (Fr. ed. 1962), esp. chap. 14. In his more recent *Late Capitalism* (New York: Monthly Review, 1976), Mandel's views are somewhat equivocal but can still reasonably be described as stagnationist.

4. A good sampling of relevant radical writings reflecting these factors can be found in Mermelstein, *The Economic Crisis Reader* in *Radical Perspectives on the Economic Crisis of Monopoly Capitalism* (Union for Radical Political Economics, 1975),* and *U.S. Capitalism in Crisis* (New York: Union for Radical Political Economics, 1978).*

5. Perhaps most notably by Paul Hoffman, former chief executive of Studebaker, in a series of speeches in the fifties, after he turned public "servant."

6. Theresa Hayter's *Aid as Imperialism* (Baltimore: Penguin, 1971), provides a more wholesome perspective on this aspect of exploitation.

7. A crude reproduction of the calculation procedure used by Joseph Phillips in the Appendix he wrote to *Monopoly Capital*, based on data taken from the *Economic Report of the President* for 1976 and for 1973, gives the following: From 1963 to 1973 surplus as a share of national income increased from 67.8 to 68.7 percent. Surplus absorbed by government increased from 34.7 to 38.0 percent of national income. National defense expenditures increased by a little over 50 percent in the decade, but as a share of gross national product declined from 8.8 to 5.8 percent. Thus the increased relative surplus absorption is accounted for by nondefense government activity. Notable in this latter area is a more than tenfold increase in federal health expenditures and a more than trebling of total government expenditures on education and manpower training. The relevant data can be found in the 1976 *Economic Report*, (Washington, D.C.: U.S. Government Printing Office) tables B-11, B-12, B-64, and B-69.

Chapter 16

1. Karl Marx, *Early Writings* (New York: McGraw-Hill, 1963).*
2. For an analysis of Marx's views, see Bertell Ollman, *Alienation, Marx's Conception of Man in Capitalist Society*, (Cambridge: Cambridge University Press, 1971).* A useful if non-Marxist account of the problem under contemporary capitalism is Walter A. Weisskopf, *Alienation and Economics* (New York: Dutton, 1971). For the "Marxist-Humanist" perspective, see Howard Sherman's *Radical Political Economy* (New York: Basic Books, 1972), esp. chap. 11 and 21 and references.
3. Herbert Marcuse, *One-Dimensional Man* (Boston: Beacon, 1964),* esp. chapters 1–4, 10. The concepts in quotations in the next few paragraphs in the text are all taken from those chapters.
4. The last two chapters of Branko Horvat's *Essay on Yugoslav Society* (New York: IASP, 1969) contain some relevant arguments. A selection of readings edited by Horvat, the Yugoslav philosopher Rudi Supek, and Mihailo Marković (White Plains, New York: IASP, 1975) * *Self-Governing Socialism, A Reader*, 2 vols., contains a number of selections relevant for alienation and disalienation, several of which are by Yugoslavs. See vol. 1, pp. 327–50, 363–65, 405–37.

Chapter 17

1. Several of Horvat's works have been cited in chapters 1, 10, and 16. The present chapter is a revised and shortened version of my "Marxism-Horvatism, A Yugoslav Theory of Socialism," *American Economic Review* 57 (June 1967).
2. The issue of workers' control has been much discussed in recent years and interest in the topic seems to be still rising. In addition to the already cited book of readings edited by Horvat, Supek, and Marković, there are two other interesting collections: Gerry Hunnius et al., eds., *Workers' Control* (New York: Vintage, 1973),* and Jaroslav Vanek, ed., *Self-Management* (Baltimore: Penguin, 1975).*
3. Issues related to the efficiency of worker-managed enterprises are appraised by Vanek in his *General Theory of the Labor-Managed Market Economy* (Ithaca, N.Y.: Cornell University Press, 1969). Vanek and Horvat both believe that such enterprises will prove to be very efficient; for a less positive view, see my *Socialist Economy, A Study of Organizational Alternatives* (New York: Random House, 1967), chap. 8–10.
4. Paul Sweezy and Charles Bettelheim, *On the Transition to Socialism* (New York: Monthly Review, 1971).*

Chapter 18

1. This elitist character of neoclassical economics is described and analyzed in my *What's Wrong With Economics* (New York: Basic Books, 1972), esp. Parts I and III–IV.
2. The standard work of contemporary mathematical Marxism is Michio Morishima, *Marx's Economics* (Cambridge: Cambridge University Press, 1973). For an alternative and perhaps more nearly Marxist though still technical formulation of the issue of discrimination, see John Roemer, "Differentially Exploited Labor: A Marxian Value Theory of Discrimination," mimeo, 1976; this and other of Roemer's papers show this genre at its most productive. The controversy with neoclassical economists over capital and the theory of growth is described in G. C. Harcourt, *Some Cambridge Controversies in the Theory of Capital* (Cambridge, England: Cambridge University Press, 1972).* A very good introduction to economic theory from a radical but not really Marxist perspective is Joan Robinson and John Eatwell, *An Introduction to Modern Economics* (London: McGraw-Hill, 1973).* For an application of value theory to international trade, see Arghiri Emmanuel, *Unequal Exchange* (New York: Monthly Review, 1972).
One of the most interesting of recent controversies among radical economists concerns the role of financial as opposed to industrial interests in controlling monopoly capitalist economies. The discussion has taken place principally in the pages of *Socialist Revolution*, issues 4–6 (1970–71), 8 (1972), 11–12 (1974), and the main protagonists are Robert Fitch and Mary Oppenheimer, James O'Connor, Paul Sweezy,

and others. An empirical appraisal of finance power has recently been completed by David Kotz, *The Role of Financial Institutions in the Control of Large Nonfinancial Corporations* (Berkeley: University of California Press, 1977). Other controversies, such as that over the prospects for continued cooperation among leading capitalist countries in international affairs or the importance of political factors in the business cycle, have flared up in recent years and been discussed constructively, offering clear evidence that radical economic scholarship is now established on a firm base of agreement on most fundamentals.

Suggestions for Further Reading*

Baran, Paul. *The Political Economy of Growth.* New York: Monthly Review, 1957, rev. ed. 1962.*
  Probably the single most important Marxist work of the postwar era, it must be understood and appraised by every serious student of radical economics.
Baran, Paul, and Paul Sweezy. *Monopoly Capital.* New York: Monthly Review, 1966.*
  The radical textbook in the United States in the later sixties, it is still a useful guide to the "surplus-absorption" theory of capitalist crisis.
Barnet, Richard J., and Ronald E. Miller. *Global Reach, The Power of the Multinational Corporations.* New York: Simon and Schuster, 1974.
  The best book on this difficult and controversial subject.
Bowles, Samuel, and Herbert Gintis. *Schooling in Capitalist America.* New York: Basic Books, 1976.
  A powerful and scholarly account of the effect of class on American education.
Braverman, Harry. *Labor and Monopoly Capital, The Degradation of Work in the Twentieth Century.* New York: Monthly Review, 1974.
  The one best book on this central topic.
Brown, Michael Barratt. *The Economics of Imperialism.* Baltimore: Penguin, 1974.*
  A solid, modern, Marxist analysis of the issue.
Dobb, Maurice. *Studies in the Development of Capitalism,* rev. ed. New York: International, 1963.*
  A key work in economic history by one of the great radical economists of the era of relative stagnation in radical economic research (1920–55).
Dowd, Douglas. *The Twisted Dream, Capitalist Development in the United States since 1776,* 2nd ed. Cambridge, Mass.: Winthrop, 1977.*
  A passionate and useful account.
Eaton, John. *Political Economy.* International, 1963.*
  One of the two best primers of the economics of Karl Marx.
Edwards, Richard, Michael Reich, and Thomas Weisskopf, eds. *The Capitalist System,* 2nd ed. Englewood Cliffs, N.J.: Prentice-Hall, 1978.*
  A collection of readings that comprise the best introductory textbook on radical political economy currently available.
Frank, Andre Gunder. *Capitalism and Underdevelopment in Latin America.* New York: Monthly Review, 1967.*
  In this and other works Frank has attempted to flesh out Baran's "creation of underdevelopment" thesis, using evidence, in this case, from Chile and Brazil.
Gordon, David, ed. *Problems in Political Economy: An Urban Perspective,* 2nd ed. Boston: Heath, 1977.*
  A very useful collection on political economic issues of labor, race, crime, poverty, education and health.
Gurley, John. *China's Economy and the Maoist Strategy.* New York: Monthly Review, 1976.
  A collection of essays by a leading defender of Maoist political economy.
Hinton, William. *Fanshen, A Documentary of Revolution in a Chinese Village.* New York: Random House, 1966.*
  Probably the one best place to get a grass-roots understanding of the meaning and process of revolution in the countryside.
Horvat, Branko. *An Essay on Yugoslav Society.* White Plains, N.Y.: International Arts and Sciences, 1969.
  Repeats some of the material in his 1964 work, but with several chapters more specifically devoted to Yugoslavia and its relation to Horvat's "optimal regime".
——. *Toward a Theory of Planned Economy.* Belgrade: Yugoslav Institute for Economic Research, 1964.

* Starred items are available in paperback edition.

As noted in the text, one of the half-dozen seminal works of postwar radical economics.

———; Rudi Supek; and Mihailo Markovic͏̈, eds. *Self-Governing Socialism, A Reader*, 2 vols. White Plains, N.Y.: International Arts and Sciences, 1975.*
A collection of readings covering the gamut of philosophical, social, and economic issues related to economic participation by the direct producers in the decisions that affect their lives.

Huberman, Leo, and Paul Sweezy. *Socialism in Cuba*. New York: Monthly Review, 1969.*
An account that shows what revolution can mean to the peoples of Latin America.

Marcuse, Herbert. *One-Dimensional Man*. New York: Beacon Press, 1964.*
Though not an economist, Marcuse's treatment of alienation is the most relevant of recent efforts for the political economist, though perhaps an overly pessimistic appraisal.

Mermelstein, David, ed. *The Economic Crisis Reader*. New York: Random House, 1975.*
After reading this book the reader will not doubt that we are in the midst of a great crisis.

Miliband, Ralph. *The State in Capitalist Society*. New York: Basic Books, 1969.
Why reformism fails as an instrument of radical change.

Morishima, Michio. *Marx's Economics*. Cambridge: Cambridge University Press, 1973.
The standard work of contemporary mathematical Marxism. Demanding reading but does not provide real insight into the working of contemporary monopoly capitalism.

O'Connor, James. *The Fiscal Crisis of the State*. New York: St. Martins, 1973.*
How the state, while trying to serve the needs of the capitalists, has boxed itself into a corner.

Poulantsas, Nicos. *Classes in Contemporary Capitalism*. London: New Left Books, 1975.
Along with Miliband and O'Connor, one of the key contemporary works on the role of classes and the state under monopoly capitalism.

Robinson, Joan, and John Eatwell. *An Introduction to Economics*. New York: McGraw-Hill, 1973.*
A difficult, unconventional, rewarding textbook.

Schurmann, Franz. *The Logic of World Power, An Inquiry into the Origins, Currents and Contradictions of World Politics*. New York: Random House, 1974.*
A challenging work in an area of still underdeveloped radical research.

Sherman, Howard. *Radical Political Economy*. New York: Basic Books, 1972.
The best account of the subject from the "Marxist-humanist" perspective.

Sweezy, Paul. *Theory of Capitalist Development*. New York: Monthly Review, 1942.*
One of the two best primers of the economics of Karl Marx.

Tuchman, Barbara. *The Proud Tower, A Portrait of the World Before the War: 1890–1914*. New York: Macmillan, 1966.*
One can feel the enveloping crisis of capitalism through daily lives in this gripping account.

Union for Radical Political Economics. *Radical Perspectives on the Economic Crisis of Monopoly Capitalism*. New York: URPE, 1975.*
———. *U.S. Capitalism in Crisis*. New York: URPE, 1978.
Together with the Mermelstein readings, these books provide a good perspective on the current crisis.

Vanek, Jaroslav. *General Theory of the Labor-Managed Market Economy*. Ithaca, N.Y.: Cornell University Press, 1969.
The economic theory of self-management by a believer in both.

Wallerstein, Immanuel. *The Modern World-System*. New York: Academic, 1974.
A challenging account of the rise of the capitalist mode of production and of the process by which it penetrated new areas.

BOOK THREE

THE
CONSERVATIVE
ECONOMIC
WORLD VIEW

Contents of Book Three

PART I

The Optimal Conservative Economic World View

1. Introduction 325
2. What Made the Modern World? 330
3. Prosperity and Order in Ancient China and Republican Venice 337
4. England and the United States: The Thoroughgoing Market Economy 343
5. Markets and the Twentieth Century 349
6. Property Rights 355
7. Government and Property 361
8. Government and Spending 369
9. Money and Taxes 374
10. The Problem of Order 379
11. Economic Development 386
12. The International Economy 392
13. Socialism 399
14. International Order 405
15. The Future 411

PART II

Commentary

16. Introduction 419
17. Libertarians: The Pure Breed 424
18. Social Conservatives 430
19. Neoconservatives 435
20. Friedman 440
21. Hayek 445

NOTES 451
SUGGESTIONS FOR FURTHER READING 459

PART I

The Optimal Conservative Economic World View

ACKNOWLEDGMENTS

It is not so easy for a Berkeley economics professor to find a conservative with whom to talk over the issues. However, a certain number of conservative students have drifted into my classes, and some have gone out of their way to continue my education. I am particularly grateful to Paul Craig Roberts for a variety of such efforts over the years. An early interest in public choice theory has provided a number of opportunities for discussions with conservative economists. A semester of teaching at the University of Washington was both delightful and very useful. I am indebted to a helpful critic and friend, R. Joseph Monsen, for this opportunity, and also to Dwight Robinson and Trudy Murray, from whom I have learned much. Finally, I would like to thank Andrjej Brzeski of the Davis campus of my home university, a fine friend who offered a large number of penetrating criticisms of an earlier draft of the present work. Remaining failures to grasp conservative principles are, of course, my own.

CHAPTER 1

Introduction

ONE OF the ironic events of recent years has been the furor over the hiring of radical economists in some of the leading economics departments in the United States. The irony stems from the fact that many of the best-known departments already had radicals among their faculty members. Far scarcer in most departments were conservatives; indeed, a number of the highest status departments had no conservatives at all on their faculties.

Radical rhetoric and threat did in fact produce results; well-meaning liberals found ways to make appointments based de facto on a political test despite the violation of rules, perhaps even of the Constitution, that was involved. But probably this success will be short-lived, not because the radicals can also be thrown out for political reasons, though that could happen, but because they really have very little to offer economics beyond rhetoric and threats. Propinquity in this case can only breed contempt.

But what then of those absent conservatives? The truth is that conservatism is having a rather profound effect on economics, even though it has been poorly represented in many research-oriented institutions. This effect is being exercised through the competition of ideas rather than by physical confrontation. Conservatives have been in the forefront of the reappraisal of Keynesian economics, and the reappraisal has already led to substantial modifications of the doctrine as it was being so confidently asserted only a dozen years ago. Some of the most interesting developments in the new field of public choice theory are the product of conservative thinkers; indeed, it would not be far off the mark to say that the field of public choice was created by conservatives. And perhaps the most interesting new slant on economics in recent years, the burgeoning property-rights literature, is unquestionably a conservative product. These conservative ideas, since they are clearly meeting the competitive tests of an ideologically unfriendly but still open environment, will be around long after the radical confrontationists have been returned to the street-corner intellectualism that seems to be their natural habitat.

Though the above-mentioned developments have their dimensions of originality, the basic principles of conservatism are by no means new. They have grown by evolution and have been tested in generations of experience. They differ from liberal and radical views in four fundamental ways. In the first place, the conservative rejects utopian and mechanistic "solutions" to human problems. Second, conservatism is based on recognition of the individual human being as the primary element in society. Third, the conservative identifies the family as the most important social unit in human society. And finally, conservatives believe that the provision of order is an essential task of government, without which the economy cannot provide opportunities for families and individuals. A conservative interpretation of the operation of the contemporary economy will, of course, make frequent use of these primary distinguishing features of conservatism. In the remainder of this chapter the aim will be simply to explain why these principles do in fact serve to distinguish conservative from liberal and radical thoughts.

The libertarian bias of the conservative is by now generally recognized in the United States. However, the basis of the emphasis on freedom as a fundamental value is often misunderstood. For as John Stuart Mill pointed out, the most effective arguments are negative ones. Mill argued that the individual is generally the best judge of what is best for himself, partly because he knows more about his own wants than others and partly because he cares more about them than do others. The implication of the argument is that individuals are possessed of a considerable amount of self-concern, and that this self-concern is combined with a considerable degree of material self-interest. These are hardly revolutionary notions, given that they are being asserted of an organism that can neither thrive nor even survive without regular and *individual* access to a variety of material objects, including most notably food. Add one more ingredient, namely, that there are not enough of those material objects to go around, that they are scarce, and the stage is set for a good conservative analysis of the functioning of human society.

Radicals, of course, deny the relevance of these points. That an individual should exhibit a high degree of self-concern is, for a radical, a sign not of normal functioning of an animal organism but of sickness. Radical intellectual leaders before the revolution, and political leaders after, continually assert their right to speak for others, to decide what is good for whom, and to suppress dissent on the subject whenever possible. And much of their argumentation even denied the existence of scarcity. For a century now Marxists have been denouncing scarcity economics without having anything to put in its place. They used to argue that socialist societies, by abolishing the wastes of capitalism, would almost automatically be societies of abundance. When that thesis was tested and the truth was found to be closer to the exact opposite, there was put in its place a good deal of talk about creating abundance by abolishing the desire for goods!

Radicals differ fundamentally and at every turn from conservatives. But liberals, in their wishy-washy attempts to find a happy medium, are not actually so far behind the radicals. Big government in Western Europe and the United States is the creature of liberal thought and action. It is based on utopian and paternalistic notions of man. The often incredible and genuinely uncountable direct interventions in human affairs that these monstrous concoctions carry out are justified by liberals essentially on the grounds that the bureaucrat knows best what is good for his client. But, in fact, the bureaucracy is not viewed as confronting individuals directly. Everything is done on the basis of averages and on the assumption of one group facing another, as in the attempt to force poor neighborhoods to form groups, which would then be given money to spend, assuming, of course, that the money will be spent in ways that served to promote the best interests of the group rather than the interests of its leaders. And as for scarcity, one need only remember Galbraith's argument that Americans have far more goods provided them by the market system than they ought to have, and that they would be much better off if bureaucrats and politicans, advised by the sage, made most of society's consumption decisions. At times it seems as if the liberal were simply a more efficient kind of radical, one who recognized that the goal of total state control was more likely to be achieved if evolutionary rather than revolutionary means were used.

Utopianism and a mechanistic approach to social policy tend to go hand in hand. Much of the trouble that the American economy has been in for almost a decade now has been a consequence of excessive confidence in the products of the economist's art. Essential to the conservative's general position is the recognition of the complexity of the human being and of his social relations. The consequences of any given social policy cannot be predicted with much confidence, no matter how sophisticated the mathematical model or the statistical manipulations of the data. One of the basic ingredients of a conservative policy toward economic stabilization is the recognition of this fact and a consequent attempt to limit the power of the government to foul things up by limiting the power of government.

A radical cannot talk for more than five minutes about social reform without using words such as "solidarity" and "collective." Clearly, the sooner individualism is eliminated, the happier the radical will be. Liberals are a bit more subtle in their approach, but the result really is not much different. Liberal social theory has virtually eliminated the individual from consideration these days. Everything has to do with the group. There is the interest group, the workplace group, the large organization, small-group theory, and so on; the individual just doesn't seem to be of much use these liberal days. Such general trends in social theory find their reflection in economic model building, where the typical unit is the actor or agent, who can be an individual, a group, or even a hierarchic organization. Furthermore, the models tend to assign essentially the same traits to each "class" of actors, possibly with some random variation thrown in. If you can find a few individuals in this putative analogue of the real world, they will differ from one another on, at best, a few well-specified and probably randomly distributed properties. And the outcomes, "efficient" or "optimal" though they may be, do not distinguish among this mish-mash of entities.

If liberal model building has strained out the individual, leaving either a collective or a very simple robot in his place, liberal social policy has substituted, at every turn, government-vs.-group interaction for the private bargains of the marketplace.

The twentieth century has seen perhaps the greatest assault on the family in recorded history. Socialists make no bones of their desire to destroy it; clearly, the family's cohesion gets seriously in the way of their designs for a more pliant individual. But liberals seem to have a similar notion. They often lead the discussion of the death of the family, treating its problems without reference to the fact that many of these same problems stem precisely from liberal social policy. One of the central functions of the family in history has been to serve as an institution of security. When the state becomes a substitute for the family as far as the material security of its members is concerned, this is bound to have a weakening effect. Compulsory features of the substitution leave the family bereft of one of its primary functions, whether its members like the idea or not. A second central function of the family has been the education of the child to fit him for the world. This function too is largely removed from family control through a massive public education system, supported by compulsory levies, in which the parents' ideas of education are given virtually no weight. And in the welfare system, as well as at a number of other turns in a family's history, the state bureaucrat is authorized to make deep interventions in family life, of which the systematic driving away of the male head of poor families is but one notorious instance. Other aspects of liberal society often force dependence onto the children until a late age, while depriving the parents of influence over their children. There is little wonder that after all this many liberal sociologists can make a comfortable living holding seminars on the decline of the American family.

Order is a concept that has very ambivalent meaning for a radical and, in practice at least, for the liberal as well. The atmosphere in which a revolutionary can flourish is one of disorder, and this, of course, serves to set his priorities. The disturbance of others in the exercise of their rights is the principal weapon of revolutionary change; the revolutionist has decided that he knows what's best for society and sets about to sow disorder through demonstrations, strikes, riots, agitation against the government, and so forth. We have described no ambivalence as yet—that emerges only after the revolutionary comes to power, when he suddenly feels the need for perfect "order" and sets about eliminating his enemies until he gets it. There will then be no more disorder in utopia until some comrades decide they want a different policy, and have the power to confront the new boss.

The liberal, on the other hand, carries his ambivalence with him at all times. Believing as he does that behavior that isn't nice only occurs because of the environment—in other words, that criminals and rioters are victims at least as much as those they are attacking—the liberal finds it very hard to call a halt by the use of force. The result is usually application of too little force and consequently a great deal more disorder.

The conservative position on these issues is very different. For a conservative, it is possible to draw a sharp line between orderly and disorderly behavior. The line drawing must be done carefully, but once it is drawn behavior toward those on the other side of the line should be quite unequivocal. The effort should involve effective deterrence through the use of overwhelming force and punishment as an indication that the individual *will* be held responsible for his acts in a free society.

As for the family, the conservative recognizes it as containing the deepest and most central relationships in an individual's life. The capacity to love is generated and expressed most profoundly in family relationships. But the family is also a very private institution, diverse and complex and still well beyond the grasp of social theory to comprehend. This fact plus its central place in society require support from society, not harassment. But given the historical inefficiency of the state in implementing policies of support, the strongest argument exists simply for saying, Hands off! to the state where family affairs are concerned. There is a very limited place for the state in regulating affairs among family members—essentially this role only occurs where family conflicts have spilled over into the outside world.

Individuals are no less complex than families. Their behavior too is not to be understood by simple models; nor is man well enough understood to be successfully manipulated into another kind of being by "instruments of social policy." Once again, what is needed is that he be left alone to seek his own way in the world, helped by his family and by his own efforts. And, once again, the essential role of government is to intervene only when these efforts have begun clearly to cause substantial harm to others. Family, freedom, and order are the unique basis of the conservative position.

CHAPTER 2

What Made the Modern World?

AN insufficiently noticed historical fact is that we tend to know more about those societies in which trading was a major activity than about others. We know a great deal about Athens, very little really about Sparta. Rome's history is shrouded in darkness in its earliest, traditional era of kingship and in the later period of attempted direct imperial control of the economy. The great trading period of the later republic and early empire provides us with substantial documentation. In the Middle Ages we have plenty of information about the great Italian trading cities, increasing information about Britain as she emerges as a trading nation, while much of the history of centralist Byzantium is blank. And in our own era what we know about Western market societies stands in sharp contrast to the few bits of information that filter out of closed socialist societies.

Of course, this is no accident. Merchants need information as a central part of their business. Furthermore, they need to supply information to prospective customers as a necessary part of making a sale. Much of what we think of as the organization of a market consists in ways of getting information to those who may want to deal on that market. But the need for information in order to do business goes deeper than this. Successful deal making requires that the trader acquire some understanding of the wishes and motives and resources of his prospective customer, if only so that he can use the information to get the best possible deal for himself. The market tends to develop in the successful trader a sensitivity to the wishes of others, and for the most durable of motives, namely, his own benefit. The old Fuller Brush man certainly was no philanthropist, and may at times have been something of a nuisance, but he did epitomize the market in this respect. Once he got your attention by coming around to you, he then made a genuine effort to find a match between your tastes and his wares. And the customer has, to some extent, an incentive to reveal his wishes; he too may want to bargain and to simulate those wishes, but if his wants are not known they are hardly likely to be satisfied on the market.

The contrast with bureaucratic societies is striking. There the leadership has a strong desire to know a number of things about its citizenry. But the great inequality between leader and led makes the citizen much more wary of revealing his wishes, especially any that may run counter to the leader's own ideas as to what is appropriate for the citizenry. The tax collector is not a person there is much incentive to expose one's wishes and resources to, and in a bureaucracy every bureaucrat is a tax collector, in the sense that he has the power to restrict the freedom of action of his clients, which is precisely what taking money from them does. In addition, the bureaucracy has very little incentive to provide information to outsiders, since it is too likely to reveal mistakes and can serve little positive purpose, at least from the bureaucrat's point of view. The Watergate events, clearly a product of big government, are the latest illustration of this aspect of bureaucracy.

Thus the greater informational openness of the trading society tends to be accompanied by a greater freedom of action for participants. Primarily, this is a consequence of the voluntary nature of deal making, the ability of each party to say, No deal! which is present so long as bargaining power is not too unequal. This openness tends in turn to promote mobility for the citizenry. Knowledge of opportunities elsewhere is one of the trader's main stocks-in-trade, and the information gets around. It is no accident that serfdom tended to be abandoned first in those parts of Europe in which trade was beginning to flourish, and that it persisted or was even recreated in those parts of Europe in which a strong centralized regime was able to prevent by force the rise of petty trade. Another reflection of this greater freedom of action and the trader's relation to information is manifested in the relation between trade and education. Many of our earliest written documents relate to trade, alphabets may have been initially designed for traders' use, and merchants have always been among the most important groups to acquire some measure of literacy. The need to keep records of business activity and to send letters in search of information about trading opportunities have thus been among the prime stimuli to the development of literacy.

The relation between trade and the development of industry has also been very close. Actually, the artisan is best viewed as a kind of trader. His shop is likely to lie alongside that of the trader, and he too has some portion of his clientele as regular customers to whose special wishes he caters and some portion of nonrepeat business. The artisan uses his knowledge and skill to process goods so as to enhance their value; so does the trader, but by selecting and moving them to the place where they are likely to be demanded. The processes of development of industry involved the trader at every turn. In this connection one need only mention that intermediate stage in development, the putting-out system, in which the merchant controlled a series of production processes, or the early factories, which were very often financed by merchant capital.

Trade opened up the world, introduced a strong element of voluntarism into economic life, and became a prime mover in the process of creating the modern world of industry and affluent, educated citizenries. It is probably the single most dynamic social process known to history. But that, of course, is not to say that it is perfect, only that it has established itself as a far better basis for much human interaction than any other known social process.

There are very strong biases against trade in both the liberal and radical literatures. The model of trading activity that is suggested is something like Cortez conquering and slaughtering the Aztecs. "Imperialism," "merchants of death," and a variety of other slogans are used to associate trade and wars in the reader's mind. In a way this is understandable, for the study of economic history was strongly under the influence of Marxism during most of the twentieth century. Only recently has a new economic history been developing that shows just how wrong these interpretations have been.[1]

The facts are almost the opposite of those depicted by liberal and radical historians. The merchant has a strong interest in an orderly environment, for only then can he bring his skills to bear in anticipating changes in demand and in economic values, which are the basis of his operation. A few examples will serve to illustrate the general point. Consider first the merchant corporations of early modern times, such as the East India Company, which represent the liberal archetype of the predatory merchant warmonger. The truth is that these merchants went into lands where there was already great disorder. They attempted at first to trade from the margins of those societies but found that the societies were too subject to random disorders for any durable trade relations to develop. At that point some of the merchant houses embarked on conquest of the land, assisted, of course, by their home government. But the aim was to bring order, and that in fact was what happened. Liberal and radical historians tell the exciting story of the war, but lose interest when the unexciting aftermath unfolds. For example, in the Indian case, it was merely assumed that as a result of conquest the Indian economy was gutted and starved for generations. We now know that to be false, and it seems that the higher level of public order brought by the colonists permitted substantial economic development in parts of colonial Africa and Asia, development that compares very favorably with the situation in those areas that remained "free" of colonial rule.[2]

The association between trade and freedom has historically been very close. We have already mentioned Athens and Britain. The United States is, of course, another example, where the impetus for the elimination of slavery came from merchant-dominated New England. And at the opposite end of the spectrum we see the very different nature of order under a despotic rule where trade is typically despised. In such places, from ancient Egypt to Ottoman Turkey, from Byzantium to the

Incas, the soldier, the priest, the bureaucrat is continually intervening in the affairs of the citizenry in arbitrary ways. The effects are clear enough: When the citizenry comes to understand that economic success will in all likelihood be siphoned off by some governmental hanger-on, the incentive to create economic successes wanes, and the regime slips into stagnation and decay. It is generally true in history that periods of flourishing economic activity and freedom tend to coincide with periods in which trade and the merchant are near the center of things and wars and bureaucrats in the background. This story is beginning once again to be told accurately in the literature of economic history.

In the nineteenth century a new kind of society emerged and began a process of relatively peaceful conquest of the world. This was the thoroughgoing trading society, and England and the United States were its proving grounds. The particularly novel feature of this form of society lay in the marketization of land, labor, and capital. In earlier times each of these factors of production had been subject to occasional sale from time to time, but never before had an integrated market system involving all three of the basic factors developed.

The process of development of trading societies was relatively peaceful, that is to say, very peaceful when compared with the histories of bureaucratic societies, but not without some measure of exciting times. Old values change slowly, and markets themselves are complex phenomena. Markets develop with experience in trading, with the emergence of a body of traders who understand how the market works, who know its facts, and who can pass on the hard-earned wisdom to succeeding generations. For each market has its pitfalls and risks, and the conservative trader, the one who wants to be able to continue trading year after year, must acquire the prudent insight that only this accumulated knowledge can provide.

An example from labor market history will illustrate this point. Radicals claim that the marketization of labor wreaked havoc on the economic condition of the workers, removing them from the protections of feudal or semifeudal agriculture and turning them into commodities, to be bought and sold like dead fish. However, the available facts suggest that the economic condition of workers generally was improved by the shift, there being strong evidence that movement into the marketized labor force was largely voluntary and involved short-distance migration. Consequently the worker probably did know something of the terms that were being offered him in both town and country, and so could make an informed choice. Nevertheless, some problems emerged, one of these obviously being the insecurity of life in the market, where in hard times the worker was likely to be laid off. Actually, even here the move to the labor market probably did more good than harm. The worker's level of insecurity may not have been greater than it had been on the farm; in many areas the incidence of bad crop years was even more frequent than the incidence of the business cycle in town, and often led to starvation for the peasant. But, more important, as the labor market developed and became organized, workers in similar situations found it feasible to develop their own job and sickness insurance. These so-called friendly societies took voluntary contributions from the workers and offered premiums when the worker fell on certain kinds of hard times. Thus the development of markets generated the opportunity for the development of voluntary insurance schemes by which workers could *protect themselves* against insecurity. In fact, as marketization spread to the countryside a similar phenomenon developed there too in the form of voluntary farm credit unions.[3]

The story of the rise of real wages in England and the United States is too well known to need repeating. The horror stories that have been told of the industrial revolution deal mainly with transient phenomena associated with the transition to marketization and with problems in declining industries. These problems have always been with us; *what the market system did was make the facts widely known*. In some few cases there was a good argument for limited government intervention. But there was never a case that on balance the condition of labor was worsened by the market system. Not only did the workers' real economic situation improve, but the market created opportunities for upward mobility for the more energetic that were far greater than history had known before. The openness of the society, its dynamic quality, and the structuring of energies in the direction of helping oneself by providing goods and services others were willing to make material sacrifices to obtain: These were the central ingredients of this new social form.

Clearly, the family is the most ubiquitous of history's social institutions. It comes in various forms, but at the heart of every form are parenthood and durable sexual relations. In the West in particular, and in trading societies in general, the conventional husband-wife, natural parent-child form of the family has been dominant. Less close ties of kinship often are reflected in cooperative relations for economic purposes, as in the extended family of agricultural and merchant fame.

Obviously, these relationships are the closest ones humans can have. That the conventional family has proved historically to be the dominant form for supporting central emotional needs speaks well of it as a basic social institution. But the family has also served other functions as well. Already mentioned has been its great significance as a private social-security institution. It has also often served as a support for more mobile members of the family. A common pattern of migration has the first established family member in the city create a sort of base to which later other family members can come in order to ease the burden of transition from country to city. Also familiar is the custom in poorer families of concentrating the family savings on giving a special advantage, such as professional education, to one member. In these and a number of other ways family relations have provided a secure base for further advance by members of the family, and not infrequently for the family as a whole.

Down to the nineteenth-century political history could be told essentially in terms of family relations, except perhaps in one or two of the largest of bureaucratic states. Political factions tended to be united around a central family and its clients or prospective beneficiaries. Once again the warmth of family relations served as a basis for alliance on the wider scene of political competition. Of course, that does not mean that there were never rifts within families, only that on the whole it proved to be the most secure amalgam for political alliance.

Throughout much of history larger economic units were essentially households, operating either as family farms or merchant businesses. In both cases a large number of hired or servile hands might be employed, but the central positions of influence within the unit would be family members, and the operation would tend to be headed by the family head. Some of the larger and more successful economic units have played a vital role in the development and testing of political institutions compatible with the thoroughgoing trading economy. Everyone knows the story of Magna Carta, the first great bill of rights growing out of resistance by aristocratic families to attempted usurpations of power by the king. Less well known these days, but of central historical significance, is the story of the organization of the Venetian state. An elaborate system of checks and balances was developed to prevent the ruler from acquiring the ability to dominate the other families in the ruling oligarchy, and this system may have been the model from which the American system of checks and balances ultimately was developed.

The great feudal landlords of England and the great merchant oligarchs of Venice headed powerful, autonomous, and self-concerned family businesses. Because of their autonomy and power, they played a central role in the historical development of the idea of a free society, though they represented transitional stages in that development. Their autonomy was based in part on the security of family relations, which gave the basic unit a cohesion and durability it could not otherwise have possessed.

Yet another influence of the family relates to its role in that most creative aspect of the thoroughgoing trading economy, namely, entrepreneurship. It appears that one of the central motivations energetic and creative people bring to the marketplace is the modern version of founding a dynasty. That is, they are motivated to found a fortune by the desire to have a durable and substantial legacy to pass on to their children. This is the one central respect in which the existence of families modifies the principles of individualism. At more modest levels of economic activity it is reflected in the sacrifices parents make for the education of their children, typically motivated by the desire to improve their economic chances in life. As one of the most important of motivations, inspiring, it should be emphasized, the expenditure of much energy in economic activity as well as "sacrifice," it is one of the most important sources of dynamism in society, a resource, if you like, that one would expect a free society to treasure and support.[4]

In summary, we see that the answer to the chapter's title question is the trinity noted at the end of chapter 1, namely, freedom, family, and order. But associated closely with each of these factors is the institution of the market and trade. The profit-seeking merchant needs freedom because his profits are often to be found in doing something different, in finding some opportunity neglected by others. The family has served as both means and end; on the one hand, it serves as a source of reliable colleagues in the economic venture, while at the same time the improvement of the material condition, status, and prospects of the family provides one of the most fundamental drives of the trader. And order is the environment within which markets serve their enabling functions most effectively, providing information and opportunity to the energetic seeker after profits, and satisfying the desires of those with both wants and means. In the next two chapters we look briefly at several societies where this trinity has served as a central basis for extraordinary achievement.

CHAPTER 3

Prosperity and Order in Ancient China and Republican Venice

THE libertarian conservative position is closely associated in the historical literature with a number of root facts and ideas. It is, of course, centrally related to the ideas of the British empiricist philosophers of the seventeenth and eighteenth centuries. It is associated with the rise of the laissez-faire economy in Britain and elsewhere in the nineteenth century. Both the notion of freedom and the association of freedom with trade go back to ancient Greece. And the association of trade and the rule of law suggests the Rome of the republic. These are familiar stories. However, they are often dismissed as being but a single, now irrelevant, story of the brief expansion of markets and development of ideas in small trading societies, whose occupation of history's center stage was always of short duration. The sense often conveyed is that the fragility of the societies is a disproof of the validity of the ideas.

In this chapter we try to combat this line of anticonservative thought by discussing the features of two societies whose history confounds the liberal or radical critic. Both were among history's most durable societies, preserving essentially similar regimes over a period of many centuries. Both provided a successful amalgam of economic and political order as the basis of their durability, and in both societies the family was fostered as a central social institution. As we will see, even in their demise are found lessons of importance for conservatism. And they show clearly the lack of time- and culture-dependence of major conservative principles.

The basic social structure of China was probably established about the time of Rome's great wars with Carthage, that is, a century or two before Christ.[1] This structure persisted through two thousand years of challenging and often violent history, and even today, under communism, it exerts a strong force. Conquest and invasion at several points broke up the existing society, but when some kind of order returned to the land the Chinese went right back each time to this traditional social structure. During much of its history Chinese society was very dynamic; when Marco Polo visited China in the thirteenth century, he observed a culture that clearly was more advanced than his own. Thus the basic Chinese social structure had survived dramatic technological transformations as well.

The secret of the Chinese success did not lie in Peking. Rather it lay in a peculiar arrangement that permitted a great deal of local autonomy. Recruitment to the Chinese national bureaucracy was by means of competitive examinations, given periodically and dealing with the classics of Chinese culture. Scions of the highest status families often were able to bypass the examinations, or at least most of them, but still the element of competition in the selection procedure was very strong. It also generated, uniquely in the world for much of its history, a literate bureaucracy, which of course greatly facilitated information flow to and from the center. The basic recruiting ground for this bureaucracy, however, was the local elite, often called the gentry. These were the richer—and as a rule the more powerful—families in a given district. Their sons would typically be given some education and might pass the earlier stage examinations even though they never entered the bureaucracy. This gave them some ties of sympathy and common experience with the bureaucrats, and was the source from which renewal of the system occurred after a time of troubles.

But contrary to widespread impression, the bureaucracy did *not* run the Chinese economy. The lowest level member of the national bureaucracy might typically be the sole representative of that bureaucracy in a district roughly comparable to an American county. Basic economic activity was carried on mostly in a highly decentralized way, agriculture, of course, being its base, but with trade present and in good times even flourishing. And even in its irrigation works China did not operate as a vast beehivelike "hydraulic society." Most irrigation works were small-scale projects, organized and carried out under local aegis. That vast bureaucratic superstructure was not essential to the survival of Chinese agriculture. Local society was largely controlled by the gentry, whose power stemmed both from their wealth and from their close contacts with the bureaucracy. In time of revolt they could, of course, call on the state for assistance, but in normal times this was not necessary to the economy's successful functioning. They raised crops on their own land, no doubt were often involved in moneylending, and provided the demand side of the market for many types of luxury goods.

The competitive and intellectually stimulating life of a bureaucrat kept his central interests focused internally on the bureaucracy and his and his friends' paths through it. One of the great virtues of the system was that in normal times the bureaucrats were too busy with their own concerns to pay too much attention to what was going on in the economy. Of course, they did provide a steady flow of tax revenue to the center to support themselves, their rulers' whims, and at times to provide for the national defense. But even this operation was often tempered by the typical bureaucrat's close ties of family with some locality, a past that gave him some feel for what the traffic would bear. And this feel was kept alive by the constant risks in his career, risks that meant he might at any time be sent back home, his bureaucratic career at an end.

The secret of Chinese society thus lay in the system of elite circulation, which provided for both stability and decentralization in a combination that has rarely been achieved in world history. The gentry appear as the primary element of stability, families whose claim to influence rested on continued successful performance in the private sector of the economy. Recruitment to that class was thus somewhat open for the most energetic and fortunate local families. Bureaucratic recruitment too had this "somewhat open" feature, which preserved acquired experience through limited rates of movement up and down the status ladder, but also provided for steady recruitment of the most energetic and ambitious. Further, the preservation of ties of mutual interest between bureaucrats and gentry tempered the ever-present tendencies for tax collectors to take excessive advantage of the coercive monopoly of the state.

A major reason for the successful maintenance of the regime was, no doubt, the challenge posed by the continuing threat to national security. Northern tribes constantly threatened or actually carried out invasions of China proper. The Chinese responded by building the Great Wall and by maintaining an army that was often the world's largest. This was a major reason for the empire-wide tax collection operation; it also gave the Chinese continual confirmation of the proposition that eternal vigilance is the price of security. When the Chinese lowered their guard, a time of invasions and other troubles ensued.

Chinese social structure was, of course, far from perfect. The monarchic system was, in China as elsewhere, a major internal cause of the periodic decline of Chinese life into a time of troubles. The period of Western contact in the nineteenth century coincided with such a period of decline, which accounts for much of the negative reaction of Westerners to what they saw there. The local economies were traditional in organization and resistant to change; this was no trading economy, and it was unable to withstand substantial penetration by the outside world in the nineteenth century. But the lessons it offers, summarized above, provide some fundamental support for contemporary conservative positions.

Venice in many ways seems the complete opposite of China.[2] A mere city state at the top end of the Adriatic Sea, whose population during a good part of her history ran to not much more than a hundred thousand souls, she was located for much of that time at the center of the maelstrom of Mediterranean and European politics. She was surrounded by much larger states—Hapsburg Austria, the French and Spanish, who used Italy as their principal battleground, and the Turks, not to mention the rival Italian city states, several of whom were much larger than Venice. Nevertheless, Venice survived for a millennium as an independent and unconquered state, for over half that time with substantially the same basic social structure. Not only is this durability a record for the time and region, but even in domestic affairs Venice seemed far less disturbed by conflict and class division than any of her contemporaries. Once again we have a society with a secret weapon.

During its half millennium and more of social stability, Venice was ruled by an oligarchy of some 200 families. The chief executive, the doge, was elected for life, but his children had no right to succession. In fact, the structures of the electoral system and the system of committees that bore legislative and executive power were designed expressly to prevent the doge from acquiring the ability to dominate political life. Even so, he was available as a leader with wide powers during times of great stress.

Two additional features stand out as part of the Venetian success story. The great families were mostly engaged in trade. A typical successful career pattern would have a son engage in a number of trading voyages and then settle down in Venice to help run the family business from there. He would begin to serve on some of the less powerful governmental committees and gradually move into more serious involvement in affairs of state, perhaps leaving business affairs largely to other close relatives. When he reached the pinnacle, becoming either doge or member of the Council of Ten, he was a man rich in knowledge of both Venetian and world affairs. He was already an experienced executive, and he would have no doubt at least some experience of war, the times being what they were. And basic decisions would be taken on the basis of the collective judgment of at least a dozen men as worldly as himself. No other state could match this skill and judgment, and Venice reproduced it generation after generation for centuries.

Nowhere was this skill more severely tested than in the effort to preserve Venice's independence in the face of surrounding predator states. The Venetians successfully combined a preference for peaceful trade with a willingness to fight with all their resources to preserve independence when necessary. Only relatively rarely did this continued high level of preparedness lead to attempts at conquest, and even then the act of conquest often had a strong element of defensiveness to it, as in her relatively late and modest expansion into the territory surrounding the island city.

Another and central point about Venetian affairs: She operated with a small bureaucracy. Clerks and secretaries were needed, men who knew the law and the details of the operation of the society's political system. But not many such were needed, it turned out, especially if the bureaucracy was to function as a genuine instrument of the will of the leaders and not become an autonomous and resource-devouring body. This was no doubt something the Venetian merchant-rulers had all learned before they took up the reins of government, and they kept the bureaucracy in check for centuries.

The small bureaucracy did not imply the absence of a welfare system, however. Venice was probably less subject to famine during its history than any other comparable territory in the region. The Venetian government had a grain board that provided for distribution of grain to residents during times of food shortage. This was an essential ingredient in their famine-control program. But equally essential was the market. The Venetians, with their unequalled economic intelligence system based on traders' and consuls' reports, were able to take advantage of the wide variation in grain prices in various parts of the Mediterranean as a normal part of their trading activity. When a bad crop year came to Venice and its normal suppliers, this intelligence was used to buy up the necessary grain at the best available prices. The system functioned so well that serious deprivation came to Venice perhaps only once over these centuries, while it must have occurred a dozen or more times in even the best organized of the other lands of the region. It was a low-cost and very effective system. Accompanying it was a model—for its time—and also low-budget public health system.

The centrality of the family in Venetian society is very striking. Family members tended to be involved in the family business, and family and state affairs were conducted on the assumption of the durability of families. Building for the next generation was obviously a major incentive for the participants. And, of course, the family served as a support, a social-security agency, for its members.

Elite circulation was quite low in Venice. In fact, for centuries only members of the 200 or so families whose names were inscribed in the Golden Book could hold significant political office. Adoption was a device that provided some upward mobility, but clearly that mobility was quite limited. Nevertheless, Venice thrived as did no other state, its leaders rising to the occasion time after time. Furthermore, domestic Venetian affairs seem to have been extremely tranquil. This was not a product of brutal exploitation; on this dimension too Venice ran a quite mild-mannered regime. There were opportunities for the lower classes too, in crafts and petty trade, for example. The general prosperity of Venice created opportunities that could never have existed in more democratic but less stable societies of the time. A worker, it seems, did not aspire to be doge; but he did aspire to obtain a higher income and to leave something for his children. In Venice energy devoted to economic activity could produce this result often enough to keep such people relatively satisfied.

Venice, of course, did finally decline, sinking into a half century or more of stagnation before succumbing without a fight to Napoleon's armies. But even this decline offers its lessons. A major factor in later Venetian history was the expansion of the bureaucracy into a large and corrupt spoils system. This occurred when opportunities for the poorer nobility to make money in trade declined. Tied to their aristocratic traditions and social structure, these young nobles were not allowed to follow the market signals regarding their relative economic worth and so sink into less well-paid occupations. Instead, bureaucratic sinecures were found for them. Competition for these jobs led to the sale of offices and the usual sad tale of developing malfunction. In addition, the enriched nobles finally followed the course of aristocrats elsewhere and moved out of trade and into landholding, turning much of the trading activity over to foreigners. Estates of those times being largely self-contained, the nobles lost interest in problems of the larger society. Deterioration of the bureaucracy through growth and the separation of political and economic power seem to tell the story of Venetian decline. For the "upstart" merchants were thriving in the eighteenth century; it was not that there were no longer opportunities, but that the heart of the Venetian system had been transformed.

China and Venice may well be the two greatest national success stories of prenineteenth-century history. Certainly their social structures were among the world's most durable, and the message they pass on to us is essentially a conservative one. One might put its essence into four propositions.

1.   The primary basis for upward mobility (and downward too) should be economic performance, the creation of economic values.

2.   Those who make the basic economic and political decisions in the society should have a self-managed stake in the successful functioning of the economy.

3.   That state is governed best which is governed least.

4.   Eternal vigilance is the price of national security.

The nineteenth century was to add a fifth proposition.

5.   The most effective, dynamic, and stable economic system is based on the thoroughgoing market economy.

When properly interpreted, these propositions could stand as the basis of the conservative position; and each has been tested over the centuries in history's great success stories.

CHAPTER 4

England and the United States: The Thoroughgoing Market Economy

HISTORIANS usually place the start of the so-called Industrial Revolution at about two centuries ago. But having done this, they then point out that preparations for it were underway during the two centuries before that time and that the eighteenth-century changes came in at a modest pace. Then they add that this "revolution" is still in progress around the world. Some revolution! If they were all like that, you would never be able to tell a revolutionary from the rest of us.

A much more appropriate term for what has been going on has been suggested, namely, the Rise of Modern Industry.[1] *Modern industry* means production that requires relatively large amounts of fixed capital, such as factories and machinery and railroads and electric power stations. This emphasizes the single most important feature of modern economic times. And though, if you compare England today with England two centuries ago, "revolutionary" change has certainly occurred, that would not be the case for any two points in time that were, say, a decade or two apart. That is, there was quite steady change, so *rise* is also a more appropriate term.

The process was initiated and continued for reasons that have formed a central part of the conservative position. This should not be surprising, since important aspects of the conservatism developed as attempts to understand what was going on in this era, which posed important new problems for the individuals who were economically active. And though this new experience was largely a development of the eighteenth and nineteenth centuries, it has not lost its validity in the twentieth.

First, however, we must deal with the origins. How did it come about? It began, of course, in England, which in the eighteenth century was a great trading nation, with an economy that had considerable resemblance to that of the Venetian Republic, though writ on a larger scale. Merchants were already influential in government, and there was widespread recognition of the central role that trade played in generating the nation's prosperity. In fact, the increasing prosperity over the preceding century or two was a product of increasing trade, which of course is simply a question of merchants seeking out and finding profitable opportunities.

However, trade-based prosperity has its limits, unless increasing supplies of goods can be generated that can be profitably traded. Merchants were accumulating circulating capital, the money that was needed to buy the goods to be sold later. But this kind of investment was quickly turned over. Merchants tended to be leery of sinking their funds for long periods of time into an investment. The world seemed too uncertain a place for that. What caused them to change their minds? The answer to that question produces the key to the rise of modern industry.

Part of the answer lay in the consequences of previous success. Over time there had been a very substantial increase in the stock of circulating capital. This made the cost of money cheaper, lowered the interest rate, so that a potential factory builder found the costs of going into business cheapened. Furthermore, the richer merchants had become wealthy enough to be willing to take an occasional flyer on the more risky but potentially very profitable fixed-capital ventures.

This increased availability of capital created a favorable environment for the rise of modern industry, but could not generate the factories by itself. What had to be added was science, the systematic exploration of ways to harness nature to the satisfaction of human wants. The seventeenth-century science of Newton and others, combined with the technological development of the following century by such men as James Watt, created the technical opportunities that the economic environment made profitable. The conditions of both supply and demand had become extraordinarily favorable.

Probably the most important reason that these conditions had both become so favorable was that the institutional environment supported the developments. In the first place, there was the much-reduced impact of restrictive guild regulation as compared with the rest of Europe. For a century or more English mill owners who made use of water power had been escaping from the cities to the shores of more distant streams where the water flow permitted efficient use of water power to turn over the machines. In the countryside the guilds were relatively ineffective in controlling quantity, quality, and production methods, and of course the mill owners chose the lowest-cost methods. This is a very important factor, as can be seen from comparing the backwardness of the woolen mills, where guild regulation remained strong because mechanization came late, with the far more progressive cotton mills.

Second, there was the ability of the government to adjust successfully to new information. As the English cotton textile industry expanded by leaps and bounds, the government came to understand the institutional reasons for this success and to allow the guild regulation to die, or to abolish it. Thus additional industries were free to take advantage of the new freedom to follow the market's dictates, with similar consequences. This became vital even to cotton textiles in the early part of the nineteenth century when the advent of steam power led the industry to follow its profits nose back to the towns.

The government was flexible about these matters because it had already gone through an important adjustment in power relations.[2] The political upheavals of the seventeenth century had produced a kind of coalition and partial coalescing of the great merchant and landowning families. The British ruling circles thus had an understanding of the needs of commerce built in, so that it was not so difficult as it was elsewhere to convince them as to what needed to be done. In fact, some of the needed steps had already been taken. Among the most famous was the ending of the Patents of Monopoly, which were simply sales of monopoly rights to individuals as a revenue-generating device for the crown; a new kind of patent was allowed, namely, the right of individuals to benefit privately from selling or licensing an invention. This latter was very important to James Watt, among others, in spreading rapidly, and profitably, the new steam engine that he had invented and teamed up with Boulton to produce.

A number of changes of the above kind were developing in England in the eighteenth and nineteenth centuries; they can be summarized by saying that private property rights were being developed and publicly recognized to an extent unprecedented in the rest of the world. This produced a tremendous burst of energy within the population. A potential entrepreneur could go into business with far more confidence than elsewhere that the government would not interfere with the operation of his firm, and indeed through the developing legal system would be prepared to defend his rights against the predatory. And scientist-inventors such as Watt had some assurance that they could reap a profit from the commercial success of their inventions. This sort of stabilizing of expectations could not but further support the other forces favorable to the introduction and expansion of modern industry.

The structure of government had yet another fundamental consequence, namely, the favorable environment it offered to the advance of science and technology. England was a leader in these areas far beyond her share of Europe's population. In general, science and technology flourished where freedom flourished, and England and Holland, the great trading societies of the time, were precisely the places where freedom and science flourished most freely. These societies were refuges for those who were fleeing from tyranny; but more, they were also pragmatic societies, where the connection between science and commerce was valued, where prizes for solutions to scientific and technical puzzles of practical significance were offered, as in the prize offered for the first person to provide a practical basis for estimating the longitude of ships at sea; and where colleges were founded that were oriented toward teaching and researching the "practical arts." This connection between the trading society and political freedoms, so notable a feature of past history, has, of course, survived the rise of modern industry and today distinguishes the modern trading society from its socialist counterpart.

All these factors came into play to set the process in motion. But then, acting in combination, they tended to trigger further developments that provided still more stimulus to modern business, gave England a still greater competitive edge in international trade, and consequently increased the pressure on other countries to follow England's lead. One of the main ways in which this worked led to the improved functioning of individual markets. For example, the capital market became a steadily more effective vehicle for mobilizing and allocating resources for investment. As the volume of investment increased, the various suppliers of capital found themselves increasingly aware of the same opportunities; this, of course, meant competition among them and tended to generate uniform prices for similar types of loans. And on the other side of the market, the entrepreneurs found that the prices of the goods they purchased tended increasingly to fall under the competitive pressures of markets and improved information. All this served to stabilize expectations and to create still more favorable conditions for further progress. At the same time, devices for mobilizing capital improved. Not only were banks able to shift savings from regions where there was a surplus to deficit areas, but new forms of business developed to make investment more attractive. Most notable was the limited-liability company, legalized in the mid-nineteenth century in Britain, which permitted the smaller investor to participate in a company's profits without committing all his resources to the paying off of potential debts of a failing company. The same forces were at work producing similar changes in other major markets, for land and labor, and for products as well. In all these cases what was happening was that property rights were being developed, particularly by enhancing the ability of the owner both to use his assets without unnecessary restriction and to sell or buy goods and services at will.

There was one final development that in effect was a codification and generalization of all the other changes. This was the development of a very close interconnection among markets, and the spread of markets into nearly every nook and cranny of economic activity. The businessman could evaluate costs with confidence because each item he was likely to need could be bought on a market at a price that was readily discernible. He could evaluate his revenue, actual and potential, with relative ease because the same was true of his products, or soon would be if it was a new one. The investor had a comparable improvement in his ability to appraise profitability, since profit is the offspring of revenue and cost. Information tended to spread rapidly about new developments as those who saw the opportunity competed eagerly to obtain funds from the market, and those with funds sought out new ways to put their money to work profitably. And, of course, all this activity was generating a rapid rise in the volume and kinds of goods produced, goods that would be of no use to these capitalists unless they could find people who wanted them and could afford to buy them.

This latter point brings us to the question as to how capitalism, the regime of modern industry, has dealt with the workers who had no capital but their labor to offer. The answer is well known to every honest economic historian: The nineteenth century saw a rapid and sustained rise in the real wages of the working classes. As the last paragraph suggests, this was no accident but was a factor strongly imbedded in the logic of the system. In nineteenth- as in twentieth-century capitalism the rich got richer, the middle class got richer, and the poor got richer. The thoroughgoing market economy emerged and functioned in an environment of general enrichment.

Not only standards of living rose. Freedom too expanded and developed throughout the nineteenth century in Britain. Step by step the vote was extended until all adults were participants in the political process. The level of education continually improved, as did the supply of books and of knowledge in general. Newspapers created a general public that was better informed about national and world affairs than ever before in history. And dissidence became institutionalized in political parties. The connections between the political and economic processes are obviously intimate, and British levels of freedom were only to be approached in other thoroughgoing market economies, most notably, of course, that of the United States.[3]

The American republic, like the Venetian republic, was not conceived by its founders as a one-man-one-vote affair. Rather, it represented a development of the basic Venetian idea, calling for both the urban middle class and the small farmer to have their voices heard in the councils of power. True, the voice of the small farmer was to be based on one-man-one-vote elections to the House of Representatives, but indirect election of senators and the president were expected to give special weight to urban commercial interests. The mechanism did not quite work out as planned but essentially the desired outcome was produced over much of American history. The principles on which this result was based were those of justice and order. Justice was promoted by giving each man the right to have his interests represented politically, and order by an electoral system that was capable of adjusting to changing power balances.[4]

With no aristocratic class and no entrenched guild system to oppose, resort to the market as the basic resource allocator was almost automatic. In principle, government was primarily concerned with providing a stable framework, and was kept small enough that practice could not deviate very substantially from the ideal. An ambitious young man would not think of going into government service as a means of furthering his ambitions. Productive economic activity would be what he sought. And this in turn led to the rapid expansion of farming and trade and, later on, of manufacturing.

Thus by a different route a firm basis was laid for the development of a thoroughgoing market economy in the United States. That condition was not achieved until the second half of the nineteenth century. The system of slavery in the Old South was one hindrance to that development though, as will be seen in chapter 6, market theory offers a somewhat different interpretation of the nature of that problem than is customary. However, another drag on the emergence of the thoroughgoing market economy in the United States was simply a product of the immense size of the country and the undeveloped nature of the transport system. Markets in different regions could not develop very complex interactions with one another, and so stabilize prices and expectations over the whole system, until the transport and communications base for a national market had been laid. Throughout the nineteenth century the United States was moving strongly in that direction. It might be noted that the government had a considerable involvement in many transport developments. It may have served to hasten progress, but the cost of federal government action of this kind can be partly measured in the contribution government made to the creation of great fortunes. Much the same thing could be said of the government's involvement in land markets, though government involvement in land ownership would have been harder to avoid under the peculiar conditions in which the country was founded and expanded its territory. At least in this area the government organized a vast program of reducing its ownership of land, thus permitting market forces relatively free rein. The result was one of the most explosive episodes of economic growth and transformation known to history. The "minimal state" had proved its mettle.

In these two countries all the power of the five conservative principles mentioned at the end of the last chapter was demonstrated. The upper ranks of these societies came increasingly, in the United States overwhelmingly, to be occupied by men of experience with business, and their role in shaping government policy came to be increasingly important. The governments tended to be small—the American government's budget at the turn of the century was about 2 percent of the value of the national product, and Britain's, though relatively larger, was still miniscule by contemporary standards. The market had thoroughly penetrated every aspect of economic life. And they were free societies, the freest of their era, with a high level of domestic order.[5] The British, understanding the need for security, maintained the world's most powerful navy to provide for the island's protection.[6] The question to which we must now turn is whether this form of society can continue to function successfully in the changed conditions of the twentieth century.

CHAPTER 5

Markets and
the Twentieth Century

IN the twentieth century the economy has become much more complex. It is often argued that, as a consequence, the market does its job less well, the implication of course being that big government has been a badly needed development. However, there is no real theory to support this sort of conclusion. The theories of government that are popular these days in fact do the conservative job quite well: They point out the various ways in which government produces decisions of very poor quality. Essentially, the liberal line of argument does not use any theory of government at all. It first argues that the market cannot do the job well, and then assumes that the government, being a device to serve the people, will set everything to rights. Both theory and practice suggest that though the market is not perfect, it generally does a better job than government in delivering the desired goods.

For the moment let us concentrate on that nineteenth-twentieth century comparison. For example, some of the problems of market operation in the nineteenth century could be laid to the door of poor information flows. Problems of long communication time often led to goods continuing to be delivered to one market for some time after inventories in that market had begun to rise. It is even thought that a series of short-period business cycles in England may be attributable to the cumulative effects of communications time lag; for example, goods shipped home from India would keep piling up on British wharves for months after home demand had slackened off.[1] Letters written by hand take a long time to write, and often to read as well. Postal systems were rudimentary and in many places nonexistent. Hand delivery of messages about town was costly and time-consuming. As a consequence market decisions were often based on crude, partially informed guesses.

The reader, of course, can anticipate the twentieth-century response to all this. Typewriters, electronic data processing, radio and telephonic transmission—in a variety of fundamental ways the market has supported an incredible improvement in the speed and quality of information made available to the user. And where important problems remain, as with the postal service, the difficulties obviously are not the result of market failure; indeed at the present writing private delivery systems, such as United Parcel Service, are increasingly—and profitably—substituting for the inefficient government service. Once again, it is a market response that deals successfully with the problem, producing among other things the elimination of a whole genre of business cycles. Another thing to note is that this revolution in information if anything has improved the *relative* performance of markets vis-à-vis governments. Markets are organized to generate, process, and disseminate information of the kind and in the form that their users need; and markets are centrally concerned to keep this information flow in order. Government has a much more ambivalent attitude toward information. It wants the information in order to assist government decision making, but it does not much want the information to get out, where it might prove embarrassing; and those same motives exist for individual bureaucrats within the government. Combine this ambivalence with coercive power and you get the result noted in chapter 2, namely, bureaucracies that remain historical enigmas because they have managed to suppress so much information. Informationally speaking, they are the black holes of social space. Consequently, when there is a general improvement in information flow, much less of it will serve to improve government operation and much more of it will serve to improve market operation. Given the tremendous reduction in the cost of obtaining information, this has to represent a substantial improvement in the relative performance of market over bureaucracy in the twentieth century.[2]

There is no doubt that things have become a good deal more complex in the twentieth century. Deals tend to be bigger, the terms of contracts often contain literally thousands of clauses, and the time span of validity of contracts is often measured in years and tens of millions of dollars' worth of goods and services. What in fact has been the effect of this increasing complexity?

Accompanying it has been increasing creativity. There has been a scientific revolution coinciding with, perhaps even generating, the information revolution. The increase in scientific information has opened the door to creating new technologies; and at this point markets have come into their own as creative institutions. It is true that government has sponsored a large part of the scientific research—though it should also be noted that many of our leading universities, such as Harvard, MIT, Yale, and Chicago, are privately endowed. But it is under the pressure of market incentives that these technological possibilities have been transformed into effective realities. The comparison between Western market societies and bureaucratic socialism shows this in most striking form. The Soviet Union has a first-rate scientific establishment, fully aware of and even contributing to world scientific advance, at least when its Stalins are not instructing the scientists in their business. But despite massive efforts, the Soviets seem unable even to reproduce modern technology. In field after field, from commerical aviation to computers, from petroleum-industry equipment to chemical factories, the Soviets—and such once highly developed satellites as Czechoslovakia—must turn to the West if they are to get decent equipment to work with. Even in the space program, once supposed to be the shining example of socialism's superiority, we have recently been discovering just how crude the Soviet program was relative to the market-supplied American effort.

But the creativity of markets does not stop with the generation and commercial adaptation of technology. Organizational creativity has also been its hallmark. The structure of the modern corporation, and most strikingly the multinational, is certainly novel, and has grown out of the pressures of the marketplace to come up with an organizational form flexible enough to respond effectively to the massive new information flows, and effectively controllable under the constraints of the market environment within which it must operate. Once again socialism is either groping with crude marketlike forms of organization or attempting to emulate Western management practices, or both. The complexity of the developed twentieth-century economy has produced a variety of challenges to which the market system has clearly risen. And the secret of its success is a simple one, namely, the fact that material self-interest tends to be rewarded on the marketplace if it can generate goods and services that others want enough to be willing to give up the acquisition of other goods in order to be able to afford them. In a bureaucracy innovation is viewed with suspicion, since it is likely to be a threat to the authority of someone.

A third argument has it that the market system might be all right if it remained competitive, but that here is a built-in tendency for competitive markets to become monopolies. Consequently, government must step in either to preserve competition or to take over the operation of whole sectors of the economy.

The first and most important thing to notice about this line of argument is that the gross facts contradict it. A century or so ago there were undoubtedly far more monopolies in the United States, and probably in Britain as well, than there are today. For in those days the poor quality of the transportation system made it possible for local monopolies to abound. Especially if their products were heavy or bulky, these local monopolists were often able to extract the full monopoly price from their customers. But accompanying the information and scientific revolutions there has also been a transport revolution, which has turned these isolated markets into single markets national in scope. The result in most industries has been competition among a number of firms for the consumers' dollars and a substantial reduction in the number of monopolies.[3] During the twentieth century firms have grown, but so have markets, and by and large the one has canceled out the other.

A monopoly is defined as a single agent that has gained effective control over the total supply of some resource. If we simply take that definition and look around us in search of monopolies, our eyes will inevitably be drawn, not to the marketplace, where the monopoly is a rather rare bird nowadays, but to that biggest monopoly of all, the government. And the resource that government always legally controls the entire effective supply of is a very troubling one, namely the legitimate use of coercion. Coercion has historically been perhaps the most valuable of all resources, being the primary source of income for countless despots down through the centuries. There seems to be no alternative to concentrating its use in the hands of a monopoly, but it does throw a new light on much of the talk about monopoly. When agents of the biggest monopoly of all start talking about putting down capitalist monopolies, it sounds just a bit like using their own monopoly of coercion in order to squeeze out potential competition. This is not, of course, to claim that large private corporations lead blameless lives of public service. They are the instruments of people who are trying to get either rich or richer. But it *is* to suggest that one should always be suspicious of proposed controls that will have the effect of making the biggest and most threatening monopoly of all relatively bigger still; and one should be especially wary if the claimed goal is to reduce monopoly.

How did government come to be so overwhelmingly the dominant monopoly in American society? This certainly was not true of the nineteenth century. There are several points involved. First, there is a factor that can also serve as a sort of parable of our own time. One of the ways in which government became bigger was as a consequence of its involvement with railroad development in the West (that is, west of the Alleghenies). There was a tremendous potential market for the grain that could be produced on the endless plains, as well as for other products. But the investment required to run a railroad over such long distances was discouraging to private capital, and the profits in the medium run speculative, despite the golden longer-term prospects. Government was brought in and then used in ways that both rewarded promoters handsomely and fostered the development of monopolistic practices. Vast tracts of land were handed over to railroad companies, the roadbed grants covering a far wider swatch of land than was needed just for the railroad, while also serving as a firm base for monopolizing traffic. The attraction of this kind of operation, which involved a good deal of bribery of legislators among other things, tended to attract somewhat unsavory characters, who form a rather gaudy chapter in American history and founded some of the great American fortunes in the process.

So this joint business-government operation helped skew the income distribution as well as helping to generate some very strong monopolies. Over time the citizenry of the growing western states found these monopoly practices intolerable; they organized politically and eventually managed to impose a substantial level of regulation on the railroads. This had modest effects on railroad practices but helped make government still bigger and more powerful. Then when the railroads, gutted by those unsavory if government-favored financiers, went broke, government was brought in to help bail them out; after all, the citizenry wanted low prices, not suspension of service. And when rival modes of transportation developed, new schemes of regulation were cooked up to ensure "equitable" price structures, and the level of government involvement in the economy took a few more leaps forward. This process of interaction between economic problems and expanding government, together with mostly unneeded government aid, has continued for more than a century in this area of the economy, the latest episodes being the proposed government support for the mismanaged and bankrupt Penn Central Railroad and the government takeover and inefficient operation of railroad passenger service.[4]

The message is clear enough: Once government gets seriously involved in joint economic operations with private companies, the government role is likely to expand continually, since there will always be new opportunities for it to "help," whether by bailing out the victims of previous poor decision making or by serving as financial patsy for some new promotional venture. The appropriate line between government and business is the usual market line, and there is always a *prima facie* case against any proposal for the government to *give* a government service to some agent on the other side of that line. And, of course, that stricture does not apply only to *businessmen* who are seeking a handout.

The subject of creeping government encroachment immediately brings us to one of the most vociferous of liberal arguments. This is the claim that where there are externalities, the government must step in if good outcomes are to be generated. Externalities, which refer to "third-party" effects, or effects flowing from the implementation of a contract that fall on parties who are not a part of the deal, can be found most everywhere if one looks hard enough. So the argument for government involvement in almost every market is felt by liberals to have been established in principle. Clearly, if this line is accepted, there will soon be nothing but government operation of the economy.

Fortunately, it is not a very powerful argument. It has always been one-sided: The market is imperfect, therefore the government ought to do it. There is not any theory to show that government will do it better. But arguments to the effect that government will nearly always do it worse than the market are, in fact, quite powerful.[5] The problem facing a conservative today is in getting that message across. As will be indicated later, there are some grounds for optimism on this point, but there are also grounds for pessimism, based on the personal stake in government provision of certain services that so many individuals and businesses have today. The government has very powerful weapons in the service of buying support for a policy of government expansion.

These issues will be the subject of the next two chapters. For the present it is enough to note two things: once again the complexity and diversity of human wants and the creativity and adaptability of markets in the service of those aims; but also the unpredictability of humans, their tendency to whim and fashion as well as to wild outbursts of energy in the service of odd goals. Markets cannot be expected to deal at a very high level of effectiveness with such organisms, bureaucracies still less. But the point is, we don't really seek instruments for "dealing with" human behavior, only ways of living together that permit us to express ourselves freely while keeping the harmful effects on others within limits. A powerful and steadily growing agent who possesses a monopoly on the legal use of coercion is a very unlikely candidate for doing this successfully.

CHAPTER 6

Property Rights

IN RECENT YEARS a number of economists have begun to develop what amounts to a new field, namely, the economic analysis of property rights. Of course, the notion of property rights is an old one, and economists have written on the subject in the past. But much of this earlier work was flawed, mainly because the writers failed to appreciate the very close connection between the market and property rights.[1] We now turn to a description of the new approach together with a few examples of its application.

A private property right consists essentially of legal and social permission granted to an individual exclusively to use some resource, combined with permission to transfer that right to others. Of course, a private property right is only of interest if it is effective, that is, if the propertied individual does in fact have the ability to control the use and transfer of the resource. An individual's collection of property rights constitutes his room for independent maneuver in society, which of course relates closely both to his level of affluence and to his level of freedom.

If property rights are to be effective, they must have several key properties. Two of them, exclusivity and transferability, are mentioned in the definition in the last paragraph. In addition, a right must be well defined, so that both the owner and others know exactly what the owner does own. A right must be enforceable if it is to have any real meaning. And finally, the costs involved in defining, enforcing, and effectively transferring rights must be sufficiently low, relative to the value of the right, for owners to find it worthwhile to exercise their rights.[2]

The most obvious kind of property is real estate. In the United States today an owner has, more or less, the right to use the land himself and to sell it when and to whom he wishes. His rights in the property are defined at law and in the survey of the boundaries on file at the local land-registration office, and these rights are enforceable at law. There are, of course, costs involved in transferring the rights, and in enforcing them, but most of the time the costs are a small fraction of the value of the rights, as is evidenced by the frequency of exercise of the right of sale.

Though real estate probably represents the most typical kind of property, in fact anything that can become the subject of a deal can be viewed as property in exactly the same way. One can even have a property right to a service—for example, by signing a contract with a company to clean your office every week for the next year. Of course, in practice there are some legal restrictions on the property rights of the owners of almost all kinds of property, and property-rights analysis centers around the justification—and particularly the lack of justification for many—of these restrictions.

We will be discussing property rights in more detail in this and the next few chapters. Right now, an example or two will serve to indicate the great importance of property rights in defining an individual's economic situation and his opportunities for improvement. Consider first a farmer on a medieval manor. He and his family would be assigned the right to cultivate a tiny plot of land in some larger field, which was divided up among the other villagers. But this right was restricted in a number of ways. Every other year his land would have to lie fallow, the fences torn down and village cattle free to graze on his plot. The small size of the plot and its propinquity to neighbors meant that the timing of plowing, planting, and harvesting would all have to be controlled by joint decision, or by decision of the bailiff of the estate. So, in fact, the farmer could do very little individually to improve the productivity of his own land. He could not even sell the rights that he possessed, if he wanted to leave for town. The fact that he did not have an exclusive right to the use of the land was a serious brake on progress, and indeed the manorial economy was an especially backward one. Real progress only came after this form of holding had been abolished.

This example has some contemporary relevance, for in most socialist economies something very much like the manorial form of agricultural organization has been recreated. The peasants—the word farmer is not appropriate for such serflike creatures—are bound to the soil in this variant of socialism; that is, they are not allowed to leave the "collective" without legal permission. They are compelled legally to put in so many days a year of work on the collective farmlands. Their rewards, however, are miniscule, as is suggested by the fact that in the Soviet Union about a quarter of all agricultural output is produced on roughly the one twentieth of the land that peasants are allowed to work individually. One could hardly imagine a clearer demonstration of the inhibiting effects of the lack of an exclusive property right on incentives. Nor is there likely to be a clearer demonstration of the peasants' own view of this most common form of socialism, the collective farm, than their response to an offer to abandon the collectives and return to private agriculture. This occurred in Poland in 1956 and in Yugoslavia two or three years earlier. In both cases over 90 percent of the collectivized peasantry immediately redivided the land and returned to their former "bourgeois" ways. One last point, which relates to the rationale

for such a system: When the Nazis conquered the Soviet grainbelt province of the Ukraine in World War II, they took one look at the collective farm system and decided to retain it. Their leaders could think of no
better system for extracting a maximum of the harvest from the peasantry at minimum cost to themselves.[3] Who in his right mind, when
comparing the life of a private farmer with these beasts of burden,
would call the *former* the exploited ones?

A precise definition of any particular property right is obviously
important, since it would be difficult to either use or sell your property
if you are not sure just what it is you have in your possession. A patent
law, which gives the holder sole right to the use, licensing, and sale of
the benefits from an invention for some period of time, is an example of
a property right that has been defined by state action. Without that
definition the inventor has lost most of his material incentive to invent.
But, perhaps as important, he may also have lost access to resources
that would make the act of invention possible. Once the right is defined, those with money may be willing to subsidize certain kinds of
innovative activity. The modern university is a case in point, where
patents for the innovative work generated in its laboratories are, by
agreement with the researchers, assigned to the university.

But it is important not to exaggerate the role of the state in defining property rights. Usually the key steps are taken in the marketplace. For example, patent law could only be contemplated after it had
become widely recognized that innovative activity was often profitable,
and further that it was in the general social interest to support such
activity. Recognition of these two points requires a fairly sophisticated
knowledge of how societies work. That knowledge was to come from
business activity. Once again it was the businessman who, far more than
others, had the appropriate experiences for developing the relevant
understanding. Only in the Middle Ages in the West, and much later—if
ever—elsewhere, did this recognition spread far enough to produce
effective property-rights definitions for inventions. Not surprisingly, it
was in commerce-oriented Britain that the key steps were first taken.
And, of course, it was not just a matter of the businessman's experience, but the greater frequency of innovation in the more open environment of the commercial society that contributed to this outcome.[4]

Clearly, if property rights are not enforced, they are not worth
much. And equally clearly, there is a role for government in the enforcement of property rights. However, once again it is important to
realize that by far the major enforcement activity is generated by the
private sector itself. Historically, for example, the Law Merchant,
which governed relations between traders at the great medieval fairs,
grew up out of merchant practice and was enforced by the merchants
themselves. And today in the United States enforcement of property
rights as defined in business contracts is, by a factor of more than ten
to one, done privately and outside the judicial system. What typically
happens is that the contract itself calls for submission of disputes to
arbitration. Private arbitrators who are knowledgeable in the practices
of particular trades are organized to provide this service for a fee. The

merchant who loses such a private arbitration award has a powerful incentive to accept the decision, for otherwise his credit as a reliable businessman will suffer. And, of course, resort to the law remains as an option if the merchant feels strongly enough about the issue to bear the costs and uncertainties of legal action.[5] Throughout a market society one will have no difficulty in picking out the many other ways in which private activity dominates the enforcement of property rights.

There is one more point that is relevant in understanding the basic idea of property rights, namely, the cost of establishing them. In some cases it may simply be more trouble than it is worth to try to define and enforce some property right, in which case the right will tend to disappear. A rather striking recent example of this occurs in the older sections of some American cities. Buildings in these areas have been subject to a large variety of regulations, such as rent control, permission granted tenants to withhold rent on the basis of alleged building code violations, increasing complexity of building code rules, combined with increases in the cost of compliance, and restrictions on the right of eviction for nonpayment of rent. In many cases the landlord finds it no longer profitable to assert his property right in the building; he simply abandons it. This happens because he is no longer at all clear as to just what his property rights in the building are, and in addition he finds the cost of enforcing what rights he may have prohibitive. Interventions in the market system, which were the product of well-meaning but economically misinformed politicians and interest groups, thus ended up producing a decline in both the quantity and the quality of housing available to the poor.[6]

Having defined the concept of property rights, it is now time to point to some of the ways in which it can be used to gain insight into the fundamental issues of our day. We may begin with that basic socialist notion, enforced sharing. Many are attracted to this idea, especially when it is given more attractive names, such as "solidarity" or "commune." But in practice what it always turns out to be is enforced sharing. Even so, one might ask, surely there *is* something attractive about the idea of working together for a common goal and sharing the fruits of that labor. Indeed there is. The problem is not in that basic aim, one of the noblest of human aims. The problem lies in the particular method of implementation. When individuals are put into groups and told that their reward will be proportionate to the output of the group as a whole, the individual has lost most of his incentive to produce. The difficulty lies in the fact that he has lost his exclusive right to the fruits of his own labor.

This loss of incentive accounts for much of the lower productivity evidenced in both agriculture and industry in socialist countries. But often such collaborative effort is unavoidable. Factories in capitalist countries are often large, and involve hundreds of people operating in teams. How do they manage to attain higher efficiency levels than their socialist counterparts? The answer lies in the right to offer or withhold the use of the services they command, a right that each individual possesses in a market economy. In this case the laborer has alternative sources of employment, and the factory owner has alternative sources of labor. Performance must meet market standards or an alternative will be found for the worker. And the employer must meet market conditions of labor and reward or alternative employment will be found by the worker. The Chinese commune member and many of the more valuable and highly skilled employees of socialist factories typically do not have this opportunity, or the incentive of market competition. The lack of exclusivity and the lack of ability to transfer the resource, two key aspects of property rights, are defective or absent; the result: inefficiency and unpleasant conditions of work.

But what about that noble aim of working together and sharing the fruits of labor? The answer is that a regime of property rights, a market-based economy, is precisely the one that gives the greatest stimulus to such activity. No system of sharing is worth much unless the participants are there by their own choice; and in the long run it will not be worth much unless there *are* fruits to share. But those are the things the regime of property facilitates. Knowing what the various parts of a package will cost and will be worth, because the market prices tell them; free to enter into voluntary agreements with confidence that their property rights are protected, the participants in a market society tend to be on the lookout for just such opportunities of mutual labor for mutual benefit. The difference is in the voluntary nature of the agreement, the concern of each that he will receive a sufficiently large share of the fruits that it will justify his participation, and free to leave if things don't work out to his satisfaction: This is the sort of arrangement for cooperative work that the market generates. This is the essence of a capitalist enterprise. If results are any criterion, it is superior in every way to other arrangements, which by definition involve in some form or another coercion of the participants.

A description of the role of capital in society offers another opportunity to show the fundamental role of property rights in generating an affluent and orderly society. In Marx's view the problems of capitalism all stemmed from the monopoly of the means of production, the factories and farms that are the tools for generating output, which the capitalist class possessed. We have seen that something very much like monopoly of this kind did exist in Venice, and that it played a role in the ultimate decline of that city-state. And in nineteenth-century England it was certainly true that a relatively small number of people owned the factories, and most of the farmland too.

But that is not a monopoly. Ownership of *all* scarce resources is restricted; that is precisely what scarcity means. And no one would say that everyone ought to own a factory, for that would be an impossibly inefficient drain on our scarce resources. A monopoly occurs when *one* agent owns or controls the means of production. And only one kind of society fits that bill, namely, the socialism that Marx and his followers want to replace capitalism with. In a sense Marx's prediction has been vindicated; in socialism there is monopoly ownership of the means of production by a tiny ruling class acting in concert as the Communist party; but the results are pretty awful.

In a market economy the regime of property rights implies the very opposite of Marx's charge. The market provides access to the means of production for all who can afford to participate. And participation does not require great wealth. There are over 15 million private individuals in the United States who own shares of stock. And there are millions of capitalists who exert direct control over the means of production as owners and managers of small businesses and corporations. This occurs because the market is a voluntary mechanism, because it stimulates incentives to work and hence generates more affluence than other forms, and because it generates efficient use of the means of production since each potential use of capital must compete with others on the marketplace. It is the openness and competitiveness of the process by which capital is generated and allocated among competing uses that is the essence of capitalism. In fact, the power of these processes is illustrated by the Venetian case. Given the size of the economy, restriction of control over the means of production to some 200 families turned out to be sufficient to keep these voluntary, competitive pressures at a high pitch. Over a period of centuries these pressures dominated the distorting force of restrictionism and permitted Venice to function successfully. Some concentration of wealth actually serves to stimulate progress by increasing the supply of funds available to be put into expanding future production, as our exemplary market economies show all too clearly.

Many other examples of the role of property rights in the economy could be cited, from the development of credit to the control of pollution. Some of them will be discussed as we go along. But enough has perhaps been said at this point to establish that property rights are an essential feature of a successful market economy. Their relation to the processes of government is the subject to which we now turn.

CHAPTER 7

Government and Property

GOVERNMENT and the bureaucrat are inseparable. The latter is the fellow who operates the former, not as an elected official responsive to the needs of his constituents but as a cog in a large and complex machine. No one has much good to say about the bureaucrat, and with reason. However, there *is* one nice thing that can be said about him, and we will begin the discussion of government and property with that remark.

The bureaucrat is a human being, not different in any essential way from the rest of us. His problem is that he is put down in an environment where, behaving in a quite human way, he produces horrendous results. It cannot be a very satisfactory way of life, so eliminating as many bureaucratic jobs as possible will release both his victims and the bureaucrat himself from misery.

The problem of the bureaucrat stems from the nature of his job. A typical bureaucrat is assigned some clientele, say, applicants for food stamps or for a small business loan or for a hunting license or for a particular routing of a new highway. In all likelihood he hasn't chosen his clientele, and they certainly haven't chosen him. Second, the bureaucrat's success or failure depends not nearly so much on whether he satisfies his clientele as whether he satisfies his boss. Just what his boss wants varies from situation to situation, but, human being that he is, the boss bureaucrat typically wants a minimum of trouble. He doesn't want a lot of complaints to handle and he doesn't want to have to make a lot of tricky decisions. If there is a difficulty, bureaucrat and boss bureaucrat want to protect themselves; so as a matter of routine anything out of the ordinary will be passed up the line as far as possible for decision. The possibly devastating effect on the client is of little interest to the bureaucrat; or at least there is no way the client can make it worth the bureaucrat's while to take him more seriously without violating the laws against bribery. Actually, there is one way, namely, by exerting influence at the top of the hierarchy to get special treatment. This works quite well provided you have that kind of friends, but the result is clear enough: The bureaucracy will give little consideration to special need but will give careful consideration to the especially influential.

Finally, there is a property of the government bureaucrat that has the effect of turning the merely frustrating into the rather sinister. The government bureaucrat represents the agency that has been assigned a monopoly in the application of legalized coercion in the society. Behind the bureaucrat stands that vast panoply of process servers, inquisitors, and jails that, in a very direct way, legitimize the bureaucrat's unconcern. The bureaucrat will always want information before he acts, and the rational—but uninfluential—citizen will always feel just a touch of the fear inspired by the awful majesty of the state as he considers his responses and where they may lead.

The market is a means of getting jobs done superior to bureaucracy in each of these dimensions. The market is a voluntary mechanism—no cops lurking in the background to go into action if you say no deal. The businessman's assistants have a much more clearcut incentive to please the client, namely, if it brings in profits it makes the boss happy. Furthermore the firm—and this applies to nearly all of them in the United States—will not be a monopoly and so has a direct incentive to satisfy the customer in order to retain the business. There is no alternative government to go to for your licenses and subsidies.

Of course, the market isn't perfect, and there are some jobs it does not do too well, such as actually managing the national defense. But all we are arguing is that there should be a very strong case for letting the market do the job, given the problem of the bureaucrat, before resort to government is made. And this bias against government control of economic activities has been a central part of the conservative tradition, as earlier chapters have suggested.

Unfortunately, the matter cannot rest there, because there is built into bureaucratic government an almost irresistible tendency to grow, which tends to make a mockery of even the best intentioned conservative governments. One might remember that in Ronald Reagan's tenure as governor of California the state budget doubled. The same tendency toward growth has been observed in other conservative administrations at both state and federal levels, both in America and in Britain.

By now it is well known that this tendency toward growth is built into bureaucracies. Parkinson's famous law tells us that in a bureaucracy the number of tasks assumed tends to rise to the level of employment. And Niskanen's analysis of bureaucracies has shown how much of their behavior can be explained simply by assuming the bureaucrat is trying to maximize his budget.[1] That, of course, is quite a plausible assumption, given that the influence of a bureaucrat tends to be measured by the size of the organization he heads.

Once again the comparison with the market is instructive. The businessman too is often judged by the size of the operation he controls. But the difference is that his operation is tied far more closely than the bureaucrat's to providing services his clientele actually wants. And the size of his organization is measured in terms that reflect this level of service, namely, sales and cost, including the rate of return on the capital supplied to the business. The bureaucrat's operation will be based on only one of these, cost, for the value of his service will not be measured in a marketplace and so cannot be measured in terms of price. Move to a big new building and double your staff and you have become a much bigger success, almost regardless of the effect on the level of service provided. This is the secret of empire building in Washington and the other centers of government around the world.

Just as these lines are being written, a whole new giant bureaucracy, the Department of Energy, whose employment will run into the tens of thousands, is moving into its big new headquarters in Washington; there is a good deal of talk of a Department of Education; my state's budget, under two reputedly penny-pinching governors, Ronald Reagan and Jerry Brown, has tripled; and my home town, whose population has risen less than 20 percent in the past two decades, has just taken over two good-sized buildings to house our expanded city staff. It seems there are many successful bureaucrats these days.

Before turning to the question of how to control bureaucracies, the connection between big government, that is, big bureaucracies, and property rights needs to be pointed out. Actually, the problem is the lack of connection, for the existence of bureaucracy usually implies that important infringements of property rights are occurring. In the first place, where there is big government property rights will tend to be relatively ill-defined. This stems from the uncertainty as to just what decision a bureaucrat will render, a decision that may determine whether you have the legal right to start a business or receive some other benefit that only the bureaucracy can bestow. The uncertainty, of course, is a consequence of the situation of the bureaucrat, discussed above, and especially of the lack of mutuality in the relation between bureaucrat and client.

Second, bureaucracies have often been brought into existence for the express purpose of infringing or eliminating many existing rights. They are created to restrict your right to drive your truck on certain roads, to compel the installation of various so-called safety and anti-pollution devices, to make tax rulings that substantially increase your liability in various ways, to enforce licensing requirements that increase costs to many and deprive some of their livelihood; and so on ad infinitum. Much of this power is the product of what is known in the trade as "discretionary authority" and, given the complexity of the regulations under which the bureaucracy will almost certainly be operating, the authority that results can be very great.

Big government often creates serious problems of enforcing even those property rights it has defined and recognized because of overlapping jurisdictions among agencies; for example, the enforcing agency may be independent of the agency that confirms the right and may be unwilling to act. This sort of buck passing is familiar to everyone who has had dealings with a bureaucracy. And then too there is the tremendous increase in the cost of preserving one's property rights in the face of all these harassments. Even though success in fighting the bureaucracy may be attainable, it may not be worth the victim's time and money.

Finally, and possibly most important of all, there is a massive creation of what might be called public property rights. Each bureaucrat has his own little sphere of influence, which consists in the right to make decisions one way or another over some restricted range of problems. The bigger government gets, the greater the likelihood that any particular private property right will come into conflict with one of these bureaucrat's rights. Where does the injured individual go for redress? The answer, of course, is that he must go to government, and all too likely to the offending bureaucrat's boss. One can hardly expect justice to be done when the judge is an interested party. The Watergate events provide a long list of situations of this kind. And so the larger the government, the more massive the infringements of property rights.[2]

This is quite a depressing picture, a picture of a government that performs poorly but continually expands. Where can one look for help in bringing it under control? One place one might look is the electoral process and the legislature. In a democracy, if the people want to reduce the bureaucracy they elect legislators who are committed to doing just that, and the problem is solved, right?

Unfortunately, the correct answer is wrong. For generations now scholars have been trying to produce an analysis of democracy that shows how well it functions. But no one, however erudite or sophisticated, has managed to improve on the old saw to the effect that democratic government seems like an absolutely abysmal form—until you look at the alternatives. It wins by default, not because of its "optimality properties."

One major difficulty in the present context has to do with the relation between majority rule and property rights. If a majority can change the law at will, all property rights that are protected by the law are in constant jeopardy. And for any particular property right, it is usually not too difficult to put together a majority vote against it, since property rights can usually be categorized in such a way that only a minority holds any one of them. Nor are individuals at their best when deciding the fate of others, as opposed to their own. For all these reasons, among others, majority rule is capable of producing some very bad outcomes.

The American founding fathers were well aware of this fact, being keen students of the classical democracies—and of the history of Venice, it might be noted. Their notion was that the majority should be represented but should not rule absolutely. The system of checks and balances was designed explicitly with a view to curbing the power of the majority. The dual system of legislatures, followed at the federal level as well as in many states—which has been threatened by the recent misguided one-man-one-vote decrees of the courts—was one of the keys to their system. What this means is that the legislature represents a variety of interests. What it is supposed to produce is not an ideal outcome but a workable compromise among these interests.

Unfortunately, government has become one of the most important of those interests. Legislators can influence bureaucrats, all right, but the reverse is also true, the bureaucrats' weapons as always being harassment and delay in dealing with one's opponents and open-handedness in dealing with one's friends in Congress. Even the president often finds that if his program is being stalled in the bureaucracy he is more able to get what he wants by creating a new agency than by attempting to reform the existing agency against the opposition of the many influential friends it has carefully nurtured. That is probably an important part of the reason for the creation of the Department of Energy, and it leads to the confident prediction, based on past history, that most schemes of governmental reorganization will achieve little. And to both legislature and presidency there is the constant pressure from potential beneficiaries to provide more services. So it appears that the electoral system cannot be relied upon simply to take the will of the majority and act upon it.

Among the most interesting of recent cases of this kind of influence has to do with the Nixon proposal for providing a guaranteed minimum income to the poor. A major reason for the failure of the proposal to pass Congress was that the government "service" bureaucrats opposed the measure. And why did they oppose it? Because it bypassed them, threatening their jobs by substituting money for the administrative "services" they provide.[3]

The Law vs. the Bureaucracy

The importance of the law, from the conservative point of view, is shown by the fact that it arose as a means for adjudicating conflict involving those two basic institutions, the family and the market. Near Eastern and particularly Roman law first emerged as family law, as a set of rules for dealing with conflicts between families, particularly where some harm had been done by one family's members to those of another, leading probably to breaches of the peace if society did not impose some solution. And much of contemporary law dealing with property rights is an evolving product of the medieval—and ancient—Law Merchant, a set of rules administered at first by the merchants themselves, as noted earlier. As times have changed and societies have grown more complex, the law has changed too. Today it represents the codified experience of a hundred generations.

If markets were the place where the basis of property rights was first laid in the act of exchange of goods, it was in the law that the concept and institution of property rights was given explicit form. Rules for determining ownership and obligation were worked out as a consequence of experience that provided a firm and defensible basis for trade, and one that would not be cluttered with excessive litigation and conflict. And as experience accumulated and society changed, the rules accumulated and changed too. In Anglo-American common law this process is highly visible in the process of making and adjusting precedents in the courts. But it is present too in the civil-code countries of the European continent, where the codes have undergone a very similar process of evolution in response to similar social developments. Law has thus developed everywhere in the West into a major source of wisdom with respect to dealing with practical problems of human conflict.

One must bear in mind, of course, that by "the law" we mean a good deal more than a set of books containing all that wisdom. The court system with its judges and lawyers and—in America, at least—adversary proceedings are essential to it, as are the investigating and enforcing arms of the law, the prosecutors' offices and the police. But even the judiciary taken as a whole is minute in size as compared to the executive branch. In 1965 the federal judiciary had a total employment of 6,000, compared with 2.5 million civilians in the executive branch. It is also highly decentralized, with great care being taken to prevent encroachment by one jurisdiction on another. The judiciary is obviously a very different animal from a bureaucracy.

And this brings us to a major conservative principle, which is especially valuable in the struggle against big government: In thinking of reform the effort should be oriented toward making the system look more like the judiciary and less like the executive branch. And along with this will also go the rule: Keep it simple! A governmental apparatus restructured in accordance with these two rules has some fundamental advantages over the present state of affairs. In the first place, it is clear that such a government would have far greater respect for property rights than is possible in a bureaucracy-ridden environment. For the stock-in-trade of the law is to determine the rights of the parties and to make a judgment on the basis of what rights have been infringed.

Second, the cost of administering such a system should be a fraction of the cost of bureaucratic intervention. The law is structured to respond to conflict situations and to attempt to resolve the conflict in a way that will be both just and efficient, which means less likely to cause more conflict in the future. And the law tends to be oriented toward creating an environment within which people work out their problems on their own, again in sharp contrast with the bureaucrat's direct and active involvement in the affair.

And finally, the judiciary functions as the mirror image of the ever-expanding bureaucracy. The legal system works better the less the resort to it. A good law is one that is just, is widely understood, and whose enforcement is something everyone can reasonably expect. Under such circumstances violation of the law is likely to be infrequent. The same applies to infringement of property rights; if they are reasonable, are well defined, and enforcement is expected, they too are unlikely to be infringed. And judges have little incentive to expand their workloads, in striking contrast to the attitude toward his agency's "workload" of the ambitious bureaucrat.

Now, of course, the law is a far from perfect institution. There is such a thing as a bad law, not to mention a bad judge or an ill-trained policeman. The judiciary is a human institution. It has a number of advantages over bureaucracies, among others that because of its long tradition it tends less frequently to ask its members to do ridiculous or impossible things. But it does go astray. When that happens one is likely to note an increase in litigation in the area at issue, because when the law does go astray it is usually because of problems with definition or enforcement of property rights. But at least that provides a public sign of a problem, again in sharp contrast to the bureaucracy's tendency to keep all its dirty linen carefully concealed from the public eye.

The next two chapters will be largely devoted to offering examples of how these two principles can be applied to problems of contemporary government. In closing this chapter we suggest one classic case that illustrates the principles enunciated above in a rather pure form. The case involves federal regulation of radio broadcasts.[4]

Regulation of radio broadcasts grew out of a genuine problem. When commercial broadcasting began in the 1920s, any broadcaster was free to transmit on whatever band he chose with a transmitter of whatever power he chose. The result was a great deal of mutual interference and conflict. After considering a variety of alternative forms of control, including nationalization of the industry under the Department of the Navy, a system of regulation was established that involved the licensing of broadcasters. When the latter met the requirements set up by the new agency, now called the Federal Communications Commission, it was assigned a wavelength and permission to use it for a period of years until the license expired. As the years went by, the regulations became more detailed and all-embracing, including substantial control of the general pattern of programming and even the content of specific broadcasts. Several stations have been denied a renewal of their license because of specific programs they have broadcast. And as the years went by, of course, the agency not only expanded its competence to regulate in a variety of directions but also expanded its staff continuously—for example, in the ten relatively quiet years of regulatory activity between 1955 and 1965, the commission's staff increased by 50 percent. The typical pattern of bureaucratic operation was being followed to a T— except for the fact that the commission's programming controls are probably unconstitutional, a violation of the First Amendment right of free speech.

Now consider the judiciarylike alternative to bureaucracy. The first thing to note is that the problem that generated the initial legislation is a serious one, affecting national defense as well as private communications in a vital way. However, the basic problem is actually a very simple one, namely, a lack of definition of property rights in broadcast frequencies. New technology does not always generate a clearcut property right, and such was the case here. Supposing then that the government served as the definer, and enforcer, of such rights. A simple and effective scheme would require only that the government serve as registrar of the rights. In this case it could treat the frequencies much as it treated the billion and more acres of public land that have passed through its hands in the last two centuries. That is, instead of leasing broadcast rights, it could sell them outright and enforce the property right of the purchaser. Bands could be reserved for national defense, but an even more effective outcome might be to require the armed forces to obtain their wavelengths in the same way as private users, thus providing Congress and the public with a clear picture of the cost of this aspect of national defense. The advantage of the latter approach is that undoubtedly the armed forces would not retain the 90 percent of the wavelengths they now hold, thus substantially lowering the cost of using the airwaves to communicate.

Suppose such a system were introduced. How would it differ from the present arrangement? Clearly, it would take very little government activity; after the initial sale there might be occasional subsequent sales as new technology opened up the possibility of using additional frequencies. But aside from that very modest effort, about all that would be needed would be a register of ownership of the various frequencies at various locations. Any problems would be a matter for the judiciary.

There is no apparent reason why telecasts could not be handled in exactly the same way. This is a strong case and the result is very striking: a probable reduction in regulatory cost to perhaps 1 percent of its current level. And there may be even greater opportunities in some other areas, because in the broadcast example there actually is *some* need for government action. So the final message of this chapter can be an optimistic one: By using the property-rights approach and applying the principles of keeping it simple and using judiciarylike rather than bureaucracylike forms of organization, the government leviathan may yet be brought under control.[5]

CHAPTER 8

Government and

Spending

THE most controversial area of government spending in recent years has been the welfare program. It is a massive program, involving annual expenditures far in excess of the defense budget, and it has been growing far more rapidly than the latter for a great many years. It is also a tremendously complex operation, containing literally hundreds of substantial programs aimed, at least so it is claimed, at alleviating or—as many would say—eliminating poverty in the United States. And no one seems to be able to stop the growth.

Naturally, this gigantic mess cannot be completely disentangled in a single stroke. But it is possible to point out some frequently ignored aspects of the mess and its causes, and it turns out that the suggested cures all seem to point in the same direction. The basic mistake has been the attempt to bypass the market in areas where it can do the job perfectly well, either by itself or with a minimum of definitional and enforcement assistance from the state.

A good place to start is medical care. American per capita expenditures on health care are the largest in the world but, judging from statistics, America has far from the world's healthiest population. As one would expect, the poorer sectors of the population have the highest incidence of ill health. The liberal response to this situation has been to propose massive new programs designed to get the government involved in creating a "health-delivery system" to the poor. Examples of nationalized health systems such as those in Britain and communist China are held up as shining examples of how to do this job.

At the moment the Chinese health system, with its barefoot doctors and acupuncture, is all the rage. What never seems to be noticed is that without any revolutionary fanfare a comparable system has been in operation in noncommunist China for decades. In Hong Kong and Taiwan there are modern hospitals with a full panoply of modern doctors and methods. But side by side with this there is "traditional" Chinese medicine strongly based on herbalist cures, and distributed widely over the poorer areas of these places. There is an element of quackery to some of this traditional medicine, but what medical system is wholly free of that? Many diseases are effectively cured by traditional medicine, and there is a growing interaction with at least some modern practices.

The thing that needs to be noted about the "secondary health-delivery system," as it would be called among government policy-makers, is that it is a low-cost system. The herbalists are paid fees that semiskilled workers and peasants in Taiwan and Hong Kong can afford to pay, when they themselves feel the need for the care. And these fees cover the costs of the supply of the service, so problems of overuse and of haggling over fair prices do not absorb the time and energies of large bureaucracies. And the results are suggested by the fact that the health of these populations appears to be comparable to that of the mainland Chinese. The communists' barefoot doctors program may be a success too; but essentially it is a mimicking of a system generated and sustained without political fanfare by the market systems of the "other" Chinas.

The moral for the United States is clear enough. Our problem is that government licensing of medical practice has, as in nearly all other government licensing systems, been effectively turned over to the licensees, in this case the doctors, to administer. And they, as would anyone following his self-interest, have arranged things so that the standard of medical care that passes their requirements is millionaire-type care. In effect, every doctor becomes a Park Avenue doctor because the government is guaranteeing Park Avenue prices for the supply of medical services. The recent expansion of government subsidies has expanded the demand for this kind of medical service tremendously, thereby increasing medical prices far more rapidly than the volume of medical services. And, of course, those who get left out tend to be the poor.

The solution is to make it possible for the market to supply inexpensive medical services to those who have less to spend. We even have a considerable body of people who with little or no additional training would be well equipped to provide many of these services, namely, nurses and former armed services medical corpsmen. What many people need to understand is that this does not mean that the poor will get poor-quality service. Rather, it means that they will not get the frills unless they want to pay for them. Much medical service is dispensed for cosmetic or psychological reasons rather than to create or preserve the basic health of the body. And much diagnosis and treatment is very simple, requiring nothing like the tremendous knowledge and skill of a current M.D. The place to sort these things out is not in Washington but on the marketplace. And that will not be possible until the government stops granting to the medical profession as a property right a de facto monopoly on the supply of medical services.

The response to past suggestions that the government stop licensing doctors compulsorily has been that it will destroy the quality of medical care, leading to the entry of a lot of charlatans into the health-care field. People who argue this way have not noticed two

things. First, there are already a lot of charlatans supplying health
care, as even a casual reading of the daily papers will reveal. But
second, and more important, is the fact that the government does not
now control quality in the medical profession. The government simply
granted the monopoly right to doctors; having done that, it leaves the
administration of licensing essentially up to the profession itself, acting through its chief organizations, such as the American Medical
Association. If the government were to cancel its monopoly, the AMA
would still have a strong incentive to make sure that everyone knew
that people licensed by it are reliable, high-quality practitioners; indeed,
if anything its incentive in this direction would be enhanced, for then
there would be quality competition so that the quality price-differential
that their members' services could command would be at stake. Then
the road would be opened for the entry of lower-priced medical services.
These too would no doubt develop their own quality-control organization and make efforts to see that the public understood that such
quality control was there to back up their service. And, of course, the
usual market informational mechanisms would be at work. Once this
step was taken, one of the major problems in health care would be
solved, while at the same time current government expenditures in
this area would be reduced by a large fraction.[1]

Food, clothing, shelter, and health: These are life's necessities, a
minimum supply of which are essential for the normal functioning of
the human being. In successfully functioning societies some effort is
made to supply these services to those in great need. The most successful, such as the durable and conservative societies of Venice and imperial China, had such programs, and they seem to have contributed
substantially to domestic peace and stability. In the United States we
have these programs too, but they seem to have had the very opposite
effect. They have not even done a particularly good job of supplying
the services, while costs have become astronomical, something over
three thousand dollars a year per person on the most generous estimate
of the number of poor, and probably in fact nearer twice that figure.

Why the great discrepancy? The answer is the liberal approach
to welfare. Liberals have attempted to use the program to accomplish
too many objectives, from income equalization to providing minority
employment, from turning the poor into politicians to redesigning
urban environments. Most of these objectives are resisted by large
segments of the population, because their own interests are hurt in the
process, and the diversion of resources to these various purposes has
meant that relatively little money reaches the poor. A number of these
objectives have to do not only with controversial matters but with goals
no one even knows how to achieve. Consequently, the programs all
leave a massive trail of ill-defined and poorly enforced property rights
behind them. The inevitable, and, for a conservative easily predictable,
result is inefficient supply of services and a substantial increase in the
level of conflict.[2]

A conservative welfare program would not be operated at zero
level, but it would be limited to serving the basic aim, namely, to make

possible a relatively secure supply of basic goods and services to those in great need, and to do it at minimum cost. The medical example points out the great possibilities that exist for cost reduction by such devices as simply getting the government out of the business of granting monopolies. This approach also has great promise in the housing field, where much regulation is aimed far more at preserving the monopoly power of the building-trades unions than it is at promoting safe and efficiently built homes. We will not go into this area in detail, but one point might be worth making. Even if changes in property rights in this area merely lowered the cost of middle-class housing (it would in fact do far more than that), this would be of considerable help to the welfare program. For it would lead a number of families to move up to middle-class housing, thus in turn improving the quality and quantity of the housing available to the poor. And since the middle class is far more numerous than the poor, the relative increase in housing from any such shift would be greater for the poor than for the middle class. Once again we have an elementary point in the theory of supply and demand that is largely ignored in the current welfare program.

Of course, there are always limits to cost reduction. We are talking about scarce goods and their social cost can never be brought down to zero. Current programs are often aimed at bringing their private cost down to zero, at providing "free" medical service and the like. But the taxpayers have to pay if the recipient does not, and the overuse that such an approach generates means much higher costs, which in turn leads to big control agencies and the usual process of creeping bureaucratism. If the program is to be efficient, an attempt should be made to bring private and social costs into equality. That sounds like a subtle goal, and it would be, were it not for the fact that that is just what markets do. Marketizing the welfare program is therefore a central aspect of conservative policy.

And so we come to the final step in eliminating the welfare mess, the famous negative income tax. There is no need to nationalize the health services or to engage in massive public housing ventures. Indeed, as experience shows, there is every reason not to do that. Once normal—meaning dynamic and creative—market forces are again allowed to work in these areas, there will be a supply of services at a fraction of current costs. The income support required to make these services available to the poor would be correspondingly lower and, of course, the cost of administering such a program a tiny fraction of current costs.

One final point about the welfare program is, namely, the nature of the social obligation and the nature of the goals that can reasonably be achieved. In the first place, it is important to bear in mind that the poor will always be with us. It's a simple matter of definition. A very important aspect of poverty is *relative* lack of goods. It has been noted that as average incomes in the United States have risen, questionnaires asking people how much is needed these days just to get by produce answers that rise at about the same rate. Poverty in this sense begins at about half the current average income. The poverty war seems to go along with this in practice, with the obvious result that an anti-poverty program has to get bigger every year, and the more affluent we become the more the program will require.[3]

This is obvious nonsense. The government has an obligation, as most conservatives would concede, to eliminate any serious risk that Americans do not have access to enough of those basic goods and services to survive. And that is the end of it; to get more than the minimum of necessities is a matter of the individual's own behavior. Markets—and families and private charities—exist to deal with this situation. The markets work for those who have the willingness and capacity to produce things of value to others. Those who can find no way to get above the minimum by using these agencies may be objects of pity but not of general social obligation. The history of any welfare program designed to do more than this will bear a considerable resemblance to the recent history of the American welfare program, for it is bound to have monopoly and creeping bureaucratism and corruption built into it.

Of course, there are certain aspects of the welfare and other spending programs that we have not taken into account. For example, there probably is a place for government in certain areas of more direct action. One that particularly comes to mind is transactions costs, one of the major problems in some areas of market behavior that produces less than satisfactory results, as noted in the last chapter. The government can sometimes use its powers effectively to improve market functioning by reducing the private transactions costs. A good deal of the legislation designed to be enforced through the judicial system is of this kind, such as the laws regarding sales of goods. And, of course, the more privatized welfare system outlined above involves just such a shift in emphasis, from executive agencies to the judicial system. The individual's problems with the welfare system are then more likely to be ones that he will take to court than ones he will take to some social worker for resolution.

But the poor individual may not be aware of his rights and opportunities under such a system; certainly he will not just after it is installed. In such a situation it is a legitimate function of government to engage in a substantial informational program. This might even go as far as to provide some subsidized legal counsel during the transition period. But such activities should not be continued if there is any prospect of the service being supplied on the private market. And, of course, what this suggests is a reform of the monopoly power possessed by the legal profession in ways that correspond with the above medical revision.

There are many other areas of government activity that require substantial revision if an effective conservative policy format is to be achieved. But, aside from the question of economic stabilization, to be taken up in the next chapter, these areas, from education to agriculture, require the introduction of no new principles. Equipped with the already suggested ideas and the relevant facts, there is no great difficulty in working out the basic lines of revision needed. For Keep it simple! is one of those conservative principles.

CHAPTER 9

Money and Taxes

THERE IS a close connection between economic fluctuations and property rights. Upward and downward surges in the level of economic activity create unpredictable changes, often quite substantial ones, in the market values of various assets. This destroys some of many individuals' command over resources, and thus some of their rights to exclusive use and transfer of resources. Furthermore, the uncertainty generated tends to make transactions more costly as individuals must take additional time and effort in order to study the prospective volatility in the value of the assets they are thinking of acquiring. Even the costs of enforcing contracts are affected, because economic fluctuations continually generate unexpected outcomes, which often are not anticipated in the contract negotiations and so lead to conflict between the contracting parties. Clearly, property rights would be stabilized and their transfer made cheaper and more effective if economic stability could be achieved.

Unfortunately, nobody knows how to do it. Recessions, in the sense of a slowing down and occasional actual downturn in the level of economic activity, seem to be here to stay. This statement would have been highly controversial only a decade ago when the Keynesians and the economic planners were in their heyday. Today it is a no more than commonplace remark. This change in economists' attitudes was brought about by that most effective of all teachers of economics, experience. In the hope that this lesson once learned will not be forgotten, it will be useful to look very briefly at just what went wrong.

Planning is a word that Americans were far more suspicious of than most Europeans. But without actually using the word, the American government begin doing much the same thing that the West Europeans were calling planning. They began adapting government policies to serve the interests of economic stabilization, as those interests were interpreted by Keynesian theorists. Keynesian economists have been rather like that other well-known breed of technicians, the Dow theorists of stock-market fluctuations. Both have an esoteric line of talk based on assumptions that are not always apparent but when displayed seem to fly in the face of common sense. For the Keynesian the key notion, that of the multiplier, is based on assumptions about variations in the rate at which the economy's spenders will turn over money are in about the same class, as far as realism is concerned, as the Dow theories of breakthroughs and bases.[1] More fundamentally, the two theories are alike in trying to predict the unpredictable. It is a very common type of human endeavor and wherever it happens it leads to much the same kind of rococo elaboration of qualifications to every statement, as anyone who has looked at "systems" for playing the horses or beating the roulette wheel will know. Keynesian economics remains alive by staying at least one level of complication ahead of the facts.

But, of course, this did not stop the planners. Having made their case plausible to many and, more important, offering liberal politicians just the formula they wanted, economic planning was given its head. The formula required the government to be a big spender in the economy, or otherwise it could not be used to compensate for the presumed inadequacies of the private sector. There had to be a large government debt or it would not be possible to exercise enough influence over the capital markets. Then, once big government and big debt were achieved, fine tuning could begin. After a careful Keynesian analysis of the economic situation, the Keynesians believed that a program of corrections by government taxing and spending could be orchestrated with many other instruments of lesser importance to keep the economy on its "long-run growth path" except for quite trivial deviations. For over a decade in the United States, and for much longer in a number of other countries, this sort of policy program has been in effect; and at the present writing these countries have also been in a state of economic and financial volatility for a decade and have lived through the worst recession in forty years.

What went wrong? Part of the problem was an underestimation of the importance of monetary as opposed to fiscal policy. The Keynesians have never developed a plausible or workable theory of the relationship between real and money variables, that is, between theories explaining the financial side of the economy in its impact on the production side. Another part of the problem was political. Unless the economy were simply turned over to the experts to manage, policy measures involving a change in the level of taxing or spending had to obtain congressional and presidential approval. This often could not be obtained until after the policy had become obsolete even by Keynesian standards. Fortunately, the politicians were never sufficiently sold on the theory to be willing to turn the economy over. And part of the problem had to do with time lags built into the economy. Increased government spending, of course, is supposed to stimulate the economy. But different government spending programs require different patterns of spending, and these in turn filter through to other sectors of the economy at different rates. And individual receivers of additional money behave in different ways at different times. Particularly when decisions relating to the future—saving and investment—are at issue, the behavior is impossible to predict with any kind of accuracy, and the time lags between government stimulus and private response change from one situation to another.[2]

Often these problems, in a situation of intermittent ups and downs, produce effects that are substantially worse than doing nothing. An attempt to stimulate the economy gets its response only after the economy is on a swift upward movement, so the government policy creates not prosperity but inflation; and vice versa. It turns out that this kind of well-intentioned mismanagement was a major, perhaps the most important, factor in turning the recession that began in 1929–30 into the Great Depression of the thirties.[3] And already the chairman of the Federal Reserve Board has been castigated in the press for much the same thing in connection with our most recent recession.

What can be done to clear up this mess? Fortunately, there is an answer. It is not a panacea but it holds promise of substantial improvement. The answer involves concentrating far more on monetary than on fiscal policy in stabilizing the economy; hence it is compatible with the government-spending reforms discussed previously. Second, it involves substantially reducing the discretionary authority of monetary and fiscal policymakers. The fiscal policy measures would be substantially limited to the so-called automatic stabilizers: such things as unemployment compensation, which automatically but only partially compensate for a falling off in demand. And monetary policy in turn would be substantially limited to keeping the average growth rate of the money supply at some target figure. This in itself would be mildly stimulating to the economy. Once expectations—that the rule would be followed—were stabilized much of the threat of inflation would vanish. Thus a feature of this approach is that it meets yet another conservative rule for government, namely, Keep it simple!

Recessions will not be eliminated by such a policy, but they should be mitigated; and the policy can be defended without making claims to knowledge about how the economy works that do not exist. It is essentially a defensive strategy, and is in that sense conservative. It is in the private sector and among private individuals following their own chosen pursuits that one should look for creativity. When you get it from government policymakers, armed with their powers of coercion, it is rather frightening.

One other remark about recessions: They aren't all bad. Essentially, a recession is a time of reckoning for the overly optimistic, a time of cost cutting, a time of reestablishing a base in realism as a precondition for further progress. In a society in which the unfortunate victims of the recession are guaranteed the minimum basics of life, it is not too heavy a price to pay for this kind of readjustment. Schumpeter called it a period of "creative destruction."

Varying the tax rate is one of the standard "tools" in the Keynesian "toolkit." However, there is a good argument for throwing this tool away, aside from objections to the theory itself; namely, that its variation is a serious infringement of property rights. Uncertainty as to just what sort of exclusive rights you have to the use and control of your own resources is increased by government action. Given the partly unproven and partly false nature of the theory, the case against using taxes in this way seems decisive.

Once again as these lines are written we are being given a demonstration of the harmful effects of even a proposal for tax reform on the economy. President Carter campaigned on the issue, despite the fact that a tax "reform" had just been completed by Congress the year before. All during his first year in office uncertainties as to who would be affected and by how much clearly had a negative effect on private investment, which has failed to recover the way it has after previous recessions. Of course, other factors, such as uncertainty over new government environmental controls, also have played their role. The reform has just (January 1978) turned into a typical election-year tax-reduction showpiece, and uncertainty over its size and impact no doubt will linger for a few months more.

It is essential that taxation not destroy incentives; if it does do so, it will be by preventing an individual from enjoying the benefits of additional increments in income. In our present system a number of those in top-salary brackets pay nearly confiscatory tax rates; marginal rates in some states—California is one—reach seventy cents on the dollar. But what mostly happens is that the attempts to impose such heavy rates produce great ingenuity in finding legal ways around the burden. Ingenuity is a scarce resource and consequently expensive, and so the tax system ties up the time and energy of a great many of our most productive citizens. And the upshot is a system that becomes highly discriminatory, taxing some people very heavily while others escape taxes almost entirely.

But there is another and less well-known aspect of the tax system that is perhaps even more incentive-destroying in its effects. This is its action, in combination with the welfare system, on a large segment of the poor. A number of programs come together on people in the working-poor category. The net effect of these programs is to produce an effective marginal tax rate for a great many of these people that is very high, at times exceeding 100 percent. In other words, they would have to pay money if they want the privilege of working harder.

Once again the villain of the piece is complexity. A simple definition of income, a fixed rate above the minimum standard exemption, and a limit to permissible government spending based on the rate of economic growth, comprise the simplest possible tax system. It would not dramatically change the average pattern of actual payments; it would affect many of those singled out for special reward and punishment in the current system. It would save tremendous amounts of time and energy, perhaps most important of all. And it would define the nature of property rights in the economy far more precisely. And finally, a "welfare system" that consisted essentially in marginal subsidies ("negative taxes") to the lowest income classes would show up merely as a complication of the income tax law.

Another feature of current tax methods is worth a comment. The family, as already argued, is the most important generator of social cohesion in society, and the place where much of the quality of the next generation is determined. It is also the focus of one of the most powerful of human incentives—the urge to found a dynasty, to leave one's descendants in a more favorable situation. This institution and the energies it engenders should be fostered, not harassed. Liberals often talk as if they would prefer to eliminate inheritance entirely. But they seem to have missed these central points. An amusing aspect of the McGovern campaign of a few years ago was the senator's dramatic backtrack on the inheritance tax question when he discovered from the public opinion polls that most working-class people believe that a person of substantial means should have the right to transmit his property to his heirs.

But once again the tax system already has set up enough obstacles to inheritance to put hordes of tax and estate lawyers to work. And once again simplicity and the avoidance of confiscation and its close relatives are the answer.

No doubt many people feel that a program similar to the above does justice to the individuals concerned but would be harmful to society, because it would lead to wealth becoming concentrated in a very few hands. The feeling seems to be widespread that there is a natural tendency for markets to turn into monopoly, for wealth to become steadily more concentrated, and for government to be the only savior. We have already noted the irony of a policy that takes from the less powerful to give to the agency that is already by far the *most* powerful as the means for achieving a greater dispersion of power. But there is another, more direct argument, namely, that the available statistics do not support these claims. On the whole, industry has not been becoming more concentrated during the twentieth century. And the upper or richer tail of the income distribution shows something of a tendency to follow Pareto's law. This law says, roughly, that those who have get, absolutely but not relatively, and that throughout the upper tail of the income distribution the probability of a person, say, doubling his income in some time period is about the same regardless of his current level of income. This proposition is by no means proven, but it is in better shape empirically than any theory that claims that wealth is all flowing increasingly into a very few hands.

Once again Venice offers strong and reassuring evidence. Venice was a substantially less mobile society than our own, especially at the top where the state protected the leading families from the competition of others. Venice became wealthy and remained so for centuries as a result of producing and trading on markets, of using the market system. Taxation was low, except in times of war, and was not relatively burdensome on the rich. Nevertheless, over the centuries of the great merchants' activities, the wealth in Venice did not concentrate. People became far wealthier absolutely at the top, in the middle, and even toward the bottom of the income distribution. The evidence that we have suggests that in a dynamic market economy where private property rights are respected, well defined, and enforced, there is no reason to fear that an excessive concentration of wealth will develop.[4]

CHAPTER 10

The Problem of Order

ORDER is obviously an essential ingredient in the successful functioning of a society or an economy. If there is too much disorder, the individual loses his ability to influence his own destiny. For the understanding of conservative economic ideas, the most relevant kinds of disorder are the product of assaults on person and property; that is, they consist of the arbitrary and substantial infringement of civil and property rights.

A discussion of order must be careful to distinguish between the kinds of order. For example, a liberal would probably initially refuse to discuss the issue of order at all. But if you persuade him that this *is* a serious problem, he would no doubt try to tie order to the distribution of income. The liberal would argue that if there is not a fair distribution of income, there is bound to be social unrest. As will be argued later, this is the very opposite of the truth. At the moment it only need be pointed out that there is a close connection between order and relatively stable expectations. If the citizens are reasonably confident that their property rights will be respected in the future, the fundamental basis for order has been established. So there is a close connection between order and monetary stability, the topic of the last chapter. Once again apparently very different aspects of the conservative position turn out to be mutually compatible and even mutually reinforcing.

A liberal response to this might well be: Of course, stabilizing expectations is a good thing, and I advocate a policy of price fixing so that, say, interest group X will not have to suffer the consequences of a higher price for their favorite consumer good Y. But this misses the point completely. In the first place, there is the rather obvious fact that periods of price control have historically occurred principally during times of relative unrest, as the history of incomes policies in Europe and in the United States in recent years attests. Second, there is a good reason why this should be so. Price fixing is an infringement of property rights, on the right of an individual freely to transfer ownership of an asset. Inevitably it is done by the state to protect a favored interest group against "the market," that is, against those citizens who own the asset whose price is to be fixed. This coercive intervention in the structure of property rights is inevitably resented, the favored group thinks it has acquired the "right" to unlimited access to the good at a favorable price, and the stage is set for conflict. The more of that sort of thing there is in a society, the *less* secure expectations regarding property rights become, and so in the long run the more disorder you must ultimately endure.

The essential distinction is between human interactions in which there is a commonalty of ends and those in which there is, or need be, only a commonalty of means. Market exchanges are of the latter kind. You and I may both benefit from a mutual exchange of goods and services even though I disapprove of your motives in making the trade or your plans for the use of the proceeds. A great many market exchanges have this property, and the affirmation of rights and the rule of law is designed to protect such interactions. Such exchanges are means-connected but not ends-connected social interactions. When the state gets deeply involved with the economy, as with economic planning or extensive price fixing, it is intervening in these exchanges and imposing an ends-connectedness that can in time destroy the basis of a free society. It is thus fundamental to recognize the limits to which the state must be held in the pursuit of order.[1]

However, this is not to assert that there are no ends-connected transactions in society or that there is no role for the state in regulating them. On the contrary, the regulation, under a rule of law, of the appropriate set of ends-connected human interactions represents the primary and essential task of the state. We can perhaps best get some sense of how this works by looking at three of the most fundamental problems that societies have had to face historically and considering the appropriate ways that have been developed to regulate them. In doing so one should remember a somewhat different and more restricted notion of disorder than was used above. A situation tends to foster disorder when an increasing number of people find themselves facing a major dilemma, namely, a conflict between deeply held moral imperatives. At such times the structure of a society is in some danger of fracture or even collapse. When possible such situations should be avoided; if they cannot be avoided, some way effectively to control them must be found.

Religious wars and the persecution of people for their religious beliefs have played a major role in the history of the West. Hardly a country, hardly a religion has escaped this tragedy, and the misery and loss of life entailed is literally uncountable. However, over the last two centuries the incidence of religious persecutions in Europe and America has declined dramatically. And this in turn is obviously connected with the strong trend toward disestablishing religions. How is this result related to the means for creating a society of order?

The answer seems to go something like this. By imposing a commonalty of ends-connected transactions on a religiously diverse population, the state forced much of its citizenry to face a deep conflict between moral imperatives. The law-abiding believer in an unofficial religion was the individual who faced this dilemma most acutely. However, many enforcers of the law faced a comparable dilemma, for they could see the unpleasant consequences both of enforcing the law and of failing to enforce it. Disestablishment of the official religion did not, of course, resolve all problems of order that were related to religion. For example, the issue of abortion today is for many a religious issue, and it is certainly one of the major contemporary problems for state policy in the United States. Disestablishment did not eliminate all religion-related issues. However, it did serve to defuse them somewhat by making it possible to take the issues one at a time. Instead of a web of closely related ends-connected transactions that more or less as a unit created challenges to the social order, there is one or a few issues, each of which can be treated separately. The depth of the moral dilemma was much reduced. And often the remaining issues could be further defused by disestablishing the issue, so to speak. For example, in the case of abortion, eliminating direct government subsidy of abortion without prohibiting it to those whose moral scruples are differently engaged by the issue is one way of disestablishing a vital dimension of the dispute. Naturally, this is not the appropriate place to propose a solution to this problem; we are merely attempting to illustrate one method by which a major source of disorder can be dealt with by simply removing responsibility for regulating a realm of behavior from the sphere of state competence.

However, not all problems of "moral-dilemma" disorder can be dealt with effectively by simply removing the state from the activity. The central issue of the American Civil War exemplifies another type of problem. Here the state itself is faced with the moral dilemma. Either the civil rights of the slaves continue to be violated or the property rights of the slaveowners will be violated. A believer in freedom can have only one option in this case, and a believer in the rule of law has no way out but to extensively and systematically violate rights, either civil or property. Or is that really the only option? Consider the following hypothetical policy. The government announces the elimination of slavery within its boundaries ten years hence. At any time during that ten years a slave may buy his or her freedom or an owner may sell the slave to the government, in either case at the market price current on the first day of the offer. Any slaves remaining in bondage at the end of ten years are automatically freed without compensation. Funds for the government to purchase all offered slaves are to be raised by general taxation on the whole population of the country, including the slave population (which is to say, their masters).

This is, of course, a purely hypothetical case and no implications as to feasibility at any time before the Civil War are being asserted. It might be noted, however, that something like this was done in Cuba at about the time of our Civil War, though the conditions of barracks slavery there and the absence of an effective market-pricing system were serious weaknesses in that program and produced unfortunate results. But our point is that once the nature of the problem is properly posed—in this case a fundamental conflict among rights—it may very well turn out that there are acceptable compromise proposals that avoid shifting heavy burdens on special groups in the population and so in effect encouraging desperate responses. It might also be noted that freeing the slaves in an orderly manner and without a devastating war might have produced a much different environment for the slaves to begin their lives as free human beings. The fact that the government would have to determine the market price by administrative action rather than by the simple test of what the market would bear would lead to some coercion and some windfalls to some of the parties. This is no panacea. But one important feature should be noted, namely, the fact that such a scheme could probably only be designed by someone with some experience with the operation of markets. Once again it would seem that leaders of government who have such experience are relatively more likely to be able to deal effectively with this class of problems. And once again this particular trait goes a long way toward explaining the extraordinary condition of domestic order that existed during most of the long history of the Venetian Republic.

In our own times, one of the most fundamental issues is that of revolution. The typical socialist view of revolution is that it is the culminating act of a period of intensifying class warfare in an environment in which almost every political issue is a specific manifestation of that class warfare. Of course, the resolution of conflicting rights is a matter of no interest to socialists, who obviously favor a policy of generating public disorder as a precondition to their seizure of state power. However, the first thing to note is how wildly exaggerated the notion of class warfare is in the socialist literature. In fact, no revolution has been the product of the lower class rising up in righteous indignation over the unfairness of the distribution of wealth in society and casting out the upper class as part of their policy to redistribute the wealth in their own favor. Almost everywhere one finds that the working class feels that considerable inequality is perfectly justified. Far from viewing themselves as the victims of brutal oppression, they tend to be a mainstay of patriotism who find the general division of societies into many groups of unequal wealth quite reasonable. One remembers that the Republican party has traditionally derived a large fraction of its support from this same working class, and that working-class conservatism has forced the shelving of many a liberal and radical proposal of the Democrats, among them the McGovern inheritance tax mentioned above.

Nevertheless, revolutions do occur. Why? The answer is that revolutions have occurred only in situations in which the ruling class in that society has become unable or unwilling to govern. This is as true of the Russian revolution as it is of the Chinese revolution, as true of the Cuban as of the Angolan. One form or another of malaise, often corruption or gratuitous brutality, has served to destroy the legitimacy of the rulers. But at any rate, the one fixed factor in revolutions is the weakness of the regime. The typical revolutions of the twentieth century have been ones in which the revolutionaries are relatively few in number and weak, and have the support of only a small fraction of the working class. This is not surprising in view of the fact that the leaderships of revolutions have come not from the working class but from the middle or even upper classes, which somewhat weakens their claims to represent the downtrodden. So the problem of class warfare is a pseudo-problem, one not at all likely to occur, judging from the history of the past century. And the problem of revolution becomes a problem of maintaining a government capable of taking the basic steps needed to preserve order.[2]

However, an important qualification must be made to the above conclusion. Generally speaking, class warfare will not develop unless the government creates it. And, unfortunately, liberal governments have been busy doing just that in recent decades. One of the most obvious of such steps has been the granting of patents of monopoly to labor unions. In the United States unions are encouraged to form industry-wide organizations, they are exempt from antitrust laws if they do so, and a government body has been created, the National Labor Relations Board (NLRB), with wide powers to arbitrate, that is, to coercively decide on matters of dispute between union and business. This procedure seems deliberately designed to create powerful institutions representing a particular class and then to pit them against institutions representing the other class. One must admit that class warfare becomes much more plausible as an outcome after something like this has been going on for a while. In Britain similar developments may have already approached the crisis point. And, unfortunately, the story does not stop with unions but represents a general policy of liberal government. Great efforts have been made in recent years to establish organizations of the "poor" to create another dimension of class warfare. The government actually created the organizations and provided funds for the leaders so that they could bring some clout with them to city hall. This particular aspect of the "war on poverty" was fairly quickly aborted as a result of prompt action by mayors and local governments in a number of cities. But many programs with similar impact remain.

The message here is simple enough. Neither revolution nor class war is a natural procedure or attitude for the working class in contemporary society. Where it occurs it is the product either of a failure of will on the part of the leadership of the society or of its deliberate creation by liberal politicians. That is to say, once one understands it, this problem should not be too difficult to eliminate.

There is one other kind of disorder that is, this time with good reason, much on the mind these days. Crime, the infringement of rights by individuals and small groups acting deliberately to further their own interests, has become a problem of rapidly increasing moment.[3] Record rates of increase in crime are recorded year after year. People who twenty years ago did not even know anyone who had been victimized now have direct experience. Training and equipping the

CRIME

police force, adding computerized information systems and the like, seem to have no effect on the rates. It is as if some new epidemic illness had broken out and spread rapidly among the population.

The metaphor is not a bad one, though not everyone will appreciate it. For the metaphorical sickness that is referred to is not intended to represent the mind of the criminal. The problem, perhaps the central problem in understanding crime in America, has to do with the liberal response to it. When the question of crime comes up, the liberal responds that here is an area where he, for once, is prepared to start by emphasizing the need to protect rights against violation. Unfortunately, what he is referring to is the rights of the criminal. It is true that criminals, as citizens, have the right to a fair trial, and that that right should be protected. However, liberal actions have gone far beyond this, including extremely lenient sentencing, plea bargaining, second and third chances even for repeat offenders who have committed violent crime, and so on. Among the most striking has been the expanded use of the insanity plea, which has returned dangerous criminals to the streets with clocklike regularity. Having achieved this dramatic reduction in the rates of punishment for crime, liberals have turned to the prosecution and trial processes with similar results, so that it is now substantially more difficult to obtain a conviction than it was in the past. Most recently liberals have been at work on prisons, their efforts being devoted to making the place look more like home.

Most crime seems to be committed by people who see an opportunity to benefit materially from depriving others of their rights. Thus one would expect that, other things equal, if there is an increase in the opportunity successfully to obtain goods by theft, the crime rate for theft would increase. Basically, that is the phenomenon we have been observing in the years since the liberals have gotten effective control of the criminal justice system. Having made the expected gain from criminal activity greater by reducing the risk and cost of being punished, a large number of people have been recruited to the ranks of the criminals. Of course, that is not the whole story. Our society is more affluent now than it was twenty years ago and the mere presence of more goods tends to increase the opportunity. It is also true that the number of juveniles has increased and, no doubt due to their attitude toward risk, a disproportionate share of crime is committed by this age group. But these last two factors cannot explain the magnitude of the increase in crime. Permeating the whole environment has been the liberal notion that says in effect that the rights of criminals are to take precedence over the rights of victims.

But liberals too are victimized by crime. How then can they think as they do? It should be remembered that liberals tend to be fairly affluent and are likely to have been leaders in the move to the suburbs, so the incidence of their victimization by crime is probably much lower than for the population as a whole. It might also be noted that liberal attitudes with respect to this problem have been undergoing some changes recently as crime has come to touch the lives of all of us. But basically the liberal attitude toward crime seems to have had another root. Once again liberals have been caught trying to use crime policy in order to implement a goal that was almost entirely unrelated to the criminal justice system. That aim was the redistribution of wealth and income. Their goal of an "egalitarian" society has been pursued wherever they could find a lever that would seem to take from the rich and give to the poor. And as it turned out, once one understands the goal, making crime easier is one of the great liberal success stories. There is little doubt that liberal policies toward crime have made a large number of poor criminals substantially richer!

The appropriate measures to turn this appalling situation around seem to speak for themselves. Serious or repeated violations of the civil and property rights of others should bring the culprit into contact with a swiftly and sternly acting criminal justice system. Rules of evidence and procedure should be fair, but they must be consistent with speedy trial and sentencing. Punishment should be fairly precisely specified so that deterrence is clearly established. It should be recognized that no rehabilitation scheme has much chance so long as crime pays. Consequently, punishment should be substantially devoted to keeping obvious criminals off the streets. Evidence from other countries indicates clearly that all these things can be done without violating the accused's rights to due process. Of course, not all the effort should be devoted to the system of criminal justice. Opportunity has another dimension as well, namely, the ease of access to the desired objects. But this side of the problem of crime is not essentially a government responsibility. Citizens who leave the keys in their cars and the doors of their homes unlocked are contributing to the crime rate as well. Clearly, as crime rates have increased, citizens' interest in protecting their own goods has increased *pari passu*. What is needed now is to recognize that criminals too respond to these "price" signals in their behavior.

The problem of order is one of the central ones in any society. It is not a problem for which there are easy answers. One always feels a little reluctant to advocate the use of coercion. But the basic message *is* simple. A government that is unwilling to use force in the service of order creates far more violence through growing disorder than it does by serious efforts at deterring revolution, crime, and other rights violations. A government that has the reputation for swift, sure punishment for established rights violations will have far less need to use violence. After arming their government with those two principles, members of a society can reasonably expect to live out their lives under conditions of domestic order.

CHAPTER 11

Economic Development

THE SAME conservative principles apply to developing as to developed
countries. Liberty is a basic desideratum and is threatened by concentrations of power, whether in the economy or the polity. The special problems of developing countries stem largely from the vague-
ness with which property rights are defined and the uncertainties associated with the enforcement of property rights. In addition to this, there
is a strong tendency in many developing societies, especially socialist
ones, for institutions to be manipulated so as to create substantial
divergence between private and social costs and values, so that the
economy keeps getting pointed in the wrong direction. Once these
ideas are understood, issues relating to economic development and to
socialism become clear enough.

The conservative position on economic development probably
creates more skepticism among readers than any other topic. The
misery and corruption and brutality that seem to be so much a part
of the developing world have led even many conservatives to despair
of the validity of their principles for these countries. But advocacy of
the principles is not just a matter of defending untested abstractions.
There are, in fact, a number of countries that have been successfully
applying some basic conservative principles to their economic development. A brief calling of the roll is thus in order.

Socialists these days start with China, and so shall we. The rate
of growth of industry in Taiwan over the past two decades is substantially higher than in mainland China.[1] Agricultural development,
preceded by a land reform that made freehold peasants of most farm
families, was rapid in the first decade or so of Taiwanese growth, until
Taiwan had become a substantial net food exporter, a status mainland
China is still far from achieving. The health status of the population
is good, perhaps as good as that of the mainland population. There
has been no foreign economic aid during the past decade or so. Taiwan
has developed using the basic capitalist instruments of markets, foreign
investment, and government stimulus without overwhelming government involvement in economic activity; consequently, the prospective

entrepreneur can reasonably expect that gains achieved in the market-place will not be sucked off in large and indeterminate amounts by a corrupt bureaucracy.

Very similar stories can be told for Hong Kong and Singapore, though the environment in these places was probably substantially less favorable, given the massive population inflows and sudden structural changes that they were respectively forced to absorb.[2] Again, high growth rates, healthy and hard-working populations, and strong support for the market system, including a willingness to accept large amounts of foreign investment, have been keystones of their development policies. When the subject of China comes up, one might remember that there are four Chinas, three of them capitalist, and that the capitalist Chinas are the more rapidly growing ones.

Success stories about market-based economic development are not limited to China. Mexico has been following this route with great success for three or four decades; so has Puerto Rico, and more recently Brazil has moved to the front rank of the world's growth success stories, following the same institutional pattern. In southern Europe Greece has been a model for this approach to development since shortly after her communists were defeated in a civil war. High-level capitalist performers in other parts of the world include South Korea and Iran. And, of course, there are the older examples such as South Africa and Japan. *No other group of countries in the world, socialist, communist, or what have you, can match the growth performance of the capitalist-market group whose names we have just run through.*

During the last two decades a great deal has been learned about the process of economic modernization. One or two of these lessons is worthy of note, simply to illustrate the general tendency of this experience. Some of the most interesting learning experiences have to do with economic planning. Making plans for the development of national economies became all the rage in the years following World War II. The Soviets were popular models for emulation, and their Five-Year Plans had become symbols of the idea of planned and self-conscious economic change. Also, a large number of political leaders in the newly independent countries thought of themselves as socialists, and all socialists believe that planning has to be better than the market.

These and similar justifications appeared often in the press down through the sixties in underdeveloped countries. But probably they were not the most important reasons why planning came to countries that were not actually conquered by Soviet Russia. In fact, the talk about socialism was mostly lip service; in practice, the politicians were mostly thoroughgoing liberals. They wanted "planning" too, but for different reasons. For example, consider the Keynesian isolationists. These students of Keynes abounded on the left. Their idea was that the Keynesian economic policies could be used to manipulate the economy, but only if the economy itself could be effectively isolated from world markets. Fixed foreign-exchange rates, high tariffs and import quotas, export subsidies, stringent controls over or outright prohibition of private foreign investment: These were the devices that would serve to isolate the economy, to allow the "planner" scope to practice his trade without interference from market signals. To a considerable extent Keynesianism became a sort of power trip; you adjust the economy in such a way as to make you, the planner, most powerful. Make your appeal to independence and nationalism, and the press that supported you would make you into a national hero.

Many leaders in the underdeveloped countries chose this course. The economists they hired to defend their policies gave the policy a technical name: economic development through import substitution. And on the surface, for a while, it worked. The manufacturing sectors of economies under this kind of economic control did develop. But as time went on, a number of problems began to emerge. One of the problems with import substitution is that it concentrated scarce imported capital in industries in which the economy was just not competitive. The result was that the capital imports were not generating foreign exchange to pay off the loans and so debts began to accumulate rapidly, sometimes to the point at which a substantial portion of a country's export earnings were being used merely to pay the interest on the existing debt. Studies began to emerge showing that the economic gains from substitution of domestic manufactures for foreign goods were substantially less than the costs of obtaining the capital initially. For example, behind the high tariff barriers the domestic manufacturer was able to charge a very high price for his goods. One consequence of this was that only the relatively affluent citizen could afford to buy the domestically produced goods. This and the slower real growth meant that income distribution was becoming more skewed rather than less. And so on.[3]

But what, the reader may well be asking, became of those economic planners who were supposed to be controlling the whole process in the interests of the broad mass of the citizenry? The answer is that they never did have much control over the economy, beyond a certain ability to see that funds flowing through the government budget were misspent. Economies are far too complex things to be controlled effectively at a single place. Plans were made, to be sure. Rules and regulations were passed. Controls were slapped on this or that economic activity. The upshot of all this was that some things cost more than they would have without the controls; that some things had to be bought on the black market instead of from the shop window of some big department store; that the poor, with relatively less access to information and less mobility, probably had to pay more for many things and were unable to get others because they were being handed out by bureaucrats sensitive primarily to the interests of the influential. As I write these words the prime minister of Israel has just resigned because his wife maintained a substantial bank account in the United States, something Israeli planners have decreed is illegal. That's the way it goes everywhere under "development planning": There are a lot more rules, many prices are higher, but behavior is not all that much affected. The price is paid in the silent inefficiency caused by the diversion of effort into circumventing the rules.

Over the past ten years these problems have been coming increasingly to light. Conservative development economists, of course, were making the case from the beginning, but their arguments can no longer be ignored.[4] Keynesian economics has never worked well in developed countries; with their greater economic rigidities and generally substantial involvement in world markets, it works even less well in developing countries. Five-year plans, as important as a national airline to the sense of sovereignty of many developing countries, are now recognized as political rather than economic devices, and are rarely implemented. The power of the market to mobilize energies in the service of personal gain is coming, however reluctantly, to be recognized as the driving force behind economic development. This is most promising for the future.

However, it should also be recognized that the fight against economic planning is by its nature a battle that can never be finally ended. Politicans want power, and control of the economy is unquestionably one of the ways in which the politician's power can be increased. His schemes to "foster economic development" may do no more than win him votes from one or two interest groups, but that is basically what he is after. Continuing education in the real consequences of most market intervention can perhaps serve to keep the depredations from getting out of hand.[5]

Probably the single most effective argument used in the service of economic planning is that the market in a developing country is underdeveloped; consequently, the government must intervene to take up the slack or to point the economy in the "right" direction. Most books on economic development that stress the role of planning put principal emphasis on this assertion. It is a very dangerous half truth. There are, in fact, a number of respects in which markets are indeed defective in developing countries. Most of these are a product of deficiencies in the definition or enforcement of property rights or in the costs of establishing them. This can be very discouraging for the energetic and ambitious, for they can see their opportunity slipping away for reasons that have nothing to do with the quality of their product or potential demand. The ill-defined and ill-protected nature of property rights in underdeveloped countries is the major reason why these countries *are* underdeveloped.

Probably the most important factor in restricting property rights in developing countries is disorder. Political turmoil and the consequent risks of confiscation and destruction and weak governments make property rights all too often unenforceable. The existence of large bureaucracies means that rights are ill-defined. And corruption cuts both ways. On the one hand, it raises the costs of transactions; but on the other hand, it means that bureaucratic restrictions on rights can, for a price, be bypassed. Unfortunately, it also means that such rights can, for a price, be infringed. In such an environment peculiar and very inefficient economic arrangements result. In Chile before the junta took over in 1973, the local money, being subject to violent inflation, was saved by no one. People either held foreign currencies or invested in land. Since many landowners were using the land simply as a means of preserving the value of their assets, and the tax system reinforced such behavior, it was often uncultivated and Chile was a substantial importer of food, which diverted foreign exchange that, under a free-market regime, would undoubtedly have gone into investment. In Greece, before the anticommunist government was stabilized in the mid-fifties—and this is also true of many Latin American countries—citizens kept much of their wealth abroad because of fear of confiscation.

Weak development of the market and of property rights is not much of an argument for economic planning. One only has to think for a moment about just what is being put in place of the market. The planner's proposal is to use a bureaucracy. But bureaucracies in underdeveloped countries are also highly "underdeveloped," not in terms of their size, to be sure, but in terms of their ability to define and carry out tasks effectively. For example, the bureaucrat is being asked in effect to substitute his judgment for that of the market in modernizing the country when, obviously, he has no experience of modernization on which to base his judgment. As has been argued in just about every chapter of this book, bureaucracies work rather poorly under the best of circumstances. But a developing country with its low levels of education and experience and its traditions of opposition to trade and markets is very nearly the worst of circumstances. Though in those conventional textbooks of liberal economics it is rarely so argued, it seems clear enough that bureaucracies are an even worse choice than underdeveloped markets as vehicles for economic development. And finally, one might note that bureaucracies are the wrong medicine in a more direct sense. Bureaucracies, as was argued in chapters 6 and 7, have tended to raise the costs of establishing property rights in the United States, and in many other ways to make rights less well defined and enforceable. But if that is the major obstacle to development, applying bureaucracies to the problem can be expected to make things worse, not better!

This is not to argue that there is no role for the state in developing countries. In fact, the state has about the same role there as elsewhere, namely, to establish and protect a system of civil and property rights under the rule of law. This means that, given the relatively ill-defined nature of property rights in such countries, the state may reasonably undertake their improvement. An example or two will illustrate the point. One of the major problems in developing countries, already suggested above, is the relatively poorly developed credit and capital markets. This has led to various types of state intervention. Most successful among these have been actions designed not to substitute for the nonexistent or weak markets but those designed to foster the development of the missing markets. A well-designed development bank, such as has played a major role in Mexico's successful development experience, is a good example. The function of such a bank is to bring together capital and entrepreneurship, both foreign and domestic. The state, in addition, may endow the bank with an initial grant of capital, which the bank can use to buy shares in the new companies. As a project matures and becomes profitable, the market for its shares develops and the state can gradually sell off its holdings, using the proceeds to catalyze other projects. In the early stages there may be some state participation in management decisions, but for success these too must be limited and self-liquidating. After a few decades of intelligent administration of such an agency, it will no longer be true that the capital market is underdeveloped. And no large state bureaucracy has been created, only some new or newly effective markets.

Similar possibilities exist in other areas such as agricultural credit. In Pakistan, for example, a large government bureaucracy was created to administer the allocation of tubewells to farmers. The project bogged down in a variety of ways, none of which did anything to curb the growth of the bureaucracy. Finally, a market solution was tried. The tubewells were simply sold to local dealers. Farmers with good credit who found the tubewell a profitable investment, given the special features of their own farms, bought them, and agricultural production began to increase rapidly. There was no special secret here. The market selection process tended to get the equipment to those best able to use it instead of those who had the most political influence. And the relation of turnover to profit ensured that the wells moved quickly from the dealers' shelves to the users.[6] Some government assistance in setting up credit institutions was necessary, but basically government involvement in the operation was self-liquidating. Such are the models from which a conservative picture of the process of economic development emerges.

What is the future of the underdeveloped countries? In fact, no one can say. There are many difficult problems, and the degree of difficulty varies widely from country to country. There are self-aggrandizing bureaucracies everywhere in the developing world, and so there is still wide resort to ineffective bureaucratic "solutions" to problems. But viewers of the developing world from the United States should remember that there is no such thing as a "widening gap." Counries are moving down the path to development at almost every conceivable rate of change. The more successful of them are growing substantially more rapidly than the already-developed countries. Furthermore, as our list of success stories and their policy orientation shows, the basic ingredient in economic development is self-help. Those who would make us our brothers' keepers are those who in actual effect are hindering the natural processes that can lead to economic development.

CHAPTER 12

The International

Economy

IN RECENT YEARS most major newspapers seem to have made a substantial change in their policies regarding coverage of the international monetary situation. Time was when this was considered to be front-page news, with annual or even more frequent crises getting scare headlines, and with political feature writers giving careful attention to the grave global implications inherent in the latest moves by various governments. Recently, however, there has been a gradual removal of this news to the financial pages and a substantial decline in the amount of punditry that is devoted to such matters.

What is it, some kind of conspiracy? No, it's just another conservative principle at work. One of the most cherished of liberal and radical principles, isolation of the domestic economy from international influences, had been the major factor in generating the hullabaloo all along. In order to preserve this sense of isolation, most countries, including the United States, fixed their rates of exchange between domestic and foreign currencies. This created constant imbalances between the supply and demand for these currencies. Discrepancies had to be paid off by exchanges of gold or by borrowing. Speculators had a field day as they extrapolated an imbalance into a crisis and made the crisis more likely. Eventually, some countries would make a "once-for-all" exchange rate adjustment, and the old crisis would end. But new imbalances would arise almost immediately, thus starting up a new crisis.

For years conservative economists, and in particular Milton Friedman, have been arguing that the fixing of exchange rates has been a major destabilizing influence on international money markets. They have argued for floating exchange rates, in which the supply and demand for the various currencies determined the rates. This has two important advantages over fixed rates. The first is the obvious advantage that the market rate of exchange measures the actual, current relative scarcity of any pair of currencies and so is the most effective rate on which to base economic decisions. The other major advantage is that it gets the hands of government officials out of the monetary mechanism. The politician is bound to have interests different from those who actually trade on international markets, and those different interests have caused much of the trouble. The politician has a short time horizon and he, like others, would like to get something for nothing. This he can do with fixed exchange rates by in effect subsidizing his country's exports while delaying, perhaps through loans or domestic price manipulations and economic controls, the need to pay off the inefficiently high international obligations such a policy entails.[1]

Nowadays individual countries can still get into trouble through spendthrift policies. But the problem does not create a big political crisis. The international markets have probably already discounted most of the difficulty through exchange rate changes before this kind of "crisis" becomes a matter of public discussion. And solution of the problem now depends on the ability of the country involved to convince international lenders that it is a good credit risk. This tends to structure the problem in a way that puts the incentives to change squarely on those who can, in fact, correct it instead of in effect holding the entire international financial community hostage, as was typically done in the days of fixed rates. Britain or Italy can have a crisis now without the international money market having to have one as well. The shift to floating exchange rates did not solve all the problems of international finance, but it has created a sturdier and economically sounder structure for dealing with future problems.

The shift to floating exchange rates was forced on reluctant governments by circumstances. But the fact that conservative economists' predictions were so strongly vindicated in this area, and liberal arguments refuted, has suggested to many people that perhaps some other conservative arguments may be deserving of a hearing. In the area of international economics, there are certainly a number of fundamental differences between conservatives on the one hand and liberals and radicals on the other. Let us take a brief look at a few of them.

If the crises have made themselves scarcer, the past year or two has seen another aspect of international trade begin to grab headlines. This time it is the "problem of the falling dollar." Now, this is not a crisis in the old sense. The specific movements of foreign exchange rates and monetary media in themselves create no immediately serious problem. However, debt does accumulate in the United States and exchange reserves in Germany and Japan and Saudi Arabia, and over a sufficient period of time this could become serious. On a market, of course, such events are supposed to create their own corrective forces: All relative prices adjust until the supply and demand for foreign exchange are again brought into balance. Why is this not happening? The same old answer applies to this different situation: government action. In this case, for example, government price controls on domestically produced oil and natural gas prevent the price of oil from rising and so discouraging demand. And governments continue to intervene to "protect" their currencies and to expand their supplies through deficit spending. Eventually, no doubt, "circumstances" will force the government to recognize once again the ineffectiveness of these de facto interventions in the floating exchange rate system and allow the market to do the job. And conservatives will take what pleasure they can in delivering yet another "I told you so!" to the liberal politicians in power.

Quite possibly the most misleading word in the entire vocabulary of liberal and radical writers is "imperialism." Perhaps the best way to establish this is to remind the reader of a few relatively obvious facts about international economic interactions. Consider first the charge that imperialist countries extract the wealth of the poorer countries and ship it to the developed world at exploitative prices. On its face this is an odd line of argument, since under a market system that is precisely what will *not* happen. If the foods are valuable, the owner of the resource will be able to get a good price for his product by the usual bargaining process. Note that he will probably complain that the price he is getting is too low because, being human, he would prefer to get more for less. But where markets exist, prices tend to be established that reflect relative scarcities. Clearly, the "problem of imperialism" is not associated with the normal functioning of markets.

As a concept imperialism arose to describe the relations between a country and its conquered dependencies. This usage seems reasonable. It has not been uncommon for imperialist—in this sense—countries to impose restrictions on the trade of the colonials to the material benefit of its own citizens. England did that to America in the form of the Navigation Acts. Of course, such colonial dependencies have essentially disappeared from the contemporary free world. However, that is not true of the Soviet bloc. Today the world's great imperial power by this standard is Soviet Russia, which imposes far more extensive and effective restrictions on the international trade of its numerous colonies than capitalism has yet seen. Under capitalism this kind of colonial restrictionism is no longer a matter of significant concern.[2]

A second claim is that "international monopolies" conspire to set prices, thereby abrogating the true scarcity relationships. People who use this line of argument are, of course, referring to the multinational corporations which have grown very rapidly in the last few decades. But there seem to be several fundamental problems with this interpretation. In the first place, there are almost no monopolies among the international corporations; instead, they are in rather keen competition with one another for markets. Most multinational activity has taken place in the already developed countries, especially those of the Common Market, where the opportunities for monopolizing a market are minimal. The profits come from successful operation in a relatively free-market environment. Second, international operation tends to expand the range of competition rather than contract it. American automobile companies were forced to make a number of changes in their products in response to keen competition in the United States from European producers. Or consider East and Southeast Asia, an area where, as already noted, a number of "Third World" countries have been astonishingly successful at carrying out successful economic development, starting from a level of extreme poverty. This is an area where the multinational corporation abounds. Furthermore, American, Japanese, and even British corporations are in keen competition with one another to take advantage of economic opportunities in countries that are generally receptive to foreign investment. Perhaps it is no accident that these two things, rapid development and intense activity by multinationals, seem to go together. One rather obvious reason why this should be so is that modernization requires the transfer of technology from the developed to the underdeveloped countries. The multinationals seem to be relatively well equipped to carry out this task efficiently.

A third aspect of imperialism suggests a rather different issue, namely, the taking advantage in some sense of the weakness of an underdeveloped country. No doubt it is true that if a country is backward and ruled by a corrupt and ignorant leadership, citizens are not likely to fare too well in economic activities in which effective government action is required. But two things might be noticed about this kind of situation. The first is, you can hardly blame that archvillain of radical and left liberal rhetoric, the United States, for such a situation. We are not a colonial power and, in contrast with the situation in Eastern Europe, we are not discussing situations in which the existing government is only maintained in power by foreign troops. These are unfortunate situations, but they are not the product of contemporary "monopoly capitalist imperialism." The second and perhaps more important point is that the burden of this claim is really that the relevant government cannot be relied upon to carry out a policy effectively. This then is an argument against foreign aid, which flows from government to government. And we would be wise to learn from our errors here, where literally billions of dollars of such aid have been wasted by corrupt and inefficient governments.

One final point about "imperialism." An underdeveloped country in which market relations are not highly developed is likely to be one in which property rights are not widely respected. A government that is weak and inefficient is unlikely to be able effectively to define or enforce property rights. This explains much of the relation between, for example, mining companies and developing-country governments during the first half of the twentieth century. Unable to obtain an appropriate supply of services from the underdeveloped local markets, unable to obtain security from the governments, unable to convince the government that infrastructure projects were in the general interest, the companies simply provided these things themselves. The Chilean copper mines are a good case in point. Governments were kept at bay by those devices, including bribery, which constituted the custom of the time and place. This was the only feasible way in which the companies' legally acquired property rights could be enforced.[3]

No doubt there were abuses. Since property rights acquired in such circumstances would be quite fuzzy, the company often had the ability to define or even redefine those rights; no doubt the general tendency in the new definition favored the company's interests. It is rather pointless to attempt to assign blame in such a situation; however, if one must, the most reasonable culprit would seem to be the weak and corrupt government and the domestic population that was prepared to tolerate it. Some measure of self-help is not an unreasonable demand to make on a government and the more influential citizens of a country.

The only alternative to the above process in many countries was to keep the companies out entirely. Many seem to think this was the better alternative. However, the investigations of some development economists suggest that this is clearly false. The companies brought employment, tax revenues, technology, and a growing familiarity with the modern world and its ways. Inevitably, the infrastructure projects did begin to be built. As time went on and the population that had been exposed to these new influences expanded, pressures to reform government and to organize it to assist general domestic modernization grew steadily. It seems clear that, on the whole, these companies did play a substantial role in stimulating the process of economic development. The process can be faulted somewhat, however, if one compares countries that preserved their independence with those that came under colonial rule. In general, the latter had acquired a more substantial infrastructure base for the carrying out of further development than had the former. Obviously, property rights were better protected in the colonies and the governments more concerned with economic development than were the native rulers. Needless to say, this point is typically missed in liberal and socialist accounts of the development process.[4]

Writers in the above two genres have had to do a good deal of scrambling about to new positions in recent years. For example, the classic cases of "imperialist exploitation" inevitably used to be taken from the Middle East, and in all the Middle East no country could match Iran's claimed record of victimization, which even extended to American assistance in bringing down an Iranian government. The role of Iranians in the latter even tends to be ignored, though in fact a great many of them were seriously disturbed over the threat to property rights and, as a consequence, to economic development of the policies of the Mossadegh regime. However, that is not the main point. By no stretch of the imagination can Iran be regarded today as the victim of imperialism. Somehow she has managed to bring the oil companies into a position of collaboration with her sovereign state. She has substantially secured the rights of private investors and used oil revenues to provide the basic structure of a modernized economy. As a result, Iran has had one of the highest rates of economic growth in the world for a period now approaching two decades. Three decades ago Iran was a weak nation and the "victim" of the most powerful of the international companies. Perhaps she should be regarded as the world's healthiest victim!

There is no need to continue this line of argument. Similar stories can be told for most of the countries on the list of success stories in the last chapter. It might be noted that as development proceeds, manufacturing tends to replace mining as the major multinational activity in many developing countries. This means more interdependent involvement of the foreign companies in the economic life of the countries and, consequently, a more rapid spread and deeper penetration of the ideas of modern organization and technology. The message seems clear: Those countries that are prepared to test themselves against the world market are the ones most likely to succeed.

A final word about foreign economic aid is in order. Conservatives are not enthusiastic about the efficiency that can be achieved by government economic activity. Consequently, they tend to be positively frightened at the idea of foreign "aid," which involves economic activity by two governments. The giver's congress appropriates the funds, adjusting the proposals of the executive bureaucracy. The giver's state department negotiates receipt of the funds with the recipient's foreign ministry, which then passes the funds on to the recipient's government bureaucracy to spend. Is it any wonder that students of such programs believe the funds have been largely wasted? At no point in this system of transfers is there a serious confrontation between expected costs and benefits. What it turns out to be is the traditional pork barrel, this time internationalized. An end to foreign economic aid might result in a measurable decline in the number of Mercedes on the streets of some foreign capitals, but probably not much else.

This is not to argue that there is no role for the United States to play vis-à-vis developing countries. The security role is important and will be discussed later. There are some measures of assistance that have been helpful, of which disease control is perhaps the most important. Some assistance in training technicians, both at home and abroad, can probably be done in a way that benefits the recipient nation. Some guarantees of at least a portion of private loans for investment in developing countries may also be justified as a device to stabilize property rights while assisting the essentially private process of industry building. What should be stopped once and for all is the so-called program aid, in which the United States actually requires that the developing country produce an economic plan and we then provide funds to carry it out. This has tended to produce just about everything but the desired effects. For example, in Greece in the early fifties our efforts along this line produced not modern industry but a plethora of high-rise middle-class apartments in downtown Athens.[5]

No doubt those who got newer and cheaper housing were happy, as were the apartment owners; but was it reasonable to extract a billion dollars from the American taxpayer for such a purpose? Much the same can be said for the majority of project-oriented aid, if the mechanism is that same government-to-government transfer. On the average, money is much more wisely spent if the spender is closely associated with both aspects of the venture, its costs and its benefits.

CHAPTER 13

Socialism

SOCIALISM is supposed to be the hope of mankind, the socialist society the place where affluence, justice, equality, brotherly love, and other good things will finally accrue to all. "Socialism" first showed up in Soviet Russia sixty years ago; it has been the way of life for many hundreds of millions of Asians and East Europeans for over a quarter of a century. How well does the reality fit the paper utopia? [1]

The first thing to note about socialism is that nowhere in any socialist society today is the will of the people tested by the government to see whether they like what they've got or not. These regimes were all born in violence and coercion, and they all survive with continued oppression and the rigid suppression of basic civil rights. One is perhaps permitted to suspect that there is some good reason why no people, anytime, anywhere, has freely chosen by majority vote to go socialist.

In terms of economic organization, the most noticeable difference that socialism makes is in the nationalization of industry. However, here as elsewhere, the motivation is much more political than economic. There is, in fact, no economic theory of nationalization that concludes that nationalized industry should perform more efficiently than its privately owned counterpart. Nor is there any evidence that it does perform better. Both theory and practice come to just the opposite conclusion. But nationalization does have very important political consequences It destroys the "bourgeoisie," depriving them of their property rights, their income, and, of course, their political voice. These rights all devolve on the state creating, in place of the competition among capitalists for the consumers' favor, a single large monopoly that controls these and other rights. Judging from their literature, the technical socialist term for this monopoly is "the People," which is undeniably an esoteric use of the word.

In considering the economic aspects of the operation of a socialist economy, probably the best approach is to think of it as if it were a market economy on which has been superimposed a vast maze of constraints. For despite all the oppression and monopolization, socialist states have proven singularly unable effectively to control the giant organization they have created. They have simply bitten off far more than they could chew, organizationally speaking. There are literally millions of goods being produced in a modern economy. Finding out their names and how much of each *can* be produced and what they can be used for and how much of other goods must be used to produce each is a task well beyond the capacities of any currently known group of economic planners. But that is only the start of the task, for the planners are supposed to decide which of the almost infinite combinations of goods that might be produced is the best one from the point of view of the economy's bosses. This requires a theory of production far more sophisticated than any currently existing. It has also been pointed out that even if all the above problems were to be solved at some time in the future, centralized planning might still fail simply because the computation of the "optimal" plan would be infeasible; the numbers of goods to be produced would dissolve as rounding errors gradually dominated the massive calculations.

These facts are well known to economists East and West.[2] It is because of them that the market emerges from behind that vast maze of economic controls. Since the planners cannot do their job correctly, they do a sort of caricature of it, planning the output of groups of commodities. There are several tens of thousands of different products of the steel industry. Planners divided them into perhaps ten groups and fix the amounts of these in the plan. Intermediate-level bureaucrats are responsible for dividing these figures into smaller units, the central planners hope that the proportions among the commodities included in each bundle will remain about the same as they were last year. However, the plan calls for rapid industrial growth, which means substantial changes in the relative outputs of the various goods—much more machinery, not so much more grain. So a basic contradiction is built into the plan from the start. The planners know that it cannot reflect closely the actual outcome.

But the manager has his own set of problems. He is expected to know what is best for the economy even though the national planners themselves do not. He is expected, if there is a shortage of some input he needs, to find hidden reserves in his own production to compensate. He is expected to make adjustments in product specifications to suit the needs of his purchasers. He is expected to produce according to the assigned product mix, but not to pile up stocks of unwanted goods. These are impossible tasks as stated, and the manager soon learns that he is actually expected frequently to violate the plan, because everybody knows that it is a poor reflection of the actual needs of the economy.

But when the manager starts thinking along these lines, he needs some guidelines. In which particular direction should he violate the plan when it becomes clear that plan and reality are far apart? At this point, it turns out that there *are* some prices around to guide his choices. The manager who is unable to obtain needed inputs from the harried planners finds there is a market of sorts in inputs, where he can barter some good he has in surplus for the good he needs. He gets away with this partly because the planners and other government officials cannot look over the shoulder of every bureaucrat to make sure he is doing what he is told. He also gets away with it because higher officials wink at the procedure, knowing that it is essential to the operation of the system, given the poor quality of the planning.

However, the process does not stop there. So far we have not mentioned the worker-consumer. He—she too, for in socialism everyone gets to work whether they want to or not—gets paid wages like his capitalist counterpart and goes to stores to spend his money in the same way. But as the socialist worker approaches the store, one of the big differences between socialism and capitalism emerges. There are very few goods in the socialist store, and there are long lines waiting to get many of those. A Czech study estimated that an average urban family spent more than a dozen hours a week standing in line. However, some of the shelves will be full of goods; these are overproduced items that nobody wants, and stocks of them may grow in stores and warehouses for months before the bureaucratic process grinds out the order to stop. Faced with this environment, consumers have several possible courses of action. They can first try to set up a private information network that will give them early warning that some desired commodity is about to appear somewhere so they can get in near the front of the line. They can use influence to get moved up on the waiting lists for such things as cars and apartments. They can engage in illegal sales and trades among themselves. And they can keep an eye out for a foreign traveler, or for the opportunity to travel. Travelers from abroad are beset with offers for everything they bring with them, including literally the shirts off their backs; travelers to the "outside" come back laden like Santa Claus with the domestically unobtainable goods they have found in abundance on capitalist shelves.

But the process of market emergence does not stop here. Producer and consumer can be brought into interaction. A "second market" emerges in which goods produced illegally are among the many items for sale. Whole factories have been discovered that produce goods with inputs siphoned off illegally from a socialist factory, which are then sold for private profit on the second market. According to recent émigrés, the officials who are supposed to prevent such things from happening are among the more enthusiastic participants in the second market; no wonder, since they are more likely to have more money to spend. It is in almost everyone's interest to wink at the second market.[3] But even the government can find ways to use this emergent market. One way is to set up special stores in which only hard currency can be spent, thus getting back under government control some of the fruits of illegal trade. Visas to travel have been sold in China, as no doubt have many other kinds of government permissions.

But this second market is a very inefficient one. In particular, it should be noted that property rights are not well defined or enforced since so much of the activity is clandestine. The constraints show up in empty shelves where goods are supposed to be available, and in the ever-present queues. They also show up in poor-quality goods. Perhaps best known of the empty-shelves stories is the annual complaint heard in the Soviet Union that at the peak of the harvest season up to half of the tractors are unusable because there are no spare parts.

A few years ago, during the brief months of the "Prague spring," a Czech economist reported that Czechoslovakia produced over 200 commodity groups for export but none of them was competitive with world- (i.e., capitalist-) market quality standards.[4] All estimates of output per capita in socialist countries should be reduced by some unknown but substantial amount to take account of this tremendous waste and poor quality, for it does clearly make the output far less useful to the consumers. The basic cause of all this inefficiency is, of course, the cumbersome and ineffective system of controls. They serve to prevent arbitrage, that is, bargaining over price and quantity and quality, by the various potential producers and users of a good. The price system works fitfully and no one is very secure in his property rights. A sudden efflorescence of production in one part of the system, a sudden deterioration of quality somewhere else, a sudden crack-down by the authorities in a third, a sudden demand for a cut by some official in a fourth: By such events are property rights and efficiency whittled away and consumer wants ignored in this deformed market economy we call socialism.

If this system is so inefficient, why do socialist regimes stick with it? After all, they do want the goods for military purposes and to keep their subject peoples from becoming restive if for no others. Furthermore, in private discussions with economists from these countries, one often hears them conclude that substituting markets for bureaucracies is their personal prescription for solving these major ills. There even were some halting movements in that direction in most socialist countries during the sixties. But they were swiftly aborted and the bureaucracies retained. The reasons once again seem to be political rather than economic. A market economy is inevitably a relatively open one, and that poses a political threat to the socialist regime it is simply not willing to accept. This fear is not a figment of the leaders' imaginations. There have, after all, been several revolutions staged against socialist governments. These have been grassroots affairs, such as the Berlin riots in the early fifties, or the Polish October, or the already mentioned Prague spring of Dubcek, or the strike of the Polish dockworkers, or the recent wave of strikes and riots in China. For the regime to survive, the mixture of brutal suppression and occasional concessions must be maintained. A market would require relations with foreign countries. Mobility and communication would expand and include ever-widening sectors of the population. As socialist workers compared their lot with that of Western workers, they would come to realize the heavy material price they have had to pay for socialism. Nowhere is this contrast more striking than the comparison between Austria and Czechoslovakia. In the years just following World War II, it was clear that the standard of living in Czechoslovakia was far above that in Austria. Then in 1948 the communists staged a coup and brought the blessings of socialism to Czechosolvakia. Twenty years later it was clear that the situation with respect to living standards had been almost precisely reversed. In 1968 the Czechs tried to move back toward a more open market society. The Russians, fearing that if the Czechs succeeded all the rest of the socialists would not be far behind, intervened with their troops and put the old regime back in. Without those Russian troops, East Europe would undoubtedly be capitalist today.

One of the more amusing aspects of socialism is the fickleness of Western radical fashions with respect to the question as to which of the socialist countries is the true model for all the rest of us to follow. However, closer examination reveals that there is a rule of thumb that offers quite good predictions as to which country will be this year's Givenchy of socialism: The less information the rulers of a socialist country allow to leak out to the West, the more likely the country is to win the competition. During the days of Stalinist slaughter of the innocents, the Soviet Union was Western socialism's official darling. In Castro's early years, little was known about what was actually happening in Cuba, partly because the *lider* had not yet revealed his hand, and all kudos went to Havana. Considerable information about China was allowed out by Mao and company in the fifties. But beginning in 1959, a lid was clamped on almost all publication of useful and revealing information and, sure enough, within a few years Western socialists had leaped on the Maoist bandwagon. By the seventies, however, there was enough known about almost every socialist regime to turn even socialists off—though we must except the tiny but apparently growing band who follow our rule of thumb and believe the true leader of contemporary international socialism is the prime minister of Albania! At the moment no red god rules the sky, though perhaps some former Portuguese African colony will generate another titan, provided he can keep the newsmen at bay.

Is there any fire behind all this smoke in the form of real differences among socialist countries? It would seem not. The lack of corruption in China on the scale that is so obvious in the Soviet Union and Eastern Europe may be entirely a figment of our relative inability to observe China. Or it may be partly due to the fact that China is a much poorer country, so that there are fewer goods to purloin. Or it may be that Chinese are simply a harder-working people—they are exemplary workers wherever they are found in Asia or America. But it should be remembered that they are a strongly family-centered people and that they have demonstrated an extraordinary ability to use the capitalist system for their benefit. It would be surprising indeed if these striking features of Chinese behavior outside the area of communist control find no reflection in their behavior inside.

Perhaps the only real socialist maverick is Yugoslavia, which never collectivized agriculture and which still uses markets and trading among socialist firms. How much real "worker management" there is in that country is a matter of speculation. What one can say is that where the market is allowed to work in Yugoslavia, one sees higher efficiency and better quality goods. Where it is not allowed to work, and especially in the area of investment and finance, problems emerge. Yugoslavia is a sort of halfway house that lends further evidence in support of conservative views about the relation between markets and property rights and genuine prosperity.

CHAPTER 14

International Order

IT WOULD BE nice if the incentives of the market system were always such that the use of coercion never paid off. Unfortunately, that is not the case. Contract law and criminal law are needed to deter fraud and force in the transfer of property rights. And, clearly, the method used by the law is coercion. Of course, the aim of the law is to avoid the actual use of coercion by deterring such acts. It is conceivable, if somewhat unlikely, that a rule of law could develop that would in fact eliminate the actual use of force, in which the deterrence was always successful. But that would not imply the elimination of coercion from society; the threat of force against violations of the law would still be at the basis of deterrence.

Essentially, the same remarks apply on the international scene. There are times when it is useful for those influencing a government's policies to take coercive action. It would be nice if an international system could be devised in which it was never in a nation's interest to seize the property of others forcibly but, realistically, no one knows how to do that. An international free-market system would help a great deal, but it would not eliminate the use of force. Indeed, international as well as domestic markets have a need for some sort of deterrent force in order to function properly. And one cannot ignore the possibility, even the probability, that the entity that will need to be deterred is a nation state.

The international use of force is an area where perhaps more wishful thinking occurs than anywhere else in the study of policy. But conservative principles can serve as an effective means to break through to the basic principles that must guide policy in this area.[1] First, once again, the principle, Keep it simple! One of the greatest dangers in international affairs, when threats of force are being bandied about, is miscalculation based on misinformation or faulty expectations. Simple policies are easier to understand, easier to appraise, easier to get one's opponent to understand, and about all that a government "crisis-management team" can effectively handle.

The first element of wishful thinking and misunderstanding that we will take up has to do with the problem of order in developing countries. It can take the form of a Tale of Two Juntas, namely, those of Greece and Chile. Both these juntas came to power under conditions of rapidly deteriorating public order. Both restored public order promptly. Both took strong measures to stabilize the also deteriorating economic situation, the Greek junta with striking and quick success, the Chilean junta with less success as of the present writing, though the economic situation appears far more promising now than just before it assumed power. Both juntas have been almost universally denounced, nowhere more so than in the United States. They are particularly blamed for systematically violating human rights and for acts of violence. What lessons do these experiences have to teach us?

The first lesson has to do with the selective bias of the liberal press in the United States. How do the acts of violence of these juntas compare with those of other regimes? As far as the Greek junta is concerned, one would have to look around quite carefully to find a society that resorted less to prison and intervention in citizen rights than did this one. Even the claims of its most bitter enemies were rather modest: a few thousand Greeks jailed briefly, a few hundred for a period of years. There is no communist country with a record of jailings as light as this, but, of course, the same liberals who were busy denouncing the Greek junta were simultaneously demanding that the United States establish friendlier relations with several of these far more oppressive regimes.

The Chilean issue is somewhat different. There the junta was intervening in a genuinely revolutionary situation. The rapid deterioration of the economy and the steady spread of extralegal methods, especially including trade union controls over and siphoning of funds from industry that was still, at law, legally owned by private citizens, was moving Chile rapidly toward a point of no return. The junta turned things around and moved the country back toward the situation as it had existed some years earlier. But it faced an organized socialist and communist political movement that was sworn to revolution and to the seizure of all private capital. Unions and the far left had established paramilitary organizations, designed to control the poor and working-class neighborhoods and to resist any attempts to abort the revolution. Illegal acts were a daily occurrence. The violence that accompanied the seizure of power and the restoration of property rights to private citizens must be judged against the standards of other revolutionary situations. Once again we find liberals willing to condone thousands, even millions of deaths in places such as Russia and China and Cuba, while denouncing the deaths that occurred in Chile. Little or no notice is given of the fact of success in Chile: Instead of lingering waves of violence, terror, and assassination, Chile is quiet, in striking contrast with its neighbor, Argentina, or with the violence that has riven so many countries that have been forced under the socialist yoke. Just because the initial measures taken were strong, the amount of violence actually used was relatively modest, given the conditions, and the restoration of order swift. All this happened several years ago and was given much play in the press; however, it would not surprise me if many readers are hearing this argument for the first time.

There is one thing that must be said in favor of the general liberal attitude of vociferous condemnation of authoritarian rightist regimes in developing countries and toleration or even affection for leftist authoritarian regimes. There is an implication about the future in this attitude. Liberals, after all, *do* support the idea of democracy, and their denunciation of right-wing regimes is based on their feeling that it would be better to have democracy and that perhaps they can push these rightist regimes in the direction of more democratic processes. Their tolerance of leftist tyranny is partly based on a tacit recognition that there is no hope of democracy growing out of the rigid and all-embracing oppression of leftist dictators. The conservative shares this feeling that democracy is more likely to grow out of rightist than of leftist regimes; but he also feels that the liberals' attitude is unrealistic and counterproductive.

This point too is illustrated by the two juntas. In both countries there were leaders of the moderate left who were especially disruptive in their political activities. The Papandreous in Greece were liberal or "democratic socialist" in their orientation, while Allende in Chile represented socialists and "moderate" communists. However, by both refusing to accept the existing order and being unable or unwilling to impose a different order, their behavior served to promote disorder. After the fact it seems clear that they, rather than the far left, represented the forces that generated broad public acceptance of military rule.

This is the basic problem of moderates and democrats in most developing countries: They can't fish and they won't cut bait. For the most part, these countries have no tradition of orderly transfer of political power. Property rights and civil rights both are relatively underdeveloped. But economic development can only occur if some orderly processes can be instituted. Since modernization relies on the importation of foreign technology, an orderly relationship with world markets and the more developed world is essential. And rapid change, once it begins, may tend to make stability all the harder to achieve. In this context an authoritarian regime is often the only one that is capable of preserving order. Given the relative levels of oppression involved, the right-wing regime is generally preferable. Property rights are preserved and rightist-ruled societies tend to be more open than their leftist counterparts. Thus the prospects for a more democratic future tend to be greater.

The contrast between regimes such as Brazil and Chile and Greece and Mexico and South Korea on the one hand, and Poland or Bulgaria or Czechoslovakia or North Korea on the other is very striking. In each of the communist countries either the Russians or their local creatures have imposed a regime that more or less replicates the institutions of the Soviet Union, from national plans to secret police. Private property rights, the right to dissent, personal security: All these things disappear. Peasants are herded onto collective farms and milked of their economic surplus to support the regime and its grand designs, which always include an extremely powerful military and police system. Contact with the outside world is reduced to a bare minimum so that the local population has as little opportunity as possible to compare its lot with that of others. Punishment of dissidence is swift and severe, and the regime attempts to control even the thoughts of the populace, especially through strict indoctrination from early childhood.

There are some notable contrasts between this and the authoritarian regime of the right. Already mentioned have been property rights and acceptance of foreign investment. In general, these regimes are much more open to foreign influences and their populations have much greater opportunity to travel. The family is strongly supported as a primary social institution; as a consequence, state indoctrination is less intensive. Indeed, the typical rightist regime does not care too much what its citizens believe just so long as they do not organize against the government. And the range of political viewpoints in the literature permitted to be distributed within the country is far wider than in communist states.[2]

What should United States policy toward authoritarian regimes be? The above arguments suggest that both self-interest and humanitarian concern for the future of these peoples dictate a general policy of support for authoritarian regimes of the right but not of the left. And we have not yet mentioned another and often decisive factor. The United States seeks friends among the nations of the world, who will not only welcome economic relations with us but will serve also as friends or allies when it comes to confrontation with our enemies. And here, of course, the situation requires no argument at all. We have a common interest with most authoritarian regimes of the right in preventing the spread of communism and the expansion of the power and the influence of our enemies. In this case the most important and relevant dimensions all point in the same direction. Were due respect given to conservative principles, there would be relatively few dilemmas in constructing a proper foreign policy with respect to developing countries.

Surely enough has been said by now to lay to rest notions that developments in the world are influenced by something called "American imperialism." Authoritarian regimes come to power in developing countries for reasons associated either with internal developments or with subversion from without by communists. Under liberal aegis, American governments have by and large opposed right-wing authoritarian regimes, at least until they come to power and not infrequently thereafter. Among the most successful of developing countries (remember the list of chapter 11) are those that have had the closest relations with the United States and with American and other foreign private investment. In Greece, Mexico, and elsewhere, one can see not only economic development but a movement toward more open and ultimately democratic political orders as the process of development in close interconnection with world markets proceeds. Nowhere does one see the process of economic development moving developing countries toward greater dependence on the United States; again, the truth is just the opposite of the common view instilled by liberal pundits and media.

To this point we have been considering American relations with countries that do not have the military capacity seriously to threaten the United States.[3] We must now turn to the question of the relation of the United States to its enemies and the relation, in turn, to the problem of international order. Identifying one's enemies is a simple matter. One has only to ask: What countries have the military capability to hurt seriously the United States? The answer, good for the present and also for some years into the future is: Soviet Russia has that capacity, and China is trying hard to acquire it. And that is the end of the list, suggesting where primary attention must be devoted in thinking about national defense. What governments that have the capacity to hurt you seriously say about their intentions is always interesting, but it is never so decisive as the existence of that capacity. For intentions can be concealed, especially in a closed society, or they can change, and on much shorter notice than can the military capacity successfully to defend oneself.

The second simple question is: What should the United States do about it? Again the basic answer is as simple as the question: Deter. Create a military establishment that has the capacity to ensure that an enemy attempt to use force has no hope of producing any net advantage to that enemy. Creation of such a force, of course, implies a credible commitment to using it if necessary.

The third question is a little less simple: What do we do about international violations of the property rights of Americans? The answer can get a bit complicated, but roughly it goes: Establish a system of civil penalties to deal with such violations, using and developing international agencies of adjudication where possible, but developing a national system where necessary. An implication of this formula is that the U.S. marines are not available to enforce American property rights abroad, but that an adversary system of resolving such conflicts is available to the parties involved. Since governments that have just, say, nationalized U.S. property are not likely to be willing to submit themselves to an American court over the issue, acts of government policy are probably unavoidable. But the sanctions should be kept civil in nature so long as the violation is of rights of property rather than person.

This covers the essential points involving the use of force in international relations. Of course, in practice things are complex and uncertain. The function of simple rules such as these is to make sure that policy development and implementation is carried out with constant awareness of the *principal* goals. And these goals reflect the essentially peaceful thrust of the market system. A functioning and stable market system is one in which all the principal actors have a stake in the continuation of the status quo, with adjustments proceeding at a pace and in a way that does not threaten the stability of the system. The greater the willingness of the other states to avoid the use of force, the better the market will function. And the rewards of a better functioning market to all parties will serve to stimulate the push in the direction of peaceful resolution of disputes. The history of Soviet-American relations over the last quarter of a century can be used to illustrate the validity of the three simple answers as well as this last point.

One final question is perhaps worthy of comment, namely, the persistence throughout this chapter in putting the United States at the center of consideration, the use of the word "we" to refer only to Americans. Why not adopt an internationalist perspective? After all, markets are not at all sensitive to the nationalities of the participants.

The answer to this question is, first, that the perspective *is* internationalist, in the sense that the proposals, while serving the interests of the United States, are certainly not inconsistent with the goals of the rest of the world. An international market system operating within a world order in which the use of force is successfully deterred; who—aside from doctrinaire socialists—could reasonably object to that?

But second, the United States is an entity that is of great importance to all Americans. It serves, more than any other agency outside the market itself, to define the civil and property rights of Americans. It would be nice to have such rights defined on a worldwide basis, but nobody knows how to do that. History and technology seem to decree that this at present is the job of the nation-state. We are fortunate in having one that is large enough to permit efficient markets to function and diverse enough to give us a good taste of the benefits of a dynamic and creative society that such diversity produces, benefits far in excess of their cost in misunderstanding and conflict. There is simply no way to dispense with it at present. Without the United States, we would be missing some of the basic institutions of a thoroughgoing market economy, quite aside from the threat from external predators. The commitment to America is not one of jingoism, but one of common interest, with factors of common heritage playing a strong but supporting role.

CHAPTER 15

The Future

THOUGH it is fading in the seventies, there still remains a strong residue from the days when conservatives were thought to be people whose heads were turned fixedly toward the past. Too many conservatives' positions have been vindicated by events in the last decade or two for that claim to hold much water these days. But one still frequently encounters the view that history is against conservatism, that "the imperatives of technology and organization," as Galbraith calls it, will push us inevitably in the liberal/radical direction. In this chapter we look at a few futurology-type issues to see just how wrong those views seem to be on present evidence.

First, the issue of national defense. As our experience with the Russians increases, this issue has become quite a bit less controversial. Everyone these days is for a strong national defense, and just about everyone realizes that the Russians are our major enemy and that they pose a serious threat. What a contrast with the situation only a decade or so ago, when liberals were proclaiming the end of the cold war! But there is still a problem with pessimists who argue that there is really no hope of avoiding nuclear war, that such a war will destroy us, and who would then rather spend their energies dealing with other things than confronting this awful "fact". This can be a very dangerous position, since it probably will produce neglect of the military, which in turn would sharply increase the by no means sure chance of nuclear war.

The issue essentially hinges around the direction of technical change and its nuclear implications. From the point of view of defense policy, there are basically only three possibilities. One is that the defense wins, that is, that new technology such as laser beams will make it possible to destroy an enemy launch before the missiles have left home territory. The appropriate policy is clear enough: Any possibilities in this direction should be explored and developed posthaste, even if they should prove to be very costly. The second possibility is that we continue in the present situation as new technology emerges. That is, the offense cannot be prevented from successfully detonating nuclear weapons on American territory, but we can maintain an ability to launch a second strike, after absorbing the attack, sufficiently strong that it would make the initial attack pointless from the point of view of the enemy. To maintain this position requires that we continually monitor and develop new possibilities in weaponry. There is no price tag on this effort, but it must suffice to be a genuine deterrent to an enemy leadership that has shown its willingness to commit mass murder upon its own population. The third and most troubling possibility is that offense wins; that is, that technology begins to emerge that suggests an enemy willing to make a first strike can hit its opponent sufficiently hard that an effective second strike will be impossible. But surely the basic strategy even here is clear. If such capacity becomes feasible we can expect the Russians to try to achieve it. Our only effective counter is to try to develop it ourselves, while continuing efforts to improve second-strike efficiency. If we have kept our technological guard up, we should be able to develop such a weapons system quicker and better than the Russians, who still have quite a creaky modern technological capability. At that point negotiations might be in order; but only with secure inspection could such negotiations be allowed to produce even a slackening in our efforts to produce that first-strike-victory capability.

Those are the alternatives the nuclear age and communism have thrust upon us. Though the stakes are much larger, the basic issues are not much different from those faced by some ancient city-state, Athens perhaps, or even Troy or early Rome, when confronting the threat of an enemy who would like to obliterate them. We must face the issue squarely. What we need not do is face it from a position of weakness. Our enemy has not demonstrated a taste for war regardless of outcome. Rather, he acquires force in order to subjugate. A strong defense is the best and only incentive we can give him to avoid the use of force against us.

Information is another area where many feel the trend is inevitably toward centralization and the abridgment of freedoms. But, in fact, the recent trends suggest that Big Brother theory is wrong here. For example, the history of the computer has moved in a direction precisely opposite to these expectations. Its principal uses so far have been to support the decentralization of large organizations into a looser collection of task-oriented groups. The big computer in Washington or New York that was to provide the needed information to run the economy or the government has not yet made its appearance and perhaps never will. At the moment, even firms that have purchased large computers to centralize their operations are moving away from this sort of information system to minicomputers allotted individually to, for example, branch banks. These computers, of course, can "communicate" with one another, but the ability to store and process information in ways appropriate to the local situation is becoming more economical rather than less as a result of the trend toward computer decentralization.

More generally, the information revolution is making information cheaper to acquire, store, and use by several orders of magnitude, as compared with only a few decades ago. That trend will continue for a while in this area, which does not make heavy demands on energy as an input. But information is what markets thrive on. Making it cheaper makes them work better. And as noted in chapter 5, this latter tendency is much weaker for government, so once again the current trend of technology seems to favor the conservative idea of using government less and markets more to deal with our problems of resource allocation.

The relation between economy and government is, of course, a major place where conservatives are thought to have their heads in the sand. And if one simply looks at changes in the size of government over the last half century, one might be inclined to agree. If the share of government spending out of GNP continues at its past rate of increase, by 2019 the government will be purchasing an amount equal to the entire 1977 output of the economy. But there are growing signs that this will not happen. As the property-rights arguments for structuring and limiting government-economy relations find a wider audience, there is reason to expect a reversal of trend. That trend toward increased understanding of the problem is on a strong upturn in academic and business circles and among the general population, where it has perhaps always been strongest. The tax revolt of 1978 is only the most recent manifestation of this tendency.

There is one place, however, where the conservative may despair over the prospects of his educational campaign, and that is the Congress. A simple principle, actually a truism, is, Scarce things *will* be costly. Congress seems truly incapable of mastering this elementary point. It seems to feel that if, for example, oil becomes scarce, it can pass a law calling for rationing, and then people will not have to pay the higher price. Congressmen simply refuse to consider the costs of operating the rationing system, the taxes needed to carry the subsidies of favored consumers, or the even higher prices paid on the inevitable black market as being costs related to their law, costs that do in fact accrue in varying degrees to all citizens as a result of the use of oil.

But, of course, this is an exaggeration. Most of the congressmen who support such schemes for energy, medical care, welfare, and all the rest know very well what they are doing. They are engaged in a quite deliberate process of using issues essentially concerned with efficiency as means for the redistribution of income. They are aware that the voters will not buy direct confiscations of income and are strongly opposed to higher taxes. So congressmen turn to issues such as energy and are willing to pay a considerable price in efficiency in order to get their redistributive aims achieved through the back door. And so the problem here is not to convince the congressmen of conservative principles but to explain to the voters just what their congressmen are doing. That seems quite a manageable task.

"Environmentalism" has become the fashionable code word these days for a whole series of efforts designed to increase the size of government at the expense of the private sector. Wherever the environmentalist looks he sees troubles. People litter, factories pollute. Those are the basics, from which a detailed appraisal of the deficiencies of self-interested behavior will be supplied for any desired sub-group on demand. And, of course, the only possible correction is government prohibition of the activity, unless it is nationalization of the activity. The attractive thing about the environmentalist position is that the lists provided generally do constitute lists of things that are wrong. It can be great fun pointing out other people's defects, and, since nobody is perfect, a small amount of research will produce a rich harvest of deficiencies. Once the idea became fashionable one could be sure that the long lists would be forthcoming.

Of course, the problem with environmentalism is equally obvious. When it comes to proposing solutions for the problems, by and large environmentalists literally don't know what they are talking about. The reason for this is that they are generally referring to very complex phenomena that have many causes and many and scattered effects, none of which have been very comprehensively studied. In considering the consequences of doing one thing or another, they are dealing with something about which no one is qualified to speak.

The history of the most fashionable environmental issue, that pertaining to the automobile, is certainly a case in point, and one that has proved a bit humbling to the more honest among the environmentalists. In the first place, the trend toward smaller cars began in the United States well before the environmentalists had captured the media. The reason was simple enough: The costs of operating a large, luxurious automobile had been rising rapidly. The number of people who had other things they preferred to do with the few hundred dollars a year savings from driving a Volkswagen "bug" began to increase fairly rapidly in the late fifties. This trend has continued with only brief interruptions ever since, and does not seem to be much affected by environmentalism. Furthermore, the demands for rigid controls of emissions, which were nonnegotiable for the environmentalists in the sixties, suddenly seemed rather silly when the oil price rise showed them—and the rest of us—a very different set of relative costs, while controls served to reduce gas mileage. Their response was to demand mandated technologies that would both reduce emissions and increase gas mileage. But more or less normal technological progress in the worldwide and highly competitive automobile industry began in the seventies to yield its fruits, including cars such as the Honda, that could meet high emission standards and get excellent gas mileage without adding a lot of emission-control gadgetry to the cars. The market seems to have been able to adapt in its usual way to market signals, and most of the environmentalist agitation seems to have been either misdirected or unnecessary or both.[1]

This in itself is enough to make one sceptical of environmental proposals, but there is another problem at least as serious, namely, the institutional side of the remedies they propose. The tacit assumption is almost always that the market cannot do the job and that government can. The conservative's explicit and carefully argued thesis is that most of the time the very opposite is true. If there is, in fact, a significant environmental failure, the first place to look is to government itself, to see whether the problem is not largely a consequence of government rigging or restricting of markets. If that is not the case, the next step is to see whether the problem does not stem from inadequately defined or enforced property rights. If this is the case, government action may be feasible to correct it, but the correction will be such as to make the existing markets function better, not to substitute a government bureaucracy for the market. Rare indeed will be the environmental problem that will survive the tests of severity, understanding, market rigging, and property-rights prescription and thus become a legitimate object of direct government intervention. In all likelihood application of these tests to all known environmental problems would result in a substantial reduction in the level of government economic activity.

Yet another big fashion these days is doomsday. Leading this pack is the pseudoscience of the Club of Rome projections of future levels of economic activity, which predict something approaching total economic disaster in about the second decade of the twenty-first century if we, the world, continue on our present course. The best way to think about this problem is to recall a prediction made by a Harvard historian of science a decade or so ago. He pointed out that if the number of scientists continued to grow at its then-current rate, then at about the time of the Club of Rome catastrophe there would be seven scientists per capita in the world! The Club of Rome stuff is of a piece with this prediction with only one exception—the Harvard man was joking. Already, as the world adjusts to higher oil prices, we see the way in which the market system will provide an effective counter to the threat of "disaster" brought on by depletion of a resource. The price of that resource rises and people start seriously looking around for substitutes. Much the same happens or should happen when some problem such as pollution associated with some particular economic activity becomes unpleasant. Those harmed are having their property rights damaged, and should be able to obtain redress; most of the time the redress should consist of higher costs to the producer in order to bring his costs of doing business in line with the true social costs of doing business. Then the market system will create the incentives to improve the situation, by some combination of product substitution, industrial and human migration, and absorption of some level of unpleasantness that is more than compensated by the accompanying benefits. If it weren't for the market's periodic redirections, we would already have passed through a number of Club of Rome-type catastrophes. With its assistance we will be able to avoid this one too.

The main point of this section is a very simple one: Underlying trends in the twentieth century are not at all unfavorable to the flowering of the thoroughgoing market economy. As was noted in chapter 3, the principal technical changes, relating as they do to lowering the cost of communicating and transferring goods and men, have been very favorable toward improving substantially the quality of the market economy over its nineteenth-century counterparts. The United States is supposed to be the central place in the world for the defense of the capitalist system. But it may well be true that a substantial majority of our better-educated citizenry has never been exposed to the major arguments in favor of the system of liberty and its central social manifestation, the thoroughgoing market economy. Once this defect is corrected, by strictly voluntary actions that infringe no citizen's freedom, the potential those underlying forces have created will finally become realizable.

PART II

Commentary

CHAPTER 16

Introduction

THE BASIC PRINCIPLES of conservatism have played an important role in the history of the past millennium and more. Nevertheless, like other orientations toward society and social change, conservatism has also had its ups and downs. For example, nineteenth-century Britain and the United States were far more consonant with the principle of freedom in their economic arrangements than either nation has been thus far in the twentieth century. Much the same thing can be said, with respect to those countries and to many others, for the status of the family.[1]

Within the twentieth century there have also been marked fluctuations in the public and intellectual esteem with which conservative ideas have been held. The twenties were a peak period for the public fortunes of conservatism and the depression thirties and wartime forties a sort of nadir. The widespread public disesteem, and perhaps more fundamental difficulties as well, had their effect on intellectual conservatism, which also reached a low ebb during this period and into the fifties in the United States. This is not to say that conservative voices were silent but rather that they were dispersed and at odds with one another. Conservatism was not One but Many.[2]

In fact, it was Three, three strands of thought whose proponents came from different places, intellectually speaking, and could at first find little or no common ground. The first of these was the libertarian view. Though a main-line inheritor of the tradition of nineteenth-century laissez-faire, this view had suffered a number of apparently decisive defeats in the several decades preceding the fifties. The inability of the major countries to get back onto a normally functioning gold standard as the medium of international exchange during the interwar period had created a strong backlash in favor of "managed" currencies and foreign exchange rates. A number of scandals relating to the behavior of business leaders during the thirties had somewhat tarnished the public image of conservatism, despite the irrelevance of occasional individual malfeasance to the fundamental issues. Probably this tarnished image was more a consequence of the depression itself, which liberal intellectuals had convinced themselves was a product of the failure of the market system. And finally, there was the Keynesian "revolution," which seemed to many to have established the case for big government, big deficits, and national planning. In the increasing turmoil of depression and war, it was becoming increasingly difficult to hear the conservative voices; and, as often happens in such circumstances, these isolated voices, in their attempts to emphasize principle, tended to move toward extreme positions, leaving out the qualifications that actually strengthen the case for those willing to take the time to think about what they have heard.

A second strand consisted of the traditionalist conservatives. Their emphasis was on the role of civilization as the basis for a decent human society. The unfolding two-thousand-year tradition of Judeo-Christian civilization has been the fundamental shaper of European and American—and a number of other—ideas and institutions. In the relativistic and polyglot and materialistic environment that was growing by leaps and bounds, there seemed to be little hope for the continuation of this influence. Churches were not only disestablished but emptying. Universities were steadily sloughing off their role as the conservator and transmittor of the culture to become smorgasbords of vocational training and self-indulgence. Political institutions were in the hands of demagogues and opportunists. For the traditionalists, the basic problem was to mobilize those individuals still knowledgeable of and committed to civilized values for the effort to move conservation in this most fundamental sense to its former central place. At best this was a task for the long run, and it did not leave much time to worry about the details of economic arrangements.

The third strand was anticommunism. A number of writers, many of them formerly active on the left, had come to recognize the severity of the threat of Soviet Russia to Western civilization in general and the United States in particular. It was not just that the Soviets had through terror and organization developed a massive and predatory instrument for imperialist expansion, nor even that this was accompanied by a far more effective fifth column of subversives within the Western democracies than anything that had preceded it. There was also a fundamental lack of recognition of the nature and extent of this threat by the politically dominant liberals. This was the era in which Maoists were spoken of as mere "agrarian reformers," and in which many liberals refused to believe the truth of the great purges in Stalin's Russia, or of the massacres of Poles and others carried out by the various terrorist militias of the Soviets. The sense of desperation felt by those who did perceive the danger once again left little time or energy to devote to the issues raised by conservatives of the other strands.

These are the three strands that form the intellectual base on which the contemporary American conservative movement rests. They have been brought together both by events and by "fusionist" arguments, but also simply by a growing recognition by members of each group of the extensive common ground they share.[3] One major force in the coming together has been the Mont Pélerin Society. Founded in 1947 at a meeting in Switzerland and holding more or less annual meetings since that time, it has been a sort of rallying point for proponents of the free society. Its members have a variety of views, as befits a group emphasizing the value of individualism, but its efforts have served to bring these arguments into the mainstream of discussion and to develop that recognition of common interests and beliefs among conservatives that was essential to further progress. Friedrich Hayek and Milton Friedman, perhaps the two leading conservative economists of recent times, have been active in the society from the start.[4]

The ideas of two economists in particular were very important in this early shaping of the contemporary conservative economic world view. Ludwig von Mises, Hayek's teacher, put the idea of the market economy as man's most effective instrument for economizing, and socialism as an idea that in principle was fatally flawed, at the center of his world view. In several massive volumes Mises developed these two strands into a powerful and integrated theory that emphasizes the rationalism of the one and the irrationalism of the other. The thickness of his books may have kept Mises from reaching a wide audience, but the basic message shows the fundamental link between the first and third of the above conservative strands, between libertarianism and anticommunism.

An author whose influence was probably even greater, though not so often mentioned in this context, is Joseph Schumpeter. In a writing career that spans the first half of the twentieth century, Schumpeter articulated a unique and brilliantly defended theory of the basic political and economic forces at work in our era. His approach was dynamic and emphasized the creativity of the market, its ability to release energies both by releasing men from the trammels of traditional political restraints and by the opportunities for reward that inhere in it. A vital factor for Schumpeter is the role of the family. He sees the founding of a "dynasty" as a central human motivation and one that, again, the market supports. He developed a theory of democratic government that showed clearly the degeneration that was bound to set in if government was required to make too many decisions. We will return to some aspects of his very rich theory in chapter 18; for the moment it is enough to note that, though not an organizer, he articulated views that helped in important ways to bridge the gap between the libertarians and the traditionalists.

But most important for the emergence of a distinct and coherent conservative movement in the United States have been events. The history of the last two decades has served as the great teacher, both vindicating conservative views and pointing the way to a more integrated conservative world view. The first of these events has a simple name: 1956. That was the year in which Khrushchev described the crimes of Stalin, and the Poles and Hungarians revolted against their workers' paradise. After that no reasonable person could continue to think of the Soviet Union and its socialist society as having any moral standing or any serious claim to be a desirable part of the future. Stalin killed millions, perhaps tens of millions, and for years many liberals refused to believe the evidence. Now they could not escape it. The urban workers, the "proletariat," for whose supposed benefit all this mad slaughter was being carried out, expressed their views of their socialist lives in ways that also could not be ignored.

But it was not enough merely to recognize that the Soviet Union brutally repressed those who came under its control. There was still the need to persuade many Americans that it could happen to them too, if the United States was not willing to prepare itself actively for defense against aggression. But once again the Soviets were able to serve as teachers. The Berlin crisis of 1959–60 and the Cuban missile crisis that effectively ended it showed that both the aggressiveness and the duplicity that the Soviets had already displayed in Hungary and elsewhere would be turned against the United States as soon as they thought they could get away with it. By the end of the Cuban crisis, history had vindicated the anticommunists. Their views became part of the general conservative world view, and penetrated deeply even into liberal and radical consciousness.

A second set of events, much less dramatic but very disturbing to all, has led many to reconsider some traditionalist arguments. In particular this reconsideration has been brought about by the decline of our schools, but also by the rise of crime. Increasingly, we are wondering if these great failures of our society are not connected to the secular and relativistic nature of our socialization of children. As spiritual values come more and more to be things that teachers are forbidden to discuss with their pupils, it is perhaps understandable that the pupils adopt the standards of the streets or of the pop spiritualists of Madison Avenue, the guru business, and rock-star ethics. The abdication of our responsibility to transmit our cultural heritage has perhaps produced these shoddy substitutes, our ravaged and intellectually insipid schools, and the notion that instant gratification is some sort of absolute constitutional right. As parents and taxpayers contemplate the effects of our massive investment in education, it appears to increasing numbers of them that the essence of education, the leading-forth of new lives, is missing from the system. The search for roots is on in earnest once again and, fundamentally, that is the traditionalist's quest.

The third set of events is associated with the failure of liberal policy. The War on Poverty articulated by John Kennedy and put into effect by Lyndon Johnson represented the finest product of the liberals' art, the massive throwing of governmental resources and regulations at a series of identified social "problems." The regulations were put into effect and the money was spent, but, aside from the expenditure, things went on very much as before. There were more bureaucrats, more regulations—and more problems. Even liberals came to recognize that the approach had been a failure, and the minds of millions of citizens were opened by this failure to some of the fundamental arguments libertarian conservatives had been articulating for many years.

By the end of the sixties, events had served in a surprisingly—and distressingly—direct way to vindicate the basic judgments of all three strands of American conservatism. The essential role of property rights and the private market in a free society was now generally recognized by conservatives, as was the need carefully to prepare our defenses against communism, and the need to permit—even encourage—the social processes associated with the preservation and transmission of civilized values. But that is not to say that disagreements among conservatives vanished. Indeed, the fact that such a variety of experiences was generating conservatives, and that so many were relatively recent "converts," suggests that there would be much argument over the specifics of policies and political platforms. This will be true of any active and free association of individuals. And, in fact, much insight as to the nature and future prospects of conservatism can be gained by studying the nature and scope of these differences. In the chapters that follow, we look briefly at some of the most important areas of difference, and, of course, particularly those that impinge on the economy and economic policy. As will be seen, it is now a tale of diversity within the framework of a common central theme.

CHAPTER 17

Libertarians:
The Pure Breed

INDIVIDUALISM is not a crime or a disease. Surely in social theory it represents the highest form of respect for the human being. But radical libertarians have nonetheless been substantially isolated from the mainstream of the conservative movement. In part this is a matter of choice, for their style of argument has tended to be somewhat vociferous. In part it is because of the reaction they have frequently received, which includes outrage and moral opprobrium from the anti-communists and amused contempt from many more orthodox conservatives.

In this chapter we look at a few ideas that come from the more libertarian end of the conservative spectrum. That, in fact, is our first point: This is not a separate wing of conservatism but rather a collection of thinkers whose views vary widely among themselves as to the acceptable role of the state. The reader who finds such views unrealistic may, nevertheless, benefit from them. One of the main functions of extreme arguments is to shake one's mind free of implicit constraints to the serious consideration of certain alternatives. It is quite possible to learn a good deal from radical libertarians without actually becoming one.

James Buchanan is one of the least known of conservative economists outside professional circles, but one of the best known within the economics profession.[1] A specialist on public finance, he has always had a broad perspective on the nature and functions of economic theory as well as having a developed political philosophy. Among his most interesting and useful insights has been his critique of the modern tradition of interpreting market behavior in terms of maximizing or optimizing models. This approach has tended to encourage the manipulators of human behavior, the social engineers. The way in which this works is rather subtle. After all, the models display the market "mechanism" as producing optimal results, which sounds very much like the kind of analysis we were getting in Part I and which is a staple of conservative economics. Who could object to that?

A major problem with the approach is its misplaced precision. Having derived the properties that generate such optimal results, the student finds that, as with all models, there is some considerable idealization of what goes on in the real world built into the assumptions. So next he explores the "deviations" from optimality that result when some of the idealized assumptions are adjusted. But now, in this more realistic world of "imperfect" markets and information and adjustment processes, we find our markets generating "nonoptimal" results; we leave it as an exercise for the reader to determine who is now supposed to return the system to "optimality"! In this way a mode of analysis that looks to be conservative in its implications turns out in practice to be strongly liberal and interventionist.

There are two fundamental criticisms that can be made of this very widely practiced approach of liberal economists. The first is the excess of precision in the specification of the markets' workings. The effect of this is to give the analyst the impression that he has a kind of machine on his hands. To make it run the way he wants it to, he has only to adjust a dial here, twist a valve there, and set the throttle at the efficient point. This kind of thinking by mechanical analogy is what makes Fine Tuners and other similar types of statist economists. That is not what markets are like at all.

The second criticism, and the one emphasized by Buchanan, has to do with the implied criterion by which such markets and market systems are to be manipulated. In order to decide which valves to twist, which government interventions into the market to implement, one must have a criterion by which to contrast the outcomes. Economists call this the "social-welfare function." It is a sort of weighted average of the desires of the individual citizens of the country. Where does it come from? Straight out of the economist's or politician's head. For an individualist there can be no such thing as a social organism; but without some such entity there can be no such thing as a social-welfare function, which purports to represent the desires of society. All it can really do is represent one person's preferences for outcomes. And so the whole idea is senseless—unless one wants to think of the state (the leader?) as representing the true interests of us all.

Buchanan does not simply criticize this mechano-statist approach, he also suggests an alternative mode of market analysis. One should think of markets not as an optimizing device but as a means for resolving conflicts over scarce resources. The essence of this process is deal making, and the heart of deal making is bargaining. There is a presumption that the parties to a voluntarily entered into agreement expect to have their individual lots improved as a result. A whole set of such agreements, which might be called a market, is simply the logical sum of the individual deals. The only known general property of that set is that each deal is expected to make each participant better off. But from an individualist point of view, that is about all that is of interest for the analyst.

Buchanan's suggestion is that game theory is the right way to analyze markets, since the emphasis there is always centered on the payoffs to the individual participants and the process by which they bargain with one another for their individual benefit. It is certainly true that game theory has provided a number of insights into the bargaining process. However, one might reasonably question the productivity and even the promise of this mode of analysis in dealing with social problems. Our optimal conservative of Part I prefers the property-rights format as the appropriate basis for such analysis. This, of course, does not preclude the use of game-theoretic insights where they are relevant. But it does emphasize the structure of rights that exists at the start of any bargaining process, and so serves to focus attention quite naturally on the distinction between outcomes that alter the structure of rights voluntarily and those that do so involuntarily. And that is the heart of the matter when issues of public policy arise.

Buchanan has characterized himself as an anarchist, though a good deal of his writing on public goods economics seems quite ambiguously anarchist in its thrust. No such doubts are generated by a perusal of the works of Murray Rothbard. He represents the pure breed of radical libertarian.[2] For example, he begins a recent book with a proposal simply to abolish even the judiciary apparatus of the state. Instead he claims that as time goes on there will come to be substituted for it a voluntary system of courts. These will be set up by enterprising individuals who sell judicial services to the public. If someone robs you, you identify the culprit to your court for trial. If he has his own hired court and yours and his disagree on the judgment, a system of appellate courts will also arise to adjudicate the differences. Rothbard suggests that there be agreement that the majority decision of two levels of courts prevail; if the culprit is found guilty on appeal, then he will be punished appropriately.

The reader will have a number of questions about this procedure. Presumably the convicted culprit will have to be forcibly brought to punishment. But how to get agreement on this without some agreed-upon instrument of coercion? What if there are two different decisions at the appellate level? If that means the culprit goes free, then surely the market will generate the necessary courts to provide this service, for a fee, to criminals. And how can you get individuals to testify voluntarily, when it is not in their interest? By paying them? The questions go on, and Rothbard does not bother to answer any of them.

However, the reader who stops reading Rothbard at this early point will have made a mistake. When he turns from the functions of the state associated with the preservation of order to those associated with the control of markets, Rothbard begins to make a good deal more sense. His views are those of an anarchist; they are extreme. But they are also salutary, for even libertarians at times have unquestioningly accepted a role for the state that may not stand up to scrutiny.

We may take as an example of this latter tendency a recent work by Robert Posner that attempts to use economic criteria, and particularly the notion of efficiency, as a basis for appraising the working of the law.[3] One of his most interesting findings is that in a wide variety of cases the best defense of rules of law lies not in their justice but in their promotion of efficient outcomes. For example, if you bring me to court for having done you some wrong, the issue of justice really has to do only with our particular case, with whether I in fact should be held responsible for any harm you suffered. But from the point of view of the law as an effective social institution, Posner argues, the real issue is the effect of the decision on future actions of individuals. And this suggests strongly that the court will be much concerned with finding a decision that will promote the most efficient behavior by individuals who fall into a similar situation in the future. Even if I am not really morally responsible for the harm done, if it is much cheaper and more convenient for me to take preventive actions, the court may well be justified in finding against me.

This approach to the defense of legal rules has a great deal of promise. In particular, it seems to cut through the "judicial rhetoric," as Posner calls it, that often obscures the real reasoning behind judicial decisions. However, in the case of contract law, there appear to be several instances where Posner's analysis is flawed. It is as if he had gotten a bit carried away with the idea of defending existing rules, and had forgotten that he is also supposed to appraise them. Perhaps this has generally been true of conservatives, who have not seriously considered whether the entire body of contract law actually is necessary in a free society.

The basic issue that is posed by the efficiency approach is: To what extent are we willing to accept coercion in order to improve economic efficiency? Rothbard's answer would be straightforward—one should never accept such a tradeoff, no matter how great the improvement in efficiency. A more moderate and traditional conservative position might run as follows: You have mistaken the basic issue. Law is one of our most powerful institutions just because it represents the distillation and codification of a hundred generations of experience with human conflict. One should remember that historically the primary motivation for the state's coercive intervention in private affairs was the preservation of order. Contracts are enforced because conflicts over contract violations have been a frequent source of disorder and violence in past societies. If you agree to build me a house for a fee and I refuse to pay, hoping to retain both the house and my money, you have a strong motivation to do something about it. If the law won't help, there is some reasonable prospect of your taking matters into your own hands. Law, even contract law, interposed the state between two such parties in the interest of preserving order.

This defense of the law of contract seems much more reasonable than the efficiency defense. But it is now reasonable to ask whether the law has not gone too far in the scope of its interpositions between the disputing parties. There is some evidence that this is the case. As judicial dockets have become more crowded and the cost of litigation has increased, the tendency to resolve contract disputes by private arbitration has grown until nowadays the number of cases settled by the latter method is at least an order of magnitude greater than the number settled by the former method. The parties to the settlement have good reason to accept it; they are engaged in continual contract making and so their reputation for honesty and fair dealing is worth a good deal of money to them. Without that reputation, potential partners in deals will surely go elsewhere. This suggests that much of the efficiency gain from having contracts enforced may be achievable without the need for co-ercive interposition of the state.

This point about contract law is not being made because the law seems to be overly coercive in any fundamental sense. Instead the aims are two: first, to suggest that the radical libertarian questions can often be profitably asked by a conservative who accepts many functions for the state; and second, because an attitude based essentially on an attempt to rationalize the law in economic terms misses a rather funda-mental point. If contract law is in not too bad shape, the same defi-nitely cannot be said of the massive and rapidly growing body of administrative law. This latter poses threats to freedom both in its directly destructive impact on private property rights and in its more insidious effects in promoting the further dominance of the modern leviathan. To analyze administrative laws, one after another, in order to test them against an efficiency criterion makes a mockery of the conservative analysis of law. The general formula should be: While recognizing law's deep roots in human experience, no segment of the law should be immune from critical appraisal as to the reality of the claimed need for coercive intervention into human affairs.

The most original and stimulating work of political philosophy to appear in recent years is Robert Nozick's *Anarchy, State, and Utopia.*[4] Nozick argues that the nightwatchman or minimal state, the one in which the state is essentially limited to protecting its citizens against violence, theft, and fraud, would arise naturally out of a state of anarchy. That is to say, if we were to start from a situation in which there was no legitimate coercive power, we could reasonably decide to move from that state to the minimal state without imposing solutions on any who would not be prepared to harm others for personal gain. More important, Nozick claims, using a variety of ingenious argu-ments, we would not be able to move any farther than the minimal state in expanding state powers without being forced to impose our will on some reluctant minorities. Since we have all grown accustomed to the liberal style of argument in these matters, reading Nozick comes as something of a shock. But clearly, this is a line of argument that every thinking citizen should have the opportunity to appraise for himself.

We may take just two of Nozick's points to illustrate the rele-vance of his work. The first is a notion of justice in social arrange-ments. That situation is just, he argues, which has been reached by processes that do not involve violation of anyone's rights. At each point

in time each individual has a set of entitlements, essentially rights that
he has acquired. Only those future situations can be considered just
that preserve the entitlements that exist in today's situation. Private
agreements preserve entitlements, given the absence of fraud. Government action designed to protect and preserve entitlements is justified. Nothing else is. Clearly, we have here an argument from political
philosophy that matches the spirit and essence of the arguments about
markets and property rights that have occupied so much of the attention of conservative economists. And, in fact, a conservative economist
feels quite comfortable, intellectually speaking, as he works his way
through Nozick's book.

Now consider as an application of the above argument the contrast
between two theories of redistribution. Most arguments in favor of the
redistribution of income or assets have some sort of conception of an
ideal pattern of distribution as it should exist at any one point in time.
At one extreme is the pure egalitarian, who wants all incomes to be
equal. Liberals generally accept inequality that compensates for onerous employment or, to some extent, that provides incentives to up-
grade skills. But you will often find them saying things such as: "There
is no reason why the ratio of the highest to the lowest income in
society should exceed six or seven." That specifies a pattern. And
patterns are just what it is not possible to justify, according to Nozick.
He argues against patterning but for a historical interpretation of the
just income distribution. For that is what his entitlements theory does.
The current distribution of income or assets over the population is of
no interest whatsoever; that is, it gives us no usable information as to
whether the current distribution in just. Instead, we must look to the
process by which the income was acquired. Once again, if it was acquired through legitimate processes that did not infringe the rights
of others, then the current distribution, whatever its pattern, is justified.
Not outcomes but moral behavior is the desideratum; and surely that
is a morally satisfying rule.

In sum, the libertarians have and will continue to play an important role in conservatism. The very vigor with which they defend their
views is a good part of their strength, for they force a thinking
through of positions that all too often have been conceded by default
to liberals. Often they seem to go too far. In an important sense there
can be no such thing as a radical conservative, for the seeking out
and nurturing and transmitting of all that is valuable in our heritage
must be at the center of any conservative philosophy. But clearly, a
major problem for the preservation of a free society is to turn government around, and move it step by step back toward a more appropriate
role, paying due attention to the protection of existing property rights
in the process. In that process even the strictest libertarians are both
allies and colleagues in the conservative cause.[5]

CHAPTER 18

Social Conservatives

IN a closing note to his great work, *The Constitution of Liberty,*
Friedrich Hayek lists three criticisms of traditional conservatism that
serve to explain why he does not consider himself to fit under that
label: Conservatives fear and resist all change, they are too fond of
authority, and they do not understand economic forces. I suppose no
one would want to join such a group. Our job in this chapter is to see
whether those charges are justifiable when applied to some contemporary versions of the more traditional brand of conservatism.

In dealing with conservatism in the traditional sense, the first
thing to talk about is civilization.[1] A nation, in the old sense of that
word, takes its essence from the cultural values that are held and
passed on through a leading stratum of the society. There are only a
small number of distinct civilizations in the world, Judeo-Christian
civilization representing one of these, Chinese civilization another.
Each such civilization, of course, has a number of variants, conditioned by localisms of various kinds, and each tradition undergoes
change as it moves through the generations. But it is also coherent
and in fundamental ways recognizably the same distinct entity despite
these variations.

At the heart of every civilization, every developed and city-based
traditional culture, is a concept of order. Civilization is impossible
without a large measure of order, which in every case means a recognition that others are not to be disturbed in the exercise of their rights.
What the particular concept of order does is spell out the things that
for that civilization may be considered rights.

At the heart of the Judeo-Christian sense of order is the concept
of the rule of law. The idea of the rule of law has, in innumerable
situations in the history of the Western world, been a force that interposed itself between ruler and subject, forcing the former to recognize some right of the latter to be free of harassment. The law has, of
course, grown out of several sources. Much of family and tort law
may be a product of attempts by the ruler to impose order in the most
direct sense of preventing private wars. Much of contract law derives

from the medieval Law Merchant, which grew out of practical trading activities and whose enforcement by the state was only undertaken rather late. But the idea of a state-based but quasi-autonomous arbiter of justice is uniquely central to our civilization, and it goes far to explain why our civilization is the one that, more than any others, has fostered the idea of the society of liberty.[2]

This central concept has had a variety of other influences on our civilization. The idea of the rule of law tends to encourage rational deliberative thought and choice, for it is only through rational debate of the merits of a case, and deliberative weighing of the evidence, that reasonable choices can be made and justice done. Furthermore, distinctive ideas as to the nature of moral behavior are fostered by this deeply rooted cultural value and institution. The law codifies, summarizes, and defends the joint products of a hundred generations of weighing evidence and appraising the relative merits, in situations involving immediate human conflict, of alternative rules of law as the appropriate rule of justice. This great freight of moral wisdom has permeated the civilization and lent specific tone and character to ideas of morality.

We have been discussing only one aspect of civilization and its impact; of course there are many others. But perhaps the point has been made: There is much of direct contemporary relevance built into our traditions, which in turn are passed on, through the great cultural works of our civilization, from one generation to the next. A central requirement if we are to continue to survive and thrive is that we do preserve and spread and hand down that tradition, for if we do not much that has held our society together in the past will be lost. And surely there is no doubt but that America is a part of the Judeo-Christian civilized tradition.

Apparently not all conservatives would find the above remarks acceptable. Frank Knight, one of the founders of the Chicago School, has argued that the Judeo-Christian religion is in some respects contradictory to liberalism—what these days we call libertarianism—and does not offer moral insights of value in our rapidly changing world. Others might fear that such language opens the door to reestablishing Christianity as a state religion. And the more rationalistic among conservative thinkers seem to be almost indifferent to history as a source of contemporary understanding. Clearly, there is a substantive area of difference among conservatives in this regard.

Nevertheless, I think the extent of disagreement is much exaggerated, especially in those critical remarks of Hayek with which this chapter began. Perhaps the best way to make this point is by surveying very briefly some of Joseph Schumpeter's ideas. Here we have an economist who, though dead now for a quarter of a century, has left a strong imprint on economics that continues to influence even some young technicians. Schumpeter was a conservative; he thought of himself as one and was widely regarded as one. His most fundamental contribution to economics was the development of a sort of messy dynamics, a sense of the laws of motion of the capitalist system that took full account of the human and the unpredictable in their course. At the center of the process of change for Schumpeter was the entrepreneur, the person who sees an opportunity to break the chains of tradition by introducing new methods of production or of organizing production. The dynamics of the capitalist system were for Schumpeter largely a product of the system of private property rights, which put fewer obstacles in the way of such men's activities.

Of course, society put some obstacles in their way. Clearly, inertia and resistance to change are central survival values, essential to the preservation of any kind of order. The key to the rise of the modern world has been the striking of an appropriate balance between resistance to change and more or less graceful acceptance of it. But there is more of the conservative in Schumpeter than this. Essentially, his entrepreneurs are "breaking chains" for conservative purposes. They want to found dynasties, to promote not only their personal interests but also those of their families. Knight once said that free societies might more reasonably be called "familistic" than individualistic; that too is an exaggeration, but it captures the central notions of social cohesion and drive that operate in Schumpeter's interpretation of dynamic capitalism. Obviously, the success of such a vibrant society requires not only restraint but adaptation on the part of conservative forces

To this idea of more or less controlled change Schumpeter added an idea of democracy. He notes that in successful democracies leadership tends to come from a relatively limited stratum of society. In these people's hands lies the understanding of the processes of government, the ability to rule. What the people do in a democracy is choose from among the members of this stratum who compete in elections for their favor: They choose often not even a specific leader, but a government. Such a government can only carry out its tasks successfully if it has a rather limited number of tasks to perform. The leadership must spend part of its time competing for reelection, and the process of negotiating and implementing laws takes much time. Only if these conditions are met can democracy function successfully.

This view combines much of the heart of both libertarian and traditional conservatism. Tradition supplies and instructs the leading stratum of political leaders and sets up a flexible but systematic system of barriers to change. Private property rights provide freedom for entrepreneurial maneuver. Family provides social cohesion, a vehicle for the passing on of tradition, and a central incentive for work and change and conservation all at once. And limited government provides flexibility, some measure of efficiency, and the prospect of preservation of rights.

This summary does great damage to the richness and power of Schumpeter's thought. However, our aim was very modest, being only to suggest that here, embodied in Schumpeter's works, we find a cogent answer to the charge that traditional and libertarian conservatives have little in common. Schumpeter certainly understood economic forces as well as anyone has. He did not fear change, and he gives a meaning to the idea of resistance to change that makes it an intelligible and necessary component of the healthy society. And there seems little doubt that, whatever the extent of his "fondness" for authority, he was fully aware of both the nature and the desirable properties of democracy. While thus failing all of Hayek's tests for a traditional conservative, he nonetheless seems deeply rooted in that tradition in his own thought and analysis.

However, there is one place where perhaps differences between libertarians and traditionalists *are* reflected by Schumpeter. Schumpeter, like many traditionalists, was a pessimist who believed that the modern world was moving inevitably away from democracy and toward a social structure that would be excessively resistant to entrepreneurial efforts. Culture, the intellectuals, were being mobilized against capitalism, organized interests were forcing rapidly increasing activities on government, and bureaucracies were stifling individual initiative. In Schumpeter's system the result was wholly predictable, namely, the replacement of capitalism by some bureaucratic alternative, probably socialism.

That process has been continuing, except that private "bureaucracies" seem to have developed in a much more flexible and creative way than Schumpeter expected. But the continued movement of government in a direction that is inconsistent with the preservation of democracy is clear enough, certainly to conservatives of all kinds. Suppose the tide is not stemmed, and we pass the point of no return in which democracy's days are clearly numbered. What then? Would traditional conservatives begin to think in terms of the "second best," that is, of trying to see that that next, inevitably nondemocratic form of government, be as good as possible? If so, they will find some guidance in their tradition, which seems clearly to favor oligarchy among the nondemocratic alternatives. And perhaps the experience of the Venetian republic has some hints to offer as to the great danger to be avoided, namely, tyranny or dictatorship or communism. But the libertarian cannot reasonably follow his fellow conservative down this path. His commitment to freedom would seem to permit no discussion of a political second best, no contingency plans against the failure of democracy. If this *is* a difference, it is clearly a fundamental one.

The so-called Wallaceites constitute a group that has often been called conservative, and whose rallying to the conservative banner has been advocated occasionally by political spokesmen for conservatism. Perhaps the relationship between our optimal Part I conservatism and the problems associated with this group can serve to distinguish some relevant issues of social conservatism. In the first place, it is clear that a good many individuals who are not among America's wealthy subscribe to conservative principles. We were once a thoroughgoing market economy; the ideals of self-help, individualism, and individual responsibility were once taught as central values of our culture. There are still a great many millions of Americans around who subscribe to those values and will vote for candidates for political office who advocate them publicly.

There are both good and bad reasons for thinking of former supporters of George Wallace as potential recruits to conservatism. Many of them are troubled by the deterioration of their neighborhoods, many by rising crime, many by the continued and even escalating bureaucratic hassling of small business, which for all too many has become a survival issue. In all these cases conservatism has an answer. The protection of civil and property rights of law-abiding citizens as a central concern, the drastic cutback of government regulation, the drastic reduction in federal funds available for "urban renewal," the shifting of basic responsibility for many aspects of government, and particularly of schooling, back to the local and even neighborhood level: These are all part of the core program of a contemporary American conservative.

However, there are two areas where conservatives and Wallaceites must part company. In the first place, there is a substantial component of old-fashioned populism in the movement, and populism has been intimately associated with dramatic expansions of government intervention in the economy. And second, there has been a strong vein of racism running through the movement. On the political side there are still conservatives willing to use racism in order to get votes, and they have tended to give a tone of racism to the movement. There is no way such ideas can be reconciled with the idea of a free society; furthermore, such tactics have tended to put off many who might on grounds of principle be attracted to political conservatism. Much the same thing is true of any sort of implicit appeals for the latent populist vote, including such things as ticket-balancing with liberals. Over the longer run, which is surely the run that counts for conservatives, there must be a basic compatibility between the principles of conservatism and the practice of conservative politicians; otherwise, it is all too easy to dismiss the movement as an unprincipled front for the material interests of the wealthy.

There is an area of legitimate disagreement between libertarian and traditional conservatives. Much of it hinges in practice on the extent to which the requirements of preserving a regime of order must constrain the requirements of preserving a regime of liberty. Reasonable men can differ on such matters. But perhaps enough has been said in this chapter to convince doubting libertarian conservatives that traditional conservatives are a bit more sophisticated than Hayek gives them credit for being. And hopefully our optimal conservative position of Part I will convince both groups that their mutual interests are far geater than their disagreements, that they are, in fact, all conservatives.

CHAPTER 19

Neoconservatives

"HOW DOES a radical, a mild radical, it is true, but still one who felt closer to radical than to liberal writers and politicians in the late nineteen fifties, end up a conservative, a mild conservative, but still closer to those who call themselves conservative than to those who call themselves liberal in early nineteen seventy?" With this question Harvard sociologist Nathan Glazer introduces us to the neoconservatives. They are a fascinating phenomenon, as much for their eminence as for their numbers. They indicate in an intellectually very powerful way that conservatism is passing its current tests of relevance and plausibility with flying colors. Conservatism is gaining recruits from the hitherto dominant liberals, and among its recruits are those who have been centrally involved in creating and appraising the liberal handiwork of the preceding two decades. It seems they have come to think it doesn't work.[1]

Neoconservatives are not the same thing as conservatives. Perhaps they can most easily be distinguished from optimal conservatives by the following three tests. Conservatives tend to believe three things about public policies for the improvement of the citizenry: (1) manipulation, especially coercive manipulation by government of some people by others, is a fundamentally immoral activity. (2) We know very little about the consequences for human behavior of any given policy, which inserts a large area of unpredictability into such manipulations. (3) Even if the "productivity" of a particular public policy is known, its real effects are not because of the fundamental inefficiency of bureaucratic government, its inability effectively to implement policy.

On my reading, neoconservatives tend to reject point 1 above, and their conservatism rests more on point 2 than on point 3. In other words, neoconservatives are basically liberals who have become disillusioned by the failures of public policy, failures that they attribute in large part to their—and, of course, our—ignorance. To this they might want to add an additional point: (4) What we are learning about such basic problems as crime, welfare, and the functioning of urban communities suggests that we have very little public policy leverage in changing urban behavior and ways of life. The knowledge accumulated over the past ten or fifteen years seems to be telling us more about what we cannot do in the way of public policy than about what we can do. Conservatives might partly disagree on this one, arguing that public policy does have considerable power to do evil, but I doubt that there would be much disagreement from anyone on the latter point nowadays. The neoconservative, of course, is talking about our knowledge of how to make things better.

In other words, neoconservatives seem basically to retain their liberal orientation. Their alliance with conservatives is based on disillusion rather than conversion. If a way could be found to design effective liberal policies, they would come flocking back to the banner. At any rate they *are* allies, for the moment, and the reasons may be worth taking a closer look at. Just a few points about city life will be noted to give the flavor of their orientation.

1.   Standard fare of liberal argumentation decries the "flight to the suburbs" as something new and very disturbing in American urban life, a sort of renouncing of responsibility by the citizenry for making cities work. But it turns out that in fact this is nothing new, that the "flight" has been going on for a century and more in our older cities. Such a movement by the increasingly affluent has occurred regularly with the growth of cities, which has meant crowding and increasing land values near the center. The more affluent want space and privacy, and can afford the move; developing modes of transportation have made the commute substantially less onerous. Far from being a new and fundamental social problem, it is part of a standard pattern of urban growth.

2.   However, something new was added, mostly in the post–World War II environment. This was a change in central city job structure combined with the introduction of substantially higher welfare payments to the poor in many urban areas. The new jobs tended to be white-collar and service-sector jobs, mostly for the middle class, instead of following the older pattern of industries using cheap semi-skilled labor. So appropriate new job opportunities failed to keep up. But the increased welfare payments kept the supply of newly migrant lower-class families to the city up, or even accelerated it. The result, substantially a product of well-intentioned public policy, was to turn our central city areas into a sort of adult "sandbox" where welfare recipients were congregated and were actually encouraged by public policy to give up their sense of responsibility and live as government charges. Out of this mistaken policy, substantially reinforcing an underlying change in urban job structure, has come the major causal element in deteriorating neighborhoods and crime.

3.   One fundamental variable serves quite well to distinguish members of different social strata. This variable is the degree of present orientation or, to put it another way, the degree to which an individual is willing to defer present gratification in order to have a more affluent or secure future. The lower class, the bottom 10 to 20 percent in the American status and income pyramid, display extreme

present orientation in their behavior. What happens, then, when policies are applied that are designed to jump status, to pull members of the lower class up into the middle class in their behavior? Of course, they will fail. For a striking example, there was the attempt in the later sixties to get the poor to organize their neighborhoods for political action. Funds were made available as an incentive to participate, and the poor were thus shown the way, the blessings of participation in the democratic process. Had this been tried in an upper middle-class neighborhood, it would no doubt have been a great success. But turnouts were abysmally low in poor neighborhoods. And all too often the funds became the stakes of what looked like developing old-style precinct political machines, with all the corruption and coercion that entailed.[2]

4. It seems quite likely that the minimum-wage law, another well-intentioned attempt to prevent "exploitation," has the opposite effect from that intended. There is quite good reason to believe that raising the minimum wage reduces the number of people employers are willing to hire. Since the minimum-wage law will mostly affect entry-level job seekers, this employment effect is largely concentrated on teen-agers. And since they mostly live in families where they are not the only source of income, on the average the effects of lower wages on them should not be too severe. So what *does* happen when the minimum wage is instituted or raised? Probably there is a higher level of teen-age unemployment. That is a bad thing in itself, but indirectly it may contribute significantly to the crime rate, since teen-agers commit most of the crimes, particularly the street crimes.

5. Not all policies have the opposite effect from that intended by liberal policymakers. Probably most of them have some net beneficial effect. However, a survey of individual policies in the areas of housing, health, and education, specifically as they relate to blacks, indicates that individual policy effects, where they can be discerned at all, tend to be relatively trivial in the net benefits they generated. And, of course, they tend to be rather more than trivial in the net costs they incur.

6. Finally, one might mention the great overall panacea of the liberal economist, namely, monetary and fiscal policy. The textbooks used to say that a proper application of these twin public policy instruments could keep the economy growing at or very near full employment. No more. It does not take a professional economist to see that these instruments are not working very well, that something has gone wrong with the economist's ability to predict the consequences for prices and employment of Keynesian-type economic stimulus. Controversy is even emerging among liberal economists as to the appropriate direction of change, as in arguments over whether we would have had more or less inflation by adopting expansionary policies after the OPEC price rise.

This is an interesting and powerful line of argument. The list could certainly be extended. But it should be noted that for conservatives these points represent ammunition, specific confirmations of conservative views of the consequences of adopting the liberal relation of government to the individual. They do not represent new principles, or even basically new ideas. A conservative who believes in freedom and understands the social benefits of tradition would naturally gravitate in these directions, even without the help of the more specific studies that convinced these neoconservatives.

There is, however, an additional thread to neoconservatism. It is espoused by sociologists rather than economists, but is worth mentioning here because it represents a widespread misunderstanding of the basis of American conservatism. The argument might run something like this: There are two ways to look at the law. The first is to think of it as a sort of tied sale. Most of us, following the intent of the law, do not think we have become criminals because we have gotten, and earned, a parking ticket. Many will make a sort of rational cost-benefit calculation; if it's worth the risk of a four-dollar fine, we go ahead and park in the prohibited zone. But some, perhaps an increasing number of citizens, carry this idea over into the realm of genuinely criminal activities such as theft and even murder. If this becomes the general reaction of the population to laws, the lawmaker and the judicial system must then design and implement the law as if it were a sort of cost-benefit system. A good legal system would then be one in which potential criminals assess the costs and benefits of crime and find that crime really does not pay.

A second view of law gives it moral authority. Legitimacy is the word political scientists use; the population by and large does not stop to weigh the costs and benefits of a crime, but genuinely believes that to commit a crime is an immoral act. Only when laws are legitimated, proponents of this view argue, does the judicial system have a manageable task. Legitimacy means that simply announcing a law will have a negative effect on criminal behavior; and that is the decisive edge for a society of order.

Which view is right? In answering that question, one might remember the third point above. The more present-oriented individual is much more likely to commit a crime if he sees an immediate opportunity for gain. However, he is quite unlikely to make a careful calculation of the overall and longer term costs and benefits of the act. His behavior—and probably most criminals fall into the lower or present-oriented class on this characterization—can only be controlled by making sure that the costs are large and occur in the short run. And much of the effectiveness of the judicial system will stem simply from successfully getting such people off the streets for a reasonable period after they have committed a crime. Swift and sure punishment, not some abstract distinction between legitimacy and rationalism, is the major issue here. And so the issue does not divide conservatives in any fundamental sense. Both ideas have their place.

Surely it would be pleasant if all citizens respected the law, and we should endeavor to expose our citizens to the many good arguments in favor of doing so. And equally surely neither the government in general, nor the judicial system in particular, is capable of generating a highly "productive" set of instruments as inputs to the individual decision to commit or not to commit the crime. That part leads right back to liberalism and the issues with which we started. But clearly, there are a number of areas where simple improvements in procedure, sentencing, and parole, combined with eliminating the encouragement to crime of much other social policy, could have a dramatic effect on this and other current social problems. The valid element in the search for legitimacy is contained in the conservative concept of order as the precondition of freedom.

CHAPTER 20

Friedman

WITHOUT A DOUBT Milton Friedman is America's best-known conservative economist. He has gained this renown through his regular articles in *Newsweek* over the years and through the publicized advice he has given to politicians. But Friedman is far more than a public pundit. He has done a number of solid and scholarly studies in the economics of public policy and is recognized as a leading professional by his colleagues. If the honors he received as he moved to emeritus status had not matched those of other leading economists, it would have reflected not on Friedman but on the profession itself.[1]

Nevertheless, Friedman has not escaped criticism even from within the conservative, libertarian camp. It is true that he has not pursued the philosophical interests that engaged the previous generation of conservative scholars such as Hayek and Mises and Friedman's own teacher at Chicago, Frank Knight. He has done no serious work on political philosophy or the nature of man, and has renounced Knight's profound if eclectic view of science for a rather rigid positivism. And some have found in his various policy proposals a sort of gimmickry that seemed to them inconsistent with the conservative view that human social arrangements are not lightly to be disturbed. In combination, this set of qualities in his writing could lead to the claim that Friedman is something of a radical, whose schemes for reform are at once too drastic and too simplistic to be truly conservative and truly useful. It is this criticism primarily that we appraise in the present chapter.

As an initial example of Friedman at work, we may recall the issue of fixed versus floating exchange rates in international finance, which was discussed in chapter 12. In 1962 Friedman published a list of seven steps that should be taken to free up the international monetary mechanism, of which the switch to floating exchange rates was the key step. Most liberal economists opposed these moves, but a decade later they had all been taken, and after a half dozen years of living with floating rates we seem to be surviving quite nicely, especially considering the disturbances OPEC and other agents have inflicted on world markets.

Friedman has done a little crowing over these events, which he is certainly entitled to do. But he has also carefully noted that he himself was not the principal agent of change in the matter. Liberal economists were not convinced by his arguments during the sixties— though many of them have been persuaded by now. Instead, politicians were forced by events to switch to the more robust system. Consequently, the gimmickry charge can hardly be sustained in this case. The approach called for reducing government involvement in markets, and it was chosen by the politicians because it seemed that there was no alternative. In that context the only charge one could reasonably level at Friedman is the free exercise of common sense.

As a second example, we may consider Friedman's discussion of social security. He divides the issue into three parts: the redistribution of income entailed by the system, the nationalization of the system for the provision of the pensions, and the compulsory "purchase" of the pension-annuity by almost all citizens. The redistributions go in two directions, from younger entrants into the system to older entrants, and from general taxpayers to recipients of pensions. Neither is very easy to justify, even if one were willing to impose one of the more popular egalitarian notions of equity onto the issue. Nationalization of the annuity means that the money paid by working people into the system goes through the government budget, and the terms and organization of the system are under full government ownership and control. This despite the fact that we have in the United States a large and competitive insurance industry, which would be fully competent to provide the service on a private basis for a fee and which would keep the pressure on for efficient delivery of the service. Also, requiring people to join the system seems to be based mainly on a depression-bred misconception that people could not take care of themselves in their old age through planned saving during their working years.

We will make no attempt to appraise Friedman's arguments here, except to note that all of them have some force and all of them are of even more significance today than they were fifteen years ago, when they were first published. In particular, we are now approaching the time when a very substantial redistribution of income from current taxpayers to pension recipients will be occurring every year, while the vagaries of the various other pension plans, when combined with social security, are putting a very heavy burden on a number of budgets, including those of city governments. It might also be noted that the rise in the federal social-security budget may have played a stimulating role in the rise of other government expenditures, particularly during the years in which social security was running a substantial surplus of receipts over pension payments.

But once again it is hard to find a basis for accusing Friedman of gimmickry or of simplistic radical reformism. In this case the issue is separated into three distinct parts. One could without great difficulty devise a policy that would deal with only one of these parts, so that reform need not occur in one fell swoop. Furthermore, Friedman's implied proposals in each of the three areas are consistent with overall conservative principles. And, as with exchange rates, time seems to have made his case more cogent, not less. Once again, from our present standpoint his position looks more like common sense than anything else.

The three areas where the gimmickry charge seems to be most persistent are the negative income tax proposal, the proposed abolition of licenses to practice skills and professions, and the proposal to substitute educational vouchers for the tax-supported public school system. Each of these represents quite a dramatic change from the current situation, none is based on traditional practice, and there are some reasonable objections to feasibility that a conservative might legitimately raise. But once again, each proposal probably looks better today than it did fifteen years ago, and each has been an important issue of public policy in the intervening years.

As Friedman points out, probably the most difficult aspect of these issues stems from the extent to which any government policy is based on paternalism. The less one is willing to trust the judgment of those who receive the benefits, or their customers in the case of licensure, the less attractive are Friedman's proposals. Paternalism is a difficult question to appraise in Friedmanian terms. Part of the problem is that the libertarian's notion of social arrangements is based on trust of the individual, combined with a desire to foster that trust by making the individual responsible for the consequences of his own actions. But the negative income tax is not much better than the handout in kind in this respect: In each case, the individual becomes a ward of the state. With educational vouchers the parent is given a voucher worth the regular per-pupil allocation for public school operation for each of his children and is then allowed to send the child to the school of his choice, paying the cost with the voucher. But this too involves paternalism in a most direct way, since the child is not being given responsibility for the decision. The paternalism in licensure comes from the claim that the customer, such as a doctor's patient, is in no position to judge the quality of the service before it is administered, and so must be helped by the state. So really in all of these cases the extent to which government paternalism is required becomes a central issue.

Probably all conservatives can agree that expenditures are excessive as compared to results in the case of both welfare and education. It also seems likely that Friedman's proposals will have some beneficial effect on the cost of these services. But that is by no means a necessary outcome. One could easily think of tax and voucher rates being set at levels that far outstrip current levels of payment. This absence of built-in checks to further expansion of the government system is clearly a troubling aspect of each proposal. When combined with the reduction in the government's ability to control outcomes in areas in which it provides the money, a feature of both proposals, there is further reason for conservative doubts. For example, are tax-subsidized children to be exposed to any political and social views in the schools of their parents' choice? Is any use of the welfare funds by parents to be accepted? Would it not be better to concentrate efforts on reducing the scope and size of the present program by weeding out obvious fraud and mismanagement than on substituting an entirely different program whose size is easily varied to suit the desires of politicians?

Licensure raises somewhat similar issues. It is true that there has been much abuse of licensing and that it has often resulted in establishing a government-licensed trade union that keeps prices up by restricting entry. But there also seems to be a reasonable sense in which such systems, for example in medicine, have served to keep the general quality of medical practice quite high. Our current health-care system is criticized on many grounds, but rarely if ever on grounds of the general incompetence of physicians. Once again it might seem more reasonable to concentrate on the obvious failures of the system, many of which stem from the peculiar attempts at a mixture of public and private systems of service, rather than on the fact that doctors and nurses have to work hard to obtain licenses to practice. If the government were to concentrate its efforts on that area in which it has a clear obligation to act, namely, in the field of public health, and were to leave the art of healing to the combined efforts of the existing market mechanisms and private organizations, the health status of the American population might be substantially better. But it does not seem that licensure is particularly relevant to these more central issues.

This is not to say that Friedman's ideas are to be rejected out of hand. Rather, it is to suggest that there are reasonable and conservative arguments on the other side, and that this is perhaps an area in which the conservative position is in need of clarification by further research. No one can reasonably deny that Friedman has raised important issues, and has pointed to important areas of failure of our current social arrangements. And no conservative can reasonably appraise these areas without giving careful attention to Friedman's proposals.

There is one peculiar area of neglect in much of Friedman's work. This is his lack of use of the property rights framework in his analyses. Friedman's approach to a problem is to look at what the reasonable aims of public policy may be, then to look at the results of government action, and finally to ask how things would be if the government were to do things differently, in particular if government were forced to rely more on rules and less on discretion in its behavior. There is a clear connection between a government based on rules and the stability of a structure of private property rights. The more discretion government has, the more uncertain is the definition of the property rights of those who fall within government's purview. But that is not to say that Friedman's approach is equivalent to the property-rights approach. Government discretion may itself be limited, for example to those whose failure to function effectively in the marketplace brings them under the paternalistic wing of the welfare program. It is by no means clear that one wants to establish private property rights to the receipt of welfare largesse. Discretion in this area may, in fact, do more good than harm by decentralizing some aspects of decision making. Whether it will or not is a question of fact. But conservatives can reasonably object to the insistence on granting to the citizenry property rights to enjoy either welfare or a job. If the government is going to be paternalistic in certain areas, there is a good case for allowing it some flexibility, within the budget, in deciding where and how to act. Perhaps systematic consideration of Friedman's proposals within a property-rights framework will serve to provide the needed clarification.

One of the most striking things about the set of proposals Friedman has put forward is their mutual coherence. Each one seems to come from the same basic social orientation, and they are typically not only mutually compatible but mutually reinforcing. In combination they provide a vision of a thoroughgoing market economy functioning successfully in the twentieth century. That is a vision that conservatives badly needed fifteen or twenty years ago. And there is no question but that it is a serious vision and not some half-baked utopia. I remember in the early sixties a one-liner that was going the rounds of economists: "Friedman loses all the arguments—except for the ones at which he is actually present!" This reflected a typical liberal reaction to his work; Friedman's views were never really taken seriously, and so they were not accurately reproduced or fairly appraised by liberal economists. But when he presented them himself, the audience tended to come away from the talk in a thoughtful mood. That thinking has proved to be very subversive of the liberal values of the sixties. Even if some of the specifics of Friedman's proposals are rejected by conservatives, he is deserving of their respect and gratitude for the subversive power of his thought.

CHAPTER 21

Hayek

OF ALL contemporary conservative writers, it is Friedrich Hayek who comes closest to the positions of our optimal conservative economic world view. Such differences as do exist are essentially matters of emphasis and style, and of the desire for simplicity in the Part I presentation. However, Hayek is often misunderstood, or at least misinterpreted. Perhaps that is a burden all profound and subtle minds must bear. In the present chapter we offer a few quotes and comments from Hayek's principal works. Our aim is to suggest to the reader for whom this is a first contact with Hayek that his rather heavy tomes may well repay the effort they require. But we also hope to show that Hayek's more philosophical and historical approach to problems does in fact tend in the same direction as do the more mundane arguments of our optimal conservative economist.

1. Consider first this quote from *The Constitution of Liberty:* "Far from assuming that those who created the institutions were wiser than we are, the evolutionary view is based on the insight that the result of the experimentation of many generations may embody more experience than any one man possesses." [1] Hayek thus identifies himself with a respect for tradition and against the rationalist apotheosis of reason. But again: "To the empiricist evolutionary tradition, on the other hand, the value of freedom consists mainly in the opportunity it provides for the growth of the undesigned, and the beneficial functioning of a free society rests largely on the existence of such freely grown institutions." [2] Thus the mixture of freedom and tradition, and the emphasis on the emergence through trial and error of a complex product that far transcends the reasoning abilities of Man the Planner.

2. In chapter 19 there was some discussion of the emphasis placed especially by Irving Kristol on the need for a set of shared values if society is not to fly apart. As Hayek puts it: ". . . freedom has never worked without deeply ingrained moral beliefs and that coercion can be reduced to a minimum only where individuals can be expected as a rule to conform voluntarily to certain principles." [3] But Hayek would not go so far as to attempt to coerce the acceptance of moral

rules; by implication he would rather see less order and so, indirectly, less freedom in other spheres. He also notes that, in fact, it is at times desirable for some generally held moral rules to be broken, for they too are not forever fixed, provided the breaker is prepared to assume the consequences of his act. This passage might have provided good counsel to many who, a few years after it was written, had to face the moral dilemmas of the middle and late sixties.

3.   There is an important distinction, Hayek notes, between the situation of the giver and the taker of employment. The worker's responsibility is restricted to the performance of assigned tasks, while the giver of employment bears a general and open-ended responsibility for the success of the entire venture. Most people seem to prefer that restricted responsibility. The job and the income are relatively secure most of the time. As a result the worker tends to forget that the contract with the employer does not include permanent job security. And there is a strong tendency, when something does go wrong with the venture, when the job is threatened, for the employee to blame others rather than himself. This leads inevitably, since there are so many more employees than employers, for the former to seek protection against such risks from some outside agency. And in a democracy that means the state. This is quite a natural tendency, but it cannot be carried very far without stifling initiative; and it should always be remembered that it is based on an attempt to do what is ultimately impossible, namely, escape the unpleasant consequences of living in a risky world.

4.   "The range and variety of government action that is, at least in principle, reconcilable with a free system is thus considerable." [4] Regulation aimed at preservation of health is perfectly legitimate, and this might even include, for example, the prohibition of night work. Though it should be kept within narrow limits, there is no reason, in principle, why there could not be some state enterprise. Even such things as parks, sports facilities, and theaters can legitimately be state owned, though such control should be exercised by local, not central governments. Some provision of social security may also be justified as a legitimate function of government.

Hayek proposes not that such activities be prohibited in principle but that careful attention be given to the expected problems government action entails and the alternative possibilities. For example, he notes that "What is objectionable is not state enterprise as such but state monopoly." [5] This notion certainly accords with European experience since his lines were written. Efficiency is much higher and arbitrary political intervention much lower in those nationalized firms that must compete on private markets than in those firms that have an effective monopoly of the supply of their product. In the area of social security, Hayek is not much moved by charges such as Friedman's that forced saving for a retirement pension is an intolerable intervention into personal liberty. Instead, he emphasizes the consequences of government operation of the system, the creation of a vast and complex and relatively inefficient bureaucracy, and the co-optation of expertise into the system, so that it is virtually impossible to find some-one who is both critical of the system and understands its intricacies.

But on this subject perhaps the remark that most needs pondering is: "So far as the preservation of personal liberty is concerned, the division of labor between a legislature which merely says that this or that should be done and an administrative apparatus which is given exclusive power to carry out these instructions is the most dangerous arrangement possible." [6] The growing complexity of the executive bureaucracy in the United States and the diminishing ability of an overburdened Congress to subject it to effective control would seem to exemplify this "most dangerous arrangement."

5. Von Humboldt, the great Prussian schoolmaster, created the generally admired Prussian school system in the eighteenth century. It was a highly centralized system, and it worked, in the sense that it created a very well-trained population and was thereby widely emu-lated. But were not the consequences for both Prussia and the world catastrophic? There must be more to education than the acquisition of useful skills if it is to serve the needs of a free society.[7]

6. The Beveridge Report, submitted to the British Parliament toward the end of World War II, became a sort of bible for the creators, there and elsewhere, of the contemporary welfare state. In it are iden-tified the "five giants" that the report's proposals are designed to slay: want, disease, ignorance, squalor, and idleness. They are all great evil giants, no question. The problem, of course, is with the proposals, not the targets. As Hayek puts it, the proposals have in practice only served to generate five more giants: inflation, paralyzing taxation, coercive unions, government-run education, and the arbitrary social-security bureaucracy. Furthermore, it seems that the rise of the five new giants is now serving to promote the growth rather than the demise of the other five. Thus again have liberal good intentions backfired.[8]

7. Political philosophers are not much known for their sense of humor. Hayek confines his to an occasional footnote, as in this quote from the eighteenth-century French finance minister Turgot when ap-prised of a gentleman's proposal to institute an income tax: "One should execute the author, not the proposal."

8. Running through the discussion of many of the above points, and others as well, is Hayek's central notion that the idea of distribu-tive justice is the subversive concept that most threatens to under-mine the functioning of a free society. "Freedom is inseparable from rewards which often have no connection with merit and are therefor felt to be unjust." [9] Hayek never quite articulates a theory of entitle-ments, such as Robert Nozick's, mentioned above in chapter 17. How-ever, he is both persistent and effective in arguing the interminable difficulties when a patterned ideal of distribution becomes the object of public policy. In particular, he has this to say about welfare eco-nomics: "In judging adaptations to changed circumstances comparisons of the new with the former position are irrelevant." [10] The change in circumstances does not permit either a claim that all are benefited or the identification of those that are hurt so that they may be compen-

sated. This is why welfare economics has never provided a usable basis for the evaluation of alternative social policies. Entitlements are not affected by this caveat, however, for what is tested there are not the outcomes, in terms of supplies of goods and services to individuals, but rights, whether or not the change is a consequence of someone's rights being violated. A society, even a minimal state, has the means to deal with such violations, since the damaged individuals will themselves make their claims before the judiciary. This is the great distinction, the one that separates liberal and conservative economics.

9.   This is Hayek quoting the French conservative de Jouvenal: "We are thus driven to three conclusions. The first is that the small society, the milieu in which man is first found, retains for him an infinite attraction; the next, that he undoubtedly goes to it to renew his strength; but, the last, that any attempt to graft the same features on a large society is utopian and leads to tyranny." [11] The point the two authors are making is central to the situation in the modern free society, which is that of a very large collection of individuals. For such a society, there is no escape from a set of relatively abstract rules governing individual behavior. An impersonal rule of law is the only basis for equal treatment. We are constantly drawn back to the principles of those smaller societies where a sense of community could pervade and where propinquity gave meaning to the discretionary exercise of power by its rulers. But that is a blueprint for disaster in the modern nation, and learning that lesson will be a major task not just for our generation but for future ones, as we gradually come to terms with our new situation.

In its discussion of the future, the last chapter of Part I provides the basis for an affirmative and optimistic conservative outlook. The roots of this optimism lie partly in the power of conservative arguments, partly in their durability in severe tests over a period of many generations, partly in the special confirmations that events of more recent times have provided, and partly in the obvious resurgence of conservatism as an intellectual movement, as a political movement, and as an orientation toward economic analysis. Karl Marx once said that the function of intellectual activity was not so much to understand the world as to change it. A conservative restatement of his remark may serve as the coda to the present work:

The key step in the analysis of social arrangements is to understand the severe limits imposed on any such analysis. We do not understand well how society works. However, we have learned through bitter experience that civilization is based on order, and that order is the basis of human freedom and material affluence. We have also learned that the individual is worthy of respect as an organism capable of assuming responsibility for his own actions. And we have learned that the market, essentially a system of voluntary agreements for the cooperative production and exchange of goods and services, allows the individual maximum responsibility. Bureaucrats are a necessary evil for only a very limited range of actions mostly associated with the preservation of public order and rights. The function of intellectual activity is to serve the individual's curiosity. Hopefully, an increasing number of intellectuals will attempt to persuade their fellow citizens that the world does not need coerced change so long as rights are secure.

Notes*

Chapter 2

1. Three works have played an important role in the development of this new interpretation of history. With magnificent sweep, William McNeill in his *The Rise of the West* (Chicago: University of Chicago Press, 1963),* tells the story of world history substantially in terms of the role of diffusion of better techniques and better forms of social organization from their points of origin around the world; and, of course, trade is a major facilitator of this process. Sir John Hicks, *A Theory of Economic History* (New York: Oxford University Press, 1969),* is the place to go to understand the central role of markets in the economic history of the West. Hicks, a Nobel Prize winner who turned from economic theory to history late in life, has clearly put a lifetime of reading, plus his grasp of economic theory, into this fundamental revision of the subject. For a challenging interpretation of the rise of the Western world in which the development of property rights plays a central role, see the book of that title by Douglass North and Robert Thomas (Cambridge: Cambridge University Press, 1973). Our account in this and the next two chapters draws heavily on the ideas contained in these works.

2. For an account of the substantial economic development of colonial Africa, see Peter Bauer's *West African Trade* (Cambridge: Cambridge University Press, 1954), and his other works cited in the Suggestions for Further Reading. Morris Morris, *Emergence of an Industrial Labor Force in India* (Berkeley: University of California Press, 1965), and elsewhere, shows that there were substantial positive benefits from colonial rule in this part of the world and that the asserted destruction of native handicrafts by the colonial regime simply did not occur.

3. Friedrich Hayek, ed., *Capitalism and the Historians* (Chicago: University of Chicago Press, 1954), provides the key essays in this revision of the economic history of the industrial revolution.

4. The central economic role of the family is a major thread in the works of Joseph Schumpeter. For a good example, see Part II of his *Capitalism, Socialism and Democracy* (New York: Harper, 1944).*

Chapter 3

1. Wolfram Eberhard's *A History of China*, 3rd ed. (Berkeley: University of California Press, 1969) provides many insights into Chinese history along the lines suggested in the text. Mark Elvin, *The Pattern of the Chinese Past* (Stanford: Stanford University Press, 1973),* offers further insights into the dynamism of Chinese society, technologically as well as organizationally. The first four chapters of Frederic Wakeman, *The Fall of Imperial China* (New York: Free Press, 1975), contains a succinct and very useful description of the gentry, the merchants, the peasants, and their interactions under the dynastic cycle.

2. A beautiful account of the significance of the Venetian republic is to be found in Frederick C. Lane's *Venice, A Maritime Republic* (Baltimore: Johns Hopkins University Press, 1973),* a nicely illustrated summa of Lane's lifetime of work on the topic. An extended account of the Venetian bureaucracy and welfare system is provided by Brian Pullan, *Rich and Poor in Renaissance Venice* (Cambridge: Harvard University Press, 1971).

* Starred items are available in paperback.

Chapter 4

1. This is the term used by Hicks in his *Theory of Economic History* (New York: Oxford University Press, 1969).* This work and North and Thomas, *Rise of the Western World* (Cambridge: Cambridge University Press, 1973), provide the basis for the historical interpretations of this chapter.

2. David Thomson's *England in the Nineteenth Century* (Harmondsworth, England: Pelican, 1959),* though not conservative in orientation, clearly shows the ways in which merchant-influenced government allowed and at times encouraged the rise of the thoroughgoing market economy, and the relation between both of these and the essentially peaceful process of transition to democracy.

3. For an account of the roles of markets and public order in the development of England, France, Japan and China, see Robert T. Holt and John Turner, *The Political Basis of Economic Development* (New York: Van Nostrand, 1966).*

4. Jonathan Hughes, *The Vital Few* (Boston: Houghton Mifflin, 1966), shows the special significance of individual efforts in the development of the American economy.

5. In thinking of the effects of the rising market system on general recognition of rights, one might note that after 1838 no one in England was hanged except for murder or its attempt. This process of reducing the excessive cruelty of the criminal law is associated in many countries with the rise of a system of property rights and markets. As we will see in chapter 10, liberals pushed beyond this reform to coddling of criminals as "victims of society" with the rise of the redistributive state in the twentieth century.

6. Though the United States, protected by distance from foreign threat, still had the security lesson to learn by hard experience in the changed military environment of the twentieth century.

Chapter 5

1. This cycle, and other features of nineteenth-century dynamics, are described in Arthur Gayer, W. Rostow, and A. Schwartz, *Growth and Fluctuations in the British Economy, 1750–1850,* 2 vols. (Oxford: Oxford University Press, 1953).

2. The serious study of the role of information in making economies work dates from Friedrich Hayek's seminal paper, "The Use of Knowledge in Society," *American Economic Review* 35 (September 1945). For a contemporary statement of the issues, see Armen Alchian and Harold Demsetz, "Production, Information Costs and Economic Organization," *American Economic Review* 62 (December 1972).

3. Early American market structures in their relation to changing transport costs are discussed in part 4, and esp. chap. 32, of Harold Williamson, ed., *Growth of the American Economy* (Englewood Cliffs, N.J.: Prentice-Hall, 1951).

4. For a sobering account of the way in which government has stimulated rather than inhibited monopoly, see Alan Greenspan, "Antitrust," in Ayn Rand, ed., *Capitalism: The Unknown Ideal* (New York: New American Library, 1966).*

5. For persuasive and very readable applications of these arguments see, among others, the chapters on prostitution, medical care, the automobile, and flooding Hell's Canyon in Douglass North and Roger Miller, *The Economics of Public Issues,* 3rd ed. (New York: Harper and Row, 1976).*

Chapter 6

1. These early writers, usually identified as members of the Institutionalist School of economics, had a profound appreciation of the need for stability and evolutionary change in social arrangements. They also had many interesting things to say about the interaction between law and the economy. Had they been willing to accept the usefulness of economic analysis in generating insights into this interaction (and the need for stability), their work would have been much more influential. For a sample work that still retains some interest, see John R. Commons, *The Legal Foundations of Capitalism* (New York: Macmillan, 1924).* To appreciate the change in quality wrought by property rights analysis, compare this work with Robert Posner, *Economic Analysis of Law* (Boston: Little, Brown, 1972).

2. A succinct characterization of the basis of property-rights theory can be found in Harold Demsetz, "Toward a Theory of Property Rights," *American Economic Review* 57 (May 1967).

3. From a careful study of the German archives, Alexander Dallin in his *German Rule in Russia* (New York: Macmillan, 1957) has told this still too little known story. As Dallin recounts, Ukrainian peasants greeted the Nazi invaders as liberators from the Soviet yoke—until they discovered that the Nazis, as well as their previous Russian overlords, appreciated the brutal possibilities inherent in collective serfdom.

4. On this see North and Thomas, *The Rise of the Western World* (Cambridge: Cambridge University Press, 1973).

5. Dow Votaw, *Modern Corporations* (Englewood Cliffs, N.J.: Prentice-Hall, 1965).*

6. With his usual prescience, Milton Friedman included rent controls and publicly subsidized housing construction on his 1962 list of government "bads," long before it had become a major public scandal (or rather before the more recent scandals). See also his account of the failures of public housing in *Capitalism and Freedom* (Chicago: University of Chicago Press, 1962),* pp. 178–81.

Chapter 7

1. William Niskanen, *Bureaucracy and Representative Government* (Chicago: Aldine, 1971).

2. For a short and unforgettable account of how government and property interact, read Henry Manne, "The Parable of the Parking Lot," which can be found in the Furobotn and Pejovich collection, *The Economics of Property Rights* (Cambridge, Mass.: Ballinger, 1974).

3. Daniel P. Moynihan, *The Politics of a Guaranteed Income* (New York: Random House, 1973).

4. Ronald Coase, "The Federal Communications Commission," *Journal of Law and Economics* 2 (October 1959). This is a classic article both in its treatment of the facts and in stimulating the development of property rights theory. It is reprinted in Furobotn and Pejovich, *The Economics of Property Rights*.

5. Economic analysis of law has been developing rapidly in recent years, as the reader of the book by that title by Robert Posner (Boston: Little Brown, 1972) will see. It provides a good analytic basis for the shift from executive-type to judiciary-type treatment of externalities advocated in the text.

Chapter 8

1. Milton Friedman's most controversial proposal in *Capitalism and Freedom* is probably that to abolish occupational licensure, and particularly for medical practitioners. There are, of course, halfway houses for those not prepared to take such dramatic action, for example by sanctioning the licensing of people with smaller amounts of training for limited purposes. Movement in this direction has already occurred in the gradual development of paramedic practice, something the armed services have long had.

2. Most of the problems associated with welfare and proliferating bureaucracies are tied up with large cities. For an excellent survey of what has been learned—and unlearned—by students of public policy in this area over the past two decades, see Edward Banfield, *The Unheavenly City Revisited* (Boston: Little, Brown, 1974).* See also the discussion in chapter 19 below.

3. For a typical statement in favor of the relative poverty concept, see Richard Titmuss, ed., *Essays on the Welfare State* (Boston: Beacon, 1969).* For some conservative thoughts on these matters, see William F. Buckley, Jr., *Four Reforms, A Program for the 70's* (New York: Putnam, 1973).

Chapter 9

1. This position is well argued in Milton Friedman and David Meiselman, "The Relative Stability of Monetary Velocity and the Investment Multiplier in the U.S. 1897–1958," in E. C. Brown, ed., *Stabilization Policies* (Englewood Cliffs, N.J.: Prentice-Hall, 1963), where the difficulties with the multiplier concept are pointed out. An empirical test reveals that the multiplier is a far from constant "constant,"

and the monetarist concept of velocity is shown to be both empirically and theo-retically a more satisfying base for policy analysis.

2. A considerable minority of economists was never sold on Keynesianism. Over the last decade or so the number of dissidents has been increasing rapidly. One of the seminal books in the debate was Axel Leijonhufvud's, *Keynesian Economics and the Economics of Keynes* (New York: Oxford University Press, 1968). For a short and lucid discussion of major issues, chap. 3 of Friedman's *Capitalism and Freedom* is still hard to beat.

3. Milton Friedman and Anna Schwartz's magisterial *A Monetary History of the United States* (Princeton: Princeton University Press, 1963), provides over-whelming documentation in support of the thesis that the single most productive measure for dealing with monetary instability would be to prevent continuing mone-tary mismanagement by removing most discretionary authority from the hands of government officials.

4. See chapter 3 above and particularly Frederick C. Lane's *Venice, A Maritime Republic* (Baltimore: Johns Hopkins University Press, 1973),* pp. 331–34 and 430. After the Venetian nobility shifted from trade to landowning as the basis of its wealth, the size of the nobility declined and wealth became more concentrated within the nobility. But a whole new class of merchant outsiders arose and pros-pered. Had they been fully accepted into the society, Venice might still be around! At the very least, the indications are that a late seventeenth- or eighteenth-century distribution of income that included these outsiders—who lived and worked in Venice—would not have been so different from earlier times.

Chapter 10

1. The distinction between ends-connectedness and means-connectedness is presented and analyzed in Hayek's new book, *The Mirage of Social Justice* (London: Routledge & Kegan Paul, 1976).

2. Probably the best general account of how revolutions come about is still Lyford Edwards, *The Natural History of Revolution* (Chicago: University of Chicago Press, 1927). Though rather old, this book avoids Crane Brinton's mistake of trying to equate the American with the Russian revolution (*Anatomy of Revolution* [New York: Norton, 1938]). Thomas Greene, *Comparative Revolutionary Movements* (Englewood Cliffs, N.J.: Prentice-Hall, 1974), is somewhat tainted by sociological jargon, but clearly shows the tendency for leaders of the left to be scions of the upper class, and so more distant from their followers than are the leaders of other movements. Greene also shows the association between the unwillingness or in-ability of governments to act and the success of revolution.

3. For a very good account of the relations between crime and social policy, see chap. 8 of Edward Banfield, *The Unheavenly City Revisited* (Boston: Little, Brown, 1974).*

Chapter 11

1. A scholarly account of the economic achievements of Taiwan is provided in a forthcoming study by Walter Galenson and Nai-ruenn Chen.

2. The annual surveys of the *Far Eastern Economic Review* provide ample evi-dence of the performance of these two trading economies. Keith Hopkins, ed., *Hong Kong, The Industrial Economy,* (New York: Oxford University Press, 1971),* dem-onstrates the reluctant admiration liberals express at the success of conservative monetary and fiscal policy in Hong Kong.

3. Stanley Wellisz, "Lessons of Twenty Years of Planning in Developing Coun-tries," *Economica* 38, n.s. (May 1971), explains the rather dramatic downward re-assessment by liberal economists of the effectiveness of planning. I.M.D. Little and Tibor Scitovsky, *Industry and Trade in Some Developing Countries: A Comparative Study* (New York: Oxford University Press, 1970), have produced a scholarly, nega-tive assessment of the effects of policies of import substitution.

4. The economist who has devoted his professional career to demonstrating, in the face of almost universal academic disbelief and even hostility, that the market and free enterprise works in the "Third World" as well as elsewhere, is Peter Bauer. The range of his thought on this subject is well captured in his collection of essays, *Dissent on Development* (Cambridge: Harvard University Press, 1972). He collobo-rated with Basil Yamey in writing *The Economics of Underdeveloped Countries* (Chicago: University of Chicago Press, 1957).

5. Holt and Turner, *The Political Basis of Economic Development* (New York: Van Nostrand, 1966),* discuss the political aspects of the early development efforts.

6. This tubewell story was told in a lecture at Berkeley a few years ago by economist Robert Dorfman, who worked for a time in Pakistan for the Development Advisory Service of Harvard.

Chapter 12

1. Friedman's ideas are expounded in chap. 4 of *Capitalism and Freedom,* and the events leading up to the float are analyzed in chap. 5 of his *An Economist's Protest.*

2. Joseph Schumpeter in his essay, "Imperialism" (published in English in Schumpeter: *Imperialism and Social Classes* [New York: Meridian, 1960]) provides an account of imperialist behavior that puts the role of the market and of the businessman in a proper perspective. Though forty years old, it may still be the best thing available on the subject.

3. For a good account of Chilean copper, which evaluates the effects of the copper companies' operations on the Chilean economy, see Clark Reynolds and M. Mamalakis, *Essays on the Chilean Economy* (Homewood, Ill.: Irwin, 1965), the essay by Reynolds being the relevant one.

4. Peter Bauer and Basil Yamey, *The Economics of Underdeveloped Countries* (Chicago: University of Chicago Press, 1957), provide evidence in favor of these assertions for colonial governments.

5. For an account of this waste in the case of aid to Greece, see William McNeill, *American Aid in Action 1947–1956* (New York: Twentieth Century Fund, 1957).

Chapter 13

1. Thanks to Frank Knight and Michael Polanyi, a good basic perspective on the idea of socialism can be acquired rather quickly: see Knight's "Socialism: The Nature of the Problem," reprinted as chap. 5 in his *Freedom and Reform* (New York: Harper, 1947), and Polanyi's "Towards a Theory of Conspicuous Production," *Soviet Survey,* October 1960. George Halm, *Economic Systems, A Comparative Analysis,* 3rd ed. (New York: Holt, 1968), offers a thoughtful account of the development of twentieth-century socialism.

2. Another disturbing aspect of socialism has been developed by Frederick Pryor in his *Public Expenditures in Communist and Capitalist Nations* (New Haven: Yale University Press, 1968). He offers a striking demonstration of the similarities in public policy attitudes of liberals and radicals by showing that most of the time the patterns of public expenditures in the two types of economies are statistically indistinguishable. The difference between liberals and radicals actually is not all that great.

3. For a solid account of its workings in the Soviet Union, see Gregory Grossman, "The Soviet Second Economy," *Problems of Communism* 26 (Sept./Oct. 1977), pp. 25–40.

4. This and other assertions about Czechoslovakia are a product of the author's visit to that country during the "Prague spring."

Chapter 14

1. There does not seem to be a good analysis of the international order along conservative lines. It is unfortunate though understandable that Hayek has explicitly excluded it from consideration in his massive works on political theory. However, the basic notions used in discussing domestic order seem to be transferable to the international scene with little modification.

2. For example, in the later years of the authoritarian Salazar regime in Portugal, even the works of French communists were available, in Portuguese translation, in bookstores.

3. Albert Wohlstetter in "Racing Forward or Ambling Back," in *Defending America* (New York: Basic Books, 1977), lays out the options on this central topic.

Chapter 15

1. Joe S. Bain, in his *Environmental Decay, Economic Causes and Remedies* (Boston: Little, Brown, 1973) shows how one initial measure, for reduced compression ratios on certain cars, probably led to increased pollution.

Chapter 16

1. Freedom and family have always been central concerns of conservative thought. The major development in that thought over time, aside from the steady process of enrichment of the basic ideas through continuing accumulation of experience, has been the strong trend toward increasing the scope of freedom. The original notions were closely associated with preserving the freedoms of aristocratic families against the depredations of kings and emperors. But as time went on and social and economic development continued, it became feasible to expand the range of the population that could be included within the basic framework of freedom. The great English philosophers of the seventeenth and eighteenth centuries were concerned to bring the solid citizenry, gentry, and merchants, within the framework; the American revolution was largely inspired by these notions, together with their French counterparts. But a still larger expansion occurred in the nineteenth century as a whole series of thinkers began coming to terms with the potential of the thoroughgoing market economy. Roughly speaking, this revolutionary expansion in the applicability of conservatism was expected to embrace all those citizens of a country who were prepared to accept the established market-democratic political process as the definer of the framework of economic and political activity.

This long tradition must be sharply distinguished from another conservatizing tradition, namely, the organicists, who tended to give the state some sort of mystical identity and to think of individuals as functional parts of this larger, organic whole. That line of belief was typically associated with hierarchic societies, and is a very different thing from the drive for independence of control by others that is the cornerstone of the conservative tradition we are following in this work. The reader interested in conservatism's more distant forebears can do no better than read Friedrich A. Hayek's *The Constitution of Liberty* (Chicago: University of Chicago Press, 1962).

2. George N. Nash's extremely useful *The Conservative Intellectual Movement in America Since 1945* (New York: Basic Books, 1976), provides an overview that emphasizes the trends toward coalescence and divergence of the various strands of conservative thought. The bibliographical notes to that book give the reader an idea of the volume and scope of conservative writings, and guides to selection.

3. Frank Meyer's role as advocate for fusion among conservatives is described in chap. 6 of Nash, *Conservative Intellectual Movement*. Our optimal conservative is clearly a fusionist, though the specific arguments differ somewhat.

4. As Nash, *Conservative Intellectual Movement*, notes, Walter Lippmann's *An Inquiry Into the Principles of the Good Society* (Boston: Little, Brown, 1937) was a major stimulus to the eventual founding of the Mont Pélerin Society.

Chapter 17

1. James Buchanan's general orientation can be found in part IV of his and Gordon Tullock's *The Calculus of Consent* (Ann Arbor: University of Michigan Press, 1962). For a variety of applications of his mode of economic analysis to problems of public choice, see his *Demand and Supply of Public Goods* (Chicago: Rand McNally, 1968).

2. A glance at *Man, Economy and the State*, 2 vols. (New York: Van Nostrand, 1962) or *Power and the Market, Government and the Economy* (Menlo Park, Calif.: Institute for Humane Studies, Inc., 1970),* will convince the reader that Murray Rothbard is the purest of the pure libertarian breed.

3. Robert Posner, *Economic Analysis of Law* (Boston: Little, Brown, 1972).

4. Robert Nozick, *Anarchy, State, and Utopia* (New York: Basic Books, 1974).

5. We should not leave this topic without mentioning Ayn Rand, whose works do not contain much economics but are certainly stimulating. Of her two principal novels, *Fountainhead* (New York: Bobbs-Merrill, 1943) * and *Atlas Shrugged* (New York: Random House, 1957),* I believe the former to be the more interesting and relevant to the conservative economic world view.

Chapter 18

1. The great book in this genre, from the point of view of economics at least, is Joseph Schumpeter's *Capitalism, Socialism and Democracy* (New York: Harper, 1944). The work includes, in addition to a broad-gauge account of capitalism's historical dynamics, a theory of democracy that has served as the basis for much later work, a brilliant account of Marx's thought, and an analysis of socialist political movements. The starting point for postwar traditionalist conservatism in the United States is Russell Kirk's *The Conservative Mind* (Chicago: Regnery, 1960).

2. For an influential political philosophy, see Leo Strauss's *Natural Right and History* (Chicago: University of Chicago Press, 1953) and more recent *Political Philosophy and the Issues of Politics* (Chicago: University of Chicago Press, 1977) by his student Joseph Cropsey. A contemporary sociologist who fits reasonably well into this mold and writes persuasively is Robert Nisbet, whose *Quest for Community* (New York: Oxford University Press, 1953), and *The Twilight of Authority* (New York: Oxford University Press, 1975), are perhaps his most interesting efforts. Nash, *The Conservative Intellectual Movement in America Since 1945* (New York: Basic Books, 1976), offers a number of additional suggestions. William F. Buckley, Jr.'s magazine, *National Review*, provides wit and argument that falls mostly within this genre, but unfortunately gives relatively little weight to the economic side.

Chapter 19

1. Perhaps the single best place to go to get the general line of argument of members of this group is Edward Banfield's *The Unheavenly City Revisited* (Boston: Little, Brown, 1974).* Though Banfield does not seem to be a "recusant liberal," his views are quite close to where the others are tending, and though he is a political scientist rather than an economist, he emphasizes in his writing aspects of urban life that are economically relevant. The first five of our six points describing neoconservative views are taken from this work. Daniel Patrick Moynihan's more recent works, including *The Politics of a Guaranteed Income* (New York: Random House, 1973) and *Maximum Feasible Misunderstanding* (New York: Free Press, 1969), Nathan Glazer's *Remembering the Answer: Essays on the American Student Revolt* (New York: Basic Books, 1970), and Irving Kristol's *On the Democratic Idea in America* (New York: Harper and Row, 1972), are central works in the genre. The quarterly *Public Interest* is a sort of unofficial gazette of this group and regularly includes pieces dealing with the economy.

2. Of course, to be future-oriented does not imply that one must favor a policy of governmental attempts to increase the longer-run rate of growth. Ezra Mishan, *Technology and Growth, The Price We Pay* (New York: Praeger, 1970), represents effectively the economist who feels that growth is tending to become too costly in terms of amenities foregone.

Chapter 20

1. Friedman has, of course, become a Nobel laureate. His writings of special interest for the purposes of this book have already been cited a number of times. It might be noted here, just as a reminder, that Friedman as a leading professional economist has produced a large body of writings at a more technical level, and that these are the basis for his reputation within the profession. But, of course, the two genres are connected, and in Friedman's case they form a mutually compatible whole. The specific issues raised in this chapter are all discussed in *Capitalism and Freedom*, especially in chaps. 6 and 11. The list of steps proposed in reforming the international monetary system appear in chap. 4 of the same work.

Chapter 21

1. Frederich A. Hayek, *The Constitution of Liberty* (Chicago: University of Chicago Press, 1962), p. 62.

2. Ibid., p. 61.

3. Ibid., p. 62.

4. Ibid., p. 123.
5. Ibid., p. 231.
6. Ibid., p. 224.
7. See ibid., pp. 378–79 for a discussion of Humboldt.
8. See ibid., pp. 305 and 516n. 2 for a discussion of the Beveridge Report.
9. Fredrich A. Hayek, *The Mirage of Social Justice* (London: Routledge & Kegan Paul, 1976), p. 120.
10. Hayek, *Constitution of Liberty*, p. 261.
11. Hayek, *Mirage of Social Justice*, p. 191n. 15.

Suggestions for Further Reading*

Alchian, Armin, and William Allen. *University Economics,* 2nd ed. Belmont, Calif.: Wadsworth, 1968.
> From a conservative perspective, probably the best full-scale principles textbook on the market.

Banfield, Edward. *The Unheavenly City Revisited.* Boston: Houghton Mifflin, 1974.*
> A first-rate account of the successes and failures (mostly the latter) of government policies with respect to the cities, welfare, and so on, and a very plausible explanation as to why such policies by their nature can have little effect on the problems.

Bauer, Peter, and Basil Yamey. *The Economics of Underdeveloped Countries.* Chicago: University of Chicago Press, 1957.
> A treatise on development whose first author is perhaps the most distinguished contemporary student of the subject in the conservative tradition.

Black, Angus (pseud.). *A Radical's Guide to Economic Reality.* New York: Holt, Rinehart and Winston, 1970.*
> A sort of "Chicago School" put-on. What is radical about this 100-page book is that, in contrast to the radical diatribes that were so popular at the time of its publication, it takes the market seriously as a resource allocator. In these liberal days that is in fact radical.

Buchanan, James, and Gordon Tullock. *The Calculus of Consent.* Ann Arbor: University of Michigan Press, 1962.*
> Another classic that characterizes what might be called the position of contractarian anarchism.

Friedman, Milton. *Capitalism and Freedom.* Chicago: University of Chicago Press, 1962.*
> A classic survey and analysis of major public policy issues. Though it deals explicitly with the issues of its day, it seems to have become increasingly relevant over the years.

Friedman, Milton. *An Economist's Protest.* Glen Ridge, N.J.: Horton, 1972.*
> A collection of Friedman's essays taken from *Newsweek,* and consistently applying his ideas to current economic events.

Furobotn, Eirik, and Svetozar Pejovich, eds. *The Economics of Property Rights.* Cambridge, Mass.: Ballinger, 1974.
> A collection of some of the best writings on property-rights analysis in recent years, including the main essays on the subject cited in our footnotes.

Hayek, Friedrich, A. *The Constitution of Liberty.* Chicago: University of Chicago Press, 1962.
> Hayek's magnum opus, a powerful integration of both the political and economic ideas of conservatism.

———. *Studies in Philosophy, Politics and Economics.* Chicago: University of Chicago Press, 1967.*
> Chap. 11 in this collection of essays is entitled "The Principles of a Liberal Social Order." It provides a comprehensive list of those principles and succinct commentary.

———. *Law, Legislation and Liberty.*
> This is a projected three-volume treatise of which the first two volumes, *Rules and Order,* London: Routledge & Kegan Paul, 1973, and *The Mirage of Social Justice,* London: Routledge & Kegan Paul, 1976, have already appeared. Though dealing more with law and political theory than with economics, they represent Hayek's latest thinking on the interrelation among these three, and the second volume is an especially useful refutation of contemporary liberal theories of justice.

Holt, Robert T., and John Turner. *The Political Basis of Economic Development.* New York: Van Nostrand, 1966.*
> Emphasizes the role of governmental nonacton in contributing to the early

---

* Starred items are available in paperback edition.

stages of economic development, taking evidence from pre-twentieth-century economies.

Kirk, Russell. *The Conservative Mind*. Chicago: Regnery, 1960.
> The starting point for postwar traditionalist conservatism in the United States. Interesting in that Kirk combines this version of conservatism with a relatively libertarian attitude toward the economy.

Knight, Frank. *Freedom and Reform*. New York: Harper, 1947.
> A collection of essays by the great Chicago teacher. The essay "Freedom as Fact and Criterion" is most percipient on this issue and its relevance for economics. The same can be said for "Socialism: The Nature of the Problem."

Nash, George N. *The Conservative Intellectual Movement in America Since 1945*. New York: Basic Books, 1976.
> An excellent, detailed, and dispassionate account of the subject.

North, Douglass, and Roger Miller. *The Economics of Public Issues*, 3rd ed. New York: Harper and Row, 1976.*
> An introductory survey of economic issues viewed from the property-rights perspective, it provides a very good and brief introduction to economic analysis that is fully compatible with conservative principles.

North, Douglass, and Robert Thomas. *The Rise of the Western World: A New Economic History*. Cambridge: University of Cambridge Press, 1973.
> Tells the story of the transformation of medieval into modern Europe in terms of the development of property rights.

Nozick, Robert. *Anarchy, State and Utopia*. New York: Basic Books, 1974.
> Defends the "minimal state" and argues cogently that there cannot be any connection between the idea of justice and the idea of a morally correct distribution of income or wealth.

Posner, Robert. *Economic Analysis of Law*. Boston: Little, Brown, 1972.
> An already classic work that uses the new property-rights theory and economic theory to analyze legal concepts in terms of their efficiency, as measured on the market.

Rothbard, Murray. *Power and the Market, Government and the Economy*. Menlo Park, Calif.: Institute for Humane Studies, 1970.*
> The libertarian position carried to its extreme limit, where it merges with anarchy.

Schumpeter, Joseph. *Capitalism, Socialism and Democracy*. New York: Harper, 1944.
> A classic work on the dynamics of capitalism, and on the stultifying effects of socialism, written by one of the great conservative economists of this century. It is perhaps understandable, given the time of writing, that he was unduly pessimistic as to capitalism's future.

———. *Imperialism and Social Classes*. New York: Meridian, 1960.*
> Another of Schumpeter's classic accounts of a much-misunderstood phenomenon.

Thomson, David. *England in the Nineteenth Century*. Harmondsworth, England: Pelican, 1959.*
> Without being conservative in orientation, it tells the conservative story of the inseparable connections between economic progress, freedom, and order in the development of the thoroughgoing market economy.

Epilogue: A Final Personal Note

SEVERAL YEARS AGO, as I began trying to put together these characterizations of economic world views, an annoying problem began to emerge. I found that it was not possible to work simultaneously on more than one of them. There is an important sense in which a world view is a separate world; moving from one to another when engaged in writing up the world view from the inside entails some kind of mental effort that I could not make in a matter of a few minutes or even an hour or two. That, of course, is not very surprising. But as work on a given world view continued, I found that I began to develop an intuition that served as a reasonably effective guide to appropriate positions within that particular framework. A few days of reading liberal works and thinking about economic development or socialism from within the liberal framework seemed to sort of turn me into a liberal. In particular, I found it became increasingly easy to develop "liberal" bridges and minor modifications to my arguments in areas where existing liberal work seemed to me unsatisfactory. And exactly the same thing began to happen when I switched to the radical book and, finally, to the conservative one. These switches were fairly dramatic and spilled over into other aspects of my life, affecting the way in which I answered students' questions and reacted in political discussions.

Given the environment of the early seventies, switches in political orientation were not viewed as unusual and so this movement, when noticed by friends, was perhaps not viewed with alarm. But the final phase of the process was harder to live with. As each of the world views became internalized and my efforts turned from construction to revision, I found that it became increasingly easy for me to switch from one to the other. Soon I could more or less pop in or out of one, sometimes at will, sometimes as a consequence of the way a remark or a passage in the book I was reading was phrased. Unfortunately, each switch was total, in that the intuitional elements and the emotional tone of my approach to problems switched at the same time. It now became a matter of some curiosity to me to discover what my immediate reaction to any conversational situation would be, and it was indeed distressing not to know whether it would come out more like Lenin or Colonel Blimp. A certain reputation as an eccentric, or simply a liar, began to be hard to escape.

Some might think that this was the appropriate time to seek help from another profession. But I persist in the belief that my problem was one that should be shared in part by all economists who make any claim to being objective or dispassionate in their professional capacity. We just happen to live in a time in which economics is trifurcated, and in which these splits have considerable impact on the nature of professional understanding, instruction, and counsel. The three sections of this book are a sort of measure of the extent of these splits and of their effects on the professional mind. I do not mean to say that all economists ought to be able to perform the tri-schizoidal switches I have just described, but a serious effort at sympathetic understanding of the consequences of *internalizing* opposing world views would seem to be a minimal test of scholarly seriousness. The same, of course, applies to the student who seeks a liberal education; ideology is something more than an object of study.

The reader who does not find the prospect of reliving my experience particularly appealing can be reassured in another way. I had a peculiarly virulent form of the disease of ideological polysociation, stemming from a deliberate immersion in each world view over a period of years. Such an extended effort is hardly necessary if one's aim is simply to understand what is going on in relevant parts of the discipline. Furthermore, the disease does not seem to be chronic. As the constructive effort on this book ends, I find the schizoidal aspects of my understanding receding without, at least on my own appraisal, any falling back into bigotry. The most enduring price is a kind of tentativeness as to what economists have really established, but that, I think, reflects reality more than it distorts.

It is in this spirit of tentativeness that the following few comparative comments on the three economic world views are offered. There is no intention to denigrate any of them, or to claim that anyone who replicated my method of study would come out free of ideological taint. That did not happen to me. Though with views somewhat modified by the experience, I emerge from the process with a primary adherence to the same world view with which I began the project. Nevertheless, there were a few surprises along the way.

The organizing strategy for this book tends to minimize the differences among world views. Each optimal economic world view has to address itself primarily to the same phenomena, the major economics-related problems that beset the contemporary world. For example, the conservative must offer a set of general policy prescriptions for developing countries, even though this has not been a major concern of economists who support that world view. Radicals are under the same constraint with respect to existing socialist societies, though here too scholarly work by radicals is something less than massive. In addition, little attention has been devoted to world view changes over time, so that the process of adaptation of general perspectives to changing world conditions is missing from the study, and this too is a major differentiator of world views.

But even when account is taken of these constraints, there are still important areas of similarities untainted by this strategic bias that cut across the three optimal world views. For example, the liberal and conservative have essentially the same picture of human nature: rationalist, hedonist, atomistic. This reflects common philosophical origins, but also probably a certain lack of interest in such "fundamentals" by liberal economists. Basic characterizations of human nature serve both liberal and conservative as a basis for defense of the market. Beyond that the liberal loses interest, since there is very little need for a characterization of human nature to support discussions of marginal change as the primary adjustor of social outcomes. Certainly the characterization suffices in defense of the market-correction interpretation of the rise of big government that our optimal liberal espouses. For conservatives the need for fundamentals is greater. Not only must the market be defended, but the charge that existing regimes of political economy are fundamentally flawed must also be defended. The vision of a society based on very substantially different proportions of governmental and private economic activity must be argued in terms of the fundamental structure of the human material that makes the system go. Consequently, the traditional libertarian conception of human nature is essential to the success of arguments couched in terms of property rights or entitlements.

There is similarity in the orientation of liberal and radical world views toward the poor. In both there is recognition of a social obligation to do something about this problem, and in both a willingness to make the rich and more affluent bear the burden of redistribution. But there is also something else, a kind of ambivalence, that expresses itself in muted discussion of the condition and needs of the more disadvantaged members of society. One can read basic radical works on political economy that devote no attention at all to the condition of the poor—this in striking contrast with Marx. Much the same has been true of liberal writings,[1] at least until the War on Poverty provided substantial opportunities for research funding. Probably the ambivalence is related to the common class origins of both radical and liberal economists. Perhaps it is partly political as well, since it seems that the segments of society nearest the bottom are politically among the most apathetic. However, the economic world views of both nowadays give considerable emphasis to devising means for improving the lot of the poor.

Conservatives and radicals share some orientations simply because both are under strong pressure to define themselves in relation to the dominant liberalism. Each as a result tends to interpret liberalism as being close to the more extreme opponent in its underlying orientation. Each is much concerned to deflate liberal pretensions. And each looks to some time other than the present for sources of inspiration; history is more important for both these groups than it is for liberals. The range of beliefs held within each of these two world views seems to be substantially wider than is the case with contemporary liberalism. Conservatism has recently made substantial moves toward a dominant core position; this seems much less true of radicals, but in both cases tendencies toward convergence are weaker than for liberals.

Each of the world views is beset by a more or less symmetric tension between what might be called rationalists and counterrationalists. For radicals, the dichotomy might be expressed traditionally as Ricardo vs. Hegel, a tension that was never fully resolved in Marx's own writing. But for the contemporary radical economist, the tension is more that between Marxian analytics and the more sociological approach that is represented in the writings of Baran, the postwar Sweezy, and Mandel, and including most of the articles in leading radical journals of the last few years. For conservatives, it might simply be called the traditionalist-libertarian split, but there is within the libertarian tradition a more rationalist, technical approach, typified by Friedman and Nozick, to contrast with, for example, the somewhat fuzzier treatment of property rights that has been typical of some writers, for example, Demsetz, and the much less rationalistic position of Frank Knight. For liberals, the central historical division might be expressed as Bentham vs. Mill, but nowadays it separates conventional, technical neoclassical economics from the more institutionally oriented types, among whom Galbraith represents a kind of extreme.

There are two other issues that seem to cut across world views in a rather striking way. The issue of nuclear war has at the moment only one short-run or even medium-run solution: the balance of terror. I cannot find a central rejection of this policy approach in serious writings that lie within any of the three world views, since pacifism at the moment does not seem to offer any sort of coherent alternative. Balance of terror is essentially a liberal policy. Because of its long-run dangers [2] the supporter of balance of terror tends to ignore the longer run and to concentrate on marginalist policies aimed at limited defusing of potential conflicts. The result is that, by and large, liberals hold the field in serious discussions of nuclear strategy.

Ecology in general is an area of rapidly changing ideas, but there are indications of a common split within each world view, depending on how seriously the author views the various risks. A Britisher like E. J. Mishan, who seems to combine rationalism and traditionalism to defend substantial social intervention in order to preserve "amenities," can stand for one kind of apocalyptic conservatism on this issue. The liberal and radical counterparts have been discussed in the relevent commentary sections. But all three world views also contain ecologists who do not view the issues with such fundamental alarm. For liberals and conservatives of this bent, the compatibility with other aspects of the world view is clear enough. For radicals, it seems to stem from a belief that ecological problems are a product of the social system rather than one of nature's givens, so once again compatibility is achieved. Probably the radical orientation is least sensitive to the decision taken on this issue. That is, our optimal radical tends to locate the origins of ecological problems in the relations of production. However, a shift in the optimal position to an emphasis on nature's limits would have little effect on other arguments made by the optimal radical.

These points of inherent commonalty raise the question of possible tendencies toward convergence *among* the world views (as opposed to *within* them). There are two relevant issues in appraising possible convergence: the extent to which there is a spectrum of world views rather than three basic ones, and the depth of the differences between pairs of world views. The first question might be posed as one of inclusiveness: Are there any identifiable groups of economists who seem to be left out of our trichotomy? The most serious possible omission is that of the institutionalists. Somewhat to the surprise of a number of commentators who in recent years have written off this group, the appearance and rapid growth of the Association for Evolutionary Economics and of its publication, the *Journal of Economic Issues*, suggests this is a serious omission.

However, I disagree. It is true that the institutionalists have a rather distinctive general framework, but its structure is far more critical than constructive. I am unable, for example, to point to a few key works that identify a distinctive institutionalist interpretation of contemporary problems. The nearest thing to such a collection is the works of Galbraith himself, but as we have seen, he comes out as a close relative of the optimal liberal view. Some of the distinctive features of past institutionalism, such as the acceptance of a kind of institutional Keynesianism (not too far from what Joan Robinson has called "bastard Keynesianism") have not withstood the test of time. Institutionalist strictures on price theory, often quite perceptive, did not lead to the development of a constructive alternative, and in fact many of their ideas have been incorporated into recent work in price theory without substantially altering the basic neoclassical framework. Structural interpretations of rigidities (barriers to arbitrage) have constituted their stock-in-trade—provided they are small enough in scale —but these are usually capable of incoporation into the liberal framework.[3] Politically speaking, institutionalism has become a support for liberalism with a more interventionist political stance than is perhaps typical of the hard-nosed neoclassical; but when stripped of its critical assertions, the constructive portion of institutionalism looks very liberal.

Of course, there are a number of individual scholars whose relation to the world views as characterized is ambiguous. Some of the classificatory difficulty stems from the tendency of world views not to travel too well: Even the British structure may be rather different from the American, and when one moves to the continent or to Third World countries, the relative roles of Marxism, liberalism, and traditionalism may change considerably. We have obviously concentrated on an American classification and have avoided international comparisons. But that is not to say that these three world views do not manifest themselves elsewhere. Perhaps most striking of all has been the emergence of liberalism among the younger economists of the Soviet Union and Eastern Europe.[4] This is an issue worthy of further analysis. But it should be remembered that our aim is not to tuck everyone neatly into some Procrustean bed but to characterize powerful tendencies of thought within the economics profession with a view to exposing the extent to which barriers to communication among economists have arisen. It is consoling to realize that some have managed, at least partially, to bridge these gaps, but that is not to say that the gaps are not real and substantial.

A few comments on the extent of inter-worldview differences offer some basis for appraising this latter point. A first and surely one of the most prominent differences has to do with class. Class is probably the central factor that divides radicals from the other two world views. Attitudes in favor of or against trickle-down or enclave-expanding growth exemplify the way this difference works. But of course, class also has its ambivalences. On the one hand, the last do wish to become first, and on the other hand, our optimal liberals and conservatives are not bereft of concern for the downtrodden. Nevertheless, this difference does permeate the world views and lends radicalism its distinctive overtones.

The locus of power, in economics and among intellectuals generally, is what separates the liberals from the others. As was noted already, liberal dominance serves to generate some similarities in the stances of radicals and conservatives, but it also serves to divide them from liberals. The tone of liberal writing is cooler, less given to attacks on those outside the world view, and more optimistic, since more of the same is both what they want and a rather likely outcome. The dominance of liberals, of course, extends beyond politics to the media and to the social sciences themselves. The vast majority of research projects are carried out by identifiable liberals, with consequences that are not well explored in any scholarly sense, but which it is plausible to characterize as very substantial. They are a truly formidable opponent and the style of the world view writers reflects this fact strongly.

Only the radicals are revolutionary in their policy orientation. Though conservatives would like to see dramatic changes in society, there seems to be little sentiment in favor of immediate realization of the goals. This don't-rock-the-boat aspect of the traditionalist position seems to have survived the twentieth century quite well. However, as a result, there are often rather striking similarities in the policy principles enunciated by liberals and conservatives. A conservative who would like to set in motion a process of major reduction of the size of government may often seem indistinguishable from a liberal who supports marginal movements in the same direction; their real differences will not emerge until the process has actually gone on for a while. Once again the distinctiveness of the radical views is apparent from the start.

Conservatives and radicals differ from liberals in their appraisal of the effectiveness of government. The role of defender of the status quo is inevitable for the liberal. But, of course, the radicals and conservatives differ as to the real cause of ineffectiveness, which might be sloganized as class vs. coercion.

And again radicals differ from both liberals and conservatives in their conception of human nature, the collective spirit serving as the central defining quality for radicals. Its implications thoroughly permeate the radical perceptions and prescriptions, especially when the time comes to discuss socialism.

Clearly, the radical view is very much different from the views espoused by liberals and conservatives in many fundamental respects. But perhaps the conservative-liberal differences have been exaggerated? When I first began this effort, it was my view that conservatism was simply a variant of liberalism, and I planned to treat it as such in a few chapters in the commentary section on liberalism. I believe that interpretation is widely held, and some support for it is provided by the neoconservatives who, as noted in the commentary to Book III, seem to occupy a sort of marginal position between the two views. That is to say, the distinction between a "right-wing" liberal and a "moderate" conservative may often be hard to draw. This reflects the common origins of the two world views, the clear ability of many economists to communicate across this world view barrier on a number of topics, and the acceptance by conservatives of the status quo as a base from which further movements of society should start.

Nevertheless, I do think that a quite distinctive conservative orientation toward economics and economic policy has emerged and acquired some central tendency over the last two decades. Within economics it has been expressed especially in terms of anti-Keynesianism and property-rights analysis. These two thrusts have served to redefine a number of questions in both macro- and microeconomics in distinctive ways. Practitioners identified by this orientation tend to select rather different problems for investigation. There is much more overlap with liberals in the technical tools they bring to bear on their research, but even there, especially in microeconomics, conservative analyses seem more reminiscent of an older, Marshallian era. There is a kind of implicit bias toward the manipulation of human subjects in liberal analysis that the style of these conservative economists seems designed to combat. In addition, there is the "evidence" of my tri-schizoidal experience. At any rate, all this has served to convince me that there are at present not two but three quite distinctive world views operative in economics.

Let us suppose, in conclusion, that the reader accepts the basic thesis of this work that there are three distinctive world views held by economists in at least the United States these days, and that they produce the distinctive interpretive and policy orientations ascribed in the three parts of the work. What follows? Surely the major implication is that economics as presently taught in American universities fails a fundamental test of scholarly objectivity. In one or two economics departments the message conveyed may have a substantial radical component, in some it is basically conservative, but in the overwhelming majority of the better-known departments the message is almost purely liberal. If ideologies are powerful, our scholarly approach has been transformed into a system of indoctrination in liberal values and how to use such values in dealing with economic policy and the interpretation of society. The usual counter to this—that a scholar can give an honest account of views with which he disagrees—fails. A liberal scholar can be expected to give an honest account of *liberal* views with which he disagrees, but not of those which transcend his world view. There are many examples to illustrate this point, but the liberal and radical receptions accorded Assar Lindbeck's *Economics of the New Left* [5] are perhaps the most convenient illustrative example. Lindbeck receives rave notices from leading liberal economists, who recommend him to anyone who wants to know what the "New Left" is all about, despite the fact that radicals disown the account. The reason liberals persist in their praise is basically that Lindbeck has redefined the radicals' questions into liberal questions. By doing so, the questions change their nature; in particular, the major structural-institutional aspects of the problems, as the radicals see them, begin to look like things that can be divided up into a number of little problems that can be dealt with one at a time and by familiar methods. That may or may not be true, but it is a gross distortion of the radical position, which emphasizes the interconnectedness of the problems in the context of monopoly capitalism. What the student who is sent to Lindbeck gets is a liberal version of radicalism, one that does not suggest a challenge to the other things being instilled by the students' liberal teachers. And, judging from their comments, our leading liberal economists are unaware of this fact.[6]

Of course, the problem cannot be solved by having the student transfer to a radical or conservative department. In fact, just because they are more embattled, such departments are likely to be less tolerant of opposing world views. Lindbeck's is a very good liberal account of radical economics. I have not found it difficult to encounter very bad accounts of liberalism from illiberal hands. The problem is, so to speak, a barrier to arbitrage across world views, a problem of communication. That this entails strong pressures on researchers to conform to mainly liberal canons of performance is surely plausible and is probably, as I have argued elsewhere,[7] a principal reason for the overselling of the results of liberal economics during the sixties. The liberal "club," by a variety of rather indirect devices, effectively silenced dissent with respect to its results. Only pressures from outside the club, combined with much more manifest failures of the research, opened the door. The thing now is to prevent it from closing again.

How can this be done? The principles are easy enough to state. Given the peculiar nature of ideology, the fact that almost every attempt to communicate across world views is an attempt to alter value systems, reliance on liberals to characterize radical or conservative positions is clearly not enough. Some opportunity to penetrate alternative world views should be given to students, and should be required of budding professionals. Whether that can be done by reading alone, without personal instruction from someone committed to the world view, is an open question. Whether serious scholars can succeed in internalizing alternative world views to the point at which they can give reliable accounts of them is an open question. Whether either they or students can be motivated to take alternative world views seriously is an open question. Whether these presently distinctive world views will all survive the stresses ahead is an open question. But I believe that at present, economists as a group stand convicted of looking more like advocates than scholars, of being members of a profession in which the most esteemed practitioners are unwilling to take into professional account the full range of seriously posed alternatives relevant to their research and teaching.

Notes

1. This is the case with the key radical work, *Monopoly Capital*, by Baran and Sweezy (New York: Monthly Review, 1966), and with the seminal liberal work on economic development by Walt Rostow, *Stages of Economic Growth* (Cambridge: Cambridge University Press, 1960).

2. Consider the following argument: In each year there is a positive probability of major nuclear war occurring as the result of accident, conspiracy, or confrontation. In a balance-of-terror mode there is no known way to reduce that probability to zero. Consequently, the probability of at least one nuclear war occurring in a given time period is a positive function of the length of the time period; and by choosing a period of suitable length, that probability can be brought as close to unity—that is, to certainty—as desired. Crude as it is, this is a powerful argument that, to my knowledge, has never been refuted. In fact, I know of no serious attempt to refute it.

3. There is ambivalence in some institutionalist thought that is worthy of mention. The analyst who tends to picture a world of barriers inhibiting more satisfactory behavior may react in either a liberal or radical way. That is, the policy prescription may be either a series of modest changes or one big, revolutionary change. The analysis itself may not require dramatic alteration as a consequence of a shift in advocacy from one to the other policy. This is quite noticeable in reactions to Galbraith: Liberal and radical interpretations of *The New Industrial State* tend to fit the orientations of the reviewers. But more fundamentally, I think this ambivalence was closely associated with an earlier generation of institutionalists who were involved in the process of establishing labor as a politically effective interest group. Success in this endeavor tended to mute the more revolutionary side of these analysts' views, and perhaps it accounts for their substantial failure to reproduce themselves in the students of the first two postwar decades. Like Galbraith, they had effectively merged with mainline liberalism, despite some continuing peculiarities of style. Their more recent resurgence reflects different times and, I believe, a rather different orientation from that of the older generations.

4. For a discussion of this issue, see my *What's Wrong with Economics* (New York: Basic Books, 1972), part II.

5. Assar Lindbeck, *Economics of the New Left*, 2nd ed. (New York: Harper and Row, 1977).

6. Paul Samuelson's foreword to Lindbeck's book, and comments on the book by George Bach and James Tobin, which are also included in the second edition, are very revealing on this score. Their strong recommendation of the work to students clearly implies that they prefer radical arguments to be sanitized a bit before exposing students to them. Paul Sweezy's comment, also included, is rather casual but captures the essence of the problem in one sentence: "The biggest difference between Lindbeck and us is that we see two totally different realities" (p. 140).

7. Ward, *What's Wrong with Economics*, parts I and IV.

Index

Abandoned buildings, 358
Adams, Walter, 164
Adaptability of affluent capitalism, 46
Adaptation to organization, 110
Affluent capitalism, 8–9, 12–35; consumption and leisure and, 13–16; markets and, 22–35; organization of social life and, 17–18; in other countries, 19–21; politics and, 36–47; risk and, 16–17
Affluent Society, The (Galbraith), 108, 120
Age of Discontinuity, The (Drucker), 126
Agriculture, 127; historical development of, 188–90
Aid, economic, 77–78, 129; international economy and, 397; development and, 234
Albania, Western socialists and, 403
Alchian, Armen, 452
Algeria: overthrow of reactionary government in, 256, 257; social effects of colonialism in, 184
Algerian war, 81
Alienation, 288–92; expenditures related to, 210
Allende, Salvatore, 254, 407
Alperovitz, Gar, 315
Althusser, Jean, 307
American Capitalism (Galbraith), 108
American Economic Review, The, 164
American Medical Association (AMA), 162, 371
American Rural Small-Scale Industry Delegation, 315
Anarchism, libertarian conservatism and, 426
Anarchy, State and Utopia (Nozick), 428
Anarchy of market, 226
Anglo-American common law, 366
Angola: cause of revolution in, 382; Soviet support of, 228
Anticommunism, 420
Arab-Israeli war, 147
Argentina, internal violence in, 406
Arbitration of property disputes, 357–58
Armed forces, management of, 55
Arms Control and Disarmament Agency, 308
Association for Evolutionary Economics 465
Athens, 330, 332; military defense of, 412
Atomism, 102
Australia, affluence in, 19
Austria: affluence in, 19; standard of living in, 402–3

Authoritarian regimes, 406–8; in developing countries, 64–65
Automobile industry: demand manipulation by, 118–19; dominance of, 127; environmentalism and, 414; foreign competition in, 395; pollution control and, 90; waste in 208–9
Availability of goods, 26
Aztecs, 332

Bach, George, 470
Balance of terror, 464
Banfield, Edward, 453, 454, 457
Bain, Joe S., 166, 456
Bangladesh, capitalist institutions in, 229
Baran, Paul, 177, 207, 236, 270, 271, 274–83, 285–87, 296, 299, 307, 310–13, 315, 316, 464, 470; on political economy of growth, 275–78
Bargaining power, unequal, 29–31
Barnet, Richard J., 313
Basic liberal values, 102–7; compatibilities of, 105–7
Bauer, Peter, 451, 454, 455
Baumol, William, 110
Belgium, affluence in, 19
Bellamy, Edward, 315
Benassy, J. C., 312
Bendix, Reinhard, 161
Bentham, Jeremy, 8, 105, 464
Berg, Alan, 308
Berkeley, Lord, 8
Berlin crisis, 83, 146, 422
Bettelheim, Charles, 281, 298, 307, 313, 314, 316, 317
Beveridge Report, 447
Big business, power of, 136, 137
Birth control, 63
Blacks: individual policy effects related to, 437; as interest group, 46; wage rates for, 183; *see also* Racism
Block, Fred, 312
Bloomfield, Lincoln, 310
Boddy, Raford, 312
Bolivia: "growth facism" in, 234; overthrow of reactionary government in, 256, 257; radicalism in, 176
Bolsheviks, 239, 243
Bottomore, T. B., 311
Boulton, William, 345
Bowles, Samuel, 311
Braverman, Harry, 281, 282, 310

Brazil: authoritarian regime in, 407; economic growth in, 69, 163, 236; development in, 387; "growth fascism" in, 234; United States imperialism and, 182

Briffault, Robert, 308

Brinton, Crane, 454

Britain: affluence in, 19; class warfare in, 383; emergence of trading nation, 330, 332; feudal, 335; foreign investments by, 395; government regulation of business in, 198; Great Depression in, 217; health care in, 369; imperialism of, 230, 232; industrial revolution in, 191, 192; intermittent crisis in, 227; international money market and, 393; labor based political parties in, 42; laissez-faire economy in, 337; liberalism in, 9; monopolies in, 351; nineteenth century, 194, 333; occupation of Murmansk by, 201; ownership of means of production in, 359; patent law in, 357; political coalitions in, 136; principle of freedom in, 419; restrictions on trade by American colonies of, 394; rise of Labour party in, 195; rise of modern industry in, 343–47; rise of real wages in, 334; short-period business cycles in, 349; welfare system in, 447; worker control in, 294

British Africa, 81

Brookings Institution, 164

Brown, E. C., 453

Brown, E. H. Phelps, 309

Brown, Jerry, 363

Bruce-Briggs, B., 164

Buchanan, James, 424–26, 456

Buckley, William F., Jr., 453, 457

Bukharin, Nikolai, 309

Bulgaria: authoritarian regime in, 407; industrial base of, 68; life of average citizens in, 244

Bureau of the Census, U.S., 308

Bureaucracy, 18; in ancient China, 338–39; information and, 33; internal organization and behavior of, 110; law vs., 365–68; mode of functioning of, 361–62; property rights and, 363–65; Third World, 295; in Venetian Republic, 340–41

Business interests, 41

Business Week, 276

Byzantium, 330, 332

Cadre-building, 257

California: state budget of, 362; tax rates in, 377

Cambridge Journal of Economics, 177

Canada, affluence in, 19

Cancer, 155

Capital (Marx), 163, 303

Capital market, improved functioning of, 346

Carr, E. H., 313

Carter, Jimmy, 164; tax reforms proposed by, 377

Carthage, 338

Castro, Fidel, 403

Caves, Richard, 161, 165

Central Intelligence Agency (CIA), 234

Centralization, technology, and 218

Centrally planned economies, 72

Chad, capitalist institutions in, 229

Chandler, Alfred D., 162

Chen, Jack, 314

Chenery, Hollis, 162, 163

Chiang Kai-shek, 79, 182

Chicago, University of, 350

Chicago School, 431

Childe, V. Gordon, 309

Chile: Allende government in, 254–55; authoritarian regime in, 406–7; capitalist institutions in, 229; copper mines in, 395–96; counterrevolution in, 304; landowners in, 390; politics and economic development in, 65; radicalism in, 176; United States imperialism and, 182

China, 67; ancient, 188, 338–39, 371, 430; British imperialism and, 230; cadre-building in, 257; cause of revolution in, 382; collectivized agriculture in, 243; decentralization in, 251; détente with, 143; development in, 248, 386–87; economic education of peasants in, 302; English language publications from, 178; families in, 283; health care in, 369–70; illegal trade in, 401; internal violence in, 406; international relations of, 70; military capability of, 408; Nationalist, *see* Taiwan; participation in, 249; political position of military in, 162; property rights in, 359; reversal of cultural revolution in, 260; socialist revolution in, 79, 238, 256; social transformation in, 70; Soviet boycott of, 80; Soviet conflict with, 279; surplus extraction in, 236; technology in, 69, 264; transformation of man in, 252–53; vanguard-party thesis and, 297; violent revolution in, 304; Western socialists and, 403; in world market, 76

Choice: consumer, 118; increased complexity of, 14–15

CIA, 234

Cipolla, Carlo, 310, 313

Civil rights, 258

Civil War, 381

Class, 183; Marx on role of, 187; radical view of, 466

Class struggle: instability and, 224–225; urbanization and, 222–223

Class warfare, 383

Clausewitz, 45

Club of Rome, 164, 415

Coase, Ronald, 453

Cohen, Benjamin, 164

Cohen, C. D., 312

Cold War, 202

Collectivization, 242–43; abandonment of, 356; in Yugoslavia, 247

Colonial regimes, 277

Colonialism, 184; war and, 81

Cominform, 247
Commerce Department, U.S., 131, 161, 310
Common law, 366
Common Market, 21, 28
Commoner, Barry, 89, 154, 166
Commons, John R., 452
Communes: Chinese, 248; Yugoslav, 250
Communications, 223; access in United States to, 258–59; development and, 232; in nineteenth century, 349; technological revolution in, 79
Communist party, Russian, 240
Communist party, Yugoslav, 250
Competing capitals, 225–26
Competition, 24; oligopoly and, 114
Comprador regimes, 277
Concept of Corporation, The (Drucker), 126
Congress, U.S., 40, 122, 123, 162; bureaucratic influence in, 365; domination by business interests of, 197; executive bureaucracy and, 447; redistribution of income and, 413; tax reforms in, 377
Constitution of Liberty, The (Hayek), 430, 445
Consumption, 13–16; demand manipulation and, 117–21; in developing countries, 59; per capita, 208; under socialism, 401
Contract law, 427–28
Control, planning and, 52–54
Corporations: dominance of large, 17–18; organization of, 351
Cortez, Hernando, 332
Council of Ten, 340
Counterrationalists, 464
Creativity: affluent capitalism and, 56–57; of markets, 350–51
Crime, 383–85
Crisis, 222–28; government, 219–21; monopoly capitalism as response to, 196–99; nineteenth century, 193–95
Cropsey, Joseph, 457
Crotty, J., 312
Cuba, 67; American boycott of, 80; cause of revolution in, 382; elitism of leadership of, 260; internal violence in, 406; Leninist party in, 257; publications on, 178; revolution in, 256; slavery in, 381; social transformation in, 70; Soviet support of, 228, 242
Cuban missile crisis, 83, 146, 422
Cyprus confrontation, 147
Czechoslovakia: authoritarian regime in, 407; availability of goods in, 26; collective farming in, 243; consumers in, 401; foreign troops in, 21; political controls in, 69, 70; revolution in, 79; Soviet suppression of uprising in, 244; standard of living in, 402–3

Dahl, Robert A., 162
Dallin, Alexander, 453
Dandekhar, V. M., 313
Deals, 22–25

Debt peonage, 190, 191
Decentralization: of corporations, 51; of government, 91
Decolonization, 81
Defense, management of, 55
Defense interests, 43–44
Degradation of environment, 89–90
Demand: domestic, 60–61; manipulation of, 117–21; patterns of, 20; volatility of, 223
Democracy: affluence and, 19, 65; traditional conservative view of, 432–33; *see also* Parliamentary democracy
Democratic party, 38, 135; working class influence in, 382
Demsetz, Harold, 452, 464
Denison, Edward, 161
Denmark, affluence in, 19
Dependence, economic, 75–77
Détente, 146–48
Developing countries, *see* Development
Development, 386–91; agricultural credit and, 391; differing views on, 149–53; discontinuities in, 128–29, 132–33; economic imperialism and, 77–78, 229–37; main line, 58–66; market-based, 386–87; order and, 406–8; planning and, 387–89; property rights and, 389–90; socialism and, 68–69; trade and, 75–76; uneven, 235–37
Dewey, John, 163
Dietary deprivation, 151–52
Discontinuities, 126–34
Discretionary authority, 363
Discrimination, 183
Distributive justice, 447
Dobb, Maurice, 299, 300, 309, 313
Domestic demand, 60–61
Domhoff, G. William, 311
Dominican Republic: United States intervention in, 182, 234, 235
Doomsday projections, 415
Dorfman, Robert, 164, 455
Dow, J. C. R., 312
Dowd, Douglas, 309, 312
Drucker, Peter, 126–34, 138, 139, 162, 165, 312; liberal overview and, 131–34
Drug industry: waste in, 208–9

East Germany: foreign troops in, 21
East India Company, 332
Eaton, John, 308
Eatwell, John, 317
Eberhard, Wolfram, 451
Ecological problems, 154–60, 264; commonality of views on, 464
Economic aid, 77–78
Economic dependence, 75–77
Economic development, *see* Development
Economic imperialism, 77
Economic instability, *see* Instability
Economics and the Public Purpose (Galbraith), 108
Economics of the New Left (Lindbeck), 468

Education, 138–41; government expenditures for, 216; Hayek on, 447; spiritual values and, 422; trade and, 331

Edwards, Lyford, 454

Edwards, Richard, 162, 308, 310, 315

Egypt: ancient, 188, 332; overthrow of reactionary government in, 256, 257

Ehrlich, Anne, 166

Ehrlich, Paul, 89, 126, 154, 166

El Salvador Ministry of Public Health, 313

Elvin, Mark, 451

Emmanuel, Arghiri, 317

Ends-connected social interactions, 380

Energy Crisis, 63; resource exhaustion and, 87

Energy Department, U.S., 363

Engels, Friedrich, 309

England, *see* Britain

Entrepreneurship, 335; traditional conservatism and, 432, 433

Environmental degradation, 89–90

Environmentalism, 413–15

Equal opportunity, 16–17

Establishment, political, 37–41

Eurocommunism, 255

Exchange rates, 392–94; Friedman on, 440

Executive agencies of government, interests of, 43

Exegetics, Marxist, 303

Exhaustion of resources, 86–89

Exploitation under monopoly capitalism, 205–13

Externalities, 32–33; ecological problems as, 155; government encroachment and, 353; government response to, 138

Factory system, development of, 192

Family: changes in, 17; as private institution, 329; social change and, 263; taxes and, 377–78; in trading societies, 334–35; in Venetian Republic, 341

Family law, 365

Fanon, Franz, 308

Fascism, 201, 217; "growth," 234

Federal Communications Commission (FCC), 367

Federal Reserve Board, 376

Feudal property rights, 356

Field, Alexander, 311

Financial markets: development of, 194; volatility of, 223

Finland, affluence in, 19

First Amendment rights, 367

Fiscal policy, 375; neoconservatism and, 437

Fishing, ocean, 88

Fitch, Robert, 317

Five Year Plans, 387

Fixed exchange rates, 392; Friedman on, 440

Floating exchange rates, 392–93; Friedman on, 440

Flynn, Dennis O., 311

Food and Agriculture Act (1965), 38

Food distribution, 152

Ford Motor Company, 208

Foreign aid, 77–78; development and, 234; international economy and, 397

Foreign investment, 75; development and, 233–34; Soviet Union and, 80

France: affluence in, 19; domestic communism in, 202; imperialism of, 232; inflation in, 227; political crises in, 20; population of, 251; transition to socialism in, 255

Frank, Andre G., 312

Franklin, Raymond, 308

Free-rider imbalance, 136

Freedom: relation of stability to, 140; trade and, 332–33

Freeman, Orville, 38

French Africa, 81

French Revolution, 176

Friedman, Milton, 392, 421, 440–44, 453–55, 457, 464

Friedmann, W., 165

Furobotn, Eirik, 453

Galbraith, John Kenneth, 95, 97, 99, 108–25, 138–40, 161, 164–66, 327, 411, 464, 465; 470; on demand manipulation, 117–21; on economic policy, 122–23; on market system, 113–16; on motivation of management, 109–11; on planning system, 111–16

Galenson, Walter, 454

Game theory, 426

Gayer, Arthur, 452

General Motors, 51

Gerassi, John, 178, 307

Germany: counterrevolution in, 304; government regulation of business in, 197–98; under Hitler, 69; revolutionary struggles in, 201; social democracy in, 195, 255; worker control in, 294; in World War II, 202; *see also* East Germany; West Germany

Gintis, Herbert, 311

Girvetz, Harry, 164

Glazer, Nathan, 4, 35, 457

Goldberg, Marilyn, 310

Golden Book of Venice, 341

Goods and services, supply of, 13–14

Gordon, David, 310, 311

Government: alliance of business and, 203; appraisals of effectiveness of, 466; basic liberal values and, 103–4; discontinuities and, 129–30; flexibility of British, 345; Hayek on, 446–47; inefficient, 223–24; liberal view of, 103–4; management in, 55–56; markets and, 352–53; monopoly capitalism and, 214–21; normal and crisis, 219–21; overcentralization of, 91; power and, 135–41; principles of United States, 347–48; property rights and, 361–68; protection of consumers by, 119–20; relation between economy and, 413; role in affluent nations of, 19; spending and, 367–73; *see also* Politics; State

Grange, 38
Gratification, deferment of, 436–37
Gray, Jack, 162
Great Britain, see Britain
Great Depression, 201, 216–17; government policy and, 376
Greece: aid to, 77, 397; ancient, 25, 189, 337; authoritarian regime in, 406–7; capitalist institutions in, 229; civil war in, 202; development in, 387; fear of confiscation of wealth in, 390; "growth fascism" in, 234; movement toward democratic order in, 408; politics and economic development in, 65; United States imperialism and, 182
Green, Mark J., 311
Green Revolution, 153, 232
Greene, Thomas, 454
Greenspan, Alan, 452
Griffin, Keith, 313
Griffin, Keven, 166
Gross, Bertram, 310
Grossman, George, 455
Growth: political economy of, 275–78; surplus extraction and, 207–11; see also Development
"Growth fascism," 234
Guevara, Ché, 178
Guilds, 344–45
Gurley, John G., 308, 314

Habermas, Jürgen, 307
Halm, George, 455
Handfield-Jones, J., 309
Harcourt, G. C., 317
Harris, Seymour, 310
Harvard University, 350, 415, 435
Hayek, Friedrich A., 421, 430, 431, 433, 440, 445–49, 451, 452, 454–58
Hayter, Theresa, 316
Health care: government and, 369–71; reduction of risk and, 16
Hedonism, 102
Hegel, Georg Friedrich Wilhelm, 289, 464
Heilbroner, Robert, 163, 164
Hicks, Sir John, 451, 452
Hinton, William, 308, 314
Hitler, Adolf, 69
Hobshawm, Eric, 309
Hoffman, Paul, 316
Holland: affluence, in, 19; science and technology in, 345
Holt, Robert T., 452, 455
Honda cars, 414
Honduras, capitalist institutions in, 229
Hong Kong: development in, 387; health care in, 369–70
Hopkins, Keith, 454
Horvat, Branko, 177, 178, 293–98, 300, 307, 309, 313, 314, 317
House Agriculture Committee, 38
House of Representatives, U.S., 38, 347
Huberman, Leo, 316
Hughes, Jonathan, 452
Human nature, similarity in view of, 463, 466–67

Hume, David, 8
Hungary: decentralization in, 250; factory committees in, 294; refugees from, 70; revolution in, 79; Soviet suppression of uprising in, 244, 421
Hunnius, Gerry, 317
Hussein, King of Jordan, 146

Ibsen, Henrik, 308
Identification with aims of organization, 110
Ideology, nature of, 462, 468
Illegal activities, 209
Illegal trade under socialism, 401
Imbalance, social, 136–37
Imperialism, 182–83; development and, 229–37; economic, 77–78; international economy and, 394–97; rise of, 194; of Soviet Union, 244
Implicit Big Deal thesis, 116
Import substitution, 388
Incas, 333
Incentives: division of, 25–26; in socialist countries, 72
Income, reduced risk of loss of, 16
Income distribution, 209–10, 413; development and, 61; discrimination and, 183; in socialist countries, 69; stability and, 46–47
Income tax, negative, 372, 377, 442
India: ancient, 188; British imperialism in, 230; capitalist institutions in, 229; increasing poverty in, 236; parliamentary democracy in, 59; politics and economic development in, 65; population control in, 150; in war with Pakistan, 81
Individualism, 424; emphasis on, 326–28
Industrial regulation, involvement of business interests in, 197–98
Industrial revolution, 191–93; British imperialism and, 230; labor conditions and, 334; start of, 343; surplus extraction and, 206
Industrial Workers of the World (IWW), 195
Industrialization, trade and, 331–32
Inequality, 181–82
Information: bureaucracy and, 331; for consumers, 118; future trends in availability of, 412–13; markets and, 33–34, 349–50; organization in market economy of, 26; in socialist countries, 72; trade and, 330
Inheritance taxes, 378, 382
Insecurity of modern life, 211–12
Instability, 222–28; crisis and, 227–28; of markets, 31–32; in nineteenth century, 194; tendencies promoting, 222–24; underlying forces of, 224–27
Institutionalist economists, 113, 452; on development, 149–50
Interest groups, 37, 41–44; government policy responses to, 137
International economy, 392–98; foreign aid and, 397; imperialism and, 394–97; rates of exchange in, 392–94

International order, 405–10; authoritarian regimes and, 406–8; markets and, 409–10; military capability and, 408
International relations, 74–85; aid and intervention and, 77–78; prospects for peace and, 81–84; socialist revolutions and, 79–81; trade and economic dependence and, 75–77
Internationalization of capital: instability and, 223; during nineteenth century, 194
Interstate Commerce Commission (ICC), 197
Intervention, 77; socialist, 79–81
Investment, foreign, 75; development and, 233–34; Soviet Union and, 80
Iran, development in, 387, 396–97
Iraq, overthrow of reactionary government in, 256
Israel, 83, 146; development planning in, 388
Issue structure, failure of, 142–48
Italian trading cities, 330; *see also* Venetian Republic
Italy: domestic communism in, 202; international money market and, 393; transition to socialism in, 255
ITT, 255
IWW, 195

Jalée, Pierre, 310
Japan: affluence in, 19; development in, 387; economic growth in, 69, 163, 203; exchange reserves in, 393; foreign investments of, 203, 395; industrialization of, 229, 277; United States boycott of, 201; in World War II, 202
Jews, Soviet, 70
Job structure, urban, 436
Johnson, Chalmers, 163
Johnson, Lyndon Baines, 422
Johnston, Bruce, 166
Johnston, Kenneth, 162
Journal of Economic Issues, 465
Jouvenal, Henri de (French conservative), 448
Judeo-Christian civilization, 420, 430, 431
Judiciary, libertarian conservatism and, 426
Justice: criminal, 384–85; distributive, 447; libertarian conservative notion of, 428–29; principle of, 347

Kahn, Herman, 164
Kennedy, John F., 422
Kershaw, Joseph, 308
Keynes, John Maynard, 226
Keynesianism, 198, 202, 312, 420, 454, 465; conservative reappraisal of, 325; development and, 387–89; economic fluctuations and, 374–75; neoconservatism and, 437; taming of business cycle and, 226–27
Khrushchev, Nikita, 421

Kilby, Peter, 166
Kindleberger, Charles, 164
Kirk, Russell, 457
Kissinger, Henry, 31; boycott of Chile organized by, 255
Kneese, Allen V., 166
Knight, Frank, 431, 440, 455, 464
Knowledge: discontinuities and, 130–32; organization of, 129; *see also* Information
Kolko, Gabriel, 309
Kolko, Joyce, 312
Kondratiev cycle, 316
Korea: United States imperialism and, 182; *see also* North Korea; South Korea
Korean war, 227
Kotz, David, 311, 318
Kristol, Irving, 445, 457
Kuznits, Simon, 161, 163, 308

Labor, establishment politics and, 41, 42
Labor market, history of, 333–34
Labor and Monopoly Capital, The Degradation of Work in the Twentieth Century (Braverman), 281
Labor struggles: nineteenth century, 195; twentieth century, 198
Labour Party of England, 195
Land-management issues, 157
Lane, Frederick C., 451, 454
Late Capitalism (Mandel), 177
Law: bureaucracy vs., 365–68; coercion and, 405; concept of rule of, 430–31; libertarian conservatism and, 426–28; neoconservative view of, 438
Law Merchant, 357, 365, 431
Law of value, 206
Learning process, 130–31
Lebanon: intervention in, 234; United States imperialism and, 182
Legitimacy, 438, 439
Leijonhufvud, Axel, 312, 454
Leiss, Amelia, 310
Leisure, 13–16
Lenin, V. I., 68, 240, 243, 262, 309, 315
Leninist parties, 256–57, 261
Lerner, Michael P., 315
Lewis, Oscar, 313
Libertarian conservatism, 10, 419–20, 424–29; law and, 426–28; market analysis and, 425–26; models of market behavior and, 424–25; notion of justice in, 428–29; redistribution of income and, 429; social-welfare function and, 425
Licensure, 443
Lindbeck, Assar, 272, 315, 468, 470
Lindblom, Charles, 140, 162, 166
Linder, Staffan, 161, 165
Lippitt, Victor, 315
Lippmann, Walter, 456
Lipset, S. M., 161
Little, I. M. D., 454
Liu Shao Chi, 309
Locke, John, 8

Loss-producing economic activity, 209
Lowenthal, Richard, 163
Lyons, Nancy, 308

McGovern, George, 378, 382
Machlup, Fritz, 131, 166
McNeill, William, 451, 455
Magna Carta, 335
Main line development, 58–66; causal factors of, 60–62; state and, 63–65
Majority rule, property rights and, 364
Malnutrition, 181
Malraux, André, 308
Mamalakis, M., 455
Management, 48–57; of corporations, 49–51; in government, 55–56; motivation of, 109–11; planning and control and, 52–54; under socialism, 400–1
Mandel, Ernest, 177, 300, 307, 309, 313, 464
Manne, Henry, 453
Mansfield, Edwin, 161
Mantoux, Paul, 310
Mao Tse-tung, 71, 163, 177, 178, 307, 309, 403
Maoism, 248; anticommunism and, 420
Marcuse, Herbert, 235, 300, 308, 317; on alienation, 289–92
Marginal adjustment: development and, 61; limits of, 47; of market, 23, 24; in political system, 38–39; stability and, 45
Marglin, Stephen, 309
Markets, 22–35; deals and, 22–25; development based on, 386–87; externalities and, 32–33; imperialism and, 394; improved functioning of, 346–47; information and, 33–34, 330; instability of, 31–32; international order and, 409–10; libertarian conservative analysis of, 425–26; malfunctions of, 28–34; monopoly of, 28–29; planning vs., 113–16; social interactions of, 380; socialist, 72; in twentieth century, 349–54; unequal bargaining power in, 29–31; welfare and, 373
Markovic, Mihailo, 314, 317
Marris, Robin, 110, 165
Marx, Karl, 163, 187–88, 262, 293, 299, 303, 306, 308–9, 315, 317; on alienation, 289; on function of intellectual activity, 448; on ownership of means of production, 359–60; theory of exploitation of, 212–13
Marxism, 68, 269; alienation and, 289; exegetic, 303; influence during twentieth century of, 332; mathematical, 302; modifications of, 294; neoclassical economics and, 301; recent works based on, 177; scarcity economics and, 326; social democrats and, 255; on technology, 263, 264
Marxism-Leninism, 309
Marxist Economic Theory (Mandel), 177
Mass media, *see* Communications

Massachusetts Institute of Technology (MIT), 350
Mathematical Marxism, 302
Means-connected social interactions, 380
Means of production, ownership of, 359–60
Media, *see* Communications
Medical care: government spending for, 369–71; reduction of risk and, 16
Medicare, 162
Meiji Restoration, 277
Meiselman, David, 453
Meritocratic interests, 42–43, 48
Mermelstein, David, 310, 316
Mesopotamia, 188, 189
Meyer, Frank, 456
Mexico: authoritarian regime in, 407; development in, 387, 390; economic growth in, 163; movement toward democratic order in, 408
Middle Ages, trade during, 330
Middle East conflict, 83, 88, 146–48; stabilization and, 146–47
Militarization, 183; Pax Americana and, 203–4
Military capability, 408
Military expenditures, 214
Mill, John Stuart, 8, 326, 464
Miller, Herman P., 308
Miller, John, 164
Miller, Roger, 452
Miller, Ronald E., 313
"Minimal state," 348
Minimum-wage laws, 437
Mises, Ludwig von, 294, 421, 440
Mishan, Ezra J., 457, 464
MIT, 350
Models of market behavior, 424–25
Modern industry, rise of, 343
Modernity, 65
Modernization, process of, 151–52
Monetary policy, 375; neoconservatism and, 437
Monetary stability, 374–78; order and, 379–80
Monopoly, 28–29, 351–52; overcentralization and, 91
Monopoly Capital (Baran and Sweezy), 177, 274, 279, 280, 287
Monopoly capitalism, 180–86; alienation and, 183–85; exploitation under, 205–13; family and, 263; government and, 214–21; growth of surplus under, 207–11; imperialism and, 182–83; inequality of, 181–82; insecurity of life under, 211–12; irrationality of, 185; racism and sexism under, 183; revolutionary process and, 258–60; structure and tendencies of, 196–204; underdevelopment and, 229
Monthly Review, 177
Moral dilemmas, 380–82; Hayek on, 445–46
Morgan, J. P., 196
Morishima, Michio, 317
Morocco, capitalist institutions in, 229
Morris, Morris, 451

Morris, William, 262, 315
Moss, Stanley, 310
Mossadegh regime, 396
Motivation of management, 109–11
Mount Pérelin Society, 420, 456
Moynihan, Daniel P., 453, 457
Multinational corporations, 78; competition among, 394–95; organization of, 351; in Third World, 386
Murmansk, British occupation of, 201
Myrdal, Gunnar, 150, 166
Myrdal, Jan, 308, 314

Nader, Ralph, 120, 311
Nai-ruenn Chen, 454
Napoleon, 341
Nash, George N., 456, 457
National defense, 409, 411–12
National Farmers' Union, 38
National Labor Relations Board (NLRB), 383
Nationalization, 399; in capitalist countries, 123
NATO, 21
Navigation Acts, 394
Navy, U.S., 55, 367
Nazis, 243; occupation of Ukraine by, 357
Near Eastern law, 365
Negative income tax, 372, 377; Friedman on, 442–43
Neoclassical economics, 301–3; Galbraith on, 108
Neoconservatives, 435–39
Netherlands, inflation in, 227
New Deal regimes, 277, 278
New Europeans, The (Sampson), 51
New Industrial State, The (Galbraith), 108, 109
New Left, 178, 281; liberal account of, 468
New Left Review, 177
New York City, fiscal crisis in, 220
New Zealand, affluence in, 19
News from Nowhere (Morris), 262
Newsweek, 440
Newton, Isaac, 344
Nexö, Martin Anderson, 308
Nicaragua, life of average citizens in, 244
Nieburg, H. L., 164
Nineteenth century capitalism, crisis of, 193–95
Nisbet, Robert, 457
Niskanen, William, 362, 453
Nixon, Richard M., 143; economic mismanagement under, 224; fall of, 218; guaranteed minimum income proposed by, 365
NLRB, 383
North, Douglass, 451–53
North Korea, authoritarian regime in, 407
Norway, affluence in, 19
Nozick, Robert, 428–29, 447, 456, 464
Nuclear family, 263
Nuclear war, 258; balance of terror and, 464

Nuclear wastes, 157
Nuclear weapons, 411–12
Nurkse, Ragnar, 149

Objectivity, scholarly, 467–68
Occupational structure, changes in, 48
Occupations, wasteful, 209
Ocean fishing, control of, 88
O'Connor, James, 311, 317
October Revolution, 262
Oil states, 22; bargaining power of, 88
Old Left, 178, 281
Oligarchy, Venetian, 340
Oligopoly, 114
Ollman, Bertel, 317
OPEC, 225, 437, 440
Open societies, 9, 19
Opium War, 230
Oppenheimer, Mary, 317
Optimality, 424–25
Order, 379–85; in ancient China, 338–39; concepts of, 328; crime and, 383–85; international, 405–10; monetary stability and, 379–80; moral dilemmas and, 380–82; revolution and, 382–83; United States electoral system and, 347; in Venetian Republic, 339–42
Organization: creativity of markets and, 351; of social life, 17–18
Ottoman Turkey, 332
Output per capita, 207
Overcentralization, 90–91

Pakistan: agricultural development in, 391; in war with India, 81
Palestinian guerrillas, 146
Papandreou (Greek leader), 407
Paris Commune, 239
Parkinson's law, 362
Parliamentary democracy, 36–37; development and, 59–60; socialism and, 249–50
Pateman, Carole, 314
Patent law, 357
Patents of Monopoly, 345
Pax Americana, 198, 203
Peace, prospects for, 81–84
Peasantry, development of, 188–90
Pejovich (author), 453
Penn Central Railroad, 353
Pentagon Papers, 144
Perlman, Janice, 313
Perlo, Victor, 308, 312
Peru, overthrow of reactionary government in, 256
Phillips, Joseph, 311, 316
Planning, 48–57, 374–75; control and, 52–54; development and, 61, 387–89; socialism and, 71–72, 400; system for, 111–16
Plato, 116
Poland: anticommunism and, 420; authoritarian regime in, 407; factory committees in, 294; private agriculture in, 356; Soviet suppression of uprising in, 421

Polanyi, Michael, 455
Policy, Galbraith on, 122
Political Economy (journal), 178
Political Economy of Growth (Baran),
Political Economy of Growth (Baran), 177, 274, 279
Politics, 36–47; economic development and, 62–65; establishment, 37–41; interest groups in, 41–44; stability in, 44–47; *see also* Government
Pollution, 89–90; taxation to control, 157
Polo, Marco, 338
Population distribution, 193
Population growth, 62–63; development and, 149–50
Populism, 434
Populist economists, 113
Portugal, imperialism of, 232
Portuguese Africa, 256
Posner, Robert, 427, 452, 453, 456
Poverty: inequality and, 181; relativity of, 372–73; similarities in orientation toward, 463
Power: liberal view of, 466; survival of liberal government and, 135–41
Practical embodiments of liberal ideas, 8
Pragmatic approach to problems, 9
Prats, General, 254
Preobrazhensky, Evgeniy, 309
Present orientation, 436–37
Price controls, exchange and, 394
Price fixing, 379–80
Pricing, 23–24; control and, 53–54
Private property rights, *see* Property rights
Production: forces and relations of, 192; ownership of means of, 359–60; socialization of, 218
Productivity under socialism, 358–59
Progress, liberal orientation toward, 105
Property rights, 355–60; development and, 389–90; economic fluctuations and, 374; Friedman on, 443–44; government and, 361–68; imperialism and, 395–96; international violations of, 408; order and, 379–80; ownership of means of production and, 359–60; patent law and, 357; public, 364; real estate and, 355–56; socialism and, 356–59
Prosperity: in ancient China, 338–39; in Venetian Republic, 339–42; *see also* Affluence
Prussian school system, 447
Prussian state bureaucracy, 49
Pryor, Frederick, 161, 163, 455
Public policies, benefits of, 437
Public property rights, 364
Public-transit delivery systems, 121
Puerto Rico, development in, 387
Pullan, Brian, 451

Racism, 183; traditional conservatism and, 434
Radical scholarship, 300–1
Radio broadcasts, federal regulation of, 367

Railroads, 194
Rand, Ayn, 452, 456
Rates of exchange, 392–94; Friedman on, 440
Rationalism, 102, 464
Reagan, Ronald, 362, 363
Real estate, 355–56
Real wages, stagnation of, 210
Recessions, 374–76
Redistribution of income, 413; libertarian conservatism and, 429
Reich, Michael, 162, 308, 310, 315
Religious persecution, 380–81
Reprivatization, 130, 133, 138
Republican party, 123; working class support for, 382
Resnick, Solomon, 308
Responsibility, 446
Resources, exhaustion of, 86–89
Review of Radical Political Economy, 177
Revolutions, 79–81, 256–58; nineteenth century, 193; ordre and, 382–83; role of, 304–6
Reynolds, Clark, 455
Ricardo, David, 464
Risk, affluence and, 16–17
Riskin, Carl, 313
Rivalry among capitalists, 193–94
Robinson, Joan, 317, 465
Roemer, John, 317
Roman law, 365
Rome, ancient, 189; markets in, 25; military defense of, 412; trade and, 330, 337; in wars with Carthage, 338
Rostow, Walt W., 73, 162–63, 452, 470
Rothbard, Murray, 426, 427, 456
Rule of law, 430–31
Rumania: economic growth in, 69; industrial base of, 68
Russia, 19; price of bread in, 26; *see also* Soviet Union
Russian Revolution, 79, 238–40, 294; cause of, 382

Salazar, Antonio, (Portuguese dictator), 455
Sampson, Anthony, 51, 162, 165, 312
Samuelson, Paul, 470
Saudi Arabia, exchange reserves in, 393
Scarcity economics, 326
Scholarly objectivity, 467–68
Schmidbauer, P. L., 310
Scholarship, radical, 300–1
Schultze, Charles L., 166
Schumpeter, Joseph, 421, 431–33, 451, 455, 457
Schurmann, Frank, 308, 314
Schwartz, Anna, 452, 454
Science: British, 345–46; markets and, 350–51
Scientific management, 130
Scitovsky, Tibor, 454
Serfdom, 189
Sexism, 183
Share tenancy, 190
Shelly, Alan, 312

Sherman, Howard, 312, 317
Shoshone Indians, 205
"Shuttle diplomacy," 31
Siberia, United States occupation of, 201
Silk, Leonard, 311
Skinner, B. F., 315
Slavery, 348; moral dilemma of, 381
Slavic family structures, 263
Sloan, Alfred P., 51
Smith, Adam, 8, 105; invisible hand of, 226
Snow, Edgar, 163
Social change, 10
Social conservatives, *see* Traditionalist conservatism
Social democracy, 255–56
Social-harmony expenditures, 216–18
Social imbalance, 136–37
Social life, organization of, 17–18
Social security, 441
Social-welfare function, 425
Socialism, 399–404; defense against capitalist depradations of, 176; development and, 68–69; differences in countries under, 403–4; international relations and, 79–81; managers under, 400–1; planning and, 71–72, 400; property rights and, 356–57; rise of, 238–53; second market under, 401–2; size and power of movements for, 176; in Soviet Union, 238–45; transition from capitalism to, 254–61; utopia and, 67–73; worker-consumers under, 401
Socialist party of United States, 195
Socialist Revolution (journal), 177
Socialization of production, 218
Solow, Robert, 165
Solzhenitsyn, Alexander, 313
South Africa, development in, 387
South Korea: authoritarian regime in, 407; development in, 387; foreign aid to, 129
South Vietnam, 79
Soviet Union, 67, 201, 238–45; achievements of socialism in, 240–42; agricultural output in, 356; anticommunism and, 420–22; authoritarian regime of, 407; Chinese conflict with, 279; in Cold War, 202; Communist Party of, 177–78; demand manipulation in, 119; détente with, 143, 145; economic growth in, 69; failures of, 242–44; Five Year Plans in, 387; industrial policy of, 68; internal violence in, 406; international relations of, 70, 79–80, 83; Jews in, 70; liberal economists in, 465; military capability of, 82, 408, 412; oppressive bureaucracy in, 260; political position of military in, 162; pollution in, 264; science and technology in, 69, 350–51; socialism in, 399; support of national liberation struggles by, 228; suppression of dissent in, 273; trade restrictions imposed by, 394; unavailability of goods in, 402; United States relations with, 410, 411; Western socialism and, 403; in world market, 76; in World War II, 202

Sparta, 330
Spending, government, 369–73
Stability: affluence and, 20; economic, 31–32; markets and, 26–27; political, 45; relation to freedom of, 140
Stagflation, increasing tendency toward, 224
Stagnation, surplus absorption and, 284–87
Stalin, Josef, 69, 243, 420, 421
Stalinism, 243–44, 403
Starr, John, 163
State: liberal view of, 103; *see also* Government; Politics
Status quo, maintenance of, 45
Steel industry, dominance of, 127
Steinbeck, John, 308
Steindl, J., 279, 316
Stigler, George, 164
Strauss, Leo, 457
Suburbs, flight to, 436
Sugar Trust, 196
Supek, Rudi, 314, 317
Superpowers, relations between, 83
Supreme Court, U.S., 202
Surplus absorption, 284–87
Surplus extraction, 205–7; in developing nations, 235; growth of, 207–11; insecurity of modern life and, 211–12
Sweden: affluence in, 19; inflation in, 227; labor-based political parties in, 42; political coalitions in, 136
Sweezy, Paul, 177, 270, 271, 274–83, 285–87, 296, 298–300, 307, 309–12, 314–17, 464, 470
Switzerland, affluence in, 19
Syria, overthrow of reactionary government in, 256, 257
Syrquin, M., 162
Szechuan, population of, 251

Taiwan: aid to, 77, 129; capitalist institutions in, 229; development in, 387; economic growth in, 69; "growth fascism" in, 234; health care in, 369–70; United States imperialism and, 182
Taxes: economic policy and, 376–78; negative, 372, 442; on polluters, 157
Taylor, Frederick, 130
Technology, 18, 60–61; affluence and, 20; availability of goods and, 14; of birth control, 63; centralization and, 218; development and, 60, 232; foreign investment and, 233–34; industrial revolution and, 192; markets and, 350–51; military, 191, 192; resource exhaustion and, 87; rise of modern industry in Britain and, 345–46; socialism and, 263–64; trade and, 75–76; weapons, 411–12
Technostructure, motivation in, 110
Terror: balance of, 464; use by socialist regimes of, 69
Thieu, General, 182
Third World: bureaucracies in, 295; capitalist institutions in, 57; decolon-

ization of, 202, 227; delegitimization of United States policies toward, 259; economists from, 178; losses imposed by imperialism on, 230–31; influence of Communist parties in, 242; interventions in, 78; living conditions in, 236; multinational corporations in, 286, 395; resource constraints and, 285; social development processes of, 232; surplus extraction in, 270–71

Thomas, Hugh, 315

Thomas, Robert, 451–53

Thomson, David, 452

Thoroughgoing market economy: in Britain, 343–47; in United States, 347–48

Tinbergen, Jan, 163

Titmuss, Richard, 453

Tobacco Trust, 196

Tobin, James, 470

Tolerance, 9

Top management, 51

Toward a Theory of Planned Economy (Horvat), 177

Trade, 330–36; among affluent nations, 21; in ancient times, 330; development and, 233; economic dependence and, 75–77; freedom and, 332–33; industrial development and, 331–32; restrictions imposed on, 394

Traditionalist conservatives, 420, 430–34; civilization and, 430–31; controlled change and, 432; democracy and, 432–33; Wallacites and, 433–34

Transformation of man, 70–71, 252–53

Transportation, 223; development and, 232; technological revolution in, 76; urban, 120–21

Troy, military defense of, 412

Trust-busting, 197

Tuchman, Barbara, 309

Tullock, Gordon, 456

Turgot (French finance minister), 447

Turner, John, 452, 455

Ukraine, collective farms in, 243, 357

Underdeveloped nations, *see* Development

Underdevelopment: continuance of 231–35; creation of, 229–31

Unequal bargaining power, 29–31

Uneven development, 235–37

Union of Soviet Socialist Republics, *see* Soviet Union

Unions, 383

United Kingdom, *see* Britain

United Nations, 77, 161, 162; Economic Commission for Latin America, 313; Food and Agriculture Organization, 308

United Parcel Service, 350

United States: access to communications media in, 258–59; affluence in, 7, 12–13, 19, 21; alienation in, 184; attitude of government toward consumers in, 119–20; average incomes in, 372; bureaucratization of universities in,

134; consumption per capita in, 208; cost of establishing property rights in, 390; debt accumulation in, 393; decline of radicalism in, 176; defense interests in, 43; détente and, 145; disestablishment of religion in, 380–81; economic aid from, 202; economic policies of, 375; elimination of slavery in, 332; enforcement of property rights in, 357; executive bureaucracy in, 447; foreign aid programs of, 77, 397; foreign investments by, 395; foreign policy of, 83, 142; government expenditures in, 214–21; government regulation of business in, 197; growth of output per capita in, 207; health care in, 369–71; hegemony of, 227; imperialism and, 182, 232; income policies in, 379; industrial policy of, 68; industrial revolution in, 191, 277; internationalism and, 410; interventions by, 78; labor struggles in, 195, 198–99; legal system in, 366; liberalism in, 8–10; markets in, 30; monopolies in, 351; nineteenth-century, 194, 333; nuclear capacity of, 82, 258; occupation of Siberia by, 201; opposition to Allende government by, 255; planning system in, 115, 135; policy toward authoritarian regimes of, 408; policy toward enemies of, 408; pollution in, 264; potential use of force by, 305; poverty in, 181; power of business interests in, 41; principle of freedom in, 419; public policy issues in, 140; rate of exchange for, 392; rise of modern industry in, 347–48; rise of real wages in, 334; tax revision in, 133; top management of government agencies in, 55; unions in, 383; worker control in, 294

Upton, Letitia, 308

Urban job structure, 436

Urbanization: changes caused by, 14–15; intensification of class struggle and, 222–223

U.S.S.R., *see* Soviet Union

U.S. Steel, 28–29; emergence of, 196

Utopias, 69–72, 262–63; planning and, 71–72

Value, law of, 206

Values: liberal, 102–7; transmission of, 422, 423

Vanek, Jaroslav, 317

Venceremos (Gerassi), 178

Venetian Republic, 364, 371, 382; organization of, 335; ownership of means of production in, 359; prosperity and order in, 339–42; taxation in, 378; United States compared with, 347

Vernon, Raymond, 164

Vietnam: overthrow of reactionary government in, 256; refugees from, 70; socialist revolution in, 79; Soviet support of, 228; United States imperialism and, 182

Vietnam war, 44, 227, 235; issue structure in, 143–45
Vogel, David, 311
Volatility of demand, 223
Volkswagens, 414
Von Humbolt, 447
Votaw, Dow, 453

Wage labor, generalized system of, 206
Wakeman, Frederic, 451
Wall Street Journal, 40
Wallace, George, 434
Walras, Leon, 112
Wang, George, 307
War, 142–48; expenditures for, 215–16; increased risk of, 16
War on Poverty, 422
Waste: in occupations, 209; in production, 208–9
Watergate, 220, 331, 364
Watt, James, 344, 345
Wealth, ownership of, 181
Weapons technology, 411–12
Weber, Max, 70, 163, 294
Weimar Germany, 255
Weinstein, James, 309
Weisskopf, Thomas, 162, 308, 310, 315
Weisskopf, Walter A., 317
Welfare, 9; government expenditures for, 216–17, 371–73; Hayek on, 447; urban job structure and, 436
Wellisz, Stanley, 454
West Germany: affluence in, 19; Berlin and, 146; exchange reserves in, 393; foreign investments of, 203; as hard-currency nation, 227; political interests in, 41; population of, 251
Wiener, Anthony, 164
Wiles, Peter, 163

William, William A., 308
Williamson, Harold, 452
Wohlstetter, Albert, 455
Women, wage rates for, 183
Wood, Adrian, 165
Worker control, 294
Working class: organized, 198; revolution and, 382–83; rise of modern industry and, 347; under socialism, 401
World Bank, 162, 163
World War I, 127; causes of, 199; economic controls during, 198; full employment during, 207; military expenditures during, 214
World War II, 55, 79, 280, 310, 447; changes in United States economy during, 207; military expenditures during, 214; monopoly capitalism and, 201–2; Nazi occupation of Ukraine in, 357

Yale University, 350
Yamey, Basil, 454, 455
Youth movement, radical, 178
Yugoslavia: aid to, 77, 182; alienation and, 290–91; cadre-building in, 257; commercialism in, 260; decentralization in, 250–52; economic development in, 247–48; markets in, 403–4; participation in, 249–50; political controls in, 69; private agriculture in, 356; publications on, 178; socialist revolution in, 79, 238, 256; Soviet boycott of, 80; transformation of man in, 252; worker control in, 294

Zammit, Ann, 315
Zevin, Robert, 316